The

Works of Plato

IN FIVE VOLUMES

Volume II

Translated by

Thomas Taylor

and

Floyer Sydenham

Published by

The Prometheus Trust

Volume X

of

The Thomas Taylor Series

The Prometheus Trust

Huan House, 17 Rossiters Hill,
Frome, Somerset BA11 4AL, UK.

A registered charity,
number 299648.

The Works of Plato, volume II.

This Edition published in 1996.

ISBN 1 898910 09 X

First Edition published in 1804.

British Library Cataloguing-in-Publication Data.
A catalogue record for this book is
available from the British Library.

Printed in England by Antony Rowe, Chippenham, Wiltshire.

* * *

For the preface to the Thomas Taylor Series, a short note on Thomas Taylor, and the Prometheus Trust's introduction to Taylor's *Plato*, see the first volume of the *Works of Plato* (Thomas Taylor Series volume IX).

CONTENTS

Changes to the original text

i.   Where Taylor had *the one, the one itself, the good* or *the good itself* this edition gives these names capital initials; this to distinguish them as the highest names the Platonists gave to God.   Other principles have been left in lower case.

ii.   A few very obvious grammatical errors and archaic spellings have been corrected; wherever there is any doubt as to the validity of possible errors the original has been followed.   A few mistakes in translation (or Taylor's printer's errors) have been corrected - on each occasion the correction is footnoted.

iii.   We have followed Taylor's explicit method of printing Greek characters without accents or breathings (see his defence of his Greek at the end of his *The Fable of Cupid and Psyche* and also his reference to this in the Introduction of *Proclus' Commentary on Euclid*).

iv.   Many references to works quoted are added, and some original references are given more precise indicators.

v.   Stephanus line numbers have been added to the dialogues throughout; these are for guidance and are not exact, as Taylor's translations verge towards paraphrase rather than literal, on occasions. The ancient commentaries are also line numbered where possible.

vi.   Page numbers in references: Taylor normally quotes page numbers to his own works whenever he refers to texts he had already published and these we have kept (*i.e.* they refer to the original publications' numbering).   However, in cases where works have been republished in this Thomas Taylor Series we have changed these page numbers so that they refer to the numbering within the Series; see over for a full list of these works.

vii.   Some notes have been rearranged: several long footnotes are now to be found in the Additional Notes.

The Thomas Taylor Series

Volume I - *Proclus' Elements of Theology.*

Volume II - *Select Works of Porphyry.*

> Abstinence from Animal Food; Auxiliaries to the Perception of Intelligibles; Concerning Homer's Cave of the Nymphs; Taylor on the Wanderings of Ulysses.

Volume III - *Collected Writings of Plotinus.*

> Twenty-seven treatises, being all the writings of Plotinus translated by Taylor.

Volume IV - *Collected Writings on the Gods and the World.*

> Sallust On the Gods and the World; The Sentences of Demophilus; Ocellus on the Nature of the Universe; Taurus and Proclus on the Eternity of the World; Maternus on the Thema Mundi; The Emperor Julian's Orations to the Mother of Gods and to the Sovereign Sun; Synesius on Providence; Taylor's essays on the Mythology and the Theology of the Greeks.

Volume V - *Hymns and Initiations.*

> The Hymns of Orpheus together with all the published hymns translated or written by Taylor; Taylor's essay on Orpheus.

Volume VI - *The Dissertations of Maximus Tyrius.*

> Forty-one treatises from the middle Platonist, and an essay from Taylor - The Triumph of the Wise Man over Fortune.

Volume VII - *Mysteries and Oracles.*

> A Collection of Chaldean Oracles; Essays on the Eleusinian and Bacchic Mysteries; The History of the Restoration of the Platonic Theology; An essay on A Platonic Demonstration of the Immortality of the Soul.

Volume VIII - *The Theology of Plato.*

> The six books of Proclus on the Theology of Plato; to which is added a further book (by Taylor), replacing the original seventh book by Proclus, now lost. Extensive introduction and notes are also added.

Volume IX - *The Works of Plato I*

The Five Volumes of the Works of Plato

THE LAWS

INTRODUCTION

Plato, in composing the following books of *Laws* after his *Republic*, appears to have acted in perfect conformity to the genius of his philosophy, which every where ascends to things more universal and thence descends to things more particular, and contends that the latter can only be accurately known by contemplating the former. As, therefore, in his *Republic*, or, the great polity, he assigned all things in common, so here he distributes land and a habitation, a wife and children, to every individual.

The Athenian guest, the chief speaker in this Dialogue, is Plato himself, as is well observed by the Greek Scholiast, whom we have frequently cited in the Notes to the *Republic*. For this guest observes, in the course of the *Laws*, that he had already completed two polities; so that either these must be the polities of Plato, or, if this is not admitted, Plato will be the same with the Athenian guest. Plato, therefore, travelling to Crete, met near Cnossus with Megillus the Lacedæmonian, and Clinias the Cretan, whom, together with nine others, the Cnossians had invited to their country that they might there establish a colony, build a city, and give it laws. Megillus then and Clinias, says the Scholiast, betook themselves to the sacred cavern of Jupiter, which was the most holy of all others, and in which the most venerable and arcane of the mysteries were performed.[†] The Athenian guest meeting with these two, and having asked them in what design they were engaged, they replied, In the establishment of laws. However, as they had been asked many things concerning laws by the guest, and had by no means satisfactorily answered his questions, and as he appeared to them to be well skilled in the subject, they request him to assist them in framing laws for the city.

The genius of Plato in composing these laws is truly admirable; for, prompted by a philanthropy of which a resemblance has from time immemorial been rarely seen, he has devised certain exhortatory introductions, which he calls prefaces, to the several laws, that the citizens may be led by persuasion, and not by terror, to act legally, and that they may spontaneously obey the laws as paternal injunctions, and not unwillingly submit to them as the mandates of a tyrant. The

---

[†] προσεχως δ' ωρμημενοις επι το του Διος αντρον ιερον, τουτο γενομενον αγιωτατον, εν ᾧ τα σεπτοτατα και αρρητοτατα των μυστηριων επιτελειτο. - Schol. Græc. in Plat. p. 214.

observation, therefore, of Seneca,[†] that 'nothing can be more trifling, nothing more frigid, than a law with a prologue,' is frigid and trifling in the extreme, when applied, as Seneca does apply it, to Plato's prefaces to his *Laws*. But Seneca was ignorant of the benevolent intention of the divine philosopher, in this instance, and perfectly unskilled in his doctrines. Can the objections, therefore, of such a *Roman* be of any weight against such a *Greek*?

In short, Plato, in this work, appears to have most happily blended the Socratic philanthropy with the Pythagoric intellectual elevation. Hence, besides an easy accommodation to familiar discourse, and the ethical peculiarity, in the tenth book, in perfect conformity to the dogmas of the Pythagoreans, he demonstrates the existence of the Gods and Providence, and shows that the divinities possess immutable perfection. This book, indeed, may be considered as forming one of the most important parts of the writings of Plato, as it indisputably proves that he was a firm believer in the religion of his country, and that, when properly understood, the theology of the Pagans is the *ne plus ultra* of sublimity. An introduction, therefore, of considerable extent will be prefixed to that book, which I earnestly recommend to the diligent perusal of the liberal reader.

[†] Senec. Epist. 94.

THE LAWS

BOOK I

PERSONS OF THE DIALOGUE

AN ATHENIAN GUEST
CLINIAS THE CRETAN, AND
MEGILLUS THE LACEDÆMONIAN

624a GUEST. Do you think, O guests, that a God, or some man, was the cause of the establishment of laws?

CLIN. A god, O guest, a God, as it is most just to assert: with us, indeed, Jupiter; but, with the Lacedæmonians (whence originated this our guest), I think, Apollo dictated the laws. Is it not so?

MEGIL. It is.

GUEST. Whether, therefore, do you speak according to Homer, *viz.*
b that Minos[†] every year, for the space of nine years, went to converse with his father, and established laws for your cities, according to his conceptions?

625a CLIN. It is so said by us: and, likewise, that his brother Rhadamanthus (you have heard the name) was most just. We Cretans, therefore, say that he obtained this praise, from his distributing, at that time, things pertaining to justice in a proper manner.

GUEST. His renown is indeed beautiful, and highly becoming the son of Jupiter. But since both you and this other have been educated in
b legal institutions of this kind, I persuade myself, it will not be unpleasant to us to speak and hear about the establishment of cities and laws, at the same time that we are proceeding on our journey. But the

---

[†] Minos was an intellectual hero, or, in other words, a hero who energized according to intellectual virtue; and, as he was illuminated by Jupiter, from whom he proceeded, he is on this account said to have conversed with his father. For an ample account of heroes, see the Notes to the *Cratylus*.

way from Cnossus to the cavern[†] and temple of Jupiter is, as we have heard, sufficiently long; and the resting-places along the road are, as it is proper they should be during the present hot weather, shady, from their position under lofty trees. It will likewise be suitable to our age, to rest in them frequently; and thus, by the allurements of discourse, render the whole of our journey easy.

CLIN. Indeed, O guest, in the course of our journey, we shall meet in
c the groves with cypress trees of an admirable height and beauty, and meadows in which while we rest we may discourse.

GUEST. You speak rightly.

CLIN. Entirely so. We shall however speak with more confidence when we become spectators of these. But let us now proceed on our journey with good fortune.

GUEST. Let it be so. But inform me, why the law instituted for you public feasts, gymnastic exercises, and the custom of using arms.

CLIN. I think, O guest, that these particulars respecting us may be apprehended with perfect ease. For you see that the nature of the whole region of Crete is not plain, like that of Thessaly. On this account,
d with them, horses are more used, and, with us, courses on foot. For this, irregularity of the ground is more adapted to the exercise of pedestrial races. Hence, for this purpose, it is necessary that the arms should be lighter, that they may not hinder the race by their weight. But lightness of bows and arrows seems to be adapted to this purpose. All these particulars, therefore, are subservient to our use in war; and the legislator, as it appears to me, looking to this, established every
e thing. For he seems to have instituted public banquets, in consequence of perceiving that all men, when they engaged in war, were compelled by the thing itself, for the sake of their own defence, to feast at that time together. But he appears to me to be charged with folly by the multitude, in consequence of their not having learnt that cities are
626a perpetually at war with each other. But if during the time of war it is necessary to feast together for the sake of defence, and that certain governors and men governed should be the armed defenders of them, this also should be done in the time of peace. For that which most men call peace, is only a name; but, in reality, war is perpetually proclaimed
b according to nature, by all cities, against all. And thus considering, you will nearly find that the Cretan legislator established for us all the laws, both public and private, as if looking to war; and ordered them to

---

[†] According to the Greek Scholiast, not only the greatest mysteries of Jupiter but also those of the Curetes were performed in this cavern.

defend these laws in such a manner as if nothing else was useful, either of possessions or studies, unless a man became victorious in war; and as considering that all the goods of the vanquished become the property of the victors.

GUEST. You appear to me, O guest, to be well exercised for the purpose of explaining the Cretan laws. But explain this yet more clearly to me. For you seem to me to say that a city is then well established when it is so constituted as to be able to vanquish other cities in war. Is it not so?

CLIN. It is perfectly so; and I think that this our other guest will be of the same opinion.

MEGIL. How can a Lacedæmonian, O divine man, answer otherwise?

GUEST. Whether, therefore, is this right from cities towards cities, but not from one village towards another?

CLIN. By no means.

GUEST. Is it therefore the same?

CLIN. It is.

GUEST. But what then? Is it likewise the same from one house to another in the same village, and from one man to another?

CLIN. The same.

GUEST. But what shall we say of one man towards himself? Shall we consider the relation as that of an enemy to an enemy? Or, how shall we say?

CLIN. O Athenian guest! for I am not willing to call you Attic, because you appear to me rather to deserve to be called by the surname of the Goddess Minerva.[†] For, rightly reducing the discourse to its principle, you render it more clear; and, by this mean, are able to find with facility that which has now been rightly asserted, - I mean, that all men are enemies to all, both publicly and privately, and likewise, that each individual is an enemy to himself.

GUEST. How do you say, O wonderful man?

CLIN. This, O guest; that for a man to vanquish himself if the first and best of all victories, but to be vanquished by himself is a thing the most shameful and vile. For these things signify that there is war in each of us against ourselves.

GUEST. Again, therefore, let us resume the discourse. For, since each of us is either better or worse than himself, whether shall we say that a house, a village, and a city, have this same thing in them, or not?

CLIN. Do you mean that one is better, and the other worse than itself?

---

† Alluding to Minerva being called the Goddess of Wisdom.

GUEST. I do.

CLIN. Concerning this also you have rightly inquired. For this does not less happen to cities, but in the highest degree. For, in those in which the better vanquish the multitude and the worse, such a city is with propriety said to be better than itself, and may with the greatest justice be praised for such a victory. But the contrary must be the case with a contrary city.

b　GUEST. Whether, therefore, here, the worse is at any time more excellent than the better, must be left uninvestigated; (for it would require a prolix discussion;) but I understand what is at present asserted by you, thus: That sometimes citizens who are allied to each other, and of the same city, being unjust and numerous, will forcibly attack the just, being fewer in number, that they may subject them to slavery; and that, when they conquer, the city may be justly said to be inferior to itself, and at the same time depraved, but, when they are conquered, better than itself, and good.

c　CLIN. What is now said, O guest, is wonderful in the extreme; but, at the same time, thus to confess is most necessary.

GUEST. Come then, let us again consider this. Many brothers may be born from one father, and from one mother. Nor is it at all wonderful that the greater part of them should be unjust, and the lesser just.

CLIN. It is not wonderful.

GUEST. Nor will it be proper for me and you to investigate this, that when the base vanquish, both the house and every kind of alliance may be called inferior to themselves, but better than themselves when the
d　base are vanquished. For we do not investigate these things at present for the sake of an elegant or inelegant arrangement of words, according to the manner of many, but for the sake of discovering what is natural rectitude and error concerning laws.

CLIN. You speak most truly, O guest.

MEGIL. It appears to me, too, that what has hitherto been said is beautiful.

GUEST. Let us besides consider this: Can any one become a judge of such brothers as we have just spoken of?

CLIN. Doubtless.

GUEST. Which therefore will be the better judge? he who cuts off
e　those that are unworthy, and orders the worthy to govern themselves? or he who causes the worthy to govern, but suffers the unworthy to live, when they are willing to be governed? But we will say that a third is a judge with respect to virtue, if such a one can be found, who, receiving one discordant alliance, will not destroy any one, but,

628a reconciling the disagreeing parties, will establish for them laws by which they may be enabled to preserve friendship towards each other.

CLIN. Such a judge and legislator will be by far the best.

GUEST. And he will frame laws for them, by acting in a manner contrary to looking at war.

CLIN. This indeed is true.

GUEST. But what - Whether does he who aptly constitutes a city look to external war, and by this mean principally adorn the lives of the

b citizens, or to the war produced within the city, which is called sedition, which every one would particularly wish not to arise in his city; and that, when it arises, the city may be liberated from it with the utmost celerity?

CLIN. It is evident that he would look to the latter.

GUEST. Whether would any one choose that peace should be the result of sedition, in consequence of one part of the citizens being destroyed, and the other part being victorious, or rather that peace and friendship should be the consequence of reconciliation, and thus the

c mind of the citizens be necessarily directed to external wars?

CLIN. Every one would rather wish that the latter should happen to his city, than the former.

GUEST. Would not a legislator in a similar manner?

CLIN. He would.

GUEST. Does not every one establish all laws for the sake of that which is best?

CLIN. How should he not?

GUEST. But neither war nor sedition is the best of things (for to be in want of these is execrable), but mutual peace and benevolence. Nor

d is that victory by which a city vanquishes itself, one of the best of things, but it ranks among things necessary. But to think that the best state of a city consists in fighting and conquering, is just as if any one should think that a wearied body, when undergoing medicinal purification, then acted in the best manner, but should pay no attention to a body which was not at all indigent of medical assistance. And if any one thinks in a similar manner, either of the felicity of a city or of a private man, he will never become a politician, while he thus alone and primarily looks to external war; nor will he be an accurate legislator, unless he establishes laws respecting war for the sake of peace, rather than laws respecting peace for the sake of war.

e CLIN. These things, O guest, appear in a certain respect to be rightly said. But I should wonder to find any one contending that our laws, and likewise those of the Lacedæmonians, were not with all possible attention framed for the sake of war.

629a GUEST. Perhaps this is the case. We ought not, however, to investigate the present affair in a contentious but in a quiet manner; the greatest diligence being employed, both by us and them, about things of this kind. Attend therefore to my discourse. In the first place, we shall adduce Tyrtæus,† who was by birth an Athenian, but afterwards a citizen of Lacedæmonia, and who most of all men applied himself to

b these particulars: "I shall not then (says he) consider that man as worthy of being mentioned, or of any consequence, though he should be the most wealthy of all men, and should possess abundance of goods (and he enumerates almost all goods), who does not always conduct himself in the most excellent manner in warlike affairs." These poems perhaps you also have heard. For this other associate of ours is, I think, satiated with them.

MEGIL. Entirely so.

CLIN. And these also have reached us, being brought from Lacedæmonia.

GUEST. Let us, therefore, in common interrogate this poet thus: O most divine poet, Tyrtæus! for you appear to us to be wise and good, because you have in the highest degree celebrated those who in the

c highest degree excel in war. I, therefore, and this Clinias the Cnossian, appear very much to agree with you in this particular. But we wish clearly to know, whether or not we speak about the same men. Inform us, therefore, whether you also as well as we are clearly of opinion, that there are two kinds of war? Or how do you say? For I think that a

d man much worse than Tyrtæus would answer that there are two kinds; one, which we all denominate sedition, and which we consider as the most grievous of all wars; but the other kind, I think, is that which we all consider as milder than the former, and which we employ against those who do not belong to the city, and who are of a different tribe.

CLIN. How is it possible he should answer otherwise?

GUEST. Inform us, therefore, who were the men, and what the kind of war, in which you have so transcendently praised some, and blamed

e others. For you appear to have praised those that fought in external

---

† Tyrtæus was an elegiac poet, lame, and despised by the Athenians. The Oracle of Apollo, however, ordered the Lacedæmonians to use him as their general, in the war in which they were then engaged with the Messenians. Tyrtæus therefore coming to Lacedæmon, and being inspired by the God, so animated the Lacedæmonians that they vanquished the Messenians. He flourished 684 years before Christ.

wars. Thus, you say in your poems, that you can by no means endure those who are not hardy enough to behold bloody slaughter, and to aspire after fierce battle, hand to hand. From this, O Tyrtæus, we should infer, that you praise those who have been eminently illustrious in waging external war. Shall we say that Tyrtæus would grant this?

CLIN. Certainly.

GUEST. But we, since these are good, shall assert that those are far 630a better who evidently excel in the greatest war. We have too the poet Theognis[†] a witness in our favour, who was a citizen of the Megarensians in Sicily. For he says:

> Who faithful in insane sedition keeps,
> With silver and with ruddy gold may vie.

We say, therefore, that such a one will conduct himself in the most difficult war in a manner nearly as much superior to the other, as b justice, temperance, and prudence, when conjoined with fortitude, are superior to fortitude alone. For no one can be found faithful and sound in seditions, without the whole of virtue. But, as Tyrtæus says, there are a great number of mercenaries who fight intrepidly and die willingly in battle, most of whom are ferocious, injurious, reproachful, and, with a very few exceptions, are the most stupid of all men. But to what does all this tend? And what did he perspicuously intend to signify by these c assertions? It is evidently this, that both he who framed laws here from Jupiter, and every other legislator who profits cities in the smallest degree, establishes laws by always looking as much as possible to the greatest virtue. But it is, as Theognis says, confidence in dire events, which may be denominated perfect justice. But that which Tyrtæus so highly praises is indeed beautiful, and opportunely celebrated by the d poet; yet it may most rightly be said to be honourable, the fourth in number, and in power.

CLIN. Shall we, therefore, O guest, rank our legislator among remote legislators?

GUEST. Not him indeed, most excellent man, but ourselves, since we are of opinion, that both Lycurgus and Minos established all the laws in Lacedæmon, and here, in consequence of especially directing their attention to war.

CLIN. In what manner then ought we to speak?

[†] This poet flourished about 549 years before Christ. [The lines quoted from him are Theog. 77-78.]

GUEST. As truth and justice, I think, require those should speak who
e discourse about a divine republic; for such ought not to be considered
as looking to a certain part of virtue, and that the most abject, but as
regarding the whole of virtue, and inquiring after laws, according to the
species of virtue; - not, indeed, investigating those species which many
at present propose; for, at present, every one proposes to inquire after
that which he is principally in want of. Thus, one inquires about an
inheritance, another about women who are left the only heirs, another
about an injury, and others about ten thousand things of a similar kind.
631a But we say that inquiries about laws rank among good inquiries, when
they are such as we have just now begun. And, indeed, I in every
respect approve of the manner in which you have entered on the
discussion of laws. For you are certainly right in beginning from virtue,
and asserting that for its sake laws are framed. But you do not appear
to me to be right in saying, that the legislator framed all his laws by
regarding a part of virtue, and this the least; and this has been the cause
b of all that was afterwards said by me. Are you, however, willing I
should tell you in what manner I wish you to distinguish in this affair?
CLIN. Entirely so.
GUEST. It is proper, O guest, to assert that the laws of the Cretans are
not rashly approved by all men, and particularly by all the Greeks. For
they are rightly framed, since they render those who use them happy;
and this because they impart every good. But there are two kinds of
goods, one human, and the other divine; and the former is suspended
from the latter. And if any city receives the greater goods, it also
c possesses the lesser; but if not, it is deprived of both. But the lesser
goods are those of which health is the leader, beauty the second in
order, and strength for the course, and all the other motions pertaining
to the body, the third. But riches rank in the fourth place, which are
not blind,† but perceive acutely, if they follow prudence. However,

---

† "Theophrastus (says the Greek Scholiast) observes, that if wealth had life, it would
come only to the good. For every thing desires its proper good; but this is the good of
wealth, to become an instrument to the worthy: since that which is the good of any
thing is the object of desire to that thing, and this also is according to nature to it. But
all things aspire after a disposition according to nature. However, since wealth is
without life, it now also falls among the evil." Ο Θεοφραστος φησιν· ει ζωην ειχεν ο
πλουτος, προς μονους αν απηλθε τους αγαθεως· εκαστον γαρ του οικειου εφιεται
αγαθου· τουτο δε τω πλουτω εστιν αγαθον, το τοις αγαθοις οργανον γιγνεσθαι· το γαρ
εκαστω αγαθον, τουτο και εφετον υπαρχει· τουτο δ᾽ αυτω και κατα φυσιν· παντα δε της
κατα φυσιν ορεγεται διαθεσεως· νυν δε επειδη ο πλουτος ουκ εχει ζωην, εμπιπτει και εις
τους κακους. - Schol. Græc. in Plat. p. 227.

that which is the first leader of all divine goods is prudence.[†] That which ranks in the second place after intellect is a temperate habit of the soul. From these mingled with fortitude, the third in order will be justice. And the fourth will be fortitude. All which are to be placed, according to nature before those human goods. A legislator, therefore, ought to follow this order, and should command the citizens to look to these divine goods in all their actions. But, of these, human should be referred to divine goods, and all divine goods to their leader intellect. After these things he ought to pay attention to the marriages of the citizens, and to the procreation and education of children, both male and female, and likewise to the young, and those who are advancing to old age. Such too, among these, as behave well, he should honour as they deserve, but should reprobate in all the conversations of these, their pains, pleasures, and desires. He should likewise consider, and act as a guardian over, the studies of all lovers; and, through the laws, praise such as are worthy, and blame the contraries to these. With respect to anger and fear, too, he will show what in each of these is laudable, and what to be avoided; likewise what perturbations are produced in the soul through misfortune, and what the means by which these are avoided in prosperity. Lastly, he will show what passions men are subject to, through disease, war, poverty, or the contraries to these; and in all such things he will teach and define what is beautiful, or otherwise, in the disposition of each. After this, it is necessary that the legislator should pay attention to the possessions and expenses of the citizens, so as to know how they are conducted, together with societies, and their dissolutions, whether voluntarily or involuntarily instituted; where justice is found among these, and where it is wanting, that by these means he may distribute honours to those that obey the laws, and punish those who cannot be persuaded to obey them. In the last place, having instituted every thing as far as to the end of every polity, it is necessary he should establish the manner in which the monuments of the dead should be raised, and what honours are to be paid to them. The legislator, having established all these particulars, should place over them guardians, some of whom conduct public affairs according to prudence, but others according to true opinion; so that intellect, binding

[†] Meaning intellectual prudence, through which we obtain a knowledge of things good and advantageous, of things beautiful and the contrary; and which, in short, is the governor of man, referring cities and houses, and the life of every individual, to a divine paradigm. Plato immediately after this calls it intellect, because it is generated from a pure and perfect intellect.

all these together, may evince that the city follows temperance and
d   justice, and not riches or ambition. After this manner, O guests, I have
wished, and am now desirous, you would explain how all these
particulars are to be found in those laws which are called the laws of
Jupiter, in those of Pythian Apollo, and in those which Minos and
Lycurgus established; and how, being assumed in a certain order, they
may become evident to one who is skilled in the legislative science,
either by art or from certain customs, though to us they are by no
means apparent.

CLIN. How then, O guest, ought we to discuss what follows?

GUEST. It appears to me that we ought to commence our discussion
e   from the beginning (as we began to do); considering in the first place the
pursuits of fortitude, and afterwards discussing another and another
species of virtue, if you are willing: and that we may discuss the first
object of our inquiry, we will endeavour to establish a paradigm, and
refer to it the other particulars, that by mutual converse of this kind we
may beguile the tediousness of the way. But afterwards we will consider
the pursuits of the whole of virtue, and evince that our present
discussion, if divinity is willing, looks thitherward.

633a   CLIN. You speak well. Endeavour therefore, in the first place, to
judge of us respecting this praiser of Jupiter.

GUEST. I will endeavour to do this, both for you and myself. For the
discourse is common. Speak therefore. Shall we say that common
banquets and gymnastic exercises were invented by the legislator, for the
purposes of war?

CLIN. They were.

GUEST. And is this the case with a third or fourth thing? For,
perhaps, it is proper thus to enumerate in the things pertaining to
another virtue, whether it is right to call them parts, or any thing else,
for the sake of perspicuity.

b   MEGIL. I, therefore, as well as every Lacedæmonian, should say that
hunting was invented as the third thing. But we should endeavour, if
possible, to discover the fourth or fifth thing. I therefore shall
endeavour to evince that the fourth thing consists in the endurance of
pain. For we are much exercised in this, in fighting with each other
with our hands, and in certain violent seizures, each of these being
attended with a multitude of wounds. Besides this we have an exercise,

c   which is called a certain concealment,[†] which is wonderfully laborious, and is undertaken for the purpose of strengthening our endurance. Besides, in winter, without shoes, without any covering to our body, and without servants, waiting indeed on ourselves, we wander both night and day through every region. Further still: in the exercises of naked young men, severe endurances take place among us, when we contend with the strength of suffocating heat; and there are many other things of this kind among us, which it would not be easy to enumerate.

GUEST. You speak well, O Lacedæmonian guest. But whether or not

d   shall we place fortitude as simply consisting in a contest alone with fears and pains? or, shall we say that it likewise consists in opposing desires and pleasures, and certain vehement flatteries, which soften the minds of those who are considered as venerable persons, and besides this render them like wax?

MEGIL. I think it likewise consists in opposing all these.

GUEST. If, therefore, we call to mind what was advanced above, this our other guest said, that some city was inferior to itself, and some man to himself. Was it not so, O Cnossian guest?

CLIN. Entirely so.

e   GUEST. Now, then, which ought we to call the inferior, - he who is subdued by pain, or he who is subdued by pleasure?

CLIN. It appears to me, he who is subdued by pleasure. And, in every respect, we should rather say that he who is vanquished by pleasures is disgracefully inferior to himself, and, prior to this, to him who is vanquished by pains.

634a   GUEST. Did therefore the legislators of Jupiter and Apollo establish by law fortitude as lame, and consider it as alone able to oppose things on its left hand, but incapable of resisting elegancies and flatteries on its right hand? or, did they consider it as able to oppose both?

CLIN. Both, I think.

GUEST. Let us, therefore, again relate what those pursuits are, in both your cities, which taste of pleasures, and do not avoid them, in the same

---

[†] A young man was sent from the city, in order that he might not be seen for a certain time. He was therefore compelled to wander round the mountains, and could neither sleep without fear, lest he should be detected, nor employ servants, nor carry food for his subsistence. There was also another form of exercise for the purpose of war: for, stripping every one of the young men naked, they ordered them to wander for a whole year out of the city, among the mountains, and to support themselves by theft, and other stratagems, but in such a manner that no one might detect them. Hence this was called κρυπτεια, a concealment: for they were punished if they were at any time discovered. - Schol. Gr. in Plat. p.225.

manner as they do not avoid pain, but bring them into the midst, and cause the citizens to vanquish them, partly by force, and partly by the
b   allurements of honour. But, inform me where the same thing is ordained in your laws respecting pleasures, as respecting pains; and what that is which renders you similarly brave both with respect to pain and pleasures; which renders you victorious over those things which you ought to vanquish, and by no means suffers you to be inferior to your neighbouring and most grievous enemies?

c   MEGIL. I cannot, O guest, so easily adduce a multitude of laws opposite to pleasures, as I can a multitude opposite to pains. Nor perhaps is it easy to speak of pleasures according to great and apparent parts, but only according to such as are small.

CLIN. Nor am I able in a similar manner to render the same apparent in the Cretan laws.

GUEST. This, O best of guests, is by no means wonderful. If any one, therefore, who is desirous of perceiving that which is true and at the same time most excellent, should find something to reprehend in the laws of our respective countries, we should behave towards each other with mildness, and not with severity.

CLIN. You speak well, O Athenian guest; and therefore we ought to follow your advice.

d   GUEST. Indeed, Clinias, a conduct of this kind becomes men of your age.

CLIN. Certainly.

GUEST. The next question, therefore, will be, whether or not the Laconian and Cretan polity is reprehensible. Perhaps indeed, I can better relate what is said by the multitude on this occasion, than either of you. As to your laws, though they should be but of a moderate degree of excellence, yet you certainly have one most beautiful law,
e   which forbids any youth from inquiring whether the laws are well or ill established, but orders them all to accord, with one voice, and with one mouth, that they are all beautifully constituted, as if they had been established by the Gods; and that, if any young man asserts the contrary, no one shall by any means listen to his discourse: but that an old man, if he has any thing to urge against them, shall relate his objections to the rulers, and his equals in age, yet not in the presence of any young man.

635a CLIN. You speak most properly, O guest: and though at the time this law was established you was absent from the thought of the founder, yet you appear to me to conjecture his intention sufficiently, as if you were a prophet, and to speak the truth in the most eminent degree.

GUEST. At present, therefore, let us be free from young men, but we, on account of our old age, are permitted by the legislator to speak about the laws among ourselves, without committing any offence.

CLIN. We are so. Do not spare, therefore, but freely reprove our laws. For it is not dishonourable to know if any thing is not beautifully established; but, by this mean, a remedy is applied, when what is

b   asserted is received with a benevolent, and not an envious mind.

GUEST. You speak well. I shall not, however, reprehend the laws till I have diligently considered them to the utmost of my ability; or rather, I shall proceed in this affair by doubting. For you alone, of all the Greeks and Barbarians with whom we are acquainted, the legislator has ordered to abstain from the greatest pleasures and sports, and not to taste them. But with respect to pains and fears, which we have lately

c   discussed, he was of opinion, that if any one avoided them from his infancy, when he came to endure necessary pains, fears, and labours, he would avoid those who are exercised in them, and would become their slave. This legislator ought, in my opinion, to have thought the same respecting pleasures, and to have said to himself: If the citizens should from childhood be unexperienced in the greatest pleasures, and never be taught how to sustain the attacks of pleasure, or informed that they should never be compelled to do any thing base for the sake of the sweetness with which pleasure is attended, they would be induced to act

d   in the same manner as those who are vanquished by fear, and would become servile in a different and yet baser manner than those who are able to endure the assaults of pleasure, but yet procure pleasures for themselves, and are sometimes the worst of men. The soul of such, likewise, is partly a slave, and partly free; and they do not deserve to be called simply brave, and free. Consider, therefore, whether any thing that has been now said appears to you to be proper.

e   CLIN. It does. But immediately and readily to assent to things of such great importance would be the province of young men, or rather of stupid men.

GUEST. Shall we then, O Clinias and Lacedæmonian guest, after this, discuss what we at first proposed; (for after fortitude we shall speak of temperance,) I mean, what difference there is between these polities and those which are governed by chance, in the same manner as we have now spoken about war?

636a   MEGIL. This is not very easy to accomplish.

CLIN. Yet it appears that the common banquets, and gymnastic exercises, were beautifully invented by both polities.

GUEST. It appears, O guests, to be a difficult undertaking to introduce, in reality as well as in discourse, the indubitable, respecting polities. For it seems that, as in bodies it is not possible to accommodate any one pursuit to any one body, because the same thing is seen to injure some and benefit others, the like takes place in cities.

b For gymnastic exercises, public banquets, and a multitude of other things, at one time are beneficial to cities, but in seditions they are hurtful. The truth of this is evinced by the Milesians, Bœotians, and Thurians. But this ancient, legal, and natural pursuit appears to have perverted the venereal pleasures, not only of men, but of beasts. And

c your cities may be first accused of this, and such others as have particularly applied themselves to gymnastic exercises. And whether things of this kind ought to be considered jocosely, or seriously, still we must be convinced that, when the male and female unite for the purpose of producing offspring, the pleasure attending such a conjunction appears to be imparted according to nature; but, that the conjunction of males with males, or of females with females, is contrary to nature. We must likewise assert, that he who first dared to act in this manner was induced by the incontinence of pleasure. We all of us, indeed, blame the fable

d of the Cretans about Ganymedes, as discoursing about these particulars. For, as they believe that their laws were given by Jupiter, they have devised this fable against Jupiter, that they may give themselves up to this pleasure, following the example of the God. But let us bid farewell to the fable. Again, with respect to those who make the laws the subject of their speculation, almost all their attention should be directed to pleasures and pains, both in the manners of cities and of individuals. For these two fountains are permitted to flow by nature; of which, he

e who draws whence, when, and as much as he ought, is happy; and this is equally true of a city, an individual, and of every animal: but he who draws unscientifically, and at an improper time, will, on the contrary, live unhappy.

MEGIL. These things, O guest, are so beautifully said, as to render us incapable of urging any thing against them. But, at the same time, the Lacedæmonian legislator appears to me to have very properly forbidden the avoiding of pleasure. But this our other guest can, if he pleases,

637a assist us with respect to the Cnossian laws. For it appears to me that the institutions in Sparta about pleasures are the most beautiful of all institutions; since that through which men principally fall into the greatest pleasures, the most injurious conduct, and every kind of folly, our law exterminates from the whole of our country: nor will you see in the fields, nor in any of the Spartan cities, banquets, nor such other

particulars attendant on these, as excite, according to their power, every
b   kind of pleasure. Nor is there any one who, happening to meet with a
person wanton through intoxication, would not immediately inflict on
him the greatest punishment. Nor would the pretext of celebrating the
festival of Bacchus absolve him from chastisement, as I once saw was the
case with your people in carriages. And in Tarentum, with those of our
colony, I have seen all the city intoxicated during the Bacchic festival.
With us, however, there is nothing of the kind.

GUEST. O Lacedæmonian guest, all such things as these are laudable
where they are attended with certain endurances; but, where they are
c   permitted, they are of a most slothful nature. For some one, defending
our institutions, would very readily reprove you by showing the
licentiousness of your women. But one answer appears to liberate all
such particulars, in Tarentum, with us, and with you, from not being
base, but upright. For every one who answers may say to an admiring
stranger, on his beholding things unusual in his own country: Wonder
not, O guest, that this law is established among us, but with you a
different law, perhaps about the same things. At present, however, O
d   friends, our discourse is not about different men, but about the vice and
virtue of the legislators. But let us speak more fully about all
intoxication. For it is not a thing of a trifling nature; nor is the
knowledge of it the province of a depraved legislator. I do not mean to
inquire, whether wine ought to be drunk or not, but about intoxication
itself, - whether it is to be used, as the Scythians and the Persians use it,
and besides these the Carthaginians, Celtæ, Iberians, and Thracians, who
e   all of them are warlike nations; or, as it is used by you; for you (as you
say) entirely abstain from it. But the Scythians and Thracians use it
unmingled with water, women as well as men, and pour it on their
garments, thinking that thus they are engaged in a beautiful and blessed
pursuit. But the Persians are very much given to other luxuries, which
you reject; yet, O best of men, they are more orderly in these than the
Scythians and Thracians.

638a   MEGIL. All these, however, we shall put to flight, when we take up
arms.

GUEST. O best of men, do not speak in this manner. For many
flights and pursuings have taken place, and will take place, of which it
is impossible to form any conjecture; on which account, we cannot at
any time give an evident definition, but are involved in doubts about
beautiful and base pursuits, when we speak of victory and flight in war;
especially since the greater vanquish in battle, and enslave the lesser
b   cities. Thus, the Locrians were vanquished and enslaved by the

Syracusans, who appear to have possessed the best laws of all the neighbouring nations; and the Cei by the Athenians; and innumerable instances of the same kind may be found. Neglecting, therefore, the consideration of victory and being vanquished, we will endeavour to speak and persuade ourselves about every pursuit; and to show how this thing is beautiful, and that is not so. But, first of all, hear me, how we ought to consider what is good or bad in things of this kind.

c   MEGIL. How do you say?

GUEST. All those who introduce any dispute in their discourse, and immediately propose to praise or blame it, appear to me to act by no means in a proper manner, but to do just the same as if, any one praising a piece of bread as good, another should immediately discommend it, without either understanding its operation or utility, and without knowing after what manner, by whom, and with whom it was prepared, and the past and present habit of the bodies to whom it ought

d   to be offered. But we appear to act in the very same manner, at present, in our discourses. For, upon only hearing intoxication mentioned, some of us immediately blamed, and others praised it; and this very absurdly. For, employing witnesses and those who praise, we likewise praised; and some of us thought that we advanced something seasonable, because we adduced a multitude of witnesses; but others, because those who make

e   no use of wine conquer in battle. This, however, is to us ambiguous. If then we proceed in this manner in the discussion of other particulars pertaining to laws, we shall not in my opinion proceed rationally. But adducing intoxication as an instance, I will endeavour to the utmost of my ability to point out a right method for us, about all such subjects of inquiry; since innumerable nations, who are doubtful about these particulars, will verbally contend with your two cities.

639a   MEGIL. We must not through sluggishness refuse to hear, whether we possess any right consideration about these affairs.

GUEST. Let us, therefore, thus consider. If any one should praise the employment of nurturing goats, and the possession of that species of animals, as a beautiful thing, but another should blame it, in consequence of seeing that goats are fed in cultivated places without a shepherd, and that every kind of cattle is either without a shepherd, or is under the direction of bad shepherds; should we consider the accusation of such a one as sane, or not?

MEGIL. How is it possible we could?

GUEST. But, whether will a pilot be useful in a ship, if he alone possesses the nautical science, whether he is troubled with sea sickness

b   or not? or how shall we say?

MEGIL. This passion which you speak of is not in any respect connected with the nautical art.

GUEST. But what shall we say of the general of an army? Is he to be considered as sufficient to the purposes of commanding, if he possesses the warlike science, though, being timid in dangers, yet through intoxication he should loath fear?

MEGIL. How can he?

GUEST. But what shall we say, if he does not possess art, and is timid?

MEGIL. You speak of one in every respect depraved, and who is by no means a ruler of men, but of some extremely weak women.

c   GUEST. But he who praises or blames a community, which is naturally capable of being governed, and which with a proper governor is a useful society, but, at the same time, has either never seen it well governed, or has always beheld it without governors, can he with propriety ever praise or blame such a community?

d   MEGIL. How is it possible he can, who has never beheld a society well governed?

GUEST. Attend then: do we not consider guests and banquets as one certain association out of many communities?

MEGIL. We do in the highest degree.

GUEST. Has no one, therefore, ever beheld this subsisting in a proper manner? But it is easy for you to answer, that this has never in any respect been beheld (for this is neither according to the manner of your country nor your laws). But I have met with many, and in many places,

e   and have diligently inquired, as I may say, about all of them. And, indeed, I have scarcely seen or heard of one whole community that has been established in a proper manner; but I have seen that this has been the case with certain few and small parts, while many have, as I may say, been entirely faulty.

CLIN. How do you say, O guest? Speak still more perspicuously. For we, as you say, being unskilled in such things, and perhaps not having met with them, cannot immediately know what in them is right or wrong.

640a   GUEST. You speak probably: but, while I speak, endeavour to learn. Do you then acknowledge, that, in all associations and communions of actions whatever, it is proper for each to have a governor?

CLIN. How is it possible I should not.

GUEST. But we have already said, that the governor of warlike affairs ought to be brave.

CLIN. We have.

GUEST. But the brave will be less disturbed by fear than the timid man.

b CLIN. And this also will be the case.

GUEST. If any method could be devised by which a general of an army might be rendered neither timid, nor subject to perturbation, should we not accomplish this by all possible means?

CLIN. In the greatest degree.

GUEST. But now we do not speak of an army which is governed in the inimical associations of inimical men, in war, but of the benevolence of friends communicating with each other in peace.

CLIN. Right.

c GUEST. But an association of this kind, if it is attended with intoxication, will not be without perturbation. Or, do you think it will?

CLIN. How should it be without?

GUEST. In the first place, therefore, these have need of a governor.

CLIN. Most of all.

GUEST. Whether, therefore it is proper to choose for them, if possible, a governor who is free from perturbation?

CLIN. How can it be otherwise?

GUEST. And, indeed, as it appears, he ought to be prudent with respect to association. For he should be the guardian of their friendship, and should take care that it may be increased through this their association.

CLIN. You speak most truly.

GUEST. It is proper, therefore, to place over the intoxicated a sober and wise governor, and not the contrary. For, if the governor of the intoxicated is himself intoxicated, young, and not wise, he must be abundantly fortunate if he does not accomplish some mighty evil.

CLIN. Abundantly indeed.

e GUEST. If, therefore, any one should blame drinking associations, though they should be as well instituted as possible in cities, while he accuses the thing itself, he will perhaps very properly blame them. But if he should blame all drinking associations, merely because he had seen one defective; in the first place, it is evident he is ignorant that this was not well instituted; and, in the next place, every thing after this manner

641a will appear base, although the master and governor should be sober. Or, do you not perceive, that when the pilot is intoxicated, or any other governor, he will subvert every thing, whether it is a ship, or a chariot, or an army, or any thing else that is governed by him?

CLIN. You speak, O guest, in every respect, true. But inform me what advantage can be derived from drinking associations when they are well conducted. As that which we just now asserted, that an army well commanded would procure victory in war, which is no small good: and

b in the same manner we must judge of other things. But what great advantage will accrue either to individuals, or cities, from drinking associations being properly instituted?

GUEST. What great advantage can a city derive from one boy, or one company being properly educated? or shall we not reply to him who asks this question, that the city derives but very little advantage from the education of an individual, or a company? But, if you inquire universally about the education of youth, of what great advantage it is

c to a city, it is not difficult to reply, that, when boys are well educated, they will become good men; and that, in consequence of becoming good men, they will both act in other respects in a beautiful manner, and will vanquish their enemies in battle. Discipline, therefore, will give victory, but victory sometimes produces ignorance. For many becoming insolent through victory in war are filled, in consequence of their insolence, with a thousand other evils. And discipline indeed has never at any time been Cadmeian; but there have been, and will be, many victories of this kind among men.

d CLIN. You seem to say, O friend, that associations for the purpose of drinking wine form a great part of discipline, if they are properly conducted.

GUEST. Certainly.

CLIN. Will you after this be able to prove that your assertion is true?

GUEST. To contend, O guest, that these things are true, since many doubt about them, is alone the province of divinity; but, if it be requisite to assert what appears to me, I think no one will be envious, since our intention, at present, is to discourse about laws and a polity.

CLIN. We will therefore endeavour to learn what is your opinion with respect to these ambiguities.

e GUEST. It is proper to do so; and, besides this, that you should endeavour to learn, and I to teach, and that this should be the whole business of our discourse. But, first of all, hear what follows. All the Greeks consider this city of ours as philological, and abounding in words. But with respect to Lacedæmon and Crete, the former is considered as sparing of words, but the latter, as more remarkable for

642a abundance of sagacity than abundance of words. But I am afraid I shall appear to you to speak much about a small affair, - I mean intoxication. An emendation of it, indeed, according to nature cannot be accomplished with perspicuity, without musical rectitude, nor be sufficiently handled in discourse. But music cannot be discussed without the whole of erudition. And all this requires a multitude of words.

b Consider, therefore, what we shall do: whether we shall omit these things at present, and pass on to some other question about laws.

MEGIL. Perhaps you do not know, O Athenian guest, that our family is the public guest of your city. Perhaps, therefore, a certain benevolence will immediately enter into the minds of all boys towards a city, when they hear that they are the public guests of that city; and they will consider it as another native country, which ranks in the second place after their own. And this is the case with myself at present. For I have heard the Lacedæmonian youth, as often as they praised or blamed any thing belonging to the Athenians, say, Your city,

c O Megillus, has been the cause of this evil, or that good. But, on hearing this, I have fought against those who blamed your city, in consequence of possessing all possible benevolence towards it. And now, indeed, your voice is grateful to me; and that which is said by many, that such of the Athenians as are good are so in a remarkable degree, appears to be most truly asserted. For they alone, without necessity, spontaneously, and from a divine allotment, are truly and not fictitiously

d good. Therefore, for my sake, my friend, you may boldly say whatever you please.

CLIN. And hearing and receiving, O guest, what I have to advance, you may confidently speak what you please. For you have perhaps heard, that Epimenides was a divine man, who was of our family, and who ten years prior to the Persian war came to your city through the admonition of an oracle, and performed certain sacrifices which the God

e had enjoined. And besides this, he told the Athenians, who were terrified at the Persian expedition, that the Persians would not come for the space of ten years; and that, when they came, they would depart without accomplishing any thing which they hoped to accomplish, and would suffer greater evils than they caused. At that time our ancestors hospitably received yours; and in consequence of this, both myself and our parents are benevolently disposed towards you.

643a GUEST. You therefore, as it appears, are prepared to hear; but I am indeed prepared so far as relates to my will, but not altogether with respect to my ability. I shall however endeavour to gratify your request. In the first place then, as preparatory to our discourse, let us define what discipline is, and what power it possesses. For we say that through this the discourse proposed by us at present must proceed, until it arrives at divinity.

CLIN. We ought entirely to act in this manner, if agreeable to you.

b GUEST. While, therefore, I assert what it is proper to say discipline is, do you consider whether my assertion accords with your opinion.

CLIN. You may begin when you please.

GUEST. I say, then, that those who are hereafter to become great men ought from their very childhood to meditate both in sport, and when acting seriously, things accommodated to the objects of their pursuit. Thus, if any one is to become a good husbandman or architect, he ought from childhood, even in play, either to till the ground, or build certain puerile houses. And he who is intrusted with the education of both

c these should provide each of them with small instruments, which are imitations of the true ones. And besides this, he should learn such disciplines as are necessary to be previously learned. Thus, a workman should learn how to measure, or use a rule. He who is destined to be a warrior should in sport ride on horseback, or do something else of a similar kind. And the master of the children should endeavour, by sports, to turn the pleasures and desires of the children thither, where when arrived, it is proper they should receive their consummation. But

d we say that the head or summit of discipline is a right education, which especially leads the soul of him who sports to a love of that which it will be requisite for him to do when he has arrived at manhood, and has acquired perfection in the virtue of his art. Consider therefore, now, whether (as I said) what has been thus far asserted pleases you.

CLIN. How is it possible it should not?

GUEST. Neither, therefore, should that which we have said discipline is, be left indefinite. For now, when we blame or praise the education of particular persons, we say that such a one is endued with discipline, but another is undisciplined, although he may possess the greatest skill

e in cooking, or navigation, and other things of this kind. For we do not, as it appears, consider these to be discipline, but that which causes a citizen from his childhood to desire and love virtue, and through which acquiring perfection, he may know how to govern and be governed with justice. This is what our discourse defines to be education; from which

644a it appears, that this alone ought to be called discipline, according to our sentiments; but that the education which tends to the acquisition of wealth, or bodily strength, or any other particular wisdom, without intellect and justice, is mechanical and illiberal, and does not in any respect deserve to be called discipline. We shall not, however, contend about a word. But let what we have just now assented to remain, that those who are properly disciplined become nearly all of them good. So that it is by no means proper to despise discipline, because it is present b   to the most excellent men, the first of all beautiful things. And if at any time one properly disciplined should depart from right conduct, he is capable of being put in the right way; and this he may always accomplish according to his ability, through the whole of life.

CLIN. Right: and we assent to what you say.

GUEST. But we formerly granted, that those are good who are capable of governing themselves, but those bad, who do not possess this ability.

CLIN. You speak most rightly.

GUEST. We will therefore resume this assertion, that what we say may

c   become more clear. And receive me through an image, if in any respect I may be able to manifest to you a thing of this kind.

CLIN. Only speak.

GUEST. Do we not consider each of us as one?

CLIN. We do.

GUEST. But that we contain in ourselves two counsellors, contrary to each other, and foolish, which we denominate pleasure and pain?

CLIN. This also we admit.

d   GUEST. With these are connected the opinions of things future, the common name of which is hope. But, properly speaking, the hope prior to pain is fear, but that which is prior to its contrary is confidence. But in all these there is a reasoning process, determining which of them is better or worse; and which, when it becomes the common dogma of the city, is denominated law.

CLIN. I can scarcely follow you. However, proceed with what remains, as if I were able to follow you.

MEGIL. I likewise am affected in the same manner.

GUEST. But we should thus think about these things. We should consider that each of us is reckoned a prodigy by divine animals,[†] whether we were produced as their sport, or as the result of a serious

e   operation: for of this we are ignorant. This however we know, that these passions are inherent in our nature like nerves or ropes, that they draw contrary to each other, being themselves contrary, and that they draw us to contrary actions, where virtue and vice are situated apart from each other. For reason says, that we ought always to follow one of the drawings, and should never abandon it, but through this draw in

645a a contrary direction to the other nerves; and that this is the golden and sacred guidance of the reasoning energy, which is called the common law of the city. It adds, that the other drawings are hard, and of an iron

---

† Plato, by divine animals, means the mundane, or, as he calls them in the *Timæus*,[42d] the junior Gods.

nature; but that this is soft, as being golden. That it is besides uniform, but that the others are similar to all-various forms. It is necessary, therefore, that we should always follow the most beautiful guidance of law. For, since the energy of reasoning is beautiful and gentle, but not violent, servants have need of its guidance, that the golden race[†] in us

b   may vanquish the genera of a different kind. And thus the fable, since we are beings of a wonderful nature, will be preservative of virtue; and we shall be able to understand more clearly how any one may be said to be superior and inferior to himself: and both cities and individuals, apprehending the true reason respecting these drawings, ought to live conformable to it. We shall likewise be convinced that a city, whether it receives reason from some one of the Gods, or from him who knows these particulars, will establish it as law, and employ it in its own transactions, and in its transactions with other cities. For thus vice and

c   virtue will appear to us more clearly distinct; and this distinction becoming more conspicuous, both discipline and other studies will perhaps be rendered more apparent. This will likewise be the case with respect to the custom of drinking societies, about which it might appear despicable to discourse any further.

CLIN. Perhaps it will appear not to be unworthy of a long discourse.

GUEST. You speak well. We will therefore endeavour to relate what appears to be praise-worthy in a custom of this kind.

CLIN. Speak then.

d   GUEST. If to this wonderful thing we should add intoxication, what sort of a thing shall we fashion him?

CLIN. What thing do you look to in asking this question?

GUEST. To nothing particular. But if this prodigy or wonderful thing should become connected with intoxication, what would happen to be the result? But I will endeavour to explain more clearly what I mean. For this is what I ask: Does the drinking of wine more vehemently excite pleasure, pain, anger, and love?

CLIN. It does very much so.

e   GUEST. Does it in a similar manner render the senses, memory, opinion, and prudence, more vehement? or does it entirely extinguish these, when any one has drunk of it to intoxication?

CLIN. It entirely extinguishes these.

[†]   *Viz.* the intellectual form of life, or a life according to intellect. See the Additional Notes to the *Republic* for an account of the different ages. [TTS vol. IX, p. 562.]

GUEST. Such a one, therefore, returns to that habit of soul which he possessed when he was a boy.

CLIN. Entirely so.

GUEST. Hence such a one has at that time the least possible command of himself.

CLIN. The least.

646a GUEST. Shall we, therefore, call such a one most depraved?

CLIN. Very much so.

GUEST. Not only then, as it appears, does an old man become twice a boy, but this is likewise the case with a man when intoxicated.

CLIN. You speak, O guest, in a most excellent manner.

GUEST. Is there any reason which can persuade us that we ought to taste this liquor, and not to the utmost of our power avoid it?

CLIN. It appears that there is; and you just now said you was prepared to show it.

b GUEST. You have very properly reminded me; and I am now prepared, since you have both said that you are willing to hear me with alacrity.

CLIN. How is it possible we should not hear you, if on no other account, yet for the sake of the wonderful and the absurd which it contains, if it is necessary that a man should at any time voluntarily hurl himself into every kind of depravity?

GUEST. Do you speak of the soul?

CLIN. I do.

GUEST. But what? Shall we wonder, my friend, if at any time some c one should voluntarily arrive at depravity of body, - I mean leanness, deformity, and imbecility?

CLIN. How is it possible we should not?

GUEST. Shall we, therefore, think that those who go to a dispensary for the sake of obtaining medicines, are ignorant that, in a short time after they have taken the medicines, their body will for many days be so affected, that, if they were to remain in that condition to the end of life, they would not wish to live? or, Do we not know that those who undergo gymnastic exercises and labours are immediately rendered weak?

CLIN. All this we know.

GUEST. And that they willingly tend to these things, for the sake of consequent utility?

d CLIN. Most beautifully said.

GUEST. Is it not, therefore, necessary to think after the same manner about other pursuits?

CLIN. Entirely so.

GUEST. In the same manner, therefore, we ought to think about the employment of drinking wine, if it is admitted that this among other employments may be considered in a proper light.

CLIN. Certainly.

GUEST. If it should, therefore, appear to us to possess any utility, which is not inferior to corporeal exercise, - in the first place, it will vanquish this, because corporeal exercise is attended with pain, but the employment of drinking wine is without pain.

e CLIN. You speak very properly. But I should wonder if we were able to perceive any such thing in it.

GUEST. This, therefore, as it appears, I must now endeavour to explain to you. Tell me then, are we able to understand two species of fear, which are nearly contrary to each other?

CLIN. Of what kind are they?

GUEST. They are such as these. We are afraid of things evil, when we expect they will arrive.

CLIN. We are.

647a GUEST. And we are often afraid of opinion, thinking we shall be considered by others as depraved characters, when we do or say any thing which is not becoming; which fear, I think, both we and all others denominate shame.

CLIN. Doubtless.

GUEST. These are the two fears I spoke of, - one of which is contrary to pain, and other fears, and is also contrary to the greater part and the greatest of pleasures.

CLIN. You speak most rightly.

GUEST. Will not therefore a legislator, and every one who is in the least degree useful, reverence this fear with the greatest honour, and call it shame, - but denominate confidence the contrary to this, impudence, and consider it as the greatest evil that can befall men, both in public and private?

CLIN. You speak rightly.

GUEST. This fear, therefore, will preserve us in many other and great concerns, and nothing will so much procure for us victory and safety in war, one being opposed to one, as this. For there are two things which procure victory, confidence of the enemy, and the dread of friends with respect to base infamy.

CLIN. It is so.

GUEST. It is necessary, therefore, that each of us should become intrepid, and, at the same time, timid. But we shall show, by division, on what account we ought to become each of these.

CLIN. By all means.

GUEST. When we wish to render any one intrepid, we shall accomplish this by leading him, according to law, to the dread of many terrible things.

CLIN. It appears to.

GUEST. But, what, - when we endeavour to render any one justly terrified, ought we not, by exercising him in impudence, to cause him

d to be victorious in contending with pleasures? Or, by contending with and vanquishing his usual mode of living, ought he not thus to obtain perfection in fortitude? And will not he who is unexperienced and unexercised in contests of this kind remain, as to one half of himself, destitute of virtue? But how can any one be perfectly temperate, who has not contended with and vanquished, by reason, labour and art, in sport and in earnest, many pleasures and desires, which urge him to act impudently and unjustly; but who is impassive with respect to all such things?

CLIN. It is by no means probable that he can.

e GUEST. But what, - has divinity given men any medicine of fear, so that by how much more desirous any one is of drinking it, by so much the more unhappy will he think himself from every draught; so that he will dread every thing, both present and future, and will at length, though he should be the bravest of men, be filled with every kind of dread; and, after having slept, and being freed from the potion, will

648a again every day be equally terrified?

CLIN. And what potion of this kind, shall we say, O guest, is found among men?

GUEST. None. Yet if such a potion should be found, would it be useful to the legislator with respect to fortitude, so that we might thus speak to him respecting it: O legislator, whether you have given laws to

b the Cretans, or to any other nation, are you willing to make trial of your citizens with respect to fortitude and timidity?

CLIN. He would doubtless say, that he was willing.

GUEST. But what, - are you willing to do this with safety, and without great danger; or the contrary?

CLIN. Every one must acknowledge, he would wish to do this with security.

c GUEST. Would you use this potion, leading them to terrors, and accusing them during their perturbation, so as to compel them to become intrepid, by exhortations and honours; disgracing him who will not be persuaded to become in all things such a one as you wish; and dismissing him with impunity who exercises himself in a proper and valiant manner, but punishing him who acts otherwise? or, Would you by no means use this potion, though you could find nothing else in it to accuse?

CLIN. Why should he not use it, O guest?

d GUEST. An exercise, therefore, O friend, different from those at present will possess a wonderful facility, both with respect to one person and a few, and as many as you shall always wish to be exercised. And whether any one, being alone in solitude, should place ignominy before his eyes, thinking that he ought not to be seen till he has made sufficient advances in virtue, and should thus exercise himself against fear, preparing this potion alone, in preference to ten thousand other things, he would do something proper: or whether some one, confiding in his own nature, and being properly prepared by meditation, should not refuse to exercise himself with many drinking associates, and should

e evince, in the necessary consumption of the liquor, a power so transcendent and strong, as neither greatly to err through impudence, nor to be changed through virtue, but towards the end of the liquor should depart without being intoxicated, fearing any human potion the least of all things; - in this case, he would do something well.

CLIN. Certainly. For such a one, by thus acting, would conduct himself with temperance and modesty.

649a GUEST. Again, let us thus address the legislator: Neither, O legislator, has any God given to mankind such a medicine, nor have we devised such a one: (for I do not consider witches at a banquet) but whether or not, is there a potion capable of producing intrepidity, together with vehement and unseasonable confidence? Or how shall we say?

CLIN. There is, and he would say that it is wine.

GUEST. But this produces contrary effects to the potion of which we have just now spoken. For, when a man drinks of it, it makes him at

b first immediately more cheerful than he was before; and by how much more he drinks of it, by so much more is he filled with good hope, and an opinion of his own power; till at length, as if he were a wise man, he becomes replete with all possible freedom of speech and behaviour, and intrepidly both says and does whatever he pleases.

CLIN. I think every one will admit this.

MEGIL. Certainly.

GUEST. But do we recollect that we said there were two things in our

c souls which ought to be cultivated; - the one, that we may possess confidence in the highest degree; but the other, which is the very contrary, that we may be afraid in the highest degree?

CLIN. I think you said this of shame.

GUEST. You very properly remember. But since it is necessary that fortitude and intrepidity in fear should be the subjects of meditation, let us consider whether it will be proper that the contrary should be cultivated in the contrary to fear.

CLIN. It is probable.

GUEST. In those things, therefore, in which, naturally suffering, we are remarkably confident and audacious, in these it will be proper, as it appears, to meditate how we may become in the least degree impudent and audacious, but timid with respect to daring to speak, or suffer, or do any thing base.

CLIN. It appears so.

GUEST. Are not all these, therefore, the things in which we are thus affected, *viz.* anger, love, petulance, ignorance, the love of gain, and timidity; and besides these, riches, beauty, strength, and all such things as, intoxicating men through pleasure, render them delirious? In order to make an easy and innocent trial of all these, and afterwards meditate upon them, what pleasure have we more convenient than that which explores the disposition of men by means of wine, when it is attended with prudent caution? For, let us consider: whether ought we to make trial of a morose and rustic soul, from which a thousand injuries germinate, in his contracts with others, or from his being present at the shows of Bacchus, or from his soul being vanquished in venereal affairs, so as to behold the manners of his soul when his sons, daughter, and wife, are exposed to danger? In short, among ten thousand things, you will not find any thing in which in jest, and without any danger, you can so well contemplate the disposition of any one, as by wine. We ought, therefore, to think that neither the Cretans, nor any other nation, would ever doubt but that this trial of the disposition of each other is convenient, and above all others safe and easy.

CLIN. You speak truly.

GUEST. This, then, will be one of the most useful things, to know the natures and habits of souls by that art whose province it is to procure a remedy for these. But this, as I think, is the province of the politic art. Or is it not?

CLIN. It is entirely so.

BOOK II

652a After this, as it appears, we should consider respecting these particulars, whether this alone is beneficial, to contemplate after what manner we possess certain natures, or whether also some great advantage which deserves much attention is inherent in the proper use of drinking wine in conjunction with others. What then shall we say? Our discourse would seem to insinuate that it is inherent. But when, and after what manner, let us attentively hear, lest we should be impeded in our inquiry by this affair.

CLIN. Speak then.

653a GUEST. I am desirous, therefore, of again recalling to our memory our definition of proper discipline. For the safety of this, as I conjecture at present, consists in the employment we are now speaking of, when well conducted.

CLIN. You speak largely.

GUEST. I say then, that the first puerile sense of boys is pleasure and pain; and that these are first inherent in the soul, in which vice and virtue subsist. But he is happy who in old age acquires the firm possession of prudence† and true opinions. And that man is perfect

b who possesses these, and all the goods they contain. But I call discipline that virtue which first accedes to boys. When pleasure, love, pain, and hatred, are properly produced in the soul, before it is able to receive these attended with reason; if, when they are attended with reason, they accord with it in consequence of being properly accustomed by well adapted manners, then this consent is the whole of virtue. But the proper nurture of the soul, with respect to pleasure and pain, so as that

c it may hate what it ought to hate, immediately from the beginning to the end, and love what it ought to love, - this, if it is considered separately, and is denominated discipline, will, according to my opinion, be properly denominated.

CLIN. What you have said, O guest, formerly and at present, about discipline, appears to be well said.

GUEST. It is well, therefore. For these pleasures and pains, which when properly nurtured are disciplines, are often loosened and corrupted

d by men in the business of life. But the Gods, commiserating the

---

† The prudence of which Plato speaks in this place is intellectual; for this is peculiarly adapted to old age, or the Saturnian period of life.

naturally laborious race of men, ordained for them remissions of labours, and gave them the vicissitudes of festivals[1] in honour of the Gods, together with the Muses, Apollo the leader of the Muses, and Bacchus, as their associates in these celebrations; that in these festivals they might rectify the education of youth, in conjunction with the Gods. Consider, therefore, whether it is proper to say, that our discourse at present is celebrated as true according to nature, or how shall we say? But it asserts, in short, that every youth is incapable of

e being at rest, either in body or voice, but that he always seeks to be moved and to speak; sometimes exulting and leaping, dancing and sporting as it were with pleasure, but at other times uttering sounds with every kind of voice. Other animals, indeed, have no sensation either of order or disorder in motions, which order is denominated rhythm and harmony; but those Gods whom we call associates in the

654a choir have bestowed upon us a rhythmical and harmonic sense, which might agitate us with pleasure, by connecting us with each other through singing and dancing. But the word choir was denominated from joy, as its natural name. In the first place, however, it is necessary to ask, whether we admit that discipline first subsists through the Muses and Apollo? or how shall we say?

CLIN. That it does.

b GUEST. He, therefore, who is void of discipline, is with us one who has never joined a choir; but he who is disciplined is to be considered as one who has sufficiently engaged in a choir.

CLIN. Certainly.

GUEST. But the whole of a choir consists in dancing and singing.

CLIN. It is necessary it should.

GUEST. He, therefore, who is properly disciplined will be able to sing and dance in a becoming manner.

CLIN. It appears so.

GUEST. But let us consider what it is that we have now asserted.

CLIN. What is that?

GUEST. We have spoken of singing and dancing in a becoming manner. But whether or not is it proper to add, that things beautiful

c ought to be the subjects of singing and dancing?

CLIN. This ought to be added.

GUEST. But what, - will he who considers things beautiful, as beautiful, and things base, as base, and who uses them as such, - will such a one be better disciplined for us, with respect to the choir and music, than he who is sufficiently able to become subservient to that

d which he considers as beautiful in body and voice, but yet does not rejoice in things beautiful, nor hate such as are void of beauty? Or he, who, though he is not altogether able to act or think rightly, with respect to his voice and body, yet acts rightly with respect to pleasure and pain; embracing such things as are beautiful, and hating such as are base?

CLIN. You speak, O guest, of a mighty difference of discipline.

GUEST. If, therefore, we three possess a knowledge of the beautiful in singing and dancing, we also know when any one is properly or improperly disciplined: but, if we are ignorant of this, we shall not be
e able to know what is the defence of discipline; and where it is to be found. Is not this the case?

CLIN. It is.

GUEST. Let us, therefore, in the next place, like dogs on the scent, investigate beautiful figure, melody, singing and dancing. For, if these elude our pursuit our discourse about proper discipline, whether Grecian or Barbarian, will be in vain.

CLIN. It will.

655a GUEST. What figure, therefore, or melody, is it proper to call beautiful? Shall we say, that in the same and equal labours the figures and voices of a brave and timid soul are similar?

CLIN. How can they, since neither are their colours similar?

GUEST. Well observed, my companion. But in music there are both figures and melody, since music is conversant with rhythm and harmony. So that melody or figure may possess proper rhythm or harmony, but not a proper colour, that we may speak in the assimilative way, as the masters of the choir are accustomed to assimilate. But there
b is a certain figure or melody of a timid, and of a brave man; and it will be proper to call these things in brave men, beautiful, but in the timid, base. And that we may not be prolix about these particulars, all the figures and melodies which simply adhere to the virtue of the soul or body, or to a certain image of it, are beautiful; but the contrary must be asserted with respect to the vice of the soul or body.

CLIN. You are right; and we judge that these particulars subsist in this manner.

c GUEST. But we must still further consider, whether all of us are similarly delighted with all choirs, or whether this is far from being the case?

CLIN. It is far from being the case.

GUEST. What then shall we say is the cause of our error? Is it because not the same things are beautiful to all? Or shall we say that they are the same things, but do not appear to be the same? For no one will say that a vicious is better than a virtuous choir; or that he is delighted with depraved figures, but others with a muse contrary to this. Though, indeed, most men assert, that the rectitude of music consists in a power which imparts pleasure to the soul. This, however, is neither to be endured, nor is it holy by any means to make such an assertion. But this is more probably the cause of our error.

CLIN. What?

GUEST. Since the particulars respecting choirs are imitations of manners and of actions which take place in all-various fortunes and habits, those by whom the imitations of manners, whether expressed by discourse, or melody, or dancing, are approved, either from nature or custom, or from both, must necessarily rejoice in and praise these, and denominate them beautiful. But those to whom they appear contrary to nature, or manners, or custom, can neither rejoice in nor praise them, but must necessarily denominate them base. And those, again, to whom these particulars happen right by nature, but the contrary from custom; or right from custom, but the contrary from nature; - these will denominate things contrary to pleasures, laudable. For they will assert that each of these is pleasant, but at the same time base. Hence, before others, whom they consider as intelligent persons, they will be ashamed that their body should be moved after that manner, and will blush to sing, and to call such things beautiful, or deserving serious attention; but, by themselves, they will be delighted with them.

CLIN. You speak with the utmost rectitude.

GUEST. Does he then suffer any injury who is delighted with base figures or melodies; or do they receive any advantage who are pleased with the contraries to these?

CLIN. It is probable.

GUEST. Is it only probable, or also necessary, that the same thing should happen as takes place when any one, being conversant with the depraved habits of depraved men, does not hate, but rejoices in and admits them; and yet blames them in jest, having a dreaming perception of his own depravity? For, in this case, it is necessary that he should be assimilated to the things in which he rejoices, although he should be ashamed to praise them. But what greater good, or evil, shall we say, can possibly happen to us than a thing of this kind?

CLIN. I think, none.

GUEST. But where laws are beautifully established, or will be in some future period of time, can we think it will be lawful for poets, in discipline and sport respecting the Muses, to teach in their poetical compositions whatever delights them, by rhythm, or melody, or verse, and to form in choirs the boys and young men of well instituted polities, either to virtue or vice?

CLIN. It is contrary to reason to suppose this would be allowed.

MEGIL. For how is it possible it should be?

d GUEST. But, in short, it is lawful to act in this manner at present in all cities, except Egypt.

CLIN. But how do you say a thing of this kind is established by law in Egypt?

GUEST. It is wonderful to hear. For, as it appears, they formerly knew what we have now said, that young men in cities should be accustomed to beautiful figures and beautiful melodies; and it is one of

e their institutions to exhibit in their temples what these are, and what the qualities which they possess; and besides these, it is not lawful, either for painters or other artificers of figures, to introduce any that are new, or even to think of any other than those belonging to their country: nor is it lawful at present to do this, either in these particulars or in the whole of music. If you observe, therefore, you will find that paintings and sculptures there, which were executed TEN THOUSAND YEARS ago,

657a as if they were not of such great antiquity, are neither more beautiful, nor more deformed, than paintings or carvings of the present day, but are fashioned by just the same art.

CLIN. You speak of a wonderful circumstance.

GUEST. It is, however, a circumstance pertaining to law and politics in a transcendent degree. You will likewise find other things there of a trifling nature. But this respecting music is true, and deserves attention, because the legislator could firmly give laws about things of this kind, and with confidence introduce such melodies as possessed a natural rectitude. But this must be the work of a God, or of some

b divine person. Just as they say there, that their melodies, which have been preserved for such a length of time, are the poems of Isis. So that, as I said, if any one is able to apprehend the rectitude of them, he ought to have the courage to reduce them to law and order. For the search of pleasure and pain, which is always directed to the use of new music, perhaps possesses no great power of corrupting the consecrated choir by an accusation of its antiquity. It appears, therefore, that the choir of the Egyptians was by no means capable of being corrupted, but that the contrary was entirely the case.

c CLIN. From what you have now said, it appears that it must be so.

GUEST. May we not, therefore, confidently say, that a choir is after a certain manner properly connected with sports and music; and, that we rejoice as often as we think that we do well, and, when we rejoice, think we do well? Is it not so?

CLIN. It is.

GUEST. But, rejoicing in a thing of this kind, we are incapable of being at rest.

CLIN. We are so.

d GUEST. Are not, therefore, those among us that are young men prompt to dance? And do not we who are old men think that we conduct ourselves in a becoming manner in beholding these, while we rejoice in their sports, and in their celebration of sacred festivals, since lightness of body fails us at our time of life, - through the desire of which, we thus establish games for those who are able in the highest degree to excite in us the memory of our juvenile period?

CLIN. Most true.

GUEST. Shall we therefore consider that which is said by many of
e those who celebrate sacred festivals, as said in vain, that it is proper to reckon him most wise, and to judge that he will conquer who causes us to be delighted and to rejoice in the greatest degree? For it is proper, since we permit sport in things of this kind, that we should particularly honour him who causes the greatest number and in the greatest degree to rejoice; and, as I just now said, that we should pronounce him victor.
658a Is this, therefore, rightly said, and will a conduct of this kind be right?

CLIN. Perhaps so.

GUEST. But, O blessed man, we should not hastily judge a thing of this kind, but, dividing it into parts, consider after this manner: If any one should at any time simply establish a certain game, but without defining whether it is gymnastic, or equestrian, or musical; and, collecting together all the inhabitants of the city, should proclaim, that he was going to establish a contest for the sake of pleasure alone, in
b which (without expressing the mode of contest) rewards would be assigned for him who gave the spectators the greatest delight, and that for this he would be considered as victor, and as the best of all those engaged in the contest, - what do we think would be the consequence of this proclamation?

CLIN. Of what are you speaking?

GUEST. It is proper that one should exhibit, like Homer, a rhapsody, another the modulation of the harp, another tragedy, and another
c comedy. Nor will it be wonderful, if some one, by exhibiting prodigies, should think that he is especially victorious. But, these and an innumerable multitude of other champions assembling together, can we say which of them is justly the victor?

CLIN. You ask an absurd thing. For, who can give you an answer to this question, unless he has himself been an auditor of each of the champions?

GUEST. Are you therefore willing that I myself should reply to this absurd question?

CLIN. How is it possible I should not?

GUEST. If, therefore, very little children were to judge in this affair, they would give the palm of victory to him who exhibited prodigies: or would they not?

d CLIN. How should they do otherwise?

GUEST. The greater boys, however, would give the preference to those that exhibited comedies; but such women as are better educated than others, young men, and perhaps almost the whole multitude, would prefer to tragedians.

CLIN. Perhaps so.

GUEST. But perhaps we old men should hear with the most pleasure the rhapsodist when properly handling the *Iliad* and *Odyssey*, or some of the works of Hesiod, and should by far proclaim him the victor of all the others. Ought we not, therefore, after this to show who is properly the victor in these contests?

CLIN. Certainly.

e GUEST. It is evident that both I and you ought necessarily to confess, that he will be properly the victor whom those of our age judge to be so; for the skill which we derive from age appears to be every where by far the best of all political concerns.

CLIN. Doubtless.

GUEST. I therefore grant thus much to the multitude, that music ought to be judged by pleasure, yet not by the pleasure it imparts to
659a every man, - but that, nearly, that is the most beautiful muse which delights the best of men, and such as are sufficiently disciplined; but especially when it delights a man who excels in virtue and discipline. On this account we say that judges of these things require virtue, because they ought to participate of prudence and fortitude. For a true judge ought not to learn how to judge from another, and thus become as it were stupefied by the clamours of the multitude, and his own ignorance. But he ought to possess fortitude, because, though he should
b be endued with knowledge, he ought not, through sloth and timidity, to give an unjust decision from the same mouth with which when about to judge he invoked the Gods. For a judge does not sit as a disciple, but rather, as it is just he should, as a master of the spectators, and as one who is averse to things which do not afford the spectators a fit and

proper pleasure. For it was allowed by the ancient and Grecian law, as by that of Sicily and Italy at present, that the multitude of spectators should decide who was victor, by holding up their hands: but this corrupted the poets themselves, who wrote according to the depraved pleasure of vulgar judges: so that the spectators both disciplined themselves and the poets. It likewise corrupted the pleasures of the theatre. For, as it is here proper that the spectators should always hear of manners better than their own, and thus obtain a more excellent pleasure, the very contrary to this takes place at present. What then does the present discourse wish to signify? Consider whether it is this.

CLIN. What?

GUEST. My discourse appears to me to have thrice or four times revolved to the same thing, that discipline is the drawing and leading of youth to that which is called by the law, right reason, and which the most worthy and ancient men have found by experience to be truly right. That the soul of a youth, therefore, may be accustomed by law, and by those who are persuaded by law, not to rejoice in things contrary, but to be delighted or afflicted with the same things as an old man; for the sake of this, those poetical compositions called odes, and which are truly epodes, or incantations to the soul, are composed at present, and which hastily tend to that kind of symphony of which we are speaking. But since the souls of boys are incapable of engaging in serious pursuits, sports and odes were instituted by the legislator. Just as, in curing diseased and imbecil bodies, physicians endeavour to introduce useful food in pleasant meats and drinks, but noxious food in such as are bitter, that they may be rightly accustomed to embrace the one, and hate the other. A proper legislator will persuade the poet to do the same in beautiful and laudable words; and will compel him, if he cannot be persuaded, that when he produces figures of temperate, brave, and, in short, of all good men, in rhythms, and melodies in harmonies, he shall produce them properly.

CLIN. By Jupiter, O guest, does it appear to you that this is done at present in other cities? For I do not know of any city in which what you speak of takes place, except ours, and that of the Lacedæmonians. But in other cities there are always some new regulations about dancing, and the rest of the music; and this not from any mutation in the laws, but from certain inordinate pleasures, which are very far from remaining perpetually the same, like those Egyptian regulations which you related, but continually vary.

GUEST. Most excellent, O Clinias! But if I have appeared to you, as you say, to assert these things as existing at present, I shall not wonder that I have done this in consequence of not clearly unfolding my meaning. But having spoken about certain particulars, which I wished to take place, respecting music, I perhaps appeared to you to speak as if they actually existed at present. For, to blame a thing which is incurable, and which is very far advanced in error, is by no means pleasant, though sometimes necessary. But, as we are thus far agreed, will you not say that these things subsist among us, and those, more than among the other Greeks?

CLIN. Certainly.

GUEST. But if they should also take place among others, would they not be better conducted than at present?

CLIN. By far better, if they subsisted as you just now said they ought to subsist, and as they subsist among those and with us.

GUEST. Shall we then agree at present, that the things asserted by you, in every kind of discipline and music, are these: that poets should be compelled to assert that a good man, being temperate and just, is happy and blessed, whether he is large and robust, small and weak, rich or poor; but that an unjust man is miserable, and passes his days in sorrow, though he should be richer than Cinyras or Midas? A poet, therefore, if he speaks rightly, will say to us: I shall never mention nor consider him as a man, who does not perform with justice, and possess every thing which is denominated beautiful in conduct. Such a one too, being just, will desire to contend with his enemies in close engagement. But he who is unjust will neither dare to behold bloody slaughter, nor to vanquish, running, the Thracian Boreas, nor will he acquire any of those things which are denominated good. For the things which are called by the many good, are not rightly denominated. For it is said that health is the best thing; beauty the next; strength the third; and riches the fourth. And an innumerable multitude of other things are called good. Thus, to see and hear acutely, and to possess in a proper manner all such things as belong to the senses; likewise to do in a tyrannical manner whatever you please, appears to be good. And besides this, it is considered as the end of all blessedness to become in the most rapid manner immortal, while possessing all these. But you and I say that all these are the best of possessions to just and holy men, but that to unjust men they are the worst of all things, beginning the enumeration from health. For to be well, to see, hear, and possess the other senses, and, in short, to live, is the greatest evil, though a man should be immortal through the whole of time, and possess every thing that is called good, if all these are not attended with justice and every virtue. But it is a less evil to live in this manner for the shortest time. I think that your poets should speak in this manner, and that you should persuade and compel them to do so, and to instruct the youth, through rhythms and harmonies, consequent to these assertions. Do you perceive this? For

d   I clearly assert, that the things which are called evil are good to the unjust, but evil to the just; but that things good are truly good to the good, but evil to the wicked. Do, therefore, you and I agree in what is said, or not?

CLIN. We appear partly to agree, and partly not.

GUEST. Perhaps I have not persuaded you that he is not happy, but clearly wretched, who alone possesses in himself injustice and insolence, though he should be healthy and rich, and a tyrant to the end of life; and, besides all these, should be endued with uncommon strength of

e   body, in conjunction with immortality, and should never experience any of these things which are called evils.

CLIN. You speak most truly.

GUEST. Be it so then. But what ought we to say after this? If he is valiant, and strong, and beautiful, and rich, and accomplishes through

662a the whole of life whatever he desires, - will he not necessarily appear to you, if he is unjust and insolent, to live in a shameful manner?

CLIN. Entirely so.

GUEST. Will he not also appear to you to live badly?

CLIN. This will not in a similar manner appear to me.

GUEST. But will you not admit that he must live unpleasantly, and in a manner contrary to his interest?

CLIN. How can I admit this?

b   GUEST. How? If a God, my friends, should cause us to agree in sentiment, as we now nearly dissent from each other. For these things appear to me so necessary, that Crete, O friend Clinias, does not more clearly appear to be an island. And if I were a legislator, I would endeavour to compel the poets, and all the other inhabitants of the city, to speak in this manner: and I would ordain, that nearly the greatest of

c   all punishments should be inflicted on him who should assert, in the country to which he belonged, that there are certain men of a base character who lead a pleasant life; or that some things are advantageous and lucrative, but others more just. And I would persuade my citizens to assert many other things, contrary to what are now advanced by the Cretans and Lacedæmonians, as it appears, and, indeed by the rest of mankind. For, by Jupiter and Apollo, O best of men! if we should ask those Gods who gave us laws, whether the most just is the most pleasant

d   life, or whether there are two certain lives, one of which is most pleasant, and the other most just: - if, in answer to our inquiry, they should say there are two lives, we might, perhaps, again ask them (if we inquire properly) which we ought to call most happy; those who lead the most just, or those who lead the most pleasant life. If they should say, those who lead the most pleasant life, their answer would be absurd. But I am desirous that a thing of this kind should not be said by the Gods, but rather by our fathers and legislators. I shall therefore put the same question to my father and legislator, and I shall suppose him to reply, that he who lives the most pleasant life is the most blessed. After this, I shall thus interrogate him: O father, do you not wish me to live most happily? But you never cease exhorting me to live most justly. He, therefore, who acts in this manner, whether he is a legislator or a father, acts I think absurdly, and speaks inconsistently. But if he should evince that the most just life is the most blessed, every one who hears him may, I think, inquire what it is which the law praises in that life as good and beautiful, and better than pleasure. For, what good separate from pleasure can be present to the just man? Can it be said that renown and praise, both from men and Gods, are good and beautiful, but at the same time unpleasant? and that the contrary is true with respect to infamy? We shall say, By no means, O legislator. But is neither to do an injury, nor to suffer one, unpleasant indeed, but at the same time good, or beautiful? And are other things pleasant, but shameful and base?

CLIN. How can they?

GUEST. The reason, therefore, which neither separates the pleasant and the just, nor the good and the beautiful, is persuasive, if to nothing else, yet at least to the wish to live a holy and just life. So that the discourse of the legislator will be most shameful and discordant, if he denies that these things are so. For no one will voluntarily wish to be persuaded to do that which is not attended with more joy than sorrow. But that which is beheld afar off affects every one, as I may say, and even boys, with a dark vertigo. The legislator, therefore, dispersing the darkness, shall establish for us an opinion the contrary to this; and shall persuade the citizens, by custom, and praise, and arguments, that both things just and unjust are involved in shade; and that things unjust, which appear contrary to the just, being surveyed by the unjust and depraved man, seem to be pleasant, but things just, most unpleasant: but when they are surveyed by the just man, they appear to be entirely the contrary.

CLIN. It appears so.

GUEST. But which of these decisions, shall we say, is most true? Whether is it that of the worse, or of the better soul?

CLIN. Necessarily that of the better soul.

d   GUEST. It is necessary, therefore, that an unjust life should not only be more base and depraved, but, in reality, more unpleasant, than a just and holy life.

CLIN. It appears so, my friend, according to the present reasoning.

GUEST. A legislator, therefore, who is in the least degree useful, though what we have now asserted should not subsist in this manner, - yet, as there is not any thing else which can be more advantageous to youth, he will venture to assert it, though false, for their good; because

e   he will thus be enabled to lead them to act justly, not by force, but willingly.

CLIN. Truth, indeed, O guest, is beautiful and stable: but it does not appear easy to persuade.

GUEST. Be it so. But that fable of the Sidonian, though improbable, yet easily persuades, as well as an innumerable multitude of others.

CLIN. What fable?

GUEST. That, teeth being once sown, armed men were produced from

664a   them. For this may serve as a great example to a legislator, that any one may persuade the souls of young men to whatever he pleases. So that he ought, by considering, to find out nothing else than by what means he may confer, through persuasion, the greatest good on the city; and should, by every possible contrivance, discover after what manner the whole of such an association may always speak one and the same thing about these particulars, through the whole of life, in odes, fables, and discourses. But if it appears to you to be otherwise, no discord will arise from this difference in opinion.

b   CLIN. It does not appear to me that either of us can doubt about these particulars.

GUEST. I will, therefore, continue my discourse. I say then, that it is necessary to insinuate, as by enchantment, all the choirs, which are three, into the young and tender souls of boys, together with all such other beautiful things as we have spoken of, and which yet remain for us to discuss. But the principal thing among them is this: that if the life

c   which is pronounced by the Gods to be the most pleasant, and the best, appears to be the same with that which we have described, we shall have spoken most truly, and shall more persuade those whom we ought to persuade, than if we had asserted anything else.

CLIN. What you say must be granted.

GUEST. In the first place, therefore, the puerile choir of muses should enter, being about to sing things of this kind, with all possible earnestness to the whole city. In the second place, that choir which consists of men thirty years old shall invoke the God Pæan as a witness of the truth of what is said, and shall beseech him, together with the divinity Persuasion, to be propitious to the youth. But it is necessary that there should be a third choir, consisting of those who are between thirty and sixty years old. But the mythologists about the same odes, who are more advanced in years than these, as they will no longer be able to sing to the harp, ought agreeably to a divine oracle to be dismissed.

CLIN. Who do you mean, O guest, by these third choirs? for I do not clearly understand what you wish to say about them.

GUEST. These are nearly those for whose sake most of the above assertions were made.

CLIN. We do not yet understand: endeavour therefore to speak yet clearer.

GUEST. We said, if I remember, in the beginning of this discourse, that the nature of every youth was so ardent, that it could not be at rest either in body or voice, but that it was always speaking and leaping without order; and that no other animal possessed a sense of the order of both these, but that this was alone the province of the nature of man. We likewise said, that rhythm was the name given to the order of motion, but harmony to that of the voice, when the sharp and the flat are mingled together; and that both together are denominated a choir. We still further asserted, that the Gods, commiserating our nature, gave us Apollo and the Muses as our associates in and leaders of the choir; and Bacchus (if we recollect) as the third.

CLIN. How is it possible we should not remember?

GUEST. We have therefore spoken concerning the choir of Apollo and the Muses: and hence it is necessary that we should speak respecting the third and remaining choir, or that of Bacchus.

CLIN. Inform me how you mean: for a Bacchic choir of old men appears, on the first hearing, to be very absurd; if those who form this choir exceed thirty, so as to be from fifty to sixty years old.

GUEST. You speak most truly. But I think reason is requisite, that it may appear how this may be opportunely accomplished.

CLIN. Certainly.

GUEST. Do we therefore agree in what has been previously said?

CLIN. Respecting what?

GUEST. That every man and boy, those who are free, and those who are slaves, the male and the female, and in short the whole city, should sing these things to the whole city without ceasing, according to all the varieties of harmony, so as that those who sing the hymns may experience an insatiable pleasure.

CLIN. How is it possible not to acknowledge that these things ought to be so?

d GUEST. But by what means will the best part of the city, and which is most capable of persuading by age, in conjunction with prudence, be able, by singing the most beautiful things, to be the cause of the greatest good? or shall we foolishly omit that which will be the most principal thing in the most beautiful and most useful odes?

CLIN. In consequence of what has been just now said, it is impossible to omit it.

GUEST. How then will it be accomplished in a becoming manner? Consider, if in this way.

CLIN. How?

e GUEST. Every one who is more advanced in age, being full of sluggishness with respect to odes, will be less delighted with these; and by how much the older and more modest he is, by so much the more will he necessarily be ashamed to sing. Will it not be so?

CLIN. It will.

GUEST. He will therefore be still more ashamed to sing, standing upright in the theatres, before an all-various multitude of men; especially if the choir, like those that contend for victory when exercising their voice, should be compelled to sing though lean and fasting; for, thus circumstanced, they will not sing without molestation and shame, and,

666a when they do, it will be without alacrity.

CLIN. You speak of things most necessary.

GUEST. How then shall we render them disposed to engage in odes with alacrity? Shall we not ordain by law, in the first place, that boys shall not by any means taste wine till they are eighteen years old? For we ought to teach them, that it is not proper to deduce like a river, fire to fire, into the body and soul, before they begin to engage in manly labours; but that we should dread the furious habit of youth. In the

b next place, we should inform them that wine is to be moderately used till they are thirty years old, and that young men should by all means avoid intoxication and abundance of wine. But when they have attained the fortieth year, then they may be allowed to attend feasts, to invoke the other Gods, and beseech Bacchus to be present at the mystic ceremonies and sports of the old men; for this divinity bestowed wine upon men as a remedy against the austerity of old age, that through this we might acquire a second youth, forget sorrow, and render the manners

c of our soul softer, - just as iron is softened by the actions of fire. In the first place, therefore, will not every one who is thus affected, be willing, with more alacrity and less shame, not indeed in a great but in a moderate multitude, nor among strangers, but his familiars, to sing, and, as we have often said, to enchant?

CLIN. Very much so.

GUEST. This mode then will not be altogether improper to induce them to join with us in singing.

d   CLIN. By no means.

GUEST. But with what voice, and with what muse, will these men sing? or is it not evident that it will be with such a one as is adapted to them?

CLIN. Undoubtedly.

GUEST. But which will be adapted to divine men? Will it not be that of choirs?

CLIN. We indeed, O guest, and these, are not able to sing any thing else than that which we have learnt in the choirs, having been accustomed thus to sing.

GUEST. It is reasonable it should be so. For you have not in reality

e   been partakers of the most beautiful singing; and this because your government is rather military than civil. Hence your young men are like a compact multitude of colts feeding together in herds. And no one of your people, taking to himself his own offspring, commits him as it were to a groom, that his fierceness may be tamed, and that he may be gently and mildly educated, and from whom he may receive every thing proper to the discipline of youth; whence he may not only become a good soldier, but an able governor of a city, and one who, in

67a   the beginning we said, would be more warlike than the soldiers of Tyrtæus, and would always and every where, both in private and public, honour the possession of fortitude, as ranking in the fourth, and not in the first place among the virtues.

CLIN. I do not know, O guest of ours, for what reason you again degrade our legislators.

GUEST. It is not my intention, excellent man, to do so, if I do it; but where reason leads, there, if you are willing, we will direct our course. For if we possess a muse more beautiful than that of the choirs, and the

b   common theatres, we will endeavour to impart this to such as we said were ashamed of that muse, and endeavoured to participate of one more beautiful.

CLIN. Entirely so.

GUEST. In the first place, then, it is proper that this should be present to all whom a certain grace follows, that either the grace itself alone should be the most approved, or a certain rectitude, or, in the third place, advantage. Thus, for example, a grace follows food and drink, and every kind of aliment, and this grace we call pleasure: but if it contributes to health, we denominate it rectitude and utility.

CLIN. Entirely so.

GUEST. Thus, too, a grace follows discipline, which is also called pleasure; and the truth resulting from discipline is denominated rectitude and advantage, the beneficial and the becoming.

CLIN. It is so.

GUEST. But what? In the artificial production of similitudes, when pleasure is the result of such productions, may not such pleasure be most justly denominated a grace?

CLIN. Certainly.

GUEST. But, in short, the equality of such things, rather than pleasure, renders them such and so great.

CLIN. It is well said.

GUEST. Hence that alone can be rightly judged by pleasure, which neither affords a certain advantage, nor truth, nor similitude; nor yet again is the cause of any injury, but which alone subsists for the sake of that grace which follows other things, and which may be most beautifully denominated pleasure, when none of these attend it.

CLIN. Do you alone speak of innoxious pleasure?

GUEST. I do; I say that this is sport, when it is neither the cause of any thing detrimental or advantageous, which deserves serious consideration.

CLIN. You speak most truly.

GUEST. Shall we not then assert, from what has been now said, that it is fit all imitations should be judged in the least degree by pleasure and false opinion, and in like manner, all equality? For it does not follow, that because *this* thing appears to some one to be equal, or some one is delighted with *that*, that therefore *this* thing is equal, or *that* possesses symmetry; but it is so from truth, the most of all things.

CLIN. Entirely so.

GUEST. Do we not therefore say, that all music is assimilative and imitative?

CLIN. Certainly.

GUEST. In the smallest degree, therefore, when any one says that music is to be judged by pleasure, is such an assertion to be admitted, and in the smallest degree is such a music to be inquired after as a serious thing, if it is any where to be found; but that music alone is to be explored which possesses similitude by its imitation of the beautiful.

CLIN. Most true.

GUEST. Those, therefore, that inquire after the most beautiful singing, and the most beautiful muse, ought, as it appears, to explore not that which is pleasant in each of these, but that which is right. For the rectitude of imitation, as we have said, consists in expressing the magnitude and quality of that which it represents, such as they are.

CLIN. How should it not be so?

GUEST. But every one will acknowledge this with respect to music, that all poems are an assimilation and imitation of it. Or, do you think that all poets, auditors, and players, will not assent to this?

CLIN. Very much so.

GUEST. But it is proper, as it appears, to know respecting every poem, what kind of a thing it is, if any one wishes not to err in deciding upon it. For he who does not know what the essence of it means, nor of what it is the image, will never understand the rectitude or erroneousness of its intention.

CLIN. It is impossible he should.

GUEST. But can he who does not know the rectitude of a performance ever be able to know whether it is well or ill accomplished? I do not indeed speak in a manner perfectly clear; but, perhaps, I shall thus speak with more perspicuity.

CLIN. How?

GUEST. There are ten thousand similitudes which have reference to the sight.

CLIN. Certainly.

GUEST. What then? If any one is ignorant what each of the imitated bodies is, can he ever know whether it is properly represented? as, for instance, whether the representation possesses the joints and respective members of the body, their positions, number, and quality, such as they ought to be, and besides all these, the proper colours and figures; or, on the contrary, whether all these are exhibited in a disordered manner. Do you think that any one can at all know these particulars who is unacquainted with the animal which is imitated?

CLIN. How should he?

GUEST. But if any one knows that it is a man who is painted, or otherwise represented, and that he has received all his parts, colours and figures, from art, would it be necessary that he who knows this should likewise readily know whether the representation is beautiful, or whether it is in any respect defective in beauty?

CLIN. We should all of us, O guest, as I may say, know the beautiful parts of animals.

GUEST. You speak with perfect propriety. Is it not therefore necessary, that a prudent judge should possess these three things about every image, both in painting and music? In the first place, that he
b   should know what the thing is; in the second place, that it possesses rectitude; and, in the third place, that the image is properly executed in words, melodies, and rhythms?

CLIN. It appears so.

GUEST. We should not, therefore, omit to speak concerning the difficulty which is in music. For, since it is more celebrated than other images, it requires more caution than the rest. For he who errs in this will be injured in the greatest degree, since he will thus conciliate to himself depraved manners. But it is most difficult to be known, because
c   poets are more depraved than the Muses. For these are incapable of erring to so great a degree as, in fashioning the words of men, to give the figure and melody of women; or, in composing the melody and figures of those who are free, to harmonize together the rhythms of slaves and the free-born; or, in exhibiting rhythms and liberal figures, to
d   assign a melody or discourse contrary to the rhythms. Besides this, they will never place together the voices of beasts, and men, and instruments, and every kind of noise, as imitating one certain thing. But human poets combine things of this kind together in the greatest degree, and irrationally mingle them with each other, exciting such men by these means to laugh, who, as Orpheus says, "are allotted the elegance of delight." For they perceive all these particulars mingled together: and, besides this, the poets dilacerate rhythm and figures separate from
e   melody, arranging naked words in measure; producing melody and rhythm without words; and employing the naked sound of the harp and the pipe. Among which particulars, it is very difficult to know the intention of the rhythm and harmony which subsist without words, and to which of the imitations deserving to be mentioned they are similar. But it is necessary to consider every thing of this kind as replete with rusticity; as immoderately loving swiftness without falling, and the voice
670a   of wild beasts, and on this account using the melody of the harp and the pipe for other purposes than dancing and singing. But to use either of these instruments unaccompanied with words, is full of all unskilfulness and legerdemain. But the reason of this is as follows: We do not consider that we ought not to employ our Muses when we are fifty, or thirty, years old, but we ought to find out when it is proper. Our discourse, however, appears to me, from what has been said, to signify thus much concerning the muse belonging to choirs, that it is necessary
b   those who are fifty years old should be better instructed than others in

the particulars belonging to singing. For they must necessarily possess a proper sensation and knowledge of rhythms and harmonies. Or how can they know the rectitude of melodies; to what the Doric harmony is proper or improper; and whether the rhythm which the poet has united to it is right, or not?

CLIN. It is evident that they cannot by any means.

GUEST. But the numerous vulgar are ridiculous in thinking that they sufficiently know what is well harmonized, and possesses proper rhythm, and what is not so: for these have been *compelled* to sing and walk in rhythm. But in consequence of doing each of these ignorantly, they would not syllogize as follows: Every melody, when it possesses things which accord, subsists in a proper manner; but when it does not possess things which accord, it is defective.

CLIN. Most necessarily so.

GUEST. What then? Can he who does not understand what it possesses, and what its definition is, know, as we have said, how it properly subsists at any time in any one?

CLIN. How is it possible he should?

GUEST. This then, as it appears, we have now discovered, that those singers which we have now called upon, and have after a manner compelled to sing voluntarily, ought from necessity to be disciplined thus far, as to be able each of them to follow the progressions of the rhythms, and the chords of the melodies, that, perceiving the harmonies and the rhythms, they may choose such as are fit to be sung by so many, and by such particular persons; and, thus singing, may themselves immediately be innocently delighted, and thus induce young men to embrace worthy manners. But, being thus far instructed, they will participate of a more accurate discipline than that which is directed to the multitude, and to poets themselves. For, in the third place, it is by no means necessary that a poet should know whether the imitation is beautiful or not; but it is nearly necessary that he should know this of harmony and rhythm. But all the three ought to be known for the sake of choosing the most beautiful, and the second; for otherwise they will never become a sufficient enchantment to youth to the acquisition of virtue. And thus, that which our discourse intended in the beginning, *viz.* that it might afford proper assistance to the choir of Bacchus, has been accomplished by us to the utmost of our ability. But let us consider whether this should be accomplished in this manner. For such an assembly must necessarily be tumultuous, in consequence of the compotation proceeding to a greater degree, which we supposed in the beginning of our discourse must necessarily happen to drinking associations of the present day.

CLIN. It is necessary it should.

GUEST. But every one becoming lighter than himself will be elevated and delighted; will be filled with freedom of speech; and in this condition will not hear him who is near him, but will consider himself sufficient both to govern himself and others.

CLIN. Certainly.

GUEST. Have we not said, that, when these things take place, the souls of the drinkers, being rendered fervid, will become more soft and c juvenile, like iron heated in the fire? so that they may be easily led, as when they were young, by those who are able and know how to instruct and fashion them: but that he who is able to fashion them is the same as he who was then said to be a good legislator, by whose laws respecting compotation he may be restrained who is confident and audacious, and more impudent than is proper, and who is unwilling to endure order with respect to silence, discourse, drinking, and the muse; and may be willing to act in a contrary manner in every respect; sending out against advancing and base confidence, the most beautiful opposing d fear, in conjunction with justice; which divine fear we have denominated shame and modesty.

CLIN. It is so.

GUEST. But the guardians and fabricators of these laws ought, as leaders of those that are not sober, to be themselves free from perturbation and ebriety; without which it is more difficult to fight against intoxication than to contend with enemies without unterrified leaders. But he who is unwilling to be persuaded by these, and by the e leaders of Bacchus who are more than sixty years old, sustains an equal, and indeed a greater disgrace than he who is unpersuaded by the leaders of Mars.

CLIN. Right.

GUEST. If such ebriety and such sport were adopted, would not such 672a drinking associates derive great utility from thence, and be more conjoined in friendship than before, and not be enemies as at present? Would not likewise the whole of their association be according to law, in consequence of the sober being the leaders of the intoxicated?

CLIN. Certainly, if the ebriety was conducted in the manner you now speak of.

GUEST. We ought not, therefore, to blame the gift of Bacchus simply, as if it were evil, and not worthy to be received into the city. For much more might yet be said to this purpose; though I should be fearful to disclose to the multitude the greatest good which this divinity imparts, because men when they hear it will not receive and understand it as they ought.

CLIN. What is that good?

GUEST. A certain narration and rumour has devolved to us, that this God was once disordered in his mind by his mother Juno, and that on this account he introduced the Bacchic rites, and the whole of the insane choir, that he might take vengeance on the Goddess. It is further reported, that for this purpose he bestowed wine upon mankind. But I leave things of this kind to be said by those who think that they can assert them with safety respecting the Gods. Thus much, however, I know, that no animal is born with such, and so much, intelligence as is proper to it, when it acquires a perfection of intellect. But every animal, during the time in which it has not yet obtained its proper prudence, rages and vociferates in a disordered manner; and when any one slays it rapidly, it again leaps without order.[†] But we may recollect that we said these were the principles of music and gymnastic.

CLIN. We do recollect.

GUEST. Did we not also say, that this principle imparted to us the sense of rhythm and harmony? and that Apollo, the Muses, and Bacchus, were the causes of these?

CLIN. Certainly.

GUEST. But wine, according to the assertions of some, was given to men as a punishment, that they might be rendered, through it, insane. Agreeably, however, to what has now been asserted by us, it is on the contrary a medicine; and was imparted that the soul might acquire shame, but the body health and strength.

CLIN. You have very beautifully, O guest, reminded us of what has been said.

GUEST. But now the half of the particulars pertaining to the choir is complete. Shall we finish or omit the remaining part?

CLIN. What parts do you speak of; and how do you divide each of them?

GUEST. According to us, the whole of the choir is the whole of discipline. But, of this, one part consists in vocal rhythms and harmonies.

CLIN. Certainly.

[†] *Viz.* in another life: for the soul carries with it into another the habits and manners which it possessed in the present life.

GUEST. But the other in the motion of the body, which has rhythm in common with the motion of the voice, but figure peculiar to itself: but, in the former part, melody is the motion of the voice.

CLIN. Most true.

673a GUEST. I know not, therefore, after what manner we have denominated things pertaining to the voice, which extend as far as to the soul, and contribute to the discipline of virtue, music.

CLIN. They were rightly called so.

GUEST. But things pertaining to the body, which we have called dancing in sport, if such a motion should extend as far as to the virtue of the body, we should denominate the artificial leading of it to this purpose, gymnastic.

CLIN. Most right.

GUEST. But we appear to have spoken sufficiently of that part of music, which we have said is the half of the choir. Shall we, therefore,
b speak of the remaining half, or how shall we do?

CLIN. O most excellent man, who art discoursing with Cretans and Lacedæmonians, as you have spoken sufficiently about music, but gymnastic remains yet to be discussed, what do you think each of us ought to reply to your interrogation?

GUEST. I shall say that you have perspicuously answered by your question. For I understand that your present interrogation is, as I have
c said, an answer, and, besides this, a mandate to discuss the particulars about gymnastic.

CLIN. You apprehend my meaning excellently well; and therefore discuss these particulars.

GUEST. We shall do so: for it is not very difficult to speak about things known to both of you. And besides, you are far more skilled in this art than in that of music.

CLIN. You nearly speak the truth.

d GUEST. Is not, therefore, the principle of this sport, every animal being naturally accustomed to leap? But man, as we have said, receiving a sense of rhythm, generated and brought forth dancing. And melody, recalling to mind, and exciting rhythm, these two, communicating with each other, brought forth the choir and sport.

CLIN. Most true.

GUEST. One part of this we have said we have already discussed, and that we should in the next place endeavour to discuss the remaining part.

CLIN. Entirely so.

GUEST. We will, therefore, first of all bring to a conclusion the choir of intoxication, if it is agreeable to you.

CLIN. Of what are you speaking?

GUEST. If any city should use drinking associations as a serious concern, with law and order, and as an exercise to the acquisition of temperance, and should not at the same time avoid other pleasures, but in a similar manner should engage in them for the sake of subduing them, after this manner it may be allowed to use all these. But if it uses drinking associations as sport, and gives permission to any one to drink when he pleases, and with whom he pleases, and to engage in any other pursuit without restraint, I should not be of this opinion, that this city, or any individual in it, ought, at any time, to make use of intoxication. But I should much prefer the law of the Carthaginians to the custom of the Cretans and Lacedæmonians. For their law forbids any one belonging to the camp to taste of wine, but orders water to be drunk during all this period. I likewise would not permit it to be drunk in the city by either male or female slaves; nor by magistrates during the year of their office; nor by pilots, nor judges, when engaged in their respective employments; nor, in short, by any one when deliberating about things of importance. Again, I would not permit it to be drunk by any one in the day-time, unless for the sake of bodily exercise or disease; nor by a man and woman at night, when they intend to beget children. And many other circumstances might be adduced, in which those who possess a sound mind, and conform to good laws, will abstain from wine. So that, according to this reasoning, no city has occasion for a multitude of vineyards. But other concerns of agriculture, and every thing respecting diet, should be orderly disposed: and wine should be nearly used in the most moderate and least degree of all things. And this, if it is agreeable to you, O guests, shall be the conclusion of my discourse respecting wine.

CLIN. Beautifully said: and it is agreeable to us it should be so.

BOOK III

676a And thus much concerning these particulars. But shall we say that civil government had a certain beginning? And may not any one behold it hence with ease, and in the most beautiful manner?

CLIN. Whence?

b GUEST. Whence any one may behold the progress of cities to virtue, and at the same time to vice.

CLIN. Whence do you say?

GUEST. I think, indeed, from a length and infinity of time, and from the mutations in it.

CLIN. How do you say?

GUEST. Do you appear to have ever understood what a multitude of time has elapsed since cities and the politic institutions of men commenced?

CLIN. This is by no means easy to understand.

GUEST. It is indeed infinite,† and impossible to be expressed.

CLIN. Entirely so.

GUEST. Will not myriads upon myriads of cities have subsisted in this time? and, in consequence of the same temporal infinity, have not as many been destroyed? and will they not every where have been governed according to every kind of polity; and at one time pass from the lesser to the greater, and at another from the greater to the lesser; and have become worse from the better, and better from the worse?

CLIN. It is necessary.

GUEST. Let us therefore assign, if we are able, the cause of this mutation: for perhaps it may exhibit to us the first generation and mutation of polities.

CLIN. You speak well. It is therefore necessary that you should readily unfold what you conceived to be the truth concerning them, and that we should at the same time follow you.

677a GUEST. Do ancient discourses then appear to you to possess any truth?

CLIN. Of what kind?

---

† From hence it is evident that they are not genuine Platonists, who contend that according to Plato the world had a beginning. See the *Timæus*.

GUEST. That there have been many destructions of the human race, through deluges, diseases, and many other things, in which a very small part of mankind was left.

CLIN. Every thing of this kind must be very probable to every one.

GUEST. Let us then consider one of these destructions out of many, - I mean that which was caused by a deluge.

CLIN. What ought we to think about this?

b GUEST. That those who then escaped the destruction were nearly mountain shepherds, a few dormant sparks of the human race, preserved on the summits of mountains.

CLIN. Evidently so.

GUEST. But such as these must necessarily have been ignorant of other arts, and of those artifices in cities of men towards each other, with a view of prerogative and contention, and other base ends.

CLIN. It is likely.

c GUEST. But we shall also suppose that the cities which were situated in plains, and those bordering on the sea, entirely perished at that time.

CLIN. We will suppose so.

GUEST. We must assert, therefore, that all instruments were destroyed at the time, together with every invention pertaining to art, politic discipline, or any other certain wisdom.

CLIN. For how, O most excellent man, if these particulars remained through the whole of time in the same perfection as at present, could anything new have ever been invented? It is because an innumerable d multitude of years was unknown to the inventors. But one or two thousand years have elapsed since some things were invented by Dædalus, others by Orpheus, and others by Palamedes. The particulars indeed respecting music were discovered by Marsyas and Olympus; but those relating to the lyre by Amphion. And a multitude of other things were, as I may say, invented by others but yesterday.

GUEST. Do you not perceive, O Clinias, that you have omitted to mention the friend who was yesterday present?

CLIN. Do you mean Epimenides?

e GUEST. I do. For he far excelled all among you in inventions; and, as you say, brought to perfection in reality what Hesiod had formerly divined in his writings.

CLIN. We do say so.

GUEST. We must assert, therefore, that when that devastation by a deluge took place, human affairs were in a state of infinite and dreadful solitude; that a prodigious part of the earth was unprolific; and other 678a animals having perished, some herds of oxen, and a few goats, which were rarely found, supplied those men with food that escaped the devastation.

CLIN. Doubtless.

GUEST. But are we of opinion that there was then any memory of a city, politic discipline, and legislation, which is the subject of our present discourse?

CLIN. By no means.

GUEST. From these people, therefore, thus circumstanced, all the particulars which exist at present derived their subsistence; *viz.* cities and polities, arts and laws, many vices and many virtues.

CLIN. How do you say?

b GUEST. Can we be of opinion, O wonderful man, that as those who then existed were ignorant of many beautiful things pertaining to citizens, and many of a contrary nature, they could ever become perfect either in virtue or vice?

CLIN. You speak well; and I understand what you say.

GUEST. In consequence, therefore, of the progression of time, and the increase of the human race, all things advanced to the condition of all things at present.

CLIN. Most right.

GUEST. But this was probably not effected suddenly, and in a short, but in a very extended period of time.

c CLIN. It is very proper it should be so.

GUEST. For I think that fear would prevent all the inhabitants from descending from their elevated abodes to the plains.

CLIN. Certainly.

GUEST. Would not likewise those who lived at that time be delighted in beholding each other, on account of their paucity? And would they not have nearly lost, as I may say, all the artificial means of passing over to each other, either by land or sea? I do not therefore think it would

d be very possible for them to mingle with each other. For iron and brass and all metals would have perished, confused together; so that it would be impossible to separate and bring them into light. Hence trees would be but rarely cut down. For, if any instrument should happen to be left on the mountains, these rapidly wearing away would vanish; and no other could be made, till the metallic art should again be discovered by men.

CLIN. How indeed could it?

GUEST. But in how many generations afterwards do we think this would take place?

e CLIN. It is evident, in a great many.

GUEST. The arts therefore which are employed about iron and brass, and all such things, must at the same time be involved in darkness, and indeed in a still greater degree.

CLIN. Undoubtedly.

GUEST. Sedition, therefore, together with war, must at that time be every where extirpated.

CLIN. How so?

GUEST. In the first place, they will be benevolent towards and love each other, on account of their solitude. In the next place, food will not be the cause of war to them: for pastures will be rare; a few only perhaps remaining from the first, in which the inhabitants of that time will for the most part live. For they will not by any means be in want of milk and animal food. Further still, hunting will supply them with food, neither of a bad kind nor in a small quantity. They will likewise possess abundance of clothing, beds and habitations, together with apparatus pertaining to fire, and such as has no occasion for fire. The plastic too and weaving arts will not be indigent of iron. But divinity imparted all these together with these arts to men, that, if at any time they should fall into so great a calamity, they might be able to propagate the human race. On this account, at that time they were not very poor, nor were they compelled by poverty to quarrel with each other. But neither could they ever become rich, because they were without silver and gold. But in any association where neither riches nor poverty take up their abode, in this the most just manners will nearly be found. For neither insolence nor injustice, neither emulation nor envy, can subsist in such a society. From these causes, and through their innocence which we have spoken of, they were good. For, whenever they heard that any thing was beautiful or base, they thought, in consequence of their innocence, that it was most truly said to be so, and were persuaded. For no one was suspected of lying, through his wisdom, as is the case at present; but, believing all that was asserted about Gods and men to be true, they lived conformably to what they heard; on which account they were altogether such as we a little before represented them to be.

CLIN. These things appear both to me and this other to be so.

GUEST. We say moreover, that many generations living in this manner, both of those prior to the deluge and of those at present, they must be less skilful and less learned both in warlike and other arts, which at present are exercised by land and sea; likewise in judicial affairs and seditions, which men have devised both in words and works, with every possible subtilty of contrivance, in order to injure and act unjustly e   towards each other. That besides this they must be more innocent, brave, and at the same time modest, and in every respect more just. But of these things we have already assigned the cause.

CLIN. You speak with rectitude.

GUEST. These things, therefore, have been asserted by us; and we shall
680a speak of every thing consequent to these particulars, for the sake of understanding what occasion they had at that time for laws, and who was their legislator.

CLIN. You have spoken well.

GUEST. Were they, therefore, neither indigent of laws, nor was any such thing adopted at that time? For men of that period were unacquainted with letters, but lived following the manners and laws, as they were called, of their ancestors.

CLIN. It is probable.

GUEST. But the manner of their polity was this.

CLIN. What?

b   GUEST. All of that period appear to me to have called a polity, a dynasty, which even at present subsists in many places, both among the Greeks and Barbarians. And Homer says that it was adopted in the habitation of the Cyclops; for he thus speaks:

> By these no statutes and no rights are known,
> No council held, no monarch fills the throne;
> But high on hills or airy cliffs they dwell,
> Or deep in caves whose entrance leads to hell.
> Each rules his race, his neighbour not his care,
c   Heedless of others, to his own severe.[†]

CLIN. Homer appears to you to have been an elegant poet. We have also met with other pieces, though not many, of his composing, extremely elegant. For we Cretans do not very much make use of foreign poems.

MEGIL. We however do make use of them. And Homer appears to me to excel poets of this kind, though he does not describe a Laconic,
d   but rather throughout his poems an Ionic life. At present, indeed, he appears to give a good testimony to your discourse, mythologically referring the ancient condition of mankind to rusticity.

CLIN. Certainly.

[†] Odyss. lib. ix. 112 et seq.

GUEST. For he testifies the truth of our assertion: and we shall therefore admit him as one who indicates that polities of this kind once subsisted.

CLIN. It is well said.

GUEST. Were not polities of this kind formed from families and kindred dispersed through the want arising from these devastations, - polities, in which the oldest person rules over the rest, on account of
e   their origin being derived from father and mother; and who following these like birds produce one herd, are obedient to paternal mandates, and are governed in a kingdom, the most just of all?

CLIN. Entirely so.

GUEST. But after this, more of them collecting together into one body, they will form larger cities: and first of all betaking themselves to
681a agriculture, at the roots of mountains they will make certain enclosures from hedges, as defensive walls against the attacks of wild beasts, and thus produce one common and mighty habitation.

CLIN. It is probable that this would be the case.

GUEST. But is not this also probable?

CLIN. What?

GUEST. That since these more increased habitations are composed from such as are lesser and first, each of the small ones should be present, having at the same time its most ancient governor, according to
b   alliance, together with its own proper manners; and this on account of their living separate from each other, and having had different parents and preceptors, by whom they have been accustomed to reverence the gods, and attend to themselves, the more modest by the more modest, the braver by the more brave, and so in all the rest, according as each has fashioned their sons and grandsons, who, as we have said, will bring with them to this greater habitation the peculiar laws under which they have lived.

CLIN. How is it possible this should not be probable?

c   GUEST. It is likewise necessary that every one should be pleased with his own laws in the first place, and with those of others in the second place.

CLIN. Certainly.

GUEST. But we appear to be ignorant that we are entering as it were on the beginning of legislation.

CLIN. Entirely so.

GUEST. After these things, therefore, it is necessary that those who thus assemble together should choose among themselves in common some who know the legal institutions of all of them, and that they should openly show such of these as they most approve of, to the common rulers and guides of the people, as to kings, who themselves d approving these institutions will be called legislators. But, having appointed their rulers, they will form in this mutation of their polity a certain aristocracy, composed from dynasties, or a certain kingdom.

CLIN. This will doubtless afterwards be the case.

GUEST. In the next place, therefore, let us speak of a third form of polity, in which all the forms and passions of polities, and at the same time of cities, happen to be found.

CLIN. Of what kind is this?

e GUEST. That which Homer signifies, asserting that the third was thus produced after the second:

> Dardania's walls he rais'd; for Ilion then
> (The city since of many-languag'd men)
> Was not. The natives were content to till
> The shady foot of Ida's fount-full hill.[†]

682a These verses, and those above, about the Cyclops, are in a certain respect divinely written, and are conformable to nature. For the poetic genus is divine, being agitated with sacred fury, celebrating many things which have happened according to truth, and handling each of them with certain graces and muses.

CLIN. And this very much so.

GUEST. We will therefore now proceed to consider the preceding fable: for, perhaps, something of our intention may be signified by it. Will it not be proper to do so?

b CLIN. Undoubtedly.

GUEST. We say then that Troy was built from elevated places, in a large and beautiful plain, upon a hill not very lofty, and having many rivers which rush from mount Ida.

CLIN. So it is said.

GUEST. Must not we think that this happened a long time after the deluge?

CLIN. How could it be otherwise?

GUEST. A dreadful oblivion, therefore, of the devastation we are now speaking of, must, as it appears, have been then present with them, as c they thus built their city under many rivers, and which descended from lofty places, and were not afraid to trust themselves to hills of no great altitude.

[†] Iliad. xx ver. 216.

CLIN. It is perfectly evident, therefore, that they existed a long time after this devastation.

GUEST. And I am of opinion that many other cities were at that time inhabited, in consequence of the increase of mankind.

CLIN. Certainly.

GUEST. And these indeed fought against Troy; and perhaps by sea, all of them now intrepidly using that element.

d   CLIN. It appears so.

GUEST. But the Achaians, who warred on Troy, subverted it in the tenth year.

MEGIL. Entirely so.

GUEST. In this time, therefore, or the space of ten years, in which Troy was besieged, many evils happened to the besiegers through the seditions of the young men, who received the commanders, when returning to their cities and houses, neither in a becoming nor just

e   manner, but so that many were slain, and many were exiled. Those that were exiled, however, returned, changing their names, and being called Doriens instead of Achaians, through one Dorieus, who at that time collected together the exiles. And hence you Lacedæmonians mythologize about, and thoroughly discuss, all these particulars.

MEGIL. Certainly.

GUEST. Hence, as, while discoursing about laws in the beginning of this conversation, we made a digression to music and intoxication, so now we are led to the same thing as it were by divinity; and our discourse presents us as it were with a handle for this purpose. For it

683a has brought us to that politic discipline which you said was properly instituted both in Lacedæmon and Crete, as by fraternal laws. But now we obtain this prerogative from the wandering of our discourse, that, while we pass through certain polities and habitations, we behold a first, second, and third city, following each other, according to our opinion, in immense extensions of a certain time. But now this fourth city, or

b   if you please nation, presents itself to us, which was once inhabited, and is so at present; from all which, if we are able to understand what is beautiful or the contrary, respecting its being inhabited, and what laws of the inhabitants preserve what is preserved, or corrupt what is corrupted among them, and what change of political institutions renders the city happy, we shall think, O Megillus and Clinias, that we have done enough. But all these particulars must be discussed by us from the beginning, unless we call to account what has been said.

c   MEGIL. If, O guest, any God will promise us that, if we enter a second time on the business of legislation, we shall hear neither worse nor fewer things than what have now been said, I would make a long journey, and the present day would appear to me to be short, though the God is now turning from the summer to the winter solstice.

GUEST. It is proper, as it appears, to consider these things.

MEGIL. Entirely so.

d   GUEST. Let us then be present in thought at that time when Lacedæmon, and Argos, and Messene, and the cities which were in alliance with them, were, O Megillus, in subjection to your ancestors. For then, as it is said in the fable, they thought proper, having triply divided their army, to inhabit three cities, Argos, Messene, and Lacedæmon.

MEGIL. Entirely so.

GUEST. And Temenus, indeed, was made king of Argos, but Cresphontes of Messene, and Eurysthenes in conjunction with Patrocles of Lacedæmon.

CLIN. They were so.

GUEST. But all these took an oath that they would give assistance, if e   any one should destroy any of these dominions.

MEGIL. Undoubtedly.

GUEST. But inform me, by Jupiter, whether their kingdom or government was ever destroyed by any one; or whether it was not subverted by others, but by themselves? or shall we say, that a little before, when we entered on this discourse, we thought it was so, but have now forgotten it?

MEGIL. By no means.

GUEST. Now, therefore, we shall be more able to establish a thing of this kind; for we are led to the same conclusion, as it appears, by the history of past transactions; so that we do not pursue in our discourse 684a   any vain thing, but that which has happened and is true. But the following particulars have taken place: Three kingdoms, and three cities, having a kingly government, mutually swore, respecting the laws which they had established about governing and being governed, that kings should not reign by violence as time and race continued to advance, and that the people, while the kings observed their oath, should not at any b   time destroy the kingdoms, nor endeavour that they might be subverted by others; but that kings should defend both kings and the people when injured, and the people, both kings and the people. Was it not so?

MEGIL. It was.

GUEST. That therefore which is of the greatest importance in the establishments of polities was present with the legislators in these three cities, whether the kings themselves gave laws, or any other persons.

MEGIL. What was this?

GUEST. That two cities should always rise up against one which would not be persuaded to obey the established laws.

MEGIL. It is evident.

c   GUEST. This also many advise legislators, that they should establish such laws as the people and the multitude will willingly admit; which is just as if some one should advise the masters of gymnastic exercises, or physicians, to take care of and cure the bodies under their direction in an agreeable manner.

MEGIL. Entirely so.

GUEST. It is, however, often a desirable circumstance, when with no great degree of pain any one is able to procure for bodies a good habit and health.

MEGIL. Certainly.

d   GUEST. This also was at that time present with them, and contributed in no small degree to the facility of establishing laws.

MEGIL. What was that?

GUEST. The legislators had not to procure an equality of possessions, which causes the greatest of all accusations, and which takes place in other cities established by laws, when any one endeavours to disturb the possession of land, or to dissolve what is due; perceiving that equality can never sufficiently subsist unless these things take place. For against him who endeavours to disturb every thing of this kind, all men exclaim, that he must not move things which are immoveable. Imprecations likewise are uttered against him who introduces divisions

e   of land, and the cancelling of debts; so that every man is involved in difficulty on this account. This, however, was not the case with the Doriens. For land was distributed to them, without envy or controversy; and they had no large and ancient debts.

MEGIL. True.

GUEST. How therefore came it to pass, O most excellent men, that their settlement in houses and legislation came to be so bad?

685a   MEGIL. How do you mean? and of what is it you accuse them?

GUEST. That three house-establishments taking place, two of them swiftly corrupted the polity and the laws, and one alone, which was your city, remained.

MEGIL. You ask a question which it is not very easy to answer.

GUEST. But it is proper that, considering and exploring this at present, concerning laws, with aged and prudent sport, we should accomplish the

b   journey we have undertaken without molestation.

MEGIL. We ought certainly to do as you say.

GUEST. Can we therefore speculate concerning laws in a more beautiful manner, than by considering the laws which adorned cities of this kind? or can we think of any cities and habitations more illustrious and larger than these?

MEGIL. It is not easy to speak of others that are preferable to these.

GUEST. It is nearly evident, therefore, that, thus prepared, they would not only be able sufficiently to defend Peloponnesus, but all Greece, if it should be injured by any of the Barbarians; in the same manner as those that dwelt about Ilion, who, trusting to the power of the Assyrians descended from Ninus, dared to excite war against Troy. For the form of that government, which was still preserved, was by no means despicable. And as we at present fear a mighty king,[†] in like manner all at that time feared that collected coordination of people. For the destruction of Troy a second time raised a great accusation against them; because the Trojan power was a portion of the Assyrian government. Against all these, therefore, the army at that time was divided into three cities, under the brother kings, the offspring of Hercules, and appeared to be beautifully regulated, and far more so than that which came against Troy. For, in the first place, they were of opinion that the commanders who descended from Hercules were better than those that derived their origin from Pelops; and in the next place, that this army far surpassed in virtue that which came against Troy. For these conquered, but those were vanquished by these, the Achaians by the Doriens. Ought we not thus to think, and that at that time they prepared themselves for battle with this intention?

MEGIL. Entirely so.

GUEST. It is probable therefore, that they would consider this their constitution to be firmly established, and that it would endure for a long time, in consequence of their mutually undergoing many dangers and labours, and being under the orderly government of one race, their kings being brothers. And besides this, it is further probable that they used many prophets, and among these the Delphic Apollo.

MEGIL. It is highly probable.

GUEST. But these particulars, which appear to be thus great, glided away, as it seems, at that time rapidly, except, as we just now said, a small part situated about the place of your abode; and this part has not ever ceased warring on the two other parts even to the present day. For, if the several parts of the constitution at that time had unanimously

---

† *Viz.* the king of Persia, who, as is well known, was usually called *the great king.*

conspired to one end, they would have possessed an irresistible power in war.

MEGIL. Undoubtedly.

GUEST. How, therefore, and on what account, was it dissolved? Does it not deserve to be considered what fortune subverted a constitution so great, and of such a kind?

MEGIL. Indeed, he who considers any thing else will not be able to understand either other laws or polities, which preserve beautiful and great concerns, or on the contrary destroy them, if he neglects these things.

c

GUEST. It seems, therefore, that we have been fortunately led to this consideration, which is so well adapted to our purpose.

MEGIL. Entirely so.

GUEST. Are not therefore, all men ignorant, and at present we ourselves, while each of us thinks that he beholds a certain beautiful thing, and which will produce admirable effects, when any one is not ignorant how it should be properly used? But we ourselves, perhaps, neither think rightly about this, nor according to nature. And shall we not say, that all men err respecting all other things about which they think in a similar manner?

d

MEGIL. How do you say? And about what especially are you now speaking?

GUEST. O, good man, I now laugh at myself. For, looking to that army about which we have been speaking, it appeared to me to be very beautiful, and that a wonderful possession would fall to the lot of the Greeks, as I have said, if any one should at that time have used it in a proper manner.

e

MEGIL. Did you not say all these things well and prudently; and, did not we properly praise them?

GUEST. Perhaps so. But I think that every one who perceives any thing great, and which is endued with much power and strength, will be immediately convinced, that if he knows it to be used by its possessor, being such and so great, its possessor will be happy through accomplishing many and admirable things.

MEGIL. Is not this therefore right? or, how do you say?

687a

GUEST. Consider now to what he looks, who, in praising every thing of this kind, speaks rightly. And in the first place concerning that of which we are now speaking, how will those commanders of that time, who knew properly how to marshal an army, fortunately make use of occasion? Will it not be from their establishing it in safety, and preserving it perpetually, so that they themselves may be free, and that

they may rule over others whom they please? And, in short, that both
b they and their progeny may obtain from all men, both Greeks and
Barbarians, whatever they desire? Will they not desire it for the sake of
these things?

MEGIL. Entirely so.

GUEST. He, therefore, who beholding either great wealth, or the
illustrious honours of a family, or any thing else of this kind, says the
very same things, will he not say so looking to this, as if through this
kind he should obtain all that he desires, or the greater part, and such
as are of the most consequence?

MEGIL. It appears so.

c GUEST. But there is one common desire of all men, which is signified
by our present discourse.

MEGIL. What is that?

GUEST. That all things should especially happen according to every
one's mandate; but, if not all, at least human affairs.

MEGIL. Undoubtedly.

GUEST. Since, therefore, all of us perpetually wish a thing of this
kind, both when we are adults and advanced in years, we necessarily
pray for this to the end of life.

MEGIL. Certainly.

d GUEST. But we also pray that our friends may obtain the same things
as ourselves.

MEGIL. Certainly.

GUEST. But the son is a friend to the father, viz. the boy to the man.

MEGIL. How can it be otherwise?

GUEST. But many of those things which the boy prays may happen
to himself, the father will beseech the Gods to grant that they may not
happen according to the prayers of his son.

MEGIL. Do you say that this will be the case when he who prays is
foolish, and while he is yet a youth?

e GUEST. Yes; and when he is a father, either very old or very young,
while he knows nothing of things beautiful and just, but, being affected
like Theseus to the unfortunate Hippolytus, when dying, will pray with
great alacrity. But if the son knows what is beautiful and just at the
same time, does it appear to you that he will join in prayer with the
father?

MEGIL. I understand what you say. For you appear to me to assert,
that we ought not to pray, nor endeavour that all things may be
conformable to our wish, but that our will rather may be obedient to

our prudence; and that both cities and each of us ought to pray for, and
688a endeavour to obtain, the possession of intellect.

GUEST. Certainly. And that the politician who is a legislator ought always to establish legal orders, looking to this, as I remember to have said before, and as I now remind you. For, in the beginning of this conversation, you gave it as your opinion, that a good legislator ought to establish all laws for the sake of war; but I said that this was to exhort him to compose laws according to one virtue only, when, at the
b same time, there are four virtues; and that he ought to look to every virtue, but especially towards the first, which is the leader of them all, and which is prudence, intellect and opinion, with love and desire attendant on these. But our discourse returns again to the same thing;
c and what I then said, I now again say, either if you please jesting or seriously - I assert then, that it is dangerous to pray without the possession of intellect, but that in this case it is better the contrary to what we ask should come to pass. If you are of opinion that these things are asserted by me seriously, consider them to be so. For I now entirely expect to find you consenting to what we a little before advanced, that timidity was not the cause of the destruction of kings, and of the whole of that constitution, nor yet the ignorance in warlike
d concerns of the governors and governed, but the whole of depravity, and especially ignorance about the greatest of human affairs. That these things thus happened at that time, and must so happen now, if they any where subsist, and that in following times they will no otherwise happen, I will endeavour, if you please, to discover, taking reason for our guide, and unfold it to you as friends to the utmost of my ability.

CLIN. To praise you, O guest, in words, would be troublesome, but we shall vehemently praise you in the thing itself. For we shall cheerfully follow you in what you have to say, and in so doing a liberal and true encomiast is particularly apparent.

e GUEST. You speak most excellently, O Clinias! and we shall do as you say.

CLIN. These things will be so, if God pleases. Only speak.

GUEST. We say then, proceeding according to the remaining road of our discourse, that the greatest ignorance destroyed that power at that time, and that at present the same thing is naturally capable of effecting this. So that, if this be the case, the legislator ought to endeavour as far as he is able to impart prudence to cities, and exterminate in the highest degree ignorance.

CLIN. It is evident.

689a   GUEST. What then may be justly called the greatest ignorance? Consider whether you agree with me in what I am going to say. For I establish it to be such as this.

CLIN. What?

GUEST. When any one does not love, but hates that which appears to him to be beautiful, or good; but loves and embraces that which appears to him to be base and unjust. I assert that this dissonance of pain and pleasure, with rational opinion, is *extreme* ignorance. But it is the *greatest*, because it belongs to *the multitude* of the soul. For that part of

b   the soul which is conversant with pain and pleasure corresponds to the common people and the multitude in a city. When, therefore, the soul opposes sciences or opinions, or reason, all which naturally govern, this I call ignorance: and it then takes place in a city when the multitude will not be persuaded by the rulers and the laws. The same thing happens to one man, when though beautiful reasons reside in his soul, yet he does not at all act conformably, but does every thing contrary to them.

c   I should establish all these most inordinate ignorances as belonging to a city, and to every citizen, but not as belonging to the artificers, if, O guest, you understand what I say.

CLIN. We understand you, my friend, and assent to what you say.

GUEST. Let this then be thus fixed, that to citizens who are after this manner ignorant, nothing pertaining to government is to be committed, but that they are to be reproached as ignorant, though they should be very skilful in argument, and possess every thing pertaining to the elegance and celerity of the soul. On the other hand, that those who are

d   affected in a contrary manner are to be called wise, though, as it is said, they should neither know their letters, nor how to swim, and dominion should be given to these as to prudent persons. For how, O friends, can the least form of prudence subsist without consent?

CLIN. It cannot.

GUEST. But the most beautiful and greatest of mutual agreements may be most justly called the greatest wisdom; of which he participates who lives according to reason. But he who is void of this, who destroys his own house, and is in no respect a saviour to the city, but every thing of

e   a contrary nature, - such a one appears to be ignorant with respect to these particulars. These things, therefore, as I just now said, must subsist in this manner.

CLIN. Entirely so.

GUEST. But ought there not, necessarily, to be in cities governors and the governed?

CLIN. Undoubtedly.

690a   GUEST. Be it so. But of what kind, and how many, are the axioms respecting governing and being governed in great and small cities, and in a similar manner in families? Is not this one of them, that father and mother, and universally a begetter should rule over the thing begotten? Will not this be every where a right axiom?

CLIN. Very much so.

GUEST. But the next in order is this, that the ingenious should rule over the ignoble. The third, that the more aged ought to govern, and the younger to be governed.

CLIN. Undoubtedly.

b   GUEST. But the fourth will be, that slaves should be governed, and masters govern.

CLIN. How can it be otherwise?

GUEST. The fifth will be, I think, that the better character should rule over the worse.

CLIN. You speak of a dominion which is extremely necessary.

GUEST. And of a dominion, which for the most part subsists in all animals, and is according to nature, as the Theban Pindar says. But the

c   greatest axiom, as it appears, will be the sixth, which orders the unscientific to follow, but the prudent to lead and govern. And this government, O most wise Pindar, I should nearly say was not contrary but according to the nature of law, subsisting spontaneously and not by violence.

CLIN. You speak most rightly.

GUEST. The seventh government we shall produce to a certain allotment, speaking of a thing grateful to divinity, and subsisting with good fortune. And we shall say it is most just, that he who is chosen by lot should govern, but that he who is rejected should be governed.

CLIN. You speak most truly.

d   GUEST. We shall say then jocosely to some one of those who proceed with great facility to the establishment of laws, Do you see, O legislator, how many axioms there are respecting governors, and how they are naturally contrary to each other? For now we have discovered a certain fountain of seditions, which it is necessary you should cure. But, in the first place, consider with us how, and in what respect, the kings of Argos and Messene, acting contrary to these axioms, destroyed the

e   power of the Greeks, which at that time was wonderful. Was it not because they were ignorant of that which is most rightly said by Hesiod, That the half is often more than the whole?[†] That is to say, when the

---

† *Works and Days* 38 et seq.

possession of the whole is noxious, but that of the half is moderate: for, in this case, he considered the moderate as more than the immoderate, as being better than the worse.

CLIN. Most right.

GUEST. But will this, when happening to kings, destroy each of them, prior to its happening to the people?

691a CLIN. It is probable that this is mostly the disease of kings, who live proudly through luxuries.

GUEST. It is evident, therefore, in the first place, that the kings at that time arrogated to themselves authority over the established laws, and that their actions did not accord with what they had celebrated both in discourse and by an oath. But dissonance, as we have said, being the greatest ignorance, though appearing to be wisdom, subverted all those particulars through confusion and bitter unskilfulness.

CLIN. It appears so.

b GUEST. Be it so then. But why is it necessary that the legislator of that time should be fearful respecting the generation of this passion? Shall we say, by the Gods, that to know this is a thing of no great wisdom, and that it is not difficult to assert; but that, if any one at that time had foreseen it, he would have been more wise than we are?

MEGIL. How do you say?

GUEST. We may now, O Megillus, understand that which was formerly transacted by you, and, in consequence of knowing this, easily relate what ought then to have been accomplished.

MEGIL. Speak yet more clearly.

GUEST. This then will be most clear.

MEGIL. What?

c GUEST. If any one gives a greater power to lesser things, so as to neglect mediocrity, - as, for instance, sails to ships, food to bodies, and dominion to souls, - he would subvert all things. For, becoming insolent, some of these would rush to diseases, and others to injustice, the offspring of insolence. What then do we mean to say? It is this, my friends, that the nature of a mortal soul is such, that no one of these can, when young and unrestrained, bear the greatest dominion without

d having its dianoëtic power filled with folly, which is the greatest disease; and that, besides this, it will hate its nearest friends; which circumstance, when happening, will swiftly destroy it, and obscure the whole of its power. To be afraid of this, in consequence of knowing the moderate, is the province of great legislators. Hence, that which it is easy to see was at that time transacted appears to be this.

MEGIL. What?

GUEST. Some God, as it seems, took care of you; who, foreseeing future events, planted for you a twofold generation of kings, from one, and by this mean more contracted you to the moderate. And further still, after this a certain human nature, mingling with a certain divine power, and perceiving the effervescence of your government, conjoined the prudent power of old age with the proud strength of noble birth, equalling the decision of men eighty years old, in affairs of the greatest concern, with the power of kings. But your third saviour, perceiving your distended and raging government, hurled upon it, as a bridle, the power of the Ephori, and led it near the power which is determined by lot. Hence, your kingdom being mingled from such things as are proper, and possessing measure, was both preserved itself, and became the cause of safety to others. For the faction of Aristodemus had never taken place under the government of Temenus and Cresphontes, and other legislators of that time; for they were not then sufficiently skilled in legislation. For, had they been so, they never would have thought that a juvenile soul, when receiving a dominion from which it might be possible to become a tyrant, should be kept within the bounds of moderation by oaths. But now a God has shown you what kind of government is necessary; and such a one ought especially to subsist. But that these things should be known by us, (as I said before) now they have been accomplished, is not a thing replete with wisdom. For it is not difficult to see from a paradigm a thing which has been transacted. But if any one could then have foreseen these particulars, and had been able to moderate the governments, and to form one from the three, he would have preserved all the beautiful conceptions of that time, and neither the Persian fleet, nor any other which has been despised by us as of no account, would have sailed with hostile intentions into Greece.

CLIN. You speak the truth.

GUEST. Hence, O Clinias, they made a shameful resistance. I say shameful, not because those who at that time vanquished by sea and land did not conquer in a becoming manner, but what I call shameful at that time is this: in the first place, because one of those three cities only fought in defence of Greece, but the other two were so basely corrupted, that one of them hindered Lacedæmon from assisting Greece, by warring against it with all its strength; and the other obtaining the chief authority in those times, respecting distribution, or about Argos, would neither hear, nor give any assistance when called upon to repel the Barbarian. But many things might be adduced relative to the transactions of those times, about that war, by which the conduct of the two cities towards Greece might be accused as shameful. For those who

assert that they defended Greece do not speak rightly; since, unless the
693a common opinion of the Athenians and Lacedæmonians had resisted the
approaching slavery, all things would nearly have been mingled together,
the race of Greeks with Greeks, the Barbarians with Greeks, and the
Greeks with Barbarians; just as at present, in consequence of the Persians
tyrannizing, Greece being separated in a disorderly manner is badly
inhabited. These are the things, O Clinias and Megillus, which we have
to urge against ancient politicians and legislators, and likewise those of
the present day, that, exploring the causes of these, we may discover
b what else ought to be done. Such as is that which we now assert, that
it is not proper to establish great nor unmingled governments;
considering this, that a city ought to be free and prudent, and a friend
to itself; and that a legislator ought to give laws looking to these
particulars. But we must not wonder, if we often propose other things,
and assert that the legislator ought to regard these in giving laws, though
c they are not the same with what we have previously delivered. But it
is proper to infer, that when we say the legislator ought to look to
temperance, or prudence, or friendship, our design is not different, but
the same: and you must not be disturbed on finding us using many
other words of this kind.

CLIN. We shall endeavour to do so by repeating your discourse. But
now inform us what you meant by saying that a legislator ought to look
d to friendship, liberty, and prudence.

GUEST. You shall now hear. There are as it were two mothers of
polities, from which he who says that others are produced will speak
rightly. It is necessary to call one of these a monarchy, but the other a
democracy. The race of the Persians possesses the summit of the one,
but that of the other is possessed by us. But all other forms of polities
e are nearly, as I have said, variously composed from these. It is proper,
therefore, and necessary, that a city should participate of both these, if
it is to be free, and friendly in conjunction with prudence. But this our
discourse wishes to ordain, when it says, that a city can never be
beautifully governed while it is destitute of these.

CLIN. For how can it?

GUEST. When, therefore, the one embraces monarchy, but the other
liberty, more than is proper, neither will preserve the mediocrity of
these. Your cities, however, Laconia and Crete, possess it more than
others. And this was the case with the Athenians and Persians formerly,
but now they possess less of this mediocrity. But shall we discuss the
causes of this, or not?

694a CLIN. Entirely so, if we wish to accomplish our proposed design.

GUEST. Let us hear therefore. The Persians under the reign of Cyrus, possessing more of the mediocrity of slavery and freedom, were in the first place themselves free; and in the next place they were the lords of many others. For the governors imparted liberty to the governed, and by leading them to equality the soldiers had a greater friendship for the commanders, and conducted themselves with alacrity in dangers. And if any one among them was prudent, and able to give advice, as the king was not envious, but permitted liberty of speech, and honoured those who were able to advise, he openly exhibited the common power of prudence. And at that time he gave them all things, through liberty, friendship, and a communion of intellect.

CLIN. It appears that the particulars which you have now mentioned thus subsisted at that time.

GUEST. How then came that government to be almost destroyed under the reign of Cambyses, and again nearly restored under that of Darius? Are you willing that we should speak as if we used divination?

CLIN. Certainly; for this will contribute to our design.

GUEST. Respecting Cyrus, therefore, I thus divine; that in other particulars he was a good commander, and a lover of his country, but that he did not at all apply himself to right discipline, nor attend to economy.

CLIN. But why must we say so?

GUEST. He appears from his youth to have passed his life in the army, and to have committed the education of his sons to women. But these educated them as persons happy and blessed from their childhood, and as indigent of nothing. Hence, as being sufficiently happy, they forbade any one to oppose them in any respect, and compelled every one to praise all their words and actions. After this manner were they educated by certain women.

CLIN. You speak, as it seems, of a fine education.

GUEST. Of a feminine one indeed, introduced by royal women, who became suddenly rich; and which took place during a scarcity of men, who through wars, and a multitude of dangers, had not leisure to attend to the education of youth.

CLIN. It is probable that this was the case.

GUEST. But the father of these children possessed cattle and sheep, and herds of men, and of many other animals; but he was ignorant that those to whom he was to leave all these, were not instructed in their paternal or Persian art (the Persians being shepherds, the offspring of a rough country, and the methods being hard by which they rendered the shepherds very strong, able to pass the night out of doors, to be vigilant, b   and to fight if there was occasion). But he suffered women and Median eunuchs to educate his sons, who corrupted discipline through what is called felicity. Hence they came to be such as it is likely those must be who are educated without reproof. The sons, therefore, on the death of Cyrus taking possession of the government, and being full of luxury and unacquainted with reproof, in the first place, one slew the other in consequence of indignantly bearing equality: and in the next place, Cambyses, raging through intoxication and ignorance, destroyed the kingdom through the Medes, and a certain person who was then called the eunuch, and who despised his folly.

c   CLIN. These things also are reported; and it appears that they nearly happened in this manner.

    GUEST. And it is likewise said, that the government came again to the Persians through Darius and seven others.

    CLIN. Undoubtedly.

    GUEST. But let us behold, following the order of discourse. For Darius was neither the son of a king, nor educated in a luxurious manner. But coming to the government, and receiving it as the seventh, he divided it into seven parts, of which at present some small dreams

d   remain. He likewise was of opinion that men should live under laws which contribute to a certain common equality; and made that distribution legitimate, which Cyrus had promised the Persians; thus imparting friendship and communion to all the Persians, and alluring the vulgar among them by money and gifts. Being thus beloved by his soldiers, he subdued regions not less in number than Cyrus had left. After Darius, Xerxes reigned, who was again educated in a royal and luxurious manner. But, O Darius! we may, perhaps, most justly say you

e   was not warned by the evil conduct of Cyrus, but educated Xerxes in the same manners in which Cyrus educated Cambyses. He, therefore, as being the offspring of the same discipline, acted in a manner similar to Cambyses. And, indeed, from this time scarcely any of the Persian kings were truly great, except in name. But the cause of this, according to my reasoning, was not fortune, but a vicious life, which the sons of those who were remarkably rich and tyrannical for the most part lived.

696a   For neither boy, nor man, nor old man, can ever become illustrious in virtue from such an education. And these are the things which we say should be considered by a legislator, and by us at present. But it is just, O Lacedæmonians, to confer this praise upon your city, that you never distribute any remarkable honour or nutriment to either a poor or rich

b   man, to a king or a private person, which the oracle of some God has not from the first ordered you to distribute. For it is not proper that he who excels in riches, or swiftness, or beauty, or strength, without the possession of some virtue, should obtain the highest honours in a city; nor even if he possesses some virtue, if it is not attended with temperance.

CLIN. What do you mean by asserting this, O guest?

GUEST. Is not fortitude one part of virtue?

CLIN. Undoubtedly.

GUEST. Do you, therefore, judge, on hearing what I shall advance. Would you be pleased with any domestic or neighbour who was excessively brave, yet not temperate, but the contrary?

CLIN. Predict better things of me.

GUEST. But what? Would you be pleased with one who was an artist, and wise in things of this kind, but at the same time unjust?

CLIN. By no means.

GUEST. But justice is never produced without temperance.

CLIN. How can it be otherwise?

GUEST. But neither did he who was just now considered by us as wise, because he possessed pleasures and pains, according with and following right reason, become so without temperance.

CLIN. Certainly not.

GUEST. But, further still, we should also consider this, that we may behold how honours are properly or improperly distributed in cities.

CLIN. What?

GUEST. Whether temperance, if it subsists alone in the soul without every other virtue, can with justice become either honourable or dishonourable?

CLIN. I know not what to answer.

GUEST. You speak modestly. And I think you would reply, that in this case it would subsist inharmoniously.

CLIN. You have very properly answered for me.

GUEST. Be it so then. But the addition which we made use of, of honourable and dishonourable, did not deserve a reply, but ought rather to have been passed over in irrational silence.

CLIN. You appear to me to speak concerning temperance.

GUEST. I do. But that which is of more advantage to us than other things, if it is especially honoured with an addition, it will be most rightly honoured; that which is second in utility, when honoured in a secondary manner; and thus every thing will be properly honoured when it receives consequent honours in the order of succession.

CLIN. This will be the case.

697a GUEST. What then? Shall we not say that it is the province of the legislator to distribute these?

CLIN. And very much so.

GUEST. Are you willing that we should invest him with the power of distributing all things, both pertaining to every work, and to trifling particulars? And shall we not endeavour to give a triple division, since we also are in a certain respect desirous of laws; dividing things greatest, second, and third, apart from each other?

b CLIN. Entirely so.

GUEST. We say then that a city, in order that it may be preserved, and may be happy to the utmost of human power, ought necessarily to distribute honours and dishonours in a proper manner.

CLIN. Right.

GUEST. Proper distribution, therefore, is this, to establish the goods pertaining to the soul, as the most excellent and first in rank, temperance at the same time being present with the soul: but as second in rank, things beautiful and good pertaining to the body; and in the third place, things pertaining to possessions and riches. If any legislator

c or city proceeds without these, and either causes riches to be honoured, or through honours renders something which is posterior, prior, they will act neither in a holy nor in a political manner. Shall these things be said by us, or how?

CLIN. Entirely so.

GUEST. A consideration of the Persian polity caused us to speak more copiously about these particulars. But we found that they became still worse; and we say that this was owing to their depriving the people of liberty in an immoderate degree. Likewise, by introducing the despotic

d more than was proper, they destroyed friendship and society in the city. But, these being corrupted, the deliberation of the rulers is not directed to the governed and the people, but to the advantage of their own government. Indeed, for the sake of a trifling benefit which might accrue to themselves, cities have been entirely subverted, and friendly nations destroyed by fire. Hence, hating in an hostile manner, and without pity, they are also hated. And when there is occasion for the people to fight for them, and they assemble for this purpose, they do

e not find in them a general consent to undergo danger, and fight with alacrity. But though they possess myriads, and indeed innumerable subjects, yet they are all useless for the purposes of war. Hence, as if they were in want of men, they procure some for hire; and thus think they shall be safe under the protection of mercenary and foreign soldiers.

698a Besides all this, they are compelled to be unlearned, asserting seriously, that whatever is called honourable or beautiful in the city is a mere trifle when compared to silver and gold.

MEGIL. Entirely so.

GUEST. But we have spoken sufficiently concerning the affairs of the Persians, which do not subsist in a proper manner, through excessive slavery and despotism.

MEGIL. Entirely so.

GUEST. But, after this, it is proper in a similar manner to discuss the Attic polity, that it may appear how perfect liberty, exempt from all government, is in no small degree worse than that which is moderately in subjection to others. For at that time in which the Persians invaded Greece, and perhaps nearly all Europe, our polity was ancient, and we had certain governments composed of four divisions. A certain shame, too, at that time was a despot, through which we were then desirous to live in subjection to the laws. Besides this, the magnitude of that military force, which spread itself over the land and sea, produced an immense fear, and caused us to be in still greater subjection to the governors and laws then existing. And from these causes the highest degree of friendship subsisted between us. For nearly ten years before the naval battle in Salamis, Datis, being sent by Darius, led a Persian army against the Athenians and Eretrienses in order to reduce them to slavery; Darius at the same time threatening him with death unless he enslaved these nations. Datis, therefore, in a very short time entirely subdued them with an innumerable multitude of forces; and a certain dreadful rumour reached our city, that not one of the Eretrienses had escaped, but that the soldiers of Datis had bound the hands of the Eretrienses together, and plundered all their city. This rumour, whether true or not, terrified both the other Greeks, and also the Athenians, who in consequence of this sending ambassadors to every part of Greece for the purpose of procuring assistance, no one aided them except the Lacedæmonians. And even they, indeed, whether they were hindered by being engaged in a war at that time against Messene, or by some other circumstance (for we are unacquainted with the true reason), did not come till one day after the battle at Marathon. After this, mighty preparations and innumerable threats of the king are said to have taken place. In the mean time Darius is said to have died, who was succeeded in the government by his son, at that time extremely young, and who in no respect abandoned his father's undertaking. But the Athenians were of opinion, that the whole of his preparation would be directed against them, on account of the battle at Marathon. And hearing that mount Athos was dug through, the Hellespont joined, and a great

80

multitude of ships collected, they thought that there was no safety for
them by land or by sea. For they were unwilling to confide in the
assistance of any one, recollecting that, when on the first invasion of the
b   Persians the Eretrienses were vanquished, no one gave them assistance,
or exposed themselves to danger by fighting in their defence. But it
appeared to them that the same thing would then take place by land.
And again, when they looked to the sea, they saw that all safety was
excluded there, since more than a thousand ships were coming against
them. They perceived, therefore, only one mean of safety, and that was
slender and dubious. For, looking back upon former transactions, and
considering how they had fought without any prospect of success, -
c   being borne along by this hope, they found their only refuge was in
themselves and the Gods. This, therefore, united all of them in
friendship with each other. I mean the fear which was then present,
together with that which before this the laws had produced in those that
were obedient to them. This in our former discourse we have
frequently called shame, and to which we have said all those must be
subservient who desire to become worthy characters. For he who is a
slave to this is free and intrepid. Unless this fear, therefore, had been
then present, they would never, collecting themselves together, have
defended their temples, their tombs, and their country, together with
their other familiars and friends, as at that time they defended them, but
d   we should have been widely separated from each other.
    MEGIL.   And very much so, O guest. You likewise speak very
properly, and in a manner becoming both yourself and your country.
    GUEST.   Be it so, O Megillus! For it is just to discourse with you
about the particulars which happened at that time, because you retain
the nature of your parents. But do you and Clinias consider whether
we say any thing accommodated to legislation. For I do not discuss
these things for the sake of fables: but behold on what account I speak.
e   For, in a certain respect, the same thing happens to us which happened
to the Persians: for they led the people to every kind of slavery; but we,
on the contrary, invite the multitude to every kind of freedom. But
how and what we shall speak respecting this affair, our former
discourses after a manner beautifully demonstrate.
700a   MEGIL.   You speak well. But endeavour to signify to us in a still
clearer manner what you have now said.
    GUEST.   Be it so. The people, O friends, with us according to ancient
laws, were not the lords of any thing, but after a manner they were
voluntarily subservient to the laws.
    MEGIL.   What laws do you speak of?

GUEST. Those which were then established about music, that we may show from the beginning how liberty came to be bestowed in an extreme degree. For then music was divided by us into certain species and figures; and one species of the ode consisted in prayers to the Gods, which are called by the name of hymns. But another species of the ode, contrary to this, may be said especially to consist in lamentations. Again, another species consists in pæons, another celebrates the generation of Bacchus, and is, I think, called dithyrambos: and another species is denominated laws pertaining to the harp. These, and some others, being established, it was not lawful to use one species of melody instead of another. But the authority of knowing these, and, at the same time, judging respecting them, and condemning them when improper, was not invested in the pipe, nor in the ignorant clamours of the multitude, as at present, nor yet in those who express their applause by clapping their hands, - but in men illustrious for their erudition, and who were permitted to hear to the end in silence. But boys, pedagogues, and the numerous vulgar, were admonished to behave orderly by a rod. These things being established in so orderly a manner, the multitude of citizens willingly submitted to be governed, and did not dare to judge in a tumultuous manner. But after this, in the course of time, the poets themselves became the leaders of this unlawful privation of the muse. These, indeed, naturally possessed the poetic genius, but were unskilled to a degree of folly in what is just and lawful respecting music. They likewise celebrated the orgies of Bacchus, and pursued pleasure more than was becoming. Besides this, they mingled lamentations with hymns, and pæons with dithyrambic compositions. They imitated with harps the sound of the pipe and mingled all things with all, involuntarily deceiving through their ignorance of music. For they asserted that it did not possess any rectitude whatever; but that any one, whether he was a worthy or a worthless man, might judge with the greatest rectitude from the pleasure which it produced in the hearer. Composing, therefore, poems of this kind, and thus speaking publicly, they caused the multitude to act in an unlawful and daring manner with respect to music, by persuading them that they were sufficient judges of harmony. Hence theatres, from being silent, came to be noisy, as if capable of hearing what in the muses was beautiful, or the contrary: and thus, instead of an aristocracy, a certain depraved theatrical dominion was produced. For, if only a democracy of free men had subsisted, nothing very dire would have taken place: but now, through music, an opinion came to us of the wisdom of all men in all things, and a transgression of law in conjunction with liberty followed. For they became intrepid, b   as if endued with knowledge; and this privation of fear produced impudence. For when the opinion of a more excellent person, through confidence, is not dreaded, this is nearly base impudence, and is produced from a certain liberty vehemently daring.

MEGIL. You speak most true.

GUEST. An unwillingness to become subservient to governors is the consequence of this liberty: and this is attended with a desertion of the service and admonitions of father, mother, and elders. After this follows, as now being near the consummation of the whole, disobedience to the laws. When arrived at this extremity, oaths and

c   faith, and the cultivation of the divinities, are neglected. Hence they exhibit and imitate that ancient Titanic nature, which is celebrated by poets; and again returning to the manners of that period, they lead a life involved in difficulties, and find no end to their evils. But on what account have these things been said by us? It appears to me that discourse, like a horse, should be restrained on every side, lest, having its mouth unbridled, and rushing onward, we should at length, according

d   to the proverb, fall from an ass. It is proper therefore to ask, on what account these things have been said.

MEGIL. It is so.

GUEST. On what account, therefore, have we asserted these things?

MEGIL. On what account?

GUEST. We have said that a legislator ought to give laws regarding three things; that the city which receives his laws be free, friendly to itself, and endued with intellect. Was not this what we said?

MEGIL. Entirely so.

e   GUEST. For the sake of these things we adduced two species of government, one most despotic, and the other most free; and we have considered which of these was rightly administered. But, receiving a certain mediocrity in each, in the one of despotism, and in the other of liberty, we have seen that a prosperous condition of affairs will by these means be produced; but that the contrary will be the case when each is carried to an extreme, the one of slavery, and the other of liberty.

702a   MEGIL. You speak most true.

GUEST. But, for the sake of these things, we considered the nature of the Doric army, the roots of the Dardan mountains, and the maritime habitation. We likewise considered, on the same account, those first men who escaped the devastation of the deluge; and discoursed about music and intoxication, and things yet prior to these. For all these particulars have been discussed, for the purpose of perceiving how a city may be inhabited in the best manner, and how every private individual b in it may lead the most excellent life. But if by all this we have accomplished any thing of consequence, what can be said against us, O Megillus and Clinias?

CLIN. I seem to myself, O guest, to perceive something. For it appears that we have fortunately discussed all these particulars. For I nearly am at present in want of them; and both you and Megillus here have very opportunely met with me. For I will not conceal from you that which has now happened to me, but I will make it serve as an omen. The greatest part of Crete, then, endeavours at present to establish a certain colony, and commits the management of it to the Cnossians. But the city of the Cnossians appoints me and nine others to manage this affair; and at the same time orders us to establish those laws which please us Cretans, and which may be collected from other nations. And if those of other nations shall appear to be better than our own, it enjoins us not to reject them because they are foreign. We shall now, therefore, bestow this favour both upon ourselves and you. For, making a selection out of what has been said, we shall establish a city in our discourse, and consider it from the first time of its being inhabited. For thus a consideration of the object of our inquiry will take place, and which at the same time may be useful to me in the establishment of my future city.

GUEST. You do not announce war, O guest. Unless, therefore, it should not be agreeable to Megillus, be persuaded that I shall give you every assistance in my power.

CLIN. You speak well.

MEGIL. You may likewise depend on my assistance.

GUEST. You both speak in the most becoming manner. Let us therefore endeavour, in the first place, to built a city in discourse.

BOOK IV

704a Come then, what kind of a city is it proper to think this should be? I do not now ask about its present or future name (for this, perhaps, may be owing to its colonization, or some particular place; or, perhaps, the surname of some river or fountain, or of the Gods there resident,

b may have given a denomination to the new city by its celebrity); but this is rather what I wish to ask concerning it, whether it is situated near the sea, or on the main land?

CLIN. The city, of which we are now speaking, O guest, is distant from the sea about eighty stadia.

GUEST. Are there any ports near it, or is it entirely without a port?

CLIN. It is furnished with ports, O guest, in the greatest possible degree.

c GUEST. Strange! What do you say? But is this region likewise all-prolific, or is it indigent of some things?

CLIN. It is nearly indigent of nothing.

GUEST. Is any city situated near it?

CLIN. Not very much so; on which account it became colonized. For, an ancient expulsion of the inhabitants having taken place in this city, the country was rendered desolate for an immense space of time.

d GUEST. But how is it circumstanced with respect to plains, mountains, and woods?

CLIN. It is similar to the whole of the rest of Crete.

GUEST. Do you mean to say that it is more rough than plain?

CLIN.   Entirely so.

GUEST. It is not therefore incurably unfit for the acquisition of virtue. For, if it was situated near the sea, and abounded with ports, but was not all-prolific, but indigent of many things, it would require for itself some mighty saviour, and certain divine legislators, that it might be preserved from many various and depraved manners to which it would be naturally disposed. But now its distance of eighty stadia becomes its consolation. It is indeed situated nearer the sea than is becoming, on

705a which account it abounds as you say with ports; but, at the same time, this is a desirable circumstance. For the vicinity of the sea to this region renders it every day pleasant, though this proximity is in reality extremely salt and bitter. For, filling it with the desire of gain, through merchandize, it produces in the souls of the inhabitants craft and unfaithfulness; and thus renders the city both unfaithful and unfriendly to itself, and in a similar manner to other nations. As a consolation, however, under these disadvantages, it possesses an all-prolific soil; but, being rough, it is evident that it will not be abundantly, though it is all-prolific. For, if this were the case, in consequence of great exportation, it would again possess gold and silver coin in abundance; a greater evil than which cannot, as I may say, exist, if one thing is compared with another, nor can any thing in a city be more adverse to the possession of generous and just manners, as, if we recollect, we said before.

CLIN. We do recollect; and we allow that what was then and is now said is right.

GUEST. But what? Does this region possess materials proper for building ships?

CLIN. It has not any fir-trees which deserve to be mentioned, nor yet any pines. It likewise has not many cypress trees; and very few plane- or pitch-producing trees are to be found in it, which shipwrights necessarily use in constructing the interior parts of ships.

GUEST. In this respect likewise the nature of the country is not badly disposed.

CLIN. How so?

GUEST. Because it is good for a city to be incapable of easily imitating its enemies in base imitations.

CLIN. On account of which of the things that have been advanced do you speak in this manner?

GUEST. Observe me, O divine man! I am looking to that which was asserted in the beginning about the Cretan laws, which you said regarded one particular, *viz.* war; but I said that such laws, because they were established with a view to virtue, were well established; but because they regarded only a part, and not the whole of virtue, I did not altogether approve of them. Do you therefore observe me in the present business of legislation, and consider whether I legally establish any thing tending to virtue, or to any part of virtue. For it is with me a fundamental position, that he only establishes laws in a proper manner, who, like an archer, always directs his attention thither where alone something of the beautiful in conduct will always follow, but who leaves all other things, whether riches or any thing else of this kind, when they subsist without beautiful manners. But I call the imitation of enemies then vicious, when any one residing near the sea is injured by enemies, as in the following instance. For I will relate a circumstance to you, though not with any intention of calling to mind a past injury. Minos, in consequence of possessing great power by sea, imposed a heavy tribute on the Attic region. But the Athenians at that time had not ships of war as at present; nor did their country abound in wood well adapted for building ships. Hence they could not, through nautical imitation, becoming themselves sailors, immediately at that time defend themselves against their enemies. And they would have done better if c   they had often lost seven young men, instead of suffering that which happened to them. For, instead of fighting on land, and in a legal manner, in consequence of becoming sailors they were accustomed to leap running in close array into the ships, and again rapidly to abandon them; and appeared to themselves to act in no respect base, in not daring to die, and wait for the attacks of the enemy. But they had a plausible d   pretext at hand, asserting that, by throwing away their arms, they could not be accused of shameful flight. They say, that language of this kind came to be adopted in consequence of naval engagements; language by no means worthy of infinite praise, but the contrary. For it is never proper to be accustomed to base manners, and especially for the best part of the citizens. But it appears from Homer, that a conduct of this kind is not beautiful. For Ulysses reproves Agamemnon for exhorting the Greeks, who at that time were engaged in fight against the Trojans, to draw their ships to the sea. But Ulysses thus reproves him:

e

> Is this a general's voice, that calls to flight
> While war hangs doubtful, while his soldiers fight?
> What more could Troy? What yet their fate denies
> Thou giv'st the foe: all Greece becomes their prize.
> No more the troops (our hoisted sails in view,
> Themselves abandon'd) shall the fight pursue;
> But thy ships flying, with despair shall see,

707a

> And owe destruction to a prince like thee.[†]

Homer therefore knew that three-banked galleys prepared for flight were bad in naval engagements. For lions, by using manners of this kind, might be accustomed to fly from stags. Besides this, the naval powers of cities do not together with safety bestow honours on the most beautiful of warlike concerns. For, in consequence of naval affairs b   subsisting through piloting, the government of fifty men, and rowing, men of all-various descriptions and of no great worth being employed for these purposes, no one can bestow honours upon individuals in a proper manner. Though deprived of this, how can a polity be in a good condition?

[†] Iliad, lib. xiv, 96.

CLIN. It is nearly impossible. But, O guest, we Cretans say that the naval battle at Salamis of the Greeks against the Barbarians preserved Greece.

GUEST. And, indeed, many both of the Greeks and Barbarians assert the same thing. But we, my friend, *viz.* I and Megillus here, say, that the pedestrious battle at Marathon and Platææ was the one the beginning, and the other the end, of safety to the Greeks. And, in short, that we may speak of the battles which at that time preserved us, some of them were advantageous, but others not so, to the Greeks. For to the battle at Salamis I add that at Artemisium. But now, looking to the virtue of a polity, let us consider the nature of the region, and the order of the laws; not thinking, with the vulgar, that to be preserved, and to exist, is alone to mankind the most honourable of all things, but to become and continue to be the most excellent characters during the whole period of their existence. And this I think has been said by us in the former part of our discourse.

CLIN. Undoubtedly.

GUEST. We will therefore alone consider this, if we are in that path which is best for a city, respecting habitations, and the establishment of laws.

CLIN. And we are very much so.

GUEST. Inform me, therefore, as that which is consequent to these things, who the people are that are to inhabit your colony; whether such as are willing from every part of Crete, so as that a great multitude will be collected from its several cities; or whether they are such as are chosen for the purpose of cultivating the land? For you do not collect such of the Greeks as are willing; though I see that some of you from Argos, and Ægina, and other parts of Greece, inhabit this region. But inform me at present whence you will derive this army of citizens.

CLIN. I think it will be procured from the whole of Crete. And it appears to me that those from Peloponnesus will be received for inhabitants, in preference to the other Greeks. For, what you said just now you said truly: I mean, that these are from Argos: for the race which is most celebrated here at present is Gortynic, because it migrated hither from the Peloponnesian Gortyna.

GUEST. This establishment of a colony, therefore, is not similarly easy to cities, since it does not take place after the manner of a swarm of bees, one race of friends proceeding from one region, and from friends, in order to form a settlement, being as it were besieged by a certain narrowness of land, or forced by other inconveniences of a similar nature. But it sometimes happens that a part of a city, being violently urged by seditions, is compelled to settle in some other place. And sometimes a whole city is forced to fly, in consequence of being vanquished in war. It is, therefore, partly easy for these to be colonized, and governed by laws, and partly difficult. For, when a colony is of one race, speaking the same language, and obeying the same laws, it is united by a certain friendship, and has a communion of priests, and every thing else of a similar kind; but it will not easily endure different laws, and a polity foreign to its own. But such a colony, having been forced to sedition through the badness of its laws, and still desiring through custom those pristine manners by which it was corrupted, becomes, in consequence of this, refractory and disobedient to its colonizer and legislator. But when a colony is composed of all-various tribes, it will perhaps be more willingly obedient to certain new laws; but to conspire together, and, like horses under one yoke, to blow as it is said the same blast, requires a long time, and is extremely difficult. But legislation and the establishment of cities are the most perfect of all things with respect to the virtue of men.

CLIN. It is probable; but inform me in a yet clearer manner why you asserted this.

GUEST. O good man, I appear to myself, while praising and speculating about legislators, to have said something vile. But, if we have spoken opportunely, there will be no difficulty in the affair. Though, indeed, why should I be disturbed? for nearly all human affairs appear to subsist in this manner.

CLIN. Of what are you speaking?

GUEST. I was about to say, that no man ever at any time established laws, but that fortunes and all-various events, taking place in an all-various manner, gave us all our laws. For either war by its violence has subverted polities and changed laws, or the anxiety of severe poverty. Diseases also have caused many innovations; and these have often been produced through pestilences, and unseasonable times enduring for many years. He who considers all these things will think it fit to exclaim, as I just now did, that no mortal ever established any laws, but that all human affairs are nearly governed by fortune. But he who asserts all this respecting navigation, piloting, medicine, and military command, will appear to speak well. This also may be properly asserted respecting these things.

CLIN. What?

GUEST. That divinity, and, together with divinity, fortune and opportunity, govern all human affairs. But a third of a milder nature must be admitted, - I mean, that art ought to follow these. For I am of opinion, that it would make a great difference, during a storm, whether you possessed the pilot's art, or not. Or how do you say?

CLIN. That it would.

GUEST. Will not the same consequence ensue in other things? But, indeed, we must attribute the same thing to legislation; that, other things concurring which are requisite to the living happily in a country, a legislator endued with truth ought not to be wanting to such a city.

CLIN. You speak most true.

GUEST. Ought not, therefore, he who possesses art in each of the above-mentioned particulars, to pray that something may be properly present with him through fortune, that he may not wholly trust to art?

CLIN. Entirely so.

GUEST. And would not all the rest that we have just now mentioned speak in this manner, if any one should call upon them to disclose their prayer?

CLIN. Undoubtedly.

GUEST. And I think that a legislator also will do the same.

CLIN. So I think.

GUEST. Come then, legislator (for we will now address him), What, and after what manner, shall we give you a city, so that from the things which are left in it you may be able sufficiently to govern the city? What will he rightly assert after this? Shall we not say, that the legislator will thus speak?

CLIN. How?

GUEST. Thus. Give me a city governed by a tyrant, he will say. But let the tyrant be a young man, of a good memory, docile, brave, and naturally magnificent. And let that which, we said before, ought to follow all the parts of virtue, take place in the soul of the tyrant, in order that some advantage may be derived from other things being present.

CLIN. Our guest, O Megillus, appears to me to say that temperance should follow the other virtues. Is it not so?

GUEST. I speak, O Clinias, of popular temperance,[†] and not of that which any one extolling would call prudence; but I mean that temperance which immediately and naturally blossoms forth in boys and savage animals, so that some are incontinent with respect to pleasures,

---

† Plato here means that temperance which belongs to the physical virtues, or those virtues which we possess from our birth, and may be said to be the forerunners of the moral, political, cathartic, and theoretic virtues; for an account of which see the Notes to the *Phædo*.

b   but others continent. And this temperance, when subsisting separate from the multitude of things which are called good, I do not consider as worthy to be mentioned. Do you understand me?

CLIN. Perfectly.

GUEST. This nature, therefore, our tyrant must possess in addition to the other natures we have mentioned, if the city is to receive a polity, through which it may live most happily in the swiftest and best manner possible. For no disposition of a polity can ever be more rapid or more excellent than this.

c   CLIN. But how, O guest, and by what arguments, may any one who asserts this persuade himself that he speaks properly?

GUEST. It is easy to understand, O Clinias, that this is naturally so.

CLIN. How do you say? Do you not mean to assert, if the tyrant is a young man, temperate, docile, of a good memory, brave, magnificent, and fortunate?

GUEST. Add nothing else, except that he proves to be a legislator
d   worthy of praise, and that a certain fortune leads him to this. For, this taking place, every thing will nearly be accomplished by a divine nature, which it brings to pass when it is willing that any city should be eminently prosperous. But this will happen in the second degree, when two such characters are the governors: in the third degree, when three: and the difficulty of a prosperous government will be increased in proportion to the number of such governors. But, on the contrary, the facility will be increased in proportion to the paucity of such governors.

CLIN. You appear to assert that the best city is produced from a tyranny, in conjunction with a most excellent legislator and a modest
e   tyrant; and that it is easily and rapidly changed into the former from the latter: that the best city in the second degree is produced from an oligarchy; and in the third degree, from a democracy. Or how do you say?

GUEST. Not this, by any means. But that the first is produced from a tyranny; the second, from a royal polity;[†] the third, from a certain democracy; and in the fourth place, an oligarchy[‡] will be able to receive a generation of this kind with the utmost difficulty. For, in this mode of government, the powerful are very numerous. But we say that these

---

[†] According to Plato, a *royal polity* is produced when every thing is administered according to reason, and the supreme governor is the best of men.

[‡] An oligarchy takes place when a few only, and those the worst, govern the city. See the *Republic* viii, 550c ff.

things will then take place, when a true legislator, and who is naturally
711a such, shall be found; and when a certain strength shall happen to him
in common with those in the city, who are able to accomplish that
which is of the greatest consequence. But where the governors are the
fewest in number, and at the same time the most strong, as in a tyranny,
there this mutation is accustomed to take place in a rapid and easy
manner.

CLIN. How do you mean? For I do not understand you.

GUEST. And yet I think you have heard this, not once, but often.
But perhaps you never saw a city under the dominion of a tyrant.

CLIN. Nor am I desirous of such a spectacle.

b GUEST. But you may see that in it which we have just now spoken
of.

CLIN. What?

GUEST. That a tyrant who wishes to change the manners of a city has
no occasion either of great labour, or a long time, for the
accomplishment of his purpose. For, if he wishes to exhort the citizens
c to the study of virtue, it is necessary that he should be the first who
proceeds in the road leading to it; but if to the contrary, he should first
set them the example. For he ought to express all things in himself by
acting; praising and honouring some things, but blaming others, and
disgracing those who in their several actions are disobedient to his
commands.

CLIN. How is it possible not to be of opinion that the other citizens
will rapidly follow him who is endued with such persuasion and force?

GUEST. No one will be able to persuade us, O friends, that a city will
change its laws swiftly and easily by any thing else than the command
of its governors. For this does not happen at present by any other
means, nor ever will. Indeed, this is neither difficult for us, nor
impossible to be accomplished. But another thing is difficult to be
d accomplished, and rarely takes place in a long time; though, when it
happens, it produces in the city in which it is found ten thousand
advantages, and, indeed, every good.

CLIN. Of what are you speaking?

GUEST. When a divine love of temperate and just pursuits is inherent
in certain mighty authorities, whether they govern according to a
monarchy, according to transcendency in wealth, or nobility of race.
e Or when any one restores the nature of Nestor, who is said to have
excelled all men in strength of speaking, and still more in the
temperance of his life. This man, therefore, they say, was born in the
Trojan times, but by no means in ours. If, then, such a man either

formerly was, or will be, or at present subsists among us, he must himself live in a blessed manner, and those must be blessed who hear the words proceeding from his temperate mouth. In a similar manner we must reason respecting all power; as that, when the greatest power in a man falls into the same with acting prudently and temperately, then the generation of the best polity and the best laws is produced, but never otherwise. These things, therefore, which are spoken as if they were a certain fable, have been uttered in an oracular manner: and it has been shown, that it is partly difficult for a city to have good laws; and that partly, if what we have spoken of should take place, it would happen the most rapidly of all things, and in the shortest time.

712a

CLIN. Undoubtedly.

GUEST. Let us therefore now endeavour, adapting these things to your city, like old men to boys, to fashion laws in discourse.

b CLIN. Let us endeavour to do this, and no longer delay.

GUEST. But let us invoke Divinity in constituting the city. And may he hear, and hearing be present with us, in a propitious and benevolent manner, adorning, in conjunction with us, the city and the laws!

CLIN. May he, therefore, come!

GUEST. But what kind of polity have we in our mind to impart to the city?

c CLIN. Inform me yet more clearly what you wish to say; whether it is a certain democracy, or oligarchy, or aristocracy, or a royal government. For we do not think that you will speak of a tyranny.

GUEST. Come, then, which of you is willing first to answer me, and declare which of these is the government of his country?

MEGIL. Is it more just that I, who am the elder, should speak first?

d CLIN. Perhaps so.

MEGIL. When I consider then, o guest, the polity in Lacedæmon, I cannot tell you what it ought to be called; for it appears to me to be similar to a tyranny. For the power of the ephori in it is wonderfully tyrannical. Though sometimes it appears to me to be the most similar

e of all cities to a democracy. But yet, again, not to say that it is an aristocracy is perfectly absurd. There is also a kingdom for life in it, and which is said to be the most ancient of all kingdoms, both by all men and by us. I therefore, being thus suddenly asked, cannot, as I have said, definitely inform you which of these polities it is.

CLIN. I too, O Megillus, appear to be affected in the same manner as yourself. For I am perfectly doubtful which of these I should call the polity in Cnossus.

GUEST. For you, O most excellent men, truly participate of polities; but those which are now so called are not polities, but habitations of cities, in which one part is subject to the dominion of another, and each is denominated from the power of the despot. But if a city ought to be denominated after this manner, it is fit that it should be called by the name of a divinity, who is the true ruler of those that are endued with intellect.

CLIN. But who is this God?

GUEST. Shall we then for a little while make use of a fable, in order that we may unfold in a becoming manner the object of our inquiry? Will it not be proper to do so?

CLIN. By all means.

GUEST. A long time then prior to those habitations of cities which we have before discussed, a certain government and habitation is said to have subsisted under Saturn;† a government extremely happy, and of which the present aristocracies are an imitation.

MEGIL. It is proper, as it appears, to attend to this vehemently.

GUEST. It appears so to me; and on this account I have introduced it into our discourse.

MEGIL. It is well done: and you will act very properly by proceeding with the fable as far as is necessary to your design.

GUEST. I shall do as you say. We learn, then, from the report of the blessed life of the inhabitants of that time, that they possessed all things in abundance, and spontaneously produced; of which the following is said to be the cause: Saturn, well knowing (as we have already observed) that no human nature, when endued with absolute dominion, is so sufficient to itself as not to be filled with insolence and injustice, in consequence of understanding this, placed over our cities, as kings and governors, not men, but dæmons of a more divine and excellent kind; just as we do at present with flocks of sheep and herds of tame cattle. For we do not make oxen governors of oxen, nor goats of goats; but we ourselves rule over them, as being of a better race. In a similar manner this God, who is a lover of mankind, placed over us the race of dæmons, as being more excellent than our species. But these taking care of our concerns, with great facility both to themselves and us, imparted to us peace and shame, liberty and abundance of justice, and rendered the human race exempt from sedition, and happy.   This our present discourse, therefore, employing truth, asserts, that such cities as are not governed by a divinity, but by some mortal, will never be exempt from

---

† Saturn is a deity with an intellectual characteristic. - See the Notes to the *Cratylus*.

evils and labours: but it is of opinion that we ought, by all possible means, to imitate the life which is said to have been under Saturn; and that, being obedient to as much of immortality as is inherent in our 714a nature, we should govern both publicly and privately our houses and cities, calling law the distribution of intellect. For, if one man, or a certain oligarchy, or democracy, possessing a soul aspiring after pleasures and desires, and requiring to be filled with these, but not being able to retain them, should be tormented with an insatiable vicious disease; - such a one, when governing either a city or an individual, would trample on the laws; and, as we just now said, under such a dominion there could be no possibility of obtaining safety. But it is necessary to b consider, O Clinias, whether we ought to be persuaded by this discourse, or not.

CLIN. It is necessary that we should be persuaded.

GUEST. You understand, therefore, that they say there are as many species of laws as of polities. But we have already related how many species of polities there are said to be by the multitude. Nor should you think that our present inquiry is about something vile, but that it is about a thing of the greatest moment. For, to what the just and the unjust ought to look, again becomes to us a thing of an ambiguous nature. For they say that the laws ought not to look either to war, or c to the whole of virtue, but rather to that which is advantageous to the subsistence of a polity, so that it may always govern, and never be dissolved: and they say that the definition of the just will thus be naturally beautiful.

CLIN. How?

GUEST. Because it is advantageous to that which is more excellent.

CLIN. Speak yet more clearly.

GUEST. That which has dominion, say they, always establishes the laws in a city. Is not this what they say?

CLIN. You speak truly.

d GUEST. Do you think, therefore, say they, that ever at any time, whether the people are victorious, or any other polity, or a tyranny, he who establishes the laws will voluntarily establish them, looking to any thing else in the first place than his own advantage, *viz.* the stability of his dominion?

CLIN. For how should he?

GUEST. He, therefore, who transgresses these laws when established, will be punished by the legislator (who will denominate his laws just) as acting unjustly.

CLIN. It appears so.

GUEST. This, therefore, will always be the case, and in this manner the just will subsist.

CLIN. According to this doctrine it will be so.

e   GUEST. For this is one of those iniquities which take place about government.

CLIN. What iniquities?

GUEST. It is one of those which we then considered when we discoursed about governors and the governed. And we then said, that parents ought to rule over their progeny, the older over the younger, the noble over the ignoble; and other things, in short, some of which, if you remember, were a hindrance to others, among which this was one. We likewise mentioned that Pindar said, it was both according to nature and just that the most powerful should lead.

715a   CLIN. These things, indeed, were then said.

GUEST. But consider to what persons our city ought to be committed. For a circumstance of this kind takes place ten thousand times in certain cities.

CLIN. Of what kind?

GUEST. When a contest about dominion happens, those who are victorious so vehemently usurp the affairs of the city, as not to
b   communicate any part of the government to the vanquished, nor to their progeny; always being careful lest any one of these, if invested with authority, should cause an insurrection, through a remembrance of the evils which he had formerly suffered. At present, we doubtless say, those are neither polities, nor upright laws, which are not established in common for the sake of the whole city. But those who establish these for the sake of any parts of the city, we denominate seditious, but not citizens; and we say that the things which they call just are called so by them in vain. But these things are asserted by us on this account, because we shall not give your city any magistrate who is rich, or who possesses any thing else of this kind, such as strength or magnitude, or illustrious birth; but we shall give it one who will be most obedient to
c   the legislator, and who will surpass all in the city in this respect. We likewise say that the greatest attention to the worship of the Gods must be attributed to the first in power; the second degree of attention to him who is second in authority; and that every thing consequent to this must be distributed in an orderly manner. But those that are called governors
d   I have now denominated servants to the laws, not for the sake of innovation with respect to names, but because I think that the city will obtain safety from this more than from any thing; and that by neglecting it the contrary will take place. For I see that destruction

hangs over that city in which law does not govern the magistrates, but magistrates the law. But in that city in which the law possesses absolute dominion over the governors, and the governors are slaves to the law, I behold safety, and such other goods as the Gods impart to cities.

CLIN. By Jupiter, it is so, O guest! For, through your age, you perceive acutely.

MEGIL. For every man, while he is young, perceives these things obtusely; but, when old, most acutely.

e CLIN. Most true.

GUEST. But what is next to be done? Ought we not after this to consider the inhabitants of our city as having arrived, and being present, and to finish the remaining part of our discourse to them?

CLIN. Undoubtedly.

GUEST. Let us, therefore, thus address them: Divinity,[†] O men, according to an ancient saying, containing in himself the beginning, end, 716a and middle of all things, bounds by a circular progression that which is direct according to nature. But justice always follows him, the punisher of those who desert the divine law, and which will be followed in a humble and composed manner by him who intends to be happy in future. But he who is elevated by arrogance, either because he excels in riches or honours, or in the form of his body, having his soul inflamed with insolence in addition to his youthfulness and privation of intellect, b as one who is not in want either of a governor or a leader, but is himself sufficiently able to lead others, - such a one is left destitute of divinity. But being thus left destitute, and meeting with others similar to himself, he exults, at the same time causing a general confusion. And to many, indeed, he appears to be a person of consequence; but in no long time

---

[†] Plato here, as it is well observed in the Greek Scholium on this place, by *Divinity*, means the Demiurgus of the universe; and, by the *ancient saying*, appears to allude to these Orphic verses:

Ζευς αρχη, Ζευς μεσσα, διος δ᾿ εκ παντα τετυκται.
Ζευς πυθμην γαιης τε και ουρανου αστεροεντος.

i.e. "Jupiter is the beginning and the middle; and all things were fabricated from Jupiter. Jupiter is the profundity of the earth, and of the starry heavens." He is the beginning, indeed, as the producing cause; but the end, as the final cause of the universe. He is the middle, as being equally present to all things, though all things participate him differently. But by *that which is direct according to nature*, Plato signifies desert according to justice, and undeviating energy, and as it were by one rule. And by *a circular progression*, he signifies the eternal, and that which is perpetually after the same manner, and according to the same; for circulation in sensibles possesses this property. See the Notes on the *Cratylus*, for a further account of Jupiter.

afterwards suffering an unblameable punishment from justice, he entirely subverts himself, his house, and his country. Since these things, therefore, are thus disposed, what ought a prudent man to do, or to think, and from what ought he to abstain, both in action and thought?

CLIN. It is evident, that every man ought to think how he may be of the number of those who follow divinity.

c   GUEST. What action, therefore, is friendly to and attendant on divinity? One indeed, and which possesses an ancient reason, is this, that the similar will be friendly to the similar which is moderate; but that the immoderate are neither friendly to each other nor to the moderate. But divinity, indeed, is in the most eminent degree the measure to us of all things, and much more, as it is said, than any man. He, therefore, who becomes friendly to a nature of this kind must necessarily become such to the utmost of his power. But, according

d   to this reasoning, every temperate man is a friend to divinity, for he is similar to him. But the intemperate man is dissimilar, different, and unjust; and other things from the same reasoning will take place in a similar manner. But we should understand that which is consequent to these things, and which in my opinion is *the most beautiful,* and THE MOST TRUE[†] of all assertions, that for a good man to sacrifice to and be conversant with the GODS, is of all things the most beautiful, the best, and the most useful to the possession of a happy life; and that, besides

e   this, it is *in the highest degree becoming;* but the contraries of these things naturally happen to the vicious man. For the vicious man is unpurified in his soul, but the contrary character is pure. But to receive gifts from one who is defiled, can never become either a good man or a God. In

717a   vain, therefore, do the unholy bestow much labour about the Gods; but such labour is most opportune to all holy men. Such then is the scope which we ought to regard. What therefore shall we say the arrows are, and what the impulse by which they will be most properly directed? In the first place we must say, that he who after the Olympian Gods, and those who preside over the city, honours the terrestrial Gods, by attributing to them things even, secondary, and on the left hand, will in

b   the most proper manner reach the mark of piety. But to the Gods superior to these he will attribute things according to the odd number,

---

[†] This passage, among many others in the writings of Plato, sufficiently proves that philosopher to have been a firm believer in the religion of his country; and that he did not secretly despise it, as has been asserted with no less impudence than ignorance by certain sophistical priests, whose little soul (in the language of Julian) was indeed acute, but saw *nothing* with a vision healthy and sound.

and dissonant to the particulars we have just now mentioned. But after these Gods a wise man will celebrate the orgies of dæmons, and after these of heroes. In the next place, statues must follow of the household Gods, which must be severally sacrificed to according to law. After these things, such honours as are lawful must be paid to living parents. For to these the first, greatest, and most ancient of all debts are to be

c   paid. For every one ought to think, that the whole of his possessions belongs to those by whom he was begotten and educated, and that he ought to supply their wants from these to the utmost of his power; beginning in the first place from his external possessions; in the second place, supplying them from those of his body; and, in the third place, from those of his soul: imparting all these, in order to discharge the debt which he owes his parents for the care they have bestowed upon him, and the pangs of labour which his mother formerly endured on his account. He must support them too in old age, when they want assistance in the highest degree. It is likewise requisite through the

d   whole of life to speak of our parents in the most honourable manner, because there is a most heavy punishment for light and winged words. For Nemesis, the angel of justice, is the inspector of all men in things of this kind. It is necessary, therefore, to be submissive to them when they are angry and full of rage, whether their anger shows itself in words or in deeds, as not being ignorant that a father may very properly be angry with his son, when he thinks that he has been injured by him. But, on the death of parents, the most decent and beautiful monuments are to be raised to them; not exceeding the usual magnitude, nor yet less than those which our ancestors erected for their parents. Every year,

e   too, attention ought to be paid to the decoration of their tombs. They ought likewise to be continually remembered and reverenced - and this

718a with a moderate expense, adapted to the condition of our fortune. By always acting, therefore, and living in this manner, we shall each of us be rewarded according to our deserts, both by the Gods and those natures superior to our own, and shall pass the greatest part of our life in good hope. But the course of the laws themselves will show in what manner we ought to behave towards our offspring, relations, friends, fellow-citizens, and strangers, so as to conduct ourselves piously towards

b   all these, and render our life pleasant, and adorned according to law; and this it will accomplish, partly by persuading, and partly by punishing through violence and justice, such manners as will not submit to persuasion; and thus, through the favouring will of the Gods, will render our city blessed and happy. But what a legislator whose conceptions are the same as mine ought necessarily to say of these things, but which c   cannot be adapted to the form of law, it appears to me an example should be presented, both to the legislator and those to whom he gives laws; and that, having discussed what remains to the utmost of our ability, we should after this commence the thesis of laws. Such things, indeed, cannot be easily comprehended in one description, so as to explain the manner in which they subsist; but we may thus be able to assert something stable respecting them.

CLIN. Inform me how.

GUEST. I should wish them to be obedient to virtue: and it is evident that the legislator should endeavour to accomplish this in the whole of legislation.

d   CLIN. Undoubtedly.

GUEST. What has been said, therefore, appears to me to contribute something to that end; so that, if the soul of the hearer is not perfectly savage, it will attend with greater mildness and benevolence: hence, though we should not accomplish any great but a small matter, by rendering the hearer more benevolent, and by this means more docile, we ought to be perfectly satisfied. For facility is rare, nor is there an abundance of those who endeavour to become the most worthy characters in the greatest degree, and in the shortest time. But many

e   proclaim Hesiod to be wise for asserting that the road to vice was smooth, and easy to be passed through, as being very short: "but (says he) the immortal Gods have placed sweat before virtue, and the road which leads to it is long and arduous, and, at first, rough; but, when we

719a arrive at the summit, the path which before was difficult becomes easy."†

CLIN. And it appears to be well said.

GUEST. Entirely so. But I am willing to explain to you the intention of my discourse.

CLIN. Explain it then.

GUEST. We will thus therefore direct our discourse to the legislator.

b   Inform us, O legislator, whether, if you knew what we ought to do and say, you would not say so?

CLIN. He necessarily would.

GUEST. Did we not a little before hear you saying, that a legislator ought not to suffer poets to say just what they pleased? For they are ignorant that, when they assert any thing contrary to the laws, it will injure the city.

CLIN. You speak truly.

---

† Hesiod. Op. et. Di. lib. i, 287 et seq.

GUEST. But if we should thus speak to him respecting the poets, shall we have spoken moderately?

CLIN. On what account do you ask this question?

c   GUEST. There is an ancient saying, O legislator, which is common among us, and is confirmed by all other nations, that a poet, when he sits on the tripod of the muse, is not in his right senses, but, like a fountain, readily pours forth the influx which he has received: and that, his art being imitative, he is often compelled, when representing men

d   that are contrary to each other, to contradict himself; and does not know whether these things, or those, are true. But a legislator must not act in this manner in law, *viz.* he must not assert two different things about one thing, but always make one assertion about one thing. And you may perceive the truth of this from what you have just now said. For, since of sepulchres some exceed, others are deficient, and others are moderate, you, having chosen the last of these, have ordered them to be adopted, and have simply praised them. But I, if my wife was remarkably rich, and should order me to bury her, I would celebrate in

e   a poem her magnificent sepulchre: but a parsimonious and poor man would praise a tomb which was, in some respect or other, deficient; and he who is moderately rich would praise a moderate sepulchre. But it is not proper that you should only speak of the moderate as you did just now, but that you should inform us what the moderate is, and how far it extends; for otherwise you will not as yet understand that a discourse of this kind is a law.

CLIN. You speak most true.

GUEST. Whether, therefore, will he who presides for us over the laws order nothing of this kind in the beginning of the laws, but immediately inform us what ought to be done, and what not, and, having appointed

720a   a fine, will turn himself to the establishing of another law, adding nothing of exhortation and persuasion to the promulgators of the laws? Just as different physicians cure in a different manner. But we will recall to our mind the methods which they employ; that, as boys entreat the physician to cure them in the gentlest manner, so we may implore the legislator to cure us by the mildest means. That I may explain, however, what I mean - we say that some are physicians, and others the servants of physicians; and these last we likewise call, in a certain respect, physicians. Do we not?

b   CLIN. Entirely so.

GUEST. And do we call them so, whether they are free, or servants, who, through the orders of their masters, have acquired the art of medicine, both according to theory and experience, but are not naturally physicians like those who are free, who have both learnt the art from themselves, and instructed their children in it? Or do you consider these as forming two kinds of physicians?

CLIN. Why should I not?

c GUEST. Do you, therefore, understand, that when in a city both servants and those who are free are sick, servants are for the most part cured by servants, who visit the multitude of the sick, and are diligently employed in the dispensatories; and this without either assigning or receiving any reason respecting the several diseases of the servants, but what they have found by experience to be efficacious they tyrannically prescribe for their patients, as if they possessed accurate knowledge; and thus, in an arrogant manner, hurry from one diseased servant to another; by this mean facilitating their master's attention to the sick?

d But the freeborn physician, for the most part, heals and considers the diseases of those who are freeborn; and this, by exploring the disease from the beginning, and proceeding according to nature; conversing both with the sick man and his friends, and, at the same time, learning something himself from the sick, and teaching him something, so as not to order him to do any thing till he has persuaded him of its propriety.

e But after this he always endeavours, in conjunction with persuasion, to lead him in a gentle manner to health. Which of these appears to be the better physician and exerciser, he who in this manner heals and exercises, or he who in that? He who accomplishes one power in a twofold manner, or he who accomplishes it in one way, and this the worse and more rustic of the two?

CLIN. The twofold method, O guest, is by far the more excellent.

GUEST. Are you willing, therefore, that we should consider this twofold and simple method as taking place in the establishment of laws?

CLIN. How is it possible I should not be willing?

721a GUEST. Inform me then, by the Gods, what the first law will be which the legislator will establish. Will he not first of all adorn by his mandates the principle of the generation of cities?

CLIN. Undoubtedly.

GUEST. But are not the mutual mixture and communion of marriages the principle of generation to all cities?

CLIN. Undoubtedly.

GUEST. Nuptial laws, therefore, being first of all established, they will appear to be well established with respect to the rectitude of every city.

CLIN. Entirely so.

GUEST. We will, therefore, first of all speak of the simple law, which,

b perhaps, will subsist in the following manner. Every one should marry from thirty to thirty-five years of age; but he who did not should be fined both with money and disgrace; with money to a certain amount, and with disgrace of this or that particular kind. Let this then be the simple law respecting marriages; but let the following be the twofold law. Every one should marry from thirty to thirty-five, considering, at the same time, that the human race participates from a certain nature of immortality, of which every one is naturally desirous in the extreme.

c For the endeavour of mankind not to remain after death without a name is a desire of this kind. The human race, therefore, is something connate with the whole of time, following and being conjoined with it to the end, becoming immortal by leaving children of children, and participating of immortality through being one and the same by generation. For a man willingly to deprive himself of this, is by no means holy. But he intentionally deprives himself of this who neglects

d children and wife. He, therefore, who is persuaded by this law shall be liberated from the punishment of a fine. But he who is not obedient to it, and who is not married when he is thirty-five years of age, shall be fined every year a certain sum of money, that his solitary life may not appear to be profitable and pleasant to him; and that he may not partake of those honours which the younger in a city pay to the elder. These laws being compared with each other, it will be possible to judge of every particular law, whether it ought to be double, and of the smallest

e extension, on account of mingling threats with persuasions; or whether, alone employing threats, it should become simple in length.

MEGIL. Agreeably to the Laconic mode, O guest, the shorter ought always to be preferred. But if any one should order me to become a judge of these writings, I should, if it were left to my choice, adopt the

722a longer law for a city. And according to this paradigm, if these two laws were proposed, I should choose the same respecting every law. It is, however, proper that the laws which we have now instituted should be approved by Clinias; for the city belongs to him for whose use these laws have been conceived by us.

CLIN. You speak well, O Megillus.

GUEST. To pay great attention, therefore, either to prolixity or brevity of writing is foolish in the extreme. For I think that the best writings, and not the longest or the shortest, are to be preferred. But,

b in the laws which we have just now spoken of, the one is not by the double alone more conducive to virtue than the other; but that which we said respecting the twofold kind of physicians was most properly adduced. This, however, no legislator appears at any time to have considered. For, as it is possible to use two things in the establishment of laws, *viz.* persuasion and force, they alone employ one of these in

c managing the crowd who are void of erudition. For they do not mingle persuasion with force, but alone employ unmingled violence. But I, O blessed man, perceive that a third thing also should take place respecting laws, but which is not at present adopted.

CLIN. Of what are you speaking?

GUEST. Of something arising, through a certain divinity, out of things which we have now discussed. For we began to speak about laws in the morning, and it is now noon; and, reposing in this all-beautiful retreat,

d we have discoursed of nothing else than laws. And we appear to me to have entered just now on the business of legislation; but all that has been said before by us was nothing more than a preface to laws. But to what purpose do we say this? It is because I wish to say, that of all discourses, and other things which participate of sound, that is the preface, and, as it were, prelude, which possesses any artificial argumentation, and is useful to the intended discussion. And, indeed, of the laws, as they are called, of the ode belonging to the harp, and of

e every muse, prefaces precede which are wonderfully elaborate. But of true laws, which we say are political, no one has ever at any time led forth into light a preface either spoken or written; as if there were not naturally any such thing. But our present conversation appears to me to signify that there is one. The laws, however, which we just now called twofold, are not simply so; but the law, and the preface of the law, are a certain two. However, that which we assimilated to a tyrannic mandate, and to the mandates of servile physicians, is mere, or

723a unmingled, law. But that which was said prior to this, and was called persuasive, was in reality persuasive, but, with respect to discourse, had the power of a preface. For, that the mandate of the legislator, which is law, might be received more benignantly, and, through this, in a more docile manner, the whole of that discourse, which was calculated to

b persuade, was introduced by me. Hence, according to my decision, that discourse is a preface, and cannot properly be called a discussion of law. But, after this, what is it I am desirous should be said by me? It is this: that a legislator ought to introduce prefaces prior to all laws, and prior to each particular law, so far as they differ from each other, in the same respect as the two which we have just now mentioned.

CLIN. For my part, I should never exhort a man skilled in these things to establish laws in any other manner.

c GUEST. You appear, therefore, to me, O Clinias, to speak well, so far as you say there should be a preface to all laws; and that, on commencing the business of legislation, it is requisite to prefer to every discourse an exordium naturally accommodated to the several laws. For that which is to be said after this is not a thing of small importance, nor is the difference trifling, whether such things are commemorated in a clear, or in an obscure, manner. If, therefore, we should order legislators to preface in a similar manner about great and small laws, we

d should not act properly. For this is not to be done either in every song or in every discourse; because, though it may naturally belong to all, yet it is not useful to all. A thing of this kind, however, is to be allowed the rhetorician, the singer, and the legislator.

CLIN. You appear to me to speak most true. But let us make no longer delay, but return to our proposed discourse, and begin, if it is agreeable to you, from those things which, not as prefacing, were asserted by you above. Again, therefore, as those that are engaged in sports say, let us revolve better things from a second beginning, as finishing a preface, and not a casual discourse, as was the case just now.

e Let us begin, then, acknowledging that we preface. And the particulars, indeed, respecting the honour of the Gods, and reverence of our ancestors, have been sufficiently discussed. Let us, therefore, endeavour to speak about what follows, till it shall appear to you that our preface is complete. And after this you may enter on the business of laws.

724a GUEST. About the Gods, therefore, and the attendants on the Gods, together with parents both when living and dead, we then sufficiently prefaced, as we now say. With respect to what remains, you appear to me to order that it should be led forth into light.

CLIN. Entirely so.

GUEST. But, after these things, it is proper to discourse in common

b about our souls, bodies, and possessions, together with serious pursuits and remissions of labour, in such a manner that both the speaker and the hearers may, to the utmost of their power, be partakers of discipline. After what has been said, therefore, these things are to be truly spoken and heard by us.

CLIN. You speak with the utmost rectitude.

BOOK V

26a   Let every one then hear who has already heard what we have said respecting the Gods, and our dear progenitors. For, after the Gods, a man's soul is the most divine of all his possessions, as being his most intimate property. But a man's possessions are in every respect twofold. 27a And the more excellent, and the better, possess dominion, but the inferior, and worse, are subject to command. The former, therefore, are always to be honoured before the latter. Hence, I properly exhort every man, when I say that he ought to honour his own soul in the second place, after our lords, the gods, and their attendants. But, in short, no one honours his soul properly, though he appears to do so. For honour is, in a certain respect, a divine good: but nothing evil is honourable. He, therefore, who thinks that he enlarges his soul by certain discourses or gifts, when, at the same time, he does not render it better than it was before, appears indeed to honour it, but by no means does so. For every man, from his very childhood, thinks himself sufficient to know all things, and that he honours his soul by praising it, and by freely permitting it to do whatever it pleases. But we now say that he who acts in this manner injures, and does not honour, his soul. And yet it is necessary, as we have said, that it should be honoured in the second place after the Gods. Nor does he honour it who does not consider himself as the cause of his own errors, and of his numerous and mighty vices, but lays the blame upon others, and is always careful to exonerate himself. Such a one appears, indeed, to honour it, though this is far from being the case: for he injures it. Nor does he in any respect honour his soul who gratifies himself with pleasures contrary to reason, and the praise of the legislator: for he dishonours it, by filling it with vice and repentance. Nor yet does a man honour his soul, when he does not strenuously endure labours that are praised, fear and pain, but sinks under them: for by doing all these things he dishonours his soul. Nor, again, does he honour his soul, who thinks that to live is a thing in every respect good: for by such a conception he dishonours it. For he assents to him who thinks that every thing in Hades pertaining to the soul is bad; nor does he oppose and teach him, that he is ignorant whether, on the contrary, the things about the Gods that dwell there are not the greatest of all goods. Nor yet, when any one honours a certain corporeal beauty before virtue, is it at all different from truly and entirely dishonouring the soul. For such a one falsely asserts, that the

body is more honourable than the soul. For nothing earth-born is more
e honourable than things Olympian. But he who entertains an opinion
different from this, respecting the soul, is ignorant that he neglects this
admirable possession. Nor, again, does he adorn his soul with gifts, who
728a desires to possess riches in an unbecoming manner, or who is not
grieved when he possesses them unjustly; but such a one entirely fails of
accomplishing this. For he gives up that which is honourable, and at
the same time beautiful, in his soul, for the sake of a little gold; when
at the same time all the gold, which is both upon and under the earth,
is in no respect of equal worth with virtue. In short, he who is not
willing, by all possible means, to abstain from such things as the
legislator ranks among the base and vicious, and to pursue to the utmost
b of his power such things as he places among the good and beautiful, does
not perceive that, in all these things, he renders his soul, which is a most
divine possession, in the highest degree dishonourable and base. For, in
short, no one considers what is the greatest punishment of evil conduct;
which is the becoming similar to vicious men. But he who becomes
similar to them avoids good men and good assertions, separates himself
from the good, becomes agglutinated to the vicious, and earnestly desires
their conversation. But, in consequence of intimately associating with
c these, he must necessarily do and suffer such things as they naturally do
and say to each other. Such a passion, therefore, is not justice (for the
just and justice are beautiful), but punishment; this being a passion
attendant on injustice, of which both he who is a partaker, and he who
does not partake, are miserable: - the one, because he is not cured; but
the other, because, while many are saved, he perishes. But, that I may
sum up the whole, our honour consists in following things of a more
excellent nature, and in rendering such things as are worse, but yet are
capable of being made better, as good as possible. No possession,
therefore, belonging to a man is more naturally adapted to fly from evil,
d and to investigate and choose that which is the best of all things, than
soul; nor, when it has chosen to associate with it in common for the
remainder of life. On this account, it must be honoured in the second
degree. But every one will understand, that the third honour according
to nature is that of the body. It is however requisite to contemplate
these honours, and to consider which of them are true, and which
adulterated. And this is the business of a legislator. But he appears to
me to announce, what, and what kind of honours these are; as, that the
body is honourable, not when it is beautiful, or strong, or swift, nor yet
e when it is large or healthy, (though under these circumstances it appears
to be so to many,) nor when it has the contraries of these. But those

things which, being in the middle, touch upon the whole of this habit, are by far more moderate and safe. For the former render the soul arrogant and confident, but the latter humble and servile. The like takes place with respect to the possession of riches and property of every kind. For the possession of each of these, in a transcendent degree, produces hatred and sedition, both among cities and individuals. But slavery is for the most part the consequence of a deficiency of these. No one, therefore, should apply himself to the acquisition of wealth for the sake of his children, that he may leave them rich in the extreme: for this will neither be better for them, nor for the city. For the property of young men, which is neither attended with adulation, nor indigent of things necessary, is the most harmonious, and the best of all. For, symphonizing and harmonizing with us in all things, it renders our life free from pain. It is proper, therefore, to leave children, not abundance of gold, but of modesty. But we think that we shall accomplish this by reproving impudent young men. this, however, is not to be accomplished by exhorting young men in the manner adopted at present, - I mean, by telling them that they ought to be modest in every thing; but a prudent legislator will rather advise old men to behave modestly before youth, and above all things to take care that no young man, at any time, either sees or hears them doing or saying any thing base. For, where old men are void of shame, there young men must necessarily be most impudent; since the most excellent discipline, both of young and old, consists, not in admonishing, but in acting through the whole of life agreeably to the admonitions of others. But he who honours and venerates the whole of his kindred, who participate of the same blood, and the same household Gods, will deservedly find those Gods propitious to him in the procreation of children. And besides this, he will obtain the benevolence of his friends and associates through life, who considers the attention which they pay him greater and more venerable than they do, but his own kindness towards them less than they do. But he will by far behave in the best manner, both towards his country and fellow citizens, who prefers the glory of being subservient to the laws of his country, to conquest in the Olympian games, and to all warlike and peaceful contests; and who is subservient to them in the most becoming manner through the whole of life. The associations, too, with strangers should be considered as things most holy. For nearly all the crimes of strangers towards strangers are more noticed by avenging Deity than those of citizens towards each other. For, a stranger being destitute both of companions and kindred is an object of greater commiseration both to men and Gods. He, therefore, who is more capable of taking vengeance is more readily disposed to give assistance. But the hospitable dæmon and divinity of every one, being the attendants of hospitable Jupiter, are capable of taking vengeance in the most eminent degree. Every one, therefore, who is endued with the least portion of consideration, should be very fearful through the whole of life of acting in an inhospitable manner. But, of all crimes which are committed both towards strangers and natives, those are the greatest which are committed towards suppliants. For the Divinity with whom the supplicant forms a covenant, becomes eminently the guardian of him in his affliction. So that no one who injures suppliants will go unpunished. And thus far we have nearly discussed the duties of children towards their parents, of a man towards himself, and the things belonging to himself; likewise of his duty towards his country, friends, kindred, strangers, and fellow citizens. It now follows that we show what qualities a man ought to possess so as that he may pass through life in the most becoming manner; and so that, not law, but praise and blame, instructing every one, they may by these means be rendered more benevolent and obedient to those who are about to establish laws. And these are the things which after this must be subjects of our discourse. But *truth is the leader of every good both to Gods and men:* of which he who in futurity will be blessed and happy, must participate from the beginning, that for the greatest part of time he may pass through life in truth. For such a one is faithful. But he is unfaithful who is a friend to voluntary falsehood. And he who is a friend to involuntary falsehood is deprived of intellect: neither of which is an object of emulation. For he who is unfaithful and void of discipline is unfriendly. And in progress of time, his character being known, near the end of life there is prepared for him the grievous solitude of old age. So that, whether his associates and children live or not, he nearly leads, in either case, an orphan life. Indeed, he is honourable who acts in no respect unjustly: but he who does not suffer the unjust to act unjustly, deserves more than double the honour of the former character. For the former is of equal worth with one man, but the latter, with many men; since he announces to the governors the injustice of others. But he who punishes injustice, in conjunction with the governors, to the utmost of his power, such a one will be proclaimed a great and perfect man in the city; for he will be victorious in virtue. It is proper also to give the same praise to temperance and prudence. And he who possesses other goods, and is not only able to possess them himself, but to impart them to others, is to be honoured as one who has attained the summit of excellence. But he who is not able to accomplish this, and yet is willing,

31a   is to be ranked in the second place: and the envious man, and he who will not impart any good for the sake of friendship, are to be blamed. We ought not, however, to dishonour the possession on account of the possessor, but should endeavour to obtain it with all our might. Every one too should contend with us for virtue, without envy. For every character of this kind enlarges cities, in consequence of striving himself, and not impeding others through calumny. But the envious man, while he thinks to surpass others by detraction, tends less himself to true virtue, and renders those who mutually tend to it despondent, by blaming them unjustly. Hence, depriving the city of strenuous exertions in the acquisition of virtue, he, at the same time, lessens its renown. It is proper, besides, that a man should be ardent in every thing, and particularly that he should be mild. For it is impossible to avoid the unjust actions of others, which are either difficult to be cured, or are entirely incurable by any other means than contest, defence, victory, and by suffering no remission in punishment. But it is impossible for any soul to accomplish this without generous ardour.

With respect to such unjust actions as are curable, it is requisite to know, in the first place, that no unjust man is voluntarily unjust. For no one would, at any time, willingly possess any of the greatest evils, and much less in those things respecting himself which are most honourable. But soul, as we have said, is in reality in all things the most honourable. No one, therefore, would at any time voluntarily receive the greatest evil in that which is most honourable, and live through the whole of life possessing it. But the unjust man, and he who is vicious, are in every respect miserable. It is proper, however, to pity him who is capable of being cured, and to restrain our anger against him, lest, by an effeminate effervescence of anger, we should exhibit all the bitterness of wrath. But it is requisite to employ anger against those who are incontinently and incurably bad. Hence, we have said that every good man ought to be ardent, and at the same time mild. But an evil, which is the greatest of all evils, is implanted in the souls of many men, which (every one pardoning himself) they do not devise any means of avoiding. And this is what is usually said, that every man is naturally a friend to himself, and that it is proper a thing of this kind ought to be. But, *in reality, a vehement love of self is to every man the cause of all his errors.* For he who loves is blind with respect to the object of his love. So that

2a   he who thinks he ought always to be honoured in preference to truth, judges of things just, good, and beautiful, in a depraved manner. For it is proper that he who is destined to be a great man should neither love himself, nor the things pertaining to himself, but that he should love just actions, whether they are accomplished by himself or by another. In consequence of this error, every man's ignorance appears to himself to be wisdom. Hence, in short, though we do not know any thing, we are of opinion that we know all things. But, not permitting others to do that of which we ourselves are ignorant, we are compelled to err from their conduct. On this account every man ought to avoid the vehement love of himself, and to follow one better than himself, without paying any attention to shame. There are also certain lesser things, which are often said, and which, as they are not less useful than what has been already asserted, it is proper, recollecting ourselves, to mention. For, as if something was always flowing away from us, it is necessary that, on the contrary, there should be a perpetual influx of something. But recollection is an influx of prudence which had deserted us. It is proper, therefore, to restrain unbecoming laughter, and that every man should announce to every man the propriety of concealing all joy and sorrow, and of keeping the body in a becoming habit, whether the dæmon of any one establishes him in felicity, *or whether his fortune is such that he is obliged, with dæmons opposing him, to engage in actions of an elevated and arduous nature.* But it is proper always to hope for those things which divinity imparts to the good; and when we are oppressed with heavy labours, we should hope that Divinity will diminish their weight, and change the present condition of our circumstances into one more favourable; and with respect to good things, the contraries of these, that they will always be present with us, with good fortune. With these hopes every one ought to live, and with the recollection of all these things; not with a parsimonious recollection, but always, both seriously and in sport, perspicuously reminding each other and ourselves of these particulars. And now we have nearly said all that is proper respecting those divine duties which every one ought to perform, but we have not yet spoken concerning human duties. It is, however, necessary so to do: for we speak to men, and not to Gods. But pleasures, pains, and desires, are naturally in the highest degree human, from which it is necessary that the whole mortal animal should, with the greatest earnestness, be suspended. And it is requisite to praise the most becoming life, not only because in its form it excels in glory, but because, if any one is willing to taste of it, and not when a youth to fly from it, he will also excel in that which we all are in search of, I mean the possession of more joy than sorrow through the whole of life. That this will clearly be the case, if any one tastes of it in a proper manner, will readily and vehemently be apparent; but how this may be accomplished, and whether it is inherent in us naturally, or contrary to nature, it is requisite now to consider. We ought, however, to consider one life compared with another, the more pleasant and the more calamitous, in this manner. We wish that pleasure may be present with us, but we neither choose nor wish for pain. And we never wish for a middle condition instead of pleasure, but we desire it in preference to pain. We also wish for less pain with more pleasure, but we do not desire less pleasure with greater pain. But we can clearly show that we are unwilling to possess each of these in an equal manner. All these both differ and at the same time do not differ in multitude and magnitude, in intensity, equality, and such things as are contrary to all these, with respect to the choice of each. And as these particulars are thus circumstanced, we wish for that life in which many of both these greatly and vehemently subsist, but in which pleasures transcend; but we do not desire that life in which the contraries to these are inherent. Nor, again, do we wish for that life in which a few of these, of a trifling and solitary nature, subsist, and in which afflictive circumstances transcend; but we desire that life in which the contraries to these are found. However, as we have said before, we ought to consider that life as subsisting in an equilibrium, in which these possess equal power. For we desire the life which surpasses in the things with which we are pleased; and we are unwilling to possess that which exceeds in the contraries to these. But it is necessary to consider all our lives as naturally bound in these; and besides this, what the things are which we naturally desire. If, therefore, we should say that we wish for any thing besides these, we must say that it is through an ignorance and unskilfulness in lives. What then, and of what kind are those lives, in preferring which it is necessary that he who perceives what is the object of desire, and voluntary, and what are the contraries to these, should prescribe a law to himself, that thus having chosen that which is friendly, pleasant, the best, and the most beautiful, he may lead the most blessed life possible to man? We call then one life temperate, another prudent, another brave; and we rank in the fourth place a healthy life. We likewise establish four other lives contrary to these, *viz.* the imprudent, the timid, the intemperate, and the diseased. He, therefore,

4a who knows what a temperate life is, will assert that it is mild in all things, and that it imparts quiet pains, quiet pleasures, placid desires, and loves not insane; but that an intemperate life is impetuous in all things, so that it imparts vehement pains, vehement pleasures, strenuous and furious desires, and the most insane loves. But in a temperate life the pleasures surpass the pains, and in an intemperate life the pleasures are surpassed by the pains, in magnitude, multitude, and density. Hence,

the one of these lives is necessarily more pleasant to us, according to
b   nature, but the other is more painful. And nature does not permit him,
who wishes to live pleasantly, to live voluntarily in an intemperate
manner. But it is evident, if what we have now asserted is right, that
every intemperate man is necessarily unwillingly so. For the vulgar
every where live indigent of temperance, either through the privation of
discipline, or through incontinence, or through both. The same things
are to be considered respecting a diseased and healthy life: as, that they
c   possess pleasures and pains, but that the pleasures surpass the pains in a
healthy life, but the pains the pleasures in diseases. Our will, however,
in the choice of lives, does not consent that pain may transcend pleasure;
but we judge the life in which it is surpassed to be more pleasant. And
we say that the temperate man possesses in every respect things fewer,
d   less, and more attenuated than the intemperate, the prudent than the
imprudent, the brave than the timid; and that the one surpasses in
pleasures, but the other in pains; so that the brave man surpasses the
timid in pleasures, and the prudent the imprudent. And, in short, the
life which participates of virtue, either pertaining to the body or the
soul, is more pleasant than the life which participates of depravity; and
besides this, it transcends other lives in beauty and rectitude, in virtue
e   and glory; so that he who possesses it lives more happily than he who
possesses the contrary life, in every respect, and totally. Here then let
the preface to laws end.

But, after the preface, it is necessary that law should follow; or rather,
according to truth, the laws of a polity are to be written. As, therefore,
735a things which are woven are not all woven from the same threads, but
there is a difference in the quality of the threads, for some are more firm
and strong, but others softer and of a more yielding nature; in like
manner it is necessary to judge of those that have great dominion in
cities, and those that act only in every thing from trifling discipline.
There are, however, two forms of a polity: the one, the establishment
of governors; the other, that which gives laws to the governors
themselves. But prior to all these things it is necessary to consider as
b   follows: When a shepherd and herdsman, one who takes care of horses,
and others of this kind, engage in their respective offices, they never
attempt to take any care of them till they have first administered a
purification adapted to each of them. And, besides this, choosing out
the healthy and the sick, the noble and the ignoble, they send the
former to other herds, but take care of the latter; considering that
c   otherwise their labour would be vain about those bodies and souls
which a depraved nature and aliment have corrupted; since, without

separating in each of these herds the healthy and diseased manners and bodies from each other, they would perish by contagion. The attention, however, which is paid to other animals is indeed less, and is alone worthy to be mentioned for the sake of an example. But the legislator ought to pay the greatest attention to men, and should investigate and assert that which is accommodated to every one, both respecting purification and all other actions. For that which concerns the purification of a city should subsist as follows: As there are many purifications, some of them are easy, but others difficult; and he who is both a tyrant and a legislator may be able to use such purifications as are difficult, and such as are the best. But the legislator who establishes a new polity and laws without the assistance of a tyrant, may rejoice, if he is able to purify with the mildest of purifications. The best purification is however painful; just as those medicines which unite justice with punishment, produce at length in the offending party either exile or death. For it is customary to free the city from those men who have perpetrated the greatest crimes, when they are found to be incurable, and have in the greatest degree injured the city; but with us the following is a milder purification. For those that through want of food readily offer themselves to certain leaders, in order to assault those that are not in want, these, as being naturally the disease of a city, should be benignantly sent away,[†] under the honourable appellation of a colony. Every legislator, therefore, should do this in the beginning of his legislation. But more difficult things than these happen to us at present. For it is not necessary to devise at present either a colony or any select purification: but as if there was a conflux of water, partly from fountains and partly from torrents, into one lake, it is necessary to observe how the confluent water will be most pure; partly by drawing, partly by deducing it into another channel, and partly by diverting its course. But labour and danger, as it appears, are to be found in every political establishment. However, since we are now engaged in discourse, and not in action, our selection is accomplished, and purification takes place according to our desire. For, having by every kind of persuasion, and for a sufficient length of time, examined those evil men who endeavour to enter our city in order to govern it, we shall forbid their entrance. But we shall admit the good, rendering them

---

† The laws of Plato, being perfectly equitable, consider the good of the offender in the punishments which they enjoin, and not the good of the community alone; but our laws, especially in crimes pertaining to money, alone consider the good of the community. This is one among many of the baneful effects of commerce.

benevolent and propitious to the utmost of our power. The felicity, however, which has happened to us ought not to be concealed. For, as we say that the colony of the Heraclidæ was happy, because it escaped the dire and dangerous strife respecting the division of land and the discharge of debts, about which a city of the ancients being compelled

d to give laws, it did not permit any thing to be immoveable, nor yet after a manner was it possible for any thing to be moved; in like manner, the same thing appears nearly to have happened to us. But, in short, prayer alone remains, and a trifling mutation cautiously and slowly made in a great length of time; so that, in these mutations, the citizens, together with many debtors, will possess abundance of land, with which they will

e give assistance to many, humanely imparting their land to the indigent, and contenting themselves with moderate possessions. They will likewise consider poverty as consisting, not in a diminution of property, but in an insatiable desire of acquiring more. For this is the greatest beginning of safety to a city; and upon this, as a stable foundation, every politic ornament, which is accommodated to an establishment of this kind, may be raised. But when this mutation is debile, no political action will afterwards be easily accomplished by the city. This, indeed,

737a as we have said, we should avoid; but, at the same time, it may more properly be said, that, if we do not avoid it, we should show by what means this flight may be accomplished. We say then, that it is to be accomplished by cultivating justice, and banishing the desire of gain: but, besides this, there is no other, either broad or narrow, passage for flight. Let this then be established by us as a prop of the city. For it is necessary that the possessions which the citizens prepare for themselves

b should be blameless; or, that those should desist from advancing any further in the acquisition of property, who have an ancient enmity towards each other, and who participate but a small degree of intellect. But those to whom Divinity imparts, as it does to us at present, the establishment of a new city, in which the inhabitants have no enmity towards each other, - if through the distribution of land and habitations hatred should arise among them, - in this case it will not be human ignorance, but ignorance accompanied with every vice. What then will

c be the mode of proper distribution? In the first place, the quantity of the number ought to be determined. In the next place, it should be agreed into how many and what kind of parts the distribution to the citizens should be made. In the third place, the land and habitations should be distributed equally, in the most eminent degree. But the quantity of the multitude cannot otherwise be properly assigned than by paying attention to the land and cities of the neighbouring inhabitants.

And the land, indeed, should be as much as is sufficient to afford nutriment for so many moderate men; but of more than this there is no occasion. But the number of these moderate persons should be sufficient to defend themselves against the incursions of their unjust neighbours, and likewise to give assistance to their neighbours when injured. Having then considered these things, we may be able to define both actually and verbally the land and the neighbouring inhabitants. But now, for the sake of a scheme and description, that the thing itself may be accomplished, our discourse proceeds to legislation. The number of the husbandmen, and those that defend the distribution of the land, should be five thousand and forty, this being a number adapted for the purpose. In like manner the land and the habitation should be distributed into the same parts, so that the man and his portion of land may accord in distribution. And in the first place, indeed, the whole number should be divided into two parts, and afterwards into three. It is likewise naturally capable of a division into four, five, and so in succession as far as to ten. Thus much, indeed, ought to be understood by every legislator respecting numbers; I mean, that he should understand what, and what kind of number will be most useful to all cities. But we say that that number is best adapted for this purpose, which possesses in itself many distributions, and these orderly disposed. For every number is not allotted sections into all things. But the number five thousand and forty, both for the purposes of war and peace, for all conventions and communions, for tributes and distributions, cannot be cut into more than one of sixty parts; but you may continue the division of it from one as far as to ten. These things, however, ought to be more firmly considered at leisure, by those to whom they are committed by the law; for they cannot subsist otherwise than in this manner. But it is necessary that they should be mentioned to the founder of a city, for the sake of what follows. For, whether any one establishes a new city from the beginning, or whether he restores an ancient one that has perished, - if he is endued with intellect, he will not attempt to make any alterations in any thing which ought to be performed respecting the Gods, their temples, and their sacred concerns, or the names of certain Gods or dæmons, which ought to be given to temples; whether these ceremonies are derived from Delphi, or Dodona, or Ammon, or from certain ancient discourses, by which some persons have been persuaded; or whether they have been the result of divine visions and inspiration. For, in consequence of being persuaded of their truth, the ancients established sacrifices mixed with mystic ceremonies; whether these originated from the natives themselves, or whether they are of Tyrrhene, or Cyprian, or of any other origin. But, from these ancient discourses and rumours, they consecrated statues, altars and temples, and placed each in a sacred grove. In all these the legislator should not make the

d   smallest innovation; but should attribute to each of the parts, a God, a dæmon, or a certain hero. And in the distribution of the land, he should in the first place select a portion for illustrious groves and other sacred purposes, so that the inhabitants of each of the parts, assembling at stated times, may with facility prepare themselves for their respective employments, so as during the sacrifices to associate benevolently with

e   and recognize each other. For *nothing is more advantageous to a city than for the citizens to be known to each other; since, where each has no light in the manners of each, but darkness,*[†] *there neither honours nor governors are properly appointed, nor can any one obtain, in a becoming manner, the justice which is due to him.* But every man, one towards one, ought earnestly to endeavour in all cities, that he may never appear insincere to any one, but may be always artless and true, and that, being

739a such, no other person may deceive him. But the throw which follows this, in the establishment of laws, like that of chess-men, according to the proverb, from a temple, since it is unusual, may perhaps cause him who hears it at first to wonder. But to him who has reasoned upon, and tried it, it will appear that the city will thus, in the second place, be inhabited in the best manner. Some one, however, perhaps, will not approve of this city, because it does not employ a tyrannic legislator. It will, indeed, be most proper to speak of the best polity, and likewise of a second and third, and then leave it to every one's option to choose

b   that which pleases him the most. We therefore shall act in this manner; and, after we have spoken of a polity which is first, of one which is second, and of another which is the third in virtue, we shall leave it to the option of Clinias, and any other who may be present at the selection of these, to attribute to his country whichever of them he pleases. The

c   first city and polity, therefore, and the best laws, subsist there where through the whole city that ancient proverb takes place in the most eminent degree, that all things are common among friends. This then must be asserted, whether it now is or ever was adopted, that women, children, and all possessions should be common; and that private property should by all possible means be exterminated from life. Things too which are private by nature should every where, as much as possible, become common; such as the eyes, the ears, and the hands. For seeing, hearing, and acting, should be employed for common

† As in London, and all great modern cities.

advantage. In like manner, all men should praise and blame the same things, rejoice in and be afflicted with the same circumstances, and as much as possible adopt such laws as will unite the city in the most eminent degree. No one can establish any bound or virtue more transcendently proper than this. The inhabitants of such a city, whether they are Gods[†] or sons of the Gods, by living together in this manner, will lead a joyful life. On this account it is not proper to consider any other paradigm of a polity, but, inspecting this, we ought to explore such a one to the utmost of our power. But this, which is the subject of our present discussion, if it should subsist, would most nearly approach to immortality. And if it does not rank in the first, it certainly will in the second place. However, if Divinity is willing, we will after this discuss the polity, which is the third in order. Let us now then consider the nature of this polity, and how it may be established. In the first place, land and houses should be distributed to them, and they should not be suffered to cultivate the ground in common; since a thing of this kind is greater than their generation, nutrition, and education will admit. Land, however, and houses, should be distributed to them with this intention, that each may consider the portion allotted him, as common to the whole city. But, this region being their country, they ought to reverence it in a greater degree than children their mother; for, being a goddess, she is the sovereign mistress of mortals. The same should be our conceptions of the indigenous Gods and dæmons. But that these things may subsist in this manner, through the whole time, the following particulars are to be considered: As many Vestal hearths as are distributed to us at present, so many ought always to be distributed, and neither more nor fewer in number. But a thing of this kind will be firmly established in every city, if every one always leaves that child to whom he is most attached, the only heir of his allotted portion, his successor, and cultivator of the Gods, of his race, his country, of the living, and the dead. But those who have more children than one should for this purpose portion the females according to the established law, but commit the males to the care of those citizens that have no children of their own, and this in a very benevolent manner. However, if benevolence is wanting, or each of the citizens has a numerous progeny of male or female children, or on the contrary but a few children, owing to the barrenness of the women, then that greatest

---

[†] *Viz.* Gods according to similitude. For, as intellect is called a God by Plato, according to union, and soul according to participation, so the most exalted characters among men are called by him Gods according to similitude.

and most honourable governor whom we have established, must consider what is proper to be done in either of these cases, and, whether there is an abundance or a defect of children, must devise some method by which five thousand and forty habitations alone may always remain. But there are many methods by which this may be accomplished. For procreation may be restrained, which is the cause of this abundance; and, on the contrary, by diligent attention, an increase of offspring may be obtained, when it is requisite. For what we are speaking of may be accomplished by honour and disgrace, and by the admonitory discourses of the old to the young. Lastly, every defect arises from the number of

e   five thousand and forty houses not being preserved. But, if our city should have a superabundance of citizens, through the familiarity of those that dwell together, and by this means it should be oppressed with poverty, that ancient device must be adopted which we have often mentioned, that a friendly colony should be sent from friends; for it

741a   appears that this will be advantageous to the city. But if, on the contrary, at any time an inundation of diseases, or the ravages of war, should reduce the citizens to a less than the established number, such citizens as have been educated in an adulterated manner are not to be voluntarily admitted to supply the place of those that are wanting. But it is said that even Divinity is not able to force necessity. We should way, therefore, that our present discourse speaks in an exhortatory manner as follows: O best of all men, who honour according to nature

b   similitude and equality, sameness, and general consent, never relax in honouring these, both according to the number, and all the power of things beautiful and good. And, in the first place, preserve through the whole of life the above-mentioned number. In the next place, do not despise the moderate elevation and magnitude of the possessions which were first distributed to you, by buying and selling with each other. For, if you act in this manner, neither Divinity, the distributor of your allotted portion, nor the legislator will be your associate in war. For now the law announces in the first place, that he who is willing to

c   receive the allotted portion shall receive it, but that he who is unwilling shall be deprived of it: and this, because in the first place the land is sacred to all the Gods; and in the next place, because the priests and priestesses pray during the first, second, and third sacrifices, that both the buyers and sellers of allotted houses and lands may be properly disposed in such transactions. But they should write on cypress monuments in temples, for the benefit of posterity. And besides this,

d   for the purpose of preserving these, they should commit them to the care of that magistrate who appears to have the most acute vision, that those may be detected who act fraudulently, and that he who is disobedient both to law and divinity may be punished. But, according to the proverb, no vicious man will ever understand how much all cities will be benefited by acting in the manner we have prescribed, but he only who is skilful and of equitable manners. In this city there is no ardent pursuit of gain; nor is it lawful for any one to apply himself to the acquisition of illiberal wealth, because the disgraceful mechanic art, as it is called, which is employed for this purpose, subverts liberal manners. Riches, therefore, are not to be accumulated by any such means. Besides this, another law follows all these, which forbids any private person the possession of either silver or gold. But because there is daily occasion for money for the sake of commutation, which is nearly necessary to artificers, and to all those that have similar wants, in order to pay the wages of mercenaries, servants, and husbandmen - for the sake of these things we permit the use of money in the city, but order it to be such as may be honoured by our citizens, but despised by other men. For the sake of war, indeed, and travelling to other countries, as when ambassadors are sent to foreign nations, or for some other necessary purpose, the city should possess a quantity of the common coin of Greece. But when any necessity obliges a private person to leave the city, having begged permission of the magistrates, he shall be suffered to depart; but the foreign coin, which he possesses on his return, he shall change for that of his own country. And if any one is detected converting the money of another city to his own private use, such money shall become public property. He who has been an eye witness of such conduct, but has not divulged it, shall be disgraced, and pay the same fine as he who endeavoured to enrich himself with foreign coin. Besides, no one shall be permitted to give or receive a marriage portion, nor to deposit money with a man who cannot be trusted, nor to put money out to use. And it shall be lawful for him with whom money is deposited at interest, to pay neither interest nor principal. That a conduct of this kind is best for a city, will be rightly judged by him who always refers these particulars to the intention of the legislator. But we say that the intention of a politician who is endued with intellect, is not that which the multitude say is the intention of a good legislator, - I mean, that the city may be greater and richer than others, and that it may for the most part have dominion over the land and sea. To which they add, that he who establishes laws properly, ought to wish that the city may be the best, and the most happy. But of these, some are capable of taking place, but others not. The legislator, therefore, will wish that the possible, but he will not wish that the impossible, may take place. For in the latter case his wish would be vain; neither, therefore, would he attempt it. For it is nearly necessary that they should be happy, and at the same time worthy. This then will be the object of his wish. But it is impossible that they should be rich in the extreme, and at the same time good; I mean rich in the vulgar acceptation of the word. For the vulgar call those rich, who being few in number possess a great quantity of money, which even a bad man 743a may possess. If this be the case, I should never grant them, that a rich man, who is not at the same time worthy, can be truly happy. But I assert that it is impossible a man can be at the same time eminently good, and eminently rich. Some one, however, may perhaps say, Why not? Because we say, The possession which is obtained both from just b and unjust conduct is more than double of that which is alone justly obtained; and that the expenses which are neither becoming nor base are doubly less than those which are becoming, and which are performed in a becoming manner. He, therefore, who acts in a contrary manner will never be richer than him who acquires more than double, and spends less than half. But of these, the one is worthy, but the other not worthy, because he is parsimonious. Sometimes, indeed, this latter character is perfectly vicious; but, as we have just now said, is never good. For he who receives both justly and unjustly, and spends neither justly nor unjustly, is indeed rich, because he is parsimonious: but he who is perfectly vicious, as being for the most part prodigal, is c extremely poor. And he who spends in a becoming manner, and alone acquires justly, will never at any time become remarkably rich, nor yet excessively poor; so that our assertion is right, that very rich are not good men. But, if they are not good, they are not happy. With us, however, the establishment of laws looks to this, that the citizens may become most happy, and in the highest degree friends to each other. But the citizens will never be friends where there is much judicial controversy and unjust transactions with each other, but where the least d of these is found. We have said too, that there ought to be neither gold nor silver in the city, nor yet an anxious pursuit of gain through mechanical arts and usury, or base cattle, but that wealth should be acquired from such things as agriculture imparts and affords; yet in such a manner, as that it may not compel the citizens to neglect those things e for the sake of which riches are desired: but these are the soul and body, which without gymnastic and the other disciplines will never be of any worth. On this account, we have said more than once, that an attention to money ought to be honoured in the last place. For, since all the concerns in which every man is seriously engaged are three, an attention to riches properly ranks in the last and third place: but the concerns of the body possess the middle; and those of the soul the first place. And, indeed, the polity which we are now considering will be governed by proper laws, if it distributes honours in this manner. But if any one of the laws which are established in it shall appear to prefer the health of the body to temperance, or riches to both health and temperance, it will appear to be improperly established. A legislator, therefore, ought often to signify his intention to the people in this manner: I am desirous that this particular thing should take place, which if it does, my intentions will succeed; but if it does not, they will be rendered frustrate. And thus, perhaps, he might both liberate himself and others from the burthen of legislation; but never by any other means. He, therefore, who receives an allotted portion should possess it on the conditions we have mentioned. But this will take place in a becoming manner, when each person who becomes an inhabitant of the colony possesses every thing else equally. Since, however, this is not possible, but one coming to settle in it will possess more money, and another less, it is requisite, for the sake of many advantages, and of equality in the city, that property should be unequally possessed: that, in consequence of each receiving magistracies, tributes, and distributions, according to the honour annexed to each, and not according to his own virtue only, and that of his ancestors, nor yet according to the strength or beauty of his body, but receiving these equalized as much as possible, *viz.* unequally, but commensurably distributed, they may not disagree with each other. For the sake of these things, it is requisite that there should be four divisions in magnitude of possessions; and that these should be called first, second, third, and fourth divisions, or should receive some other appellations: so that, both when they remain in possession of the same property, and when they become most rich from being poor, or poor from being rich, each may pass to the possession of property accommodated to each. For this purpose, I shall lay down the following scheme of law:

We say, that in a city which in future is to be void of that greatest disease, which may be more properly called discord, or sedition, none of the citizens should either be extremely poor, or extremely rich: for both these produce both. It is therefore now requisite that a legislator should say what is the bound of each. Let, then, the bound of poverty be the honour of the allotted distribution, which ought to be stable, and which no magistrate, nor any one who loves honour for the sake of virtue, will ever suffer to become less to any one. The legislator, establishing the measure of these distributions, will permit the double, triple, and quadruple of this to be possessed. But, if any one possesses more than these, whether they are found, or bestowed, or procured by mechanical arts, or possessed by any other such like fortune, - if he imparts what remains to the city, and to the Gods, the guardians of the city, he will act in a blameless and laudable manner. But he who accuses one that is not obedient to this law shall obtain the half of his possessions; and, at the same time, the half of the accuser's property shall be dedicated to the Gods. An account too shall be openly given, in writing, of all such property as surpasses the allotted portion, to the magistrates who are appointed guardians by law, that all the judgments respecting riches may be easy and extremely clear. In the next place, the city ought to be built as much as possible in the middle of the country, and in a place possessing other things accommodated to the city, which it is not difficult to understand and relate. After this, it should be divided into twelve† parts, the temple of Vesta, Jupiter, and Minerva, being first of all raised under the appellation of the Acropolis, or tower of the city. This temple should be circularly enclosed; and from this enclosure, the city and all the region should be divided into twelve parts. But the twelve parts ought to be equalized in such a manner, that the portion of the prolific land may be small, but that of the unprolific great: and the allotted portions should be five thousand and forty. Again, each of these should receive a twofold division. The two divisions, likewise, should be associated allotments, and each should participate of the near and remote distributions, *viz.* the division near the city should communicate with that which is situated in its extremity; that which is at the second distance from the city, with that which is the second from its extremity; and after this manner with all the rest. It should likewise be so contrived in the twofold divisions of which we are now speaking, respecting the fecundity and barrenness of the region, that there should be an equality of distribution in multitude and paucity. It is likewise necessary that the streets should be divided into twelve parts, and, indeed, every other possession, equality being preserved in the greatest degree, and a description made of every particular. After this, the twelve allotments should be attributed to the twelve Gods; each allotted portion being denominated after, and consecrated to, its presiding deity, and called a tribe. The twelve sections too of the city ought to be divided in the same manner as the rest of the region, *viz.* so

745a

b

c

d

e

---

† The reason why Plato adopts this division is, because the number 12 is an image of all-perfect progression, being composed from the multiplication of 3 by 4, both which numbers, according to the Pythagoreans, are images of perfection.

that each section shall have two habitations, one near the middle, and the other near the extremity. And thus much respecting the habitations. This, however, we ought by all means to consider, that all the particulars which we have just now spoken of will never so opportunely
746a   concur as they have happened to do in our discourse; and that the inhabitants will not be indignant at living together in this manner, but will be satisfied with their allotted and moderate portion of wealth through the whole of life. The procreation too of children will take place with each in the manner we have mentioned: and they will be deprived of silver and gold, and other things, which it is evident, from what has been said, the legislator will forbid. Besides this, the habitations will be circularly enclosed in the middle of the city and the region, as we have mentioned above. All which particulars have nearly been asserted by us as dreams: and we have fashioned, as it were, from
b   wax a certain city and citizens. But these particulars in a certain respect have not been badly asserted. It is now proper, therefore, to attend to the legislator, addressing us in the following manner: - You must not consider me, O friends, as ignorant that what has been now said has been after a manner truly asserted. But I think it will be most just in each of the following particulars, that he who exhibits a paradigm, according to whose similitude that which he wishes to accomplish should be formed, ought not to omit any thing which is most beautiful
c   and true. And he to whom it is impossible something of these should happen, should desist from attempting to accomplish this; but he should devise some means by which he may produce that which is most proximate and allied to these; and should permit the legislator to bring his wish to an end. This being done, he should consider, in common with him, which of the above mentioned particulars contributes, and which is adverse, to legislation. For even an artificer of the most trifling
d   thing ought every where to produce a work in consent with itself, if he wishes to obtain praise for its execution. But now, after the distribution of the twelve parts, we should consider, that since these twelve parts contain in themselves many distributions, and things consequent to, and produced from, these, as far as to five thousand and forty; whence they possess tribes, and towns, and streets, warlike orders and discipline, money, dry and wet measures, and weights; - all these the law should establish commensurate and according with each other. Besides this, we
e   ought not to fear lest we should be thought to bestow too much attention on things of a trifling nature, when we order that no one shall possess furniture of any kind which is destitute of the proper measure,
747a   and consider the divisions and varieties of the numbers as useful to all

things; to such particulars as are various in themselves, and such as receive a variety in length and depth, or in sounds and motions, whether the motions are upwards and downwards, in a right line, or circular. For the legislator, looking to all these, should enjoin all the citizens to preserve this order to the utmost of their power. For no one discipline belonging to youth possesses such a mighty power, in economies, polities, and all arts, as the study of numbers. And that which is

b   greatest of all is, that this discipline excites even the sleepy, and those that are naturally rustic, and renders them docile, of a good memory, and sagacious; benefiting them, by a divine art, beyond what their own nature is able to accomplish. All which things, when they are possessed sufficiently and usefully, illiberality and avarice being extirpated from the mind of their possessor, become beautiful and properly adapted studies: but, when these are not extirpated, instead of wisdom they

c   secretly produce that which is called craft; as we see at present is the case with the Egyptians, Phœnicians, and many other nations, through the illiberality of their pursuits and possessions; whether things of this kind were occasioned by a depraved legislator, or by adverse fortune, or by any other similar nature. For, O Megillus and Clinias, this ought not

d   to be concealed from us, that there is a great difference in places,[†] with respect to producing men of a more or less excellent character; and that laws should be established accommodated to such places. For some places, through all-various winds and storms, are inhabited with difficulty; others through water; others through nutriment from the earth, which not only imparts to bodies food of a more and less

---

† It is well observed by Proclus, "that a change is produced in different nations from the places themselves which each inhabits; from the temperament of the air, and from habitude to the heavens; and still more partially from spermatic reasons. But they most especially differ according to the gregarious government of the Gods, and the diversities of inspective guardians; through which (says he) you will find colours, figures, voices, and motions changed in different places. Hence emigrants often change their colour and their voice, when they settle in other countries; just as plants are changed with the quality of the region, if they happen to be transplanted into a foreign land." Δει γινωσκειν οτι τοις διαφοροις εθνεσιν η εξαλλαγη γινεται μεν και παρα τους τοπους αυτους ους εκαστα κατοικει, και παρα τας των αερων κρασεις, και παρα την προς τον ουρανον σχεσιν, και ετι μερικωτερον, ει βουλει, παρα τους σπερματικους λογους· πολυ δ' αν μαλιστα διαφερειν ειποις αυτα, κατα την αγελαιοκομικην των θεων επιστασιαν, και τας των εφορων διαφοροτητας, παρ' ας και χρωματα, και σχηματα, και φωνας, και κινησεις εξαλλαττομενας ευροις αν εν τοις διαφοροις τοποις, ως τε και τους αποικους πολλακις μεταβαλλειν, το τε χρωμα και την φωνην, ωταν εις αλλους αφικωνται τοπου· καθαπερ τα φυτα τη ποιοτητι της χωρας συμμεταβαλλονται, καν εις αλλοτριαν γην μεταβληθεντα τυγχανη· Procl. in Tim. p.31.

e   excellent nature, but is no less able to accomplish this, with respect to souls. But those places in a country possess the greatest difference, in which there are a certain divine inspiration, and allotments of dæmons who are either always propitious to the inhabitants, or the contrary. Which things the legislator, who is endued with intellect, considering as much as it is possible for man to speculate things of this kind, will thus endeavour to establish laws. And this must be done by you, O Clinias! for, before you cause the city to be inhabited, you must direct your attention to these particulars.

CLIN. But, O Athenian guest! you speak in an all-beautiful manner: and, therefore, this must be done by me.

BOOK VI

751a   After all that has now been said, the next thing that remains for you to do will be the establishment of magistrates in the city.

CLIN. It will so.

GUEST. These two species are found to subsist respecting the ornament of a polity. In the first place, the establishment of magistrates, how many there ought to be, and in what manner they ought to be appointed. In the next place with respect to the laws, which are to be given to the several magistrates, what, how many, and what kind will

b   be accommodated to each. But, previous to choosing the magistrates, let us mention some particulars pertaining to the election of them.

CLIN. What particulars are these?

GUEST. These. It must be perfectly evident that, since legislation is a great work, he who does not appoint proper magistrates in a well regulated city, though the laws are well established, will find no advantage derived from them, but abundance of ridicule; and such a one

c   will be the mean of oppressing the city with the most weighty injuries and calamities.

CLIN. Undoubtedly.

GUEST. We will therefore consider this, as now happening to you, O friend, respecting this polity and city. For you see it is necessary, that those who undertake in a proper manner the office of magistrates should from their youth have been sufficiently tried, as likewise their race, till the time of election. In the next place, that those who are to choose the magistrates should be educated in legitimate manners, so that they may

d   be able to judge in a proper manner, who should be admitted, and who rejected. But with respect to those that have recently met together, as they are unacquainted with each other, and, besides this, are void of erudition, how can they ever be able to choose magistrates in a blameless manner?

CLIN. They nearly never will be able.

GUEST. But the contest, as they say, does not easily admit of excuses.

e   This then must now be accomplished both by you and me; since you have willingly undertaken the office of establishing a city for the Cretans, and are, as you say, the tenth in this employment; and I have

752a   promised to assist you in the present fabulous narration. I shall not therefore willingly leave this discourse without a head. For, wandering every where in this condition, it would appear deformed.

CLIN. You have spoken most excellently, O guest.

GUEST. Let us, therefore, accomplish this to the utmost of our power.

CLIN. Let us indeed, do by all means as we have said.

GUEST. Be it so, if divinity is willing, that in this respect we may vanquish old age.

b CLIN. But it is reasonable to suppose that he is willing.

GUEST. It is reasonable. Following him, therefore, let us attend to this.

CLIN. To what?

GUEST. In how bold, and at the same time dangerous, a manner our city will at present be established.

CLIN. To what circumstance adverting do you thus speak?

GUEST. To the easy and intrepid manner in which we have given laws to unskilful men, and have ordered them to receive such laws. Thus

c much, indeed, O Clinias, is nearly perfectly evident, even to one who is not very wise, that no one will easily admit these laws at first. But if we wait so long till boys tasting of, and being sufficiently disciplined in, the laws, and accustomed to them, are able to give their votes in conjunction with the whole city, and this by a certain manner and device is properly accomplished, I then should think that a city so disciplined would remain after the present time abundantly secure.

d CLIN. It is reasonable to suppose this will be the case.

GUEST. Let us consider, therefore, whether we can afford assistance sufficient for this purpose. For I say, O Clinias, that the Cnossians, far more than the other Cretans, ought not only to make an expiation about the region which you have now caused to be inhabited, but should be strenuously careful that the first magistrates may be appointed as much as possible in the most secure and best manner. In appointing others, indeed, there will be less labour; but it will be most necessary

e that the guardians of the laws should be chosen with the utmost attention.

CLIN. What method then shall we adopt in order to accomplish this?

GUEST. The following. I say, O sons of Crete, that the Cnossians, since they are the most ancient of many cities, ought to choose in common from themselves, and those that settle with them in the same habitation, thirty-seven men in all; nineteen indeed of these from the inhabitants, but the rest from Cnossus itself. The Cnossians should give

753a these to your city, and should cause you to be a citizen of this colony, and one of the eighteen men; and this, either by employing persuasion or moderate force.

CLIN. But what? Will not you, O guest, and Megillus, partake with us of this polity?

GUEST. The Athenians, O Clinias, are men of lofty thought, and so also are the Spartans, and each dwell at a great distance. But, both by you and the other inhabitants, every thing will be elegantly possessed, conformably to what you have just now said. However, in the course of time, and the polity remaining, the magistrates should be chosen in the following manner: All such as are capable of bearing arms, whether horsemen or footmen, and when age has given them sufficient strength to engage in war, all these should give their vote; and the election should be made in that temple which is considered by the city as the most honourable. But every one, from whatever part of the country he may come, should place the name which he derived from his father, and that of his tribe and nation, written on a small table on the altar of the God. He should likewise, in a similar manner, write on it his own name. But it shall be lawful for every one to take away that table which does not appear to him to be properly written, and place it in the forum, where it shall remain for not less than thirty days. After this, the magistrates shall expose to the view of the whole city three hundred approved tables; and in a similar manner the city shall approve out of these whichever it pleases. In the second place, they shall again show to every one a hundred chosen out of these: and, in the third place, every one shall name out of the hundred men that person whom he most approves. But the thirty-seven men shall declare those to be the magistrates who are chosen by the greatest number of votes. Who, therefore, O Clinias and Megillus, will establish all these things for us in the city, respecting magistrates, and the examination of them? Do we, therefore, understand, that in cities so constituted from the first, there ought to be such persons, but that they will never be found among those that are chosen for magistrates? It is however necessary that these should not be men of a depraved character, but of the most exalted virtue. For the beginning, according to the proverb, is the half of the whole work; and all men praise him who begins a thing well. But, as it appears to me, the beginning is more than the half, and that no one has sufficiently praised it when properly accomplished.

CLIN. You speak most properly.

GUEST. Since, therefore, we know this, we should not pass over it in silence, and leave it involved in obscurity. Indeed, at present, I have nothing to say respecting it, except this one necessary and advantageous thing.

CLIN. What is it?

GUEST. I say, that no one is the father or mother of this city which we are about to establish, except the city which gives it inhabitants. Nor am I ignorant that there often has been, and will be, strife between colonies and their parent countries. At present, therefore, as a child, who, though he sometimes opposes his parents, yet, through his indigence of education, loves and is beloved by them, and, always flying to his own, finds in them alone protection; in like manner, I say, the Cnossians will be readily disposed to give assistance to the new city, and the new city to the Cnossians. I repeat then what I have just now said (for there is no harm in twice saying that which is well said), that the Cnossians ought carefully to attend to all these particulars, and choose no fewer than a hundred of the oldest and best men out of the colony, and another hundred from the Cnossians themselves. I say too, that these coming to the new city should be careful that the magistrates are established according to the laws, and that they are approved of when established. When these things are accomplished, the Cnossians should return to Cnossus, but the new city should endeavour to preserve and render itself prosperous. But the thirty-seven men, whom we have chosen, should both at present and in futurity attend to the following particulars: In the first place, they should establish guardians of the laws; and, in the next place, of those writings in which every one must give an account to the magistrates of the multitude of his possessions. The greatest estate should be that of four minæ; the second, of three; and the third of two minæ; but the fourth should consist of one mina. But if any one shall be found to possess more than he has given an account of in writing, all such overplus shall become public property; and, besides this, it shall be lawful for any one to accuse him as acting in neither a becoming nor legal manner, when he is found to despise the laws, through the love of gain. He likewise who is desirous of accusing such a one shall accuse him to the guardians of the laws, under the appellation of one addicted to base gain. And he who happens to be condemned shall not partake of the public property; but, when any distribution is made in the city, he shall possess nothing but his first allotment. It shall likewise be signified in writing, that such a one is condemned as long as he lives; and the writing shall be placed where any one who is willing may read it. The guardian of the laws shall not govern more than twenty years, and shall not hold this office if he is less than fifty years of age. But, if he is sixty years old when he enters on this employment, he shall only govern for ten years. It shall likewise be established, that he who has lived more than seventy years shall not hold an office of such great importance. These three mandates, therefore, are to be attended to, respecting the guardians of the laws. But, as the laws advance, any one may order these men what they ought to attend to, in addition to what we have already said.

Let us now, therefore, speak about the election of other magistrates. For, after these, it is necessary that the commanders in chief of the army should be chosen, and such as are ministrant to these in war, as, for instance, the masters of the horse, the military tribunes, and those who c orderly arrange the foot; and who may very properly be called, as they are in common, governors of tribes. The guardians of the laws, therefore, should draw out of the city the commanders of all these, and should approve all such as, being of a proper age, either have been, or now are, engaged in war. But if it shall appear that any one of those who are not drawn out is better than some one of those that are, it shall d be lawful to choose the former in preference to the latter, on condition that this preference is confirmed by an oath; and the choice, when he is named, shall be determined by the greater number of votes. Three amongst these, who are found to have the most votes, shall be chosen as the commanders of the army, and as those that are to take care of warlike concerns, just in the same manner as the guardians of the laws e were chosen. These shall appoint twelve præfects of the military orders, and assign one to each tribe. It shall likewise be here lawful to prefer one who is not nominated, to one who is, in the same manner as was observed respecting the election of the commanders in chief. But this assembly, before the præfects are deliberately chosen, shall be held by the guardians of the laws in a place the most holy and best adapted for the purpose. Here the foot and the horse shall be seated separate from each other; and in the third place, after these, the rest of those who are employed in warlike concerns. And every one, indeed, shall give his vote in the choice of commanders in chief and masters of the horse. 756a The præfects of the bands shall be chosen by those alone that carry shields, but the commanders of tribes by all the horse. The commanders in chief shall choose for themselves the light-armed soldiers, the archers, and the rest of this kind. In the next place there remains for us the establishment of the masters of the horse. These, therefore, must be appointed by those who appoint the commanders in chief; and the election must be conducted in a similar manner. But the horse shall give b their vote, the foot being placed opposite to them, and those two that have the most votes shall be the commanders of all the horse. Disputes about votes shall be allowed to take place twice; but, if any one doubts about them a third time, the votes shall be determined by those whose province it is to fix the measure of voting. The council shall consist of thirty twelves; for the number three hundred and sixty will be found accommodated to the distributions. And it is capable of being distributed into four parts by ninety, so that ninety counsellors may be obtained from each of the divisions of land. And in the first place all the counsellors will necessarily be obtained from the largest possessions; and he who is unwilling to be chosen shall be fined; and after information has been given respecting him, he shall be noted. On the following day the same method shall be adopted with possessions of the second rank. And on the third day, whoever is willing shall be obtained from possessions of the third order. This mode with respect to three orders of possessions is necessary; but the fourth and smallest possession should be exempt from fine, if any one whose property is of this order is unwilling to act as a counsellor. On the fourth day all shall be obtained from the fourth and smallest order of possessions; but he who is unwilling to be chosen from third and fourth possessions shall be exempt from fine. But he who refuses from possessions of the second and first order shall be fined, so as that he who belongs to the second rank shall undergo a fine triple of the first fine, and he who belongs to the first quadruple. On the fifth day the magistrates shall exhibit to the view of all the citizens the names of the counsellors. Every man belonging to these shall act as a counsellor; or, if any one refuses to act in that capacity, he shall be fined the first fine. But the half of those that are elected out of all the possessions, *viz.* one hundred and eighty, shall be chosen by lot as counsellors for a year. The election, therefore, subsisting in this manner, will be a medium between a monarchical and democratic polity, which medium a polity ought always to preserve. For slaves and despots can never become friends, nor the depraved and worthy, when they are equally honoured. For, by unequal things, such as are equal will become unequal, unless they partake of measure; because, through both these, polities are filled with seditions. That ancient saying, indeed, being true, that equality produces friendship, is asserted with the greatest propriety and elegance. But, as it is not very evident what the equality is which is able to accomplish this, we are on this account vehemently disturbed. For, as there are two equalities which have the same appellation, but are in reality nearly contrary to each other in many respects, every city and every legislator may sufficiently employ one of these in the distribution of honours by lot, *viz.* the equality consisting in measure, weight, and number;[†] but it is

---

[†] *Viz.* arithmetical equality, which takes place when a series of numbers have the same common difference; as 1, 2, 3, 4, &c. or 1, 3, 5, 7, &c.

not easy for every one to perceive the most true and the best equality. For it is the judgment of Jupiter, and but little of it is at all times employed by men; though as much of it as is employed either by cities

c or private persons produces every good. For it distributes more to the greater, and things smaller to the less;[†] imparting to each that which is moderate according to the nature of each. It likewise always attributes greater honours to those who are greater in virtue, but less to such as are less in virtue and discipline; and imparts to each the becoming according to reason. For this is, doubtless, always with us the politically just itself; which we ought at present to aspire after, and, looking to this equality, O Clinias, establish our now rising city. Whoever, likewise, establishes any other city ought to give laws with his eye directed to

d this, and not to a few tyrants, or to one, or to any strength of the people, but always to the just itself. And this is what has just now been said by us, *viz.* a distribution of the equal, according to nature, to unequal particulars. But it is, indeed, necessary, that every city should make use of these two equalities, which are similar in denomination, if it wishes to continue entirely free from sedition. For the equitable and

e the lenient judgment of the perfect and accurate, when it takes place contrary to upright judgment, is broken. On this account it is, perhaps, necessary to use election by lot, for the sake of avoiding the moroseness of the multitude, and to invoke on this occasion divinity and good fortune, and beseech them to direct the lot to that which is most just. In this manner, then, it is necessary to use both the equalities; but that equality which is indigent of fortune ought to be used on very few occasions. These things, O friends, must be accomplished by the city

758a which is to be established on a sure foundation. But as a ship, while sailing on the sea, requires a perpetual guard both night and day; in like manner a city, while situated in the tempest of other cities, subject to all-various stratagems, and in danger of captivity, is continually indigent of protection. Hence, the magistrates and guardians of a city ought mutually to succeed each other from night to day, and from day to

b night, so as that this interchange of office may never cease. But the multitude is not able to accomplish any of these things with celerity. It is, however, necessary that the multitude of the counsellors should be

---

[†] The true equality which Plato here speaks of is geometric equality, which is identity of ratio, and according to which the merits of individuals are to be estimated; so that as merit is to merit, so should gift be to gift. The equality, therefore, here is that of ratio, and not of number; as, for instance, in the numbers 2, 4, 6, 12, which form a geometric proportion.

permitted to employ the greatest part of their time in properly managing their own private affairs; but that a twelfth part of them, a distribution being made into twelve months, should succeed each other, one by one,

c in the office of guardians. These should readily attend to every one, whether coming from the city or elsewhere, whether he wishes to give any information, or to ask respecting those particulars about which a city ought either to ask or answer other cities, or receive answers from them. And this, for the sake of those all-various innovations which are always accustomed to happen; so as to prevent them, as much as possible, from not happening; and that, when they do happen, the city

d may perceive them with the utmost celerity, and apply a remedy. This ought always to be accomplished by an assembly of the governors of the city, together with a dissolution of the difficulties which suddenly happen to the city and the laws. All these particulars must be under the direction of the twelfth part of the council, who are to cease from their office eleven parts of the year. But this part of the council ought always

e to defend the city in common with the other magistrates. And the particulars, indeed, respecting the city, when subsisting in this manner, will be orderly disposed. But what care, and what order, must there be of all the rest of the region? Will it not be necessary, since all the city, and the whole region, is distributed into twelve parts, that there should be inspectors of the roads, habitations, edifices, ports, forum, fountains, sacred groves, and temples, and other things of this kind belonging to the city?

CLIN. Undoubtedly.

759a GUEST. We must say, then, that there ought to be purifiers of the temples, and priests and priestesses. But that three species of magistrates ought to be chosen for the purpose of taking care of the roads and buildings, and the ornaments belonging to things of this kind, and of preventing men from being injured by each other, or by wild beasts; and that, both within the walls and in the suburbs of the city, every thing may be conducted in a proper manner. And those that take care of the above mentioned particulars should be called ædiles; but those that attend to the ornament of the forum, præfects of the market; and those

b that take care of the ornament of the temples, priests. But the priesthood which is paternal, whether sustained by men or women, is by no means to be moved. if nothing of this kind happens to none, or but to a few, which is likely to be the case with the inhabitants of a new city, then priests, priestesses, and the purifiers of temples are to be appointed. But all these things are to be instituted partly by election, and partly by lot. In every region, too, and city, the common people, and those that are not common, should mingle in a friendly manner with each other, that they may be concordant in the highest degree.

c The particulars, therefore, pertaining to the priests are to be committed to the care of Divinity, that, as it pleases him, so the lot may be referred to a divine fortune. But he who is allotted the priesthood ought always to be examined, and proved to be in the first place a man of integrity, and legitimately begotten; in the next place, one from a pure habitation, and who is free from slaughter, and all crimes of this kind against divine natures, and whose father and mother have lived with similar purity. The laws too relative to divine concerns ought to be procured from

d Delphi; and, interpreters of them being appointed, these should be used. But the priesthood should not be of longer continuance than a year; nor should he be less than sixty years of age who is to attend to divine concerns for us, sufficiently, according to sacred laws. The same things are to be established respecting priestesses. The four tribes should appoint thrice four interpreters; three being taken from each tribe: and three being approved, that are chosen by the greatest number of votes, the other nine must be sent to Delphi, that one may be chosen out of

e each triad. But the examination and approbation of these, and their age, must be such as that of the priests which was mentioned above. These should be established as interpreters for life; and, on the decease of any one of them, the four tribes to which he belonged must choose another in his place. There ought likewise to be, in each of the temples, dispensators of the sacred money, who should possess absolute authority

760a over the sacred groves, and their fruits, and over things let out to hire: and three should be chosen for the greatest temples out of the three largest possessions; but two for the smaller temples, and one for such as are the most elegant. The choice, too, and examination of these should be made in the same manner as in the election of the leaders of the army. And such are the particulars which should take place respecting sacred concerns. But the utmost care should be taken that nothing is left without a guard. The guards of the city, too, should be these: the commanders in chief of the army, the præfects of the military orders, the masters of the horse, the governors of tribes, the dispensators, the

b inspectors of roads and buildings, and the magistrates who preside over the markets, when all these are properly chosen. The rest of the region should be defended as follows: - The whole region was divided by us, as much as possible, into twelve parts. But one tribe being allotted to each division, it should choose every year five, as it were, inspectors of the lands, and governors of tribes. Each of these should choose out of his

c own tribe twelve young men, not less than five-and-twenty years of age, and not more than thirty. Each of these should be allotted each part of the region for the space of a month, that all of them may be skilful and knowing in every part of the region. But the guardians and governors should defend and govern the city for the space of two years. And when first they are allotted their respective divisions, they should change their places every month, and the governors of the guard should lead them to the places next in order, and to the right hand parts in a circular progression. But I mean by the right hand parts, those which are towards the east. Afterwards, in the second year, they should change to the left hand parts, that they may not only be skilled in the nature of the country for one part of the year, but may know, for the most part, what happens in every season, to every part of the country. In the third year, five other inspectors of the land, and governors of the guard, should be chosen, as curators of the twelve young men. But the following care should be bestowed in the several occupations in each place. First, that the region may be, in the highest degree, well fortified against the incursions of the enemy; trenches being dug where they are requisite, and buildings raised for the purpose of restraining those who may endeavour to injure the country and its possessions. Animals subject to the yoke, and the servants belonging to each place, should be employed for this purpose, when they are not engaged in their usual respective employments; those that preside over these disposing every part of the country in such a manner, that it may be difficult of access to the enemy, but easy to friends, animals subject to the yoke, and cattle. They should likewise take care that the waters from Jupiter[†] do not injure the country, but that they may rather be useful to it, when descending from lofty mountains into hollow valleys; and this by restraining their course in edifices and ditches; so that, being received and imbibed by these places, they may produce streams and fountains for all the subject lands and places, and may thus render the most dry parts of the country moist, and abounding with water. They should likewise adorn fountains and rivers with trees and edifices; and, conducting streams through metal pipes, should cause them to be distributed in great abundance. In like manner, they should send these streams into thickets and sacred groves, as an ornament to the temples of the Gods. But every where, in things of this kind, young men ought to procure gymnastic exercises, both for themselves and the aged, preparing senile hot baths, and placing dry wood in abundance; that an easy remedy may by these means be obtained for the diseased, and the

---

† *Viz.* rain.

d   bodies of husbandmen, when wearied with labour, may be refreshed; which remedy is, indeed, far better than any which can be adopted by a physician who is not very skilful in his art. These things, therefore, and every thing of this kind, should be introduced into these places, as both ornamental and useful, in conjunction with sport by no means unpleasant. But let the attention which is to be paid to things of this kind be as follows: - Sixty men should each of them defend their own place, not only on account of enemies, but for the sake of those who call themselves friends. And if any one, whether he is a servant or free,

e   injures his neighbour, or any other citizen, if the offence is small, he shall be judged by those five governors, but if great, by seventeen men, together with the twelve, and shall be fined as far as to three minæ. But no judge or magistrate ought to be exempt from giving an account of his conduct when called upon, except such as like kings bring things to a conclusion. Besides this, the præfects of the land, if they behave insolently towards the subjects of their care, by enjoining them unequal

762a tasks, or taking any thing by force from the husbandmen, or if they receive any thing which is given through flattery, or distribute justice unjustly, in consequence of yielding to adulation; - in any of these cases, they shall be disgraced by the whole city. But for other injuries which they may commit in their office, they shall voluntarily be fined by the inhabitants of the same village, and by their neighbours, as far as to one

b   mina. If, however, they are unwilling, either for greater or smaller injuries, to pay the proper fine, in consequence of believing that, during their transitions from place to place every month, they shall escape punishment, - in this case, they shall be sentenced by a common judgment to pay the injured person the double of his loss. But both the governors and the præfects of the land shall live for the space of two years in the following manner: In the first place, the convivial associations in the different places shall be in common. But he who is

c   absent from these for one day or night, without orders from the governors, and without being compelled by any necessity, - if the five men condemn him, and write in the forum that he has abandoned his guard, he shall be disgraced, as betraying his part of the polity. He shall likewise be chastised with stripes by any one who may meet him; and whoever is willing to punish him shall do it with impunity. All the

d   sixty men, likewise, should carefully observe whether any one of the governors acts in this manner: and he who perceives or hears that any one of these does so, but yet does not accuse him, shall be subject to the same punishment as the offending governor; and, being more severely punished by the young men, shall be despised by all their magistrates.

The guardians of the laws too should diligently attend to all these particulars, either that they may not take place, or that, when they do, the offenders may be properly punished. But every man ought to think respecting all men, that he who has never been a servant will never be a master worthy of praise. So that he who has acted in a becoming manner as a servant, ought to glory in his conduct more than he who has properly exercised the authority of a master: - in the first place, as having been properly subservient to the laws, which is the same as being a servant to the Gods; and in the next place, to old men who have conducted themselves in an honourable manner towards youth. After this, the præfects of the lands should, during the space of these two years, live on humble and poor food. For, when the twelve magistrates think proper to assemble together with the five, they should not join with themselves the other servants and slaves, nor employ husbandmen, and the inhabitants of the same village, for their own private concerns, but alone for public utility. In other particulars, they may attend to their own advantage. Besides this, they should explore every part of the region in summer and winter, armed, for the sake of perpetually defending and becoming acquainted with every place. For it appears, that for all men to have an accurate knowledge of every place is a discipline inferior to no study. And for the sake of this, young men ought to apply themselves to hunting with dogs, and the capture of wild beasts, no less than for the sake of any other pleasure or advantage which is derived from pursuits of this kind. Every man too should, to the utmost of his power, apply himself to that study, which may either be called concealments, or inspection of the lands, or by any other name at pleasure, if he is desirous that the city should be sufficiently secure.

After this, it follows that we should speak concerning the election of the governors of the markets, and the præfects of cities. Three præfects of cities, therefore, should follow the governors of markets, who are to be sixty in number; and should preside over the twelve parts of the city according to a triple distribution, in imitation of those twelve parts. These should inspect the roads about the city, and the public ways which lead from the country to the city: likewise the buildings, taking care that all of them are raised according to law; and the streams of water which are sent by the guardians into the city, that they may be deduced into pure fountains, and such as are sufficient for use, and may become both an ornament and advantage to the city. These too ought to be such as are capable, when at leisure, of employing their attention on public affairs. On this account, every man should nominate from the largest estate him whom he wishes to be a præfect of the city. And out e   of six that have the most votes, three shall obtain this office by lot. Lastly, when they have been examined and approved, they shall discharge the duties of their office according to the laws which are prescribed to them. After this, the governors of markets shall be chosen, five in number, from possessions of the second and first order; and they shall be elected in the same manner as the præfects of the city. For out of ten that have the most votes, five shall be chosen by lot, and,

764a   when they are approved, shall be declared to be governors. But every individual shall give his vote. And he who is unwilling to vote, if he is brought before the magistrates, shall be fined fifty drachms, and shall, besides this, be considered as a bad man. Likewise, every one shall be permitted to enter into the assembly and common convention; and all those shall be compelled to do this whose possessions are of the first and second order. And he who is absent from these shall be fined ten drachms. But those whose possessions are of the third and fourth order

b   shall not be compelled to be present at the common convention. Hence, if any one is absent from these, he shall not be fined, unless the governors shall find it necessary to order all the citizens to assemble. But the office of the governors of markets consists in preserving the forum in that order which is established by law; and in taking care of the temples and fountains about the forum, and that no one acts unjustly with respect to them: likewise in punishing him who acts unjustly, with stripes and bonds if he is a slave and a stranger; but if it is a native who acts in a disorderly manner, with respect to things of this kind, he shall be condemned by these governors to a fine of one hundred drachms: but they shall not be allowed to condemn him to a greater fine, as far as to the double of this, unless the governors of the

c   city are present on the occasion. The governors of the city too should adopt the same mode of fining and punishing in their department; fining offenders as far as to a mina by their own authority, but the double of this in conjunction with the governors of markets. After this it will be proper that the governors of music and gymnastic should be established, so as that there may be a twofold order of each of these; some of them being appointed for the sake of discipline, and others for the sake of

d   exercise. And the law is desirous of asserting with respect to those who preside over discipline, that they should be careful of the ornament pertaining to exercises and doctrines, erudition, and the attention requisite to things of this kind; and likewise of the conduct of males and females, both at home and abroad. Those who reward the athletæ should have the care of gymnastic exercises and music. And these should be twofold; one kind being employed about music, and the other about gymnastic exercise. The same persons should preside over the agonistic exercises of both men and horses. But, with respect to music, some should preside over the monody, and the imitative art, *viz.* over the rhapsodists, harpers, pipers, and all of this kind, but others over the singing of the choir. And in the first place, with respect to the sport of the choir, where men, boys, and girls are exercised in the dance, and in the whole order of music, the governors of this ought to be properly chosen. But one governor will be sufficient for these, who is not less than forty years of age. One also will be sufficient for the monody, who is not less than thirty years old, and who must perform the office of an introducer, and be able to judge sufficiently the merits of the contending parties. But the governor and moderator of the choir ought to be chosen in the following manner: Those who are attached to things of this kind should go to the assembly, and, if they did not go, should be fined: and the guardians of the law should be the judges in this case. No one, however, should compel others to join this assembly if they are not willing. The candidates should be chosen from among skilful persons; and the skilfullness or unskilfulness of the candidate should be the only thing attended to in his examination. But he who, out of ten that have the most votes, is approved of on being examined, shall, according to law, preside for one year over the choir. The election and approbation respecting the monody, and the melody of the pipe, should be accomplished in a similar manner; and he who is finally chosen should preside over these for a year; his election at the same time being confirmed by the judges. After these things, it is proper that the dispensators of rewards to the gymnastic exercises, both of horses and men, should be chosen in the following manner from possessions of the third and second order. Three estates should be compelled to the election of these, but the smallest estate should be exempt from fine; and three being selected out of twenty that have the most votes, are after examination to be chosen as dispensators. But if any one happens to be rejected, according to any election by lot, and judgment of the magistrate, another shall be chosen in his place, and the examination of him performed in a similar manner. There now remains the governor, who is to take care of the whole of the above-mentioned discipline, both of males and females. Let there then be but one governor of this kind established by law. Let him be not less than fifty years of age; one who is the father of lawful children of both sexes, but, if not of both, at least of one sex. But both he who chooses and he who is chosen ought to think that this magistrate is by far the greatest of the chief magistrates in the city. For the first blossom of every plant, when it tends in a becoming manner of the virtue of its nature, possesses the highest power of arriving at its proper end; and this is true, both with respect to other 766a plants, and to tame and savage animals. But we say that man is a tame animal; who, when he partakes of proper discipline, in conjunction with a prosperous nature, is wont to become a most divine and mild animal: but when he is not sufficiently or not properly educated, he is the most savage of all the animals which the earth produces. On this account the legislator ought not to suffer the education of youth to be a secondary thing, or to be attended to in a careless manner. But, in the first place, he who is desirous of bestowing a proper attention upon youth, ought to choose out of the citizens him who is the most excellent in all things, b and establish him as one who is to educate children with the utmost attention and care. All the magistrates, therefore, except the counsellors and præfects, coming into the temple of Apollo (the guardians of the laws privately receiving the votes), shall each of them choose him whom they consider as calculated to educate youth in the best manner. And he who has most votes, after he has been approved of by the magistrates c that choose him (the guardians of the laws being excepted), shall act in this capacity for five years. And in the sixth year another shall be chosen to succeed him in a similar manner. But if any public magistrate dies before he has governed more than thirty days, another shall be similarly chosen by those to whom this province belongs. And, when any one who is the guardian of orphans dies, the kindred of both father and mother, as far as to cousins, who may at that time be present, shall appoint another within the space of ten days, or each shall be fined every day a drachma till they have appointed another guardian. But d every city will become a privation of a city, in which courts of justice are not properly established; and a mute judge, and who in his interrogations does not speak more than the litigants, will never be sufficient to us for the purpose of deciding justly. On this account, neither can judges when they are many judge well, nor when they are e few and of a depraved character. But it is proper that the object of inquiry should be clearly enunciated by both parties. Time however, delay, and frequent interrogation contribute to the resolution of doubts. On this account litigants ought first of all to betake themselves to their neighbours and friends, and discuss with them the subject of their 767a complaints. But, if they are not able to determine their cause sufficiently by the assistance of these, they should go to another court of justice. And, if they cannot be reconciled by the two former, a third shall bring the affair to a conclusion. In a certain respect, indeed, the establishments of courts of justice are the elections of magistrates; for every magistrate is necessarily a judge of certain things. But every judge is not a magistrate; though, in a certain respect, a judge on the day in which he acts as a judge, is no contemptible magistrate. Considering, therefore, the judges as magistrates, let us show which of them will be adapted to our purpose, of what things they are to be judges, and how many for every particular. Let then the most principal court of justice be that which they exhibit among themselves, when they choose certain judges by common consent. But let there be two criteria of the rest: the one, when, any private person accusing another of acting unjustly, and leading him to justice, he is willing that he should be judged; the other, when any one thinks that the public minister has been injured by some one of the citizens, and is willing to assist the community at large. Let us say then who are the judges, and what kind of men they ought to be. In the first place, there should be a common court of justice for all those that contend the third time with each other; and this should subsist in the following manner: All the magistrates, as well those that govern for a year as those that govern for a longer time, ought to assemble into one temple, on the day before the first day of that month in which after the summer solstice the new year begins. Here taking an oath, and making a first-fruit offering as it were, out of every order of magistrates, they should choose one judge, who appears likely to be the best in every magistracy, and to judge the citizens on the following year in the best and most holy manner. When the judges are chosen, the examination and approbation should be made by those that chose them. And if any one is rejected, another shall be chosen in a similar manner. But the persons approved shall judge those that fled from other courts of justice, and give their decision openly. The counsellors, however, and the other magistrates that chose these, must necessarily be hearers and spectators of these decisions. With respect to men of another description, any one of these who is willing may be present. But, if any person accuses any one of these judges, as voluntarily judging unjustly, he shall accuse him before the guardians of the law; and he who is condemned in consequence of such accusation shall pay the half of the fine to the injured party. But if he shall appear to deserve a greater fine, the judges by whom he is condemned shall determine what he ought to suffer, or to restore, either to the community, or to the person who has suffered the injury. With respect to public accusations, it is necessary in the first place that the multitude should participate of the decision. For, when any one acts unjustly towards a city, all the citizens are injured; and hence the multitude will justly be indignant, when they are excluded from such judgments. The beginning likewise and end of such a

decision ought to be referred to the people, but the examination of the particulars in which the litigants accord, to the three greatest magistrates. But if they cannot agree, the council itself shall judge the election of
b each of them. It is requisite likewise that all men should participate to the utmost of their power of private judgments. For he who is deprived of the power of judging with others must be considered as in no respect participating of the city. On this account courts of justice must necessarily subsist in the tribes, and the judges should immediately give sentence by lot, uncorrupted by entreaties. And, finally, that court of justice should judge of all these particulars which we have said should be established incorrupt to the utmost of human power, for the purpose of determining those disputes which can neither be decided by neighbours
c nor by the courts of justice belonging to the tribes. And thus, concerning courts of justice, which we say can neither easily be indubitably called magistrates, nor yet denied to be such, this description, which is as it were externally induced, has asserted some things, and nearly left others undiscussed. For, towards the end of legislation, the accurate position, and at the same time division of
d judicial laws, will be by far most properly discussed. We shall, therefore, till then defer the consideration of these. But the establishment of other magistrates has nearly taken up the greatest part of legislation. The accurate, however, respecting all civil and politic administrations will not become perspicuous, till the discussion, receiving from the beginning things secondary, middle, and all its parts, has arrived at the end. For at present, indeed, proceeding as far as to the
e election of magistrates, it becomes a sufficient end of what has been previously delivered, so that the beginning of the position of laws is no longer indigent of sluggishness and delay.

CLIN. All that you have asserted above is entirely, O guest, agreeable to my sentiments; but your discourse will be still more pleasing to me, when you have conjoined the beginning of what is now to be said, with the end of what has been already asserted.

769a GUEST. Thus far then we have played in a becoming manner the game of prudent old men.

CLIN. You appear to have evinced a beautiful pursuit of men.

GUEST. It is probable. But do we understand whether this appears to you as it does to me?

CLIN. What do you allude to?

GUEST. Do you know that the art of painting has no boundary with respect to the several animals, but never ceases adorning, either by
b inumbrating or deumbrating, or by whatever name a thing of this kind

may be called by painters, that the picture may continually become more beautiful and conspicuous?

CLIN. I scarcely understand what you say, since I am by no means conversant with this art.

GUEST. This will be no detriment to you. But we will employ this similitude which fortune has presented to us. If then some one should design to paint a most beautiful animal, and which might not become worse but better by length of time, do you not perceive that in consequence of such a one being a mortal, unless he leaves behind him a successor who may prevent the damages which the picture might sustain from time, by frequently retouching the piece, or who may supply what was omitted by the artist, through the imbecility of his art, and thus daily render the picture more splendid, the laboured piece will last but a short time?

CLIN. True.

GUEST. What then? Does not this appear to you to be the wish of the legislator? In the first place, that laws may be written for him as accurate as possible? In the next place, can you think that in the course of time, and after having made an actual trial of the thing, any legislator can be so insane as not to know that many things must necessarily be left, which will require amendment from some successor; that a polity may by no means become worse, but always better and more adorned?

CLIN. It is probable. For how is it possible he should not wish a thing of this kind?

GUEST. If then any legislator possesses any method by which both in words and in reality he can teach another, whether he is a man of greater or of less consequence, how laws ought to be preserved and corrected, he will not cease speaking about a thing of this kind till he has accomplished his purpose.

CLIN. For how is it possible he should?

GUEST. Ought not this, therefore, to be done, both by you and me, at present?

CLIN. Of what are you speaking?

GUEST. As we are about to establish laws of which we have chosen the guardians, but we ourselves are in the decline of life, and the guardians are with respect to us young men, it will, as we have said, be necessary that at the same time we should both establish laws, and endeavour to make these very men, as much as possible, both legislators and guardians of the laws.

CLIN. Undoubtedly, since we are sufficient for the purpose.

GUEST. Let us then cheerfully endeavour to effect this.

CLIN. By all means.

GUEST. We will, therefore, thus address them: O friends, saviours of the laws, we have necessarily left many things unfinished, respecting the several particulars of which we have established laws, and which are not indeed inconsiderable; and we have endeavoured to the utmost of our power not to leave the whole unexplained by a certain circumscription. This deficiency it is your business to supply. But it is proper you should hear where you ought to look in order to accomplish a thing of

c this kind. For Megillus, I, and Clinias, have often said the same things to each other, and we are agreed among ourselves that we have spoken in a becoming manner. We are likewise desirous that you should both be favourable to our undertaking, and become our disciples; and the same time looking to those things which, we have agreed among ourselves, a guardian of the laws and a legislator ought to make the

d objects of his consideration. But this agreement, which has one head or summit, is this: That we should endeavour to find the means by which a man may become a worthy character, possessing that virtue of the soul which is accommodated to his nature, either from a certain study, or certain manners, or from some kind of possession or desire, or opinion; or, lastly, from certain disciplines; and this, whether the nature of the inhabitant of our city is male or female, youthful or aged. Likewise, that every one, through the whole of life, should tend with all possible earnestness to this of which we are now speaking; neglecting at the same time every thing which may become an impediment to this acquisition.

e Besides this, too, he should be disposed to die for his country if it is necessary, rather than either to see it entirely subverted, and becoming subject to the yoke of bondage, governed by bad men, or desert it by flight. For every thing of this kind is to be endured rather than the polity should be changed, which men of a worse character are naturally disposed to effect. These things have been already mutually assented to by us, and do you now, looking to both these, praise and blame the laws; blaming such as are not able to accomplish these particulars, but,

771a embracing and receiving in a benevolent manner such as are, live in them. But it is proper that you should bid farewell to other studies which tend to other things that are called good. Let this, then, be the beginning to us of the subsequent laws, commencing from sacred concerns. For we ought in the first place to resume the number five

b thousand and forty, because it had, and now has, convenient distributions, both the whole number, and that which was assigned to the tribes; which we established as the twelfth part of the whole, this producing with the greatest rectitude the number four hundred and twenty. And as the whole number has twelve distributions, so also that of the tribes. But it is proper to consider each division as a sacred gift of divinity, as following both the order of months and the period of the universe. On this account, that which is connate should lead every city, rendering them sacred. Some, indeed, are perhaps more properly distributed than others, and more prosperously dedicate their distributions to the Gods. But we now say, that the number five thousand and forty is most properly chosen, as that which has all distributions as far as to twelve, beginning from one, except that into eleven parts. This, however, has the easiest remedy. For it will be restored to health, if two houses are distributed to the other part. But that these things are true, may be evinced with facility when at leisure. Believing, therefore, in the present conception and discourse, let us distribute this number; and ascribing a God, or a son of the Gods, to each part, likewise dedicating altars, and things pertaining to these, let us make two conventions for the purpose of sacrificing every month; accommodating twelve to the distribution of the tribes, and twelve to the division of the city. But all this should be done, in the first place, for the sake of the Gods, and things pertaining to the Gods; in the second place, for the sake of our familiarity with, and knowledge of, each other; and likewise for the sake of every kind of association. For it is necessary, in the communion and mixture of marriages, that ignorance should be taken away, so as that every one may know with whom he is connected, and that all deception in things of this kind may, as much as possible, be taken away. For the sake of this, therefore, it is necessary that sports should be instituted, boys and girls together forming a choir, mutually beholding and being beheld by each other, being properly paired, as to their age, and having as much of their bodies naked as modesty will permit. All these should be taken care of, and properly ornamented by the governors of choirs, and likewise by the legislators, in conjunction with the guardians of the laws, that they may supply what we have left deficient. But it is necessary, as we have said, respecting all such things as are small and numerous, that some particulars should be omitted by the legislator, in which the magistrates becoming every year skilful, and being admonished by experience, they may be able every year to supply what is deficient; till it shall appear that these discussions and legal institutes have obtained a sufficient bound. The space of ten years, therefore, will be a length of time both moderate and sufficient for obtaining an experience in sacrifices and choirs, and every other particular. But in order to accomplish this, he who supplies these deficiencies should live in common with the

legislator: and on his death, the several magistrates having informed the
c   guardians of the laws of his decease, must supply his place in correcting
what is amiss, till every thing shall appear to have attained the
consummation of excellence. When this period arrives, having given
stability to these institutes, they are to be used in conjunction with
other laws which the legislator has ordained from the beginning;
respecting which, nothing should ever be voluntarily changed. But if
any necessity shall, at any time, appear to urge a mutation, all the
magistrates ought to consult together on this occasion, all the people
d   should be assembled, and all the oracles of the Gods explored. If all
these accord, then a change in the laws may be made, but by no means
unless this is the case; but that which impedes, shall always obtain
dominion according to law. Whenever, therefore, any one who has
arrived at five-and-twenty years of age, beholding and being beheld by
others, believes that he has found one of his own disposition, and
adapted for the communion and procreation of children, he shall marry
e   within thirty-five years of age. But, in the first place, let him hear how
the becoming and adapted are to be investigated. For it is requisite, as
Clinias says, prior to the laws, to give a preface accommodated to each.

CLIN. You very properly remind us, O guest; and your discourse
appears to me to be both seasonable and highly fitting.

773a   GUEST. You speak well. Let us, therefore, speak as follows: O young
man, born of good parents, it is proper to contract those marriages
which appear honourable to prudent men. But these exhort neither to
avoid marriage with the poor, nor to pursue with avidity marriage with
the rich, but, cæteris paribus, always honouring the inferior, to enter
into communion with it. For, both to the city and families which are
united, this will be advantageous. For the equable and commensurate
infinitely surpasses the immoderate with respect to virtue. He,
b   therefore, who in all his actions is more rash and hasty than is
becoming, should desire that the daughter of parents of more composed
manners may be united to him in marriage: but he who is naturally of
a contrary disposition should enter into alliance with a contrary
character. And in every marriage this one thing should be observed,
that every one should enter into such a matrimonial connexion as is
advantageous to the city, and not such a one as is most pleasant to
himself. For every one always naturally tends to that which is most
similar to himself; whence the whole city becomes anomalous both in
wealth and manners, when it partakes in the highest degree of those
things which we are unwilling should happen to ourselves. If, then, in
c   our discourse we should order by law that the rich should not marry

with the rich, nor the powerful with the powerful, but should compel those whose manners are more hasty to marry those whose manners are more slow, and the more slow to marry with the more hasty, we should not only appear ridiculous to, but excite the anger of, the multitude. For it is not easy to understand that a city ought to be like a cup, in which the mad wine, when first poured forth, effervesces; but, being corrected by another deity,[†] who is a sober God, and thus obtaining a beautiful conjunction, it becomes a good and moderate drink. But no one, as I may say, is able to see this taking place in the formation of children by the mingling of the sexes. On this account, therefore, we should not compel the citizens to things of this kind by law, but endeavour to charm them into the persuasion, that they ought to prefer equability in the natural disposition of their children to the equality of the most opulent alliance; and that we ought to deter, by disgrace, him who makes riches the object of his pursuit in marriage, and not compel him to a contrary mode of conduct by a written law. Let these, then, be the exhortations respecting marriages, together with what we have previously asserted, - I mean, that we ought to aspire after perpetuity of nature, by always leaving behind us children of children, as servants of divinity, instead of ourselves. All these particulars, therefore, and still more than these, some one may with propriety preface, respecting the manner in which marriages ought to be conducted. But he who cannot willingly be persuaded to act in this manner, but lives in the city alienated, without connexion, and unmarried, for five-and-thirty years, such a one shall be fined every year. And if he possesses the largest estate, he shall be fined one hundred drachms; if that which is second in order, seventy; if that which is third, sixty; and if that which is fourth in order, thirty drachms. Let all these fines be sacred to Juno. And let him who does not pay his fine every year be made a debtor of ten times that sum. Let this money too be exacted by the dispensator of the Goddess; which unless he exacts, he himself shall be the debtor. He, therefore, who is unwilling to marry, shall be thus punished with respect to a fine; but with respect to honour as follows: In the first place, let him be deprived of all honour from his juniors, nor let any young man voluntarily obey him in any thing. In the next place, if he should attempt to chastise any one, every one shall be permitted to assist and defend the injured person. And he who does not in this case give assistance, shall be considered by the law as a timid and vicious citizen. Concerning the marriage portion we have spoken before, and we again

---

[†] *Viz.* water.

say, that equal things are to be given for equal things, since neither he who receives, nor he who bestows, will grow old in the want of money. For in this city every one is supplied with necessaries. Besides, women will be less insolent, and men will have less of humble and illiberal slavery, through riches. And he who is obedient to this law will

d accomplish one among the number of things beautiful; but he who is disobedient to it, and either gives or receives more than the worth of fifty drachms for the sake of a garment, shall either pay one mina, or three half minæ, or two minæ, according to the magnitude of his possessions. He who possesses the largest estate shall pay another such sum to the public treasury: and whatever is given or received shall be sacred to Juno and Jupiter. But the exactors of this money should be the dispensators of these divinities, just as we said, when we spoke of

e those that refused to marry, that their fine should be exacted by the dispensators of Juno, who, if they neglected to exact it, should pay it themselves. With respect to suretiship, the first shall be that of a father, the second, that of a grandfather, and the third, that of brothers by the same father. If no one of these survives, the suretiship shall, in a similar

775a manner, be equally valid on the mother's side. But if, through an unusual fortune, none of these should survive, the authority in this affair must always be vested in the nearest kindred, in conjunction with the guardians. If any thing preparatory to initiation, or other sacred operation, shall be found necessary for things future, present, or past, pertaining to marriage, it will be proper to interrogate the interpreters of sacred concerns; and each person, being persuaded by these, should think that he has accomplished every thing sufficiently. With respect to nuptial feasts, not more than five male and five female friends should be

b invited; and as many of both sexes of kindred and familiars. But the expenses on this occasion should not exceed the possessions. He, therefore, who has the largest estate shall spend one mina, another half a mina, and so on in succession, according to every one's respective property. And he who is obedient to the law in this respect ought to be praised by all men; but he who is disobedient shall be chastised by the guardians of the laws, as one who is ignorant of the becoming, and unskilled in the laws respecting the sponsal muses. To drink, however, to intoxication, is never at any time becoming, nor safe, except in the festivals of that God who is the giver of wine. Neither, therefore, is it

c proper that this should take place at the nuptial feast, when the bride and bridegroom ought particularly to be in a sound state of mind, as having changed the former condition of their life in no small degree; and in order, at the same time, that offspring may always be produced as much as possible from prudent parents. For it is nearly immanifest what night or day may generate offspring in conjunction with divinity. Children, therefore, ought not to be begotten when the body is in a relaxed and diffluent state through ebriety, but when it is compact, stable, and quiet. But he who is filled with wine hurries and is hurried away every where, being agitated with insane fury both in body and soul. Hence, he who is intoxicated, as being delirious, must disseminate in a vicious manner. So that it is probable such a one will beget offspring anomalous, unfaithful, and void of rectitude, both in their manners and corporeal frame. Hence, it is requisite to guard against intoxication, both through the whole year, and through the whole of life, but especially at the time of procreation, and neither to do such things as spontaneously introduce disease, nor such as participate of insolence or injustice. For, these being necessarily impressed in the souls and bodies of the offspring in a fœtal state, the impressions become worse than their originals. But especially on the wedding day and night it is requisite to abstain from all such things. For the principle and divinity† established in men preserves all things, when he is allotted that honour which is accommodated to his nature by the respective individuals by whom he is employed. But it is proper that the bridegroom should consider one of the two houses assigned by lot as set apart for the procreation and education of children; and that he should celebrate his nuptials in that house, and reside there with his children separate from his father and mother. For, where there is a certain desire in friendship, it agglutinates and binds together all the manners; but where association is attended with satiety, and has not any desire through time, it causes a mutual separation through transcendency of repletion. Hence, leaving his parents and kindred, the bridegroom should depart as it were to a colony, observing, and being at the same time observed by, them; procreating and educating children; transmitting to others, like a lamp, the life which he received from others, and always honouring the Gods according to law. In the next place, it is requisite to consider which among the number of possessions is the most elegant. With respect to many of these, therefore, it is neither difficult to understand nor to possess them; but with respect to servants the difficulty is extreme. But we may assign the cause of this in a certain respect properly, and in a certain respect not properly. For our assertions concerning slaves are contrary to, and yet conformable to, use.

† Plato, by the divinity in men, means intellect; for this is the divine part of our nature.

MEGIL. How do you mean? For we do not, O guest, understand what you assert at present.

GUEST. And it is very reasonable, O Megillus, to suppose you do not. For that servitude of the Lacedæmonians which is called Hilotia is nearly the source of the greatest doubt and contention to all Greece; because it appears to some to be well instituted, and to others not. But the slavery of the Heraclidæ is a subject of less contention than that of

d the Mariandyni.[†] And besides this, the nation of the Thessalians is servile. However, looking to these, and all such particulars as these, what ought we to do respecting the possession of servants? As the subject, therefore, is so ambiguous, you very properly asked me what I meant. But my meaning is this: - We know that we all say that it is requisite to possess slaves of the most benevolent and best dispositions. For many slaves, conducting themselves in every respect with more virtue towards certain persons than brothers and sons, have preserved

e their masters, together with their possessions and the whole of their habitations. We know that these things are said of certain slaves.

MEGIL. Undoubtedly.

GUEST. The contrary to this, likewise, is asserted, *viz.* that nothing in the soul of a slave is in a healthy condition, and that the race of slaves is not to be believed in any particular. The wisest of the poets too seems to be of this opinion, when he says respecting Jupiter:

> Jove fixed it certain, that whatever day

777a
> Makes man a slave takes half his mind away.[‡]

In consequence of these different conceptions, some place no confidence in slaves, but with spurs and whips, as if they had to manage wild beasts, not thrice but often, enslave the souls of their servants; but others act entirely contrary to these.

b CLIN. Undoubtedly. Since, then, the opinions respecting slaves are so different, how shall we act in our region as to the possession and correction of them?

GUEST. It appears to me, O Clinias, since man is an animal difficult to be managed, and one that by no means patiently endures that the

---

[†] Mariandynum was a place near Bithynia, where, according to the poets, Hercules dragged Cerberus out of Hades. Perhaps, therefore, the contention which Plato alludes to, was that of the inhabitants of Mariandynum respecting the particular spot where Hercules performed this achievement.

[‡] Odyss. lib. ii, 17, 322 *et seq.*

necessary distinction between a slave and one who is free and a master should be made in reality, - that on this account he is a difficult possession. The truth of this is actually evinced in the frequent rebellions of the Messenians, and by the mighty evils which happen to those cities that possess many servants of the same language; and further still, by the all-various thefts which are committed by pirates about Italy. All which particulars, when they are considered, may render it doubtful what ought to be done in things of this kind. Two methods, therefore, alone remain to be adopted, namely, that those who are to act with ease in the capacity of slaves should not be of the same country, and that as much as possible they should be discordant with each other. And in the second place, that they should be properly educated, not only for their own sakes, but much more for the sake of their masters. But the proper education of these consists in not behaving insolently, but in acting less unjustly towards them, if possible, than towards our equals. For he is perfectly manifest who reverences justice naturally and not fictitiously, and who truly hates to act unjustly towards those men whom he might easily injure. He, therefore, who is never defiled by acting in an unjust and unholy manner, with respect to the manners and actions of slaves, will be most sufficient to sow the seeds of virtue. The same thing may with rectitude be asserted of a despot, and a tyrant, and of all authority, when exercised by the more powerful over the more imbecil. But slaves ought justly to be always punished, and not to be made effeminate by admonishing them like those that are free. Every thing too that is said to a slave should nearly be a command, nor should they ever in any respect be jested with, whether they are of the male or of the female sex. Many, however, very foolishly jest with their slaves; and, thus making them effeminate, render it more difficult to their slaves to be governed, and to themselves to govern.

CLIN. Right.

GUEST. After this manner, therefore, servants may be acquired as much as possible sufficient both in multitude and aptitude to assist in the necessary employments of life. But, after this, it is requisite to describe the habitations.

CLIN. Entirely so.

GUEST. In a new city, therefore, and which had never before been inhabited, edifices are in the first place to be attended to, and particularly the temples and walls of the city. The buildings too of the city, O Clinias, ought to precede the marriages. But, now since the city is raised in discourse, we may very properly admit these particulars to subsist in the manner we have delivered them. When, indeed, the city is raised in reality, we shall attend to the buildings prior to the marriages, if divinity is willing, and afterwards accomplish every thing

c   pertaining to matrimonial connections. We shall now, therefore, in a cursory manner, discuss these particulars.

CLIN. Entirely so.

GUEST. The temples, therefore, ought to be built round all the forum, and the city should be built in a circle, in elevated places, for the sake of defence and purity. The houses of the governors and judges should be situated near the temples; and in these, as most holy places, sentence

d   should be given and received; partly, as about holy concerns, and partly because the temples of the judicial Gods are there situated. Courts of judgment too should be built in this place, in which proper sentence shall be passed on murder and other crimes which deserve death. With respect to the walls, O Megillus, I agree with the Spartans, that they should be permitted to lie sleeping on the earth, and not be raised. For

e   that poetical assertion respecting them is deservedly praised, that walls ought to be of brass and iron, rather than of earth. With us, indeed, the custom of sending young men every year into the fields to dig trenches and raise buildings, for the purpose of restraining the incursions of the enemy, may justly be considered as extremely ridiculous. We likewise inclose our city with walls, which in the first place by no means contributes to the health of the citizens; and, in the next place, it usually produces an effeminate disposition in the souls of the inhabitants. For

779a it incites them to fly within these for shelter, and not repel the enemy; and leads them to think that the safety of the city does not consist in guarding it perpetually both night and day, but that, sleeping under the protection of walls and gates, they shall be truly safe; as if they were born for sloth, and not to labour. They are, indeed, ignorant that ease is truly produced from labour; and, as it appears to me, labour is again the natural result of base ease. But, if there is any occasion of walls for

b   men, the houses of individuals should be so raised from the first, that the whole city, by its equality and similitude, may be one wall, and that all the houses may have a sufficiently secure passage to the different roads of the city. And in this case, indeed, the city, having the form of one house, will be no unpleasant spectacle, and will be in every respect adapted to the ease of its guards and the safety of the whole. The citizens who are to inhabit this region should be particularly careful that these things are constructed in this manner from the first. They should

c   also take care that ædiles are provided, compelling them to be chosen, and punish with fines those that neglect this office. Attention too should be paid to the purity of every thing in the city; and that no private person occupies any public property, either by building or digging. They should likewise take care that the waters from Jupiter may be imparted with facility to the inhabitants; and that every part, both within and without the city, may be fit to be inhabited. But all these particulars the guardians of the law, becoming skilled in by experience, must legally establish, together with such others as the law omits, through its incapacity of providing for all things. But since these things, the buildings about the forum, the particulars respecting gymnasia, theatres, and all that pertains to discipline, are instituted, let us now proceed to marriages, as following next in the business of legislation.

CLIN. By all means.

GUEST. Marriages, therefore, O Clinias, must be instituted for us in the manner we have described above. But, after this, the mode of living which should be adopted prior to the procreation of children must not continue a less time than a year. However, it is by no means easy to say, after what manner a bride and bridegroom ought to live in a city which transcends the multitude of cities. But, as many things that have been already advanced are difficult, this will appear to the vulgar still more difficult to determine. Nevertheless, O Clinias, that which appears to be right and true must be asserted.

CLIN. By all means.

GUEST. He, therefore, who is of opinion that things public and common only, in a city, should be established by law, but does not think it requisite that the necessary concerns of private persons should be attended to, but that they should be permitted to live as they please; and that it is not necessary every thing should subsist in an orderly manner; but that, private affairs being neglected by the law, men should only live legally in public and common concerns; - he who thinks in this manner does not think rightly. But on what account are these things asserted by us? On this: Because we say that the bridegrooms in our city ought to live at public tables, at other times no less than prior to their nuptials. And, indeed, when first eating in public was instituted by you, Lacedæmonians, it appeared a wonderful thing; being legally established, in consequence of a certain war, or something else endued with the same power, and which the paucity of men rendered necessary. But this mode of eating in public having been adopted by necessity, when it was found to contribute greatly to the safety of the city it was established by law.

CLIN. It appears that this was the case.

GUEST. As I said, therefore, this was at first a thing of a wonderful nature, and dreadful to enjoin; but, at present, the legal establishment of it would not be attended with the like difficulty. But that which follows this is both arduous to relate and accomplish. It is a thing which is naturally capable of taking place in a proper manner, but which

d   by no means subsists at present, and in establishing which the legislator would appear like jugglers to pluck fire, and to accomplish ten thousand other impossible things.

CLIN. What is this, O guest, which you appear to be so vehemently afraid of mentioning?

GUEST. You shall hear, that I may not any longer needlessly detain you. For every thing in the city that participates of order and law produces every good. But such things as are deprived of order, or are badly disposed, dissolve the multitude of those things which are orderly

e   disposed. And this happens with respect to the subject of our present discussion. For, O Clinias and Megillus, the public banquets of the men are instituted for you in a beautiful, and, as I said, wonderful manner, from a certain divine necessity; but those of the women are by no means properly left unestablished by law, and not led forth into light. For the

781a   female sex is another kind of men, more occult and fraudulent than we are, through the imbecility of its nature. But the legislator did not act rightly in omitting it, on account of the difficulty of managing it in an orderly manner. For, this being neglected, many things in your city will be dissolved, which would subsist far better than at present if it was

b   regulated by law. For the particulars relative to women are not only the half (as they may appear to be) of human concerns, if they are left in a disordered manner; but, by how much the feminine is worse than the masculine nature with respect to virtue, by so much it surpasses in multitude the double. This, therefore, must be resumed and corrected; and all employments and studies should be established as common, both to men and women, as that which will more contribute to the felicity of the city. But at present mankind are so unhappily circumstanced in

c   this respect, that no prudent man would even mention a thing of this kind, in other places where eating in common is by no means approved. How then can any one attempt, without rendering himself ridiculous, to force women to eat and drink openly? For there is not any thing which the sex would more difficultly endure than this. For, being accustomed to live timorously, and obscurely, when forced into light they will make every possible resistance, and greatly overpower the legislator. Women, therefore, as I have said, will not elsewhere endure

d   even the most rational discourse, without extreme vociferation; but here perhaps they will. If then it is agreeable to you, for the sake of conversation, lest our discourse about every kind of polity should be incomplete, I am desirous of informing you, how good and becoming a thing this is, - if, as I said, it is agreeable to you to hear it: - if not, I shall dismiss it.

CLIN. But, O guest, we are wonderfully desirous of hearing it.

GUEST. Let us then hear it. But you must not wonder if I appear to
e   you to derive what I shall say from an elevated source. For we are now at leisure, and there is nothing to prevent us from considering every thing pertaining to laws.

CLIN. Rightly said.

GUEST. Again, therefore, we will recur to what was first asserted by us. For it is highly proper that every man should know, that the generation of men either never had any beginning, nor ever will have an
782a   end, but always was and always will be; or that, if it had a beginning, the length of time from its commencement is immense.

CLIN. Undoubtedly.

GUEST. What then? Should not we think that there have been all-various establishments and subversions of cities, studies and employments of every kind, some attended with and others without order, and all-various desires of food and drink, in every part of the
b   earth; likewise all-various revolutions of seasons, in which animals have undergone a prodigious number of mutations?

CLIN. It is reasonable to think so.

GUEST. What then? Shall we believe that vines at a certain period rose into existence, and in a similar manner olives, and the gifts of Ceres and Proserpine; and that a certain Triptolemus supplied things of this kind? And shall we not think that during the time in which these had no existence animals devoured each other, as at present?

CLIN. We ought doubtless to think so.

c   GUEST. But we see at present that men sacrifice each other in many places; and we hear, on the contrary, that there was a time when we did not dare to taste the flesh of oxen, and when we did not sacrifice animals to the Gods, but cakes, and fruits moistened with honey, and other pure offerings of a similar kind: but we entirely abstained from flesh; considering it as neither holy to feed on it, nor to defile the altars of the Gods with blood. But we then lived an Orphic† life, feeding on
d   all inanimate substances, but on the contrary abstaining from all animals.

---

† The Orphic sacrifices were unbloody, as the hymns of Orpheus which are now extant abundantly testify. [See TTS vol. V.]

CLIN. These things, as you say, are every where reported, and persuade belief.

GUEST. But some one may say, What is the meaning of all this?

CLIN. You very properly conjecture what is likely to be the case, O guest.

GUEST. I shall endeavour, therefore, if I am able, O Clinias, to unfold what is consequent to this.

CLIN. Speak then.

GUEST. I behold all things suspended to men, from a triple indigence and desire, through which virtue is produced if they are properly conducted, but the contrary if they are improperly burdened. These are,

e from the very period of their birth, meat and drink, of which every animal having an innate love, if is full of fury, and refuses to listen to him who says that something else is to be done besides replenishing the pleasures and desires, with which all such things as these are conversant,

783a and perpetually avoiding every kind of pain. But a third, and this the greatest indigence, and the most acute desire, afterwards excites us, producing in mankind the most fiery furies. This is the desire of propagating the species, which burns with unbounded insolence. These three diseases should be turned from that which is called most pleasant, to that which is best, by three the greatest of all things; *viz. fear, law,* and *true reason;* at the same time employing the muses, and the agonistic

b Gods, in order to extinguish this influx and increase. But after marriages we should place the procreation of children, and, after this, education and discipline. For, our discourse proceeding in this manner, the law will perhaps at length lead us to public banquets, when we have arrived at associations of this kind; and then perhaps we shall see more clearly than before, whether this mode of eating in public ought to be adopted by women alone, or by men, together with the particulars preceding this

c mode, and which are not yet legally established. These things, as I just now said, we shall then behold more accurately, and establish respecting them more becoming and convenient laws.

CLIN. You speak with the greatest rectitude.

GUEST. Let us, therefore, preserve in our memory what we have just now said: for perhaps we shall have occasion for it hereafter.

CLIN. What are the things which you exhort us to remember?

d GUEST. Those which we defined by three words; *viz.* meat, drink, and the astonishment about venereal concerns.

CLIN. We shall by all means, O guest, be careful to remember these things.

GUEST. It is well. But let us proceed to matrimonial concerns, and instruct the bride and bridegroom in what manner children ought to be procreated; and if we cannot persuade them to comply with our instructions, we will threaten them with certain laws.

CLIN. How?

GUEST. It is proper that the bride and bridegroom should consider, that children are to be exhibited to the city, as much as possible, the most beautiful and the best. But all men who produce any thing in common, when they attend both to themselves and the work, produce the whole beautiful and good: but when they do not attend, or are not endued with intellect, the contrary takes place. The bridegroom, however, should attend both to the bride and to the procreation of children: and in a similar manner the bride should attend to the bridegroom, especially at that time when children are not yet begotten by them. Certain women chosen by us shall be inspectors of this particular, whether many or few, just as it may seem fit to the governors. These shall assemble every day in the temple of Lucina, and continue there for the third part of an hour. Here they shall inform each other, if they have seen any married man or woman looking to any thing else than what the sacrifices and sacred ceremonies pertaining to marriage order to be done. Let the procreation of children and the inspection of the women above mentioned continue for ten years, but not for a longer time, when there is an easy flux of generation. But if some continue unprolific for this space of time, after having consulted with their kindred, and the women that superintend them, they shall be divorced in such a manner as is advantageous to both. However, if any altercation ensues respecting what is proper and advantageous to each, ten guardians of the law, chosen by the contending parties, shall take cognizance of and determine the affair. after this, the inspecting women shall enter into the houses of the young men, and, partly by admonitions and partly by threats, liberate them from their error and ignorance. But if they are unable to accomplish this, they shall speak to the guardians of the law, who shall then take the affair into consideration. If they too are incapable of applying a remedy, they shall make the people acquainted with the case; at the same time giving in the offenders' names in writing, and affirming by an oath that they are unable to render them better. But let him whose name is committed to writing be disgraced, unless he can confute his accusers in the court of judgement. If he is unable to do this, he shall neither engage in a matrimonial connection, nor in the procreation of children. And in case he attempts it, any one that pleases shall punish him with impunity.

The same laws too must be established respecting women. For such shall not participate of female egressions and honours, and shall not be permitted to go to weddings, and labours, if they are in a similar manner condemned in a court of justice. But when children are begotten according to law, if any one has connection with another man's wife, or a woman with any man but her husband, while children are begotten by them, let them be punished in the manner mentioned above when they did not beget children. In the next place, let the married men and women that live temperately with respect to all such things as these, be honoured, but those that live in a contrary manner be disgraced. And if the greater part of the citizens conduct themselves with moderation in things of this kind, let these particulars be passed over in silence, without being established by law. But if the conduct of the greater part is disordered in things of this kind, let them be legally established, and a judgement made of such conduct according to the established laws. The first year is the beginning of the whole of life to every one. This ought to be written in paternal temples, as the beginning of life, both to boys and girls. In every tribe, too, the number of the governors that are reckoned by years should be written on a white wall. Next to these, the names of those that are living in the tribe should always be written; and on their decease their names should be blotted out. The boundary of marriage for girls should be from sixteen to twenty years of age; and this should be the longest definite time: but for boys, from thirty to thirty-five. The time for acting in the capacity of magistrates should be limited: for women, to forty years of age; but for men, to thirty. With respect to war, men should engage in it from twenty to sixty years of age; but women, when it shall appear necessary to employ them for warlike purposes, and after they have brought forth children, to the fiftieth year of their age: at the same time being mindful to prescribe the possible and the becoming to each.

BOOK VII

788a Children, therefore, both male and female, being begotten, we shall act with the greatest propriety in speaking in the next place about their education and discipline; for to pass this over in silence is perfectly impossible. However, when it is discussed, it will appear to us to be rather similar to a certain doctrine and admonition than to laws. For the numerous small and unapparent circumstances which happen privately, and in every house, since they easily take place through the

b pain, pleasure and desire of the respective individuals, contrary to the intention of the legislator, render the manners of the citizens all-various, and not similar to each other. But this is an evil to cities. For, on account of their smallness and frequency, to punish them by a legal fine would be unbecoming, and at the same time unseemly. It would likewise be the means of destroying written laws, in consequence of men being accustomed to act contrary to law in things small and numerous.

c So that it is difficult indeed to establish laws concerning them, and impossible to pass them over in silence. But I will endeavour to render what I say manifest, leading forth an example, as it were, into light; for what is said at present seems to be involved in obscurity.

CLIN. You speak most truly.

GUEST. That a proper education, therefore, appears to be capable of rendering both souls and bodies most beautiful and excellent, has been rightly asserted by us.

CLIN. Undoubtedly.

d GUEST. But I think that the most beautiful bodies are simply those which immediately from infancy grow in the most proper manner.

CLIN. Entirely so.

GUEST. But what? Do we not understand this, that the first blossom of every animal is by far the greatest and most abundant; so that it is the source of contention to many, that human bodies at twenty do not receive twice the increase in length which they had at five years of age?

CLIN. True.

789a GUEST. What then? When there is an influx of abundant increase without many and moderate labours, do we not know that it produces ten thousand maladies in bodies?

CLIN. Entirely so.

GUEST. Many labours, therefore, are then necessary, when abundant nutriment is introduced into bodies.

CLIN. What do you say, O guest? Shall we order those who are but just born, and the youngest, to undergo the greatest labours?

b   GUEST. By no means: but still prior to these, those that are nourished in their mother's womb.

CLIN. How do you say, O best of men? Do you really speak of those that are yet carried in the womb of their mother?

GUEST. I do. But it is not at all wonderful that you should be ignorant of the exercise of such as these; which, though it appears to be absurd, I am willing to unfold to you.

CLIN. By all means, do so.

GUEST. By us, indeed, a thing of this kind can be more readily comprehended, because children there engage in certain sports more than is proper. For, with us, not only children, but certain old men, nourish

c   the young of birds, and exercise them in fighting with each other; but they are far from thinking that the labours, in which by exercising they excite them, are moderate. For, besides this, taking each of them by the wing, they walk many stadia with the lesser young in their hands, and the larger under their arms; and this, not for the sake of the good habit of their own bodies, but for that of the birds. And by this, indeed, they signify thus much to him who is capable of understanding what is said,

d   that all bodies are benefited by motion and agitation when not continued to weariness, whether these are produced from themselves, or by carriages, or by the sea, or horses, or by whatever other means bodies are moved. Hence, through these vanquishing the nutriment of food and drink, they are able to impart to us health, beauty, and strength. This being the case, what shall we say we ought to do in the next place? Are you willing that we should say, laughing, while we are establishing laws, that the pregnant woman should take the exercise of walking, and, after she is delivered, fashion the infant like wax, while he

e   is moist, and during the space of two years bind him with rollers? Likewise, that we should compel the nurses, by legal fines, to carry the children either into the fields, or to the temples, or their acquaintance, till they are sufficiently able to stand alone? And that then they should be careful lest their legs become distorted through the violence of resting on them; and, for this purpose, should carry them in their arms till they are three years old? That the nurses, likewise, ought to be as strong as possible; and that there should be more than one for each child? And, lastly, that a punishment shall be ordained by a written law for neglect in each of these particulars? Or shall this by no means be the case? For

790a   that which we just now mentioned will happen to us in great abundance.

CLIN. What is that?

GUEST. We shall expose ourselves to abundant laughter, because the effeminate and servile manners of the nurses will be unwilling to obey us.

CLIN. For whose sake, therefore, shall we say these things ought to be asserted?

b GUEST. For the sake of the manners of the masters and free persons in the city, who, perhaps, when they hear these things, will rightly conceive, that unless private affairs are properly conducted in cities, it is in vain to expect that such as are common can have any stability by the promulgation of laws; and who, in consequence of such a conception, will use as laws what we have just now advanced. And further still, by a proper use of these assertions they will govern both their families and the city in such a manner as to render them happy.

CLIN. What you say is very likely to be the case.

c GUEST. We should not, therefore, desist from a legislation of this kind till we have delivered the particulars of those studies which pertain to the souls of very young children, and thus bring our discourse to a conclusion in the same manner as when we spoke concerning their bodies.

CLIN. Perfectly right.

GUEST. Let us receive this, therefore, as an element with respect to both the body and soul of very young children, that nutrition and motion, when applied every night and day, are profitable to all juvenile bodies and souls, but especially to the most youthful; so that, if it were possible, they should be in such a condition as if they were always sailing on the sea. But as this is impossible, it is requisite to approach as near to this as we are able in our treatment of infants. Indeed, that we ought to do so, may be conjectured from this, that both the nurses

d of infants, and those who are initiated in the remedies of the Corybantes, know experimentally that it is useful. For, when mothers are desirous that their children who sleep with difficulty may sleep soundly, they do not attempt to accomplish this by quiet, but, on the

e contrary, by gently moving them in their arms; nor yet by silence, but by singing to them. And, in short, they charm their children by the melody of their voice, as if by that of a pipe; just in the same manner as the remedies of mad Bacchanalians employ this choir, and, at the same time, Muse of motion.

CLIN. What then, O guest, is especially the cause of this to us?

GUEST. It is not very difficult to know.

CLIN. How so?

GUEST. Both these passions consist in fear: and they are certain terrors arising from a depraved habit of the soul. When, therefore, any one externally causes an agitation in passions of this kind, the exterior vanquishes the interior dreadful and insane motion: but, being vanquished, a tranquil quiet takes place in the soul, and the leaping of the heart, which was troublesome to endure, subsides. And thus it entirely causes some to receive the benefit of sleep; but it recalls others, who are awake, from insane to prudent habits, by dancing and the melody of the pipe, in conjunction with those divinities to whom suppliants sacrificed. And these things, in short, possess a certain probable reason.

CLIN. Entirely so.

GUEST. But if these things possess such a power, this ought to be understood concerning them, that every soul that has been familiar with fear from infancy will have been more accustomed to endurance. Every one, however, will acknowledge that this is an exercise of timidity, and not of fortitude.

CLIN. Undoubtedly.

GUEST. But, on the contrary, we should say that he is exercised in fortitude who, from his infancy, has made it his study to vanquish all the fears and terrors which befall us.

CLIN. Right.

GUEST. We may say, therefore, that this one thing greatly contributes to a part of the virtue of the soul, *viz.* the all-perfect gymnastic exercise of children in motions.

CLIN. Entirely so.

GUEST. And besides this, a placid or morose disposition becomes no small part of goodness or depravity of soul.

CLIN. Undoubtedly.

GUEST. But we should endeavour to relate to the utmost of our ability, after what manner we should wish that each of these may be implanted in infants.

CLIN. Certainly.

GUEST. This, then, is a dogma with us, that luxury renders the manners of youth morose, irascible, and vehemently agitated by things of a trifling nature; but that, on the contrary, excessive and rustic servitude causes them to be abject, illiberal, haters of mankind, and unfit for society.

CLIN. But how will the whole city be able to educate infants, who are incapable of understanding what is said to them, and who cannot taste of any discipline whatever?

GUEST. Thus. Every animal, as soon as it is born, is accustomed to utter certain sounds with a loud voice: and this is particularly the case with the human species, which to vociferation adds weeping.

CLIN. Entirely so.

GUEST. Nurses, therefore, being desirous to know what infants are in want of, conjecture this by the things which they offer to them. For that which causes them to be silent they consider as offered to them in a becoming manner, but that as improperly offered at which they cry and make a noise. For, in children, vociferation and tears are indications by no means fortunate of the things which they love and hate. But the time in which this takes place is not less than the space of three years, which is no small portion of life to pass through well or ill.

CLIN. Right.

GUEST. Does not a child at that period appear to you to be morose, and by no means kind, and for the most part full of lamentation and tears, more than becomes one that is good?

CLIN. It appears so to me.

GUEST. What then? If some one should endeavour, by all possible means, that during this period of three years the child may in as small a degree as possible be affected with sorrow, fear, and pain, should we not think that by this means his soul would be rendered more cheerful and kind?

CLIN. It is evident it would, O guest, and especially if the child should be supplied with many pleasures.

GUEST. This I cannot grant you, O wonderful Clinias. For with us an action of this kind would be the most pernicious of all things. But let us see whether we may assert a certain thing.

CLIN. Inform us what it is.

GUEST. Our discourse, at present, is about a thing of no small importance. Do you, O Megillus, attend and decide for us. For my discourse asserts that an upright life ought neither to pursue pleasures, nor entirely avoid pain, but should embrace the medium between these, which we just now denominated benignity; and which, from a certain oracular rumour, we all of us aptly call the habit of divinity. We say, too, that he who is desirous of becoming a divine man ought to pursue this habit, so that he may neither be wholly hurried away to pleasures in a rash manner (for in this case he would not be free from pain), nor yet suffer any other to act in this manner, whether he is an old or a young man, of the male or female sex. But he will least of all suffer this to be the case with infants. For all the manners then, through custom, inhere in every one in the most firm and powerful manner. And further still, if it were not that I should appear to jest, I should say that pregnant women ought more than other women so to be managed, that during the year of their pregnancy they may neither be engaged in certain numerous and insane pleasures, nor be agitated by pain, but lead a benignant, benevolent, and mild life.

793a CLIN. There was no occasion for you, O guest, to ask Megillus, which of us spoke in the more proper manner; for I agree with you, that all men ought to fly from a life of unmingled pleasure and pain, and that they should always pursue a certain middle condition. You have, therefore, both spoken and heard in a becoming manner.

GUEST. With very great rectitude, therefore, O Clinias. But, besides these things, let us all three consider this.

CLIN. What?

GUEST. That all these particulars which are now discussed by us are called by many unwritten laws, and that those which are denominated b the laws of a country are no other than all these. And further still, that what we just now said, that these particulars ought neither to be called laws, nor yet suffered to be passed over in silence, was beautifully asserted. For these are the bonds of every polity, subsisting between all laws that are as yet and will be hereafter written, and being as it were altogether the laws of a country, and such as are in every respect ancient. These, when established in a becoming manner, and rendered familiar, will invest the written laws with every kind of safety. But c when they are established in an unbecoming manner, confusion will be the consequence: just as in edifices, when the pillars by which they are supported are taken away, the whole falls to the ground, some things lie under others, and those parts of the structure which were beautifully raised on the pillars become a heap of ruins, through the falling of their supporters. In consequence of considering this, O Clinias, it is proper that you should bind your city on all sides, as being a new city, and that to the utmost of your power you should not omit any thing either great d or small, which may be called laws, or manners, or studies: for by all these a city is bound together; but no one of these can be stable without the rest. So that it is not proper to wonder, if, in consequence of many and at the same time small things appearing to us to be legal, or this being the case with a conflux of customs, the laws should become more extended.

CLIN. You speak properly; and we shall think in this manner.

GUEST. If any one, therefore, accurately accomplishes these things, in e both male and female children of three years old, and does not negligently make use of what has been said, he will procure no small advantage to such as are recently educated. But these things will be accommodated to the disposition of children of three, four, five, and six years of age. Luxury too should be removed from them; and they should be chastised, but not in an ignominious manner. But, as we said respecting slaves, that they should neither be chastised with insolence, as this would excite them to anger, nor yet be suffered to go unpunished, as this would render them delicate; the same mode of conduct should be observed towards those that are free. Sports, however, are to children certain spontaneous things, which when they engage in, they nearly of themselves invent. All children then of this age should assemble in the temples of the respective districts, from three to six years of age; the nurses of these still keeping a watchful eye over their orderly behaviour and incontinence. But one out of each of the twelve women should be placed over the nurses, and the whole herd, for the space of a year; and her province must consist in taking care that every thing prescribed by the guardians of the law is executed in an orderly manner. These should be chosen by the women that preside over marriages; one out of each tribe, and of the same age with themselves. She who is established in this office should go every day to a temple, and always punish the person that acts unjustly, *viz.* a male and female slave and a stranger of either sex, herself, by means of certain servants of the city; but a citizen, when she is doubtful respecting his punishment, must be taken by her to the ædiles to receive his sentence. But when the punishment which a citizen deserves is not dubious, she herself shall inflict it. After children are six years of age, the males should be separated from the females; boys should associate with boys, and girls in a similar manner with each other. It is likewise proper that the attention of each should be directed to disciplines; the males being sent to the masters of equestrian exercises, of bows, darts, and slings; likewise the females, if discipline of this kind is allowed them; and especially that they may become acquainted with the use of arms. But now almost all men are ignorant how things of this kind are circumstanced.

CLIN. What do you mean?

GUEST. That things on the right hand seem to differ naturally from those on the left, with respect to the several actions of the hands. For the feet, and the inferior parts of the body, do not appear to possess any difference with respect to labour. But in the hands we each of us become as it were lame, through the ignorance of our nurses and mothers. For each of the members naturally possesses nearly equal power; but they not properly using them, through custom we make a difference between them. For, indeed, in certain employments there is no great difference in the use of the hands. Thus, using the lyre with the left hand, and the plectrum with the right, is a thing of no consequence; and so in other things of a similar nature. But not to use these examples in other particulars is nearly folly. The law of the Scythians, indeed, evinces the truth of these observations. For they not only hold the bow in their left hand, and the arrow in the right, but similarly employ both hands for both these. And there are many other examples of this kind in charioteers and others. From all which we may learn, that those who render the left hand more imbecil than the right act contrary to nature. This, as I have said, is a thing of no great consequence in horned plectra, and such-like instruments; but in battle, where it is necessary to use iron, bows, and spears, it is of great consequence. But it is by far of the greatest importance when it is requisite to use arms against arms. There is, indeed, a great difference between one that learns and one that does not learn, and between him who is exercised and him who is not exercised. For, as he who is perfectly exercised in the pancratium, or in boxing, or wrestling, is not incapable of fighting from his left-hand parts, but becomes lame and confused in his motions when any one, causing him to change his position, compels him to exercise himself from his right-hand parts; - the same thing, in my opinion, ought to appear proper in arms, and in every thing else. For he who possesses a twofold power, *viz.* of defending himself, and vanquishing others, ought not to suffer, to the utmost of his power, either of these to remain indolent and without skill. And if any one had the nature of Geryon or Briareus, since in this case he would be capable of using a hundred hands, he ought with all these hands to hurl a hundred darts. All these particulars ought to be under the direction of the male and female governors; the female governors inspecting the sports and nutriment of the children, but the male their disciplines, that, all the boys and girls having the perfect use of both their feet and both their hands, they may as much as possible in no respect injure nature by custom. But it will happen that twofold disciplines must be used; gymnastic, for particulars pertaining to the body; and music, for such as pertain to the good condition of the soul. Again, however, gymnastic is twofold; dancing and wrestling. And of dancing, one kind imitates the diction of the muse, preserving the magnificent in conjunction with the liberal; but another kind, for the sake of the good habit, lightness, and beauty of the parts and members of the body, aptly bends and stretches each, imparting to them rhythmical motion, disseminating, and at the same time following the

796a whole order of dancing. With respect to wrestling, that which Antæus or Cercyon adopted among their arts, for the sake of useless contention, or the boxing employed by Epeus[†] or Amycus,[‡] since they are of no use in battle, they do not deserve to be mentioned. But the particulars respecting proper wrestling, by clinging round the neck or with the hands, or round the sides, when desire of victory and a good habit of
b body are applied for the sake of strength and health, - these, as they are useful to every purpose, are not to be omitted; but both masters and disciples are to be enjoined, that, when we establish the laws respecting these, all such particulars may be benevolently imparted to the one, and gratefully received by the other. Nor must such imitations in choirs as are fit to be imitated be omitted; in this place, indeed, the armed sports of the Curetes; but, in Lacedæmon, of the Dioscuri. Our virgin too and mistress Minerva, being delighted with the sport of the choir, does not think it fit to play with empty hands; but, being perfectly adorned with
c complete armour, she in this manner completes the dance. It will be proper that all the boys and girls should imitate the goddess in this respect, honouring her benevolence, in the necessity of war, and for the sake of festivals. It will likewise be proper that boys, immediately before they go to battle, should supplicate and make sacred processions in honour of all the Gods, being at the same time adorned with arms and horses, and performing their supplications to the Gods and the sons
d of the Gods, sometimes swifter, and sometimes slower in dancing, and as they proceed to battle. Contests too, and preludes of contests, should be used, for no other purpose than for the sake of these things. For these, both in peace and war, are useful to a city and to private families. But other labours, sports, and exercises respecting the body are not, O Megillus and Clinias, liberal. And thus that gymnastic, which I said in our former discourse ought to be discussed, is nearly now absolved.
e But, if you have any thing better than this, speak, and do not withhold it.

CLIN. It is not easy, O guest, omitting these, to have any thing better to say about gymnastic and contest.

---

† Epeus was the son of Endymion, and brother to Pæon, who reigned in a part of Peloponnesus. His subjects were called from him Epei. He conquered in boxing at the funeral games in honour of Patroclus.

‡ Amycus was the son of Neptune, by Melia, and was famous for his skill in the management of the cestus.

GUEST. It follows, therefore, that we should speak about the gifts of the Muses and Apollo, which we formerly thought we had so sufficiently discussed, that the particulars about gymnastic alone remained; but now it is evident that there is something respecting these which should be mentioned before every thing else. Of this, therefore, we will in the next place speak.

797a CLIN. By all means.

GUEST. Hear me, therefore; for you have heard me in what has been already discussed. But at the same time it is requisite that both the speaker and hearer should be cautious in mentioning that which is vehemently wonderful and unusual. This also should be the case at present. For I am now going to assert something which cannot be mentioned without fear; but at the same time, assuming courage, I shall not desist.

CLIN. What is this, O guest?

GUEST. I say, that all cities are ignorant that the stability or mutation of sports is the principal thing respecting the promulgation of laws. For
b   when it is so ordered, that the same persons always use, and are delighted with, the same sports, according to the same, and in a similar manner, legal institutions are then permitted to remain established in quiet. But when sports are changed, and innovations made in them, so that young men are perpetually engaged in new sports, both in the figures of their bodies and other apparatus; continually form a different
c   opinion of the becoming and unbecoming in these particulars; and in the highest degree honour the inventors of new figures, colours, and every thing else of this kind; - when this is the case, we say, and say with the greatest rectitude, that a greater mischief cannot befall the city. For it secretly changes the manners of the youthful part of the inhabitants, and causes them to despise that which is ancient, and honour that which is new. But I again say, that there is not any thing more detrimental to all cities than this assertion and dogma. Hear, however, what a mighty evil I say it is.

d   CLIN. Do you speak of blaming ancient institutions in cities?

GUEST. Entirely so.

CLIN. You shall not, therefore, find us depraved auditors of this discourse, but as much as possible most benevolent.

GUEST. It is reasonable to suppose that you will be so.

CLIN. Only speak, therefore.

GUEST. Come then, let us hear this with greater attention, and thus speak among ourselves. We find then, that mutation in all things, except such as are evil, is in the highest degree pernicious at all times in e the diet of bodies, in the manners of souls, and, in short, in every thing except, as I just now said, in things evil. So that, if any one directs his attention to bodies, and considers them as accustomed to certain kinds of food, drink, and labours, he will find that at first they are disturbed by them, but afterwards by the long continued use of these acquire flesh, become friendly, accustomed, and familiar to all this diet, and are 98a disposed in the best manner with respect to health and pleasure. He will likewise find, that if at any time they are forced to change any part of their approved diet, at first they are disturbed by disease, and do not recover their health till they are accustomed to the new food. The same thing must be considered as taking place in the thoughts of men, and the natures of souls. For every soul reverences and fears to make any change in the laws in which it has been educated, when by a certain divine good fortune those laws have remained for a long time unmoved, so that no one either recollects or has ever heard that they subsisted otherwise than at present. The legislator, therefore, ought to devise some method by which this may be accomplished in the city. But I have discovered the following method: All men, as I have said before, consider the sports of youth when changed, as nothing more than mere sports, and are far from thinking that they are of the greatest consequence. Hence, they do not resist this mutation, but comply with it. Nor do they consider, that the children who engage in these new sports necessarily become different men from what they would have been if their old sports had remained; but, becoming different, that they will pursue a different life, and thus be accustomed to different studies and laws. Hence, no one fears that what I just now called the greatest evil will by these means happen to cities. Mutations, therefore, respecting figures are less noxious. But frequent innovations in praising and blaming manners are, in my opinion, the greatest of all evils, and the most to be dreaded.

CLIN. Undoubtedly.

GUEST. What then? Shall we believe in our former discourse, in which we said that the particulars respecting rhythm, and every kind of music, were imitations of the manners of better and worse men? Or how shall we say?

CLIN. Our opinion is in no respect different from this.

GUEST. We say, therefore, that we should endeavour by every possible contrivance, that neither children in our city may desire other imitations in dancing and singing, nor any one may persuade them to this innovation by introducing all-various pleasures.

CLIN. You speak with the utmost rectitude.

799a GUEST. Has any one then of us any art better calculated for this purpose than that of the Egyptians?

CLIN. What are you speaking of?

GUEST. That every kind of dancing and melody should be consecrated; instituting, in the first place, festivals at certain times of the year, in honour of the several Gods, the sons of Gods, and dæmons; and after this, the sacrifices to the different divinities, together with the ode and choirs with which the sacrifices are to be honoured. After these things are established, all the citizens in common should sacrifice to the
b Fates, and to all the other Gods, and dedicate their several odes to each of the Gods and their attendants. But if any one introduces other hymns and choirs in honour of the Gods than those which are instituted by law, the priests and priestesses, together with the guardians of the laws, shall, in a holy and legitimate manner, repulse him in his undertaking. And he who is repulsed, if he is not willingly restrained, shall suffer the punishment of his impiety through the whole of life, from any one who is willing to inflict it.

CLIN. Right.

c GUEST. But since we are arrived thus far in our discourse, we should be affected in a becoming manner.

CLIN. About what are you speaking?

GUEST. All men, not only the old but the young, when they see or hear any thing unusual, do not immediately assent to that which is dubious respecting it, directly, as it were, running to embrace it; but, standing still, as if situated in a place where three roads meet, and not
d very much seeing the right way, inquire, and do not proceed any further till they have a firm assurance respecting the road they should take. We too should act in a similar manner at present. For, as we have now fallen upon an unusual and wonderful discourse respecting laws, we ought necessarily to make every possible inquiry, and not readily decide, being such men as we are, on things of such great importance, or attempt to assert any thing immediately, as if the subject was perfectly clear.

CLIN. You speak most truly.

e GUEST. We will, therefore, give the subject time, and then firmly decide upon it, when it has been sufficiently considered by us. But lest we should in vain leave the order consequent to laws unfinished, let us proceed to the end of them. For, perhaps, if divinity is willing, and this discussion obtains its completion, what is at present dubious may become sufficiently clear.

CLIN. You speak most excellently, O guest, and we shall do as you say.

GUEST. We say, then, that this wonderful thing must be granted, - I mean, that odes must be established for us by law; just as the ancients, as it appears, proclaimed respecting singing to the harp. So that they, perhaps, did not entirely dissent from what is said by us at present; but in a dream, as it were, or roused to a vigilant state, they either dreamt or prophesied this. Let this then be the decree respecting it: - No one shall dare to sing any thing besides the public and sacred songs, or make any alteration in the whole choir of the young men, or utter any thing contrary to the other laws. And he who complies with this decree shall be liberated from fine; but he who does not comply, as we said just now, shall be punished by the guardians of the laws, and by the priests and priestesses. Let these things, therefore be now established for us in discourse.

CLIN. Let them be established.

GUEST. But after what manner can any one so establish them by law as that he may not appear perfectly ridiculous? It appears to me that it will be the safest way to fashion them first of all in our discourse like certain images. I say, then, that one of the images is as follows: The sacrifice being performed, and the victims burnt according to law, if some private person, a son for instance, or a brother, should approach the altars and sacred rites blaspheming with every kind of blasphemy, should we not say that he uttered a sorrowful and bad omen and prophecy, both to his father and the rest of his kindred?

CLIN. Undoubtedly.

GUEST. This, therefore, in short, must nearly take place in all our cities. For, when any magistrate performs any sacrifice in common, not one choir, but a multitude of choirs assemble on the occasion; and standing not far from the altars, but sometimes close to them, they utter every kind of blasphemy respecting the sacred concerns, exciting the souls of the hearers with words, rhythms, and the most lamentable harmonies: and he who causes the city to weep most abundantly immediately after the sacrifice is finished, bears away the palm of victory. Shall we not abrogate this law? And if, at any time, it is necessary that the citizens should hear lamentations of this kind, it should not be on certain sacred, but rather on inauspicious days: and then it will be proper that rather certain foreign choirs, conducted by hire, should sing on this occasion, as is the case at funerals, where those who are hired for the purpose walk before the dead with a certain *Caric*

Muse.† A thing of this kind may very properly be adopted about such odes as these. A long robe too will be proper for funeral odes, and not crowns or golden ornaments. But, in short, every thing of a nature contrary to these should be employed on this occasion, that I may dismiss all further discourse about these particulars with the utmost celerity. I again, therefore, ask if it is agreeable to you, that this first image should be established for odes?

CLIN. What kind of image?

801a GUEST. A good omen. And, indeed, the genus of the ode should every where, and in every respect, be employed in prognosticating well. Or shall I not at all ask your opinion, but thus establish it?

CLIN. By all means, establish it: for this law will vanquish by the unanimous votes of all men.

GUEST. What then, after good omination, will be the second law of music? Will it not be, that prayers should be offered to the respective Gods to whom we sacrifice?

CLIN. Undoubtedly.

b GUEST. But the third law, I think, will be, that since poets know that prayers are petitions addressed to the Gods, they ought to be careful in the highest degree, lest they should ignorantly request what is evil, as if it were good. For I think the condition of him who prays in this manner would be ridiculous.

CLIN. Undoubtedly.

GUEST. Did we not a little before agree, that neither silver nor gold ought to be considered as riches in our city?

CLIN. Entirely so.

GUEST. Of what then shall we say this discourse is the paradigm? Is it not of this, that not every genus of poets is sufficient to know, in the highest degree, things good and evil? If, therefore, any poet, either in prose or verse, shall compose for us improper prayers, he shall be made c by the citizens to pray for the contrary to what he asked in his prayers, in things of the greatest importance: though, as we have already said, we shall not find many offences greater than this. But we shall establish this as one of the laws and forms respecting the Muse.

CLIN. Which? Speak to us more clearly.

GUEST. That a poet shall not compose any thing, either beautiful or d good, different from the legal and just institutions of the city. Nor shall he be permitted to show what he has composed to any private person,

---

† That is, says the Greek Scholiast, a lamentable Muse: for the Carians appear to be of a mournful disposition, and for hire lament over the dead bodies of foreigners.

before the judges and guardians of the law, appointed for this purpose, have seen and approved it. But it has nearly been shown by us, who those are whom we have chosen to preside over music and discipline. Shall I then, as usual, ask whether this law, formula, and third image, is to be established for us? Or how does it appear to you?

CLIN. That it should be established, undoubtedly.

GUEST. After these things, it will be most proper that hymns, and encomiums of the Gods, should be sung mingled with prayers; and after the Gods, in a similar manner, that proper prayers, with encomiums, should be offered to dæmons and heroes.

CLIN. Undoubtedly.

GUEST. But, after this law, the following will take place without envy. It will be proper that those citizens who have accomplished beautiful and laborious works, pertaining either to bodies or souls, and who have been obedient to the laws, should after their decease be celebrated.

CLIN. Undoubtedly.

GUEST. But to honour those who are yet alive, with encomiums and hymns, and before, having completely run the race of life, they have arrived at a beautiful end, is not safe. Let all these particulars be established for us, common both to men and women that have been illustriously good. But it will be proper that odes and dancings should be established in the following manner:- There are many ancient and beautiful poems about music, and in a similar manner about dancing. Out of these to choose that which is becoming and adapted to an established polity, cannot be the means of exciting envy. The electors of these shall not be less than fifty years old. These shall choose that poem out of the ancient poems which appears to be sufficient for the purpose. But that which is insufficient, or altogether unfit, they shall either entirely reject, or commit to poets and musicians to be properly corrected, employing for this purpose their poetical abilities. They shall not apply to these for the gratification of desire, or for pleasures, except in a very few cases; but, the will of the legislator being made known, all dancing, every ode, and every choir, shall be instituted according to their determination. For every employment about a Muse, which is conducted in an orderly manner, though a sweet Muse is not added, is ten thousand times better than every disorderly pursuit of a Muse. The pleasant, however, is common to all the Muses. For every one considers that to be pleasant with which he has been conversant from infancy to mature age. And if he has been familiar with a prudent and orderly Muse, when he hears one of a contrary character, he hates, and calls it illiberal. But he who has been educated in a familiarity with a common and sweet Muse, calls the contrary to this frigid and unpleasant. So that, as I just now said, neither the pleasant nor the unpleasant has any peculiar privilege. But the case is different with respect to emolument and detriment: for the one renders those who are educated in it better, and the other worse.

CLIN. It is well said.

e GUEST. Further still, it will be proper to separate the songs which are adapted to the women from those which are adapted to the men, defining them by a certain formula, and accommodating them to harmonies and rhythms. For to be dissonant from the whole of harmony, or foreign from rhythm, attributing to melodies nothing adapted to each of these, is a dire circumstance. It is necessary, therefore, that the figures of these should be established by law, and both be properly attributed to both. But that which is accommodated either to men or women ought to be rendered manifest from the difference of the nature of each. That which is magnificent, therefore, and verges to fortitude, must be called virile: but that which more inclines to the ornamental and the moderate must be delivered, both in law and in discourse, as of a more feminine nature. This, then, is the

803a order. In the next place, let us declare after what manner, by whom, and when, each of these are to be accomplished. But as a shipwright, when he lays down that which is the principle in the construction of a ship, describes the form of the keel; in like manner, I appear to myself

b to do the same thing. For, while I endeavour to distinguish the figures of lives according to the manners of souls, I in reality lay down the keels of them, and very properly consider by what device, and after what manner, we may transport in the best manner life over this sea of life. Human affairs, indeed, are not worthy of great attention; yet it is necessary that they should be attended to. But this is not an unfortunate circumstance. Since, however, we are here, if we can in a certain respect accomplish this in a convenient manner, it will, perhaps, be sufficient for us. But some one may, perhaps, very properly inquire what it is that I now say.

CLIN. Some one may.

c GUEST. I say, then, that a thing of a serious nature ought to be seriously studied, but that this ought by no means to be the case with that which is not of a serious nature. And that divinity, indeed, is naturally worthy of every blessed study, but that man, as I said before, was fashioned to be a certain sport[†] of divinity. This, indeed, is truly the most excellent thing which he possesses. It is necessary, therefore, that every man and woman, pursuing this mode, and engaging in the most beautiful sports, should thus pass through life, thinking, in a manner, entirely contrary to what they do at present.

CLIN. How?

GUEST. Now, indeed, they think that serious pursuits ought to subsist for the sake of sports. For they consider that warlike concerns, which are things of a serious nature, ought to be well disposed for the sake of peace. But neither does sport naturally belong to war, nor was there ever any discipline in it which deserves to be mentioned, nor is there at present, nor will be. But we say that this is a thing of a most serious nature, - I mean, that every one ought to pass through life, for the most part, and in the most excellent manner, in peace. What the proper manner, therefore, is of sporting through life, and what the sports are which should be employed in sacrifices, in singing and dancing, so that the Gods may be rendered propitious, and enemies opposed and vanquished in battle; likewise, by what songs and dances both these may be accomplished; - of all these particulars we have delivered the formulæ, and, as it were, cut the paths in which we should proceed. The poet too appears to speak well when he says: "You will conceive, O Telemachus, some things from yourself, but others the dæmon will suggest to you. For I do not think that you were born and nourished with unfavourable Gods."[‡] Such too ought to be the conceptions of our pupils. For they should think that what we have already said has been sufficiently said; and that the dæmon and divinity will suggest other things to them respecting sacrifices and choirs, *viz.* what divinities they ought to render propitious in their sports, and when; at the same time living in a natural manner, and being themselves, for the most part, prodigies, but participating certain small portions of truth.

MEGIL. You vilify, O guest, in every respect the human race.

GUEST. You should not wonder at this, O Megillus, but pardon me. For, looking to divinity, and being affected with the view, I have said that which I just now said. But let our race not be any thing despicable

---

[†] Ancient theologists and intellectual philosophers were accustomed to call the energy of divinity proceeding into the sensible universe sport, on account of the delusive, fictitious, and ever-gliding nature of matter, and the forms which it contains. So that in this sense man, considered as connected with body, may be said to be the sport of divinity.

[‡] Odyss. lib. iii, 26 *et seq.*

c   (if it is agreeable to you), but worthy serious attention. After these things the public buildings for gymnastic exercises and disciplines have been spoken of, and placed in a tripartite manner in the middle of the city. The gymnasia too of the horses have, in a similar manner, been assigned a tripartite distribution in the suburbs of the city, together with ample places adorned for the sake of the young men, that in these they may exercise themselves with the bow and arrow, and in other jaculations; and may be properly disciplined and attended to. If, therefore, we did not then sufficiently speak about these particulars, let us now discourse about them in conjunction with the laws.

d   Of all these, then, foreign masters should be hired, who, residing in these ample places may teach every one that shall come to be instructed, the warlike and musical disciplines; not only instructing those whom their parents wish to be taught, and rejecting others, but, as it is said, teaching every man and boy to the utmost of their power, as being those

e   who from necessity discipline the city rather than children. My law too asserts the same things about females as about males; and says, that the former ought to be equally exercised with the latter. Nor shall I be afraid to say, that both the gymnastic and equestrian disciplines are adapted to women as well as to men. For I am persuaded of this through hearing ancient fables. But, in short, even at present, I know

805a that there are innumerable myriads of women about Pontus, called Sauromantides, who are ordered equally to use, and equally to be exercised in, horses, bows, and other arms, in common with the men. But besides this I reason in the following manner about these particulars: I say, if it is possible that these things may subsist in this manner, the custom of our country, which excludes women from engaging with all their strength in the same pursuits as men, is the most foolish of all

b   customs. For thus every city is nearly rendered half instead of double, from the same effects and labours. Though, indeed, this is a wonderful error of the legislator.

CLIN. So it appears. Yet, O guest, many of the things asserted by us at present are contrary to the custom of a polity.

GUEST. But we ought to permit the subject of our discourse to be well discussed; and, when discussed, it is requisite to select that which appears to be best.

CLIN. You have spoken very elegantly, and you have made me reprove myself for what I just now said. Speak, therefore, after this, whatever is agreeable to yourself.

c   GUEST. That is agreeable to me, O Clinias, which I said above; that, if it should appear these things could not be sufficiently accomplished, they may perhaps be contradicted in discourse. But now, if some one is by no means disposed to admit this law, he ought to inquire after something else. Nevertheless, our exhortation will not cease to assert that women ought in the highest degree, in our city, to participate in common with the men of discipline and other particulars. For in a certain respect it is requisite to think as follows on this subject. Admit that women are not to participate in common with men, in every thing pertaining to life, will it not be necessary that another order should be assigned to them?

CLIN. It will be necessary.

GUEST. What other order then among those which exist at present, shall we assign them in preference to that of our communion? Shall we adopt that of the Thracians and many other nations, who use women for the purposes of agriculture, and in the place of herdsmen and shepherds, in the very same manner as they use their slaves? Or shall we adopt the custom of our country, and that of all our neighbouring cities? For, with us, all possessions, as they are called, are collected together into one habitation, and the care of provisions, shuttles, and every thing pertaining to the manufacture of wool, is committed to women. Or shall we, O Megillus, choose a medium between these, the Laconic mode? so that virgins shall engage in gymnastic exercises and music; but women, during the time of peace, shall take care of the manufacture of wool, at the same time leading an active, but by no means a depraved and abject life? And further still, shall they bestow a certain kind of middle attention to the care of provisions and the education of children, but shall not engage in war; so that, if it should be necessary at any time to defend the city and their children, they may neither be able to use bows like certain Amazons, nor be skilled in any other kind of jaculation, nor yet to imitate the Goddess with spear and shield, and make a generous resistance for their besieged country, so as to be able, when beheld in a certain order, at least to terrify the enemy, if they can accomplish nothing greater than this? But, if they live in this manner, they will by no means dare to imitate the Sauromantides, who will appear to these women to be men. Let him, therefore, who is willing to praise your legislators for these things, praise them: but my opinion respecting them will never alter. For a legislator ought to be a perfect and not a half character, who suffers the female sex to be lost in luxury, and to use improper diet, but takes consummate care of the male sex, and thus nearly leaves for the city the half instead of the double of a happy life.

MEGIL. What shall we do, O Clinias? shall we suffer our guest thus to censure the Spartans?

d CLIN. Certainly. For, since liberty of speech is given to him, he must be suffered to go on, till laws have in every respect been sufficiently discussed.

MEGIL. You speak very properly.

GUEST. It is, therefore, nearly my province to endeavour to discuss what is subsequent to this.

CLIN. Undoubtedly.

GUEST. What then will be the mode of life by which necessaries may be moderately procured for men? so that arts may be left to others, but agriculture committed to slaves, who may procure the first fruits of the e earth, so as to be sufficient for men that live in a moderate manner; likewise, that eating in common may be adopted, the men being placed apart, and their domestics situated near them; also the female offspring, together with their mothers. Further still, that male and female governors may be placed over these public banquets, so as to dissolve them every day, and inspect the behaviour of all those that eat in 807a common; and who may return home after the governor and the rest have made libations to those Gods to whom that day or night is dedicated. To men governed in this orderly manner, will no necessary work, and which is in every respect adapted to them, be left? But is it necessary that each of them should live after the manner of cattle, paying attention to nothing but growing fat? This therefore, we say, is neither just nor beautiful: nor is it possible that a man who lives in this b manner can obtain that which is adapted to his nature. But to a sluggish animal, and which grows fat through indolence, it belongs to be torn in pieces by another animal who is vehemently exercised by fortitude and labours. If, therefore, we investigate these things with the accuracy which we employ at present, we shall perhaps find that they will never take place as long as women and children, private houses, and every thing else of this kind, are made to be private property. But those particulars which are secondary to these, and have just now been mentioned by us, if they take place, should be established in a very c moderate manner. We say then that a work remains for those that live in this manner, which is neither the smallest nor the most vile, but the greatest of all things which are ordained by a just law. For, as he who aspires after victory, in the Pythian or Olympian games, neglects every other pursuit, so his soul is filled with a double, or more than a double employment, who devotes himself in the most proper manner to the d virtue of the soul and body. For no other employment ought to become an impediment to a proper attention to the body, and to the disciplines and manners of the soul. But, indeed, every night and every day are scarcely sufficient for him who does this, to accomplish his end in a perfect and sufficient manner. Since these things, therefore, naturally subsist in this manner, the whole time of employment ought to be always orderly assigned to liberal men, in a continued succession, from one rising of the sun to another. The legislator, indeed, will appear ungraceful, who says many and trifling things about domestic government, and among these about the necessity of nocturnal vigilance, in order that the whole city may be continually defended with accuracy. For it ought to be considered as base, and not liberal, by all men, for any citizen to pass the whole night in sleep, and not to be always the first that is roused and seen by all his domestics; whether it is proper to call a thing of this kind a law or an institute. Besides this, it ought to be reckoned base by female slaves, for the mistress to be roused by them, instead of being herself the first to rouse the rest, *viz.* both male and female slaves, her children, and in short, if possible, the whole house. All free persons, therefore, rising by night, should perform the many necessary political and economic duties of their stations; the governors, those pertaining to the city, and masters and mistresses, those pertaining to their families. For much sleep is neither naturally adapted to bodies nor to souls, nor to the actions of these. For he who is asleep is of no more worth than that which is destitute of life; but, whoever among us is careful in the highest degree that he may live and be wise, will be vigilant for the greatest part of his time, sleeping no longer than is necessary to the preservation of health. But much of this will not be requisite for him who is familiar with good habits. Magistrates, indeed, who are vigilant by night in cities, are a terror to evil men, whether they are enemies or citizens, but are admired and honoured by the just and the wise; and are both useful to themselves and the whole city. The night being passed through in this manner, besides all the above-mentioned advantages, produces likewise a certain fortitude in the souls of the citizens. On the dawn of day it will be proper that boys should go to their masters. For neither cattle nor any thing else should live without a shepherd; nor boys without certain teachers, nor slaves without masters: but *a boy is the most difficult to manage of all wild beasts.* For, in consequence of the fountain of prudence in him not being yet perfect, he becomes insidious and vehement, and the most insolent of wild beasts. On this account it is necessary to bind him with a multitude of chains: and as soon as he is freed from his nurse and mother, he should be committed to the care of pedagogues, on account of his childishness and infancy, and afterwards to preceptors, that, as a free-born animal, he may be instructed in proper disciplines. But if the boy is born a slave, let it be lawful for any free-born man to punish the child, pedagogue, and preceptor, whenever he detects them acting improperly. But whoever is present on this occasion, and does not justly punish the offenders, shall in the first place be subject to the greatest reproach; and, in the next place, he who was chosen by the guardians of the law to preside over boys, shall take notice whether he whom we have mentioned does not chastise these offenders, when it is fit they should be chastised, or does not chastise them in a proper manner. For he must be an acute inspector, and one who diligently attends to the education of boys, and regulates their natures, always converting them to that which is legally good. But in what manner will the law furnish us with sufficient instruction in this particular? For this has not yet been delivered either clearly or sufficiently, but only in a partial manner. It is however necessary, that to the utmost of our power, nothing should be left incomplete, but that every thing should be unfolded, that our discourse may be to others both an interpreter and a nourisher. We have, therefore, already spoken concerning the form of a choir of singing and dancing, which among these are to be chosen, corrected, and dedicated to divinity. But we have not yet spoken concerning prose compositions, which of these, and in what manner, O most excellent superintendent of boys, they are to be delivered to those under your tuition. Though you have in our discourse the particulars which they ought to learn and study, respecting war. For the things, my friend, pertaining to letters have in the first place been sufficiently discussed by the legislator. In the next place, those pertaining to the lyre, and such as are of a memorable nature, which we said it was necessary to mention, together with warlike and economical concerns. After this, the legislator discussed those particulars respecting the periods of divine bodies, *viz.* of the stars, the sun, and the moon, which ought to be established by every city. But of what particulars are we speaking? I answer, Of the order of days with respect to the periods of months, and of months with respect to years, that seasons, sacrifices, and festivals, receiving that which is accommodated to them, and being disposed in a natural order, may render the city alive and vigilant, attributing proper honours to the Gods, and causing men to be more wise about the worship of divinity. These things, O friend, have thus been sufficiently discussed for you by the legislator. Attend, therefore, to what follows: We say that all has not been said about letters that might be said, because it has not yet been determined whether he who

809a

b

c

d

e

is to become a moderate citizen ought to possess an accurate knowledge of discipline, or by no means apply to it. In a similar manner, too, respecting the lyre. Boys, therefore, of ten years of age should apply to letters for nearly the space of three years. And those who are thirteen years old should bestow in like manner three years on the study of the lyre. Nor shall it be lawful for a father to keep his children to these studies for a shorter or longer space of time, nor for a child to apply to them, whether he is a lover or a hater of discipline. But he who is not obedient to the law in this respect, let him be deprived of those youthful honours which we shall shortly mention. However, in the first place, hear what masters ought to teach, and youth to learn, during this period. They should labour at letters till they are able to read and write. But we should not be at all concerned that those who are not naturally quick make neither rapid nor beautiful advances in allotted portions of time. With respect to those monuments of the poets destitute of the lyre, which are partly written in measure, and are partly without the sections of rhythm, O ye best of all guardians of the laws, what use will ye permit to be made of those writings, which, being destitute of rhythm and harmony, are deceitful compositions, and are left us by certain men of this description? It appears to me, that the legislator himself will very much doubt what is to be done in this case.

CLIN. What is this, O guest, which you appear to say, doubting with yourself?

GUEST. Your question is very pertinent, O Clinias. But to you, who speculate in common with me respecting laws, it is necessary that I should speak both that which appears certain, and that which appears dubious.

CLIN. What, therefore, do you now say respecting these? And what is it that moves you to speak in this manner?

GUEST. I will tell you. For it is by no means easy to speak contrary to what has been often said by ten thousand mouths.

CLIN. But what? Does it appear to you that the few and inconsiderable particulars which have been above mentioned by you respecting laws, are contrary to the sentiments of the multitude?

GUEST. You have spoken this with the greatest truth. For, as it appears to me, you exhort me to proceed confidently in this road, though it is arduous and odious to many, and advance through the path of laws which our present discourse has unfolded, without omitting any particular. And, perhaps, a journey of this kind will be pleasing to no less a multitude of a different description; but, if to a less, it will not be a worse multitude.

CLIN. Undoubtedly.

GUEST. I shall not therefore desist. I say, indeed, that we have many poets who have written in hexameter, and many how have written in trimeter[†] verse; among which the intention of some has been serious in these compositions, but of others jocose. An innumerable multitude too of such as are skilled in these writings have often said, that children who are properly educated must be abundantly nourished with those poetical compositions by often hearing them read; and, in short, must be made 811a learned by committing all the poets to memory. But others say, that a selection should be made of the principal things in all the poets, and that certain entire sentences collected for this purpose should be committed to memory, if any one among us is desirous of becoming a wise and good man through much experience and skill in a multitude of particulars. Do you, therefore, now order me to explain what is beautifully said, and what not, among these assertions?

CLIN. Undoubtedly.

GUEST. Shall I, in one word, therefore say what I think sufficient b about all these? I am of opinion, indeed, that every one will allow me to say that many things are beautifully asserted by the poets, and many things quite the contrary. But, if this be the case, I say that polymathy is dangerous to youth.

CLIN. How then, and what would you advise the guardian of the law to do?

GUEST. Of what are you speaking?

CLIN. Of the paradigm, by looking to which the guardian of the laws c may permit some things to be learnt by all boys, and may forbid others. Speak, and do not be remiss in answering this question.

GUEST. O good Clinias, I appear in a certain respect to be fortunate.

CLIN. About what?

GUEST. Because I am not entirely destitute of a paradigm. For, now looking to the particulars which we have discussed from the rising of the sun to the present hour, *but not in my opinion without divine inspiration*, it appears to me that they are similar to a certain poesy. Nor perhaps d is it wonderful that I should be very much delighted, on beholding our assertions collected as it were together in one. For, of all those above-mentioned numerous sentences which I have learnt and heard, those which we have collected in the present discourse appear to me to be the most moderate, and most fit to be heard by youth. So that I think I cannot propose a better paradigm to the guardian of the laws, and to the

---

[†] A trimeter is an Iambic verse of three measures, or six feet.

e   preceptor of youth, than this, that they should exhort the masters to teach boys these things, together with such particulars as are consequent and similar to these, whether they are written in prose or verse, or are simply asserted without being written, but are conformable to these laws, and are, therefore, by no means to be neglected, but committed to writing. And, in the first place, the teachers themselves should be compelled to learn and praise these assertions: but those teachers must not act in the capacity of teachers by whom they are not approved. And, finally, boys must be committed to the care of those preceptors by

12a   whom these assertions are approved and praised. And thus much concerning letters, and the masters of letters.

CLIN. We do not appear to me, O guest, to have wandered from the design of our discourse: but whether or not we are right upon the whole, is perhaps difficult to determine.

GUEST. But this, O Clinias, will become more apparent (as it is

b   proper it should) when, as we have often said, we arrive at the end of this discussion of laws.

CLIN. Right.

GUEST. Should we not, after having discussed the particulars about letters, speak concerning the master of the harp?

CLIN. Undoubtedly.

GUEST. If we call to mind what has been already said by us, we assigned to the masters of the harp the province of imparting discipline and every kind of instruction about things of this sort.

CLIN. Of what kind of things are you speaking?

GUEST. We said, I think, that the Dionysiacal singers of sixty years of age ought to become remarkably acute in their perception of rhythms, and the compositions of harmonies; so that, in those melodies which imitate the passions of the soul, they may be able to distinguish good from bad imitations, - rejecting the latter, but singing to and enchanting the souls of youth with the former, and thus inciting them through imitations to the possession of virtue.

CLIN. You speak most truly.

GUEST. It is requisite, therefore, for the sake of these things, that both the harper and his pupil should use the sounds of the lyre, and likewise for the sake of the distinction of the chords; rendering sounds consonant to sounds. But it shall not be lawful to exhibit to those who, through the quickness of their apprehension, would in three years experience the utility of music, the different sounds, and variety of the lyre; the chords themselves producing certain melodies, and others being produced by the poet who composes the melody, so as to connect the dense with the

rare, the swift with the slow, the acute with the grave, and the consonant with the dissonant, and in a similar manner harmonizing to
e the sounds of the lyre all the varieties of rhythms. For contraries when confused with each other are difficult to be learnt. But it is proper that youth should be taught with the greatest possible facility. For the necessary disciplines which they must acquire are neither small nor few. However, our discourse as it advances in conjunction with time will show what these are. And such are the particulars respecting music,
813a which must be attended to by the master of youth. But the particulars respecting those melodies and words which ought to be taught by the masters of choirs, we have already discussed. These we said ought to be consecrated in festivals, in an accommodated manner, so as that they may be advantageous to the city, in conjunction with prosperous pleasure.

CLIN. These things too have been delivered by you, conformable to truth.

GUEST. He, therefore, who is chosen as governor respecting the Muse, must attend to these particulars in conjunction with benevolent fortune. But, as we have delivered what remained to be discussed respecting
b music, we shall do the same respecting dancing, and the whole of gymnastic pertaining to the body. For it is necessary that both boys and girls should learn to dance, and to be exercised. Is it not?

CLIN. Certainly.

GUEST. Dancing-masters therefore must be chosen for boys, and dancing-mistresses for girls, that they may not be unaptly exercised in this art.

CLIN. Be it so.

c GUEST. Again, we call that man who engages in a variety of employments, the curator of youth, and who, since he attends to both music and gymnastic, cannot have much leisure.

CLIN. How is it possible that, being advanced in years, he can attend to so many things?

GUEST. Easily, my friend. For the law has permitted, and will permit him to choose, as his associates in these employments, such men and women among the citizens as he pleases. But he knows who ought to
d be chosen, and will desire to choose worthy associates, as prudently knowing and reverencing the magnitude of government, and being well convinced that all our affairs will sail prosperously over the sea of life when youth are properly educated. But, when this is not the case, the consequence neither deserves to be mentioned, nor shall we mention it, as in the highest degree venerating the lovers of prophets in a new city.

Much, therefore, has been said by us respecting dancing and all gymnastic motions. For we consider as gymnastic, all corporeal exercises in war, such as that of the bow, and every kind of hurling,
e likewise with the shield, and all the battles with arms; together with tactic evolutions, the conducting of armies, the positions of camps, and such particulars as pertain to equestrian disciplines. For it is proper that there should be common teachers of all these, procured by hire for this purpose by the city;, and that both boys and girls, men and women, should be their disciples, that they may be skilled in all these particulars. And girls indeed should apply themselves to every kind of dancing and
814a fighting in armour; but women to military evolutions, and the taking up and laying down of arms, if on no other account, yet that, if at any time there should be occasion for all the men leaving the city to march to battle, the women may be able sufficiently to defend the children and the rest of the city. Or, on the contrary, that they may take up arms for the city, if it should be attacked by foreign enemies, with a certain mighty strength and violence, whether they are Greeks or Barbarians; this being an event that may easily happen. For it is certainly a great
b fault in a polity, to educate women in so shameful a manner as to be inferior even to birds, who fight for their offspring with the strongest of savage animals, are willing to die, and expose themselves to every danger in their defence. But women, according to the present mode of education, in time of danger immediately run to sacred places, and fill all the altars and temples, and thus give rise to an opinion that man is naturally the most timid of all animals.
c CLIN. By Jupiter, O guest, this is both disgraceful and detrimental to a city.

GUEST. We will, therefore, establish this as a law, that women shall not neglect warlike concerns, but that all the citizens, both male and female, shall pay attention to them.

CLIN. I agree with you that it should be so.

GUEST. With respect to wrestling, therefore, we have said some things, but we have not discussed that which I should call the greatest thing, nor is it easy to discuss it without uniting gesticulation to the discussion. This, therefore, we shall then determine when our discourse,
d following things, indicates something clear about other particulars of which we have spoken, and shows that such a wrestling is, in reality, of all motions most allied to contention in battle: and, besides this, that such wrestling ought to be studied for the sake of war, but not war for such wrestling.

CLIN. This assertion of yours is beautiful.

GUEST. Thus much, therefore, may suffice at present concerning wrestling. But with respect to every other motion of the body, the greatest part of which may be properly denominated a certain dancing,

e it must be divided into two species; one of which imitates that which is venerable in more beautiful bodies, but the other, that which is depraved in baser bodies. And again, of each of these there are two species. For, of the worthy motion, one kind takes place when beautiful bodies and brave souls are entangled in war and violent labours: but the other, in the prosperous condition of this temperate soul in moderate pleasures.

815a And he who calls a dancing of this kind pacific, denominates it according to nature. But of these, the dancing in battle, which is different from the pacific, may be properly called Pyrrhic; which imitates the avoiding of all blows and hurlings by declinations, every kind of yielding, leaping on high, and dropping on the ground; and likewise attempts to imitate the motions contrary to these, tending to efficacious figures, in the hurling of bows and spears, and in all kinds of

b blows. But the rectitude and proper tone both of good bodies and souls takes place for the most part when an imitation is employed which is advantageous to the members of the body. This, therefore, should be admitted as proper, but the contrary to this, as improper. This also should be considered in the pacific dancing of every one, *viz.* whether, engaging in beautiful dancing, according to nature, he conducts himself in the choirs in a manner conformable to those who are subservient to good laws. In the first place, therefore, it is necessary to distinguish the ambiguous from the unambiguous dancing. What then is this, and how

c is each to be distinguished? The ambiguous dancing is Bacchic, and belongs to those that follow the Bacchuses, *viz.* the Nymphs, Pans, Silenuses, and Satyrs, who, as they say, imitate those that are intoxicated with wine, and perform purifying and certain mystic ceremonies. The whole of this kind of dancing cannot easily be defined, either as pacific, or adapted to war; nor, in short, is it easy to say what is the intention

d of it. But it appears to me that it may with the greatest rectitude be distinguished as follows: We must place the military dancing separate from that which is pacific, and assert that this kind of dancing is not adapted to war. Leaving it, therefore, thus situated, let us return to the military and pacific dancing, which may be praised as indubitably ours. But that kind of the pacific Muse which subsists in an opinion of a prosperous condition, and which honours the Gods and the sons of the Gods, in dancing, may receive a twofold division. For one kind is

e adopted when we have escaped certain labours and dangers, and have obtained good; and this contains greater pleasures. But the other kind subsists when the goods which we before possessed continue to be safe, and become increased; in which case the pleasures are of a milder nature. But in things of this kind every man, with respect to the motions of the body, is moved in a greater degree when the pleasures are greater, but 816a in a less degree when they are less. And he who is more modest, and more exercised in fortitude, is moved in a less degree. But he who is timid, and unexercised in temperance, sustains greater and more vehement mutations of motion. And, in short, every one that emits a sound, whether in singing or in speaking, is not entirely able to accomplish this with a quiet body. On this account the imitations of words by figures of the body produced the whole of the art of dancing. Some of us, therefore, in all these move elegantly, but others inelegantly. b And as many of the ancient names ought to be praised by us as posited well, and according to nature; in like manner it is proper to believe that he, whoever he was, rightly and musically denominated the dancings of prosperous men, who conduct themselves moderately with respect to pleasures; and that, assigning all of them a name according to reason, he denominated them *modulations*. Likewise, that he established two kinds c of beautiful dancing; calling the military dancing *Pyrrhic*, and the pacific *modulation*, giving to each a becoming and adapted name. These things, indeed, the legislator ought to explain by representations: but the guardian of the laws ought to investigate dancing; when he has discovered it, unite it with the rest of music; and in all festivals distribute that which is adapted to each of the sacrifices; so consecrating every thing in order, that no innovation may be made either in dancing d or singing, but that, both the city and citizens persevering as much as possible after the same manner in the same pleasures, they may live well and happily. And thus we have determined what the particulars respecting the choirs of beautiful bodies and generous souls ought to be. But it is necessary to contemplate and know the motions of base bodies and thoughts, and those motions which are conversant with the defamations of laughter, in words, singing, dancing, and the reviling imitations of all these. For it is not possible that serious things can be learnt without such as are ridiculous, or contraries without all contraries, if any one is desirous of becoming prudent. But it is impossible to do e both, if we wish to participate even a small portion of virtue. These things, however, ought to be learnt, lest through ignorance we should either do or say something ridiculous, which is at all times unbecoming. Servants, therefore, and hired strangers, should be appointed to imitate things of this kind: but no free person should ever study, or be seen learning them, neither woman nor man; but some novelty of imitation about them should always present itself to the view. And thus let the sports pertaining to laughter, which we all denominate comedy, be established both in discourse and law. But if any of the tragic poets,

817a who, as they say;, write about things of a serious nature, should thus interrogate us: - O guests, will you allow us, or not, to come to your city and region, and present you with our poesy? or how are you determined to act about things of this kind? what answer, then, shall we give to these divine men about these particulars? For it appears to me

b that we should reply as follows: O most excellent of strangers, we ourselves are, to the utmost of our power, poets of the most beautiful and best tragedy. For the whole of our polity is an imitation of the most beautiful and most excellent life, which we say is, in reality, the most true tragedy.[†] You, therefore, are poets, and we also are poets of the same description, being your competitors and antagonists in the most beautiful drama, which, as we hope, true law alone is naturally capable of effecting. But do not think that we shall easily suffer you to

c fix your scenes in the market-place, and, introducing players of elegant utterance, who speak louder than we do, to discourse to our children, wives, and the vulgar, about things for the most part different from those which they have heard from us. For we ourselves, and the whole city, would be nearly perfectly insane, if we should permit you to do what we have just now mentioned, before the magistrates have seen

d what you have composed, and have judged whether it is fit or not to be spoken before the people. Now, therefore, O boys, offspring of soft Muses, we shall, in the first place, show your odes, together with ours, to the governors; and if the things said by you shall appear to be the same, or better than those which are said by us, we will give the choir to you: but if this should not be the case, we shall never, O friends, be

e able to give you the choir. Let these particulars, therefore, be instituted by law respecting every choir, together with the discipline and manners of choirs, those pertaining to slaves being separated from those pertaining to masters, if it is agreeable to you.

CLIN. How is it possible it should not be so?

GUEST. Three disciplines, however, still remain for the freeborn. One of these is computation, and the particulars respecting numbers. But the second is that which measures length, breadth, and depth. And the third

---

† For he who leads the most excellent life will, like another Ulysses, purify his soul from the dominion of the passions, those baneful suitors, whose aim is to dethrone reason and debauch philosophy. He who destroys these secret foes may be justly said to perform the most true tragedy.

is that which contemplates the circuit of the stars, and the order in which they are naturally formed to move with relation to each other. 818a With respect to all these particulars, it is not proper that the multitude should labour in obtaining an accurate knowledge of them, but a certain few, of whom we shall speak when we arrive at the end of our discussion. But it is shameful for the multitude not to know such particulars among these as are necessary, and which, in a certain respect, b are asserted with the greatest rectitude. However, it is neither easy, nor altogether possible, to investigate all things accurately: but whatever is necessary among them must not be rejected. Indeed, it appears that he who first spoke proverbially respecting divinity, looking to these things, said, that God was never at any time seen contending with necessity; which I think must be understood of such necessities as are divine. For, if this was asserted of human necessities, to which the multitude looking speak in this manner, it would be by far the most stupid of all assertions.

CLIN. What are those necessities of disciplines, O guest, which are not human, but divine?

GUEST. It appears to me that they are those, which he who does not practise, nor in any respect learn, will never become either a God, a c dæmon, or a hero among men, so as to be able to be a consummately diligent curator of mankind. But he will be very far from becoming a divine man who is neither able to know one, nor two, nor three, nor, in short, the even and the odd, nor in any respect knows how to number, nor is capable of numbering night and day;, but is unskilled in the revolutions of the moon, the sun, and the other stars. He, therefore, d who is of opinion that all these are disciplines not necessary for one who is about to know the most beautiful disciplines, will think in a very stupid manner. But what the nature is of each of these, how many they are, and when they are to be learnt; likewise, what that is which is to be learnt with some other, and what without others, together with all the mixture of these, - these are the things which ought in the first place to be learnt; and, with these disciplines as leaders, a transition is to be made to other things. For, thus necessity subsists naturally, which we e say no divinity opposes at present, nor ever will oppose.

CLIN. What you assert at present, O guest, appears to be truly asserted, and according to nature.

GUEST. So it is, O Clinias: but it is difficult to establish laws respecting these things, when previously disposed in this manner. If, therefore, it is agreeable to you, we will establish laws concerning them in a more accurate manner at some other time.

CLIN. You appear to me, O guest, to be afraid of our ignorance in things of this kind; and, indeed, not improperly. However, endeavour to speak, and do not conceal any thing on this account.

GUEST. I fear, indeed, what you now say: but I am much more afraid of those who have, indeed, touched upon these disciplines, but in a depraved manner. For, the being ignorant of all things is by no means a circumstance vehemently dire, nor yet the greatest evil; but much skill and great erudition, when improperly employed, are much more pernicious.

CLIN. True.

GUEST. Freeborn men, therefore, ought to learn those things which a great multitude of boys in Egypt learn, together with their letters. For, in the first place, with the Egyptians the art of reckoning is so inartificially devised for children, that they learn it in sport, and with pleasure. For a distribution is made of apples and crowns to many, and at the same time to a few, the same numbers being adapted for the purpose. The fitting together too of the pugilists and wrestlers, and the alternate and consequent order of their conjunction, are determined by numbers. Likewise, when they play, mingling together vessels of gold, brass, and silver, and other things of this kind, or distributing them separate, they adapt, as I said before, to their sports the use of necessary numbers; and thus render their pupils fit to conduct armies, to fix camps, and become good economists; and, in short, to be more useful and vigilant than other men. In the next place, since a certain ridiculous and base ignorance respecting the measures of length, breadth, and depth, is naturally inherent in all men, they take care to liberate them from this.

CLIN. Of what kind of ignorance are you now speaking?

GUEST. O friend Clinias! I formerly heard, but after a long time began to wonder at, the manner in which we are affected about these things; and it appears to me, that it is not human, but rather the passion of certain swine and cattle. I therefore not only blush for myself, but for all the Greeks.

CLIN. About what? Inform us, O guest, what it is you mean.

GUEST. I will tell you. Or, rather, I will point it out to you interrogating. And do you answer me a trifling question. Do you know what length is?

CLIN. Undoubtedly.

GUEST. And what breadth is?

CLIN. Entirely so.

GUEST. And do you know that these are two things, and that the third of these is depth?

CLIN. How is it possible that I should not?

GUEST. Does it not, therefore, appear to you that all these may be measured by each other?

CLIN. It does.

GUEST. I mean length by length, and breadth by breadth; and that, in 820a a similar manner, depth is naturally capable of being measured by depth.

CLIN. Very much so.

GUEST. But, if some among these can neither do this vehemently, nor remissly, but some are able, and others not,[†] and yet you think it can be effected by all, in what manner are you circumstanced with respect to these?

CLIN. Badly, it is evident.

GUEST. But again, do not all the Greeks, after a manner, think that length, breadth, and depth, can be mutually measured by each other?

b CLIN. Entirely so.

GUEST. But if this is by no means possible, and yet all the Greeks, as I have said, think that it is possible, is it not fit, that, being ashamed of all them, we should thus address them: O best of the Greeks, this is one of the things which we said it was base not to know; but is it not in every respect beautiful to know things necessary to be known?

CLIN. How is it possible it should be otherwise?

GUEST. And further still, there are other things allied to these, in c which many errors are produced in us, the sisters of the above-mentioned errors.

CLIN. What are these?

GUEST. The reason why some things are commensurate and others incommensurate with each other. For it is necessary that these things should be known, or that he should be in every respect depraved who is ignorant of them. In these things, therefore, we should always be mutually engaged. For this aged game will be much more pleasant, and more worthy of a free-born man, than that of chefs.

d CLIN. Perhaps so. It appears, therefore, that the game of chess, and these disciplines, are very different from each other.

GUEST. These things, then, I say, O Clinias, ought to be learn by youth. For they are neither noxious nor difficult: and when they are learnt in conjunction with sport, they will be advantageous, but never detrimental to the city. But, if any one says otherwise, let us hear him.

[†] That is to say, some quantities are incommensurable, and others not.

CLIN. Undoubtedly.

GUEST. If, then, it should appear that these things are so, it is evident that we should embrace them; but if it should appear that they are not so, that we should reject them.

e   CLIN. Evidently so. Ought not, therefore, O guest, these to be now established by us as necessary disciplines, that the particulars pertaining to laws may not be discussed by us in vain?

GUEST. Let them, indeed, be established, but as pledges from another polity, which may be dissolved if they should in no respect please us who establish them, or you for whom they are established.

CLIN. The condition you propose is just.

GUEST. But, consider after this the discipline of the stars, whether this being chosen for youth pleases us, or the contrary.

CLIN. Only speak.

GUEST. A great prodigy takes place in these, and which can by no means be endured.

821a   CLIN. What is this?

GUEST. We say that the greatest God, and the whole world, ought not to be investigated, and that the causes of things ought not to be diligently and anxiously explored; because a conduct of this kind is not holy. It appears, however, that the very contrary to this is proper.

CLIN. How do you say?

GUEST. What I have said is a paradox, and some one may think it is not adapted to old men: but when any one is of opinion that a discipline
b   is beautiful, true, and advantageous to a city, and likewise in every respect friendly to divinity, it is perfectly impossible he should not mention it.

CLIN. You speak probably. But shall we find a thing of this kind about the discipline of the stars?

GUEST. O good man, all we Greeks, as I may say, conceive falsely of THOSE MIGHTY DIVINITIES THE SUN AND MOON.

CLIN. Of what kind of falsehood are you speaking?

GUEST. We say that the sun and moon never move in the same path, and that this is likewise the case with certain other stars which move together with these, and therefore we denominate them planets.

c   CLIN. By Jupiter, O guest, what you say is true. For, in the course of my life, I have often seen the morning and the evening star, and certain other stars, by no means moving in the same track, but entirely wandering. But we all know that the sun and moon perpetually wander.

GUEST. These are the things, therefore, O Megillus and Clinias, which
d   we say our citizens and boys ought to learn respecting the celestial Gods,

so far as this, that they may not blaspheme in speaking of them, but may celebrate them in a proper manner, by piously sacrificing and praying to their divinities.

CLIN. This indeed is right, if in the first place it is possible to learn that which you speak of; and in the next place, if we should not at present speak properly about these particulars, yet we shall when we are instructed in them. This being admitted, I grant that a thing of this kind should be thus far learnt. Do you, therefore, endeavour to evince that these things are so, and we will follow you as your disciples.

GUEST. It is not easy to learn what I say, nor is it again in every respect difficult, nor does it require a great length of time. As a proof of this, I myself have heard these things, neither recently nor formerly, and yet I am able to render them manifest in a short time; though, if they were difficult, I who am aged should not be able to explain them to you, who are likewise aged.

CLIN. True. But what is this discipline which you call admirable, which you say it is fit youth should learn, but we are ignorant of? Endeavour to speak about it with the utmost perspicuity.

GUEST. I will endeavour. The dogma then, O best of men, respecting the sun and moon and the other stars, that they have at any time wandered, is not right; but the very contrary of this is true. For each of them perpetually passes through, in a circle, one and the same path, and not many paths; though they appear to pass through many. But that which is swiftest in them is not rightly conceived to be slowest, nor contrarily the contrary. And these things, indeed, naturally subsist in this manner; but we are of opinion that they subsist otherwise. If then, beholding in the Olympic games the course of horses or of men that run the longest race, we should call the swiftest the slowest, and the slowest the swiftest, and, making our encomiums, should celebrate the vanquished as the victor, I do not think that we should adapt our encomiums properly, nor in a manner agreeable to the racers. But now, when we err in the same manner respecting the Gods, shall we not think that, as such a conduct in the instance just alleged is ridiculous and not right, this is likewise true in the present case?

CLIN. It is ridiculous indeed.

GUEST. We are not, therefore, acceptable to divinity, when in hymning the Gods we celebrate them falsely.

CLIN. Most true, if these things are so.

GUEST. If, therefore, we can show that they are so, all these particulars as far as to this are to be learnt; but, if we cannot show it, they must be dismissed. Let these things then be thus determined.

CLIN. By all means.

d GUEST. It is proper, therefore, now to say, that the legal institutions respecting the disciplines of erudition have obtained their consummation. But it is requisite to conceive in a similar manner respecting hunting, and every thing else of this kind. For it appears that the office of a legislator is something more than of merely establishing laws, and that he ought to make use of that medium which naturally subsists between admonition and the laws, and which has often occurred to us in the course of our discussion, and especially when we spoke concerning the education of children. For we said there were many
e things pertaining to this which could not be established by law, and that it was folly to attempt it: but laws being thus written, and the whole of a polity established, that is not the perfect praise of a citizen excelling in virtue, which says that he submits to the laws in the best manner, and
823a is persuaded by them in the highest degree; but the praise is more perfect which asserts that he is one who leads a pure life, in consequence of being obedient to the writings of the legislator, in which he establishes, praises, and blames laws. For this is the most proper praise of a citizen. And the legislator, in reality, ought not only to write laws, but should subjoin to them what appears to him to be beautiful and not beautiful. The citizen too, that has arrived at the summit of virtue, should no less observe these, than those particulars which are punishable by the laws. But we will adduce for this purpose, as a witness, the subject of our present discussion; for it will render our intention more
b manifest. For hunting is a thing of a great extent, and which is now nearly comprehended in one name. For there is much hunting of aquatic, much of aërial, and still more of terrestrial animals, not only of wild beasts but of men; and, of this last, one kind respects war, and another friendship; and the one is laudable, but the other blameable.
c The thefts too of robbers and camps are huntings. The legislator, therefore, who establishes laws about hunting, can neither leave these unnoticed, nor impose fines and menacing laws on each, in a certain order. What then is to be done respecting things of this kind? The legislator ought to praise and blame what is laudable and blameable in hunting, with a view to the labours and studies of youth. And young men, when they hear, should be obedient to him, and should not suffer either pleasure or labour to prevent them from acting contrary to the directions of the legislator. But they should rather honour what is said
d and enjoined with praise, than what is established with threatenings and fines. These things being premised, the praise and blame of hunting will follow in a becoming manner. For that hunting is to be praised which

improves the souls of young men, but that which has a contrary tendency is to be blamed. Let us therefore discuss what follows, calling as follows upon young men through prayer: O friends, may never any desire or love of marine fishing, or of fishing with a hook, seize you; nor, in short, of labouring to catch any aquatic animals with a bow net, either by day or by night?! May you likewise be void of all inclination of piracy, by which you would become unjust and atrocious hunters of men on the sea! And may you never in the least desire to commit theft in the region and city to which you belong, or to hunt birds, which, though a fascinating, is not a very liberal pursuit! The hunting, therefore, of pedestrial animals alone remains for our athletæ. But, of this, that kind which is performed by sleeping in turns, and is called nocturnal, as it belongs to sluggish men, is not worthy of praise. Nor yet that which during a remission of labours vanquishes the fierce strength of wild beasts by nets and snares, and not by patient endurance. That hunting, therefore, of wild beasts alone remains as the best of all, which is accomplished by horses, dogs, and corporeal strength and skill. For those that are anxious to obtain divine fortitude will vanquish savage animals by hunting them in the course, and with wounds, darts, and their own hands. And thus much may suffice respecting the praise and blame of all these particulars. However, let the law be this: No one shall impede these truly sacred hunters from hunting wherever they please. But no one shall suffer any person to engage in nocturnal hunting with nets and dogs. Fowling shall be permitted in uncultivated places and in mountains; but any one who may happen to be present shall forbid it in cultivated and sacred places. A fisherman shall not be suffered to hunt, either in ports or sacred rivers, marshes, or pools; but in other places he may be permitted to hunt so long as he does not use a mixture of juices. Now, therefore, it is proper to say, that the legal institutions respecting discipline have obtained their completion.

CLIN. You speak well.

BOOK VIII

828a   It now follows that we should legally establish festivals, in conjunction with the Delphic oracles, and show what are the sacrifices, and who the divinities to whom it will be better for the city to sacrifice. But when and what number of sacrifices should be performed, it is perhaps nearly our business to establish by law.

CLIN. Perhaps so, as to the number.

b   GUEST. Let us therefore first speak as to the number. I should establish then three hundred and sixty-five; so that some one of the magistrates may always sacrifice to some God or dæmon for the city, and for their possessions. But, the interpreters being assembled together with the priests, priestesses, prophets, and guardians of the laws, all these shall ordain such particulars as were necessarily omitted by the legislator. For it is requisite that these should take notice of things omitted. For

c   the law indeed says that there should be twelve festivals to the twelve Gods, from whom each tribe is denominated, and that the citizens should perform sacred rites to each of these monthly, together with choirs, musical contests, and gymnastic exercises, in such a manner as is properly adapted both to the Gods themselves and the several seasons. Female festivals too must be orderly disposed in such a manner, that it may appear which should be celebrated with, and which without men. Further still, the festivals of the terrestrial, and such as are denominated celestial Gods, together with the attendants on these, must not be

d   mingled with each other, but must be separated in the twelfth month, which is sacred to Pluto, that they may be legitimately celebrated. For a God of this kind must not be indignantly treated, but honoured by warlike men, as always being the best of divinities to the race of men. For *the communion between, is not better than the solution of soul and body, as I affirm, speaking seriously.* Besides, it is requisite that those who intend to distinguish these things sufficiently should think that this our city is such with respect to vacation of time, and the possession of things

829a   necessary, as no other city is found to be at present. But it is requisite that it should live well in the same manner as an individual of the human species. To those however that live happily, this must necessarily be present the first of all things, - I mean, that they neither injure others, nor are injured by others. But, of these, the former is not very difficult; but the latter is difficult in the extreme, and cannot be perfectly acquired otherwise than by becoming perfectly good.[†] The same thing also takes place in a city. For, when it is good its life is pacific; but, when depraved, it is infested with external and internal war. But, this being nearly the case, cities should not exercise themselves in war during the time of war, but in a life of peace. It is necessary, therefore, that a city endued with intellect should every month exercise itself in war, for not less than the space of one day, but more frequently as it may seem fit to the magistrates, and this without fearing either heat or cold; and that the magistrates, together with women and boys, should be exercised in it, that every inhabitant of the city may be prepared when it shall appear to the governors proper to lead forth all the people. For this purpose, too, certain beautiful games are to be devised, together with sacrifices, that certain festive battles may take place, perspicuously imitating in the highest degree the contentions of war. It is likewise necessary that the rewards of valour should be distributed to each of these; and that the victors should be praised, and the vanquished blamed, in a degree corresponding to the manner in which they have conducted themselves in the contests, and through the whole of life. However, let not every one be a poet of things of this kind. But in the first place let him be a poet who is not less than fifty years of age; and in the next place who not only sufficiently possesses the poetic muse, but who has accomplished something beautiful and illustrious. The poems, therefore, of good and honourable men in the city, and who have performed illustrious actions, should be sung, though they may not be naturally musical. But let the judgement of these be given to the instructors of youth, and to the other guardians of the laws. These shall attribute this honour to worthy men, that they alone shall be allowed freedom of speech in the Muses; but they shall not grant this liberty to others. No one, therefore, shall dare to sing a Muse which is not approved by the guardians of the laws, though it should be sweeter than the hymns of Thamyris and Orpheus: but such sacred poems shall be sung as have been examined and approved, and are dedicated to the Gods; together with the poems of worthy men, in which certain persons are praised or blamed, and which are judged to do this with moderation. The same things ought in a similar manner to take place, both among men and women, respecting war, and poetic liberty of speech. But it is requisite that the legislator should thus reason with himself: In properly

---

[†] For a perfectly good man cannot be injured; because he who is injured is deprived of some good: but virtue is the proper good of a truly worthy man, and this cannot be taken away.

830a arranging the whole city, what citizens shall I educate? Ought they not
to be the athletæ of the greatest contests, who have ten thousand
antagonists? Entirely, some one speaking with propriety may say. But
what? If we should educate pugilists, or pancratiasts, or others of this
kind, shall we lead them forth to the contest before they have contended
with any one? Or, if we were pugilists, should we not have learned to
fight, and laboured in it, many days prior to the contest, imitating all
such particulars as we should adopt in a real contest when we contend

b for victory? And should we not, as approaching in the nearest manner
possible to a similitude of real contention, instead of thongs, gird
ourselves with the cestus, that we may be able sufficiently both to give
wounds and with premeditation avoid them? And if it should happen
that there are none with whom we can contend, should we not, without
dreading the laughter of the foolish, dare to suspend an inanimate image,

c and exercise ourselves against it? And if we were in want both of
animate and inanimate adversaries, should we not venture to contend
even with our own shadows? Or, would any one say that this particular
motion of the hand was devised for any other purpose?

CLIN. For nearly no other purpose, O guest, than that which you
have just now mentioned.

GUEST. What then? Will the warlike part of the city dare to engage
in the greatest of contests, worse prepared than combatants of this kind?

d I mean, when they are to fight for life for their children, possessions,
and the whole of the city. Will not, therefore, the legislator be afraid
lest these mutual gymnastic exercises should appear to certain persons
ridiculous? And will he not establish by law, that military concerns
should be engaged in every day in an inferior degree, without arms,
exciting to this purpose the choirs, and the whole of gymnastic exercise?
Will he not likewise order, that both greater and lesser gymnastic
exercises should be performed every month at least, that each may
contend in taking possession of places, or acting on the defensive in

e every part of the city; truly imitating every thing pertaining to war, and
fighting with balls and with darts, which approach as near as possible to
true and dangerous darts? And this, that the sportive contests of the
citizens with each other may not be entirely destitute of fear, but may
excite terror, and thus, after a manner, evince who is magnanimous, and

831a who is not? For, thus he may be able in a proper manner to honour
some, and disgrace others, and render the whole city through the whole
of life useful for true contention. But, if any one should happen to die
in these contests through involuntary slaughter, let it be established that
the homicide, when he has made an expiation according to law, shall be

considered in future as pure. For the legislator ought to think that, in the place of a few who may happen to die, others again will succeed not worse than the slain: but that fear becoming, as it were, extinct in all these, he will no longer be able to distinguish the better from the worse;

b   which is, in no small degree, a greater evil to the city than the involuntary destruction of a few individuals.

CLIN. We agree with you, O guest, that these things ought to be legally established, and attended to by all the city.

GUEST. Do we, therefore, all of us now the reason, why in cities at present there is scarcely any such choir and contest, or, at least, in a very small degree? Shall we say that this happens through the ignorance of the multitude and of the legislators?

CLIN. Perhaps so.

c   GUEST. By no means, O blessed Clinias! But it is proper to say that there are two causes of this, and those very sufficient.

CLIN. What are they?

GUEST. One is, that, through the love of riches every thing else being at all times neglected, the soul of every citizen is incapable of applying to any thing but the daily accumulation of wealth. Hence every one with the greatest alacrity learns and exercises himself in that discipline or study which leads to this, but ridicules other things. It is proper therefore to say, that this is one reason why citizens are unwilling to

d   engage seriously in this, or any other beautiful and excellent pursuit; but, through an insatiable desire of silver and gold, every man willingly embraces every art and artifice, both the more beautiful and the more base, that he may become rich, acts both in a holy and unholy manner, and is not indignant at any kind of conduct, however base, by which he may be able like a wild beast to eat and drink abundantly, and enjoy venereal pleasures to satiety.

e   CLIN. Right.

GUEST. This, therefore, I assign as one reason why cities are prevented from being sufficiently exercised in any thing else beautiful, and in war-like particulars: but those that are naturally modest have their attention directed to merchandize, navigation, and servile offices; and those that are naturally brave, to theft, house-breaking, sacrilege, warlike stratagems, and tyranny. These indeed are naturally well disposed, but

832a   become unfortunate through this pernicious custom.

CLIN. How do you say?

GUEST. Why should I not call those in every respect unfortunate, who are compelled by hunger through the whole of life to torment their own soul?

CLIN. This, therefore, is one reason. But what do you assign, O guest, as the second reason?

GUEST. You have very properly admonished me.

CLIN. One reason, as you say, is the insatiable desire of riches, in the accumulation of which all men are so busily engaged, that they have not
b leisure to attend in a proper manner to warlike concerns. Let it be so. But inform us what is the second reason.

GUEST. Do I appear to you to have dwelt too long upon the first reason, through an incapacity of assigning the second?

CLIN. You do not. But you appear to us to reprobate through hatred a custom of this kind more than is becoming.

GUEST. You accuse me, O guests, in a most proper manner. You shall therefore hear what is consequent to this.

CLIN. Only speak.

c GUEST. I say, therefore, that those polities which we have often mentioned in the preceding part of our discourse are the causes of this, *viz.* a democracy, oligarchy, and tyranny. For no one of these is a polity, but all of them may with the greatest rectitude be called seditions; because in these the willing never rule over the willing, but over the unwilling, and this always with a certain violence. And as in these the governor fears the governed, he never at anytime suffers men to become voluntarily good, rich, strong, brave, or altogether warlike. These two reasons are nearly the causes of all things in cities, but particularly of those which we have enumerated. But the polity to
d which we are now giving laws avoids both these. For it possesses the greatest leisure; its inhabitants are free, and I think will from these laws be lovers of money in the smallest degree. So that it seems probable, and may reasonably be concluded, that such an establishment of a polity alone of all that exist at present can bring to perfection that warlike discipline, and warlike sport, which we have already rightly discussed.

CLIN. It is well said.

e GUEST. Does it not follow, therefore, that we should now speak concerning all gymnastic contests; so that such of them as are conducive to war may be studied, and the rewards of victory assigned them; but such as are not, may be dismissed? But it is better to relate from the beginning what these are, and establish them by law. And, in the first place, should we not establish the particulars pertaining to the course, and to swiftness?

CLIN. We should establish them.

GUEST. The celerity of the body, therefore, is universally the most warlike of all things; one kind being of the feet, and the other of the hands; that of the feet consisting in flying and pursuing; but that of the hands being indigent of strength and vigour in fighting and wrestling.

33a CLIN. Undoubtedly.

GUEST. But neither of them without arms possesses the greatest utility.

CLIN. For how should they?

GUEST. The crier, therefore, must first announce to us the race of the stadium in the contests, as at present: but he who runs the stadium must enter armed. For we do not place rewards for one that contends unarmed. In the first place, therefore, he that runs the stadium must enter armed. In the second place, he that runs the twofold course, *viz.* from the barriers to the goal, and from the goal to the barriers. In the third place, the equestrian racer. In the fourth place, he who runs twenty-four stadia. And, in the fifth place, he who is lighter armed, whom we shall order to run for the space of sixty stadia to a certain temple of Mars. Afterwards we shall enjoin another, who is heavier armed, to run a shorter and smoother space of ground. And again, another who is an archer, and has all the apparatus belonging to archery, shall, contending, proceed through mountains and all-various places, for a hundred stadia, to the temple of Apollo and Diana. Having established the contest, therefore, we must wait for these till they arrive, and bestow on the several victors the rewards of victory.

CLIN. Right.

GUEST. These contests we must conceive to have a tripartite division: one of boys; another of beardless youths; and a third of men. And for the beardless youths we shall establish two out of three parts of the course: but for boys the halves of these, who shall contend with archers and armed men. With respect to females, for naked girls not yet fit for marriage, we shall establish the stadium, the twofold course, the equestrian course, and the long course, or that of four-and-twenty stadia. But those that are thirteen years of age shall not, prior to their marriage, contend in the course longer than their twentieth, nor shorter than the eighteenth year of their age. At the same time care must be taken that their clothing is adapted for the purpose. And thus much concerning the contests of men and women in the course. As to the particulars respecting strength, instead of wrestling, and such things as are adopted at present, such as are more difficult must be instituted. And one should contend with one, two with two, and so on, as far as to ten with ten. But the things which the victor ought neither to suffer nor do, and the number of these, must be legally established by those that are skilled in the contests of arms; in the same manner as, in wrestling, those that

834a preside over this exercise determine what is beautifully performed in wrestling, or the contrary. Let the same things too be legally established respecting women till they are married. But it is requisite that the whole of the peltastic† should be opposed to the pancratian contest; and that those who engage in this contest should use bows, half-mooned shields, darts, and the hurling of stones both from the hand and slings. Laws too shall be established respecting these particulars, by which the rewards of victory shall be given to those that behave well in these

b contests. After these things, it is requisite we should establish laws respecting equestrian contests. But we have not much occasion for horses in Crete; so that the Cretans must necessarily pay less attention to the rearing of horses, and contests with them. For no one of you is in any respect a curator of chariots, or ambitious of acquiring renown through them. So that it would be foolish to establish contests of this kind. We must, however, establish an equestrian sport with single

c horses, with colts that have not yet shed their teeth, with those that are situated between these, and with those that have attained the perfection of their nature, according to the condition of the country. Let, therefore, contention and desire of victory with these be according to law; and let a common judgment of all these contests, and of those that contend with arms, be attributed to the governors of tribes, and the masters of horses. But it will not be proper to give laws to the

d unarmed, neither in gymnastic exercises nor in these contests. However, he who hurls an arrow or a dart on horseback is not useless for Crete. So that let there be strife and contention with these for the sake of sport. But it is not fit to force women by law to engage in this contest. However, if nature is not averse to girls or virgins contending in this manner, in consequence of their former disciplines and habits, it may be admitted. And thus much may suffice for gymnastic contest and discipline, whether it is such as takes place in contests, or such as we

e daily engage in under proper masters. We have likewise, in a similar manner, discussed the greater part of music. But the particulars respecting rhapsodists, and those that follow these, together with those contests of choirs which must necessarily take place in festivals, days, months, and years being assigned to the Gods and their attendants, -

835a how all these are to be disposed, and whether they are to be instituted for three or for five years, must be referred to the conceptions imparted by the Gods respecting their order. Then also it is proper that the contests of music should alternately take place, according as the athletæ,

---

† *Viz.* fighting with bucklers.

the instructor of youth, and the guardians of the laws, assembling together for this purpose, shall determine. For these shall order when, and with whom, the several contests in all dancing and singing assemblies shall take place. But of what kind each of these ought to be, both with respect to the odes and harmonies mingled with rhythms and dancing, has been often said by the first legislator; conformably to which, succeeding legislators should establish contests in such a manner that they may be properly adapted to the several sacrifices and stated times; and should ordain sacred festivals for the city. With respect to these, therefore, and other such particulars, it is not difficult to know what legitimate order they should be allotted; nor would the transferring of them be greatly advantageous or detrimental to the city. There are, however, some particulars of no small consequence, which it is so difficult to establish, that divinity alone is equal to the task; but now they require some bold man who, honouring in the highest degree liberty of speech, will declare what appears to be best for a city and citizens, and will establish it in such a manner, as to introduce into the corrupted souls of the citizens that which is becoming and consequent to the whole polity. He will, likewise, assert things contrary to their most ardent desires; and this without any human assistance, and singly following reason alone.

CLIN. What is it you now say, O guest? for I do not understand you.

GUEST. It is likely. But I will endeavour to speak to you in a yet clearer manner. For, when my discourse led me to discipline, I saw the youth of both sexes associating in a benevolent manner with each other. But I was alarmed, as it was reasonable to suppose I should, when I considered who would use a city in which young men and women are delicately educated, and never engage in those vehement and sordid labours which in the highest degree extinguish petulance, but through the whole of life are at leisure for sacrifices, festivals, and choirs. How, therefore, in this city will they abstain from those desires which hurl many of both sexes into the extremity of danger, so that those things may be forbidden by law which reason orders us to abstain from?: Indeed, it is not wonderful if the laws which were above established vanquish a multitude of desires. For the law which forbids the possession of riches in an immoderate degree, contributes not a little to the acquisition of temperance: and the whole of discipline possesses laws accommodated to this purpose. And, besides this, the eye of the governors is compelled not to look elsewhere, but always to observe youth. These things, therefore, possess measure with respect to such other desires as are human. But the unnatural connexion with boys and girls, with women as if they were men, and with men as if they were women, whence innumerable evils arise both to individuals of the human species and to whole cities, how can any one prevent? And what medicine can be found by which the danger in each of these may be avoided? This is by no means easy, O Clinias. For, in other things, and these not a few, all Crete and Lacedæmon will afford us no small assistance in establishing laws foreign from the manners of the multitude; but, with respect to amatory affairs, they will entirely oppose

c us. For, if any one, following nature, should establish the law which existed prior to the times of Laius,[†] and should assert it was proper not to have connexion with men and boys as if they were females, adducing as a witness the nature of wild beasts, and showing that, among these, males are not connected with males, because this is unnatural, perhaps he would use a probable reason, but he would by no means accord with our cities. In addition to this, likewise, he would not agree with them in that particular which we have said ought always to be observed by a legislator. For he ought always to observe among legal institutions,

d what contributes to virtue, and what does not contribute. Thus, for instance, he should consider whether what we have just now asserted would, when legally established, be beautiful, or at least not base, and how far it would contribute to the acquisition of virtue. Whether, when it takes place, it will produce the habit of fortitude in the soul of him

e who is persuaded, or a species of temperance in the soul of him who persuades? Or shall we say that no one will be persuaded of these things, but rather of every thing contrary to them? For every one will blame the effeminacy of him who yields to pleasures, and is incapable of endurance. But will not every one reprobate the similitude of the image in him who imitates the female sex? What man, therefore, will legally establish such a thing as this? Scarcely no one who has true law

837a in his mind. How, therefore, do we say it is true, that the nature of friendship, desire, and the love which we have spoken of, must be necessarily beheld by him who would properly consider these things? For, since they are two, and there is another third species arising from both, and which is comprehended in one name, the greatest doubt and darkness are produced.

CLIN. How?

GUEST. We call a friend one who is similar to the similar according to virtue, and equal to the equal. We likewise denominate him a friend

---

† A son of Labdacus, and king of Thebes. He was the father of Œdipus, by whom he was slain.

who is indigent of a rich man, through he is contrary to him in genus. But, when each of these friendships becomes vehement, we call it love.

CLIN. Right.

GUEST. The friendship, therefore, which arises from contraries is dire and rustic, and is not often mutual: but that which arises from similars is mild and mutual through life. But as to that which is mixed from these, in the first place, it is not easy to learn what his wish may be who possesses this third love: and, in the next place, being drawn by both to that which is contrary, he himself is doubtful what he should do; the one exhorting him to use the flower of his age, and the other dissuading him from it. For, he who is a lover of body, and hungers after its flower, as if it were ripe fruit, endeavours to be satiated with it, and confers no honour on the manners of the soul of his beloved. But he who possesses a careless desire of body, and rather beholds than loves it with his soul, such an one, since he is a lover of soul in a becoming manner, considers the satiety of body, with respect to body, as disgraceful; but, reverencing and cultivating temperance, fortitude, magnificence, and prudence, he always wishes to live chastely with a chaste lover. But the love which is mixed from both these is the love which we just now discussed, as ranking in the third place. Since, therefore, there are three kinds of love, ought the law to forbid all of them, and prevent them from subsisting in us? Or, is it not manifest we should be willing that the love which is of virtue, and which desires that youth may arrive at the summit of excellence, should subsist in the city; but that, if possible, we should expel the other two? Or how shall we say, O friend Megillus?

MEGIL. You have spoken, O guest, about these particulars in a manner perfectly beautiful.

GUEST. I was right in my conjecture, O friend, that you would accord with me in sentiment. But it is not proper that I should inquire what your law conceives about things of this kind, but that I should receive what you admit; and, after this, that I should endeavour to persuade Clinias to be of our opinion. Let, however, that which you have granted me be admitted, and let us now diligently discuss the laws.

MEGIL. You speak with the utmost rectitude.

GUEST. I possess an art at present relative to the establishment of this law, which is partly easy, and partly in every respect difficult.

MEGIL. How do you say?

GUEST. We know even at present many men, who, though they act illegally, yet in a becoming manner and diligently abstain from a connection with beautiful persons, and this not involuntarily, but for the most part willingly.

MEGIL. When does this take place?

b   GUEST. When any one has a beautiful brother or sister. The same law too, though unwritten, sufficiently defends a son or a daughter, and prevents their parents from having any connection with them, either openly or secretly. Indeed, it prevents the vulgar from even desiring a connection of this kind.

MEGIL. True.

GUEST. A small word, therefore, extinguishes all such pleasures.

MEGIL. What word is that?

GUEST. That which says these things are by no means holy, but that

c   they are odious to divinity, and the most base of all base things. But does not this take place, because the contrary to this is never asserted, but each of us from our childhood hears the same things said both jocosely and seriously; and often in tragedies, when a Thyestes† or Œdipus is introduced, or a certain Macareus,‡ who being secretly connected with their sisters, but detected, immediately suffered death, as

d   the punishment of their offence?

MEGIL. This is said with the greatest rectitude. For rumour possesses a certain wonderful power; since no one attempts even to breathe in a manner contrary to law.

GUEST. That which we just now said, therefore, was right; that it was easy for a legislator, who wished to enslave some one of those desires which in a remarkable degree enslave men, to know in what manner this must be accomplished. For, if this rumour becomes consecrated among slaves and the free-born, men and women, and the whole city,

e   it will cause this law to be most firm and stable.

MEGIL. Entirely so. But how can it be brought to pass that all men shall willingly speak in this manner?

GUEST. Your question is a very proper one. For this is what I said, that I had an art relative to this law, by which men might be induced to use copulation according to nature, and in order to produce offspring.

839a Let them, therefore, abstain from connection with males, and not designedly cut off the race of men, nor disseminate in rocks and stones, where the prolific nature of that which is sown can never take root. Let

---

† A son of Pelops and Hippodamia, and grandson of Tantalus. He debauched Ærope, the wife of his brother Ægeus.

‡ A son of Æolus, who debauched his sister Canace, and had a son by her.

them, likewise, abstain from every feminine field in which the seed is unwilling to germinate. This law, if it was established, and possessed the same authority in other things as in the connection of parents, would produce innumerable benefits. For, in the first place, it would be established according to nature. And, in the next place, it would restrain men from amatory fury and madness, from all adulteries, and the immoderate use of meats and drinks. It would likewise cause men to be familiar and friendly with their wives; and many other benefits would arise if this law was diligently observed by every one. But, perhaps, some very young man, and who is full of seed, on hearing that this law is to be established, will immediately revile us, as framing laws which are foolish, and impossible to be observed, and will fill every place with his vociferations. It was in consequence of looking to this, that I said I possessed a certain art, which was partly easy and partly difficult, by which this law might be firmly established. For it is easy to understand that this is possible, and in what manner it is possible. For we have said that, when this legal institution is sufficiently consecrated, it will subdue every soul, and entirely cause them, through fear, to be obedient to the established laws. But at present it appears to be impossible that it should ever take place: just as the institution of eating in common is considered as a thing impossible to be perpetually observed by a whole city; yet it is adopted by you, though it appears impossible to persuade women to this, nor does it seem to be naturally adapted to your cities. Hence, through the strength of this belief, I said that both these could not without great difficulty be legally established.

MEGIL. And you was right in saying so.

GUEST. Are you, therefore, willing that I should endeavour to mention to you a thing endued with a certain persuasive power, and which is not beyond human ability to accomplish?

CLIN. Undoubtedly, we are willing.

GUEST. Will, therefore, any one more easily abstain from venereal concerns, and be willing to observe in a moderate manner, and not like the vulgar, the order imposed on him, when his body is in a good condition, or when it is badly affected?

CLIN. Doubtless, when his body is in a good condition.

GUEST. Have we not, therefore, heard of the Tarentine Iccus, who, for the sake of Olympic and other contests which he applied himself to, through a desire of victory and art, and in conjunction with temperance and fortitude, never had any connection either with a woman or boy during the whole time of his exercise? The same thing too is reported of Crysson, Astyllus[†] Diopompus, and many others; though their souls were much worse disciplined than those of your and my fellow citizens,

b O Clinias, and their bodies much more luxurious.

CLIN. You give a true account of what the ancients say respecting the conduct of these athletæ.

GUEST. What then? Could they for the sake of victory in wrestling, in the course, and such like things, have the courage to abstain from that affair which is called blessed by the multitude; and shall our youth be incapable of a similar continence, for the sake of a far more excellent victory, which we sing to them from their very childhood, as a thing

c most beautiful, in fables, in prose and in verse, and charm them into a persuasion of this, as it is fit we should?

CLIN. What victory are you speaking of?

GUEST. Of the victory over pleasure, - that, being continent in this, they may live happily: for, if they are vanquished by pleasure, the very contrary will take place. Besides this, will not the dread lest it should be a thing by no means holy, enable them to subdue those things which others worse than themselves subdue?

CLIN. It is probable it will.

GUEST. Since, therefore, we have arrived thus far about this law, and

d have fallen into doubt through the depravity of many, we now say with confidence, that our citizens ought not to be worse than birds, and many wild beasts: for many herds of these live a single, pure, and incorrupt life till the time of procreating offspring; and when they arrive at this age, the male benevolently uniting with the female, and the female with the male, they live for the remainder of their time in a holy

e and just manner, firmly abiding in the first compacts of friendship. But it is requisite that our citizens should be better than wild beasts. If, therefore, they are corrupted by other Greeks, and the grater part of Barbarians, and are incapable of restraining themselves when they see and hear that the Venus which is called inordinate is capable of accomplishing in them that which is greatest, - in this case, it is requisite that the guardians of the laws, becoming legislators, should devise for them a second law.

841a CLIN. What law would you advise should be established for them, if they reject the present?

GUEST. Evidently that which follows this, O Clinias.

CLIN. What law do you mean?

[†] Astyllus is mentioned by Pausanias as a victor in the Olympic repeated course. See vol. ii. of my translation, p.119.

GUEST. That they should especially cause the strength of pleasures to be unexercised, altering the course of its infusion and aliment through labours of the body. But this will take place if the use of venereal pleasures is not attended with impudence. For, these being more rarely used through shame, the mistress of them will possess a more imbecil dominion. Custom, therefore, and an unwritten law, should privately persuade them to act in this manner, and dissuade them from a contrary mode of conduct as base. For thus, in the second place, we shall preserve the becoming; and one race of men comprehending three genera, will compel those of a depraved nature, and who, we have confessed, are their inferiors, not to act in an illegal manner.

CLIN. What three genera are these?

GUEST. Those that venerate divinity, the lovers of honour, and those that do not desire corporeal beauty, but are lovers of the beautiful manners of the soul. And these things, perhaps, which are now asserted by us, are like prayers in a fable. But they will by far subsist in the most excellent manner, if they should be adopted by all cities. Perhaps, too, if divinity pleases, we may by force accomplish one of the two in amatory affairs: either that no one shall dare to touch any free and well-born woman besides his wife, or have any connection with concubines, or disseminate contrary to nature in the barren soil of males: or else we must entirely take away connection with males; and if any one has connection with other women than those which came to his house in conjunction with the Gods, and sacred marriages, whether such women are bought, or acquired by any other means, - such an one, unless he is concealed from all men and women, may perhaps with propriety be deprived by law of all the honours in the city, as being one who is truly a foreigner. This law, whether it is proper to call it simple or twofold, should be established respecting all venereal and amatory concerns, which are transacted by us with each other through suchlike desires, and this both in a proper and improper manner.

MEGIL. I very much approve, O guest, of this law: but let Clinias here inform us what is his opinion respecting these things.

CLIN. I shall do so, O Megillus, when it appears to me that a proper opportunity presents itself for this purpose: but let us now permit our guest to proceed forward in his discussion of laws.

MEGIL. Right.

GUEST. But we have now proceeded so far, that we are nearly arrived at the establishment of eating in common; which in other places we have said it is difficult to establish, but no one will suppose but that it ought not[†] to be adopted in Crete. After what manner, however, must it be established? Shall we say as here, or as in Lacedæmon? or is there a third mode better than both these? It appears to me to be difficult to discover this third mode, and that when found it will not be productive of any great good. For what we have now instituted appears to have

c been accomplished in an elegant manner. After this, it follows that we should speak respecting the apparatus of food, and show in what manner it should be procured for our citizens. Food then in other cities is all-various, and procured from many places, but especially from two places. For food is obtained for the greatest part of the Greeks from the earth and sea; but to our citizens from the earth alone. This, therefore, will be easy for the legislator. For much less than half of the laws will be sufficient; and these will be more adapted to free-born men. For the legislator of this city will have nothing to do with naval and mercantile

d affairs, or with inn-keepers, publicans, victualling-houses, miners, borrowing money, usury, and ten thousand other things of this kind. But he will only have to give laws to husbandmen, shepherds, the curators of bees, and the guardians and superintendents of things of this

e kind: and his principal business as a legislator will consist in attending to marriages, the procreation, education, and discipline of children, and the establishment of magistrates in the city. it is, therefore, now necessary that we should direct our attention to nutriment, and to those who by their own labour procure it. let the laws, therefore, called georgic be first established. And let this be the first law of Jupiter Terminalis:[‡] No one shall move the boundaries of land, neither that of a neighbouring fellow-citizen, nor of a neighbouring stranger, if he should possess the extremities of the land; but he should consider that

843a the saying, 'This is to move things immoveable', is true. And every one should rather wish to move a mighty rock, than a boundary, or small stone, which terminates friendship and hatred by an oath. For Omophylus[§] Jupiter is a witness of the one, and Hospitable Jupiter of the other; and these divinities are roused in conjunction with the most hostile battles. He, too, who is obedient to the law shall be free from condemnation: but he who despises it shall be obnoxious to a twofold punishment; one, and that the first, from the Gods; but the second from

---

[†] In Taylor's original this *not* is omitted.

[‡] i.e. Jupiter the guardian of bounds.

[§] i.e. Jupiter the guardian of a tribe or kindred.

b the law. For the law says that no one shall voluntarily move the boundaries of his neighbour's land. But of him who does move them, any one that is willing may inform the husbandmen, who shall lead him to the court of judgment. Here he shall be condemned by the judges to make restitution, as one who distributes land privately and by force, and shall be otherwise punished in such manner as the judges shall determine. But, in the next place, many and small injuries of neighbours, when often taking place, produce great enmities, and render vicinity difficult and vehemently bitter. On this account a neighbour ought to be extremely cautious of injuring his neighbour, both in other things, and in every thing pertaining to agriculture. For to do an injury is by no means difficult, but is in the power of every man; but to profit is not in the power of every one. But he who, passing beyond his own boundaries, cultivates his neighbour's land, shall make a restitution, and, suffering the punishment of his impudence and illiberality, shall pay the injured person the double of his loss. Of all such like particulars, husbandmen should be the judges and censors. And of such as are greater, as I have said before, the whole order of the twelfth part; but of the lesser, those that preside over the guardians of these. And if any one distributes cattle, the husbandmen, considering the injury, shall judge and condemn accordingly. Likewise, if any one usurps a swarm of bees belonging to another, alluring the bees by the sound of brass, and thus rendering them familiar to him, he shall make a restitution to the injured person. And if any one sets fire to certain materials, without paying any attention to his neighbour's property, he shall pay that fine which the magistrates think fit to impose. In like manner, he who in planting does not leave the measure of his neighbour's land, shall be

4a punished in such a manner as would be said to be sufficient by many legislators; whose laws we ought to use, and not think that the many and trifling particulars which are instituted by any casual legislator are to adopted by a greater moderator of a city. For ancient and beautiful laws respecting water are established for husbandmen, which yet do not deserve to be recited. But he who wishes to deduce water to his own place, should so deduce it from common fountains as not to cut off the apparent fountain of any private person. He may likewise be permitted to conduct the water where he pleases, except through houses, or certain temples, or sepulchres, at the same time being cautious not to do any damage, except what may arise from the derivation of the stream. But if the natural dryness of the ground in certain places should be incapable of retaining the waters from Jupiter, and there should be a defect of necessary drink, any one may dig in his own ground till he comes to chalky earth. And if in this depth he meets with no water, he may draw as much from his neighbours as his necessities require. But if there should be a scarcity of water with his neighbours, the quantity that should be daily used must be determined by the præfects of the land.

c However, if the waters from Jupiter abound and those that inhabit or cultivate the lower places restrain the flux of the water, so as to injure those in the higher grounds; or, on the contrary, if the inhabitants of the higher places, inconsiderably permitting the waters to flow, injure the inhabitants of the lower grounds, and disagreement arises between the two respecting this particular, - then, in the city, the city surveyor, but, in the country, he who presides over the land, shall order what each ought to do in this case. But he who is not obedient to this order shall

d suffer the punishment of his envy and moroseness, and shall give the injured person the double of his loss. A participation of the fruits of autumn should be made by all men as follows: - The God of autumn imparts to us two gracious gifts; one Dionysiacal, which does not require to be concealed; but another, to which concealment is natural. Let this law then be established respecting autumnal fruits. Whoever tastes of

e the rustic fruit of grapes, or of figs, before the time of vintage, which concurs with Arcturus, shall be fined fifty drachms sacred to Bacchus, if he has gathered these fruits from his own land; but if from that of his neighbour's, a mina; and if from other lands, two parts of a mina. Grapes and figs, which we denominate generous, may be gathered by any one, after what manner and when he pleases, if they are his own; but not when they belong to another, unless he obtains leave of the possessor; and this in conformity to the law which says that no one shall move that which he has not deposited, and that he who does so shall be

845a fined. But if a slave, not complying with the orders of his master, gathers fruits of this kind, he shall receive as many lashes with a whip as the number of the grapes and figs which he gathered. When a native has bought any generous autumnal fruits, he may eat them if he pleases; but if a stranger as he passes along desires to eat these autumnal fruits, whether he is alone or with one companion, he may eat them as hospitable property: but the law forbids strangers from eating those

b fruits which are called rustic. If any one ignorantly gathers these, or if they are gathered by a slave, the slave shall be punished with stripes; but the free person shall be dismissed with an admonition that he may gather other autumnal fruits, but that those from which raisins, wine, and dry figs are made, are not fit to be gathered. With respect to pears, apples, pomegranates, and all such fruits, let it not be considered as base

c to gather them secretly. But if any one who is less than thirty years of age is detected gathering them, let him be chastised, but without wounds; and let not the free-born man suffer any punishment for inflicting this chastisement. Let it likewise be lawful for a stranger to partake of these fruits in the same manner as of generous autumnal fruits. If any person more advanced in years tastes of these, but does not take them away, let him, in the same manner as a stranger, be permitted to partake of all these: but if he is not obedient to the law, let

d   him be considered as one who does not contend for virtue; - if any one gives information of this to the judges of these particulars. Again, water is the most nutritive of every thing pertaining to gardens, but it is easily corrupted. For neither the earth, the sun, nor the air, which together with water nourish things germinating from the earth, can be easily corrupted either by medicaments, turnings aside, or thefts: but all such things as these are able to take place respecting the nature of water; and on this account it requires the assistance of law. Let this, then, be the law respecting it: If any one voluntarily corrupts water belonging to

e   another person by medicaments, or ditches, or thefts, whether such water is fontal or collected, he shall be taken before the ædiles; and, if convicted, he shall be punished adequately to his offence. With respect to the conveyance of all seasonable fruit, let it be lawful for any one

46a who is willing, to carry his own fruit any where, so long as he does not injure any one, or so long as a gain arises to himself triple of the damage which his neighbour has sustained. Let the magistrates be the inspectors of these things, and of all such injuries as are either committed by violence or secretly, against a person himself, or his property. Let all such particulars be laid before the magistrates, if the injury does not

b   exceed three minæ; but if it does, let the case be brought before the common courts of justice, and let him who has committed the injury be punished. But if any magistrate shall be found to condemn an accused person unjustly, let him be considered as a debtor to the injured person of twice the loss which he sustained. And, in short, let the unjust conduct of the magistrates be brought before the common courts of justice by any person that is willing. But as there are ten thousand small legal institutions, according to which punishments ought to be inflicted respecting the allotments of justice, citations, and the persons cited,

c   whether the citation ought to be made between two, or between many; - all such particulars as these must not be left destitute of law, nor yet do they seem worthy to be noticed by an aged legislator. Let young men, therefore, give laws respecting these, imitating prior legal institutions, understanding small things from such as are great, and becoming experienced in the necessary use of them till every thing shall appear to be sufficiently established. After this, causing these institutions to be immovable, let them be used as such.

d With respect to other artificers, it is requisite to act as follows: In the first place, let no citizen labour about artificial works, nor yet a servant of any citizen. For a citizen who preserves the common ornament of the city, is engaged in an art which requires long continued exercise, and, at the same time, many disciplines, and the possession of it is not to be obtained by indolent application. But to labour accurately in two studies, or two arts, nearly surpasses the ability of human nature. Nor

e can any one sufficiently exercise one art, and at the same time direct his attention to one who exercises another. This, therefore, ought first of all to take place in the city, that no one shall at the same time be a coppersmith and a builder; and that a builder shall not attend more to the coppersmith's, than to his own art, under a pretext that, because he has many servants who work for him, he very properly bestows more attention upon them, that greater gain may thence accrue to him from

847a his own art: but every artist in the city shall exercise one art only, and from this derive his support. This law the ædiles should particularly attend to; and should punish with disgrace and infamy any one who inclines a citizen to a certain art more than to the study of virtue, till they have converted the citizen to his right course. But, if any stranger is found to apply himself to two arts, he shall be punished with bonds,

b fines, and expulsions from the city, and shall be compelled to exercise one art alone. With respect to the wages of workmen, and the destruction of works, and the injuries which workmen may either suffer or commit, the ædiles shall judge of these as far as to fifty drachms. Offences which merit a greater fine than this, shall be judged according to law in the common courts of justice. There shall, likewise, be no revenue in the city arising from the exportation and importation of

c goods. But, with respect to frankincense, and other foreign aromatics, from which fumigations are made to the Gods, together with purple, and other dyed colours, which are not produced in this region, or any other article of foreign importation, let no one introduce any of these, nor yet again export any thing which the region necessarily requires. All these particulars must be attended to, and taken care of, by the twelve guardians of the laws, five of the elder being excepted. With

d respect to arms, and all warlike instruments, if there should be a necessity of any foreign art, whether relative to plants, or metals, or bonds, or animals which are subservient to war, the care of the importation and exportation of these must be committed to the masters of the horse, and the generals of the army; but the guardians of the law e must establish respecting these becoming and sufficient laws. No victualling-houses shall be suffered, either in the city or in any part of the region for the sake of accumulating wealth. But it appears that the mode established by the law of the Cretans of distributing the food which is the produce of the country, is a proper one: for a general distribution into twelve parts is made of the whole produce of the land,

348a which also is consumed. Every twelfth part of barley, wheat, all autumnal fruits, and vendible animals, should be triply divided according to proportion; one part being given to free-born persons, another to the servants of these, and a third part to artificers and strangers, whether such strangers have taken up their residence in the city through the want of necessary sustenance, or for the sake of any advantage to the city, or any individual in it. This third part, therefore, of all necessaries, should be alone vendible from necessity; but nothing belonging to the

b two other parts should be necessarily sold. How, therefore, are these to be distributed in the most proper manner? In the first place, it is evident that we should distribute them partly equally, and partly unequally.

CLIN. How do you say?

GUEST. It is necessary that every land should produce and nourish things better or worse than each of these.

CLIN. Undoubtedly.

GUEST. As, therefore, there are three parts, let no more be distributed either to masters or slaves, or strangers, but let the distribution be made to all, according to the same equality of similitude. But let each citizen since he receives two parts, have the power of distributing both to slaves and free-born persons, as much, and such things, as he pleases. It is however proper that a greater quantity than these should be distributed in measure and number, and that a distribution should be made after an account is taken of all the animals which derive their nourishment from the earth. After this, it is necessary that habitations should be separately assigned them in an orderly manner. But the following order will be adapted to things of this kind. There ought to be twelve streets in the middle, and one in each of the twelve parts; and in each street a forum, and temples of the Gods, and of dæmons the attendants of the Gods, should be raised; and whether there are statues of certain inhabitants of Magnesia, or of other ancients whose memory is preserved, to these the honours of ancient men should be paid. The temples of Vesta, Jupiter, Minerva, and of him who is the leader of each of the other divinities that preside over the twelve parts, should be every where established. But first of all buildings should be raised about these temples in the highest place, as well defended receptacles for the guards: but the rest of the region should be distributed for the artificers into thirteen parts. And one part of these shall reside in the city, this part being distributed into the twelve parts of the whole city; but another part shall be circularly distributed about the environs of the city. In every street artificers shall reside that are adapted to the purposes of husbandmen.

849a The governors of the husbandmen, too, shall take care of all these particulars, and of such things as each place may require; and shall provide such places as will be most advantageous to the husbandmen. The ædiles in like manner shall take care of the artificers in the city. Things pertaining to the forum ought likewise to be taken care of by the præfects of the markets. After attention to sacred things, they should be careful, in the first place, that no one acts unjustly in buying or selling; and, in the next place, they should punish every one that deserves punishment, as being the inspectors of modesty and insolence. With respect to things vendible, they should, in the first place, consider, whether the citizens sell to foreigners in a manner conformable to law. But let the law be this: On the first day of the month, those that take care of foreigners shall exhibit a part of what is to be sold; viz. in the

b first place a twelfth part of the corn: and foreigners during the space of the whole month shall buy corn, and such things as pertain to corn, in the first market. But on the twelfth day of the month, the selling and buying of most articles shall take place through the whole of the month.

c And on the twenty-third day of the month, let such animals be sold as may be wanted, together with such articles as husbandmen require, viz. skins and garments of every kind, whether knit or woven. But it is necessary that strangers should buy the possessions of others. However, let there be no buying or selling of wheat or barley, distributed into barley-meal, or of any other aliment, either among the citizens or their slaves. In the markets of the strangers, a stranger may sell and exchange

d to artificers and their slaves, wine and food, and in like manner distributed flesh, which is generally called cauponation. A stranger, too, may be permitted to buy every day the whole materials of fire, from the inspectors of places, and sell it again to other strangers, for as much as

e he pleases, and when he pleases. Let every other useful article be sold in the common forum, in such places as the guardians of the laws, and præfects of the markets, together with the ædiles, shall appoint. Here let money be exchanged for things, and things for money; no one committing the exchange to another, but performing it by himself. However, if any one thinks proper to commit it to another, whether restitution is made to him or not, he must be contented, because no

850a notice is taken in the courts of justice of such contracts. But if that which is bought or sold, has been bought or sold at a greater or less price than the law fixes upon vendible commodities, the quantity by which it exceeds the just price shall be taken an account of in writing by the guardians of the laws, and the contrary shall be expunged. Let the same things be enjoined respecting the registering of the property possessed by the inhabitants of the city. Let it likewise be lawful for any one to migrate to our city on certain conditions, *viz.* so that he is

b skilled in, and exercises, some art, and does not continue more than twenty years from the day of his being registered; during which time he shall not be forced to pay any tribute for buying and selling, nor be under any restraint, except that of conducting himself temperately. But when the twenty years are expired, he shall receive his own property and depart. However, if it should so happen during this time, that the city should be greatly benefitted by him, and he is desirous of continuing longer, or of settling for life in the city, let his request be complied with, if agreeable to the inhabitants of the city. With respect

c to the sons of the emigrants that are artists and fifteen years of age, let the time of their continuance in the city commence from their fifteenth year, so that they may stay, if they please, twenty years after this period, or longer if agreeable to the inhabitants. But if they choose to leave the city they may depart after their registers, which were committed to the care of the magistrates, are obliterated.

BOOK IX

853a　As judicial affairs are consequent to all the preceding particulars, the discussion of them at present will be agreeable to the natural order of laws. But we have partly shown what the particulars are respecting which judgements ought to take place, *viz.* respecting agriculture and the like; though we have not as yet distinctly spoken of the greatest judgments, and shown what punishments they ought to inflict, and who should be the judges. It therefore follows that we should now speak of these.

b　CLIN. Right.

GUEST. But it is after a manner base that the city which we say will be properly inhabited, and furnished with every thing adapted to the study of virtue, should observe all such laws as we are now about to establish. For to suppose that, in such a city, a man capable of the greatest iniquity will be born, so that it will be necessary to give laws by

c　anticipation, and enjoin threatenings, if such a character should arise, and this for the sake of preventing the greatest enormities, and that when they are committed, they may be legally punished, - to suppose this will, as I have said, be in a certain respect base. But since we do not, like the ancient legislators, give laws to heroes the sons of the Gods, these legislators at the same time being themselves descended from the Gods, but being ourselves men, we at present give laws to those that are born from the seed of men; - since this is the case, we may justly be afraid lest any one of our citizens should be so naturally intractable and untamed, as not to be liquefied; just as leguminous substances, when blasted by thunder, cannot be subdued by fire. The first law, therefore, which we shall establish, though it is not agreeable to us to do so, is respecting sacrilege, if any one shall dare to commit it. Indeed, we neither wish, nor do we very much fear, that a citizen, when properly educated, will ever labour under this disease. But the servants of these,

854a　strangers, and the slaves of strangers, will attempt many things of this kind; for the sake of which especially, and at the same time fearing for all the imbecility of human nature, I shall speak about the law of sacrilege, and all other such particulars as are either difficult to be cured, or entirely incurable. The preface, however, to these particulars, according to what has been formerly assented to, ought to be as short as possible. Some one, therefore, may thus address him who is excited

b　by a vicious desire both day and night to plunder temples, mingling at the same time admonitions with his speech: O wonderful man, neither a human nor a divine evil moves and excites you now to sacrilege, but a certain execrable fury, arising in men from ancient and unpurified offences, which you ought to dread with all your might. Learn, then, what this dread is. When any such opinion attacks you, betake yourself to expiations, betake yourself, in a suppliant manner, to the temples of

c those Gods that avert evils from mankind; and betake yourself to an association with good men. Among these partly hear, and endeavour yourself to say, that every man ought to honour things beautiful and just. But fly without turning back from an association with the vicious. And if, in consequence of your acting in this manner, the disease ceases, you have done well; but if not, considering that in this case it is better to die, liberate yourself from life. Since, therefore, we have sung these exordia to those whose thoughts lead them to deeds impious and destructive to the city, it is proper to dismiss him in silence who is obedient to the law: but to him who will not be persuaded, it is necessary, after the preface, to sing in a higher strain. He, then, who is

d detected in the act of sacrilege, if he is either a slave or a stranger, shall have his calamity written in his face and hands, and after he has received as many lashes with a whip as the judges shall think proper, he shall be driven naked beyond the borders of the region. For, perhaps, being brought to his right mind by this punishment, he will become a better man. For no punishment subsisting according to law is inflicted with an evil intention. But one of two things is nearly always effected: for he who suffers punishment either becomes better or less depraved. if, however, a citizen shall at any time appear to have perpetrated any thing

e of this kind, or some mighty and arcane crime towards the Gods, or his parents, or his country, the judge shall pronounce such an one to be incurable, in consequence of considering, that though he has been well nourished and disciplined from his childhood, yet he has not abstained

855a from the greatest vices. But death to such a man is the least of evils. Such an one, therefore, that others may be benefited by his example, being stigmatized with infamy, and expelled beyond the boundaries of the region, shall there be put to death. But let his children and race be honoured and praised, if they avoid this manners, as those that bravely fly from evil to good. It will not, however, be proper that the riches of any such person should become public property, in a polity in which the same and equal allotments ought to be perpetually preserved. But when any one perpetrates such things as are to be punished with a fine, he shall be fined as much as he possesses above his allotted portion, but

b the lot itself shall remain entire. The guardians of the laws, however, considering this affair accurately from written accounts, should always give a clear statement of it to the judges, that no one may be deprived of his allotments through want of money. If any one should appear to deserve a greater fine, and no one of his friends is willing to be bound for him, and procure his liberty, such an one shall be punished with lasting and apparent bonds, and with certain reproaches. But let no one

c offence ever by any means pass unpunished, nor any fugitive; but let him either be punished with death, or bonds, or stripes, or certain squalid feats, or with standing, or being exhibited in temples at the extremity of the region, or by fines, in the manner we have before mentioned. Let the guardians of the laws too be established the judges of death; and let the best among them be chosen for this purpose, who

d in the preceding year had acted in the capacity of magistrates. But the citations and accusations of these, and such like particulars, together with the manner in which they ought to take place, should be attended to by junior legislators. The manner, however, in which suffrages ought to be conducted, it is our business to determine. Let them, therefore, be given openly. But, prior to this, let the judge sit before the accuser and defendant, and as near to them as possible, in a grave and dignified manner. Let all the citizens too that are at leisure, diligently attend as

e the hearers of such causes. And, in the first place, let the accuser speak, and afterwards the defendant. After this, let the senior judge diligently and sufficiently examine what was said: and, after the elder judge, all the other judges in order ought to consider what is worthy of discussion in the speeches of the accuser and defendant. But he who does not think there is any thing worthy of discussion in either of the speeches, should refer the investigation of it to another. And, lastly, such things as shall appear to be well said, being committed to writing, and signed by all the

856a judges, shall be placed in the temple of Vesta. And again, assembling the next day into the same place, they shall in a similar manner examine and judge, and put their signatures to what shall appear to have been well said. When this has been thrice accomplished, and the proofs and witnesses have been sufficiently examined, each judge bearing in his hand a sacred pebble, and swearing before Vesta that he has judged to the utmost of his ability justly and truly, a judgment of this kind shall be thus brought to a conclusion.

b After crimes respecting the Gods, it is requisite to speak of those which pertain to the dissolution of a polity. He, therefore, who subjects government to the power of a man, enslaves the laws, makes the city subservient to factious societies, and, accomplishing all this by force, excites illegal seditions. It is proper to consider a character of this kind as the greatest of all enemies to the whole city. But he who, though he is not the author of any thing of this kind, yet possesses the greatest authority in the city, but takes no notice of these conspiracies, or if he does notice them, through timidity, suffers his injured country to be unrevenged; - a citizen of this kind ought to be considered as the second

c in wickedness. Every man who is of the smallest utility in a city should inform the judges of these particulars, and bring him to judgment who endeavours by stratagem to produce a violent and illegal mutation of the polity. But let the same judges give sentence in these cases as decided in sacrilege; and let the whole process be conducted in a similar manner. Let the suffrage too which vanquishes in multitude, be the sentence of death. And, in short, let not the disgrace and punishment of the father

d attend the children, unless the father, grandfather, and great-grandfather, of some one in succession, have deserved death. These, with their possessions, except as much as pertains to the lot, shall be sent to their ancient paternal city. But as to those citizens who shall happen to have more children than one, and these not less than ten years of age, ten out of their number must be chosen by lot, which the father, or paternal or maternal grandfather, shall approve; and after they are chosen, their

e names must be sent to Delphi. Then, with a better fortune, the possessions and habitation assigned by lot shall be restored to him whom the Delphic God approves.

CLIN. And very properly so.

GUEST. Let there be yet a third common law, respecting judges, and the mode of judgment, against those that are accused of treason. In a similar manner let there be one law respecting the abiding of children

857a in, and their egression from, their country; just as we instituted one respecting the betrayer of his country, the man who commits sacrilege, and he who by violence destroys the laws of the city. With respect to theft too, whether in great or small matters, let one law, and one punishment, be ordained for every kind of theft. For, when any one is condemned for thieving, if his own possessions, besides his allotted portion, are sufficient, he shall make a twofold restitution: and if he does not, he shall be fettered till he has either paid the appointed sum, or persuaded him to whom he is indebted to excuse him from paying it.

b But if any one is convicted of public theft, he shall then be freed from his bonds, when he has either persuaded the city, or made a twofold restitution.

CLIN. How is it that we say, O guest, there is no difference whether the theft is small or great, and whether it is from sacred or not sacred places, and such other dissimilitudes as subsist about the whole of thieving? For, since thefts are various, the legislator ought to attend to their varieties, and not inflict similar punishments on dissimilar offences.

GUEST. You most excellently repulse me, O Clinias, who am, as it
c were, hurrying along, and you likewise recall into my memory what I have formerly thought, that the particulars respecting the establishment of laws have never been by any means properly determined.

CLIN. But how, again, do we say this?

GUEST. We did not adopt a bad image when we said, that all those of the present day that submitted to laws were similar to those slaves who are cured by slaves. For it is well to know this, that if at any time one of those physicians who meddle with the medical art from experience alone, without reason, should meet with a free-born physician discoursing with a free-born patient, and very nearly philosophising, by
d investigating in a rational manner the beginning of his disease, and afterwards discoursing about all the nature of bodies, he would readily and vehemently laugh, and would address the free-born physician in language not at all different from what is generally used towards most physicians. For he would say to him, O stupid fellow, you do not cure the sick man, but you discipline him as if he wanted to become a physician, and not to be well.

e CLIN. And would he not speak properly by speaking in this manner?

GUEST. And may it not also be very properly objected against us, that whoever discusses laws in the manner we do at present, disciplines the citizens, but does not give them laws?

CLIN. Perhaps so.

GUEST. But at present a fortunate circumstance happens to us.

858a CLIN. What is that?

GUEST. That there is no necessity for us to establish laws, but that, entering voluntarily on the business of legislation, we have endeavoured to perceive in every polity what is best and most necessary, and after what manner it might take place. And now, as it seems, it is permitted us if we please to consider what is best, or, if we had rather, what is most necessary, respecting laws. We may choose, therefore, whichever is most agreeable to us.

CLIN. We propose, O guest, a ridiculous choice, and we manifestly become similar to those legislators who are compelled by a certain
b mighty necessity to give laws immediately, and are not permitted to defer this till tomorrow. But it is lawful for us to speak through divine assistance, just as it is permitted those who gather stones, or any other materials of a building, to collect abundantly, and at leisure, such things as are adapted to the future building. Like builders, therefore, who do

not raise structures from necessity, but at leisure, let us lay down some things, and join together others, so that it may be rightly said that some
c things pertaining to the laws are placed as foundations, and that other particulars are raised on them as foundations.

GUEST. For thus indeed, O Clinias, our synopsis of laws will be more natural. But, by the Gods, let us consider this respecting legislators.

CLIN. What?

GUEST. That there are writings and written discourses in cities respecting a variety of particulars, and that there are writings and discourses of the legislator.

CLIN. Undoubtedly.

d GUEST. Whether, therefore, shall we direct our attention to the writings of poets and others; writings which, whether in verse or in prose, are composed respecting the mode of conduct in life; but by no means apply ourselves to the writings of legislators? Or shall we direct our attention to these beyond all others?

CLIN. To these far beyond others.

GUEST. But will it not be necessary that the legislator should only consult writings respecting things beautiful, good, and just, and that he should teach what is the nature of these, and how they should be studied by those that intend to be happy?

CLIN. Undoubtedly.

e GUEST. But it is shameful that Homer, Tyrtæus, and other poets, should have written more beautifully respecting life and the studies of men than Lycurgus, Solon, and other legislators. Or, is it not proper that writings respecting laws should be by far the most beautiful and best of all writings in a city: but that other writings should be consonant to these; or, if they are discordant, that they should be treated with
859a ridicule? We ought, therefore, to conceive, that laws should be so written for cities that the legislator in composing them shall appear to have assumed the person of a father and mother, and the writings themselves ought to be full of benevolence and prudence, and not like those of a tyrant and despot, commanding, threatening, and written on walls. Let us consider, therefore, whether we should endeavour to speak
b in this manner respecting laws, whether we are able or not. Let us, however, attempt it with alacrity, and, proceeding in this way, patiently endure whatever difficulties we may have to encounter. And may our journey be prosperous! which it will be if Divinity pleases.

CLIN. You speak well. Let us, therefore, do as you say.

GUEST. In the first place, then, let us accurately consider, as we began to do, respecting sacrilege, every kind of theft, and all injuries. And let

us not be indignant if, while delivering laws in an intermediate manner,
c we establish some things, and deliberate about others. For we are
becoming to be legislators, but are not yet, though, perhaps, we soon
shall be. But if it is agreeable to you, as I have said, to consider
respecting the particulars I have mentioned, let us consider them.

CLIN. By all means.

d GUEST. However, respecting all beautiful and just things, we should
endeavour to consider this, in what manner we now accord, or dissent
from ourselves: for we acknowledge that we desire, though we may not
be able, to excel most others.

CLIN. What kind of disagreements among ourselves do you speak of?

GUEST. I will endeavour to inform you. With respect to justice
entirely, just men, things, and actions, we all of us, in a manner, agree
that all these are beautiful. So that, if any one should strenuously affirm
that just men, through the habit of justice, are all-beautiful, though they
should be deformed in body, there is scarcely any one who by thus
speaking would be considered as speaking in a disorderly manner. Is not
this true?

e CLIN. Perhaps so.

GUEST. But let us see whether all such things as partake of justice are
beautiful: for all our passions are nearly equal to our actions.

CLIN. How so?

GUEST. Whatever action is just, so far as it participates of the just, so
far also it nearly participates of the beautiful.

CLIN. Undoubtedly.

860a GUEST. If a passion, therefore, which participates of the just, is
acknowledged by us to be beautiful on this account, our discourse by
such an assertion would not be rendered dissonant.

CLIN. True.

GUEST. But if we should agree that a passion is just, but at the same
time base, the just and the beautiful would be dissonant, in consequence
of asserting that just things are most base.

CLIN. How is this?

GUEST. It is not at all difficult to understand. For the laws which a
little before have been established by us, appear to announce things
perfectly contrary to the present assertions.

CLIN. After what manner?

b GUEST. We established it as just, that he who committed sacrilege
should die; and likewise the enemy of well-established laws; and, as we
were about to establish many other laws of this kind, we desisted, on
perceiving that these were passions infinite both in multitude and

magnitude: and that they were the most just, but at the same time the most base, of all the passions. Do not things just and beautiful after this manner appear at one time to be the same, and at another to be most contrary?

CLIN. They do appear so.

c GUEST. By the multitude, therefore, things beautiful and just, which are so dissonant with each others, are denominated things separate.

CLIN. It appears so, O guest.

GUEST. Let us therefore again, O Clinias, see how we accord with ourselves respecting these things.

CLIN. What concord and what particulars are you speaking of?

GUEST. I think it has clearly been shown by me in the foregoing discourse.

CLIN. How

GUEST. However, if it has not been already shown by men, yet consider me as now speaking about it.

CLIN. After what manner?

d GUEST. That all vicious men are in all things involuntarily vicious; and that, if this is the case, this also must necessarily follow.

CLIN. What?

GUEST. That the unjust is a vicious man; and that the vicious man is involuntarily such. But the voluntary can by no means be done in an involuntary manner. He, therefore, who acts unjustly, will appear to act so in an involuntary manner to him who considers injustice as a thing involuntary. This also too is now acknowledged by me. For I have agreed, that all men act unjustly involuntarily, though some one, for the

e sake of contention or ambition, may say that unjust men are involuntarily unjust, but yet many act unjustly voluntarily. This, however, is not my assertion. After what manner, then, shall I accord with my own assertions, if any one, O Clinias and Megillus, should thus interrogate me? If these things are so, O guest, what would you advise us respecting the city of the Magnesians? Shall we give laws to them, or not? I say, undoubtedly. Do you distinguish injuries then by the voluntary and involuntary? And do you ordain greater punishments for voluntary offences and injuries, than for such as are involuntary? Or do

861a you punish all offences equally, as considering that no injuries are voluntarily committed?

CLIN. You speak properly, O guest. But what use shall we make of what has now been said?

GUEST. You interrogate well. In the first place, then, we shall use what has been said for the following purpose.

CLIN.   What purpose?

GUEST.   Let us call to mind that it was well said by us above, that there is great confusion and dissonance among us respecting things just. Resuming this, therefore, we again ask ourselves whether, since we have

b   neither solved the doubt about these things, nor defined what is their difference, though in all cities, by all legislators that have ever existed, voluntary and involuntary injuries are considered as forming two species of injuries, and laws are established conformable to this opinion, - whether, therefore, since this is the case, ought we to dismiss what we have now advanced, after we have asserted that it is, as it were, divinely said, without offering any arguments to show the rectitude of such assertions?   Certainly not.   But it is in a manner necessary, that before

c   we establish laws we should evince that these two things have a subsistence, and what is the difference between them; that, when any one establishes a punishment for either, every one may understand, and be able to judge, whether it is established in a becoming manner, or not.

CLIN.   You appear to us, O guest, to speak well.   For it is fit we

d   should do one of two things, *viz.* either not say that all unjust actions are involuntary, or first of all evince by defining that this is properly asserted.

GUEST.   One of these two things, therefore, I can by no means endure, I mean the denying that I think it is so, (for this would neither be legal nor holy).   But after what manner these are two, if they by no means differ with respect to voluntary and involuntary, but with respect to something else, we should endeavour to evince.

CLIN.   By all means, O guest: for we cannot otherwise understand the nature of these.

e   GUEST.   Let it be so.   Do not, therefore, many damages take place among citizens in their communications and associations with each other, in which the voluntary and involuntary abound?

CLIN.   Undoubtedly.

GUEST.   Whether, therefore, does any one, considering all damages as injuries, think, in consequence of this, that they are attended with twofold injuries, one kind being voluntary, and the other involuntary?

862a   For the involuntary damages of all men are neither in number, nor magnitude, less than the voluntary.   But consider whether I say any thing to the purpose, or not.   For, do I not say, O Clinias and Megillus, that when some one unwillingly hurts another, he acts unjustly, but involuntarily injures one who is unwilling to be injured?   And do I legally establish this as an involuntary injury?   Indeed I do not at all consider a damage of this kind as an injury, whether it is of a greater or

less magnitude. But we often say that he who assist another in an improper manner acts unjustly, if his assistance is not victorious. For,
b my friends, it is not proper, neither if any one imparts any thing, nor if, on the contrary, he takes any thing away, to call such an action simply just or unjust: but the legislator should consider whether he who benefits, or is the cause of detriment to another, is endued with worthy manners, and employed those manners justly. And he should look to these two things, *viz.* injustice, and detriment. He should likewise, as much as possible, legally indemnify the person that has sustained a damage, restore what has been lost, raise what has fallen, and repair the ravages of death and wounds. Lastly, he should always endeavour that
c the discords arising from damages may, by means of the laws, terminate in friendship.

CLIN. These things are well said.

GUEST. Unjust damages, therefore, and emoluments, if any one happens to derive emolument from injuring another, ought to be cured, if they are such as are capable of being cured, as diseases inherent in the soul. But it is requisite to say, that the cure of injustice verges to this.

CLIN. To what?

d GUEST. That the law may discipline every one who does an injury, whether it be great or small, and may entirely compel him, either that he shall never afterwards dare to do the like voluntarily, or by far less frequently, through the dread of the consequent punishment. In whatever manner any one may accomplish this, whether by works or words, pleasure or pain, honour or infamy, fines or gifts, so as that men may either love, or at least not hate, the nature of justice, but may hate injustice, - this is the business of the most beautiful laws. But those
e whom the legislator perceives to be incurable with respect to these particulars, he should punish in the extreme, as knowing that death is better than life to all such as these; and that when they are liberated from life they will doubly benefit others. For they will serve as a
863a warning to others not to act unjustly, and the city, by their death, will be freed from bad men. On this account *it will be necessary for the legislator to punish* INCURABLE *offences with death, but* BY NO MEANS *on any other account.*

CLIN. These things appear to have been spoken by you in a very sufficient manner; but we should gladly hear you relating still more clearly the difference between injustice and detriment.

GUEST. I shall endeavour, therefore, to do and say as you request me.
b For it is evident that you have both said to, and heard from, each other thus much respecting the soul, that anger naturally residing in it,

whether as a certain passion, or a certain part, and being contentious and invincible, subverts many things through irrational violence.

CLIN. Undoubtedly.

GUEST. Besides this, too, we do not call pleasure the same as anger, but we say that it possesses dominion from a contrary power, and that it persuades us, with a violent deception, to do whatever it pleases.

CLIN. And very much so.

c GUEST. He, likewise, who says that ignorance is the third cause of crimes will not be deceived. But he will be a better legislator who gives this a twofold division: considering one kind as simple, and the cause of light offences; but the other twofold, when any one is void of discipline, not only from being detained by ignorance, but by an opinion of wisdom, so as to think that he has a perfect knowledge about things of which he is entirely ignorant. Things of this kind, therefore, when followed by power and strength, are to be established as the causes of mighty and rustic crimes; but when followed by imbecility, as in this

d case they become the crimes of children and old men, they are to be considered as crimes, and laws are to be established for those that commit them; but, at the same time, they should be reckoned the mildest of all crimes, and as deserving the most abundant indulgence.

CLIN. You speak reasonably.

GUEST. We nearly, therefore, all of us speak of pleasure and anger, as things to which some of us are superior, and by which others of us are vanquished: and this is truly the case.

CLIN. Entirely so.

GUEST. But we never have at any time heard that one of us is superior to ignorance, and another vanquished by it.

e CLIN. Most true.

GUEST. But we say that all these allure us to their will, and often, at the same time, draw us to things contrary.

CLIN. Often, indeed.

GUEST. But I will now explain to you clearly what I call the just and the unjust, without any variety of distinction. For I entirely denominate

864a injustice to be the tyranny of anger, fear, pleasure, and pain, envy and desire in the soul, whether such a tyrant injures any one or not. But the opinion of that which is best, whether it is the conception of cities, or of certain private individuals, if, possessing dominion in the soul, it adorns the whole man, though it may in a certain respect lead him into error, - this I denominate justice, and call every thing which is performed from this opinion, just. And I further add, that the whole life of those who are obedient to a principle of this kind will be most excellent. But a damage of this nature is considered by the multitude as involuntary injustice. However, our business at present is not a contention about names. But since we have evinced that there are three species of crimes, let us, in the first place, still more diligently recall these into our memory. Of pain, therefore, which we denominate anger and fear, there is one species for us.

CLIN. Entirely so.

GUEST. But of pleasure and desires there is a second species, a third of hopes and a desire of true opinion about that which is best. This third species being divided into two parts, five species will be produced, for which laws are to be established, differing from each other in two genera.

CLIN. What are these?

GUEST. The one, every thing which is performed through violent and according actions; the other, which takes place with darkness and deception in a secret manner. And sometimes actions are attended with both these; which, if they are treated in a proper manner, ought to be restrained by the severest laws.

CLIN. It is just they should.

GUEST. But let us now return whence we have digressed, and finish the establishment of laws. The particulars then which we proposed to discuss were respecting sacrilege, betrayers of their country, and those who corrupted the laws, by dissolving the polity governed by those laws. Some one may perhaps commit one or other of these through insanity, disease, excessive old age, or youthfulness, which last does not in any respect differ from the other causes which we have enumerated. If it shall appear that any one thus affected has perpetrated one of these crimes, when the judges are chosen, and the crime is divulged, either by the guilty person or the inspector of the deed, he shall be judged to have acted contrary to law; and he shall be entirely fined a simple fine for the injury which he has committed. But let him be exempt from other punishments, unless, having committed manslaughter, his hands are not pure from murder: for, in this case, departing to another country, he shall be exiled for a year. If he returns before the time prescribed by the law, or shall be detected within the borders of the country, he shall be imprisoned for two years in the public gaol by the guardians of the laws, but liberated from his bonds after this period. However, as we began with murder, let us endeavour to establish laws consummately for every species of it. And, in the first place, let us speak concerning violent and involuntary homicide. If any one, therefore, in a contest, and public gymnastic exercises, shall involuntarily slay his friend, whether his death happens immediately, or some time after, from the wounds which he has received; or, if a man kills his friend in battle in a similar manner, or in warlike exercises instituted by the magistrates, whether with naked bodies, or with certain arms in imitation of warlike exercises, - in all

b these cases let him be purified according to the law about these particulars received from Delphi. But let all physicians who, in endeavouring to cure, have unwillingly been the death of any one, be considered as pure according to law. If any one with his own hand unwillingly slays another, whether with his own naked body, or with an instrument or dart, or from administering drink or food, or by the hurling of fire, or tempest, or the privation of breath, whether he does this with his own body, or through the means of other bodies, let him

c be entirely considered as one that slays with his own hand, and suffer the following punishments: if he kills a slave belonging to another person, thinking that it is his own, he shall indemnify the master of the dead slave, or be fined the double of the worth of such slave: but his worth shall be determined by the judges. The homicide, too, in this case shall use greater and more numerous purifications than those who

d commit murder in gymnastic exercises; and the proper interpreters of these things shall be those whom the Delphic God approves. But if any one kills his own slave, when he is purified according to law, let him be liberated from murder. If any one involuntarily slays a free-born person, let him be purified with the same purifications as he who cuts off a slave. And let him not despise one of the ancient sayings. For it is said, that a free-born person who is violently put to death, will soon

e after his death be angry with his murderer; and being filled with fear and terror through his violent dissolution, and perceiving the person that slew him living after his usual manner, he will terrify, and, being disturbed himself, disturb with all his might his murderer and his actions, memory at the same time contributing to oppose him. On this account, it is requisite that a homicide should be exiled from every part of his country for a whole year. But, if it is a stranger who is slain, the homicide shall be expelled from the country of the stranger for the same

866a length of time. And if any one is willingly obedient to this law, he who is the nearest relation of the deceased, and who was an inspector of all the particulars relative to the murder, shall pardon the homicide; with whom if he is entirely reconciled, it will be perfectly sufficient. But with respect to him who is not obedient to this law, and who, in the first place, being unpurified, dares to go to the temples of the Gods, and sacrifice; and, in the next place, is unwilling to be exiled for the above-mentioned time, such a one the nearest relative of the deceased shall

b accuse to the judges, and he shall suffer double the punishments which are due to the crime. If the nearest relative of the deceased does not call him to an account, the defilement, as it were, revolving on such a one, or, in other words, the slain person directing his anger towards him, he shall be accused by any one that pleases, and shall be compelled by law to leave his country for five years. But if a stranger involuntarily slays

c a stranger in the city, whoever is willing shall accuse him by the same laws. If an inhabitant slays a stranger, he shall be exiled for one year. And, universally, if a stranger slays a stranger, who is an inhabitant and a citizen, besides his purification he shall be banished for the whole of his life from the country in which laws of this kind have dominion. And if he returns illegally, the guardians of the laws shall punish him with death; and his property, if he has any, shall be given to the nearest relation of the deceased. However, if any one involuntarily returns

d before the limited time, being driven on the coast by a storm at sea, in this case, let him fix a tent on the shore, so that his feet may touch the water, and watch for a fit opportunity of sailing. But, if he should be forcibly brought into the city by any one, let him be liberated by the first magistrate he may meet with, and sent back with safety into exile. Again, if any one with his own hand shall slay a free-born person, being incited by anger to the deed, a thing of this kind ought, in the first place, to receive a two-fold distinction. For he commits murder through

e anger, who suddenly and unintentionally kills a man by blows, or any other such like means, so that immediately after the impulse penitence follows the deed. And he likewise murders another in anger, who having been previously defamed by ignominious words or deeds, and, endeavouring to be avenged, afterwards voluntarily slays the person by whom he has been injured, and is not penitent for the deed. Murder, therefore, as it appears, must receive a twofold distribution; and both of

867a them nearly are produced by anger. But they may most justly be said to subsist between the voluntary and the involuntary. In reality, indeed, they are but images of the voluntary and involuntary. For, he who retains his anger, and does not immediately and suddenly, but with stratagem, at some distance of time, avenge himself, is similar to one who murders voluntarily. But he who does not conceal his anger, but immediately follows its impulse without premeditation, is similar to one who murders involuntarily. However, he is not altogether involuntary,

b but an image of one that acts involuntarily. On this account, it is difficult to determine respecting murders committed through anger, whether they should be established by law as voluntary or involuntary actions. The best and the truest method, therefore, that can be adopted is, to consider both these kinds of murder as images, and to divide them apart from each other, so as to class the one under premeditated, and the other under unpremeditated actions. Severer punishments, therefore, are to be ordained for those that commit murder through anger, with premeditation; but milder punishments for those that murder without deliberation, and suddenly. For, that which is similar to a greater evil should receive a greater punishment, but that which is similar to a lesser

c evil, a lesser punishment. Let it, therefore, be thus established by our laws.

CLIN. By all means.

GUEST. But again returning to the subject we say, that if any one with his own hand slays a free-born person, but was incited to the deed by a certain anger, without premeditation, in other respects let him suffer the same punishment as it is proper he should suffer who kills a man without anger; but let him, from necessity, be exiled for two years, as

d a punishment for his anger. But he who commits murder through anger, but with deliberation, shall be punished in other respects in the same manner as the former character; but he shall be banished for three years instead of two, that his anger, which is greater, may be punished for a longer time. And let this be the universal establishment respecting these particulars. For it is difficult to give laws about such things with accuracy. For, sometimes, murder of this kind, which is considered by the law as of a more atrocious, will prove to be of a milder, nature; and sometimes that which is of a milder, will be considered as of a more atrocious, nature; according as the murder is committed in a more savage

e or a more gentle manner. But, for the most part, they will happen agreeably to the above-mentioned mode. Of all these particulars, therefore, the guardians of the laws should be inspectors. When the time of the banishment of these offenders is expired, the guardians of the laws must send twelve judges to the boundaries of the region, for the purpose of considering, in a still clearer manner, the actions of the exiles during this time; and that they may determine in a proper manner respecting their modesty and reception. But the exiles shall acquiesce in

868a the judgment of these magistrates. And if again, on returning from banishment, any one of these, being impelled by anger, shall commit the same offence, he shall be perpetually banished: and if he returns from his exile, he shall be punished in the same manner as a stranger for returning from exile. Let him who kills his slave purify himself. But if he kills the slave of another person in anger, let him pay to the master of the slave double the worth of his loss. If any homicide is not obedient to the laws respecting murder, but, while he is unpurified,

b defiles by his presence the forum, gymnasia, and other sacred places, -

whoever is willing may bring before a court of judgment both the homicide, and the relation of the deceased who has neglected to avenge the dead, and compel him to pay a double fine, and suffer in other respects a double punishment. And let the offending party consider the fine as legal. If a slave kills his master in anger, the kindred of the deceased shall be allowed to slay the homicide in whatever manner they please, and shall be pure from murder, so long as they do not by any means preserve the life of the slave. But if a slave does not kill his own master, but some other free-born person, in anger, he shall be given up by his master to the kindred of the deceased, who shall, from necessity, put him to death in whatever manner they please. If a father or mother shall in anger slay a son or daughter, by blows, or any other violent manner (a thing which will happen, though but rarely), let them be purified after the same manner as other homicides, and be exiled for three years. And after they return from exile, the husband shall be divorced from the wife, and the wife from the husband: and they shall never afterwards beget children together, nor shall either of these dwell together with him whose son or brother either of them slew, nor communicate with him in sacred rites. But he who is impious with respect to these things, and does not obey these laws, shall be obnoxious to the charge of impiety by any one that is willing. If a man slays his wife, or a wife her husband, in anger, they shall be purified in a similar manner with other homicides, and shall be exiled for three years. But, on returning from exile, let not either of them be permitted to join with their children in sacred rites, nor ever eat at the same table with them. And, if either the father or the child is disobedient to this law, let them be obnoxious to the charge of impiety by any one that is willing. If a brother slays either a brother or a sister, or sister a brother or a sister, in anger, let them be purified and exiled in the same manner as parents that slay their children; and, on their return from exile, let them not eat at the same table, or join in sacred rites, with those whom they have deprived of brothers, or sisters, or sons. And if any one is disobedient to this law, he shall with justice be obnoxious to the charge of impiety. If any one, through incontinent anger, is so enraged with his parents as to dare to slay one of them in his insane fury, - if the dying parent, before he expires, shall voluntarily absolve his murderer from the deed, then, being purified in the same manner as those who commit murder voluntarily, and performing such other things as they perform, let him be considered as pure. But if the dying parent does not absolve him, let him be obnoxious to many laws. For he must be subject to the extreme punishments of whipping, and, in a similar manner, of impiety and sacrilege, because he has expelled the soul of his begetter. So that, if it were possible that a man could die frequently, it would be most just that a parricide or matricide should suffer many deaths. For, how is it possible that he who is not permitted by any law to destroy his parents, who led forth his nature into light, even though he should find that he

c was going to be slain by them, but is enjoined by the legislator to endure all things rather than perpetrate a deed of this kind, - how is it possible, I say, that such a one can in any other way be properly punished? Let death, therefore, be ordained as the punishment of him who in anger slays either his father or mother. But if a brother slays a brother in his own defence, being attacked by him, through sedition taking place between them, or any other such means, let him be pure in

d the same manner as one who slays an enemy. And if a citizen slays a citizen, or a stranger a stranger, in his own defence, let him be similarly pure; as, likewise, if, in defending himself, a citizen slays a stranger, or a stranger a citizen, or a slave a slave. But if a slave, in his own defence, slays a free-born person, let him be obnoxious to the same laws as him who slays his father. Let the same thing also be understood respecting the absolution from murder in all these cases as was said concerning the

e absolution from parricide. If any dying person, therefore, among these, previous to his death, willingly absolves his murderer from voluntary murder, purifications shall be administered to the homicide, and he shall be exiled for a year. And thus we appear to have spoken sufficiently respecting murders committed by violence, involuntarily, and in anger. Let us now speak concerning such as are voluntary, and perpetrated with every kind of injustice, and from stratagems, through the tyranny of pleasures, desires, and envy.

CLIN. You speak properly.

GUEST. Again, therefore, in the first place, let us speak to the utmost

870a of our power concerning the causes of these. the greatest cause, then, is desire, which has dominion in a soul rendered savage by venereal incentives. It is this which abundantly, and in the most vehement manner, inflames the minds of the multitude, and which, through a depraved nature and want of discipline, generates ten thousand loves of infinite riches. But we say that the want of discipline is the cause why both among the Greeks and Barbarians riches are praised in a vicious manner. For they place these in the first, though they belong to the

b third, rank of things good; and, through this opinion, destroy both themselves and posterity. For, to speak the truth to all cities respecting riches, is the most beautiful and the best of all things. But the truth is, that riches subsist for the sake of the body, and the body subsists for the sake of the soul. Since, therefore, those things are good for the sake of which riches naturally subsist, they will rank in the third place after the virtue of the body and soul. This reason, therefore, will inform us as a teacher, that he who desires to be happy ought not to seek after wealth indiscriminately, but in a just and temperate manner. For thus murders would not be committed in cities, which require to be purified by murders. But now, as I said in the beginning of this discussion, this is one and the greatest cause of the greatest punishments of voluntary murder. The second is the habit of an ambitious soul, which generates envy; and this is bitter to those that dwell together, and especially to him by whom it is possessed, and afterwards to the best persons in the city. But cowardly and unjust fears rank in the third place, which produce many murders, when such things have been transacted by any one, or are at present transacted, as no one wishes to be conscious have taken place, or do take place. On this account they take away by death those that might give information of such transactions, when they cannot prevent them from making a discovery by any other means. And thus much for a preface to all these particulars. To which may be added, what many who are studious respecting the mysteries have heard about things of this kind, of the truth of which they are vehemently persuaded, - I mean, that such actions are punished in Hades, and that the perpetrators of them, again returning hither, necessarily suffer punishment according to nature, and end their days by suffering the very same kind of death which they caused another to suffer. For him, therefore, who from this preface is persuaded, and is in every respect afraid of such a punishment, there is no occasion to establish a law respecting voluntary murder: but for him who will not be persuaded by it let the following law be ordained. He who designedly and unjustly slays with his own hand his fellow-citizen, shall, in the first place, be expelled from temples, from the forum, from ports, and from every general assembly, that he may not defile any of these by his presence; and this, whether any one forbids him from these places or not. For the law forbids him, and forbids him as a perpetual injunction to the whole city. But the male or female relative, as far as to a cousin, of the deceased, who does not prosecute such a one in a proper manner, nor expel him from these places, shall first of all receive in himself the defilement, together with the hatred of the Gods, agreeably to the imprecation of the law. And, in the second place, he shall be obnoxious to any one who is willing to revenge the dead. He who is willing to do this, having performed every thing respecting washings, and such other particulars as Divinity has caused to be legal in cases of this kind, and uttered such things as must be previously announced, let him proceed, and compel the homicide to suffer the punishment of his deed according to law. But that these things ought to take place through certain prayers and sacrifices to certain Gods, who attend to such particulars, and are careful that murder may not be perpetrated in cities, will easily be apparent to the legislator. However, who these Gods are, and in what manner these judgments may be introduced, so as to take place with the utmost rectitude with respect to a divine nature, the guardians of the laws, together with the interpreters and diviners, must promulgate. But let the judges of these particulars be those to whom we have given the power of punishing sacrilege. Let him too who is condemned, be punished with death; and let him not be buried in the country of the murdered person, on account of his having acted in an impudent, as well as an impious manner. If he makes his escape, being unwilling to stand his trial, let him be perpetually exiled. And if he is ever detected in any part of the country in which he has committed the murder, he who first meets with him, whether he was the murderer of one of his kindred, or fellow-citizens, shall slay him with impunity; or shall deliver him bound to those magistrates that preside as judges over these affairs, that he may by them be put to death. But if any one should stand forth in his defence, he shall be bound for his appearance, and shall procure three bondsmen, whom the judges shall think sufficient, for the purpose. If he is either unwilling or incapable of doing this, he shall be bound by the magistrates, and properly secured, that he may be punished for his interference. If any one slays another, not with his own hand, but by consultation and stratagem, and yet, though he is the cause of the murder, and not purified in his soul, shall reside in the city where the deed was committed, such a one, being condemned, shall be similarly punished, except that he shall not be permitted to procure bondsmen, but shall be allowed his proper sepulchre. Let other things respecting him take place in the same manner as above. Let the same particulars too be established respecting strangers towards strangers, citizens and strangers towards each other, and slaves towards slaves, in murder committed with the homicide's own hand; and in that which is committed by consultation and stratagem, excepting that these latter homicides shall be obliged to give bondsmen, in the same manner as those that murder with their own hands. If a slave voluntarily murders a free-born person, whether with his own hand, or through consultation, and is condemned, the public executioner shall lead him to the tomb of the murdered person, or to a place where he may see the tomb. Here he shall be whipt as long as the person that apprehended him pleases,

and if he survives the whipping, he shall be put to death. But if any one
kills a slave who has not in any respect acted unjustly, through fear lest
he should disclose his base and vicious actions, or through some similar
cause, he shall be punished in the same manner as if he had slain a
citizen. However, if cases should happen for which it is very difficult
to establish laws, at the same time that it is impossible not to deliver
laws respecting them, such as the voluntary, and, in every respect,
unjust, murdering of kindred, whether the homicide accomplishes this
with his own hand, or by consultation and stratagem, (murders which
frequently take place in cities badly inhabited and governed, and
sometimes in a region where no one would expect to find them) - in
such cases as these, it will be proper that what was lately mentioned by
us should be repeated. For, perhaps, some one, on hearing these things,
may be induced more willingly to abstain from the most impious of all
murders. For a fable, or a discourse, or by whatever other name it may
be proper to call it, is clearly delivered by ancient priests, that Justice,
the avenger and inspector of the murdering of kindred, uses the law of
which we have just now spoken. Hence, they say, she has ordained that
he who commits any such action shall necessarily suffer the same things
as he has committed. So that, if any one has ever murdered his father,
he shall himself, in certain periods of time, be violently put to death by
his children. And, if any one has murdered his mother, he shall, in
succeeding times, partake from necessity of a feminine nature, and be
deprived of life by his offspring. For they add that, when common
blood is defiled, there is not any other purification, nor can the stain be
washed away by other means, than by the guilty soul suffering murder
for murder, and in a similar manner, and laying asleep the anger of all
the kindred of the murdered person. It is proper, therefore, that men
should be restrained from crimes of this kind, through the fear of those
punishments which are inflicted by the Gods. But if such a miserable
calamity should happen to any, as that they should designedly and
voluntarily dare to deprive father or mother, brothers or children, of
life, let the following law respecting things of this kind be established by
the mortal legislator. By a public declaration they shall be expelled from
all sacred places, and shall be obliged to give bondsmen, in the same
manner as was mentioned above. And when any one is condemned for
murder of this kind, he shall be put to death both by the servants of the
judges and the magistrates, and shall be driven naked out of the city to
an appointed place, where three roads meet. Then all the magistrates,
for the sake of the whole city, carrying each of them a stone, shall hurl
it at the head of the dead body, and thus expiate the whole city. After

this, carrying the dead body to the boundaries of the region, and hurling
c   it thence, they shall leave it unburied, according to law. - But what
ought he to suffer who slays his nearest, and, as it is said, most friendly,
relative? I mean the man who kills himself, and by violence deprives
himself of the allotment of fate; being neither compelled to do this by
the judgment of the city, nor by a grievous and inevitable chance of
fortune, nor by any extreme shame or poverty; but, through indolence
d   and effeminate timidity, unjustly punishes himself. What purifications,
and what mode of interment, ought to be legally established respecting
such a one, Divinity knows; but the nearest relatives of the deceased
must inquire what these are from the interpreters of the Gods, and the
laws about these. As to their sepulture, let them be buried in solitary
places, where no one else is buried, and in those parts of the region
which are the boundaries of the twelve divisions, and which are desolate
e   and without a name. Let them, likewise, be buried in an ignoble
manner, neither making their tombs conspicuous by the erection of
pillars, or the inscription of their names. If a beast of burthen, or any
other animal, shall kill a man, unless this happens in some public
contest, the relations of the person so killed shall avenge his death: and
the præfects of the land shall do whatever the relation of relations of the
deceased command. But the punishment shall consist in driving the
animal beyond the boundaries of the region, and there slaying him. If
any inanimate thing deprives a man of life, except thunder, or any other
such-like dart sent from Divinity, by either falling on the man, or the
874a man falling on it, he who is nearest of kin to the deceased shall appoint
his neighbour to be a judge in this case, and shall make an expiation
both for himself and the whole of his kindred. But the thing
condemned shall be exterminated the region, in the same manner as
animals that are homicides. If any one is found dead, and it is not
manifest by whom he was slain, but cannot be discovered after the most
diligent search, proclamations must be employed as in other murders,
b   and the crier must proclaim in the forum, that whoever has slain this or
that person, as being guilty of murder, must not approach any sacred
places, nor reside in any part of the region where the deed was
committed: for, if he is detected within the boundaries of the said
region, he shall be put to death, and, being hurled beyond them, left
unburied. Let this one law, therefore, be established as the principal one
respecting murder. And thus much may suffice about things of this
kind. Let the following, then, be the particular cases in which he who
commits murder will be pure. If any one detects a thief entering his
house by night, for the purpose of robbing it, and slays him, let such an

one be pure. In like manner, let him be pure who slays a highwayman in his own defence. And if any one uses force respecting venereal concerns towards a free-born woman or boy, let him be put to death with impunity, either by the injured party, or by the father, brothers, or sons of the person so injured. Likewise, if a man meets with any one offering violence to his wife, and kills him, let him be pure, according to law. And if any one, in assisting his father, or mother, or children, or brothers, or wife, in doing that which is by no means unholy, should slay some one, let him be in every respect pure. And thus far we have given laws concerning that education and discipline of the living soul, which if it is fortunately endued with, it may be suffered to live, but of which if it is unfortunately deprived, it must be put to death: and we have likewise ordained such punishments as murders deserve. We have spoken too respecting the nutrition and discipline of bodies.

It now remains that we should define, to the utmost of our power, what violent, voluntary, and involuntary actions are, and how many they are in number, and what are the punishments accommodated to each. For these, as it appears, will be properly discussed after those. But even the vilest legislator will place the consideration of wounds, and mutilations from wounds, after murder. Wounds, therefore, are to be divided in the same manner as murders. For some of them are inflicted involuntarily; others through anger; some through fear; and some voluntarily and from design. Respecting all these, the following
a observations must be premised. It is necessary that laws should be established for men, and that they should live according to law, or they would in no respect differ from the most savage animals. But this is owing to the nature of men, which is never found to be sufficient of itself to know what is advantageous to a human polity; and, when it does know this, is never always able to do and wish that which is best. For it is, in the first place, difficult to know that not private but public advantage must necessarily be attended to by the political and true art; (for that which is common binds, but that which is private dilacerates, cities,) and that it is more advantageous, both to the public and individuals, that common concerns should be well established, than such as are private. In the second place, though some one should know sufficiently from art, that these things naturally subsist in this manner, yet, after this, if he should govern the city with an unrestrained authority, he would be incapable of persevering in this dogma, and of living in the opinion that common advantage should be nourished in a city, and private follow the general good. But the mortal nature will always impel him to prerogative and private advantage: for this nature

avoids pain, and pursues pleasure, in an irrational manner; prefers both
c these to that which is more just and excellent; and, producing darkness
in itself, fills at length both itself and the whole city with evils of every
kind. Indeed, if any man, through a divine destiny, should be naturally
sufficient to comprehend what is the public good, he would require no
laws for the government of himself; for neither any law, nor any order,
is better than science; nor is it lawful that intellect should be subservient
d and a slave to any thing, but that it should be the ruler of all things, if
it is thus true, and really free by nature. But now, with respect to such
an intellect as this, it cannot be said, that it is not by any means any
where to be found, but it should be said that it is but rarely seen. that
which ranks, therefore, in the second place, must be chosen, *viz.* order
and law; of which many things are indeed perceived, but it is impossible
to view all that pertains to them. And thus much we have said for the
sake of these things. - Now, let us ordain what he who wounds or
injures another, ought to suffer or pay. For it is easy for every one to
comprehend properly, whether any one is wounded or not, who it is
e that is wounded, in what part, and after what manner. For there are an
innumerable multitude of particulars of this kind, and which very much
differ from each other. It is, therefore, alike impossible, to refer all, or
no one of these, to courts of justice. For this one thing, in all these,
must necessarily be referred to the decision of justice. I mean, whether
each of these was done, or not. That nothing, indeed, should be
determined by courts of justice respecting the fine for injuries of this
876a kind, but that all things, both small and great, should be determined by
law, is nearly impossible.

CLIN. What then shall we say after this?

GUEST. That some things should be referred to courts of justice, but
that others should be determined by the legislator himself.

CLIN. What are the particulars then which the legislator must decide,
and what those which must be decided by courts of justice?

GUEST. With the greatest propriety, after these things, the following
assertions may be made: That, in a city in which the courts of justice
b are depraved and dumb, the opinions of the judges concealed, and
sentence privately passed; and in which something still more dire than
this takes place, when each of the judges decides, not in silence, but in
the midst of tumult, as in a theatre, the rhetoricians praising and
blaming with loud exclamations; - then a heavy calamity befalls the
whole city. If, therefore, from a certain necessity, any one should be
compelled to give laws to such courts of justice, it would not be a
fortunate circumstance; but, at the same time, he who is forced to give

them, should commit only the smallest fines to the judges, but should clearly ordain the greatest part of them himself. But, in a city, in which courts of justice are established with as great propriety as possible, and the judges are well educated, and examined with the greatest accuracy; in such a city, it will be proper and becoming to refer many things to the decision of such judges, respecting the punishment of such as are condemned. No one, therefore, should be indignant with us, that we do not now promulgate to these, such things as are the greatest and most numerous, which judges that are educated in the vilest manner may be able to perceive; and who likewise may be capable of punishing every offence in a proper manner. But, as we are of opinion that those for whom we promulgate laws, will not be in the smallest degree inelegant judges of these things, we shall commit most things to their decision. However, as we have often said, in the former part of this discussion, that a description and formulæ of punishments ought to be given as examples to judges, which are never to be transgressed, and this we ourselves have accomplished, - this was then both rightly asserted and performed, and must be observed at present, as we are again returning to the laws. Let the written law, therefore, be established respecting wounds. If any one, thinking in conjunction with his will to slay his friend, (if his friend is one of those whom the law forbids him to injure) wounds, but is not able to kill him, such an one, as neither deserving pity nor regard, we shall compel to suffer the punishment of murder, no otherwise than if he had actually slain his friend: except we should reverence his fortune, if it should not be entirely bad, and also the dæmon who, commiserating both him and the wounded person, may become an averter of evil to both, and may cause the wound of the one not to be incurable, and the fortune and calamity of the other to be devoted to the Furies. Giving thanks, therefore, to this dæmon, and not opposing him, we shall take away the punishment of death from him that inflicted the wound, but order him to be exiled for life in a neighbouring city, and there enjoy the fruits of all his possessions. If the wounded person, however, has suffered any loss, he shall make him a proper restitution, and such an one as the court of justice shall determine. But those judgers that decide in cases of murder shall decide in this case. If a child designedly wounds his parent, or a slave his master, the punishment shall be death. And if a brother designedly wounds a brother or sister, or a sister a sister or brother, the punishment shall in like manner be death. But if a woman wounds her husband with an intention of slaying him, or a husband his wife with the same design, let each be perpetually banished. And, with respect to their property, if their sons or daughters are at that time but children, let persons be appointed to manage their affairs, and take care of the orphan children. But if their sons or daughters are adults, let them not be compelled to provide for their exiled parent, but let them be permitted to take possession of his or her property. If any one who has

d no children happens to fall into calamities of this kind, let his kindred, as far as to cousins, both of the male and female side, assemble, and, consulting together with the guardians of the laws and priests, in the house of the exiled person, let one family out of the five thousand and forty houses of the city be appointed as his heir: at the same time considering that no house out of this number is so much the property of its inhabitant, and his kindred, as of the city at large. it is requisite,

e indeed, that the city should possess its own houses, to the utmost of its power, in the most holy and prosperous manner. When any house, therefore, is at the same time both unfortunate and impious, in consequence of its possessor leaving no children behind him, and of having been condemned for voluntary murder, or any other crime towards the Gods, or his fellow citizens, the punishment of which according to law is evidently death, or perpetual exile; - when this is the case, in the first place, let the house be purified and expiated according

878a to law; and, in the next place, let the kindred, as we just now said, assembling together with the guardians of the laws, consider what family in the city is most renowned for virtue, and at the same time fortunate, and consisting of a numerous progeny. Let one of the children belonging to this family be adopted by the father of the deceased, and by his grandfather and great grandfather, beseeching, at the same time, Divinity that he may be a parent, master, and minister of holy and

b sacred rites, with better fortune than his predecessor. Having prayed after this manner, let him be appointed heir according to law. But let the guilty person be suffered to lie without a name, without children, and without any lot, in consequence of being oppressed by such calamities as these. Boundary, however, as it appears, is not in all things mingled with boundary. But where there is a common confine, this, being previously hurled in the middle of both boundaries, subsists between both. And we have said that crimes committed through anger are of this kind, subsisting between voluntary and involuntary crimes. If then any one is condemned for wounding another through anger, if

c the wound shall prove to be curable, he shall pay the double of the loss sustained; but if incurable, he shall make a four-fold restitution. If the wound shall prove to be curable, but at the same time becomes the cause of great shame and disgrace to the wounded person, he shall likewise pay a fourfold fine. But if any one, in wounding another, not only injures the wounded person, but the city, by rendering him incapable of assisting his country against the enemy, he shall be similarly fined, and, besides this, make restitution to the city for its loss. Besides, too, his own military duties, he shall perform those of the wounded person; or, in case of non-compliance, he shall be accused according to law, by any one that is willing, for neglect of military duty. He shall likewise make a double, triple, or quadruple restitution, according to the decision of the judges. If one near relation in a similar manner wounds another, the parents and kindred, as far as to the male and female cousins assembling together, shall decide the case among themselves, and shall deliver the offender to his parents to be punished according to nature. But if the punishment should be doubtful, it shall be determined by the kindred on the male side. And if they are incapable of deciding the case, they shall betake themselves at last to the guardians of the laws. When children inflict any such wounds on their parents, the judges shall be those that have passed beyond their sixtieth year, and whose children are truly their own, and not such as are adopted. He that in this case is condemned shall be put to death, or suffer some greater punishment, or one that is not much less; but no one of his kindred shall be permitted to judge him, though he should be of the age prescribed by law. But if a slave wounds any free-born person in anger, his master shall deliver him to the wounded person, that he may punish him in whatever manner he pleases: but if his master does not deliver him, he himself shall make a compensation for the injury. If any one has a suspicion that the slave and wounded person acted from mutual compact, he shall acquaint the judges with his suspicion; and if he does not prove that his suspicion was true, he shall be fined triple of the damage sustained; but if he does prove it, let him be obnoxious to slavery, who has acted thus artfully with a slave. But let him who involuntarily wounds another, pay a simple fine. For no legislator is sufficient to govern fortune. Let the judges also be such as were appointed for children when guilty of wounding their parents, and let these determine the proper punishment. All the above-mentioned passions, indeed, are violent; and every kind of striking likewise is violent. It is necessary, therefore, that every man and every woman should always think about things of this kind, that an elderly person is to be honoured in no small degree beyond a younger person; that they are so by the Gods; and must be so by men who design to be saved and be happy. To see, therefore, an elderly struck by a young man in a city, is shameful, and odious to Divinity. But it seems fit that every young man, when struck by an old man, should patiently

endure it, through a reverence of his age. Let it, therefore, be thus:
Every one shall reverence both in word and deed a person older than
himself; and in such a manner, that whoever is more than twenty years
d   of age, whether male or female, may be reverenced as a father or
mother; and so that every young person may abstain from offering
violence to any who are capable of begetting or bringing forth children,
through regard to the Gods that preside over births. In a similar
manner, let no violence be offered to a stranger, whether he has resided
for some time in the city, or has but recently taken up his abode in it.
For, whether he excites contention, or resists an injury, let no one dare
to chastize him with blows. But if a stranger should dare wantonly to
strike a citizen, let him who thinks he ought to be punished bring him
before the præfects of the city, but not strike him himself, that, by thus
refraining from a stranger, he may be far from daring to strike a fellow-
e   citizen. The præfects of the city, reverencing the hospitable God, shall
examine the affair; and if it shall appear that the stranger has acted
unjustly, the citizen shall give him as many lashes with a whip, as the
blows which he received from him, that he may prevent him from
daring to do the like in future. But if it shall appear that the stranger
has not acted unjustly, after threatening and disgracing the person that
brought him before the præfects of the city, let both be dismissed. If
880a one person strikes another of the same age with himself, or who is a
little older, but without children, or if an old man strikes an old man,
or one youth another, the injured parties may defend themselves
according to nature, without weapons, with their naked hands. But if
any one who is more than forty years of age shall dare to strike another,
either while the person he strikes is attacking another, or defending
himself, let him be called rustic, illiberal, and servile; and he may be
considered as sufficiently punished by this reproach. And if any one is
obedient to these admonitions, he will be of a tractable disposition: but
b   let him who cannot be persuaded by them, and who despises this
exordium, receive with alacrity the following law: If any one strikes
another who is older than himself by twenty years or more, - in the first
place, let him who happens to be present at the time, if he is neither of
an equal age, nor younger, prevent any further violence; or, if he does
not prevent it, let him be considered as unworthy according to law. But
if he is of the same age with, or younger than, the person struck, let him
defend him as if he was his brother or father, or as if he was his
superior. And, besides this, let him be obnoxious to judicial
punishment, who, as we have said, dares to strike a person older than
himself: and if he is condemned, let him be punished with bonds, for

c not less than a year; or for a longer time, if it shall seem proper to the judges by whom he is condemned. If a stranger or an inhabitant shall strike one who is twenty years older than himself, let the same law have the same power, with respect to those that are present giving him assistance. And let him who in this case shall be condemned, if he is a stranger, and not an inhabitant of the city, be punished with bonds for the space of two years. But if he is an inhabitant of the city, and is not obedient to the laws, let him be punished with bonds for three years, if

d the court of justice does not determine that he shall be punished for a longer time. Let whoever happens to be present on this occasion, and does not give assistance, according to law, be fined. And if he possesses one of the first and largest estates, let him be fined a mina; but if his estate is of the second rank, fifty drachms; if of the third, thirty; and if of the fourth, twenty. Let the court of justice too respecting all such particulars consist of the generals of the army, the præfects of the military orders, the governors of tribes, and the masters of the horse. But with respect to laws, as it appears, some are instituted for the sake of worthy men, that they may be instructed by them, how they may associate with each other in a benevolent manner; but others for the sake of those who, avoiding discipline, and being of an intractable nature, are disposed to rush into every kind of vice. It is for these that what follows is asserted, and that the legislator necessarily establishes laws; at the same time wishing, that there may never be any occasion to use them. Whoever, therefore, dares to strike his father or mother, or the progenitors of these, neither dreading the anger of the Gods above, nor the punishments which are said to be inflicted under the earth, but,

881a as one who thinks he knows that of which he is perfectly ignorant, despises assertions which are both ancient and assented to by all men, and in consequence of this acts unlawfully, - such a one requires the most extreme remedy. Death, therefore, is not the last remedy, but the punishments which are inflicted in Hades are rather ultimate remedies; and which, though they are most truly said to exist, yet are incapable of averting souls of this kind from evil. For, if they were capable, there never would be found any who would impiously dare to strike their parents. It is requisite, therefore, that the punishments for crimes of this kind in the present life, should be as much as possible in no respect inferior to those which are inflicted in Hades. Let the following law, therefore, be established: If any one who is not insane shall dare to strike his father or mother, or their fathers or mothers, - in the first place, let any one who is present (as was mentioned before) give assistance. And if it is an inhabitant that gives assistance, let him be called to take the principal seat in the games; but if he does not give assistance, let him be perpetually banished from the region. If he is not an inhabitant, but gives assistance, let him be praised; but if he does not give assistance, let him be blamed. if a slave gives assistance, let him be made free; but if he does not assist, let him receive a hundred lashes with a whip. And if this happens in the forum, let the punishment be inflicted by the præfects of the market; but if in any other part of the city, by the ædiles. In like manner, if it should happen beyond the city, let him be punished by the governors of the husbandmen. If any citizen is present when a parent is struck by his child, whether such citizen is a boy, a man, or a woman, let him give assistance, at the same time exclaiming that such conduct is impious. But if he does not give assistance, let him be obnoxious to Jupiter Omognius† and Patroius.‡ Lastly, if any one is condemned for striking his parents, let him, in the first place, be perpetually banished from the city to some other region; and, in the next place, let him be expelled from all sacred places and ceremonies; from which if he will not abstain, let him be punished with blows by the magistrates that take care of rural affairs, and entirely in such a manner as they please. And if he returns from exile, let him be punished with death. If any free-born person shall eat or drink with such a one, or have any transactions with him, or voluntarily touch him, if he should happen to meet with him, - such a one shall neither be suffered to enter into any temple, or forum, nor in short into the city, till he is purified; for he should think that he has had communication with an execrable fortune. But if, being unpersuaded by the law, he illegally defiles sacred places, and the city, - whatever magistrate, perceiving this, does not punish such an one, let him be accused as guilty of one of the greatest crimes. If a slave strikes a free-born person, whether he is a stranger or a citizen, let any one who is present give assistance, or be punished with the above-mentioned fine, according to the value of his estate. Those who are present, therefore, shall succour the injured person, and deliver to him the offender bound. Then the injured person, receiving him in this condition, shall give him as many lashes with a whip as he pleases; observing, at the same time, not to injure his master, to whom he shall afterwards deliver him, to be possessed according to law. But let the law be this: if a slave strikes a free-born person, without being ordered to do so by the magistrates, his

---

† *Viz.* who presides over nations and families.

‡ Paternal.

master, on receiving him bound from the person he has injured, shall
c   not free him from his bonds till the slave has persuaded the injured
person that he deserves to be released from them. Let the same laws be
adopted for women, in their conduct towards each other, with respect
to all these particulars; and for women towards men, and men towards
women.

INTRODUCTION

TO

THE TENTH BOOK OF THE LAWS

The following book may be justly considered as forming one of the most important parts of the works of Plato, as it demonstrates the existence of divine natures, the immediate progeny of the ineffable principle of things; and shows that they provide for all things, and govern the universe with justice. It is also important in another point of view, as it incontestably proves that Plato firmly believed in the religion of his country; though this has often been denied by those who, being ignorant of its real nature, have had no conceptions of its unequalled sublimity. As Proclus, therefore, with his usual depth and fecundity of conception, has admirably elucidated Plato's doctrine on these three important subjects, in his first book *On the Theology of Plato*,[†] the following translation from that book is subjoined for the benefit of the reader:

I. In the *Laws* these three things are asserted by Plato: That there are Gods, that they providentially attend to all things, and that they conduct all things according to justice, and receive no perversion from subordinate natures. That these, then, are the principal of all theological dogmas, is obvious to every one. For, what is more principal than the hyparxis of the Gods, or than beneficent providence, or immutable and undeviating power? through which the Gods produce secondary natures uniformly, and preserve and convert them to themselves with perfect purity: they indeed governing others, but being in no respect passive to things subordinate, nor changed together with the variety of the objects of their providential energy. We shall learn, however, in what manner these things are naturally distinguished, if we endeavour first to comprehend by a reasoning process the scientific method of Plato in each of these subjects, and, prior to the rest, by what irreprehensible arguments he proves that there are Gods; and, in the next place, consider the problems which are suspended from this.

---

† TTS vol. VIII; see p. 84 *et seq.*

Of all beings, then, it is necessary that some should move only, that others should be moved only, and that the natures which subsist between these should both be moved and move; and this in such a manner, that either they must necessarily be moved by others, and move others, or be self-motive. these four hypostases[†] succeed each other in an orderly progression. For, prior to that which is moved only, and is passive to other primary causes, is that which moves others, and is moved by others; and beyond this is the self-motive nature, originating from itself, and, in consequence of moving itself, imparting to others also the representation of being moved. And after all those which participate of efficient or passive motion the immovable nature succeeds. For every thing self-motive, as possessing its perfection in a life attended with mutation and interval, is suspended from another more ancient cause, which always subsists according to the same things, and after the same manner, and whose life is not according to time, but in eternity: for time is the image of eternity. If, therefore, all things which are moved by themselves are moved according to time, but the eternal form of motion is beyond that which is borne along according to time, the self-motive nature will be the second in order, and not the first among beings. And again, that which moves others, and is moved by others, must necessarily be suspended from a self-motive nature: and not this only, but likewise every alter-motive composition or constitution of things, as the Athenian guest demonstrates. For, says he, if every thing which is moved should stop,[‡] there will not be that which is first moved, unless the self-motive natures have a subsistence in beings. For the immovable is by no means naturally adapted to be moved, nor would it then be that which is first moved. And the alter-motive nature will require another moving power. The self-motive nature, therefore, alone, as beginning its energy from itself, will move itself, and others also, in a secondary degree. For a nature of this kind imparts to things alter-motive the power of being moved, in the same manner as the immovable inserts in all things the power of moving. And again, in the third place, that which is moved only, we must primarily suspend from the natures which are moved by another, but which move others. For

---

[†] *Hypostasis* (ὑποστασις) *is an individual subsistence.*

[‡] The force of this argument for the existence of a self-motive nature is very great. If all motion were to stop, whence could it again originate? Not from the immovable; for it is a mover only, and therefore cannot be that which is first moved. Nor could motion originate from the alter-motive nature; for this, as its name implies, derives its motion from another.

it is requisite that both other things, and the series of natures which are moved, and which extends supernally as far as to the order of things last, should be filled with their proper media. All bodies, therefore, belong to things which are naturally adapted to be moved only, and to be passive. For they are effective of nothing, on account of possessing an hypostasis endued with interval, and participating of magnitude and bulk; since whatever is effective and motive of other things naturally makes and moves in consequence of employing an incorporeal power.

Of incorporeal natures, however, some are divisible about bodies, and others are exempt from such a distribution about the last of things. The natures, therefore, which are divided about the bulks of bodies, whether they consist in qualities, or in material forms, belong to the natures which are moved by another, but which move others. For these, because they have an incorporeal allotment, participate of the power of moving; but again, because they are divided about bodies, and, in consequence of this, are deprived of the power of verging to themselves, are distributed together with their subjects, and are replete with sluggishness from these, they require a moving power which is not borne along to foreign seats, but possesses an hypostasis in itself. Where, then, shall we have that which moves itself? For things which are extended into bulks and intervals, or which are divided in these, and consist about them inseparably, must of necessity either be alone moved, or move in consequence of being moved by others. But it is requisite, as we have before said, that the self-motive nature should be prior to these, which is established in itself, and not in others, and which fixes its energies in itself, and not in things subordinate to itself. There is, therefore, some other nature exempt from bodies, both in the heavens and the much-mutable elements, from which the power of being moved is primarily imparted to bodies. If, then, it be requisite to discover what such an essence is, we shall act rightly in following Socrates, and considering what that nature is, which, by being present to things alter-motive, imparts to them a representation of self-motion, and to which of the above-mentioned natures we should ascribe the power of being moved from themselves. For all inanimate things are alone alter-motive, and their passive properties are naturally derived from a power externally moving and impelling.

If, therefore, the self-motive is more ancient than the alter-motive essence, but soul is primarily self-motive, from which the image of self-motion pervades to bodies, soul will be beyond bodies, and the motion of every body will be the progeny of soul, and of its internal motion. Hence, it is necessary that the whole of heaven, and all the bodies it contains, possessing such a variety of motion, and these moved according to nature (for to every body of this kind a circular motion is natural),[†] should have ruling souls, essentially more ancient than bodies, moving in themselves, and supernally illuminating bodies with the power of being moved. With respect to these souls, therefore, which orderly distribute the whole world, and its parts, and move and vitalize every thing corporeal, and which, of itself, is destitute of life, inspiring the cause of motion, - with respect to these, it is necessary that they should either move all things rationally, or according to a contrary mode, which it is not lawful to assert. But if this world, and every thing which has an orderly subsistence in it, and which is equably moved and perpetually borne along according to nature, are referred to an irrational soul, which both moves itself and other things, neither the order of the periods, nor motion essentially bounded according to one reason, nor the position of bodies, nor any thing else which is generated according to nature, will have a stable cause, and which is able to arrange every thing according to the same things, and after the same manner. For every thing irrational is naturally adapted to be adorned by another, since, of itself, it is indefinite and inordinate. But to commit all heaven to a thing of this kind, and a circulation which revolves according to the same reason, and after the same manner, by no means accords with the nature of things, nor with our undisciplined conceptions. If, on the contrary, an intellectual and rational soul governs all things, and if every thing which eternally revolves is under the dominion of such a soul, and there is nothing of wholes destitute of soul (for, as Theophrastus somewhere observes, no body that is honourable is deprived of this power), - if this be the case, whether has it this intellectual,[‡] perfect, and beneficent nature, according to participation, or according to essence? For, if according to essence, every soul must necessarily be of this kind, if each, according to its own nature, is self-motive. But if it is intellectual according to participation, there will be another intellect in energy more ancient than soul, which will possess intellection essentially, and which comprehends in itself, by its very essence, an uniform knowledge of wholes; since it is also necessary that the soul which is essentialized according to reason, should possess a subsistence according to intellect through participation, and that an intellectual

---

[†] See my Introduction to my Translation of Aristotle's *Metaphysics*.

[‡] Intuitive perception is the characteristic of intellect, as discursive energy of the rational soul.

nature should be twofold, - one primarily in a divine intellect itself, and another secondarily in soul, and proceeding from this divine intellect.

You may also add, if you are willing, the presence of intellectual illumination in body. For whence is the whole of this heaven either spheric, or carried in a circle, and is rolled round the same according to one definite order? How is it always immutably allotted the same idea and power according to nature, unless it participate of the effective nature of form according to intellect? For soul is the supplier of motion; but the cause of a stable condition, and which leads back the fluctuating mutation of things which are moved, to sameness, and to a life bounded according to one reason, and a circulation subsisting after the same manner, must evidently be superior to soul.

Body, therefore, and the whole of this sensible essence, belong to alter-motive natures; but soul is self-motive, binding in itself all corporeal motions; and prior to this is immovable intellect. Nor must you conceive that this immovable nature of intellect is such as that which we say is sluggish, void of life, and without spirit; for it is the leading cause of all motion, and the fountain of all life, as well of that which is converted to itself, as of that which has its hypostasis in other natures. Through these causes the world is called by Timæus an animated intellectual animal. It is denominated an animal from its own nature, and the life which pervades to it from soul, and which is divided about it; but animated, from the presence of a divine soul in it; and intellectual, from the government of intellect. For a sufficient supply of life, the government of soul, and the communication of intellect, connectedly contain the whole of heaven.

But if this intellect is intellect according to essence, since the very being of intellect consists in intellection, and Timæus, demonstrating this, calls it divine, for he says that soul,[†] receiving a divine intellect, is rightly and prudently disciplined, - if this be the case, it is necessary that the whole of heaven should be suspended from the deity[‡] of this intellect, and that motion should be present to this universe from soul, but perpetual permanency and a subsistence after the same manner from intellect, and one union, concord in itself, sympathy and an all-perfect measure, from a unity through which intellect is uniform, soul is one, and every being is a whole and perfect, according to its nature. It is also necessary that every thing secondary, together with the perfection in its

---

† i.e. the soul of the world.

‡ See the Introduction to the *Parmenides*.

own proper nature, should also participate from an order established above it of another more excellent idiom. For that which is corporeal, being alter-motive, derives the appearance of self-motive power from soul, and is through it an animal. But soul, being self-motive, participates of life according to intellect, and, energizing temporally, possesses unceasing energy and ever-vigilant life from its vicinity to intellect. And intellect, possessing its life in eternity, and in an essence ever in energy, and fixing all its intelligence collectively in itself, is perfectly divine, through a cause prior to itself, or, in other words, from the unity which it participates. For, as Plotinus says, it has twofold energies, some as intellect, and others as being inebriated with nectar:[†] and, in another place, that this intellect is a God, through that prior to itself which is not intellect. Just as soul, by that summit of itself which is above soul, is intellect; and body, through a power prior to body, is soul.

All things, therefore, as we have said, are suspended from unity through intellect and soul as media. And intellect is, indeed, uniform, or has the form of unity; but soul is mentiform, or has the form of intellect; and the body of the world is vital. Every thing, in short, is suspended from that which is prior to itself. And, with respect to the things posterior to those above mentioned, one enjoys a divine nature more nearly, and another more remotely. And deity, indeed, is prior to an intellectual essence, in which, as in a vehicle, it first rides; but intellect is most divine, as being deified prior to other things. Soul is divine, so far as it requires an intellectual medium; and the body which participates of such a soul, so far as it participates, is, indeed, divine (for the illumination of divine light supernally pervades as far as to the last dependance), but, simply considered, is not divine. But soul, by looking to intellect, and living from itself, is primarily divine.

The same reasoning, also, must be adopted with respect to each of the whole spheres, and the bodies which they contain. For all these imitate the whole of heaven, since they have a perpetual allotment. And the sublunary elements are not entirely mutable according to essence, but abide, according to their *wholenesses*,[‡] in the universe, and comprehend

---

[†] That is, as energizing super-intellectually through its unity, which is the blossom of its essence, and which abides in unproceeding union in the ineffable cause of all.

[‡] Each of the elements is a *wholeness* from the possession of one perfect form which remains perpetually the same. - See the Introduction to the *Timæus*.

in themselves partial animals: for every *wholeness* has, in conjunction with itself, more partial hypostases. As, therefore, in the heavens the number of the stars proceeds in conjunction with the whole spheres, and as, in earth, a multitude of terrestrial partial animals subsists, together with its wholeness, - in like manner, I think it is necessary, that in the wholes which are situated between heaven and earth, every element should be filled with its proper numbers. For how, in the extremes, can wholes, which subsist prior to parts, be arranged with their parts, unless there is also the same analogy in the media?

But if each of the spheres is an animal, is perpetually established after the same manner, and give completion to the universe, so far as it has life always primarily participating of soul, but, so far as it preserves its own order immutably in the world, is comprehended by intellect, and so far as it is one and a whole, being the leader of its proper parts, is illuminated by divine union,- if this be the case, not only the universe, but each of its perpetual parts, is animated, endued with intellect, and as much as possible similar to the whole. For each of these is a universe, with respect to its kindred multitude. In short, there is one wholeness with a corporeal form of the universe, but many others under this, depending on this one; one soul of the world, and after this others orderly distributing, in conjunction with it, its whole parts with inviolable purity; one intellect, and an intellectual number under this participated by these souls; and one God who connectedly contains all mundane and supermundane natures, and a multitude of other Gods who distribute intellectual essence, the souls suspended from these, and all the parts of the world. For, it is impossible that every progeny of nature should be generative of things similar to itself, but that wholes, and the first things in the universe, should not in a much greater degree extend in themselves the exemplar of such like propagation. For the similar is more allied to, and more naturally accords with, the similar, from the reason of cause, than with the dissimilar; and, in like manner, the same than the different, and bound than the infinite. And thus much concerning the first particular, or the existence of the Gods.

II. Let us now direct our attention to the second thing demonstrated in the following book, *viz.* that the Gods providentially attend both to wholes and parts. That which is self-motive, then, is the principle of motion and being to all mundane natures; and life proceeds from soul, together with local and other motions. A progression, likewise, into being is derived from this; and, by a much greater priority, from an intellectual essence, which binds in itself the life of things self-motive, and precedes, according to cause, all temporal energy. But in a still greater degree is this progression into being derived from an hyparxis, characterized by unity, which contains both intellect and soul, fills with total goods, and proceeds to the last of things. For all the parts of the world are not able to participate of life, nor of intellect and gnostic power; but all things participate of *The One*, as far as to matter itself, wholes and parts, things according to nature and the contraries to these, and nothing is destitute of a cause of this kind; nor can any thing which participates of being be deprived of *The One*. If, therefore, the Gods, who are characterized by unity, produce all things, and contain all things in their unknown comprehending powers, how is it possible that they should not also contain a providence, supernally pervading as far as to the most partial natures? For it is every where fit that offspring should enjoy the care of their causes. But all alter-motive are the progeny of self-motive natures; and things which subsist in time, either according to the whole or a part of the whole of time, are the effects of things eternal; because perpetual being is the cause of being which sometimes has a subsistence. Divine and single genera, likewise, presubsist as causes of the subsistence of all multiplied natures; and, in short, there is no multitude of essences or powers which is not allotted its generation from *The One*. It is necessary therefore, that all these should partake of the providence of preceding causes, being vivified, indeed, by the Gods that are connected with souls, and circularly moved according to temporal periods; but participating the permanent establishment of forms from the intellectual Gods;[†] and receiving in themselves the presence of union, measure, and the distribution of good, from the first[‡] Gods. Hence it is necessary, either that the Gods should know their productions, because a providential care of their own offspring is natural to them, and that they should not only give subsistence to secondary natures, and impart life, essence, and union, but also comprehend the primary cause of the good in these; or, that, being Gods, they should be ignorant, which it is not lawful to assert, of what is proper to every thing. For what ignorance can there be of things beautiful, with the causes of beauty, or of things good, with those who are allotted an hyparxis bounded in the nature of the good?

[†] It is necessary here in the original, after the word καταστασως, to add εκ των νοερων θεων.

[‡] *Viz.* from the intelligible Gods, who are wholly characterized by the superessential. See the Introduction to the *Parmenides*.

Indeed, if the Gods are ignorant of their progeny, neither do souls govern the universe according to intellect, nor are intellects carried in souls, nor prior to these do the unities of the Gods contract all knowledge in themselves, which we have granted from preceding demonstrations. But, if the Gods know their progeny, being the fathers, leaders, and rulers, of all things in the world, and to these, being such, the care of the things governed, consequent to, and generated by, them, pertains, - whether shall we say that these, knowing the law according to nature, are able to give completion to it, or, that through imbecility of providence they are deprived of their possessions or progeny, or whatever else you may think proper to call them? For, if through imbecility they abandon the care of all things, what is the cause of this imbecility? For they do not move things externally, nor are other things the causes of essence, while the Gods merely assume the government of what others have produced, but as from the stern of a ship they direct all things, imparting being, containing the measures of life, and distributing the powers of energy to energizing natures. Whether also are they incapable of providentially attending to all things at once, or do not leave any part destitute of their presiding care? And if they are not curators of all things in the world, whether do they provide for greater things, but neglect lesser? Or do they take care indeed of lesser things, but pay no attention to such as are greater? For, if we similarly deprive them of a providential attention to all things through imbecility, how, attributing to them that which is greater, *viz.* the production of all things, can we avoid granting what is naturally consequent to this, that they providentially attend to their offspring? For it is the province of a power which makes a greater thing, to direct also a lesser. But if the Gods take care of lesser things, but neglect greater, how can this mode of providence be right? For the more allied and the more similar are naturally more adapted to the communication of good, which the Gods impart. And, if the first of mundane natures are thought worthy of providential attention and of the perfection emanating from the Gods, but the Divinities are incapable of proceeding as far as to the last of things, what is that which will restrain their being present to all things? What will interrupt their unenvying energy? How can those who are capable of effecting greater things, be imbecil with respect to dominion over lesser? Or how will those who produce the essence even of the minutest things, through impotency not be the lords of their perfection? For all these things oppose our natural conceptions. It remains, therefore, that the Gods must know what is adapted to every thing, and possess a power perfective of, and a dominion which rules over, all things. But if they know what is according to nature, and this, to those that generate all things, is to take care of all things, an abundance of power is not deprived of this providential attention.

It may also be inquired, whether the will of providence is in the Gods? or whether this alone is wanting to their knowledge and power, and that, on this account, things are deprived of their care? For if, knowing what is adapted to themselves, and being able to fill the objects of their knowledge, they are not willing to provide for their own progeny, they will be indigent of goodness, will be no longer unenvious, and, by such an hypothesis, we shall subvert the hyparxis according to which they are essentialized. For the very being of the Gods is constituted in goodness, and in this they possess their hypostasis. But to provide for subject natures, is to impart to them a certain good. By depriving the Gods therefore of providence, do we not at the same time deprive them of goodness? And, depriving them of goodness, do we not also ignorantly subvert their hyparxis? By every necessity,[†] therefore, goodness is consequent to the very being of the Gods. And this being admitted, it follows that they do not depart from a providential attention to secondary natures, through indolence, or imbecility, or ignorance; and again, as consequent to this, it must be admitted, that they possess the most excellent knowledge, undefiled power, and unenvying will.

Thus providing, therefore, for all things, they appear to be in no respect deficient in the supply of goods. Let no one, however, suppose a providence of such a kind, as to extend the Gods about secondary natures, and deprive them of their exempt transcendency, or ascribe to them, who are established far remote from all mortal molestation, a busy energy, and laborious life. For their blessedness is not willing to be defiled with the difficulty of administration; since the life also of worthy men is attended with facility of energy, and is free from molestation and pain. But all labours which are the consequence of perturbation, arise from the impediments of matter. if, however, it be requisite to define the mode in which the providence of the Gods energizes, we must establish it to be spontaneous, undefiled, immaterial and ineffable. For they do not govern all things in the same manner as men when they providentially attend to their own affairs, viz. by inquiring what is fit, investigating the good of any particular by dubious reasonings, directing their view to externals, and following effects; but,

---

† In the original instead of πασαν αναγκην, we find πασαν αρετην.

previously assuming in themselves the measures of wholes, producing from themselves the essences of things, and looking to themselves, in a silent path, they lead, perfect, and fill all things with good, neither producing similar to nature, which alone energizes by its very essence without free deliberation, nor like partial souls, who energize in conjunction with will, and are deprived of essential operation, but they comprehend both these in profound union. And they will, indeed, what they are able to effect by their very essence; but, being able to accomplish, and producing all things by their very essence, they contain, in unenvying will, the cause of production. What busy energy, therefore, what molestation, what punishment of Ixion, can be said to give completion to the providence of the Gods, unless to impart good in any way is laborious to a divine nature? But that which is according to nature is not laborious to any thing: for it is not laborious to fire to impart heat, nor to snow to refrigerate, nor, in short, to bodies to energize according to their proper powers. Nor, prior to bodies, is it laborious to natures to nourish, or generate, or increase; for these are the works of natures. Nor again, prior to these, to souls: for many of the energies of these are from free deliberation; and they move many things and excite many motions by their very essence, through their presence alone. so that, if the communication of good is natural to the Gods, providence also is natural to them; and this we should say is effected by the Gods with facility, and by their very essence alone. But if these things are not natural to the Divinities, neither will they be naturally good: for good imparts good; just as life gives subsistence to another life, and intellect to intellectual illumination. And whatever is primary in every nature generates that which has a secondary subsistence.

What, however, is most illustrious in the Platonic theology is this, that neither does it convert the exempt essence of the Gods to secondary natures, through the care of things subordinate, nor diminish their providential presence to all things, through their undefiled transcendency; but, at the same time that it assigns to them that which is separate in hypostasis, and unmingled with every deterior nature, it celebrates them as extending to all things, and as taking care of and adorning their proper progeny. For the manner in which they pervade through all things is not corporeal, like that of light through the air, nor divisible about bodies, as that of nature, nor converted to things subordinate, as that of a partial soul; but it is separate from, and unconverted to, body, is immaterial, unmingled, unrestrained, uniform, primary, and transcendently exempt. In short, such[†] a mode of divine providence must be understood in the present case; since it is evident that there is a peculiar mode of providence according to every order of the Gods. For soul is said to provide for things secondary in one way, and intellect in another; but Deity, which is prior to intellect, transcendently provides for all that intellect and soul provide. And of the Gods themselves there is one providence of the sublunary, and another of the celestial. And of those beyond the world there are many orders; but the mode of providence is varied in each.

III. In the third place, let us consider how we are to understand the immutability of a divine nature, which conducts all things according to justice, without departing from undeviating rectitude, both in the providence of all other things and of human affairs. This, then, I think, must be apparent to every one, that every where that which governs according to nature, and pays every attention to the felicity of the governed, must lead and direct them to that which is best. For neither will the pilot, in governing sailors and a ship, have any other principal end than the safety of those that sail in the vessel, and of the vessel itself; nor will the physician, being the curator of the sick, either cut the body, or administer medicines for the sake of any thing else than the health of the subjects of his care; nor can it be said that the general or guardian looks to any other end, than the latter the liberty of those whom he preserves, and the former that of his soldiers. Nor does any other, to whom the government and care of any thing are committed, endeavour to subvert the good of his charge, over which he presides, and, aiming at which, he disposes every thing pertaining to the objects of his government in a becoming manner. If, therefore, we grant that the gods are the governors of all things, and acknowledge that their providence is extended to all things, goodness being the characteristic of their nature, and that they possess every virtue, how is it possible for them to neglect the felicity of the subjects of their providential energy? Or how can they be inferior to other leaders in the providence of things subordinate? since the Gods always look to that which is better, and establish this as the end of all their government; but other leaders

---

[†] *Viz.* This general mode of providence is applicable to all the Gods; but a peculiar mode is also united with it. For the providence of superior Gods is more universal, but that of the inferior Deities more particular. In short, the providence of the Gods is varied according to the subjects, times, and places of its energy; not that the diversity of the latter produces, but, on the contrary, proceeds from, the variety of the former.

overlook the good of men, and embrace vice rather than virtue, being perverted by the gifts of the depraved. In short, whether you are willing to call them leaders, or governors, or guardians, or fathers, a divine nature will not appear to be indigent of any one of such-like appellations. For all things venerable and honourable subsist in them primarily: and, on this account, here also some things are naturally more venerable and honourable than others, because they bear an ultimate resemblance of the Gods. But what occasion is there to insist any further on this? For we hear, I think, paternal, guardian, ruling, and Pæonian powers celebrated by those who are skilled in divine concerns. How is it possible, therefore, that the images of the Gods, when subsisting according to nature, and aiming at their proper end, should provide for the well-being of the subjects of their government, but that the Gods themselves, with whom the whole of good, real and true virtue, and an innoxious life, reside, should not direct their government to the virtue and vice of men? And how do they evince[†] that virtue is victorious, but that vice is vanquished in the universe? Indeed, by admitting that they attend to the worship of the depraved, we must also admit that they corrupt the measures of justice, subvert the boundary of undeviating science, and evince that the gifts of vice are more honourable than the pursuits of virtue. such a mode of providence, however, is neither profitable to those that lead, nor to those that are led. For to those that have become vicious there will be no liberation from guilt, because offenders always endeavour to anticipate justice, and decline the measures of desert. But it will be necessary that the Gods (which it is not lawful to assert) should regard the vice of the subjects of their providence, neglect their true safety, and be alone the causes of shadowy goods. This universe, too, must be filled with disorder and incurable perturbation, depravity abiding in it, and must be in a condition similar to that of badly-governed cities; though, is it not perfectly impossible that parts should be governed according to nature rather than wholes, human affairs than things divine, and images than primary causes?

So that if rulers among men rule with rectitude, honouring some and disgracing others, and every where directing the works of vice by the measures of virtue, - by a much greater necessity must the Gods, who

---

[†] Proclus here alludes to the Chaldean Oracles, of one of which the sentence, "Virtue is victorious, but vice is vanquished in the universe," is a part, as appears from his Commentary on the *Republic*, p.376.

are the leaders of wholes, be immutable; for men, through a similitude to the Gods, are allotted this virtue. But, if we acknowledge that men who corrupt the safety and well-being of those who are governed by them, imitate in a greater degree the providence of the Gods, we shall forget that, at the same time, we entirely abolish the truth concerning the Gods, and the transcendency of virtue. For this I think is obvious to every one, that what is more similar to the Gods is more blessed than that which is deprived of them through dissimilitude and diversity. So that, if here, indeed, the uncorrupted and undeviating form of providence is honourable, in a much greater degree must it be honourable with the Gods. But if with them mortal gifts are more venerable than the divine measures of justice, - with men, also, earth-born will be more sufficient than Olympian goods to perfect felicity, and the blandishments of vice than the works of virtue. Through these demonstrations, therefore, Plato, in this book, delivers to us the hyparxis of the Gods, their providential care extending to all things, and their immutable energy, which things are, indeed, common to all the Gods, but have a leading dignity and a primary subsistence according to nature in the doctrine concerning the divinities. For this triad appears supernally pervading from the occult genera as far as to the most partial progressions, in the divine orders; since a uniform hyparxis, a power providential of all secondary natures, and an intellect undeviating and immutable, subsist in all the Gods, as well in those prior to the world, as in those of a mundane characteristic.

BOOK X

After the laws respecting wounds, let the following general law be established respecting violence of every kind; that no one shall carry or take away any thing belonging to another, or use his neighbour's property, if he has not obtained the consent of its possessor. For all the above-mentioned evils have depended, depend at present, and will depend on a thing of this kind. But the greatest of the remaining evils are the intemperance and insolence of young men. The first of these consists in insolent and injurious behaviour towards sacred concerns.

And the intemperance and insolence of young men are particularly mighty evils when they take place in public and holy affairs, or in any common part of the tribes, or any other communions of this kind. But the second of these crimes, and which rank in the second place, are those committed towards private sacred concerns and sepulchres. Those of the third rank, separate from the above-mentioned particulars, consist in insolent behaviour towards parents. The fourth kind of insolence takes place when any one, despising the magistrates, takes away or uses any thing belonging to them, contrary to their intention. The fifth consists in unjustly calling to account the political conduct of any citizen. And for each of these a common law must be established. For, with respect to sacrilege, we have summarily said in what manner it ought to be punished, if it is committed with violence and secrecy. Let

b us now speak concerning the punishment which those ought to suffer who speak or act in an insolent manner towards the Gods, premising first of all the following particulars, as an atonement. He who believes that there are Gods, conformably to the laws, will never at any time voluntarily act in an impious manner, or speak illegally. But he who does so will suffer one of these three things: either he will not believe that there are Gods; or he will believe that there are, but that they take no care of human affairs; or, in the third place, he will believe that they are easily appeased by sacrifices and prayers.

c CLIN. What then shall we do, and what shall we say to them?

GUEST. O good man! let us, in the first place, hear what I prophesy they will jocosely say in contempt of us.

CLIN. What?

GUEST. They will, perhaps, in a reviling manner thus address us:- O Athenian guest, you Lacedæmonian, and you Cnossian, you speak the truth. For some of us are by no means of opinion that there are Gods:

others among us believe that they take no care of human affairs; and others, that they may easily be appeased by sacrifices and prayers, agreeably to what you said. But we think it proper, in the same manner as it appeared proper to you respecting laws, that before you threaten

d us severely you should endeavour to persuade and teach us that there are Gods, adducing for this purpose sufficient arguments; and likewise, that they are beings too excellent to be allured in an unjust manner by any gifts. For, now often hearing these, and other such particulars, asserted by the best of poets, rhetoricians, prophets, priests, and ten thousand others, the greater part of us do not turn from acting unjustly, but we

e endeavour by such conduct to obtain a remedy for our evils. But from legislators who confess themselves not to be rustic, but mild, we think it reasonable to expect that they should endeavour to persuade us that there are Gods; so that, though they may not speak better than others respecting the existence of the Divinities, yet they may speak better with respect to truth. And perhaps, indeed, we may be persuaded by you. If, therefore, we speak in a proper manner, comply with our request.

CLIN. It appears therefore easy, O guest, to show the truth of this assertion, that there are Gods.

86a GUEST. How?

CLIN. In the first place, the earth and sun, all the stars, and the seasons so beautifully adorned and distinguished by months and years, evince the truth of this assertion. To which we may add, that all men, both Greeks and Barbarians, believe that there are Gods.

GUEST. O blessed man, I am afraid for the depraved, (for I will not ever say that I am ashamed of them,) lest you should despise them. For you are ignorant with respect to the cause of the difference between them and others, and think that their souls are impelled to an impious life through the incontinence alone of pleasures and desires.

CLIN. But what other cause is there, O guest, besides this?

GUEST. One, of which you are nearly entirely ignorant, through living remote from such characters.

CLIN. What is it?

GUEST. A certain ignorance of a very grievous nature, and which appears to be the greatest prudence.

CLIN. How do you say?

GUEST. There are certain writings among us, partly in verse and partly in prose, which, as I understand, you have not, through the virtue of your polity. The most ancient of these writings assert, respecting the Gods, that the nature of Heaven, and of the other Divinities, was first generated; and at no great distance from the beginning of these compositions, the generation of the Gods, and their discourses with each other, are related. It is not easy to censure these writings, on account of their antiquity, whether they may be properly adapted to the hearers of them, or not. But I shall never praise them as useful, nor as in every respect speaking properly respecting the reverence and honour, which

d is due to parents. Let us, therefore, dismiss and bid farewell to the writings of the ancients, and speak of them in such a mánner as is pleasing to the Gods. But let us accuse such assertions of junior wise men as are the causes of evil. Their assertions, then, produce the following effect:- When you and I, as arguments that there are Gods, adduce the sun and moon, the stars, and the earth, as Gods and Divine natures, - others, persuaded by these wise men, will say that they are

e earth and stones, incapable of paying any attention to human affairs, though they are celebrated as Divinities in discourses well calculated to procure persuasion.

CLIN. Such an assertion, O guest, would be of a dangerous nature, even if I was the only one that heard it; but now, since it is heard by many, it is still more dangerous.

GUEST. What then ought we to say, and what ought we to do? Shall

887a we apologize as if we were accused by some impious person for acting in a dire manner by establishing laws as if there were Gods? Or shall we bid farewell to these, and again return to the discussion of laws, that this our preface to the laws may not become more extended than is proper? For our discourse will be far from being short, if we sufficiently exhibit what is necessary to men prone to impiety; wish to deter them from wickedness: to render them indignant with what is base; and afterwards to establish laws in a proper manner.

b CLIN. But, O guest, we have often said in the course of this short time, that in the present discussion brevity is not to be preferred to prolixity. For nothing (according to the saying) pursues us urging. But it would be ridiculous, and at the same time base, to prefer that which is shorter to that which is best. For it will be a thing of no small consequence if our discourse shall possess any persuasive arguments that there are Gods, that they are good, and that they honour justice far more than men. For this will be nearly the most beautiful and excellent

c preface to all our laws. Without any molestation, therefore, and delay, let us, to the utmost of our power, omit nothing which may tend to persuade that these things are so.

GUEST. What you have just now said appears to me to call us to prayer, since you excite yourself with alacrity to the ensuing discourse, and do not admit of any further delay. *But how can any one, without anger, speak concerning the existence of the Gods, as if it was a thing of a doubtful nature?* For it necessarily follows that we must be indignant with, and hate, those who are the causes to us of the present discussion. These, indeed, might be persuaded there are Gods, from what they heard while children, and while they were yet nourished with milk from their nurses and mothers, as it were in songs, both in sport and in earnest, in sacrifices and prayers. For in these they must have seen and heard in the sweetest manner their parents supplicating the Gods with the greatest earnestness for themselves and children, and proclaiming, by their prayers and supplications, that there are indubitably Gods. Besides this, too, they must have heard and seen both Greeks and Barbarians, during the rising and setting of the sun and moon, supplicating and adoring, as well when their affairs were prosperous as when they were adverse; by all which they might be led to conclude that there are Gods, without any suspicion to the contrary. But with respect to those who despise every thing of this kind, though not from one sufficient argument, as every one who possesses the least degree of intellect will acknowledge, and on this account compel us to speak as we do at present, how shall we be able to correct them in mild language, and at the same time, in the first place, teach them that there are Gods? Let us, however, dare the attempt. For it is not proper that, at the same time they are insane through the voracity of pleasure, we should be transported through anger with such characters as these. Laying aside all anger, therefore, let us previously address those who are thus vitiated in their dianoëtic part, and mildly speak to one of them as follows: O boy, you are as yet a youth; but time, as it advances, will cause you to change your opinions, and think in many respects contrary to what you do at present. Wait, therefore, till that period, that you may be able to judge concerning things of the greatest consequence. But to possess right conceptions respecting the Gods, though to you at present it appears to be a thing of no consequence, is of the greatest importance as to living well, or the contrary. If, therefore, I announce to you what follows as one of the things of the utmost consequence, I shall by no means speak falsely. Not you alone, nor your friends, are the first that have entertained this opinion respecting the Gods, but there always have been a greater or less number who have laboured under this disease. I will, therefore, tell you what happens to most of them, *viz.* that they do not remain in this opinion, that there are no Gods, from youth to old age. Two opinions, indeed, respecting the Gods remain, though not in many, yet in a few, - I mean, that there are Gods, but that they take no care of human affairs; or, if they do, that they may be easily appeased by sacrifices and prayers. If, therefore, you will be persuaded by me, wait, considering whether this is the case or not, till you possess as clear information in this particular as can possibly be obtained. And in order

d   to this, interrogate others, and particularly the legislator. But at the present time do not dare to act in any respect impious towards the Gods. For he who establishes laws for you will endeavour, both now and hereafter, to teach you how these things subsist.

CLIN. What has been said thus far, O guest, is most beautiful.

GUEST. Entirely so, O Megillus and Clinias; but we are ignorant that we have fallen upon a wonderful assertion.

CLIN. What kind of assertion do you mean?

e   GUEST. That which in the opinion of many is the wisest of all assertions.

CLIN. Speak yet clearer.

GUEST. Some then say;, with respect to all things that have been, are, and will be, that some subsist from nature, others from art, and others through fortune.

CLIN. And they speak well.

889a   GUEST. It is fit, indeed, that wise men should speak properly. Following them, therefore, let us consider what they meant by this assertion.

CLIN. By all means.

GUEST. It appears (say they) that the greatest and most beautiful things are produced by nature and fortune, but lesser things by art; which receiving from nature the generation of great and primary works, fashions and fabricates all smaller works, which we all of us denominate artificial.

CLIN. How do you say?

b   GUEST. I will speak still clearer. They say[†] that fire and water, earth and air, subsist from nature and fortune, and not from art. That the bodies also, which are posterior to these, *viz.* of the earth, the sun, the moon, and the stars, are generated through these, which are entirely destitute of soul. They add, that, all things being casually borne along by the impulse of fortune, they became in a certain respect properly harmonized together, *viz.* the hot with the cold, the dry with the moist,

c   the soft with the hard; and, in short, that all things of a contrary

---

† Plato here alludes to those natural philosophers Democritus, Anaxagoras, and Archelaus; the first of whom asserted, that the universe was constituted by a certain rash chance rather than by a divine intellect; and the other two, that the celestial orbs have nothing in them more divine than the sublunary elements.

temperament were, from necessity, through fortune mingled together. That, besides this, the whole of heaven, with all that it contains, all animals and plants, and the seasons of the year, were produced after this manner: not (say they) through intellect, or any divinity, nor yet through art, but, as we have said, from nature and fortune. That afterwards mortal art was generated from these by mortals, and that through its assistance certain posterior disciplines were produced, which do not very much partake of truth, but are certain images allied to each other; such as painting, music, and the sister arts, beget. They add, that if there are any arts which produce any thing of a serious nature, they are such as communicate their own power with that of nature; such as are the arts of medicine, agriculture, and gymnastic: and that the political art communicates in a certain small part with nature, but very much with art. So that, according to them, the whole of legislation does not consist from nature, but art, and its positions are not true.

CLIN. How do you say?

GUEST. O blessed man, they say in the first place, that the Gods do not subsist from nature, but from art and certain laws, and that these are different in different nations, according as the legislators by mutual agreement have determined. They likewise assert, that things beautiful or becoming are not the same by nature as by law; and that things just have not any natural subsistence whatever, but that men always dissent among themselves respecting these, and are perpetually changing them. That, when they are changed by them, they then possess authority, deriving their subsistence from art and laws, and not from any certain nature. These, my friends, are the particulars which are taught young men from the writings of the wise, both in prose and verse, and by which they learn that the most just is that which is obtained by violence. Hence, young men fall into impiety so as to believe that there are not Gods, such as the law ordains us to conceive have an existence. Hence, too, seditions arise, through which men are drawn to a life consisting in vanquishing others, and refusing subjection to others according to law, as if it was a life naturally proper.

CLIN. O guest, what a circumstance have you related, and what a pest to young men, both publicly to cities, and to private families!

GUEST. You speak truly, O Clinias. What then ought a legislator to do in this case? Ought he only to threaten every one in the city, that they shall be punished unless they assert and believe that there are Gods, such as the law says there are; and unless they conceive they ought to act in such a manner with respect to things beautiful and just, and every thing else of the greatest consequence, and whatever pertains to virtue and vice, as the writings of the legislator enjoin? If, therefore, any refuse to obey his laws, ought he to punish some with death, others with stripes and bonds, others with infamy, and others with poverty and exile? but ought he to pay no attention to persuasion and gentle methods, at the same time that he is establishing laws?

d CLIN. By no means, O guest. But if any persuasion, though small, respecting things of this kind can be obtained, a legislator who is of the last worth ought by no means to be weary, but, as it is said, with the most strenuous exertions of his voice, should give assistance to the ancient law, by asserting that there are Gods, and such other things as you have discussed; and should give his suffrage both to nature and art, that they have a natural subsistence, or a subsistence not inferior to that of nature, since they are the progeny of intellect, according to the dictates of right reason, as you appear to me to assert, and as I believe.

e GUEST. O most prompt Clinias, is it not difficult to follow by a reasoning process things asserted by the multitude, and which are of a very extended nature?

CLIN. But what, O guest? Shall we patiently endure to discourse in so prolix a manner about intoxication and music, and shall we not be equally ready to speak about the Gods, and such-like particulars? Besides, such an undertaking will be of the greatest assistance to legislation, when prudently conducted, since those written mandates pertaining to the laws, which have always been subject to reprehension,

891a will thus entirely remain undisturbed. So that we ought not to be terrified if those things should at first be difficult to hear, which, when often repeated, may be apprehended even by one whom, from his inaptitude to learning, it is difficult to instruct. These things, therefore, though they may be prolix, yet, if they are useful, they are not to be considered as of no consequence; nor does it appear to me to be holy not to assist these assertions to the utmost of our power.

MEGIL. O guest Clinias, you appear to me to speak most excellently.

b GUEST. He does very much so indeed.

MEGIL. Let us, therefore, do as he says. For, if assertions of this kind were not, as I may say, scattered among all men, there would be no occasion of arguments to prove that there are Gods: but now this is necessary. Since, therefore, the greatest laws are corrupted by vicious men, to whom does it pertain to give assistance to them more than to the legislator?

CLIN. To no one.

GUEST. But inform me again, O Clinias, (for it is proper that you

c should partake of this discourse,) does it not appear that he who asserts the above-mentioned particulars considers fire and water, earth and air, as the first of all things, and that he denominates these very things nature, but is of opinion that soul was produced afterwards from these? Indeed, it not only appears to be so, but is truly signified to us by the very assertions themselves.

CLIN. Entirely so.

GUEST. Whether or not, therefore, by Jupiter, have we found, as it were, a certain fountain of the stupid opinion of those men who have ever touched upon physical inquiries? Consider, investigating the whole affair. For it will be of no small consequence if it shall appear that those who meddle with impious assertions, and thus rule over others, do not employ good, but vicious arguments. To me, therefore, this appears to be the case.

CLIN. You speak well: but endeavour to show that it is so.

GUEST. But I shall appear to employ unusual arguments.

CLIN. Let not this make you sluggish, O guest. For I understand that you are of opinion we shall wander from the business of legislation, if we engage in a disputation of this kind. But if it is not possible to show by any other method than this that the laws speak properly concerning the Gods, let us, O wonderful man, adopt it.

GUEST. I will enter, therefore, on this discourse, which, as it appears, is so unusual. Those discourses, then, which render the soul impious, assert that the first cause of the generation and corruption of all things is not the first, but was produced afterwards; and that what was posterior is prior. On this account they err respecting the true essence of the Gods.

CLIN. I do not yet understand.

GUEST. Almost all men, O my associate, appear to be ignorant what the soul is, and what power it possesses, both with respect to other things and its generation; I mean, that it ranks among things first, that it had a subsistence prior to all bodies, and that more than any other nature it rules over the mutation and all the ornament of bodies. If this is the case, does it not necessarily follow, that things allied to soul will have an origin prior to those pertaining to body, soul itself being more ancient than body?

CLIN. It is necessary.

GUEST. Opinion, therefore, diligent attention, intellect, art, and law, will be prior to things hard and soft, heavy and light. Besides this, too, great and primary works and actions, which are produced by art, will rank among things first; but natural productions, and nature herself, (which they do not properly denominate,) will be things posterior, and in subjection to art and intellect.

c CLIN. How?

GUEST. They are not willing to say that the generation about things first is nature, though it would be right to call it so; and they place bodies in the first rank of beings. But if soul shall appear to belong to the first order of things, and not fire or air, it may nearly be said with the greatest rectitude, that soul was generated[†] prior to body; that, if these things subsist in this manner, they will subsist naturally, *viz.* if any one evinces that soul is more ancient than body; but that this will by no means be the case if they subsist otherwise.

CLIN. You speak most true.

d GUEST. Shall we, therefore, after this manner proceed to what follows?

CLIN. Undoubtedly.

GUEST. But let us by all means guard against and avoid fraudulent arguments, lest these, which are of a juvenile nature, should deceive by false persuasion us who are advanced in years, and thus render us ridiculous; and lest we should appear to attempt greater things, and wander from such as are smaller. Consider, therefore, if it were necessary that we three should pass over a very rapid river, and I, who

e am the youngest of the three, and have tried many rivers, should say it is proper that I should first of all endeavour to pass over it by myself, leaving you in safety, and should consider whether or not it may be passed over by you, who are more aged than myself; that afterwards, this being agreeable to you, I should either call you to ford the river in conjunction with me, or, if it should be too deep for you, encounter the danger by myself; - consider, I say, if in this case I should not appear to speak to the purpose. In like manner, since the discourse we are now

893a entering on is of a more vehement nature, and perhaps nearly inaccessible by your strength, lest it should cause in you a dark giddiness, by leading you to questions to which you are unaccustomed, and afterwards overwhelm you with disgrace and sorrow, it appears to me that I ought, in the present case, first to interrogate myself, while you hear in safety, and, after this, again answer myself; proceeding in this manner till the whole of this discourse respecting the soul is finished, and it is shown that soul is prior to body.

---

† Plato, when he uses the word *generation*, in speaking of the soul, does not mean to imply a *temporal origin*, but *an eternal procession from an eternally energizing cause.*

CLIN. You appear to us, O guest, to speak most excellently: do, therefore, as you say.

GUEST. Come then, let us invoke Divinity; for, it if is ever proper to do so, it will be requisite in the present case; and let us beseech the Gods with the greatest earnestness to assist us in demonstrating their existence. Holding, therefore, as by a certain secure rope, let us ascend into the present reasoning. And it appears to me that, by the following interrogations respecting these things, I shall most securely answer my opponent. If any one then should ask me, O guest, do all things stand still, and is nothing moved? Or, does the very contrary to this take place? Or, are some things moved, but others stand still? To this I should reply, Some things are moved, and others stand still. Do not, therefore, the things which stand still, abide in a certain place, and are not the things which are moved, moved in a certain place? Undoubtedly. And some things do this in a certain respect in one feat, but others in more than one. Do you mean we shall say that some things which abide, receiving the power in the middle, are moved in one, in the same manner as the periphery of circles, which are said to stand still, revolves? I do. But we understand that in this revolution a motion of this kind, leading round the greatest and the least circle, distributes itself analogously in small and large circles, and is itself, according to proportion, less and more. On this account it becomes the fountain of all wonderful things, proceeding homologous according to slowness and swiftness, in large and small circles, and thus accomplishing what to some one it might appear impossible to accomplish. You speak most true. But by things moving in many things, you appear to me to mean such as are moved locally, always passing from one place to another. And sometimes, indeed, they obtain the basis of one certain centre, and sometimes of more than one,† by being rolled round. Each too meeting with each, they are cut by those that stand still. But when they meet with each other, and are borne along in an opposite direction, then the parts situated in the middle, and those between these, becoming one, they are mingled together. I acknowledge that these things are as you say. Besides this, too, the things which are mingled together are increased; but when they are separated, they are then corrupted, when

---

† *Viz.* That which changes its place changes the centre of place, to which the circumference of the moving body is compared; and sometimes, besides changing the centre, it preserves after a manner the same centre, when, not being fixed, but transferred from one place to another, it is carried round by a certain equal circumference.

894a the permanent habit of each remains; but when it does not remain, it is dissolved through both. But the generation of all things takes place when a certain passion is produced, *viz.* when the principle[†] receiving increase arrives at a second transition, and from this to that which is near it; and when it has arrived as far as to three, it possesses sense in things sentient. Every thing, therefore, is generated by this mutation and transition. However, a thing truly is, when it abides: and when it is changed into another habit, it becomes entirely corrupted. Have we not therefore, O friends, enumerated all the forms of motion, except two?

b   CLIN. Of what kind are those?

GUEST. They are nearly those, O excellent man, for the sake of which the whole of our present discussion is undertaken.

CLIN. Speak more clearly.

GUEST. Was not the present discussion undertaken for the sake of soul?

CLIN. Entirely so.

GUEST. Let one motion then be that which is able to move other things, but is always incapable of moving itself:[‡] but let the other be c   that which is always able move both itself[§] and other things, by mingling and separating, by increase, and the contrary, and by generation and corruption; and this motion is different from all the other motions.

CLIN. Be it so, therefore.

GUEST. Shall we not, then, place that motion as the ninth, which always moves another, and is moved by another: but call that the tenth[*] motion, which moves both itself and others, which is adapted to all

---

[†] By the principle here, Plato means a motive and seminal nature. This nature by alteration proceeds through three degrees, i.e. into length, breadth, and depth, and finally arrives at vitality and sensation.

[‡] This motion belongs to nature.

[§] This is the motion of soul.

[*] Plato in this book distinguishes the genus of motions into ten species, *viz.* circulation about an immovable centre, local transition, condensation, rarefaction, increase, decrease, generation, corruption, mutation or alteration produced in another by another, and mutation produced from a thing itself, both in itself and in another. This last is the tenth motion, of which he now speaks, and is the motion of soul.

actions and passions, and which is truly denominated the mutation and motion of all things

CLIN. Entirely so.

GUEST. But which of the ten motions shall we with the greatest rectitude judge to be the most robust, and by far the most efficacious of all motions?

CLIN. It is necessary to say, that the motion which is able to move itself is infinitely to be preferred to the rest, and that all the others are posterior to this.

GUEST. You speak well. Must not, therefore, one or two of the things which have not at present been rightly asserted by us be transposed?

CLIN. What things do you mean?

GUEST. We did not altogether speak properly respecting the tenth motion.

CLIN. Why so?

GUEST. Because, according to reason, it is the first in generation and strength; but that which follows this is the second, though it has been just now absurdly called by us the ninth.

CLIN. How do you say?

GUEST. Thus. When one thing moves another, and something else always moves this, will there ever among such things as these be any thing which is first moved? But how is it possible that a thing which is moved by another can ever be the first of things changed? It is certainly impossible. But when a thing moving itself causes mutation in something else, and this latter in some other, and ten thousand things are thus moved in succession, - whether or not in this case will there be any other principle of all the motion than the mutation of that which moves itself?

CLIN. You speak most excellently. These things, therefore, must be granted.

GUEST. Further still, let us thus interrogate and answer ourselves. If all generated natures should, after a manner, stand still, as many of those we are now addressing dare to say they do, which among the above-mentioned motions would necessarily first take place

CLIN. Doubtless that which moves itself. For the motion depending on another could not by any means take place till it had previously undergone some mutation.

GUEST. We must say, therefore, that the principle of all motions, and which first subsists in things abiding and in motion, is that which moves itself; and that this is necessarily the most ancient and the most powerful mutation of all things: but that the second is that which is changed by another, and at the same time moves others.

CLIN. You speak most true.

GUEST. Since we have, therefore, arrived thus far in our discourse, let us also answer the following question.

c   CLIN. What is that?

GUEST. If we should see this first motion taking place in a terrene, aquatic, or fiery-formed body, whether simple or mixed, what passion should we say was inherent in a thing of this kind?

CLIN. Do you ask me, whether that which moves itself should be said to live?

GUEST. I do.

CLIN. Undoubtedly it should.

GUEST. But what? When we see soul inherent in any thing, do we admit that it lives through any thing else than this?

CLIN. Through nothing else.

d   GUEST. Consider then, by Jupiter, are you willing to understand three things respecting every thing?

CLIN. How do you say?

GUEST. One of these is essence, another the reason or definition of essence, and a third the name. And likewise the interrogations respecting every being are two.

CLIN. How two?

GUEST. Sometimes each of us, when a name is proposed, inquires the reason of the denomination; and sometimes, when the reason is proposed, we inquire after the name. Are you, therefore, willing that we should now speak of a thing of this kind?

CLIN. Of what kind?

e   GUEST. A twofold distinction is found in other things, and in number. Thus, for instance, in number, the name indeed is the even, but the definition is one number divided into two equal parts.

CLIN. Undoubtedly.

GUEST. My meaning is this. Do we signify the same thing in each, when, being asked concerning the name, we assign the reason, or, when, being asked the reason, we assign the name; since we denominate one and the same thing by name, even, but, by reason or definition, a number divided into two equal parts?

CLIN. Entirely so.

896a   GUEST. But what is the definition of that which is called soul? Have we any other than that which was just now mentioned by us, I mean a motion capable of moving itself?

CLIN. Do you say, that the being moved by itself is the definition of that essence which we all denominate soul?

GUEST. I do say so. But if this be the case, do we yet desire it should be more sufficiently shown, that soul is the same with the first generation and motion of things which now are, have been, and shall be; and, again, of all the contraries to these; since it appears that soul is the cause of all mutation and motion to all things?

CLIN. Certainly not. For it has been sufficiently shown, that soul is the most ancient of all things, and is the principle of motion.

GUEST. Will not, therefore, the motion which subsists through another in another, but which is never the cause of a thing moving itself, be the second in order? and ought it not to be placed after the former motion, by whatever interval of numbers any one may choose to assign, since it is truly the mutation of an inanimate body?

CLIN. Right.

GUEST. We have said, therefore, with rectitude, propriety, and in the most perfect manner, that soul was generated prior to body, but that body is posterior and secondary, soul naturally possessing dominion, and body subjection.

CLIN. With the greatest truth, therefore.

GUEST. But do we recollect, that it was acknowledged by us above, that if soul should appear to be more ancient than body, the things pertaining to soul would also be more ancient than those pertaining to body

CLIN. Entirely so.

GUEST. Disposition, therefore, manners, volitions, reasonings, true opinions, attention, and memory, must have been generated prior to the length, breadth,, depth, and strength of bodies, on account of the priority of soul to body.

CLIN. Necessarily so.

GUEST. Is it not, therefore, after this necessary to acknowledge, that soul is the cause of things good and beautiful, evil and base, just and unjust, and of all contraries, since we establish it to be the cause of all things?

CLIN. Undoubtedly.

GUEST. Is it not also necessary to assert, that soul, which governs all things, and which resides in all things that are in any respect moved, governs likewise the heavens?

CLIN. Certainly.

GUEST. But does one soul, or many, govern them?

MEGIL. Many: for I will answer for you.

276

GUEST. We should not, therefore, establish less than two, one beneficent, and the other of a contrary† nature.

CLIN. You speak with the utmost rectitude.

897a GUEST. Soul, therefore, by its motions, leads every thing in heaven, earth, and the sea; and the names of these motions are - to will, to consider, take care of, consult, form true and false opinions, rejoicing, grieving, daring, fearing, hating, loving; together with all such primary motions as are allied to these, and which, receiving the secondary motions of bodies, lead all things to increase and decay, separation and concretion, and to things consequent to these, such as heat and cold, gravity and levity, the hard and the soft, the white and the black, the sour, sweet, and bitter; and, lastly to all things which, soul employing,

b when it perpetually receives a divine intellect, as being in this case a goddess, disciplines all things with rectitude and felicity; but when it is conjoined with folly, it produces every thing contrary to these. Shall we admit that these things subsist in this manner, or shall we yet doubt whether they do not in a certain respect subsist differently?

CLIN. By no means.

GUEST. Whether, therefore, shall we say, that the genus of soul which is prudent, and full of virtue, governs heaven and earth, and the whole period of generated nature, or that which possesses neither of these? Are you wiling, therefore, that we should answer this question as follows?

c CLIN. How?

GUEST. Thus, O wonderful man. If the whole path of the heavens, and the local motion of all the natures it contains, possess a nature similar to the motion, circulation, and reasonings of intellect, and proceed in a manner allied to these, it must evidently be granted, that the most excellent soul takes care of the whole world, and leads it according to a path of this kind.

CLIN. Right.

d GUEST. But if it proceeded in a mad and disordered manner, it must be led by an evil soul.

CLIN. And this also is rightly asserted.

† Plato, by an evil soul, here means the nature or natural life suspended from the rational soul of the world, and which is the proximate *vis matrix* of bodies. As this life, without the governing influence of the rational soul of the world, would produce nothing but confusion and disorderly motions, it may be said, when considered as left to itself, to be evil.

GUEST. What nature, then, does the motion of intellect possess? To this question indeed, O friends, it is difficult to answer prudently. It is, therefore, just, that I should now answer for you.

CLIN. You speak well.

GUEST. Let us not, therefore, looking as it were to the sun in an opposite direction, and thus introducing night in midday, answer the present question, as if we could ever sufficiently behold and know intellect with mortal eyes: for, by looking to the image of the object of our interrogation, we shall see with greater security.

e CLIN. How do you say?

GUEST. Let us receive from among those ten motions, as an image, that to which intellect is similar. This motion I will recall into your memory, and answer for you in common.

CLIN. You speak in the most beautiful manner.

GUEST. We must remember, therefore, it was asserted by us above, that of all things that exist, some are moved, and others abide.

CLIN. It was so.

GUEST. But, of things which are moved, some are moved in one place, but others are borne along in more than one.

98a CLIN. They are so.

GUEST. But it is necessary that these motions, which are always borne along in one, should be moved about a certain middle, in imitation of circles fashioned by a wheel, and that they should be, in every respect, as much as possible allied and similar to the circulation of intellect.

CLIN. How do you say?

GUEST. That both of them are moved according to the same, in a similar manner, in the same, about the same, and towards the same, according to one reason and order. if, therefore, we should say that intellect, and the motion which is borne along in one, are similar to the local motions of a sphere fashioned by a wheel, we should not by any means be bad artificers in discourse of beautiful images.

CLIN. You speak with the utmost rectitude.

GUEST. The motion, therefore, which is never borne along in a similar manner, nor according to the same, nor in the same, nor about the same, nor towards the same, neither in ornament, nor in order, nor in one certain reason, will be allied to all folly.

CLIN. It will, with the greatest truth.

c GUEST. Now, therefore, it will be no longer difficult to assert openly, that since it is soul which leads all things in a circular† manner, it must necessarily follow that the circulation of the heavens must be led round, taken care of, and adorned, either by the most excellent soul, or the contrary.

CLIN. O guest, from what has been said, it is not holy to say otherwise than that either one soul, or many souls, possessing every virtue, cause the circulation of the heavens.

d GUEST. You understand my arguments, O Clinias, most excellently: but listen still further to this.

CLIN. To what?

GUEST. If soul convolves the sun, moon, and the other stars, is not each of these convolved by a soul‡ of its own?

CLIN. Undoubtedly.

GUEST. We shall, therefore, discourse about one soul, in such a manner, that what we say may be accommodated to all the stars.

CLIN. What soul is that?

GUEST. Every man perceives the body of the sun, but no one its soul; nor, indeed, does any one perceive the soul of any other body, either of

e a living or of a dead animal; but there is every reason to believe that this genus of things is naturally incapable of being seen by any of the corporeal senses, but is of an intelligible nature. Let us, therefore, by intellect alone, and the dianoëtic energy, apprehend this respecting it.

CLIN. what?

GUEST. If soul is the leader of the sun, we shall perhaps not err in asserting, that it accomplishes this by one of these three modes.

CLIN. What modes?

GUEST. That either, residing within this apparent circular body, it entirely rolls it along, in the same manner as our soul moves us, or that, in a certain respect being situated externally, and connecting itself with

899a a body of fire or air, according to the assertions of some, it violently impels body with body; or, in the third place, being itself destitute of body, it governs this visible orb through possessing certain other powers transcendently admirable.

---

† The reader must carefully remember that soul leads all things circularly, from its possession of a divine intellect; for Plato has just before shown, that a circular is an image of intellectual motion.

‡ Aristotle also, in the twelfth book of his *Metaphysics*, shows, that each of the heavenly bodies possesses a divine intellect, which is the source of its motions; to my Translation of which I refer the reader.

CLIN. Certainly.

GUEST. This then is necessary. - that all things should be governed by this soul, according to one of these modes. But whether this soul residing in the sun, as in a chariot, imparts light to all things, or whether it is situated externally, or in whatever other manner it may be connected with this visible orb, it is better that all men should consider it as a God. Or, how shall we say?

b   CLIN. *This must certainly be acknowledged by every one who has not arrived at the extremity of folly.*

GUEST. *But with respect to all the stars, and the moon, years, months, and the seasons, shall we speak in any other manner than this - That since a soul and souls, good from the possession of every virtue, appear to be the causes of all these, they should be called* GODS, *whether being resident in bodies, and thus becoming animals, they adorn all heaven, or in whatever other manner they may accomplish this? And, in the next place, can he who assents to these things deny that all things are full of* GODS?

c   CLIN. No one, O guest, is so *insane* as to deny this.

GUEST. Assigning, therefore, certain boundaries at present to him, O Clinias and Megillus, who does not believe that there are Gods, let us dismiss him.

CLIN. What boundaries do you mean?

GUEST. Either that he must teach us we do not speak rightly, in asserting that soul is the first generation of all things, together with such other particulars as are consequent to this; or, if he is incapable of

d   asserting any thing better than we have asserted, that he shall be persuaded by us, and live for the remainder of his life in the belief that there are Gods. Let us, therefore, now see whether we have spoken sufficiently or not, in our arguments that there are Gods, to those who deny their existence.

CLIN. Your arguments, O guest, are very far from being insufficient.

GUEST. Let this, then, be the conclusion of our discourse to these. But let us cure, in the following manner, him who believes that there are Gods, but that they take no care of human affairs. - O most excellent man! we shall say, because you think that there are Gods, a certain nature allied to Divinity leads you to honour, and believe in that which is connate with yourself; but the prosperous condition of evil and unjust men, both in private and public, who, though they are not truly

e   happy, yet are considered to be so in the highest degree in the inelegant opinion of the multitude, and are improperly celebrated as such in poetical, and a variety of other compositions; - this it is which leads you to impiety. Or, perhaps, on seeing impious men leaving behind them,

900a after having arrived at old age, grandchildren in the greatest honours, you are disturbed: Or from hearing, or perhaps being yourself an eye-witness, of some who, though they have acted in a most impious and dire manner, yet, by means of such actions, have arrived from slender possessions and small power to tyrannies and the greatest wealth. It is evident that, in all such cases as these, you are unwilling to blame the

b Gods as the causes of them, through your alliance with their nature, but, at the same time, being led by a certain privation of reason, and not being able to be indignant with the Gods, you have arrived at the present condition, so as to believe in their existence, but that they despise and neglect human affairs. That the present dogma, therefore, may not lead you to greater impiety, but that you may be removed further from it, we shall endeavour, to the utmost of our power, to convince you of its fallacy, conjoining the following discourse with the former, which we employed against those who entirely denied the existence of the Gods. But do you, O Megillus and Clinias, take upon

c you to answer for the young man, as you did before; and if any thing difficult should happen to take place in our discourse, I, taking hold of you as I just now did, will pass over the river.

CLIN. Rightly said. Do you, therefore, act in this manner; and we to the utmost of our power will do as you say.

GUEST. But, perhaps, it will not be difficult to evince that the Gods pay no less attention to small things than to such as transcend in magnitude. For it was just now asserted by us, that they are good from

d the possession of every virtue, and that, in consequence of this, a providential concern for all things is in the highest degree accommodated to their nature.

CLIN. This was vehemently asserted.

GUEST. Let us, therefore, in common investigate that which follows this, - I mean, what the virtue of the Gods is, since we acknowledge that they are good. Do we not then say, that to be temperate, and to possess intellect, are things pertaining to virtue, but the contraries of these to vice?

CLIN. We do say so.

e GUEST. But what? Does not fortitude belong to virtue, and timidity to vice?

CLIN. Entirely so.

GUEST. And do not we say that some of these are base, and others beautiful?

CLIN. It is necessary we should.

GUEST. And must we not say that such among these as are base belong to us, but that the Gods participate neither any thing great, nor any thing small, of such-like particulars?

CLIN. And this also every one will acknowledge.

GUEST. But what? Do we place negligence, indolence, and luxury, as belonging to the virtue of the soul? Or how do you say?

CLIN. How can we?

GUEST. As belonging, therefore, to the contrary?

CLIN. Yes.

901a GUEST. The contraries, therefore, to these belong to that which is contrary.

CLIN. To that which is contrary.

GUEST. What then? Will not he who possesses these contraries be considered by all of us as luxurious, negligent, and indolent, and, according to the poet,[†] similar to a drone bee, without a sting?

CLIN. The poet speaks with the utmost rectitude.

GUEST. It must not, therefore, be said, that Divinity possesses manners that are odious to him, nor must we permit any one to make such an assertion.

CLIN. By no means. For how can it be said?

b GUEST. But will he to whom it belongs in the most eminent degree to do and take care of any thing, will the intellect of such a one take care of great, but neglect small things? And shall we not in every respect err by praising such an assertion? But let us consider as follows: Will not he who acts in this manner, whether he is a God or a man, be influenced by two species of action?

CLIN. What are those two?

c GUEST. I will tell you: Either because he thinks the neglect of small things is of no consequence to the whole; or, if he thinks it is of consequence, yet he pays no attention to them, through indolence and luxury. Or is it possible that negligence can take place in any other way? For, when any one is incapable of taking care of all things, and, in consequence of this, neglects either such as are small, or such as are great, he is not in this case said to be negligent, whether it is a man or a God who is thus destitute of power.

CLIN. Undoubtedly not.

GUEST. But now let those two answer us three, who, though they

d both of them acknowledge there are Gods, yet one of them considers the divinities as easy to be appeased, but the other as neglecting small

---

† Hesiod Op. et Di. 303 et seq.

affairs. let us, therefore, thus address these in the first place: You both acknowledge that the Gods know, see, and hear all things, and that nothing which is either an object of sense or science can be concealed from them. Do you not say that this is the case? Or how do you say?

CLIN. That this is the case.

GUEST. But what? Are they not able to accomplish all things which both mortals and immortals are able to accomplish?

CLIN. How is it possible they should not acknowledge this?

e GUEST. We, that are five in number, also agree that the Gods are good and most excellent.

CLIN. Very much so.

GUEST. Must we not, therefore, acknowledge that it is impossible for them ever to act in an indolent and luxurious manner, since they are such as we have granted them to be? For, in us, indolence is the offspring of timidity, but sluggishness, of indolence and luxury.

CLIN. You speak most true.

GUEST. But the Gods cannot be negligent through indolence and sluggishness: for timidity is not present with them.

CLIN. You speak with the utmost rectitude.

902a GUEST. It remains, therefore, that if they neglect a few things, and such as are small in the universe, they must either do so because they know that things of this nature ought by no means to be taken care of, or because they are ignorant that they ought to be taken care of; for, can there be any other alternative?

CLIN. None.

GUEST. Whether, therefore, O most excellent and best of men, shall we consider you as saying that the Gods neglect these in consequence of being ignorant that they ought to be taken care of; or that, like the most depraved of men, they know that this is proper, but are prevented from acting agreeably to their knowledge, through being vanquished by certain pleasures or pains?

b

CLIN. But how could this be possible?

GUEST. Besides, human affairs participate of an animated nature, and at the same time man is the most religious of all animals.

CLIN. It appears to.

GUEST. We likewise say that all mortal animals are the possessions of the Gods, in the same manner as all heaven.

CLIN. Undoubtedly.

c GUEST. Whether, therefore, any one says, that these things are considered either as small or great by the Gods, it is not proper, since they are the most provident and best of beings, that they should neglect their possessions. But further still, in addition to these things, let us consider this.

CLIN. What?

GUEST. Respecting sense and power, whether they are not naturally contrary to each other, with reference to facility and difficulty.

CLIN. How do you say?

GUEST. Small things are seen and heard with greater difficulty than such as are large. But to carry, govern, and take care of a few things, and such as are small, is in every respect more easy than to carry, govern, and take care of the contraries to these.

d   CLIN. It is by far more easy.

GUEST. But since it is the province of a physician to take care of a certain whole, and he is both willing and able to do this, will this whole ever be in a good condition if he neglects parts, and such things as are small?

CLIN. By no means.

GUEST. But neither will things numerous and mighty ever be well conducted either by pilots, or commanders of an army, or certain political characters, or any others similar to these, without an attention

e   to things few and small. For builders say, that great stones cannot be well placed without small ones.

CLIN. For how can they?

GUEST. We ought not, therefore, to think that divinity is more vile than mortal artificers: for these, by how much the more skilful they are, by so much the more accurately and perfectly, from one art, do they accomplish things small and great pertaining to their peculiar works.

903a   Since this is the case, can it be supposed that divinity, who is most wise, and who is both willing and able to energize providentially, will alone take care of great things, but by no means of such as are small, which it is easy to take care of, like one indolent, or timid, or sluggish through labour?

CLIN. We can by no means admit this opinion, O guest, concerning the Gods; for this would be forming a conception neither holy nor true.

b   GUEST. It appears, therefore, to me, that we have now sufficiently spoken to him who accuses the Gods of negligence.

CLIN. Certainly.

GUEST. But we have hitherto forced him by our arguments to change his opinion.

CLIN. Right.

GUEST. It appears, however, to me that he yet requires to be enchanted by certain words.

CLIN. What words, O good man?

GUEST. We should persuade the young man, that he who takes care of the whole has constituted all things with a view to the safety and virtue of the whole, every part of which, as much as possible, suffers and acts in a manner accommodated to its nature; that over each of these parts rulers are placed, who always cause that which is smallest in every action and passion to receive its ultimate distribution; among which

c parts, O miserable creature, thou art one, and which, though *diminutive in the extreme,* continually directs its views to *The All.* But you are ignorant that every generated nature subsists for the sake of the whole, that the universe may enjoy a blessed life, and not for your sake, but that you subsist for the sake of the universe. For every physician, and every artificial fabricator, effects all things for the sake of the whole, and regards that which is best in common; fashioning a part for the sake of

d the whole, and not the whole for the sake of a part. You, however, are indignant, in consequence of not knowing how that which is best with respect to yourself happens both to the universe and yourself, according to the power of common generation. But since a soul which is connected at different times with different bodies undergoes all-various mutations, either through itself, or through some other soul, nothing else remains to be done by the *dice-player* than to transfer manners when they become better, into a better place, but, when they become worse, into a worse place, according to the proper condition of each, that they may obtain convenient allotments.

e CLIN. How do you say?

GUEST. I appear to myself to speak with reference to the facility with which the Gods take care of all things. For if any one, always looking to the whole, fashions any thing, and transforms all things, with a view

904a to this, such as animated water from fire, and not many things from one, or one thing from many, participating of a first, second, or third generation, there will be an infinite multitude of transposed ornaments. But now there is an admirable facility in the power that provides for the universe.

CLIN. How, again, do you say?

GUEST. Thus. Since our king beholds all our actions, and these are animated, containing much virtue and much vice, and since both soul and body are generated indestructible,† though not eternal, like the gods

---

† Body, when corrupted, is resolved into the elementary wholes from which it originated, but is never destroyed.

b   according to *law*,[†] (for there never would be any generation of animals if either soul or body was destroyed,) and besides, since that which is good in the soul is always naturally disposed to assist, but that which is evil in it to injure, - our king, perceiving all these things, devised in what manner each of the parts should be situated, so that virtue might vanquish in the universe, but vice be subdued, in the most eminent degree, and in the best and most facile manner. He devised, therefore, how each particular should be generated with reference to the universe,

c   what seat it should reside in, and what places it should be allotted: but he left to our will the causes of this or that generation. For where the desire of any soul is, and such as is its condition, there each of us nearly resides, and such for the most part each of us subsists.

CLIN. It is likely.

GUEST. Every thing, therefore, that participates of soul is changed, and possesses in itself the cause of this mutation; but, when changed, it is borne along according to the order and law of fate. And those souls whose manners are less changed, have a less extended progression; for they proceed no further than the superficies of the region. But those

d   whose manners are more changed, and are more unjust, fall into depth, and into the places beneath, which are denominated Hades, and the like, where they are vehemently terrified, and conversant with dreams, both living and when freed from body. A greater soul, however, when it participates either of virtue or vice, becoming in this case strong, through its own will, and converse with other natures, if, mingling with

e   divine virtue, it becomes eminently divine, then it is translated into another better place, which is entirely holy: but if it mingles itself with the contrary to divine virtue, then its life is transferred into a contrary place. This then, O boy and young man, who think that you are neglected by the Gods, is the judgment of the Olympian divinities; - that he who is more depraved shall depart to more depraved souls, but he who is better, to such as are better, both in life, and in all deaths, and that he shall both suffer and do such things as ought to be done by similars to similars. But neither you nor any other should pray that you

905a may be exempt from this judgment of the Gods. For those who ordained this established is more firmly than all judgments, and as that which ought to be venerated in every respect. Indeed, you will never be neglected by this judgment; not though you were so small, that you

---

[†] *Law* here signifies intellectual distribution. So that the Gods according to *law* are those divine natures which proceed from the intellect of the fabricator of the universe. These Gods are thus denominated in the Golden Verses of Pythagoras.

could descend into the profundities of the earth, or so elevated, that you could fly into heaven. But you will suffer from these divinities the punishment which is your due, whether you abide here, or depart to

b Hades, or whether you are removed to a place still more rustic than these. My discourse to you, likewise, will be the same respecting those impious men whom you have seen rising into consequence from small beginnings, and whom you have considered as having passed from felicity to misery. For it has appeared to you that, in the actions of these, as in a mirror, the negligence of all the Gods was visible; and this, from your being ignorant in what manner the end of such characters contributes to the good of the whole. But can you think, O most

c courageous of all men, that it is not necessary to know this, which he who is ignorant of, will neither be able to perceive, nor discourse about, the felicity of life, and an unhappy fortune. If, therefore, Clinias, and the whole of this aged company, are able to persuade you that you do not know what you say respecting the Gods, divinity will assist you in a beautiful manner; but if you still require some further reason, hear, if in any respect you possess intellect, what we shall say to our third antagonist. For, that there are Gods, and that they take care of men, I

d should say, has been not altogether badly demonstrated. But that the Gods can be moved by the gifts of certain unjust men, must not be granted to any one, but confuted in every possible way to the utmost of our power.

CLIN. You speak most beautifully; and we shall do as you say.

GUEST. Come, then, by the Gods themselves, if they are moved by

e gifts, in what manner are they moved; and what kind of beings must they in this case be? For it is necessary that they must possess sovereign authority who continually govern all heaven.

CLIN. Certainly.

GUEST. But to what rulers are they similar, or what rulers are similar to them, that we may be able to compare small things with great? Whether will the charioteers of two-yoked cars that contend in the course be such as these, or the pilots of ships? Perhaps, however, they

906a may be assimilated to certain commanders of armies, or to physicians, who are cautious respecting the war of diseases about bodies, or to husbandmen, who fear for their plants during the stormy seasons, or to shepherds and herdsmen. For, since we have granted that the universe is full of much good, and much evil, though not of more evil than good, we say that a thing of this kind is an immortal war, and requires an admirable defence. But the Gods, and, at the same time, dæmons, fight for us; and we are the possession both of Gods and dæmons. Injustice b and insolence, however, together with imprudence, corrupt us. And, on the contrary, justice and temperance, in conjunction with prudence, which reside in the animated powers of the Gods, preserve us. But that something of these resides in us, though for a short time, may be clearly seen from this; for certain souls residing on the earth, and possessing an unjust gift, are evidently savage towards the souls of guardians, whether

c they are dogs, or shepherds, or in every respect the highest of all rulers. These they attack, persuading them by flattering words and specious enchantments, (according to the rumours of the wicked,) that it is lawful for them to usurp an unjust authority among men, without any disagreeable consequences to themselves. This fault, which we denominate prerogative, is called, in fleshly bodies, disease; in the seasons of the year, pestilence; and in cities and polities, by changing the word, injustice.

CLIN. Entirely so.

GUEST. According to this reasoning, therefore, it is necessary to say,
d that he who asserts that the Gods always pardon unjust men, when a part of their unjust acquisitions is offered to them, asserts at the same time that they are like dogs, to whom wolves give a small portion of their rapine, and who, becoming mild by gifts, permit them to plunder the herds. Is not this the assertion of those who consider the Gods as easily appeased?

CLIN. It is.

GUEST. But will not he be the most ridiculous of all men, who assimilates the Gods to any of the above-mentioned guardians? Shall we
e say, therefore, that they resemble pilots, who giving themselves up to the libation of wine, and the odour of flesh, destroy both the ships and the sailors?

CLIN. By no means.

GUEST. But neither do they resemble charioteers, who, when orderly arranged in the course, through being corrupted by gifts, yield the victory to the two-yoked cars of their opponents.

CLIN. For such an assertion produces a dire image.

GUEST. But neither do they resemble the commanders of an army, nor physicians, nor husbandmen, nor shepherds, nor certain dogs seduced by wolves.

CLIN. Prophesy better things. For how is it possible they can resemble any of these?

907a GUEST. But are not all the Gods the greatest of all guardians, and guardians of the greatest affairs?

CLIN. Very much so.

GUEST. Shall we say, then, that those who are the guardians of the most beautiful things, and who, as guardians, are transcendent in virtue, are worse than dogs, and men of a moderate character, who never betray justice by receiving in an unholy manner gifts from unjust men?

b   CLIN. By no means; for such an assertion is not to be borne. And he who entertains such an opinion may most justly be considered as the worst and most impious of men.

GUEST. We may say, then, that we have sufficiently demonstrated the three things which we proposed to evince, *viz.* that there are Gods; that they take care of all things; and that they are not in any respect to be moved by gifts, contrary to what is just.

CLIN. Undoubtedly; and we assent to these reasons.

c   GUEST. And besides this, in a certain respect we have spoken more vehemently, through the contention of vicious men. But, O friend Clinias, we have employed a discourse of a contentious nature, lest our adversaries, thinking that they have vanquished, should imagine they had a license to do whatever they pleased, conformably to their conceptions respecting the Gods. Through an earnest desire of preventing this, we have spoken in a more novel manner. But if, during this short time, we have offered any thing calculated to persuade these men that they should hate themselves, and embrace contrary manners, the exordium of our laws respecting impiety will have been beautifully delivered.

d   CLIN. Let us hope that this will be the case; but if it should not, the legislator is not to be accused for this kind of discourse.

GUEST. After the preface, therefore, the discourse which is the interpreter of the laws will properly follow, proclaiming to all impious persons, that they must depart from their depraved manners, and betake themselves to such as are pious. But for those who will not be persuaded by these arguments, let the following law of impiety be established: - If any one speaks or acts impiously, let any one who is present defend the cause of piety, and give information to the magistrates of the affair: and those magistrates that are first made acquainted with it, shall bring the offender before the court of justice appointed by law for the determination of such cases. But if any magistrate, on hearing the affair, does not act in this manner, let him be accused of impiety by any one who is willing to punish him, for the sake of the laws. And if any one is condemned, let the court of justice punish him for the several impieties he has committed. Let bonds, then,

908a be the punishment of all impious conduct. And let there be three prisons in the city: one common for most crimes about the forum, for the sake of securing a multitude of persons; another situated about the place where a nocturnal assembly is held, and which is to be denominated the prison for the correction of manners; and a third in the middle of the region, and in that part which is most solitary and rustic, calling it by the name of the prison of punishment. With respect to

b impiety, there are three causes of it, as we have already mentioned; and since two things take place from each of such-like causes, there will be six genera of crimes against the Gods, which require neither an equal nor a similar punishment. For some, who though they do not in any respect believe there are Gods, yet, from naturally possessing a just disposition, hate the vicious, and, through being indignant with injustice,

c neither commit unjust actions themselves, nor associate with, but avoid, unjust men, and love the just. But others, besides the opinion that all things are destitute of the Gods, fall into incontinence of pleasures and pains, at the same time possessing strong memories and acuteness with respect to disciplines. The opinion that there are no Gods, is a passion common to both these; but they differ in this, that the one is the cause of less, and the other of more, evil than other men. The one of these

d speaks with the greatest freedom concerning the Gods, sacrifices and oaths; and, as he ridicules others, will perhaps render others like himself, unless he is punished. But the other who is of the same opinion, is considered by the vulgar as ingenious, and is full of fraud and stratagem. From these characters many diviners are produced, and such as are excited to every kind of incantation. Sometimes, too, from these tyrants, public speakers, and commanders of armies, are formed; and those who in their private mysteries act insidiously, and deceive men by

e sophistical devices. Of these, indeed, there are many species; but two of them deserve the establishment of laws: of which the ironic produces crimes that deserve more than one or two deaths; but the other requires admonition and bonds. In a similar manner, too, the opinion that the Gods are negligent, produces two characters; and the opinion that they are easily appeased, another two. Since, therefore, the impious are thus distinguished, those who become such through folly, without a vicious disposition and corrupt manners, the judge shall confine in the prison

909a for correction, for not less than five years. But, during this time, let no one of the citizens converse with them, except those that participate of the nocturnal assembly, who associate for the purpose of admonishing and procuring safety to the soul. When the period arrives that they are to be liberated from their bonds, if any one among them shall appear to be more modest in his manners, let him dwell together with the modest; but if it appears that he is not, and he is again condemned for the same

b crime, let him be punished with death. With respect to such as, in addition to their believing that there are no Gods, or that they are negligent, or easily appeased, are of a savage disposition, despising mankind, alluring the souls of many while living, and asserting that they can allure the souls of the dead; likewise, pretending that they can persuade the Gods by sacrifices, prayers, and incantations, and endeavouring by these means to destroy private persons, whole families, and cities, for the sake of their riches, - among such as these, whoever shall be condemned, let him be fettered in the prison which is in the

c middle of the region, and let no free-born person be ever allowed to visit him, but let the food appointed for him by the guardians of the laws be brought to him by servants. But, when he dies, let him be hurled beyond the boundaries of the region, and left without a tomb. And, if any free-born person shall bury him, let him sustain the punishment of

d impiety by any one who is willing to inflict it. If he leaves behind him children sufficient for the purposes of the city, let the guardians of orphans take no less care of these than of others, and from the very day on which their father was condemned. But it is proper that a common law should be established for all these, which may cause the multitude to behave less impiously towards the Gods, both in word and deed, and may render them less void of intellect, through not permitting them to make innovations in sacred concerns. Let the following law, then, be simply established for all of them; - No one shall have a temple in any private house. But when any one intends to sacrifice, let him go to public buildings raised for this purpose, and present his offerings to those priests and priestesses who take care of these particulars in a pure and holy manner. Here let him pray, together with these, and any other who is willing to join him in prayer. Let these things be adopted, because it is not easy to establish temples and statues of the Gods; but to effect a thing of this kind properly, is the work of a mighty dianoëtic power. But it is usual, with women particularly, and all such as are imbecile, or in danger, or want, or, on the contrary, when they receive an abundance of any thing, always to consecrate that which is present,

910a vow sacrifices, and promise statues to the Gods, dæmons, and the sons of the Gods; being terrified by spectres when awake, and, in a similar manner, recollecting many visions in dreams; for all which they endeavour to obtain remedies, and for this purpose fill all the pure places in houses and streets with altars and temples. For the sake of all these particulars, it is requisite that the law we have just mentioned

b should be established; and besides this, for the sake of the impious, lest they, fraudulently usurping these in their actions, and raising temples and altars in private houses, should think to make the Gods propitious by sacrifices and prayers; thus infinitely increasing their injustice, and provoking the indignation of the Gods, both against themselves, and those that permitted them to act in this manner, though men of a better character. For by this means the whole city becomes subject to the punishment of impiety, and, in a certain respect, justly. Divinity, indeed, does not blame the legislator; for the law established by him says, that no one shall possess temples of the Gods in private houses. But if it shall appear that any one possesses temples, and performs orgies in any other places than such as are public, he who detects him shall announce the affair to the guardians of the laws. And if such a one, whether a man or a woman, shall be found not to have committed any great or impious crimes, he shall be obliged to carry his private sacred concerns to public temples: and if he does not immediately comply with the law, let him be fined till he does. But, if any one acting impiously shall appear to have committed, not the impious deed of boys, but of impious men, whether by sacrificing to the Gods in private or in public temples, let him be condemned to death, as one who has sacrificed impurely. However, the guardians of the laws must judge whether his impiety is puerile or not, and thus, when he is brought before a court of justice, must inflict on him the punishment of impiety.

BOOK XI

913a It now remains that we should speak of mutual compacts, and the order which they ought to receive. But a thing of this kind is, in a certain respect, simple. I mean, that no one shall touch my property, nor move the least thing belonging to me, without my consent. And I, if I am endued with a sound mind, shall act in the same manner with respect to the property of others. In the first place, then, we shall speak about such treasures, as some one may deposit both for himself and

b those belonging to him, who is not descended from my parents, and which I should never pray that I might find, nor, if I did find, should move, nor be induced to partake of, by those who are called diviners. For I should never be so much benefited by the possession of riches, when obtained after this manner, as I should excel in the virtue of the soul, and in justice, by not receiving them. For thus I should acquire one possession instead of another, a better in that which is better; preferring the prior possession of justice in the soul, to wealth. For it is well said of many particulars, that things immovable should not be

c moved; and it may be said of this, as being one of them. It is likewise proper to be persuaded by what is commonly asserted about these things, that such particulars do not contribute to the procreation of children. But he who takes no care of children, and neglects the legislator, and, therefore, takes away that which neither he nor his grandfather deposited, such a one corrupts the most beautiful and simple law, which was established by a man by no means ignoble, and which says, You shall not take away that which you have not deposited. What then ought he to suffer, who despises these two legislators, and who

d takes away that which he did not himself deposit, and which is not a small affair, but a mighty treasure? Divinity, indeed, knows what punishment he ought to suffer from the Gods. But let us declare what he ought to suffer from men. Let him who first perceives him, give information of the affair:- if it happens in the city, to the ædiles; if in the forum, to the præfects of the markets; and, if in any other part of

914a the region, to those that take care of the land, and the governors of these. When the affair becomes apparent, let the city send to Delphi, and let what the God determines, both respecting the money and him that has moved it, be performed by the city conformable to the oracle. And if he who gives the information is free-born, let him be considered as a virtuous character; but, if he does not give information, as a vicious character. If he who reveals the affair is a slave, it will be proper that he should be made free by the city, and that the city should pay his master the price of his manumission; but, if he does not reveal it, let him be punished with death. Let a similar law follow this, respecting things small and great. If a man leaves any property, whether willingly or unwillingly, let him who may happen to meet with it suffer it to remain; considering that the dæmon who presides over roads defends things of this kind, which are dedicated to Divinity by law. When any one, being unpersuaded by this law, takes away such property to his own house, if he is but of little worth, being a slave, let him receive many lashes with a whip, from any one not less than thirty years of age who may happen to meet him. But, if he is free-born, besides being considered as illiberal, and void of law, let him pay as a fine ten times the worth of what he took away to its proper owner. When any one accuses another of holding his property, whether it be much or little, and the person who detains it acknowledges that it is in his possession, but denies that it is his who demands it, - if a written account of the affair is given to the magistrates according to law, he who detains it shall be called before a magistrate, and if it shall appear to be the property of the accuser, it shall be restored to him. But if it shall be found to belong to neither, but to some absent person, if its possessor will not engage to restore it to the absent person, let him be compelled to deposit it. If a written account of the affair is not given to the magistrates, let the property be deposited with the three oldest magistrates till sentence is passed. And, if the subject of dispute is an animal, let him who upon trial is cast, pay the magistrates the expense of its keeping; but let the affair be decided by the magistrates within the space of three days. If any one leads away another as a slave, who is going to be manumitted, let him who leads him be dismissed; but he who is thus led away, if he can procure three respectable bondsmen, shall be considered as free; but otherwise not. But if any one is led away in any other manner, let him by whom he is thus led be obnoxious to the charge of using violence, and be condemned to restore double the loss to the person led away. Every one, too, may be permitted to lead away his free-man, if he is not served by him, or not sufficiently. The attention, however, which such a one ought to pay his master consists, in the first place, in going thrice every month to his master's house, and announcing that he is prepared to do whatever is just, and in his power; and, in the second place, that he may perform, with respect to matrimony, whatever shall appear requisite to his master. But it shall not be lawful for him to possess greater wealth than the person by whom he was liberated: but, if he b does possess more, let the excess be given to his master. Let a freed person not remain in the city more than twenty years, but, in the same manner as strangers, let him after this period depart, taking with him the whole of his property, unless he can persuade the magistrates and his liberator to the contrary. But if the possessions of a freed person, or of any other stranger, exceed those of the third estate, let him, on the thirtieth day after this has been discovered to be the case, take his property and depart; and let him not, though he should request it, be

c permitted by the magistrates to stay any longer. Let him who disobeys this law be brought before a court of justice; when condemned, be punished with death; and let his riches become public property. Let the judges of the tribes take cognizance of these cases, unless the litigants have previously settled the affair among themselves by means of their neighbours or arbitrators. If any one asserts that a certain animal, or any thing else, is his own property, let him who possesses it take it

d either to the seller, or to him who properly and justly gave it, or who after some other manner delivered it of his own authority. And let it remain with a citizen, or an inhabitant of the city, for thirty days, but with a stranger for five months, so that the middle of these may be that month in which the sun is turned from the summer to the winter tropic. Let whatever one person changes with another through buying or selling, be exchanged in a place appointed for each in the forum, and

e let every thing pertaining to buying and selling be transacted in this place, and no where else. Likewise, let there be no delay either in buying or selling. But, if the commutation is made in other places, let no judgment according to law be passed upon it. With respect to feasts, in which every man pays him own share, if any difference should arise in settling the payment of the shares, let the parties so transact with each other as about a thing which is not noticed by the courts of justice. Let

916a a seller, who receives no less than fifty drachms as the price of his commodity, be obliged to wait ten days in the city, and let the buyer know the place of his abode; and this for the sake of those complaints and legitimate abatements which usually happen about things of this kind. But let lawful and unlawful abatements take place as follows: When any one sells a slave who labours under a consumption, or the stone, or the strangury, or that which is called the sacred disease, or any other disease which is immanifest to many, is of long continuance and difficult to cure, whether of the body or mind, if a physician or a master of gymnastic buys him, no abatement shall be made; nor yet when the

b seller informs the buyer of the true condition of the article of sale. But if an artist sells to an ignorant person any thing of this kind, the buyer shall be permitted to return the person bought by him, who labours under any disease but the sacred, within six months: but if he labours under this disease, he shall be permitted to return him within a year. Affairs of this kind shall be decided by physicians chosen by the common consent of the litigants. He who in these cases is condemned, shall pay to the buyer double the price for which he sold him. But if c one ignorant person sells any thing to another, let the return and judgment be made in the same manner as was mentioned above; and let him who is condemned pay a simple fine. If any one sells a homicide to another, if the transaction takes place between two skilful persons, let no return be made; but if between a skilful and ignorant person, let a return then be made when the buyer perceives the case. But let the affair be decided by the five youngest guardians of the laws. If it shall appear that the seller was not ignorant that the person he sold was a homicide, let the house of the buyer be purified according to the law of the interpreters, and let the seller pay him triple the price of the d homicide. Let him who changes money for money, or for animals, or any thing else, give and receive every thing unadulterated, agreeably to the injunctions of law. About the whole of this vice, however, it is requisite to lay down a preface, in the same manner as in other laws. e Every man, indeed, ought to consider adulteration, lying, and deception, as forming one genus, about which it is usual for the multitude to say, though very erroneously, that when each of these is opportunely adopted, the result is frequently proper. But as they leave the occasion, the where, and the when, disorderly and indefinitely, they often by this assertion both injure themselves and others. The legislator, however, should not suffer this indefinite to be unnoticed, but greater or lesser boundaries ought always to be clearly determined. Let them, therefore, 917a now be determined. Let no one tell a lie, or deceive, or adulterate any thing, calling at the same time on the Gods, unless he is desirous of becoming odious to Divinity. This, however, will be the case with him, in the first place, who, swearing falsely, despises the Gods; and, in the second place, with him who speaks falsely before those that are better than himself. But the good are more excellent than the bad, and, in short, the elder than the younger. On this account, parents are better than their offspring, men than women and children, and governors than b the governed. All these ought to be reverenced in every government, and especially in political governments, for the sake of which we have engaged in the present discussion. For he who adulterates any thing in the forum, lies and deceives, and, calling on the Gods, swears falsely before the guardians of the forum, and violates their laws, neither fearing men, nor reverencing the Gods. To be careful, indeed, not to contaminate the names of the Gods, is in every respect beautiful; for they ought not to be used in common like other names, but every thing pertaining to the Gods should be preserved in a pure and holy manner. Let the following law, therefore, be established for those who will not be persuaded to act in this manner: - He who sells any thing in the forum shall not be suffered to fix two prices to any article; but when he

c has fixed a simple price, if he does not sell it, he shall take it away, and be allowed to bring it back again on the same day, without valuing it at a higher price than before. Let praise, and taking an oath, never be employed in selling. And if any one is disobedient to this law, any citizen, not less than thirty years of age, who detects him in swearing, shall strike him with impunity; and if he neglects to do this, let him be considered as a betrayer of the laws. But let him who detects any one

d selling an adulterated article, and incapable of being persuaded by what we have now said, expose the fraud of such a one, if he is able, before a magistrate; and let a slave, or an inhabitant, bring with him the adulterated article. Let a citizen, who neglects to accuse such a one, be pronounced a bad man, as one who defrauds the Gods: but, if he accuses him, let him dedicate the adulterated article to the Gods who preside

e over the forum. Let him who openly sells things of this kind, besides being deprived of the adulterated article, receive publicly as many lashes with a whip as there are drachms in the sum for which he sold the article; a cryer at the same time proclaiming in the forum the cause of his being whipped. Let the præfects of the markets, and the guardians of the laws, endeavour to detect all the adulterations and evil practices of the sellers, by making inquiry of men skilled in vendible articles, and cause to be written on a pillar before the forum what a seller ought to do, and what not, so that men of this kind may clearly know how to act according to law in disposing of their respective articles. As to the particulars relating to the ædiles, we have spoken of these sufficiently

918a above. But if it should appear that any thing is wanting to these, let them supply the deficiency by communicating with the guardians of the laws, and afterwards let them write their first and second legal institutions on a pillar.

After adulteration it follows that we should speak of cauponation.[†] But about the whole of this we shall first of all give our advice, and the reasons for such advice, and afterwards establish a law respecting it. For

b all cauponation in a city does not subsist for the sake of injuring the

---

[†] The keeping an inn or victualling-house.

city, but naturally for the sake of the contrary. For how is it possible that he should not benefit the city who causes money, from being possessed in an incommensurate and anomalous manner, to be possessed equably, and with commensuration? It is requisite to say, that the power of money, the merchant, the mercenary character, and the inn-keeper, will accomplish this for us. For these, and others of this kind, whether they act in a more becoming or a more base manner, endeavour to supply the indigence of others, and render possessions equal. But let us consider the reason why this appears neither beautiful nor becoming, and why it is calumniated; that though we may not procure a remedy for the whole by law, yet we may for a part.

CLIN. This affair, as it appears, is of no trifling nature, and requires no small degree of virtue.

GUEST. How do you say, O friend Clinias? A small part of mankind naturally, and who are educated in the best manner, are able, when they are in want, or influenced by the desire of certain things, to conduct themselves with moderation, and, when they have it in their power to acquire great wealth, behave soberly, and prefer moderation to excess. But the vulgar conduct themselves in a manner perfectly contrary to these. For they desire without measure; and when it is permitted them to become moderately, they choose to become immensely rich. On this account, all such as are conversant with cauponation and merchandize are calumniated, and subject to shameful disgrace. For, if any one (which never did take place, nor ever will) should compel (though indeed it is ridiculous to mention it) the best of men to keep an inn for a certain time, or victualling-house, or do any thing of this kind; or if certain most excellent women, through the necessity of fate, should engage in such employments, we should know that they were honest and laudable, and that, when they are conducted according to uncorrupt reason, all such characters as these should be honoured as sustaining the part of mothers and nurses. But now, since inns and victualling-houses are raised in solitary places, and at a great distance from cities, they serve as places of shelter for those that are caught in a storm, and afford a cool retreat to those that are oppressed with heat. They do not, however, dismiss those that take refuge in them like friends, with hospitable gifts, but cruelly compel them to ransom themselves, as if they were enemies and captives, and plunder them of all their possessions. These, and other base actions of this kind, subject those employments to calumny which are calculated to assist the indigent. A legislator, therefore, ought always to devise a remedy for these. For it is a true and ancient saying, that it is difficult to fight against two things, as is evident in diseases, and many other particulars. And in the present case, indeed, there is an opposition against two things, poverty and riches; the latter of which

c corrupt the soul of men through luxury, and the former leads them through pain to impudence. What remedy, therefore, can be devised for this disease in a polity endued with intellect? In the first place, we must endeavour to the utmost, that it may use cauponation in the smallest degree; and, in the next place, we must assign cauponation to those men whose manners, when corrupt, will be no great pest to the city; and, in the third place, some method must be devised by which the souls of these men may not easily be filled with impudence and illiberality. But,

d after what has now been said, a certain law respecting these things presents itself to us, with good fortune. The city of the Magnesians, which Divinity first raised, is by Divinity again inhabited. Among these there is a law, that no husbandmen who belong to the forty-five thousand houses shall either voluntarily or involuntarily be an inn-keeper or a merchant, or act in the capacity of a servant to any private person, unless that person becomes in his turn a servant to him; a father

e and mother, with their progenitors, all his elders, and such as being free live in an independent manner, being excepted. It is not, however, easy to determine by law who is free, or the contrary; yet such as these are distinguished from the nobles by the hatred and love which they bear towards them. But let him who through a certain art is engaged in illiberal cauponation be accused before those who hold the first rank in virtue, by any one that is willing, as a disgrace to his family. And if it

920a shall appear that he has defiled his paternal house by any unworthy employment, let him, after having been fettered for a year, abstain from such employment. If, after this, he engages in it again, let him be fettered for two years. And let him always be confined in bonds as often as he is detected, twice as long as the preceding time. But a second law orders that all such as are not citizens, together with foreigners, shall exercise cauponation. And a third law ordains, that the foreigner or inhabitant who engages in this art, shall either be a most excellent character, or vicious in the smallest degree. It is proper, likewise, that the guardians of the law should consider that they are not only guardians of those who are easily prevented from acting in an illegal and

b vicious manner, viz. those who are well-born and educated; but that they are much more guardians of those who are different from these, and who engage in employments by which they are strongly impelled to improbity. Since, however, cauponation is abundantly various, the guardians of the laws should assemble together with those that are skilled in the several species of it; and, as we observed a little before concerning adulteration, which is allied to this art, they should, in the first place, establish such things as appear necessary to the city. Afterwards, having inquired into the cost and emolument attending this art, they should attend to the moderate gain resulting from it, and establish its expenses and emoluments. And some particulars should be attended to by the præfects of the markets, others by the ædiles, and others by the præfects of the land. After this manner nearly will cauponation be advantageous to every one, and injure those by whom it is exercised in the city in the smallest degree. The genus of artificers is sacred to Vulcan and Minerva, who furnish our lives by their arts. But those individuals are sacred to Mars and Minerva who preserve the works of artificers by other arts of an assistant and defensive nature. The genus of these is, indeed, justly sacred to these Gods: and all these providentially take care of the region and people. Some of them, too, preside over warlike contests; but others effect the generation of instruments, and works for hire. Reverencing, therefore, the Gods that are the authors of these arts, it will not be proper to deceive them, by lying about things of this kind. If any artificer does not complete his work in a prefixed time, through a vicious disposition, but, paying no reverence to the divinity who is the giver of life, through a blindness of intellect, thinks that his kindred God will pardon him, such a one, in the first place, will be punished by the God himself; and, in the second place, let it be established by law, that he shall be fined the worth of the work which he has not finished in the proper time, and that, beginning again, he shall complete it in the time first agreed upon. Let the same law too consult for the artificer as for the seller of vendible articles. Let care be taken, therefore, that he does not ask more than the worth of his work, but let his demand be most simple, and accommodated to its worth. For an artist knows the worth of his work. In cities, therefore, consisting of free men, it is not proper that an artist should endeavour to deceive the simple by art, which is naturally clear and void of falsehood. Hence, when this is the case, the injurer shall make a proper recompense to the injured person. If any one, in paying an artist for his work, does not pay him according to the agreement, despising Jupiter the guardian of the city, and Minerva who communicates with the polity, and, being influenced by a little gain, dissolves mighty communions; in this case, let the law assist the union of the city, in conjunction with the Gods. Let him, therefore, who, having ordered a work to be executed for him, does not pay for it in the appointed time, be fined double the price agreed upon. And let judgment be passed on things of this kind in the courts of justice belonging to the tribes. As we have, however, made mention of artificers, and as commanders of armies and military arts are artificers of safety to a city, it is but just that we should also speak of these. If, therefore, any one of these undertakes any public work, whether voluntarily or from command, and executes it in a becoming manner, let the law confer upon him the honour of unceasing praise, which is the reward of warlike men. But the law may be justly blamed which does not reward him who conducts himself well in military affairs. Let the following law, therefore, be established for these, mingled with praise, and which does not compel, but consults the multitude of the citizens: that such good men shall be honoured in the second place, as have been saviours of the whole city, whether by their valour, or by warlike devices; for the first honour must be given to those who have been remarkably obedient to the written laws of good legislators. We have, therefore, now nearly spoken sufficiently of the greatest compacts among men, except those pertaining to orphans, and the guardians of orphans. It is, therefore, necessary in the next place to speak of these. The beginning of all these is the desire of the testator, and the fortune of those that make no will. I have said it is necessary to speak of these, O Clinias, in consequence of looking to the difficulty respecting them: for it is not possible to leave them in a disordered manner. For testators would desire many things differing from each other, and contrary to the laws, to the manners of the living, and to their ancestors, if any one should simply give them permission to make their wills in whatever manner they pleased, and should ordain, that every will made near the end of life shall be properly executed. For most men, when they consider themselves as about to die, are affected with stupidity and remissness.

CLIN. What induces you to say this, O guest?

GUEST. A man when about to die, O Clinias, is morose, and is full of such language as is terrible to legislators, and difficult for them to endure.

CLIN. How so?

GUEST. Desiring to be the lord of all things, it is usual for him to speak with anger.

CLIN. What does he say at this time?

GUEST. It is a dire thing, says he, O Gods, if it is not permitted me to leave my property in whatever manner I please, and to bequeath some more, and others less, according as they were evidently well or ill affected towards me in my diseases, in my old age, and in other all-various fortunes.

CLIN. Does he not therefore, O guest, appear to you to speak well?

GUEST. Ancient legislators, O Clinias, appear to me to have been effeminate, and to have looked to a trifling part of human affairs in the establishment of laws.

CLIN. How do you say?

GUEST. That, being terrified at this language of the dying man, they made a law, that every one should be permitted to make his will as he pleased. But both you and I could answer the dying in your city in a more elegant manner.

CLIN. How?

GUEST. O friends, (we should say) who have but a short time to live, it is difficult for you to know your affairs, and likewise to know yourselves, according to the inscription of the Delphic temple. I, therefore, being a legislator, consider that neither yourselves, nor these possessions, are your own, but that they belong to the whole of your race, both past and to come, and that both the whole of your race and possessions, by a much greater priority, belong to the city. This being the case, if any one, through flattery, either when you are diseased, or in your old age, should persuade you to make your will in an improper manner, I should not admit such a will to be voluntarily made. But, looking to that which is best both for the whole city, and the whole of your race, I shall establish laws in such a manner as that the advantage of individuals may give way, as it is fit it should, to that of the public. Do you, therefore, be mild and benevolent towards us, as human nature requires you should. It will be our part to take care to the utmost of our power of every thing belonging to you, and not in a partial manner, by neglecting some things and attending to others. Let this then, O Clinias, be the consolation which we address in a prefatory manner to the living and the dead. But let the law be as follows: Let him who makes a will, and has children, in the first place appoint that child his heir whom he thinks most deserving. And, in the next place, let him signify which of his children he chooses to consign over to the care of another person. If any one of his children shall remain without an hereditary portion, and there is reason to expect that this child will be sent into a colony according to law, let the father be permitted to leave him from his other possessions as much as he pleases, except the paternal allotment, and every thing pertaining to it. But if there are many children thus circumstanced, let the father bequeath them, as he pleases, whatever remains beyond the allotment. However, if any one of these possesses a house, let him not leave such a one any money. In like manner, let him not bequeath a daughter any thing if she is betrothed to a man; but let him bequeath her something if she is not betrothed. If any allotment in the region belonging to sons or daughters shall be found after the will has been made, let it be left to the heir of the person that made the will. If the testator has no sons, but daughters, let him signify in writing what men he would wish as husbands for his daughters, and as sons for himself. And if the son of any one, whether natural or adopted, happens to die before he has arrived at manhood, let the testator mention this circumstance in the will, and signify who he wishes should be his son in his stead, with more auspicious fortune. If any one who has no children makes a will, let him be permitted to leave the tenth part of his possessions, beyond the allotment, to any one that he pleases. Let him bequeath all the rest benignantly, without blame, and according to law, to the son whom he adopts. If the children of any dying person require tutors, and the father in his will has mentioned those whom he wishes to undertake this office, let such persons enter on this employment according to his wish, if it is agreeable to them. But, if such a one has either died intestate, or has not mentioned the tutors in his will, let the next of kin undertake this office, - two on the father's side, two on that of the mother, and one from among the friends of the deceased. In this case, too, let the guardians of the law appoint the tutors. And let the whole care pertaining to orphans devolve on fifteen of the guardians of the laws that are older than the rest. And this number being divided into three parts, let three of them every year undertake this office, till the five periods are accomplished in a circle. Let the greatest care likewise be taken that this mode may never fail. If any one dies intestate, and leaves behind him children that require a guardian, let them be provided for by the same laws. But if any one dies unexpectedly, and leaves behind him daughters, let him pardon the legislator if he disposes of his daughters in consequence of looking to two things, *viz.* proximity of race, and the preservation of the allotment. The third thing which a father ought to attend to is, the choosing a proper son for himself, and a husband for his daughter: but this he omits, because the consideration of it belongs to impossibilities. Let the following law, therefore, be established about things of this kind:- If any one, dying intestate, leaves behind him daughters, let the brother on the father's or mother's side, if he is without an allotment, take care both of the daughter and the allotment of the deceased. But, if his brother is not living, let his brother's son undertake this office, if his age is sufficient for the purpose. If no one of these survives, let the charge devolve on the son of his sister; and let the fourth after these be his father's brother; the fifth, the son of this brother; and the sixth, the son of his father's sister. Let a similar process be always adopted when a

25a man leaves behind him daughters, *viz.* through brothers and cousins; first, the males, and afterwards the females, in the same family. But let the judge determine the fitness or unfitness of the time of marriages, by looking at the males naked, and at the females naked, as far as to the navel. If there is a want of kindred, as far as to the sons of brothers and grandfathers, whatever citizen the girl shall choose, with the consent of

b her tutors, shall become the heir of the deceased, and the husband of his daughter. Further still, if there should happen to be but few inhabitants in the city, and the virgin should wish to make some one who is sent into a colony her father's heir, let this person, if he belongs to her family, proceed to the allotment according to the order of law. But if

c he is a citizen, but not related to her, let him marry her if he pleases, according to her own choice, and that of her guardians; and, returning home, let him take possession of the hereditary estate. If any one dies intestate, and without children, either of the male or female sex, let other particulars take place according to the above-mentioned law, but let the males and females of the family enter as kindred the desolate house, as those to whom the allotment properly belongs. In the first place, let the sister enter; afterwards the daughter of the brother; in the third place, the daughter of the sister; in the fourth place, the sister of

d the father; in the fifth place, the daughter of the father's brother; and, in the sixth place, the daughter of the father's sister. Let these live together with those according to proximity and what is right, in the manner we have established above. But let not the weighty nature of laws of this kind escape us, and let us not be insensible to the difficulty of ordering a relation of a deceased person to marry a relation. For he who introduces such a law as this, does not appear to consider that ten thousand impediments may arise respecting mandates of this kind, so as to render persuasion to a compliance with them ineffectual. For many had rather suffer any thing than marry a person whose body is either diseased or maimed, and whose dianoëtic part is not in a sound state. The legislator, therefore, will, perhaps, appear to some, though improperly, to pay no attention to these. Let this, then, be as it were a common preface, both for the legislator, and those that are governed by his laws. Those, indeed, for whom laws are made, ought to pardon the legislator, because, while he is taking care of public concerns, he cannot at the same time attend to private calamities. We should also

6a pardon those for whom laws are made, if they are sometimes incapable of perfectly complying with the mandates of the legislator, through his ignorance of private calamities.

CLIN. In what manner then, O guest, will it be most proper to act in this case?

GUEST. Arbiters, O Clinias, must necessarily be chosen for laws of this kind, and for those that are governed by them.

CLIN. How do you say?

b GUEST. It will sometimes happen, that a rich young man given to luxury will be unwilling to marry the daughter of his father's brother, though rich, in consequence of aspiring after a greater marriage; and sometimes he will necessarily be unwilling to comply with the law which forces him to marry a girl who is disordered either in body or mind, considering this as the greatest of all calamities. Let, therefore, the following law respecting these particulars be established by us: - If c any accuse the established laws on account of wills or marriages, or any thing else, asserting that the legislator, if he were living, would not compel them to act in such a manner, or to marry such a person; and if any relation or tutor should affirm that the legislator left fifteen guardians of the laws as arbiters and fathers of the orphans, - in this d case, let the litigants apply to these, and abide by their decision. But, if it shall appear that the guardians of the law exercise greater authority than they ought, let the affair be brought before select judges; and, when determined, let him who is condemned be branded with infamy, - this being a punishment, to him who possesses intellect, of a more weighty nature than a very considerable fine. After this, a second generation, as e it were, follows with respect to orphans. For education and discipline follow the first generation, of which we have spoken. But, after the second, it is necessary to devise some means by which orphans may be oppressed with calamity as little as possible. In the first place, then, we say, that guardians of the laws should be appointed for them in the place of parents, and not worse than these; and that they should take care of them every year as if they were their own offspring. Let this, then, be 927a our preface respecting the education of orphans, and the appointment of tutors for them. For we appear to me to have spoken opportunely above, when we asserted, that the souls of the dead possessed a certain power, through which they bestowed a providential attention to human affairs. This, indeed, is true, but the confirmation of it requires a long discourse. It is likewise proper to believe in other traditions respecting things of this kind, which are both numerous and very ancient. Legislators, too, unless they are perfectly insane, ought to believe in the truth of these traditions. Since, therefore, these things naturally subsist after this manner, those that attend to the desolate condition of orphans b should, in the first place, fear the Gods above; and, in the next place, the souls of the deceased, who naturally take a particular care of their offspring, and who are, therefore, propitious to those that honour them, but hostile towards those that despise them. Add, too, that the souls of those that are living, but are in old age, and who in a city happy through good laws possess the greatest honours, and whose children and grandchildren live a pleasant life, through paying them a proper attention, - these acutely hear and perceive things of this kind, and are benevolent to those that behave justly to orphans, but in the highest degree indignant with those that injure them. For they consider the deposit of orphans as the greatest and most holy of all deposits. It is requisite, therefore, that the tutor and magistrate who possesses the smallest degree of intellect, should direct his attention to these particulars, and bestow as much care on the discipline and education of orphans as of his own offspring. He, therefore, who is persuaded by this preface to the law, and who acts in no respect unjustly towards orphans, will evidently be exempt from all anger of the legislator about things of this kind. But let him who is unpersuaded by it, and injures any one who is deprived of either father or mother, suffer twice the punishment he would have sustained from injuring one, both of whose parents were living.

The laws which follow relate to the tutors of orphans, and the attention which magistrates should pay to the tutors. if, therefore, they possessed a paradigm of the education of free children, the tutors both taking care of these and their own concerns, and if they had laws respecting these sufficiently distinct, we should not without reason establish certain laws for tutors, as very much differing from others, and distinguish, by various pursuits, the life of orphans from that of those who are not orphans. But now, with respect to every thing of this kind, the privation of parents does not with us differ much from paternal government, but is unwilling to equalize honour, dishonour, and providential care. Hence the law, through its attention to orphans, consoles and threatens. And further still, it will be very opportune for it to threaten as follows:- He who takes care either of a female or a male, and who from among the guardians of the law is appointed to observe the tutor of these, shall possess the same affection for the orphans intrusted to his care as if they were his own offspring; nor shall he bestow less attention to their affairs, but even more, than to his own. Let every one, therefore, take care of orphans conformably to this law. But, if any one acts contrary to this law in affairs of this kind, let such a tutor be condemned by a magistrate. And if it shall appear to the kindred of the orphans, or to any other of the citizens, that the tutor has acted negligently or viciously, let him be brought before a court of judgment, and make a fourfold restitution of the loss sustained, and let

c   one half be given to the boy, and the other to the accuser. When an orphan arrives at puberty, if he thinks that he has been neglected by his tutor, let him be permitted to call his tutor to an account for five years from the time that his tutorship is finished. And if any tutor is condemned, let a court of justice determine what he ought to suffer, or

d   what fine he ought to pay. If any magistrate shall appear to have injured an orphan through negligence, let a court of justice determine the restitution which he ought to make. But, if he shall appear to have injured the orphan through injustice, besides making a restitution, let him be deprived of the office of a guardian of the law; and let another common guardian of the city be appointed in his place by the region and the city. Greater discord takes place between fathers and sons, and sons and fathers, than is proper, in which fathers think that the legislator ought to permit them to renounce their sons by a public crier, so as that they may no longer be their sons according to law: and sons

e   are of opinion that they ought to be allowed to accuse their fathers of madness, when they are disgracefully circumstanced through disease or old age. These things usually take place when the manners of men are perfectly corrupt. For, if the half only of these evils took place, as that the parents alone, or the children alone, were vicious, calamities which are the progeny of such a mighty hatred would have no existence. Indeed, in any other polity, a son, when abandoned by his father, would not necessarily be deprived of the city. But, in a city governed by these laws, he who is given up by his father must necessarily take up his

929a   abode in some other place. For no one is allowed to unite himself with any family of the five thousand and forty houses. On this account it is necessary, that the son who is abandoned by his father should not only be driven from his father, but from his whole race. It is proper, therefore, in things of this kind, to act according to the following law:- When any one, through anger by no means fortunate, whether he is justly enraged or not, desires to be liberated from an alliance with him whom he has begotten and educated, let him not be permitted to accomplish his desire either in an improper manner or directly. But, in

b   the first place, let him assemble his own relations, as far as to his cousins, and, in a similar manner, those of his son on the mother's side. When they are assembled, let him accuse his son to them, and show them that he deserves to be expelled from all his kindred. Let the son also be permitted to defend himself, and endeavour to prove that he does not deserve to suffer any thing of this kind. And if the father persuades

them that his accusation is just, and all the relations, both male and
c female, except the father, mother, and the son himself, vote for his being
abandoned; when this is the case, let a father be permitted to renounce
his son, but by no means when this is not the case. If any citizen
wishes to adopt a son whom his father abandons, let him not be
restrained from adopting him by any law. For the manners of youth
naturally sustain many mutations in life. But, if no one in the space of
d ten years wishes to adopt such a son, let those whose province it is to
send offspring into a colony, take care that this rejected son is made an
inhabitant of such a colony in a proper manner. If a certain disease, old
age, or severity of manners, or all these together, more than any thing
else, render a man insane, and this is concealed from every one except
his domestics; and if such a one dissipates his substance, as being the
e master of it, but his son is unwilling to accuse his father of madness, in
this case, let the following law be established:- In the first place, let the
son go to the oldest guardians of the law, and inform them of his
father's calamity. Afterwards, let these, when they have sufficiently
considered the affair, consult whether the father should be proscribed,
or not: and, if they agree that he should be proscribed, let them be both
witnesses and patronizers of the cause. But, if the father is condemned,
let him not afterwards possess any authority over his own affairs, but
dwell at home for the rest of his life like a child. if a husband and wife,
through the wretchedness of their manners, live in discord with each
other, let ten men who subsist in the middle of the guardians of the
30a laws, and, in a similar manner, ten women who are curators of
marriages, take care of things of this kind. And if they are able to
procure a reconciliation, let their decision be valid. But, if their minds
are too vehemently inflamed to admit of a reconciliation, let them seek,
to the utmost of their power, after such persons as are adapted to reside
with each. It appears, indeed, that the manners of such as these are far
from being mild; and, on this account, we should endeavour to adapt to
them more profound and gentle manners. And such, indeed, as are
without children, or have but a few, and disagree, let these be compelled
to marry again, for the sake of procreating children. But let such as,
having a sufficient number of children, disagree, be divorced, and united
with others, for the sake of that attention which old age requires. If a
woman dies, and leaves behind her male and female children, let the law
not compel, but persuade, the husband to educate his children without
marrying again. But if there are no children, let him be compelled to
marry again, till he has procreated children sufficient both for his family
and the city. But, if a man dies, and leaves behind him a sufficient

number of children, let the mother of the children educate them, remaining a widow. If she appears, however, to be too young to live in a state of health without a husband, let her kindred, in conjunction with the women that take care of marriages, consult what is fit to be done both for her and the children. And if both these are in want of children, let them marry for the sake of having children. But let an accurate sufficiency of children be a male and female according to law.

d When it is allowed that any offspring is the progeny of the begetter, but it is necessary to have recourse to a court of justice in order to know which of the parents the child ought to follow, let the following mode be adopted:- If a female slave has connection with a slave, or with a free-born person, or with a freed-man, let the offspring be the property of the master of the female slave. But if a free-born woman is with child from a slave, let the master of the slave, in a similar manner, be the master of the offspring. If any master has a child by his own slave, or any mistress is pregnant from her slave, and this becomes apparent, let the women send the offspring of the woman, together with the father,

e into another region: but let the guardians of the law banish the offspring of the man, together with the mother of such offspring. However, neither will Divinity, nor any man who is endued with intellect, ever advise any one to neglect his parents. Indeed, the assertion, that it is proper to know how to worship the Gods, will be a proper preface with respect to the honouring and dishonouring of parents. Ancient laws concerning the Gods are among all men established in a twofold manner. For, clearly perceiving some of the Gods,[†] we honour them;

931a but we fabricate images of others; and while we rejoice in these images though inanimate, we think that the animated Gods themselves will be benevolent and propitious to us for the attention which we pay to these. He, therefore, whose father or mother, or the fathers or mothers of these, reside in his house, worn out with old age, like precious furniture, such a one will never think that any other such image, or one more efficacious, can ever reside in his house, if he pays that reverential regard to it which he ought.

b CLIN. Of what proper reverential regard are you speaking?

GUEST. I will tell you. For things of this kind, O friends, deserve to be heard.

CLIN. Only speak.

[†] Meaning the celestial orbs, which, in consequence of being divine animals, from the participation of divinity, are called Gods.

GUEST. We say that Oedipus, being dishonoured by his children, imprecated on them those things which every one is perfectly acquainted with, and has heard were inflicted by the Gods. Amyntor, too, is said to have cursed his son Phœnix in anger, and Theseus, Hippolytus, and innumerable other fathers, innumerable other sons. From which it becomes apparent, that the Gods hear the prayers of parents against their children. For it is most just that nothing should be so noxious to a child as the imprecation of his parent. Nor let any one think that the prayers of his father and mother are alone heard by the Gods according to nature, when they are despised by him, for they are also heard when they are honoured by, and are vehemently dear to, him. On this account, when in their prayers they earnestly invoke the Gods to bless their children, ought we not to think that they are similarly heard by them, and that the Gods equally impart to them such things as are good? For otherwise they would not be just distributors of what is good, which we say becomes the Gods the least of all things.

CLIN. Certainly.

GUEST. We should think, therefore, as we observed a little before, that we cannot possess any image which is more honoured by the Gods, than our fathers and grandfathers, mothers and grandmothers, when worn out with age. When any one honours these, divinity rejoices: for, otherwise, he would not hear their prayers. The image, indeed, of our progenitors ought to be considered by us, as far more wonderful than inanimate images. For animated images when they are reverenced by us, pray for us, but do the very contrary when they are despised by us. But inanimate images do neither of these. So that he who behaves properly to his father, grandfather, and all of this kind, such a one possesses the most powerful of all images with respect to procuring divine benevolence.

CLIN. You speak most beautifully.

GUEST. Every one, therefore, endued with intellect will fear and honour the prayers of his parents, as knowing that they have often been profitable and noxious to many. These things, then, are thus established by nature. By good men, therefore, their aged progenitors when living to the extremity of life, will be considered as a treasure; and, if they die before they arrive at that period, they will be vehemently desired by them. On the contrary, they will be terrible in the extreme to the vicious. Let every one, therefore, persuaded by these assertions, honour his parents according to law. But if any one is deaf to these exordia, for such the following law will be properly established. If any one then, in this city, reverences his parents less than he ought, and does not pay them more attention than he does his sons, grandsons, and himself, neglecting to comply with their will in all things beyond that of others, let parents who are so neglected, give information of the affair themselves, or by some other, to three of the oldest guardians of the law, and likewise to three of the women that have the care of marriages. And let these, after they have investigated the affair, punish the offender; if he is a young man, indeed, with stripes and bonds, if he is not more

c than thirty years of age; and let the same punishment be inflicted on a woman, if she is forty years of age. But if they are older than this, and yet do not cease to neglect their parents, but afflict them, let them be brought before a court of justice, and be tried by those citizens who surpass all the rest in age: and, if they are condemned, let the court of justice determine what they ought to suffer, without omitting any punishment which ought to be inflicted on such an occasion. If any

d one, however, who is afflicted by his children, is unable to tell his condition, let any free person who hears of his case, announce it to the governors; or let him, if he omits to do this, be considered as a vicious person, and be accused by any one that is willing of the injury sustained. But if a slave gives information of this affair, let him be made free. And if he is the slave either of the afflicting or afflicted person, let him be made free by the magistrate who is acquainted with the affair. But if he is the slave of any other citizen, let his ransom be paid for to his master, by the public. Let the magistrates, likewise, be careful that no one injures a person of this kind, on account of his giving information.

e With respect to injuries by poisons, we have already made a division of such of these as are deadly: but we have not yet distinguished other injuries, whether they are committed by means of drink or meat, or unctions, voluntarily, and with premeditation. For there are two kinds of poisons pertaining to the human species. For, as we just now clearly

933a said, bodies are naturally injured by bodies: and, in the next place, by enchantments, incantations and bindings, some who dare to injure others, are persuaded that they are able to accomplish their purpose through these, and others, that nothing is so easy as to be injured by those that possess the power of witchcraft. These particulars, therefore, and all that pertains to things of this kind, it is neither easy to know how they naturally subsist, nor, if any one does know, to persuade others. But the minds of men being dubious as to things of this kind, it is not worth while to endeavour to persuade them that, if at any time

b they see waxen images, whether in gates, in places where three roads meet, or on the tombs of their parents, they should despise every thing of this kind, as they have no clear notions concerning them. Giving a

twofold division, therefore, to the law respecting enchantments, in the
c first place, we shall exhort, admonish, and advise men, not to attempt
any thing of this kind; nor terrify the multitude, who are frightened like
children; nor compel the legislator and judge to procure a remedy for
such fears of mankind. For, in the first place, he who endeavours to
hurt another by poison, if he does not possess medical science, cannot
know what he does with respect to bodies. The same may be said of
him who endeavours to injure another by enchantment, unless he
happens to be a diviner, or an interpreter of portents. Let the following
d law, therefore, be established respecting poisons. He who employs
poison, not for the purpose of killing a man, but cattle, or swarms of
bees, or in order to injure them some other way than by procuring their
death, if he happens to be a physician, and is condemned for poisoning,
let him be punished with death; but if he is unskilled in medicine, let a
court of justice determine what he ought to suffer, or what fine he
e ought to pay. But if any one by bonds, or allurements, or certain
incantations, or such like enchantments, is found endeavouring to injure
another, if he is a diviner, or an interpreter of prodigies, let him be put
to death. But if any one is accused of witchcraft, without being a
diviner, let his punishment in a similar manner be determined by a court
of justice. Let him who injures another by fraud or force, pay a great
fine, if the injury is great, but a smaller fine, if the injury is small; and
34a let restitution in all cases be equivalent to the loss sustained. And, in all
injuries, let the injurer be fined till he is amended. If it shall appear that
any one was impelled to injure another, by a folly foreign to his nature,
through the imprudence of youth, let him be sentenced to pay a lighter
fine; but if by his own proper folly, or through the incontinence of
pleasures and pains, or through fear, envy, certain desires, or anger
difficult to cure, a heavier fine. At the same time observing, that
offenders are not to be punished because they have acted ill, (for what
is done, can never become undone,) but that afterwards both offenders,
and those that see them punished, may hate injustice, or may be in a
considerable degree liberated from a calamity of this kind. For the sake
of all these particulars, and looking to all these, the laws, like good
archers, should consider this as a mark, *viz.* the magnitude of
punishment, and the proper desert in each offence. A judge, therefore,
ought to act in this manner, as the minister of the legislature, since it is
permitted him by law to establish what punishment offenders ought to
suffer: and, like a painter, he should diligently copy his original. This,
indeed, O Megillus and Clinias, should be done by us at present, in the
most beautiful and best manner; and we should establish what

punishments ought to be inflicted, both on base actions committed by fraud, and those committed by violence; and this in such a manner as the Gods, and the sons of the Gods, will permit us to establish. Let no one then who is insane be openly seen in the city, but let the relations of the insane person keep him secure at home, in the best manner they are able. If they do not, let them be fined. And let him who possesses

d the largest estate be fined a hundred drachms, if he is negligent in securing an insane person, whether he be a slave, or free. But let him who possesses the next estate to this, be fined four out of five parts of a mina; he who possesses a third estate, three parts of a mina: and, he who possesses a fourth estate, four parts. Many, indeed, are rendered insane by various means. Some, as those of whom we have just spoken, through disease. Others through anger, and the vicious education of a

e depraved nature; who, being incited by a trifling enmity, talk loudly, and blaspheme each other. But nothing of this kind ought to take place in a city governed by good laws. With respect to every kind of slander, therefore, let the following law be established. Let no one slander another. But when one person in discourse with another is doubtful of any particular, let him with whom he discourses instruct both him and those that are present in the truth of the case, and entirely abstain from

935a slander. For men, when they slander each other with base words, are to be considered as effeminate. And, in the first place, from words, which are a light thing, hatred and grievous enmities are often produced in reality. For he who is gratified with anger, which is a thing of an unpleasant nature, and is filled with it as with noxious aliment, - such a one, being rendered as rustic and savage in this part of his soul as he was once gentle and mild through discipline, leads a morose life, and receives from anger this bitter grace. Hence, nearly all men from things

b of this kind, utter something ridiculous to their adversaries; and he who accustoms himself to a thing of this kind, either errs in every respect, or destroys many parts of magnanimity. On this account, therefore, let no one ever speak in this manner in a temple, or where public sacrifices are performed; or in places of contest, or the forum, or in a court of justice,

c or in any common assembly. But let the magistrate, who is present at the time, freely punish any one who acts in this manner: and, if he neglects to do so, let him be considered as one who pays no attention to the laws nor the mandates of the legislator, and let him never be permitted to contend for the rewards which are conferred on virtue. But, if any one uses slander in other places, either by provoking, or answering, let any more elderly person who is present, in defence of the law, restrain with blows those who are incited by a foreign and vicious

anger; or, if they do not, let them be punished in the manner mentioned
d   above. We say, too, at present, that he who is entangled with slander
will not be able to refrain from sometimes speaking ridiculously; and
this is what we condemn when it takes place through anger. But what
then? Shall we admit the jests and ridiculous slanders which comedians
employ against the citizens, if they are not accompanied with anger? Or
e   shall we give this affair a twofold division, *viz.* into the jocose and the
serious? And, indeed, any one may be permitted jocosely to employ
ridicule without anger. But let no one be allowed to employ it, as we
said before, when inflamed with anger. Let us now, therefore, establish
by law to whom this may be allowed, and to whom not. Let not then
a composer of comedies, or of iambic or musical melody, be permitted
either in words or images to slander any citizen, either in anger or
without anger. And, if any one disobeys this law, let those that
determine the rewards of ·contests drive him from the region the very
same day, or they shall be fined three minæ, sacred to the God to whom
936a   the contest belongs. But let the others, whom we mentioned above, be
permitted to employ ridicule without anger, and in sport; but let them
not be permitted to do this seriously, and in anger. Let the
determination, too, of this affair be committed to him who takes care
of the whole discipline of youth. And let him who composes any thing
be permitted to make it public, if it is approved of by this curator of
youth: but if he does not approve of it, let not the author be permitted
b   to show it to any one, or instruct in it either a slave or a free-born
person. Or, if he does, let him be considered as a vicious character, and
as one who disobeys the laws. But he deserves commiseration who,
when temperate, or possessing some other virtue, or a part of virtue, is
oppressed with a certain calamity, either from hunger, or something of
a similar kind; but this cannot be said universally of any one who falls
into such-like misfortunes. Hence it will, indeed, be a wonderful
circumstance if a man of this kind is so entirely neglected as to arrive at
extreme poverty, whether he is a slave, or free, in a polity and city
c   which is moderately inhabited. On this account, the following law may
be safely established by the legislator. Let there be no beggars in the
city. But if any one attempts to procure food by prayers which cannot
be satisfied, let the præfects of the forum expel him from the forum, and
the governor of the ways and buildings from the city: and let the
magistrate who presides over the lands expel him from every other part
of the region, that the whole country may be pure from an animal of
d   this kind. If a male or a female slave injures the property of another
person undeservedly, whether through inexperience, or intemperate

conduct, let the master of such slave either make satisfaction to the injured person, or deliver up to him the injurer. But if the master of the slave contends that the affair happened through the mutual craft of the injurer and injured, that the slave might be taken from him, let him charge with the crime of malice the person who says he has been injured; and, if he convicts him, let him receive from him double the price at which a court of justice had valued the slave. If the master of the slave is convicted, let him both make the injured person a recompense for his loss, and deliver up the slave. And, if a heifer, horse, or dog, or any other animal, injures any neighbouring property, let the master of the animal in a similar manner make restitution for the loss. If any one refuses to bear witness willingly, let him be cited by him who is in want of his evidence; and when cited, let him attend at a proper time, and bear witness to the best of his knowledge. But if he says that he is ignorant of the affair, let him swear that he is ignorant of it by the three Gods, Jupiter, Apollo, and Themis, and be dismissed. Let him who, when called to bear witness, does not attend, be obnoxious to the injury, according to law. If any judge is cited to give evidence, let him not, in giving evidence, pass sentence on the case. Let a free woman be permitted to bear witness, defend a cause, and obtain justice, if she is more than forty years of age, and is unmarried. But, if she is married let her be permitted to bear witness only. Let a male and female slave, and a boy, be alone permitted to bear witness and defend a cause in cases of murder, if they can give sufficient security for their appearance at the trial, if they should happen to be accused of bearing false witness. If any one accuses another of bearing false witness, let each of the litigants consider the testimony, both in whole and part, before sentence is passed. But let the magistrates preserve in writing the accusations of bearing false witness made by both, and bring them forward for the purpose of determining the false witnesses. If any one shall be found to have given false witness twice, let the law no longer compel him to bear witness again. But if he shall be found to have given false witness thrice, let him not be permitted ever to bear witness again. And if he dares after this to bear witness, let any one who is willing give information of him to a magistrate. Afterwards, let the magistrate deliver him to a court of justice, and, if he is convicted, let him be put to death. When in any lawsuit false witnesses are detected, and are found to be the means of an opponent gaining his cause, if more than half of the witnesses are condemned, let no judgment be passed from their evidence. But it is proper in this case diligently to inquire, whether or not any sentence should be passed; that, in whatever manner the cause may be determined, by this means justice may be done. Since, however, there are many beautiful things in the life of man, in most of them dire calamities are, as it were, naturally inherent, through which they are stained and defiled. But why should not justice among men be beautiful,

e which renders all human affairs mild? And this being beautiful, why should it not be beautiful to patronize the cause of another? This, then, being the case, a certain evil calumny gives a beautiful name to an art, which, it says, was first devised in judicial affairs; by means of which, in litigations, and the patronizing of causes, any one may vanquish another, whether the cause is just or not. They add, that the gift of this art, and

938a of the arguments proceeding from it, consists in bestowing rewards from money. This, therefore, whether it is an art, or a certain exercise void of art, must by no means be planted in our city; but, reverencing the legislator, it should be persuaded not to speak contrary to justice, and should be sent to some other region. Those, then, that are persuaded by these arguments we pass over in silence: but let the following law be announced for those that are unpersuaded by them:- If it shall appear

b that any one endeavours to give a contrary direction to the power of justice in the souls of the judges, and either excites or patronizes many unseasonable law suits, let any one who is willing charge him with acting basely in judicial matters, or with patronizing a bad cause. And let the cause be tried in a select court of justice. If, too, he is condemned, let the court of justice determine whether he acted in this

c manner through avarice or love of contention. And if through a love of contention, let the judges appoint him a certain time, beyond which he shall neither plead any cause himself, nor patronize that of another. But if through avarice, if he is a stranger, let him depart from the city without ever returning to it again, or if he neglects to do this, let him be put to death. If he is a citizen, in consequence of thus improperly honouring money, let him be immediately put to death. Likewise, let him be put to death who has been found by a court of justice to have acted twice in this manner.

BOOK XII

941a   If an ambassador or a crier deceives the city in any thing committed to his charge, or does not announce what he is sent to proclaim; or again, when returning from friends or enemies, does not truly relate the message he received from them, let a written information be drawn up
b   against such a one, as irreligiously despising, contrary to law, the denunciations and mandates of Hermes and Jupiter. And if he is condemned, let the judges determine what he ought to suffer, or what fine he ought to pay. The theft of money is, indeed, illiberal, but rapine is base. But no one of the sons of Jupiter will ever do any thing of this kind, in consequence of being delighted either with fraud or force. Let no one, therefore, acting in a disorderly manner through poets, or certain mythologists, be falsely persuaded that if he thieves either by fraud or force, he does not act basely, but does that which the Gods themselves have done. For this is neither true nor becoming: but he who illegally acts in this manner, is neither a God, nor a son of the
c   Gods. But it is proper that these things should be known by the legislator rather than by all poets. He, therefore, who is persuaded by this our discourse, is happy, and will be happy through the whole of time; but he who is unpersuaded by it, must be restrained by the following law: - If any one commits any public theft, whether it is great or small, he ought to suffer the same punishment. For he who takes away a thing of small consequence, thieves with the same desire, though with less force. But he who moves any thing of greater consequence,
d   and does not restore it to its proper place, is wholly unjust. The law, however, thinks it proper that the one should be less punished than the other, not on account of the smallness of the theft, but because, perhaps, one of these characters may be cured, but the other is incurable. If a slave, or a stranger, is accused and condemned of any public theft, let sentence be passed on him what he ought to suffer, or what fine he ought to pay, as if it were probable that he might be cured. But if any citizen, who has been properly educated, is convicted of having committed any public theft, or violence, whether he is detected in the
942a   fact or not, let him be punished with death, as one who is nearly incurable. For the sake of war, indeed, many consultations and many laws are very properly instituted. The greatest of all things, however, consists in this, that neither any male or female be at any time without a governor, nor the soul of any citizen be ever accustomed, either

seriously or in sport, to do any thing from itself alone; but that in all
b   war, and in all peace, it perpetually looks to a governor, and lives
following his mandates, so as to comply with them in the smallest
particular; to stand when he commands, walk, engage in gymnastic
exercises, wash, eat, rise by night for the purpose of keeping guard and
giving signals; and in dangers themselves, neither to pursue nor give way
c   to any one, without the mandate of the governors. And, in one word,
that it should never be taught to do or know any thing separate from
others; but that the life of all men should, in the highest degree, in all
things be collected into one, subsist together, and be common. For
nothing will ever be more excellent, better, or more artificial than this,
for the purpose of procuring safety and victory in war. In peace, too,
men should be accustomed from their childhood to govern others, and
d   to be governed by others. But anarchy should be expelled from all life,
both from that of men, and of beasts that are in subjection to men. All
choirs, too, should be celebrated, with a view to the best mode of
conducting war; and all facility, dexterity, and promptitude, should be
studied for the sake of this. On this account, too, we ought to accustom
ourselves to endurance of hunger and thirst, cold and heat, and a hard
bed. And, what is greatest of all, for the sake of this we should be
careful not to corrupt the power of the head and feet by the tegument
of foreign clothing, which destroys the generation and nature of our
e   proper hairs and shoes. For these extremities, when preserved, possess
the greatest power of the whole body, but the contrary when they are
not preserved. And one of these is in the highest degree subservient to
the whole body; but the other is endued with a principal authority,
naturally possessing all its principal senses. And this praise of a warlike
43a   life ought to be heard by young men. But the law is as follows: - Let
every one engage in war who is chosen for this purpose, or is deputed
a certain part. But, if any one, through a certain vice, deserts his post
without leave from his commander, let him be accused of desertion,
when he returns, to the principal officers of the army. Let him be
judged, too, by all the military orders, by the horse and the foot
separately, and in a similar manner by the rest. And let the foot be
introduced to the foot, the horse to the horse, and each of the other
b   orders to those of the same rank with themselves. If any one is
condemned, let him afterwards be prohibited from engaging in any
military contest, or accusing another of neglect of military duty. And
besides this, let a court of justice determine what he ought to suffer, or
what fine he ought to pay. After this, when the trial for desertion is
finished, let the commanders again assemble each of these orders, that

c military rewards may be conferred on those who have conducted themselves strenuously in battle. But any one who is willing may judge of the victory among those of the same rank with himself, so as that he neither produces arguments nor witnesses of any former battle, but alone considers the battle which has then been fought. Let a crown of olive, too, be the reward of the military champion. And afterwards, let those that have obtained these crowns suspend them in the temples of the warlike Gods, with any inscription they please, that they may be a testimony through the whole of life of the military virtue of the most valiant, and those that were valiant in the second and third degree. But,

d if any one engages in battle, and leaves the army before he is dismissed by his commanding officers, let him be tried by the same judges as the deserter was tried by, whom we mentioned above, and, if condemned, let him be similarly punished. It is proper, however, that one man,

e when he is about to judge another, should be fearful lest he should either voluntarily or involuntarily inflict punishment falsely. For justice is said, and is truly said, to be a bashful virgin. But falsehood is naturally odious to bashfulness and justice. In other things, therefore, it is requisite to be cautious with respect to judging erroneously, but particularly as to throwing away armour in battle. For, it may happen that some one may be erroneously considered as base for an action of

944a this kind, and may be punished for it undeservedly. For it is by no means easy to determine properly in this case. At the same time it is necessary that the law should endeavour to define according to parts. Employing a fable, therefore, we say, if Patroclus should have been carried to his tent without arms, and scarcely alive, as is frequently the case, and if his arms, which, as the poet says, were given to Peleus by the Gods on his marriage with Thetis, should be in the possession of Hector, would evil men in this case reproach the son of Menœtius, as if he had thrown away his arms? Further still, if any persons, being

b hurled from lofty places, either into the sea, or into places consisting of an abundant conflux of water produced through tempests, or into many other places of this kind, which might easily be adduced to free them from a suspicion of cowardice, - if, being hurled into these, they should lose their arms, ought they in this case to be blamed? But we ought to endeavour, to the utmost of our power, to separate the greater and the most grievous evil from the contrary. In slandering, therefore, the very words employed for the purpose, possess a certain division. For, as the

c throwing away arms cannot be justly asserted in all cases, but the losing them may; in like manner, he is not to be similarly called a thrower away of his shield who loses it by force, as he who voluntarily throws it away. For they totally and universally differ from each other. Let the following law, therefore, be established: - If any one, being assaulted by enemies, and having arms, does not defend himself against them, but voluntarily drops them, or throws them away, preferring a base life, in conjunction with infamy, to a beautiful and happy death, accompanied with fortitude, let sentence be passed on such a one, as a thrower away of arms, but let the judge neglect to consider the losing of arms mentioned above. For it is requisite always to punish the vicious, that they may become better, but not the unfortunate. For no advantage would be derived from an action of this kind. But what punishment will be adapted to him who is condemned for throwing away his arms in a cowardly manner? For, it is impossible to change a man of this kind into a contrary character, as they report Divinity once changed the Thessalian Cæneus from the nature of a woman into that of a man. For a contrary generation would, after a manner, be the most adapted of all others to him who throws away his shield, - I mean, that he should be punished by being changed from a man into a woman. But now, since this is impossible, let us devise a punishment which approaches the nearest to this, I mean that, in consequence of his great love of life, he shall never afterwards engage in any dangerous enterprise, but, as being a vicious character, live as long as possible, covered with disgrace. Let, then, the following law be established for these: - When a man is condemned for shamefully throwing away his warlike arms, let neither any general of an army, nor any other military officer, ever employ him as a soldier, nor admit him into the army. But if any such officer does admit him, let the judge who inquires into the reasons of conduct punish him as follows: If he possesses the largest estate, let him be fined ten minæ; if the second in rank, five minæ; if the third, three; and, if the fourth, one mina. But he who was condemned for throwing away his armour, besides being excluded from engaging in manly dangers, through his cowardice, shall, if he possesses the largest estate, be in like manner fined ten minæ; if the second, five; if the third, three; and, if the fourth, one mina. But, with respect to those magistrates who inquire into the reasons of conduct, what ought we to determine; some magistrates being chosen by a yearly lot, but others for many years, and by selection? For who will be a sufficient judge of the reasons of conduct, if it should happen that any magistrate, being bent by the weight of his government, should say or do any thing unworthy of his office? It is, indeed, by no means easy to find one adequate to the purpose. For, since one magistrate surpasses another in virtue, how shall we discover him who transcends all the rest. At the same time, we should endeavour to find certain divine men who may act for us as judges of the reasons of conduct. For the case is as follows: - There are many occasions for dissolving a polity, as there are of a ship, or a certain animal, of which, though there is one dispersed nature, yet we denominate them tones, transverse enclosures, extensions of nerves, and call them by many other names. But this is an occasion, by no means the smallest, of the preservation and dissolution of a polity. For, if the judges who require

d   of the magistrates the reason of their conduct, are better than the magistrates, and this is managed in such a manner as to take away all occasion of complaint, the whole region and city will thus flourish and be happy. But, if an inquiry is made into the conduct of the magistrates in a different manner, then, that judgment being dissolved by which all political affairs are connected in one, a divulsion of all government takes

e   place, and magistrates no longer verging to the same thing, they cause the city from being one, to be many, and filling it with seditions, bring it rapidly to destruction. On this account, it is necessary that those who inquire into the reasons of conduct should, in a wonderful manner, be endued with every virtue. We shall, therefore, thus devise the fabrication of these. Let the whole city assemble every year after the summer solstice, to a sacred grove common to the Sun and Apollo, in

946a   order to elect three men, which every one shall judge to excel all others except himself; and let these be not less than fifty years of age. Afterwards, let the half of those who are chosen by the greatest number of votes be selected, if they form an even number; but if they form an odd number, then, leaving out one who had the fewest votes, let the half of the remainder be taken, and a judgment formed by the number of votes. If some happen to have an equal number of votes, and the half

b   of these is more than three, let the excess be taken away, and the juniors rejected. Afterwards, out of these, let an election be made by votes, till three, whose votes are unequal, are obtained. But if all these, or two of them, have equal votes, then, committing the affair to good fate and fortune, let the three be distinguished by lot; and let him who is victor, together with the second and third, be crowned with leaves of olive. Afterwards, the rewards being conferred, let it be proclaimed to all men,

c   that the city of the Magnesians having again obtained safety from Divinity, consecrates three of its best citizens as common first fruits to Apollo and the Sun, conformably to an ancient law. Let these, too, in the first year, choose twelve examiners of the reasons of conduct, and continue to do this till each has accomplished his seventy-fifth year; and afterwards, let three always be added every year. Let these accurately observe all the magistrates, who are to be divided into twelve parts, with d all possible free examination. Let them reside, too, at the time in which they act as examiners of the reasons of conduct, in the grove sacred to the Sun and Apollo, in which they were elected. Here, each inquiring into every thing by himself, and all examining in common, let them signify by public writings in the forum what each of the magistrates ought to suffer, or be fined, according to their decision. But if any one of the magistrates does not acknowledge that he has been condemned justly, let him go to the chosen judges appointed to examine the reasons of conduct, and if he is acquitted by these, let him accuse, if he is willing, the examiners of the reasons of conduct; but, if he is condemned

e by the chosen judges also, and was before by the other judges condemned to death, let him die, as necessity requires. But if he was sentenced by them to pay a fine, the double of which he is capable of paying, let him be fined the double of it.

It is, however, now requisite to hear what the accusations of these judges will be, and after what manner they will take place. The first places, then, in all public spectacles should always be given to those who

947a are appointed by the common consent of the whole city to preside over all others as long as they live. And further still, when it is found necessary to send magistrates to inspect the common sacrifices, spectacles, and other sacred rites of the Greeks, let them be sent from these. Likewise, let these alone in the city be adorned with a crown of laurel; and let them all be priests of Apollo and the Sun. Let him, too, be the high-priest every year from among these, who in the former year was judged to excel the other priests; and let his name every year, as

b long as the city is inhabited, become the measure of the number of time. But when these priests die, let care be taken that their funerals and sepulchres surpass those of the other citizens. Let every one, too, on this occasion have a white robe, and let there be no weeping and lamentation. Let there be also two choirs, one consisting of fifteen girls, and the other of as many boys; and let each of these surround the bier, praising the priests, as it were, in a hymn, and each by turns celebrating

c their felicity in songs through the whole day. On the morning following, let a hundred young men, who are engaged in gymnastic exercises, carry the bier to the sepulchre which the relations of the deceased have chosen. And, in the first place, let the unmarried young men march before the bier armed in a warlike manner, together with horses and horsemen; the foot with their light arms, and others in a similar manner. But let boys, going before the bier, sing a paternal

d song; and let them be followed by girls, and women who are no longer capable of bearing children. After these, let priests and priestesses follow, as to a pure sepulchre, though they are forbidden to go to other sepulchres; if the Pythian deity likewise assents. Let the sepulchre, too, for these be built under the earth; and let it be a long arch composed of valuable and undecaying stones, and containing on each side beds of

e   stone. In this let them place the blessed deceased, and plant a grove of trees in a circular order round the monument, except in one part, that the sepulchre may be always enlarged when it is requisite. Every year, too, let musical, gymnastic and equestrian contests be instituted in honour of these deceased priests. And such are the honours which ought to be paid to those whose judgments concerning the reasons of conduct are not condemned. But, if any one of these, confiding too much in his decision, should make the imbecility of human nature apparent, and become depraved after his decision, let him be accused by

948a   any one who is willing; and let the following law respecting the mode of his accusation be established: - In the first place, let him be brought before a court of justice, and let the guardians of the laws at the same time be present. Afterwards, let the colleagues of the accused be present; and, lastly, let the court of justice be composed of select judges. Then, let his accuser signify in writing that he who is accused is an unworthy character, and that he does not deserve either the rewards, or to act in the capacity, of a magistrate. If, therefore, he is condemned, let him be deprived of magistracy, of a sepulchre, and of those other rewards which

b   pertain to his office. But if his accuser has not a fifth part of votes, let him who possesses the largest estate be fined twelve minæ; he who possesses the second, eight; the third, six; and the fourth, two minæ. Rhadamanthus, indeed, deserves to be admired with respect to his decision of judicial affairs. For he perceived that the men of that time evidently believed that there were Gods, and this very properly, because at that time many of them were the progeny of the Gods; and he is said to have been one of these. He appears, therefore, to have conceived that causes ought not to be referred to any human judge, but to the Gods; and, on this account, causes were decided by him in a simple and rapid

c   manner. For, causing the litigants in every case to take an oath, he determined causes rapidly and with safety. But now, as we have said, a certain part of mankind denies that there are Gods; others conceive that they take no care of us; and the opinion of the greatest and worst part is, that they may be appeased by trifling sacrifices and abundance of flattery, and that those who thus appease them, may with impunity defraud others of great sums of money. Hence, the art of Rhadamanthus in judicial affairs will not be adapted to men of the

d   present time. The opinions of men, therefore, respecting the Gods being changed, it is necessary that laws also should be changed. A prudent legislator, therefore, in judicial contests, will not suffer the litigants to take an oath, that as well the intention of the accuser, as the entreaty of the defendant, may be committed to writing without an oath. For if every one in the city should be freely permitted to take an oath, in consequence of many cases being every day brought before the judges, almost every one would be perjured, through connections arising from feasting together, and other associations, and from private meetings. Let it, therefore, be established by law, that he who is about to be judged shall swear to the judge, and that he who appoints the public magistrates shall either appoint them through oaths, or by suffrages. Likewise, that the judge of choirs, and all music, together with the presidents and those that confer rewards on gymnastic and equestrian exercises, shall take an oath; and, in short, in all cases in which, according to the opinion of men, perjury is not attended with gain. But let those cases in which any one may derive great advantage from perjury be judged without an oath. Likewise, in judicial cases, let not the litigants by any means be permitted either to swear for the sake of persuading, or imprecate themselves and their family, or employ base supplications or feminine excitations to pity; but let them always in an honourable manner teach and learn that which is just. But if they do not act in this manner, let the magistrates again bring them back to the affair in hand, as those who speak foreign to the purpose. When strangers, like us, quarrel among themselves, let them be permitted, if they are willing, to take an oath. For, as they are not allowed to grow old in the city, there is no reason to fear lest they should corrupt others. In the same manner, let justice be executed among free men, if any one of these is not persuaded by the city in things which are neither punished with blows, nor bonds, nor death. If any one does not attend at the celebration of a choir, or solemn procession, or any other common adornings of this kind, or public office, such as take place for the sake of pacific sacrifice or warlike tributes, - in all these cases let the damage be repaired as soon as possible; or let the pledge be taken to him to whom the city and law have committed it, and when the limited time is expired let the pledge be sold, and the money applied to public use. But, if there is occasion for a greater fine, let the magistrates bring those that refuse to pay it before a court of justice, and compel them to pay the fine enacted by the laws. It is necessary, however, to consult what ought to be done with a city which does not apply itself to the acquisition of wealth, except that which arises from agriculture, since it neither exports nor imports commodities, nor admits foreigners. The legislator, therefore, ought to consult about these particulars, employing, in the first place, persuasion to the utmost of his power. The mixture, indeed, of different 950a nations naturally causes a mixture of all-various manners; and the association of strangers with strangers produces innovations which injure in the highest degree cities that are well governed through good laws. But, to the greater part of cities, as being by no means well governed, it is of no consequence if as well the old as the young travel into other countries whenever they please, and receive foreigners in their own country. But, on the contrary, in these never to receive strangers, and b never to visit foreign countries, would appear rustic and savage to other men, who would call the city by opprobrious names, such as, that it is the enemy of strangers, and that its manners are arrogant and morose. The appearing, however, to be good, or not good, to others, ought never to be considered as a thing of small importance. For the multitude, though deprived of virtue themselves, are capable of distinguishing the worthy from the unworthy: and in certain vicious characters there is something divine, and a power of conjecturing well. So that many, and c even some that are vicious in the extreme, are able to distinguish, both in words and opinions, the better from the worse sort of men. On this account, the multitude of cities are very properly exhorted not to despise the good opinion of the multitude. For it is a thing of the greatest rectitude and magnitude, when a man is truly good himself, that he should aspire after a renowned life; since, without this, a man will by no means become perfect. On this account, it will be proper that the city d which is to be inhabited about Crete should endeavour to obtain the most beautiful and excellent reputation for virtue among other men. But there is every reason to hope, that this city in a short time will be beheld both by the Sun and other Gods, in well-governed cities and regions, living according to reason. Let the following law, therefore, be established respecting travelling into other regions and places, and the reception of guests:- In the first place, let it not be lawful for him who is less than forty years of age by any means to travel; and further still, let no person be permitted to travel privately; but let cryers, ambassadors, or certain speculators, be allowed to travel publicly. e Leaving a country, however, in order to wage war, is not to be considered as political travelling. It is likewise requisite that certain persons should be sent to Pythian Apollo, to Olympian Jupiter, and also to Nemea and Isthmus, for the purpose of communicating in the sacrifices and contests sacred to these Gods. But let as much as possible many, and these such as are the most beautiful and the best, be sent on this occasion, who may procure for the city renown, and glory

corresponding to warlike glory in sacred concerns, and things pertaining
951a to pacific communions. And when they return home, let them teach
the young men, that the legal institutions of other nations, respecting
political affairs, are inferior to their own. If any speculators, likewise,
who abound in leisure, are desirous of surveying the affairs of other
men, let no law belonging to the guardians of the laws restrain them
b from executing their desire. For a city, when ignorant of good and evil
men, cannot, in consequence of being unsociable, be sufficiently mild
and perfect. Nor, again, can it preserve its laws by manners alone,
without a knowledge of them. For among the multitude of mankind,
there are always some divine men, not indeed many, but who in the
highest degree deserve to be associated with: and these do not spring up
c in well-governed cities, more than in their contraries. Every one,
therefore, who is an inhabitant of a well-governed city, and whose
manners are uncorrupt, ought, leaving his country, to tread in the steps
of these men, exploring both by land and sea, that when he returns to
his country he may give stability to such legal institutions as are
beautifully ordained, and correct such as are in any respect deficient.
For without such a speculation and inquiry a city can never continue
perfect, nor yet if the explorers speculate badly.

CLIN. How, therefore, can both these take place?

GUEST. Thus. In the first place, let a speculator of this kind not be
more than fifty years of age. In the next place, let him be approved
both in other respects, and for the purposes of war, if he intends to
leave to other cities an example of the guardians of laws. But, when he
d is more than sixty years of age, let him no longer travel as a speculator.
Let him, therefore, return when he pleases, within the space of ten
years, and on his return go to the assembly of those that examine the
laws. But let this assembly be composed of the old and the young; and
let it be held every day from necessity, before the dawn of day, till the
sun rises. And, in the first place, let it be composed of those priests
who receive rewards, as being more excellent than the rest; in the next
e place, of twelve of the senior guardians of the laws; and, in the last
place, of the president of all erudition, together with the young, and
those who no longer act in this capacity. Let not any one of these be
alone, but let him go with some young man whom he may choose,
between thirty and forty years of age. Let these, when they assemble,
952a always discourse concerning the laws and their own city; and, if they
have heard any thing excellent respecting these, let them communicate
it to each other. Let them also discourse concerning such disciplines as
appear to conduce to this speculation, and which those who are skilled

in will be enabled to understand more clearly; but those who are not skilled in them will more darkly comprehend the things pertaining to laws. Afterwards, let such particulars among these as are approved of by the more aged, be learnt with the greatest assiduity by the younger. If any young man of the assembly shall appear to be an unworthy character, let the whole assembly blame him by whom he was brought

b   thither. But let the whole city defend and honour those young men whose conduct in the assembly is approved. If such young men as go to the assembly are worse than others, let them be more disgraced than others. Let him who speculates the legal institutions of other men immediately go to this assembly on his arrival from foreign parts; and if he has discovered any thing among others, respecting the establishment of laws, or discipline, or education, or has himself found out any thing pertaining to these, let him communicate it to the whole

c   assembly. If, too, it shall appear that he has returned neither worse nor better than he was before, let him be praised for having done his best: but if he returns much better, let him while living be greatly honoured, and, when dead, let all the assembly pay him those honours which are his due. But if it shall appear that he has returned corrupted, though he pretends to be wise, let him not dare to associate with any young or old person. And if he is obedient to the magistrates, let him live as a private

d   man; but if not, let him be put to death. Likewise, if, when he ought to be brought before a court of justice, any magistrate neglects to bring him, let such magistrate be disgraced when a contention takes place about rewards. Let him, therefore, who travels, travel in this manner, and let him be such a person as we have described. But, in the next place, foreigners ought to be kindly received. There are four kinds of foreigners, then, of whom we ought to make mention. The first is, of

e   those who are always summerly, and most of whom, like birds, fly over the sea in summer to other cities, for the sake of acquiring riches. It is proper that these should be received in the forum, in the ports and public buildings, beyond the city, by the magistrates who preside over these places; such magistrates at the same time taking care that no

953a innovation is made by any of these foreigners. Let justice, too, be properly distributed to them, and no association be held with them, beyond what is absolutely necessary. The second kind is, of those who travel for the sake of beholding what Muses are received by different cities. It is proper that all such as these should have habitations near the temples, properly constructed for hospitable purposes. Priests, too, and the purifiers of temples, ought to take care of these, that after they have staid a sufficient time, and have seen and heard all that they came to see b   and hear, they may depart without any detriment either to themselves or others. Let the priests, too, be the judges of these. And, if any one of them commits an injury, or is injured, let the priests fine the offending party as far as to fifty drachms. But it is proper that greater offences should be punished by those that preside over the markets. The third kind of foreigner that ought to be publicly received, is he who is sent from another region on some public affair. Him let the generals of the army, the masters of the horse, and the military tribunes, alone receive. And let him be alone taken care of by him with whom he

c   resides together with the chief magistrates. The fourth genus of foreigners is indeed rare. Some one, however, may come from another region with the same design that our speculators travel into foreign parts. Let such a one then be received on the following conditions. In the first place, he must not be less than fifty years of age. In the next place, he must come with an intention either of beholding what is remarkably beautiful in other cities, or of instructing other cities in

d   things of this kind. Let such a one, therefore, approach, unbidden, to the gates of the rich and the wise, since he comes under this description himself. And let him go to the house of him who takes care of the whole of discipline, believing that one who is victorious in virtue will be considered by such a character as a sufficient guest. Likewise, when he has learnt from others, and has taught others, what he considers as fit to be learnt and taught, let him depart like a friend from friends with

e   gifts and becoming honours. All foreigners, both male and female, ought to be received according to these laws, and, in a similar manner reverencing hospitable Jupiter, we should send men from our city. For foreigners ought not to be expelled with food and victims, (as the inhabitants of the Nile do at present,) nor yet are they to be driven away by savage edicts. Let every surety be responsible for another in a conspicuous manner; and let the whole transaction be acknowledged in writing, before not less than three witnesses, if the security is within a

945a   hundred drachms. But, if it is beyond a thousand, let there be five sureties at least. Let the surety, if he is a shopkeeper, be one that acts justly in his business, or else let him by no means be considered as worthy of belief. If any one desires to search in the house of another person for something belonging to himself, let him first of all swear by the legal Gods that he hopes to find there what he is in search of. In the next place, let him enter the house naked, or with no other clothing than a tunic, and ungirded. Then let him be permitted to search the house, and examine every thing, whether sealed or unsealed. But, if any

b   one refuses admittance to him who desires to search his house, let him who is forbidden access bring an action against him who refuses him admittance, for the value of what he has lost; and, if such person is condemned, let him be obliged to pay twice the value of the loss sustained. If the master of the house on such an occasion happens to be absent, let those that are present permit only such things as are unsealed to be examined; and let the person that searches the house seal with his own signet the things already sealed, and leave for five days any person he pleases as a guard in the house. But if the master of the house is absent for a longer time than this, let him who desires to search the house take the ædiles along with him, break open such things as are

c   sealed, and, after he has examined them in conjunction with the domestics and ædiles, seal them again. With respect to things of an ambiguous nature, let not a limited time for the determination of them be left dubious: for by this means there will be no altercation about houses and land. But if any one is in possession of other things, and it appears that he has used them openly for the space of a year, in the city, in the forum, and in temples, and no one has laid claim to them during

d   that time, in this case let no one be permitted afterwards to demand those things as his own. But if such person used such things, neither in the city, nor in the forum, but openly in the fields, and the proper owner of them is not found in five years, let no one be suffered to demand them after the expiration of this time. But if such person uses these things at home in the city, let the period of laying claim to them

e   be limited to three years. But if he uses them secretly in the fields, let it be limited to ten years. And, if he used them in another district, let the person who has lost them be permitted to lay claim to them at any time. If any one forcibly hinders another, whether a plaintiff or defendant, from having recourse to justice, if it is a slave that he hinders, whether his own or belonging to another person, let no notice be taken of the affair, and let the legal process be stopt: but if it is a free-born

955a person, besides the legal process being stopt, let him by whom he was forcibly detained be imprisoned for a year, and let any one who is willing accuse him of mancipation. If any one forcibly prohibits a gymnastic or musical antagonist, or an opponent in any other contest, from contending in his art, let any one who is willing inform those that confer rewards on the victors in these exercises, of the affair; and these shall be the means of procuring admittance to the contests to such as are willing to engage in them. But if it should happen that they are incapable of procuring them admittance, if he who impedes is himself victorious, let the reward of his victory be given to the person he

b   impeded, and let the name of the person so impeded be inscribed as victor in whatever temples he pleases. But let not the person that impedes be suffered to suspend an offering, or make any inscription of a victory of this kind. Likewise, let him be accused of having done an injury, whether he vanquishes in contending, or is vanquished. If any one receives stolen goods knowingly, let him suffer the same punishment as the person that stole them. Let death, too, be the punishment of him that harbours an exile. For every one should reckon

c him as a friend or an enemy, who is considered as such by the city. If any one of his own accord makes peace with, or denounces war against, certain persons, without general consent, let death be the punishment of such a one. But if any part of a city makes peace, or denounces war, by itself, let the generals of the army bring the authors of this action before a court of justice; and, when condemned, let their punishment be death. Let those that serve their country in any respect do this without gifts. And let no occasion or arguments ever induce us to believe that we

d ought to receive gifts for good offices, but not for such as are bad. For it is neither easy to know when actions are good or bad, nor to endure patiently when this knowledge is obtained. it is, therefore, more safe to listen to, and be persuaded by, the law, which says that no one shall serve his country for the sake of gifts. Let him, therefore, who is unpersuaded by this law, when condemned, be punished with death. Let public tributes, too, be disposed as follows: In the first place, every one's possessions must be considered as subsisting for the sake of many utilities. In the next place, let those of the same tribe carry a written

e account of the annual fruits to the præfects of the land; so that, in consequence of there being two tributes, the republic may choose every year whichever of the two they please, *viz.* either a part of all the estates, or the annual crop, exclusive of such things as contribute to aliment. It is likewise proper that moderate offerings to the Gods should be dedicated by moderate men. Earth, therefore, which is the hearth of habitation, is the sacred possession of all the Gods. Let no one then consecrate the same thing a second time to the Gods. But gold and silver in other cities, both privately and in temples, are an invidious possession. Ivory, too, as belonging to a body deprived of soul, is not

56a a pure offering to the Gods. And iron and brass are the instruments of war. Let, therefore, any one dedicate whatever he pleases, from wood, so as it is fashioned from one piece of wood, and, in a similar manner, any thing formed from stone, in the common temples. With respect to things woven, let nothing of this kind be dedicated which exceeds the monthly work of a woman. White colours will be adapted to the Gods, both in other things, and in such as are woven. But nothing dyed should be offered, except it belongs to warlike ornaments. The most divine gifts, however, are such birds and pictures as a painter has finished in one day. And let all other offerings be similar to these. Since, therefore, we have divided the parts of all the city, in such a manner as is proper, and have spoken in the best manner we are able respecting the laws which ought to be established in all the greatest compacts, it now remains that we should speak concerning judgments. In the first place, therefore, let there be select judges for the courts of

c   justice, and such as are chosen in common by plaintiffs and defendants. These, indeed, may more properly be called arbiters than judges. In the next place, let those of the same street and tribe, when divided according to a twelfth part, be appointed as judges. Let the contending parties, if they cannot be reconciled by the former judges, go to these, and litigate with greater loss. Here, if the defendant is a second time condemned, let him pay the fifth part of the prescribed fine. But if any one accuses these judges, and wishes to dispute the affair in a third court of justice,

d   let him refer the cause to select judges. And if he is again condemned by these, let him pay the sum that is owing, and the half of it besides. But if the plaintiff, being repulsed by the first judgment, is not satisfied, but appeals to a second, - if he vanquishes let him receive a fifth part, but if he is vanquished let him lose the same part. And if he goes to a third court of justice, not being satisfied with the former judgments, let the defendant, if vanquished, pay (as we have said) the sum that is owing, and the half of it besides; but let the plaintiff pay the half only.

e   With respect to the allotments of courts of justice, the perfection and establishment of things ministrant to the magistrates, the times in which each of these ought to take place, the particulars respecting votes, the delays, terms, citations and repulses which take place in judicial affairs, and whatever else necessarily pertains to these, - all this we have already discussed. However, according to the proverb, what is beautiful and right may be spoken twice and thrice. All such legal particulars,

957a therefore, as are small and easy to be discovered, when omitted by an aged legislator, ought to be filled up by a junior legislator. And thus much may suffice concerning private courts of justice. But such as are public and common, and which are employed by magistrates to proper purposes, are found in many cities established in no unbecoming manner by equitable men. Whence it is requisite that the guardians of the laws should procure such things as are adapted to this new polity, by reasoning, correcting, and exploring them, till they appear to them to be

b   sufficiently established; and then bringing them to a conclusion, that they should seal them as things immovable, and use them through the whole of life. With respect to the silence of judges, the praises which are given them, or the contrary, and likewise concerning things just, good, and becoming, which differ in other cities, we have already spoken, and shall again speak in the end. But it is requisite that he who in future will be an equitable judge should look to all these particulars, and being in possession of them, when committed to writing, should make them the object of his study. For written laws are more calculated to make him who learns them better, than all other disciplines, if they are properly established. For, indeed, divine and admirable law does not rashly possess a name adapted to intellect.[†] And besides this, the writings of the legislator afford us a perspicuous examination of the assertions of others respecting praise and blame, which are partly transmitted to us in verse, and partly in prose, and which likewise daily take place in all other associations, when men contend with each other through emulation, and concessions which are vain in the extreme. These a good judge should always keep in his possession, as remedies against the poison of other discourses, correcting by them both himself and the city; confirming and praising the good, and recalling, to the utmost of his power, such of the evil as are curable from ignorance, intemperance, timidity, and, in short, from all injustice. For, if they are incapable of being cured, those judges, and governors of the judges, that put them to death, as the only remedy to souls in such a condition, may be often said, with justice, to deserve praise from the whole city. After annual judgments are finished, let them use the following laws: - In the first place, let the magistrate who exercises the office of a judge consign over all the money of the debtor to the victor, leaving him only sufficient for necessary uses. And let this take place immediately after the giving of votes, the affair being announced by a cryer, and in the hearing of the judges. In the next place, if, after sentence is passed, one month has elapsed and a second commenced, and the vanquished person has not voluntarily paid what is due to the victor, let the judicial magistrate deliver up the money of the debtor to the victor. But if the debtor has not sufficient money to discharge the debt, and he is deficient not less than a drachm, let not the debtor be suffered to go to law with any other person till he has paid all that is due to the victor; but let any other person be permitted to go to law with him. If any one, when condemned by a magistrate, unjustly takes any thing from him, let the injured magistrate take the offender before the court of justice of the guardians of the laws. And if he is condemned by these, let him be

---

† For νομος, law, is properly νου διανομη, a distribution of intellect.

punished with death, as one who subverts the whole city and the laws. But a man who is born and educated, and who begets and educates children, under these laws, who engages moderately in contracts, is punished if he acts unjustly, and sees those punished that injure him, and, lastly, who grows old together with the laws, - such a one will end his days according to nature.

With respect to the funeral rites of the dead, whether male or female, and the particulars which pertain to the infernal and supernal Gods, let them be instituted according to the answers of the interpreters. Let there be no sepulchres in cultivated places, neither large nor small. But let that place alone receive the bodies of the dead which is useless for other purposes, and will in the smallest degree injure the living. For no one, either living or dying, should impede the fecundity of mother earth, and thus deprive some living person of aliment. Likewise, let no tomb be raised higher than five men are able to raise in five days. Let the stone columns, too, be no larger than are sufficient to admit an encomium of the dead in four heroic verses; and let the dead be laid out no longer a time than is sufficient to evince that they are truly dead. But, with respect to human affairs of this kind, an interval of three days before the burial will be nearly sufficient. It is likewise proper to believe the legislator in other things; and when he asserts that the soul is in *every respect* different from the body; and that, in the present life, it causes each of us to be that which each of us is; but, that body follows each of us like an image; and, that bodies may be beautifully said to be the images of the perfectly dead. That, besides this, each of us may be truly denominated an immortal soul, which will depart to other Gods to give an account of its conduct, as the law of our country asserts. This, however, is a circumstance which produces confidence in the good, but is terrible in the extreme to the evil; for no great assistance can be rendered them after death. Hence, it is necessary to give them all proper assistance while living, that they may live in the most just and holy manner, and that after the present life they may escape the punishments which await the commission of crimes. Since this, then, is the case, we ought by no means to ruin our families, in consequence of thinking that this mass of flesh which is buried is truly our relative; but we should be persuaded that the son or brother, or any person for whom we have an affection, and whom we consider as buried, has departed hence in consequence of having finished and filled up his fate. We shall, therefore, act well on these occasions by employing a moderate expense, as upon an inanimate altar of terrestrial natures. But the legislator will not, in the most disgraceful manner, divine what this moderate expense should be. Let this, then, be the law:- that he who possesses the greatest estate shall not spend more than five minæ on any funeral; that he who possesses the second estate shall spend three minæ; the third, two; and the fourth, one mina. For thus the funeral expenses of every individual will be moderate. But, as the guardians of the laws ought necessarily to take care of many things, so especially of this, that their life may be employed in attending to boys and men, and to males and females of every age. And besides this, on the death of every citizen, one of the guardians of the laws, whom the relations of the deceased shall think fit to choose, should take care that every thing pertaining to the funeral is conducted in a becoming and moderate, and not in an unbecoming and disgraceful manner. And let them be honoured when the former, but considered as infamous when the latter, is the case. Let, therefore, every thing pertaining to funerals take place according to this law. But things of the following kind ought to be committed to the care of the legislator who establishes political law: - it would be unbecoming either to order, or not, the dead to be lamented with tears; but loud lamentations on this occasion, out of the house, are to be forbidden. The dead body, likewise, should not be suffered to be carried openly in the more frequented roads, accompanied with lamentations, nor yet out of the city before day. Let such, therefore, be the established laws respecting these particulars. And let him who is obedient to them be exempt from punishment; but let him who disobeys one of the guardians of the laws be punished by all of them in such a manner a s shall appear fit to all. With respect to other particulars, which either pertain to sepulchres, or to those who through patricide and sacrilege are deprived of sepulchres, these we have spoken of before, and legally established. So that legislation has now nearly obtained its completion. But the end of all things must be considered as taking place, not from their being performed, or possessed, or inhabited, but from their being properly accomplished, and firmly established. For, in a preservation of this kind, it is proper to think, that what ought to be done is done, but that prior to this the whole is imperfect.

CLIN. You speak well, O guest. But inform me in a yet clearer manner what was your design in what you just now said?

GUEST. Many things, O Clinias, are beautifully said by the ancients, and this is true, in no small degree, with respect to the names of the Fates.

CLIN. How so?

GUEST. That the first of these is Lachesis, the second Clotho, and the third Atropos,[†] who is the preserver of what has been asserted by us. These are assimilated to things conglomerated by fire, and which possess an inconvertible power. And in a city and polity these ought not only to procure health and safety to bodies, but a good establishment of laws in souls, or rather the preservation of laws. But it appears to me that this is yet wanting to laws, - I mean, an inquiry how they may obtain an inconvertible power according to nature.

CLIN. You speak of no small affair, if it is possible to find how a thing of this kind may take place in every possession.

GUEST. But this is possible, as it appears in every respect to me at present.

CLIN. Let us not, therefore, depart hence, by any means, till we have added this to the laws we have now delivered. For it is ridiculous to labour in any thing in vain, and not to lay down something stable.

MEGIL. You exhort in a proper manner: and you will also find me to be such a one.

CLIN. You speak well. What then is this preservation, and after what manner may it be obtained in our polity and laws?

961a GUEST. Have we not said that an assembly ought to be held in our city of the following kind:- That always ten of the oldest guardians of the law, together with all such as are honoured with gifts, should make a part of this assembly? That, further still, those who have travelled over many regions in order that they might find something adapted to the preservation of the laws, should go to this assembly, if on their return their manners were found to be uncorrupted, and themselves worthy to be members of this assembly? That, besides this, each of these ought to bring with him young men, who are not less than thirty years of age, and who are judged to deserve this honour both by nature and education, and by the approbation of the whole assembly? And that if any unworthy young man should be brought to the assembly, the sentence which is passed should be of no moment? Lastly, that this assembly should be convened before day, when there is a perfect leisure from all other business, both public and private? Was not something of this kind asserted by us in the preceding discourse?

c CLIN. It was.

GUEST. Again, therefore, resuming the discourse about this assembly, we say, that if any one hurls forth this, as an anchor of the whole city,

---

[†] For an account of the Fates, see the Notes to the Tenth Book of the *Republic*, [TTS Vol. IX, p. 578 *et seq.*]

and which contains in itself every thing that can be desired, every thing will be preserved which we wish to be so.

CLIN. How so?

GUEST. We shall after this take occasion to speak with rectitude, and, to the utmost of our power, leave nothing unfinished.

CLIN. You speak exceedingly well: act, therefore, agreeably to your conceptions.

d GUEST. It is proper therefore, O Clinias, to understand, with respect to every thing, a fit saviour in every work; as in an animal, the soul and the head are naturally the greatest saviours of the whole.

CLIN. How again do you say?

GUEST. The virtue of these, doubtless, affords safety to the whole animal.

CLIN. But how?

GUEST. In soul, indeed, besides other things, intellect is inserted; and in the head, besides other things, sight and hearing. And, in short, intellect being mingled with the most beautiful senses, so as to produce one thing, the preservation of the several parts may most justly be said to be thus effected.

CLIN. It appears so.

e GUEST. Undoubtedly. But does not intellect, mingled with the senses, become the safety of ships, both in tempests and fair weather? Or, in a ship, do not the pilot and the sailors, in consequence of mingling their senses with the piloting intellect, preserve both themselves and every thing pertaining to the ship?

CLIN. Undoubtedly.

GUEST. But there is no need of many examples about things of this kind: let us consider, therefore, in an army, and in medicine, to what mark both commanders and physicians directing their attention, become the means of preservation.

CLIN. It will be proper to do so.

62a GUEST. Do not the former of these, then, direct their attention to victory, and the strength of the enemies, but the latter to the health of the body?

CLIN. Undoubtedly.

GUEST. But, if the physician is ignorant of that respecting the body which we now denominate health, or the commander of victory, or of other things which we might mention, would they appear to be endued with intellect about any of these particulars?

CLIN. How could they?

b GUEST. But what with respect to a city? If any one is ignorant of the mark at which a politician ought to look, could he, in the first place, be justly denominated a governor? And, in the next place, would he be able to preserve that, the scope of which he is perfectly unacquainted with?

CLIN. How could he?

GUEST. It is necessary therefore now, as it appears, if the establishment of this our city is to obtain its completion, that there should be some one in it who knows, in the first place, this which we call the political scope; in the next place, after what manner it is requisite to partake of this; and, in the third place, which of the laws, and who among men, will properly or improperly consult with a view to this. For, if any city is destitute of a thing of this kind, it will not be wonderful, since it must be void of intellect and sense, if all its actions are the result of chance.

c CLIN. You speak the truth.

GUEST. Now, therefore, are we able to say in what part of our city, or by what studies, any guard of this kind will be sufficiently obtained?

CLIN. I cannot clearly inform you, O guest. But, if I may be allowed to jest, it appears to me that this discourse tends to that nocturnal assembly which you said ought to be instituted.

d GUEST. You have rightly conjectured, O Clinias; and, as the present reasoning announces, this assembly ought to possess every virtue; the chief of which is not to wander, by regarding a multitude of particulars, but, looking to one thing, always to emit all things like darts to this.

CLIN. Entirely so.

GUEST. Now, therefore, we learn that it is not wonderful that the legal institutions of cities wander. For different establishments of the laws in each city look to different things. And to some, the end of what

e is just consists in certain persons governing in the city, whether they are better or worse than others. But, with others, the end consists in becoming rich, whether they are slaves or not. The attention of others again is directed to a life of liberty. Others establish laws for two purposes, that they may be free themselves, and that they may become the despots of other cities. And those that are most wise direct their attention to these, and to all such particulars, at once; but they are unable to assign any one principal thing to which the rest ought to look.

963a CLIN. Hence, O guest, that which was formerly established by us is right; for we said that the whole of our laws should always look to one thing. And we granted that this might, with the greatest rectitude, be called virtue.

GUEST. We did so.

CLIN. And it was likewise established by us that virtue was, in a certain respect, fourfold.

GUEST. Entirely so.

CLIN. And that intellect, likewise, was the leader of all these, to which all other things, and three of the virtues, ought to look.

GUEST. You have followed me in a beautiful manner, O Clinias; continue, therefore, to follow me in what remains. For we have said, b that the intellect of the pilot, the physician, and the commander, looks to one thing; but, accusing the politic intellect, we have arrived thus far, and we shall now thus interrogate it as if it were a man: - O wonderful man! to what do you tend? What is that one thing which the medicinal intellect can speak of in a perspicuous manner; but you, who, as you say, excel all prudent persons, are not able to do this in your art? Or c can you, O Megillus and Clinias, answer for him what this is, as I have often done to you for others?

CLIN. By no means, O guest.

GUEST. But should we not desire to perceive what this is, and in what things it subsists?

CLIN. In what particular things do you mean?

GUEST. As we have said that there are four species of virtue, it is evident that each of them must necessarily be one, since they are altogether four.

CLIN. Undoubtedly.

d GUEST. We likewise denominate all these one. For we say that fortitude is a virtue, and that prudence is a virtue; and, in a similar manner, the two others, as if this thing virtue was not in reality many things, but one thing only.

CLIN. Entirely so.

GUEST. So far, therefore, as these two differ from each other, and receive two names, and, in a similar manner, the other two, there is no difficulty in speaking of them; but so far as we call both of them, together with the other two, one thing, *viz.* virtue, it is not easy to speak of them.

CLIN. How do you say?

GUEST. There is no difficulty in explaining what I say. For let us only divide among ourselves the business of interrogating and answering.

CLIN. How again do you mean?

e GUEST. Do you ask me why, denominating virtue one thing, we again give this appellation to two things, one of which is fortitude, and the other prudence? For I will tell you the cause, which is this:- One of these is conversant with fear, whence savage beasts also participate of fortitude, and the manners of very young children. For the soul may be brave from nature without reason, but without reason it never was prudent and endued with intellect, nor is, nor ever will be. So that this latter differs from the former.

CLIN. You speak truly.

964a GUEST. You, therefore, understand from my discourse in what manner these are two, and how they differ from each other; but how they are one and the same do you again inform me. But think as if you were telling me how being four they are one, and as if I afterwards should show you how being one they are again four. And after this, let us consider, whether he who wishes sufficiently to understand any thing which has both a name and a definition, ought only to know the name, but should be ignorant of the definition; or whether it is base for him b who has any knowledge respecting things which transcend in magnitude and beauty, to be ignorant of all such particulars as these.

CLIN. It appears so.

GUEST. But is there any thing greater which a legislator, a guardian of the laws, and he who is thought to surpass all others in virtue, and for this receives rewards, can possess, than fortitude, temperance, justice, and prudence?

CLIN. How is it possible there can?

GUEST. Ought not, therefore, interpreters, teachers, legislators, and guardians of others, to teach those who desire to know and to perceive things of this kind, or who require punishment and reproof, what power c virtue and vice possess; and must they not, through information of this kind, in every respect excel others? Or will any poet coming into the city, or any instructor of youth, be considered as better than him who excels in all virtue? And, in the next place, will it appear wonderful if a city, in which the guardians have not a sufficient knowledge of virtue, in consequence of being without a guard, should suffer the same things which many cities at present suffer?

d CLIN. It will not appear wonderful.

GUEST. What then? Shall we do what we just now spoke of? Or shall we consider how we may enable the guardians to excel others in virtue, both in words and in reality? Or after what manner our city may become similar to the head and senses of the prudent, through possessing in itself a guard of this kind?

CLIN. How, therefore, O guest, and after what manner, shall we speak, assimilating it to a thing of this kind?

e   GUEST. It is evident that the city itself will resemble the cavity of the head; and that the junior guardians, who are ingenuous and sagacious, will be placed, as it were, on the highest summit, whence they can survey, in a circle, the whole city, and, while they defend it, deliver the senses to the memory, and announce to the elders every thing that takes
965a place in the city. But these being assimilated to intellect, through understanding in the highest perfection a multitude of things which are worthy of regard, they will consult for the city, and employ the junior guardians as agents in their consultations. For thus both will truly preserve the city in common. Whether, therefore, shall we say they are to be established in this manner, or not? Or shall we say that they are all to be considered as equal, and not accurately determine the difference between them, in education and discipline?

CLIN. But this, O wonderful man, is impossible.

b   GUEST. Let us, therefore, proceed to a more accurate discipline than the former.

CLIN. By all means.

GUEST. But is not that which we just now touched upon the very thing which we are in want of?

CLIN. Entirely so.

GUEST. We said, then, that in every thing a consummate artificer and guardian ought not only to be capable of looking to many things, but should eagerly tend to one thing, and, when he has obtained a knowledge of it, orderly dispose according to this whatever he beholds.

CLIN. Right.

c   GUEST. Can, therefore, any speculation be assigned more accurate than that which is able to look to one idea from things many and dissimilar?

CLIN. Perhaps not.

GUEST. Not perhaps, but in reality, O dæmoniacal man! there is not any human method more clear than this.

CLIN. Believing what you say, O guest, I will admit it. Let us, therefore, proceed, speaking agreeably to this assertion.

GUEST. As it appears, therefore, the guardians of a divine polity must be compelled by us to see accurately, in the first place, what that is which
d   is the same in all the four virtues; and which, being one thing in fortitude and temperance, justice and prudence, we very properly call by one name, virtue. Strenuously laying hold of this at present, O friends, if you are willing, we will not leave it till we have sufficiently said what
e   that is which is to be looked to, whether as one thing, or as a whole, or as both, or in whatever way it may subsist. Or can we think that, if

this escapes us, we can ever sufficiently possess the things pertaining to virtue, respecting which we are neither able to say whether it is many things, nor whether it is four things, nor whether it is one thing? If, therefore, you are persuaded by our advice, we shall devise some method by which this may take place in our city. Or, if it appears in every respect agreeable to you, we will dismiss it.

CLIN. A thing of this kind, O guest, is by the hospitable God by no means to be dismissed, since you appear to us to speak with the utmost rectitude. But how can any one devise this method?

966a GUEST. We shall not yet say how this is to be devised: but, in the first place, is it requisite or not that we should firmly consent among ourselves?

CLIN. It is doubtless requisite, if possible.

GUEST. But what with respect to the beautiful and the good? Are our guardians to know that each of these is alone many? Or should they, likewise, know that it is one, and how it is so?

CLIN. It nearly seems necessary, that they should know scientifically how each of these is one.

b GUEST. But what? ought they to understand this, and at the same time be incapable of evincing by arguments that they do understand it?

CLIN. But how can this be? For you speak of a certain habit belonging to a slave.

GUEST. But what with respect to all serious pursuits? Shall we in a similar manner say, that those who are to be truly guardians ought truly to know the particulars respecting the truth of laws, be able sufficiently to unfold them in discourse, and act agreeably to them, judging what things subsist beautifully according to nature, and what have a contrary subsistence?

CLIN. How is it possible we should not?

c GUEST. Is not that one of the most beautiful things which we seriously discussed concerning the Gods? As that they are, that they appear to possess a mighty power, and that this ought to be known by man, as far as he is capable of knowing it? Likewise, that we should pardon the greater part of those in the city, if they only follow the mandates of the laws, but that we should not commit the guardianship of them to any one who has not laboured to acquire all possible faith in things pertaining to the Gods? And that we should never choose any

d one for a guardian of the laws, who is not a divine man, who has not laboured in the study of the laws, and who does not excel in virtue?

CLIN. It is just, therefore, as you say, that he who is sluggish, or incapable of judging respecting things of this kind, should be far removed from beautiful concerns.

GUEST. Do we, therefore, know that there are two things which lead to a belief of the particulars concerning the Gods, which we discussed above?

CLIN. What are they?

GUEST. One is that which we asserted respecting the soul, that it is the most ancient and divine of all things, of which the motion receiving generation imparts an ever-flowing essence: but the other is concerning the orderly motion of the stars, and such other things as through the dominion of intellect adorn the universe. For he who contemplates these things neither in a negligent nor in a stupid manner, can never become so impious as not to be affected in a manner perfectly contrary to the conjectures of the multitude. For these conceive that those who apply themselves to things of this kind, I mean to astronomy and other necessary arts in conjunction with it, become atheists, in consequence of beholding things subsisting from necessity, and not from the dianoëtic energies of a will by which all things are rendered good.

CLIN. How then do these subsist?

GUEST. They now subsist, as I have said, perfectly contrary to what they would if they were conceived to be deprived of soul. For though such as more accurately investigate these things than others, in a wonderful manner touch upon the truth, and by employing accurate reasoning evince that they are not destitute of soul and intellect; and though some of these[†] dared to assert that it was intellect which adorned every thing in the heavens; yet again erring with respect to the nature of the soul, as not knowing that it is more ancient than body, but conceiving it to be junior, they again, as I may say, subverted all things, and, much more, themselves. For, believing that all such things as are obvious to the sight subsist in the heavens,[‡] they considered the celestial regions as full of stones and earth, and many other inanimate bodies, and attributed to these the causes of the whole world. It was owing to this, that many who touched upon such like particulars were accused of impiety, and of engaging in difficult undertakings. And, besides this, those who philosophised were reviled by poets, and compared by them to dogs barking in vain; and other things were said

---

[†] *Viz.* Anaxagoras and his followers. See the *Phædo.*

[‡] This is the doctrine of modern astronomers.

of them which it would be foolish to repeat. But now, as I have said, the very contrary to this takes place.

d CLIN. How so?

GUEST. No mortal man can ever become firmly pious who does not admit these two things: *viz.* that soul is the most ancient of all things which participate of generation, and is immortal; and that it rules† over

e all bodies. But, besides this, our guardian of the laws should not be ignorant of that which has been often asserted by us, that there is a true intellect in the stars; and he should likewise possess the necessary disciplines which are previous to these things; and employ a proper

968a Muse, in order to harmonize the pursuits of manners and legal institutions. And, lastly, he should be able to render a reason for such things as admit one, and to show why this is not possible with other things. He who has not these requisites for public virtues will nearly never be a sufficient governor of the whole city, but will be subservient to other governors. But it is now proper to consider, O Clinias and Megillus, whether we ought to establish the character we have been describing, as the future legal guardian of all the preceding laws, for the sake of the preservation of the whole city; at the same time, that nocturnal assembly of governors, endued with all such discipline as we

b have mentioned above, being adopted: or how shall we act?

CLIN. But, O best of men, why should we not to the utmost of our power establish him?

GUEST. We certainly ought all of us to strive to accomplish this. I, indeed, will cheerfully be your helper. For perhaps though skill in, and the consideration of, things of this kind, I may find many other assistants besides myself.

CLIN. Let us, O guest, proceed in this path rather than any other, in

c which Divinity himself nearly leads us. But let us now speak of and devise the method by which this may be properly accomplished.

GUEST. Laws about things of this kind, O Megillus and Clinias, cannot be established till the city is orderly disposed; for then their authority may be legally determined. But they cannot in any other way be adopted with rectitude than by erudition and frequent examination in conjunction with others.

CLIN. How so? Why do we again say this?

---

† As Plato, therefore, has demonstrated in the preceding Tenth Book, that the apparent orb of every star is the vehicle of a ruling soul, it follows, according to him, that no one is firmly pious who does not believe this. And hence, the gross ignorance or impudence of those sophistical priests who have dared to assert that Plato ridiculed the religion of his country is sufficiently obvious.

GUEST. In the first place, without doubt, a catalogue should be made of those men who are adapted to be guardians, by their age, by the power of disciplines, and by their manners and habits. In the next place, it is neither easy to find what ought to be learnt, nor to become the disciple of him who discovers this. Besides this, the times will be in vain prescribed in writing, in which the several particulars ought to take place. For neither will the learners be able to know when any thing may be opportunely learnt, before science of the discipline is generated in their souls. Hence, all these particulars being spoken of occultly, will not be spoken of properly: but they are occult, because they cannot be rendered clearer by narration.

CLIN. Since this then is the case, O guest, what shall we do?

GUEST. We must act, O friends, according to the proverb. For we must discuss the affair in common and publicly. And if we wish to make the dangerous trial, respecting the whole polity, we must do all things, either, as they say, throwing thrice six, or three dice. I will, however, undergo the danger with you, in speaking and explaining what appears to me respecting the discipline and education which we have now discussed. The hazardous enterprise is, indeed, neither small, nor similar to any other. But I exhort you, O Clinias, to make this the object of your care. For you, in the city of the Magnesians, or in that to which Divinity shall give a name, will obtain the greatest glory if you establish it properly. Or certainly, in this case, you cannot avoid appearing to be the bravest of all that shall succeed you. If then this divine assembly shall be established for us, O friends and companions, the city must be delivered to its care. Nor will there be any altercation, as I may say, with any of the legislators at present respecting these institutions. But, in reality, we shall nearly effect that in a vigilant state, which we touched upon in our discourse a little before, as in a dream, when we mingled together a certain image of the agreement of the head with intellect, if these men are accurately mingled together for us, are properly disciplined, and when disciplined reside in the acropolis of the region, so as to become such guardians, and possess the virtue of preservation in such a degree as we have not known any to possess it in the former part of our lives

MEGIL. O friend Clinias, from all that has been now said by us, it follows, that we must either omit the establishment of this city, or not dismiss this our guest, but by entreaties and all manner of devices make him a partaker with us in establishing the city.

CLIN. You speak with the greatest truth, Megillus. And I indeed shall act in this manner; but do you also cooperate with me.

MEGIL. I will.

End Note to The Laws

1. (See page 34, line 653d) The following account of the festivals of the ancients, from the Descriptions of Libanius, fully proves the truth of what is here asserted by Plato represents to us the liberal, philanthropic, and hospital spirit of Paganism in the most amiable point of view, and naturally leads the truly benevolent mind to regret that such philanthropy has been for so long a period banished from the earth; that the presence of divinity is no longer considered as essentially necessary to the splendour of festivity, and that a festival at present is every thing but a solemnity!

"Solemn festivals when approaching produce desire in the human race, when present they are attended with pleasure, and when past with recollection: for remembrance places men very near the transactions themselves. The recollection also possesses a certain advantage. For, in speaking of solemn festivals, it is also necessary to speak concerning the Gods in whose honour they are instituted. Men prepare themselves for these festivals, when they approach, with joy. The multitude indeed procure such things as may furnish them with a splendid entertainment, but the worthy, those things by which they may reverence the Gods. Cattle and wine, and whatever else is the produce of the fields, are brought from the country. Garments also are purified; and every one is anxious to celebrate the festival in perfection. Those that are in want of garments are permitted to borrow such as are requisite to adorn themselves on this occasion, from those that have abundance. When the appointed day arrives, the priests open the temples, pay diligent attention to the statues; and nothing is neglected which contributes to the public convenience. The cities too are crowded with a conflux of the neighbouring inhabitants, assembled to celebrate the festival; some coming on foot, and others in ships.

"At sunrise they enter the temples in splendid garments, worshipping that divinity to whom the festival is sacred. Every master of a house therefore precedes, bearing frankincense: a servant follows him, carrying a victim; and children walk by the side of their parents, some very young, and others of a more advanced age, already perceiving the strong influence of the Gods. One having performed his sacrifice departs; another approaches to perform it. Numerous prayers are every where poured forth; and words of good omen are mutually spoken. With respect to the women,, some offer sacrifices in the temples; and others are satisfied with beholding the crowd of those that sacrifice. When such things as pertain to the divinities are properly accomplished, the tables follow, at which hymns are sung in praise of the God who is honoured in the festival. Social drinking succeeds, with songs which are partly serious and partly jocose, according to the different dispositions of the company. Some likewise feast in the temples, and others at home; and citizens request strangers to partake with them of the banquet. In the course of drinking, ancient friendships are rendered more firm, and others receive their commencement. After they have feasted, rising from table, some take the strangers and show them whatever is worthy to be seen in the city; and others sitting in the Forum gaily converse. No one is sorrowful, but every countenance is relaxed with jog. The exaction of debts gives place to festivity; and whatever might cause affliction is deferred to another time. Accusations are silent, and the judge does not pass sentence; but such things as produce pleasure alone flourish. The slave is not afraid of blows from his master, and pedagogues are mild to youth.

"In the evening they sup splendidly, at which time there are so many torches that the city is full of light. There are also many revellers, and various flutes, and the sound of pipes is heard in the narrow streets, accompanied with sometimes the same, and sometimes different songs. Then to drink even to intoxication is not perfectly disgraceful; for the occasion in a certain respect appears to take away the opprobrium. On the following day the divinity is not neglected; but many of those that worshipped on the preceding day to not again come to the shows. Those that contend in the composition of verses attend on this, but those with whom the contest is in the scenes, on the preceding day. The third day also is not far short of these; and pleasure and hilarity are extended with the time of the festival. When the solemnity ends, prayers are offered for futurity, that they, their children and families may again be spectators of it; after which the strangers depart, and the citizens accompany them."

The same author likewise in his account of the Calends observes as follows: "This festival is extended as far as the dominion off the Romans; and such is the joy it occasions, that if it were possible time could be hastened for mortals, which according to Homer was effected by Juno respecting the sun, this festival also would be hastened by every nation, city, house, and individual of mankind. The festival flourishes in every plain, on every hill and mountain, and in every lake and navigable river. It also flourishes in the sea, if at that time it happens to be undisturbed by tempest; for then both ships and merchants cut through its waves and celebrate the festival. Joy and feasting every where abound. The earth is then full of honours; in consequence of men honouring each other by gifts and hospitality. The foot-paths and the public roads are crowded with men, and four-footed animals bearing burthens, subservient to the occasion; and the ways in the city are covered, and the narrow streets are full. Some are equally delighted with giving and receiving; but others, though they do not receive any thing, are pleased with giving, merely because they are able to give. And the spring by its flowers, indeed, renders the earth beautiful; but the festival by its gifts, which pouring in from every place are every where diffused. He therefore who asserts that this is the most pleasant part of the year, will not err; so that, if the whole time of life could be passed in the same manner, the islands of the blest would not be so much celebrated by mankind as they are at present. The first appearance of the swallow is indeed pleasant, yet does not prevent labour; but this festival thinks proper to remove from the days of its celebration every thing laborious, and permits us to enjoy minds free from molestation. These days free the youth from two-fold fears, one arising from their preceptors, the other from their pedagogues. They also make slaves as much as possible free, and exhibit their power even in those in chains, removing sorrow from their countenances, and exciting some of them to mirth. They can also persuade a father who expects the death of his son, and through sorrow is wasting away;, and averse to nourishment, to be reconciled to his condition, to abandon darkness, lay aside his squalid appearance, and betake himself to the bath: and what the most skilful in persuasion are unable to accomplish, that the power of the festival effects. It also conciliates citizen with citizen, stranger with stranger, one boy with another, and woman with woman. It likewise instructs men not to be avaricious, but to bring forth their gold, and deposit it in the right hands of others." He concludes with observing, "that the altars of the Gods in his time did not possess all that they did formerly, this being forbidden by the law of the Christians; but that, before this prohibition, much fire, blood, and fume of sacrifice ascended to heaven from every region, so that the banquets in honour of the Gods were then splendid during the festival."

The most remarkable circumstance in these festivals was the cause of this universal joy, which was no other than the firm persuasion that divinity was then present and propitious, as is evident from the following beautiful passage from Plutarch;, in the Treatise in which he shows that pleasure is not attainable according to Epicurus: "Neither the discourses (says he) of those that wait in the temples, nor the seasons of solemn festivals, nor any other actions, or spectacles, delight us more than those things which we ourselves do concerning the Gods, when we celebrate orgies, or join in the dance, or are present at sacrifices, or the greatest of the mysteries. For then the soul is not sorrowful, abject, and languid, as if conversing with certain tyrants, or dire avengers, which it is reasonable to suppose she then would be; but where she especially thinks and rationally conceives divinity is present, there she especially banishes sorrow, and fear, and care, and lets herself loose even to intoxication, frolic and laughter. In amorous concerns, indeed, as the poet once said,

> Remembrance of the joys that Venus gave,
> Will fire the bosom of the aged pair.

But in public processions and sacrifices, not only the old man and the old woman, not only the poor and the plebeian, but also

> The dusty thick-legg'd drab that turns the mill,

and household slaves and hirelings, are elevated with joy and gladness. Banquets and public entertainments are given both by the wealthy and kings; but those which take place at sacrifices and solemnities, when through inspiration we appear to approach very near to a divine nature, are attended with much greater joy and pleasure, in conjunction with honour and veneration. Of this, the man who denies a Providence has no portion. For it is not the abundance of wine, nor the roasting of meat, which gives delight in solemn festivals, but the good hope and belief that divinity is propitiously present, and gratefully receives what is done. From some of our festivals we exclude the flute and the crown; but when divinity is not present at the sacrifice, as the solemnity of the banquet, the rest is impious, is void of festivity, and possesses nothing of divine fury; or, rather, the whole is unpleasant, and even painful."

Ουτε διατριβαι των εν ιεροις ουτε καιροι των εορτασμων, ουτε πραξεις, ουτε οψεις ευφραινουσιν ετεραι μαλλον ων ορωμεν η δρωμεν αυτοι περι θεων, οργιαζοντες, η χορευοντες, η θυσιαις παροντες, η τελεταις. ου γαρ ως τυραννοις τισιν η δεινοις κολασταις ομιλουσα τηνικαυτα η ψυχη περιλυπος εστι και ταπεινη και δυσθυμος, οπερ εικος ην· αλλ᾽ οπου μαλιστα δοξαζει και διανοειται παρειναι τον θεον, εκει μαλιστα λυπας και φοβους και το φροντιζειν απωσαμενη τω ηδομενω μεχρι μεθης και παιδιας και γελωτος αφιησιν εαυτην. Εν τοις ερωτικοις ως ο ποιητης ειρηκε,

> Και τε γερων και γρηυς, επην χρυσης Αφροδιτης
> Μνησωνται, και τισιν επηερθη φιλον ητορ.

Εν δε πομπαις και θυσιαις ου μονον γερων και γρηϋς, ουδε πενης και ιδιωτης, αλλα και παχυσκελης αλετρις προς μυλην κινουμενη, και οικοτριβες και θητες υπο γηθους και χαρμοσυνης αναφερονται· πλουσιοις τε και βασιλευσιν εστιασεις και πανδαισιαι τινες παρεισιν αι δ᾽ εφ ιεροις και θυηπολιαις, και οταν εγγιστα του θειου τη επινοια ψαυειν δοκωσι, μετα τιμης και σεβασμου πολυ διαφερουσαν ηδονην και χαριν εχουσιν. ταυτης ουδεν ανδρι μετεστιν απεγνωκοτι της προνοιας. ου γαρ οινου πληθος, ουδε οπτησις κρεων το ευφραινον εστιν εν ταις εορταις, αλλα και ελπις αγαθη και δοξα του παρειναι τον θεον ευμενη, και δεχεσθαι τα γινομενα κεχαρισμενως· αυλον μεν γαρ ετερων εορτων και στεφανον αφαιρουμεν, θεου δε θυσια μη παροντος, ωσπερ ιερον δοχης, αθεον εστι και ανεορταστον και ανενθουσιαστον το λειπομενον, μαλλον δε ολον ατερπες αυτω και λυπηρον. The same author also observes, in his Treatise on Superstition, "that holy days, temple feasts, the being initiated in mysteries, processions, with public prayers and solemn devotions, were considered as the most agreeable things in human life."

THE EPINOMIS

or

THE PHILOSOPHER

INTRODUCTION

The *Epinomis*, or *Nocturnal Convention*, was not written by Plato, but, as we are informed by Diogenes Laertius, by Philip Opuntius, one of Plato's disciples. This dialogue, which, as its name implies, is a supplement to the *Laws*, is highly valuable, both for its great antiquity, its author being contemporary with Plato, and the recondite wisdom which it contains. However, notwithstanding its great intrinsic excellence, it appears to me that any one much conversant with the writings of Plato might easily discover that it was not written by that philosopher, though antiquity had been totally silent in this particular; for, where shall we find in it either his heroical strength and magnificence of diction, or his profundity, accuracy, and sublimity of conception?

This dialogue is also very properly inscribed *The Philosopher*, since the design of it, as the author informs us in the very beginning, is to show what wisdom is, and how it may be obtained. Before, however, he teaches us what wisdom is, he inquires what it is not; and having premised certain things necessary to its definition, he shows that the august name of wisdom can by no means accord with those arts which are subservient to the necessaries and conveniences of life, such as politics, agriculture, architecture, rhetoric, and the like. After this, he enumerates the speculative disciplines, and, in the first place, not only praises but admires arithmetic, which, according to Plato, most of all things sharpens the wit, strengthens the memory, and renders the mind prompt and adapted to every speculation and action. The arithmetic, however, which is here so deservedly praised, is not that which is commonly taught, and which is subservient to merchandize and traffic; but it is entirely speculative, and considers the properties of pure numbers unconnected with any thing sensible. Of this arithmetic Euclid and Nicomachus have transmitted to us the elements; but the study of it is at present neglected, because it is not calculated to promote gain, facilitate calculation, or expedite business. The author also adds, that number was delivered by divinity to men, as a necessary instrument of reason and discursive energy; and that, this being taken away, the soul would appear to be destitute of intellect, and arts and sciences entirely vanish. He also praises geometry, astronomy, music, and physics; and places dialectic, i.e. metaphysics, or *wisdom*, before all the other sciences, because it employs these as steps in the discovery and adoration of

Divinity. He likewise shows that there are three employments of this queen of the sciences about other disciplines. The first consists in beholding the multitude of all these; the second, in surveying the communion and connection in all of them; and the third considers in what manner this multitude and its union contributes to *The One Itself* and divine good. Lastly, the reader may learn from this dialogue, that as religion consists in the worship, so wisdom in the contemplation of Divinity; and that human felicity and the end of laws are only to be obtained in the union of both.

THE EPINOMIS

or

THE PHILOSOPHER

PERSONS OF THE DIALOGUE

An Athenian Guest,

Clinias the Cretan, and

Megillus the Lacedæmonian.

973a   According to our agreement, O guest, we are all of us rightly assembled, being three, I, and you, and Megillus here, for the purpose of considering after what manner we should investigate prudence; which when understood, we say that it causes the human habit to subsist in the most beautiful manner possible to man, with respect to itself. For we have discussed every thing else respecting the establishment of laws. But

b   we have not yet related and discovered, that which it is the greatest thing to discover and relate, I mean, what that is by the learning of which mortal man will become wise. We should now endeavour not to leave this uninvestigated: for, if we do, we shall nearly leave that imperfect, for the sake of rendering which apparent from the beginning to the end we have all of us proceeded thus far.

c   GUEST.   You speak well, friend Clinias. But I think you will now hear a wonderful discourse, though again in a certain respect it is not wonderful. For many that we meet with in life assert, that the human race can neither be blessed nor happy. Attend, therefore, and see, whether it appears to you as well as to me, that by speaking as follows about this affair we shall speak well. For I say it is not possible for men in this life, except a few, to become blessed and happy. But the hope is beautiful that after death we shall obtain every thing, for the sake of which we cheerfully live and die in the best manner we are able. Nor is my assertion novel, but that which we all after a certain manner know, as well Barbarians as Greeks. For the production of every animal is in the beginning difficult. In the first place, the participation of the

fœtal habit is difficult; and, in the next place, to be nourished and educated. And, as we all say, these things are accomplished through ten 974a thousand labours. The time, too, is short, not only with respect to the endurance of calamities, but every thing else which causes human life to take breath, as it were, about a medium. For old age swiftly arriving makes every one who is not full of puerile opinion unwilling to return to life again, when he considers the life he has lived. And is not the
b subject of our present investigation an argument of the truth of these assertions? For we investigate how we may become wise, taking it for granted that there is in each of us a power by which this may be accomplished. But wisdom then flies from us, when we apply ourselves to any of those things which are called by the name of art or prudence, or to any other such particulars as we rank among the sciences; because
c no one of these, as being conversant with human affairs, deserves to be called by the appellation of wisdom. The soul, however, vehemently confides and prophesies, that she naturally possesses this power: but what it is, and when, and how it subsists, she is not altogether able to discover. But do not our doubting and investigation respecting wisdom refer to this exceedingly, *viz.* that there is abundance of hope for such as are able to examine both themselves and others prudently, and in an according manner, through every kind of reasoning and disputation? Shall we say that these things are so, or not?

d CLIN. We admit that they are, O guest, hoping that we shall in time, together with you, entertain the most true opinions respecting them.

GUEST. In the first place, then, let us discuss those other pursuits which are, indeed, called sciences, but do not render him wise who receives and possesses them; that, removing these out of the way, we may endeavour to assign the particulars of which we are in want, and,
e when assigned, to learn them. Let us, therefore, first consider the things which the mortal genus first requires: for these are nearly most necessary, and truly such as are first.[†] But he who is knowing in these, though at first he may appear to be wise, yet now he is not considered
975a as such, but is rather disgraced by science of this kind. We shall mention, therefore, what they are, and shall show that every one who proposes to appear to others to be a most excellent man, will avoid these through the possession of prudence and accurate study. Let the first art then be that which orders us to abstain from the eating of human flesh; this, according to the fable, being the practice of mankind formerly,

---

[†] That is, they are first to man, who is naturally adapted to proceed from the imperfect to the perfect; but the perfect is first to nature.

after the manner of savage animals, and which recalls us to legal nutriment. The ancients, indeed, were and are benevolent to us. Let us,
b however, bid farewell to those whom we call the first men. The preparation, indeed, and nutriment of Cerealian food is beautiful and good, but will never render a man completely wise: for it is attended with molestation. Nor yet will the whole of agriculture he able to accomplish this. For we all of us appear to undertake the cultivation of the earth, not from art but nature, through the favour of Divinity. But neither can the construction of houses, the whole of architecture, the
c making of every kind of furniture, the art of the coppersmith, and the apparatus of tectonic, plastic, plectic, and, in short, of all instruments which are accommodated to the vulgar, but are not subservient to virtue, accomplish this. Nor, again, can the whole of hunting, though it is various and artificial, confer magnificence on the wise man. Nor yet divination, or the interpreting art; for these alone know that which
d is asserted, but they do not understand whether it is true or not. Since then we see that none of those arts by which necessaries are procured can make any one wise, after this that discipline remains which is for the most part imitative, but by no means serious. For imitation is here effected by means of many instruments, and through many gestures of bodies not altogether graceful. In discourse, too, there is imitation in every Muse; and in things of which the graphic art is the mother, where things, many and all-various, are expressed in moist and dry bodies; none of which, though fabricated with the greatest diligence, can in any
e respect render a man wise. After imitation, those arts remain which afford innumerable helps to men on innumerable occasions. The greatest of these and the most useful is the warlike art; but it is in want of abundance of felicity, and naturally rather requires fortitude than
976a wisdom. But that which they call the medicinal art affords us assistance in unseasonable cold and heat, and in all those circumstances by which the nature of animals is injured; at the same time that no one of these contributes to the most true wisdom, for they proceed by uncertain conjectures and opinions. We likewise acknowledge that pilots and sailors afford us assistance; but at the same time we do not permit any
b one of these to be called a wise man. For none of them knows the rage, or the friendship, of the winds, which is the most acceptable thing in the whole of the pilot's art. Nor yet do we call those wise who by the power of eloquence afford assistance in courts of justice; for these pay attention to the manners of opinion, through memory and experience, but wander from the truth of things just in reality. There still remains a certain absurd power with respect to the opinion of wisdom, which

many denominate nature rather than wisdom. This takes place when any one easily understands a thing which he is learning, and firmly remembers a multitude of things; and can rapidly attribute to any thing c that which is accommodated to it, when it is proper so to do. For all these some denominate nature, others wisdom, and others sagacity of nature. But no prudent person will ever be willing to call any one of these a truly wise man. It is however necessary, that a certain science should be rendered apparent, which he who possesses will be truly wise, d and not only so in opinion. But let us consider; for we are attempting a thing in every respect difficult, as we are endeavouring to find something different from the above-mentioned particulars, which many truly and with propriety called wisdom, and which he who receives will neither be vile, nor stupid, but be rendered through it wise and good, and become an elegant man in a city, whether he governs or is governed.

Let us, therefore, consider this in the first place, investigating that one science belonging to human nature, which not existing, man would e become most stupid and unwise. But this is not very difficult to perceive. For, as I may say, referring one to one, that which number imparts to the mortal race will accomplish this. I think, however, that a God himself, rather than a certain fortune, gave us this for our preservation. It is proper, however, to inform you what God I think it was, though my opinion will appear wonderful, and yet in a certain respect not wonderful. For, how is it possible that he who is the cause 977a to us of every thing good should not also be the cause of by far the greatest good, prudence? But what God am I celebrating, O Megillus and Clinias? Nearly *Heaven*, whom it is most just we should, in the highest degree, honour, and fervently pray to, since this is done by all other Dæmons and Gods. That *Heaven*, indeed, is the cause to us of all other good, we all acknowledge. But we must also assert that, at the b same time, he has given us number, and still imparts it to us, if any one is willing to follow us in what we say. For *he* will ascend to the right contemplation of this divinity (whether we may be allowed to call him the World, or Olympus, Heaven,) who attends to the variety it contains, and how, by the courses of the stars which revolve in it, it imparts the seasons and nutriment to all things; and besides these, prudence, as we have said, together with all number, and every other good. But this is the greatest thing, when any one, receiving from him the gift of number, proceeds through every circulation. Again, recurring back a little, let us c call to mind that we very rightly conceived that, by taking away number from human nature, we should be deprived of prudence. For the soul of this animal would scarcely any longer be able to receive every virtue, if deprived of reason. But the animal which does not know two and three, the even and the odd, and is entirely ignorant of number, will never be able to give a reason respecting those things of which it alone possesses sensation and memory; but nothing hinders it from possessing

d the other virtues, I mean fortitude and temperance, without this knowledge. However, he who is void of true reason can never become wise. And he to whom wisdom is not present, which is the greatest part of the whole of virtue, as in this case he will not be perfectly good, so he will never be happy. So that there is the greatest necessity that number should be established as a principle: but to show that this is necessary, a discourse longer than the preceding is requisite. It was, however, just now rightly asserted by us, that all the other arts which

e we a little before enumerated, must be entirely subverted if the arithmetical science is taken away. But some one who looks to the arts may be of opinion, that there are but few things in which mankind are indigent of number; yet, even here its utility is great. But if any one looks to that which is divine and mortal in generation, in which the cultivation of divinity and true piety are known, he will find that no

978a prophet can comprehend the mighty power which the whole of number possesses. For it is evident that every thing pertaining to music requires numbered motion and sound. And, which is the greatest thing, it may be easily known that number is the cause of every thing good, but of nothing evil, because every irrational, disordered, inelegant, and unharmonious lation, and all such things as participate of a certain evil, are deprived of all number. And this ought to be thus understood by him who is to be finally happy. To which we may add, that he who is ignorant of the just, the good, the beautiful, and all such things, and

b who has not received a true opinion respecting them, cannot employ the power of number in order to persuade himself and others.

But let us now proceed to consider how we learnt to number: Whence, then, came we to perceive one and two; so that we might understand that in order to the knowledge of which we received this

c power from the universe? Nature, indeed, has not imparted to many animals the power of numbering, derived from their parents; but Divinity first implanted in us the ability of understanding number in that which is pointed out to us. Afterwards he rendered it more apparent to us; in which unfolding of things nothing can be seen more beautiful, if one thing is compared with another, than the genus of day.

d In the next place behold the night, which possesses the greatest diversity. For, by continually revolving these things, you will see many days, and many nights, in which the heavens, without ceasing, teach men one and two, so that even the most indocile may hence learn to number. For thus each of us, on perceiving these things, may understand three and four, and the many. And from these, Divinity fabricating, made one thing the moon, which at one time appearing greater, and at another less, continually varies as far as to fifteen days and nights. And this is a period, if any one is willing to establish the whole circle as one. So that, as I may say, the most indocile animal may learn to number, if he is one to whom Divinity has imparted the ability of learning. And, as far as to these, and in these particulars, every animal has the ability of becoming skilled in arithmetic, by considering one thing itself, by itself. But always to reason about all numbers, when compared with each other, appears to be a more arduous undertaking. And for the sake of this, Divinity having made, as we have said, the moon, increasing and decreasing, fabricated months for the purpose of constituting the year, and caused us to compare every number with number, with prosperous fortune. Hence, earth bears fruit for us, and becomes prolific, so that she is the nurse of all animals; and winds and showers are produced, neither immoderate nor immense. But if any thing evil happens in these, it is proper to accuse not a divine, but human, nature, as unjustly distributing its own life. To us, therefore, investigating laws, it has appeared, that other things which are best for men, are easy to be known, and that every one can sufficiently understand and perform what we asserted respecting them, if he understands what is advantageous and what is not so. It has been shown by us, indeed, and at present it appears, that all other pursuits are not difficult in the extreme; but to assign the manner in which men may be rendered good, is perfectly difficult. And again, to possess other goods in a proper manner is, as has been said, possible, and not difficult, - I mean riches, and the body. Likewise, every one acknowledges it is requisite that the soul should be good; and every one will say that it becomes good through temperance, fortitude, and the like. Every one, too, will say that the soul ought to be wise; but what the wisdom is which it ought to acquire, is not, as we just now observed, determined by any of the multitude. Now, therefore, besides the above-mentioned kinds of wisdom, we have discovered a wisdom by no means vile; so that he who learns what we have discussed will appear to be wise. But whether he who learns these things will be in reality wise and good, must become the subject of our discourse.

CLIN. How justly, O guest, you said that you should endeavour to speak greatly about great things!

e GUEST. They are not trifling things, Clinias; and what is of still greater consequence, they are in every respect true.

CLIN. Exceedingly so, O guest; but, at the same time, do not yield to labour, but continue your discourse.

GUEST. I will. Neither do you, therefore, be weary of hearing.

CLIN. We shall not: for I will be answerable to you for both of us.

980a GUEST. It is well. But it is necessary, as it appears, to speak first of all from the beginning; and especially, if we are able, we should comprehend in one name that which we consider as wisdom. But if we are very incapable of accomplishing this, we should consider that which ranks in the second place, the quality and number of those arts, which he who receives will, according to our doctrine, be a wise man.

CLIN. Proceed, then, in this manner.

GUEST. In the next place, then, the legislator will be without envy who speaks better respecting the Gods than the ancients, and who employing, as it were, beautiful discipline, honours the Gods with hymns, extols their felicity, and thus passes through life.

CLIN. You speak well, O guest; since the proposed end of your laws consists in acquiring the best and most beautiful end of life, through reverencing the Gods, and purity of conduct.

GUEST. How, therefore, shall we speak, Clinias? Does it appear to you that we should vehemently honour by hymning the Gods, and that we should beseech them that we may proceed to speak things the most beautiful and the best respecting their divinities? Or how do you say?

c CLIN. Thus, in a wonderful manner. But, O dæmoniacal man, confiding in the Gods, pray, and begin your discourse on the beautiful things respecting the Gods and Goddesses.

GUEST. Be it so, if Divinity himself is pleased to be our leader. Do you only pray with me.

CLIN. Now, therefore, proceed with your discourse.

GUEST. As the ancients, then, as it seems, have badly delivered in images the generation of Gods and animals, it is proper, in the first place, according to our former assertion, to accomplish this in a better

d manner, by resuming our discourse to the impious. For, if you remember, Clinias, we have shown that there are Gods, that their providence extends to all things both small and great, and that they are not to be appeased by any unjust supplications or gifts. These things, indeed, you should call to mind, because they are highly true. But the greatest among those assertions is this, that every soul is more ancient than every body. Do you remember? or, rather, do you not perfectly

e remember this? For that which is better, more ancient, and more divine, is prior to that which is worse, junior, and less honourable. And, universally, that which governs is more ancient than that which is governed, and that which leads than that which is led. We must 981a admit this, therefore, that soul is more ancient than body. But, if this be the case, it is probable that what is first in the generation of the first must take the lead. We lay down this position, then, that the principle of a principle subsists in a more becoming manner, and that thus we shall most rightly ascend to the wisdom respecting the generation of the Gods.

CLIN. Let these things be so, which are asserted in the best manner we are able.

GUEST. Come, then, do we not say that an animal then subsists most truly according to nature, when one composition of soul and body produces by its junction one form?

CLIN. We do.

b GUEST. A thing of this kind, then, is most justly called an animal.

CLIN. It is.

GUEST. But it is requisite, according to assimilative reasoning, to say, that there are five solid bodies, from which the most beautiful and best things may be fashioned. But the whole of the other genus possesses one form. For there is not any thing else which can be generated immortal, and in no respect at any time possess colour, except the truly c most divine genus of soul. But this is nearly that alone to which it pertains to fashion and fabricate; but it belongs to body to be fashioned, generated, and become the object of sight. And we again assert (for it must not be said once only) that it is the property of soul to be invisible, endued with knowledge, intelligible, and to partake of memory and the reasoning power in even and odd mutations. As there are, therefore, five bodies, it is requisite to say that two of them are fire and water, that the third is air, the fourth earth, and the fifth æther. But in the several principalities of these many and all-various animals are produced. The truth of this we may thus learn in one of these bodies. d For let us, in the first place, consider the terrene genus of animals, viz. all the human kind, all such animals as have many feet, and are without feet, such as have a progressive motion, and such as are stable and connected by roots. But this one thing ought to be attended to, that though all animals are constituted from all these genera, yet the terrene genus abounds with earth and solidity. It is, however, requisite to place another genus of animals, which is generated, and, at the same time, capable of being seen. For it consists for the most part of fire; but likewise contains small parts of earth and air, and of all other things.

Hence, it is requisite to assert that all-various and visible animals are generated from this genus. It is likewise necessary to think that these genera of animals constitute all that the heavens contain; or, in other words, that they are the divine genus of the stars, consisting of a most beautiful body, and of a soul the most happy and the best. It is also requisite to consider this respecting these two genera of animals. For each of them is, from the greatest necessity, either indestructible, immortal and divine, or the life of each is so extended as not to require any longer period of duration. In the first place, therefore, as we have said, we must consider that there are these two genera of animals. And we again say that both of them are visible; the one, as it appears, consisting wholly of fire, and the other of earth. We must likewise assert, that the earthly genus is moved in a disorderly manner, but that which consists from fire, in perfect order. It is proper, therefore, to consider that which is moved without order, as stupid. But it is requisite to establish this as a great argument, that the natures which revolve in the heavens are endued with intellect, - I mean, that they always proceed according to the same and in a similar manner, and both do and suffer the same. But the necessity of a soul possessing intellect is by far the greatest of all necessities.† For it promulgates laws governing and not governed. But when soul, which is a thing of the most excellent nature, deliberates according to the most excellent intellect, then that which is perfect according to intellect takes place in reality, nor can an adamant be more firm and inconvertible than such a soul. Indeed, the three fates preserve perfect that which is deliberated by each of the Gods with the best counsel. It is requisite, therefore, men should be convinced that the stars, and the whole of this progression, are endued with intellect, from this circumstance, that they always perform the same things. For in the past time they have deliberated for a wonderfully extended period respecting their actions. But they are not, in deliberating, agitated upwards and downwards, nor do they wander and revolve in a disorderly manner, acting differently at different times. The contrary of this, however, appears to many of us, - I mean, that because they perform the same things, and in a similar manner, they are without a soul. The vulgar, too, embracing this INSANE OPINION, conceive that the human genus is intellectual and vital, because it is moved, but that the divine genus is destitute of intellect, because it abides in the same lations. But it becomes the man who attributes to the Gods things more beautiful, more excellent, and more

---

† For *persuasion* belongs to soul, but *necessity* to intellect.

friendly to their natures, to conceive that it is necessary to consider them as possessing intellect, because they always accomplish the same things, according to the same, and in a similar manner. And that this is the nature of the stars, most beautiful to the sight, and which by a progression and musical dance, the most beautiful and magnificent of all choirs, produces in all animals every thing that is proper and becoming. But that we justly consider them as animated, may, in the first place, be

983a evinced by their magnitude. For they are not in reality so small as they appear to be; but it deserves to be believed, that each of them is of an immense magnitude, as this may be shown by sufficient demonstrations. For we may rightly think that the whole sun is larger than the whole earth; and that all the stars possess a wonderful magnitude. We should consider, therefore, after what manner so great a bulk can be made to

b revolve by a certain nature perpetually in the same time. I say, therefore, that Divinity is the cause of this, and that it cannot in any other manner be accomplished. For it can no otherwise become animated than through a God, as we have evinced. As Divinity, therefore, is the cause of its animation, and all things are easy to a God, in the first place, he generated every body and every bulk in the heavens an animal; and, in the next place, he caused it to move in that manner which he conceived, by a dianoëtic energy, to be the best. And now, respecting all these particulars, we shall make one true assertion, viz. It

c is impossible that earth, heaven, all the stars, and all the bulks composed from these, could subsist, unless a soul is either present with each, or resident in each, enabling them to revolve with such accuracy according to years, and months, and days, and thus procuring for all of us every good. But it is requisite that, by how much more vile man is than celestial animals, by so much the less should he trifle, but assert something conspicuous concerning them. He, therefore, who assigns certain fluxions of bodies, or natures, or any thing of this kind, as the causes of the celestial convolutions, will not assert any thing conspicuous.

d It is, however, requisite to reconsider what we have said with the utmost attention, that it may appear whether our assertions were reasonable, or altogether futile. In the first place, then, we said, that there were two things, the one soul, and the other body; and that there were many things pertaining to each. We likewise asserted, that all these mutually differed from each other; and that there was no other third thing common to any one of them: but that soul differed from body in this, that the former possessed, and the latter was destitute of, intellect; that the one governed, and the other was in a state of subjection; and that the one was the cause of all the passions of bodies, but that the other was not the cause of any one of these. So that he who asserts that celestial natures were generated by any thing else, and that they do not consist, in the manner we have said, from soul and body, must be very stupid and irrational. If, therefore, it is requisite that the arguments respecting all such particulars as these should be victorious, and that every nature of this kind should be believed to be divine, one of these two things must follow, *viz.* we must either celebrate the celestial orbs as Gods, and in so doing we shall act most rightly; or we must consider them as images of the Gods, fabricated as statues by the Gods themselves. For these two consequences are neither absurd nor of small importance, but, as we have said, one of these must ensue; and these statues are to be honoured beyond all other statues. For no statues will ever be found more beautiful and more common to all men than these, nor any that are established in more excellent places, or which so transcend in purity, venerableness, and all life, as these, which are throughout generated the same. Now, therefore, we should also endeavour to assert this respecting the Gods, *viz.* Since we perceive two species of visible animals, one of which we say is immortal, and the whole of the other which is terrene, mortal, we should endeavour to unfold, according to probable opinion, three species of animals which subsist between these five. After fire, then, we place æther; and we assert, that from it soul fashions animals which possess, like other genera, an abundant power from their own nature, but the smallest degree of power for the sake of a mutual bond, from other genera. But, after æther, soul fashions from air another genus of animals; and a third genus from water. Soul, therefore, having fabricated all these, filled the whole of heaven with animals, employing, to the utmost of its power, all the genera, as all these participate of life. But the second, third, fourth, and fifth, beginning from the generation of the visible Gods, at length end in us men. Respecting the Gods, Jupiter, Juno, and all the rest, let any one assign them such places as he pleases, if he only distributes them according to the same law, and considers this reasoning as stable.

We must call, therefore, the nature of the stars, and such things as we perceive together with the stars, the visible Gods, the greatest and the most honourable, perceiving every way most acutely, and ranking among such things as are first. But after, and under these, in a following order, dæmons subsist, an aërial genus, possessing a third and middle seat, who unfold the will of the Gods to men, and whom it is highly fit we should honour by prayers, for the sake of obtaining their propitious intercession. We cannot, however, wholly perceive either of these two kinds of animals, one of which subsists in æther, and the other in a following order in air. For, though these dæmons are by their situations near us, yet they never become manifest to us; but they participate of an admirable prudence, as being docile and of a good memory; and they

985a know all our thoughts. They likewise love in a wonderful manner worthy and good men, and vehemently hate such as are vicious, as being themselves participants of pain. For the Gods, indeed, who possess the end of a divine allotment, are situated beyond the reach of all pleasure

b and pain, and participate, in the utmost perfection, of prudence and knowledge. And, as the heavens are full of animals, these dæmons, and the highest Gods, mutually† interpret all things to each other. For the middle animals are borne to earth and the whole heaven with a light and rapid impetus. But he who assimilates the fifth genus of animals, which is from water to a demigod, will assimilate rightly. And this genus is sometimes visible, and sometimes concealed from our sight; and, when

c it is visible, is seen in a wonderful and obscure manner. As, therefore, there are these five kinds of animals, whatever occurs to us in dreams, oracles, and divinations, and such things as we hear through the voice of the healthy or diseased, or which happen to us at the close of life, whence many sacred rites are instituted, both privately and publicly, and will be instituted hereafter, - *with respect to all these, the legislator who possesses the smallest degree of intellect, will never make innovations in any of them, lest he should turn his city to a religion which possesses nothing conspicuous.* Nor will he forbid any thing respecting sacrifices which the

d law of his country has established, as being convinced that it is not possible for a mortal nature to know any thing about such like particulars. And for the same reason MUST NOT THOSE BE THE WORST OF MEN WHO DO NOT CELEBRATE THE TRULY APPARENT GODS, AND WHO SUFFER THE OTHER GODS TO REMAIN DEPRIVED OF THEIR SACRED RITES, AND THE HONOURS WHICH ARE THEIR DUE? For this

e is just as if someone should perceive the sun and moon inspecting without receiving any honours from the whole of the human race, and at the same time should not be anxious for the celebration of their divinities by mankind, that festivals and sacrifices may be instituted, and

986a that certain parts of greater and lesser years may be often distributed in honour of them. Would not such a one, if he should be said to be evil

---

† By dæmons interpreting all things to the Gods, nothing more is implied than an energy in dæmons, by which they become fitted to receive the influence of divinity more abundantly.

both to himself and to any other by whom he is known, be justly said to be so?

CLIN. Undoubtedly, O guest: for such a one must be the worst of men.

GUEST. Know assuredly then, friend Clinias, that this very thing has now happened respecting myself.

CLIN. How do you say?

GUEST. Know that there are eight powers revolving round the whole heaven, which are sisters to each other, and which I have beheld without paying them any great attention: for this is easy for another to accomplish. Of these, the following are three; one of the sun, another of the moon, and another of all the stars, which I mentioned a little before: and besides these there are five others.[†] With respect to all these, and such natures as are contained in these, whether they have a progressive motion themselves, or are borne along in vehicles, no one of us should at any time think that some of them are Gods, and others not; nor yet, that some of them are legitimate, but others such as it is not lawful for any of us to mention; but we should say that they are all of them brothers, and that they live in fraternal allotments. We should likewise honour them, not ordaining for some a year, for others a month, and for others no allotted portion of time, in which they accomplish their revolutions, and at the same time give perfection to a world, which reason determines to be the most divine of all visible things. This world a happy man will in the first place admire; and, in the next place, he will ardently desire to learn as much respecting it as is possible to a mortal nature; thinking that he shall thus pass through life in the best and most fortunate manner, and after death arrive at places adapted to virtue; and thus being truly initiated, and participating in reality of prudence, and becoming one, will pass the rest of his time in the contemplation of things the most beautiful of all such as pertain to the sight.

It now remains that we should relate, in the next place, what and how many these are. For we may without falsehood strenuously assert as follows. I again say, then, that there are eight of these, three of which we have already discussed, and consequently five remain. But the fourth and fifth lation and transition are nearly equal in swiftness with the sun, and are neither slower nor swifter. And of these three, intellect is always a sufficient leader, I mean of the sun, Lucifer, and that third which cannot be denominated because it is not known. But the reason

---

† *Viz.* the five planets, Saturn, Jupiter, Mars, Venus, and Mercury.

987a of this is, because a Barbarian was the first spectator of these. For an ancient region is the nurse of those who first understood these particulars through the beauty of the summer season. And such was Egypt, and Syria, where, as I may say, all the stars are perpetually apparent, because clouds and rain are always far remote from that part of the world. Hence, both here, and in every other place, these things are found by the experience of an infinite length of time to be true; and on this account they ought boldly to be established by the laws. For to

b think that divine natures are not honourable, or that these things are not divine, is clearly the province of one not endued with intellect. But it is requisite to assign this as the reason why they have no names, though indeed they are denominated by certain persons. For Lucifer is called Vesper, or the star of Venus, by which it is probable that the author of this appellation was a Syrian. But the star which revolves with an equal velocity with the sun and Lucifer, is called Stilbon, or Mercury. And, besides these, there are three lations of those stars, whose course is to the right hand, in conjunction with the sun and moon. But it is requisite to call the eighth orb[†] one, which may with the greatest propriety be denominated the upper world. This orb moves contrary to the rest, and draws the others along with it, according to the opinion

c of those who have some skill in these affairs. But it is necessary to speak of such things as we sufficiently know. For true wisdom will thus in a certain respect appear to him who participates, though in a small degree, of right and divine intelligence. Three stars then remain, one of which differs from the rest by the slowness of its motion. This star is called by some Phænon, or Saturn. That which is next to this in slowness is called Phaethon, or Jupiter: and, after this follows Puroeis,

d or Mars, who has the most red colour of them all. These things, when explained by any one, are not difficult to be understood; but, when understood, we should frame such conceptions respecting them as we have mentioned above. This, also, ought to be known by every Grecian, that we inhabit a region which is nearly the best of all others for the acquisition of virtue. But it is proper to assert that its praise consists in being situated between the nature of summer and winter. However, as we have said, because we are more distant from the nature of summer than the Barbarians we understood posterior to them the orderly arrangement of these Gods; yet we must assert, that whatever

e the Greeks receive from the Barbarians, is by them carried to greater perfection. This, too, we should conceive to be the case with respect to the subject of the present discourse. For, though it is difficult to

---

† That is, the sphere of the fixed stars.

discover without ambiguity all such particulars as the present, yet the
hope is both beautiful and great, that the Greeks will reverence all these
divinities with a more excellent mode of worship than that which they
receive from the Barbarians, and that they will employ both discipline
and the Delphic oracles, and every legitimate observance, for this
purpose. Nor should any Greek be at any time fearful, that mortals
ought not busily to employ themselves about divine concerns; but, on
the contrary, he should think that neither is a divine nature destitute of
intellect, nor ignorant of human nature. For he knows that, in
consequence of Divinity acting as a teacher, those that are taught follow
and learn: and he likewise certainly knows that he teaches us number
and to numerate. For he would be the most stupid of all beings if he
were ignorant of this. For, as it is said, he would truly be ignorant of
himself, if he were indignant, and not delighted with those that are able
to learn, and who are rendered good through Divinity. But it is highly
reasonable to suppose that the first conceptions of men, respecting the
nature and actions of the Gods, were neither such as wise men would
frame, nor those that succeeded them. For they asserted, that fire and
water, and the other bodies, were the most ancient of all things; but that
the particulars belonging to that wonderful thing soul were of posterior
origin. Hence, they considered the lation of body as better and more
honourable, and as moving itself through heat and cold, and every thing
else of this kind: but they asserted that soul neither moved body nor
itself. But, now since we say, if soul subsists in body, that it is not at
all wonderful it should move and carry about both the body and itself,
there can be no reason to disbelieve its ability to carry about a certain
weight. Hence, as we now think proper to assert, that soul is the cause
of the universe; and as of things, some are good and others evil, it is not
at all wonderful, that soul should be the cause of every lation and
motion, but that a lation and motion which tends to good should
proceed from the best soul, and a lation and motion to the contrary,
from a contrary soul. But it is necessary that things good should have
vanquished, and should continue to vanquish, things which are not so.
All these particulars have been asserted by us according to Justice, the
avenger of the impious. With respect, however, to that which we have
just now examined, we ought not to hesitate in asserting, that a good
man is a wise man.

Let us however see, whether this wisdom, of which we were some
time since in search, can be acquired by discipline or art. For, if we are
destitute of the knowledge of this, we shall be ignorant of things just.
Thus it appears to me, and therefore I assert this to be the case. For,
having explored upwards and downwards, I will endeavour to evince to
you that which has become apparent to me. For, when the greatest part

b   of virtue is negligently attended to, it becomes the cause of ignorance, as what we have just now said appears to me most perspicuously to signify. But no one shall persuade us, that there is any part of virtue belonging to the mortal race, greater than piety. We must likewise assert that this is not produced in the most excellent natures through the greatest ignorance. But those are the most excellent natures which are most rarely found, and which when found benefit others in the highest degree. For the soul which moderately and mildly receives a flow, or

c   the contrary nature, is simple and ingenuous: it likewise admires fortitude, and is obedient to temperance: and, what is the greatest of all in these natures, it is able to learn, is of a good memory, is a lover of literature, and is very much delighted with things of this kind. For these things are not easily implanted by nature; and when they are innate, and obtain proper education and discipline, their possessors obtain such authority over most part of their inferiors as to cause them to think, speak, and act, in such a manner as is requisite, and when it is requisite, towards the Gods; prevent them from employing artifice in the sacrifices and purifications which are performed both to Gods and men;

d   and dispose them to honour virtue in reality, which is the most important of all things to every city. This part, therefore, we say is naturally the most principal, and, when instructed, is capable of learning in the greatest degree, and in the best manner. But no one can teach, unless Divinity leads the way. It is better, therefore, not to learn from one who teaches, but at the same time does not act after this manner. However, from what we have now said, it is necessary to learn these

e   things; and I have asserted that a nature of this kind is the most excellent. Let us then endeavour to explain what these particulars are, and how it is requisite to learn them; and this both according to my ability, who am the speaker, and the ability of those who are able to hear, that we may know after what manner certain things pertaining to

990a   the culture of divinity may be learnt. Perhaps, therefore, what you will hear is unusual: we shall, however, mention the name of the thing which, to him who is ignorant of it, would never appear to be the name. Are you then ignorant of astronomy, and that a true astronomer is necessarily the wisest of men? Not, indeed, that he is so who astronomizes according to Hesiod,[†] and all such as consider the rising and setting of the stars; but this must be affirmed of him who contemplates the eight periods, and how seven of these are contained

---

[†] Alluding to *The Works and Days* of Hesiod. He is not a true astronomer who studies the heavenly bodies with a view to the necessaries, conveniences, or elegancies of a mortal life, but he who speculates them as images of true beings.

under the first, and in what order each revolves. But no one will easily contemplate these things, unless he participates of a wonderful nature, as we have just now said, and as we shall again say, unfolding what is to be learnt, and the manner of learning it. In the first place, therefore, let this be said by us, that the moon accomplishes its period most swiftly, and thus, first of all, leads forth month and full moon. In the second place, it is requisite to consider the sun who produces the solstices through the whole of his period, and, together with the sun, those that revolve in conjunction with him. But that we may not often assert the same things about the same, the revolutions of all those natures which we mentioned before, and which it is not easy to understand, must be made the subject of contemplation; preparing human nature for this purpose by disciplines pertaining to these speculations, and this by long exercise and labour, while it is in a juvenile state. On this account, the mathematical disciplines will be necessary; of which the first and the greatest is that which respects numbers, but not those that possess a body, but which contain the whole of the generation and power of the even and the odd, as these two contribute to the knowledge and nature of things. That which is very ridiculously called geometry[†] follows these in an orderly succession. But the similitude of numbers naturally dissimilar to planes, becomes conspicuous by comparison. This circumstance, however, to him who is capable of understanding it, will evidently appear to be not a human, but a divine miracle. After this, those numbers which receive a triple increase, and are similar to the nature of a solid, are to be considered, and likewise those that are dissimilar to this nature, which is called by those that are conversant with it, geometry. But this, to those that are capable of understanding it, is a divine and wonderful thing, that as the power of things always revolves about that which is double, and in its own opposite, according to each proportion, every nature is fashioned according to genera and species. The first power, therefore, of the double proceeds according to number, in the ratio of one to two, being double[‡] according to power.

[†] Alluding to its name, which signifies the measuring of the earth, which is a mechanical operation; but geometry is a speculative science.

[‡] Of numbers, some are linear, others superficial, and others cubic and solid. The first are such as the number 2; the second such as the number 4, which is the square or second power of 2; and the third such as eight, which is the cube or third power of 2. Duple proportion also was considered by the ancients as perfect. In the first place, because it is the first proportion, being produced between one and two; and, in the second place, because it contains all proportions within it self; for the sesquialter,

But in that which is solid and tangible, the double again proceeds from one to eight. Another power of the double proceeds to the middle, but perhaps into that which is more than the less, and less than the greater; while again, another power by the same part surpasses, and is surpassed

b   by the extremities. But in the middle, of the proportion of six to twelve, the sesquialter and sesquitertian proportion subsists. And in the middle of these, a power revolving to both distributes to men an according and apt utility, which is imparted by the blessed choir of the Muses for the sake of sports, rhythm, and harmony. All these things, therefore, are produced and subsist after this manner. But their end is this, that we may betake ourselves to divine generation, and the most beautiful and divine nature of things visible, as far as divinity has conferred on men the ability of beholding them. These, however, we

c   shall never behold without the above-mentioned discipline. Besides this, in our several conversations we must refer every individual thing to its species, by interrogating and confuting when any thing is improperly asserted. For this may be rightly said to be the most beautiful and the first touch-stone which men can employ. But where only a pretended examination takes place, it is of all labours the most vain.

d   Further still, the accuracy of time must be considered by us, and the exactness with which it causes all the revolutions of the heavenly bodies to be accomplished; that he who believes the assertion to be true, that soul is more ancient and more divine than body, may also think it was beautifully and sufficiently said, *that all things are full of Gods*, and that no one of the natures more excellent than mankind, at any time forget, or pay but little attention to our concerns. But in all such things as these we should thus consider, that he who rightly apprehends each of these particulars will be benefited by them; but that it will be better for him who does not, to invoke Divinity. The manner, however, in which

sesquitertian, and the like proportions are, as it were, parts below duple proportion. The numbers which the author of the *Epinomis* here adduces are 1, 2, 4, 6, 8, 12. The ratio of 4 to 2 is duple, and that of 8 to 4 is also duple. These two excesses are equal in ratio, for that of each is duple, but they are not equal in number; for 8 exceeds 4 by 4, but 4 exceeds 2 by 2. Again, if we compare 6 to 4, and afterwards to 8, in the first case we shall have a sesquialter, and in the second a sesquitertian ratio; but these excesses are unequal in ratio, but equal in number. For the ratio of 6 to 4 = 1½, and the ratio 8 to 6 = 1⅓; but 6 exceeds 4 by 2, and is exceeded by 8 by 2. Again, compare 12 to 6, which is a duple ratio, and between these compare 8 to each. Then, 12 to 8 will be a sesquialter ratio, and 8 to 6 will be a sesquitertian ratio; but a duple ratio arises from 12 to 6; and the excesses between 12 and 8, and 8 and 6, are unequal both in ratio and number.

these particulars may be rightly apprehended is as follows: (for it is necessary to relate this also) - Every diagram, system of number, and composition of harmony, together with the one concord of all the stars in their revolutions, ought to be beheld by him who learns in a proper manner. But that of which we are speaking will become apparent to him who rightly learns looking to one thing. *For, to those who reason scientifically, there will appear to be naturally one bond[†] of all these.* But he who attempts to apprehend these in any other way ought, as we have said, to invoke Fortune. For, without these, it is not possible that any nature in cities can be happy. But this is the mode, this is the education, these are the disciplines; and through these we must proceed, whether they are difficult or easy. But it is not lawful to neglect the Gods; since the prosperous conception of all the above-mentioned particulars becomes apparent by an orderly progression. And I call him who rightly apprehends all these, most truly the wisest of men. I likewise strenuously affirm, both in jest and seriously, that such a one, when he has by death filled up his allotted time, will no longer participate of many senses, as at present, but will be a partaker of one destiny alone; and becoming one, instead of a multitude of things, will be happy, and, at the same time, most wise and blessed. And again, whether any one lives blessed on the continent, or in islands, I affirm that he will always participate a fortune of this kind; and that, whether any one living a public or a private life studies these things, he will, in like manner, obtain the same destiny from the Gods. But, as we have said in the beginning, and now the assertion appears to be most true, *it is only possible for a few of mankind to be perfectly blessed and happy.* And this is rightly asserted by us. For those that are divine and at the same time prudent men, who naturally participate of the other virtues, and who besides this have acquired all such portions of *blessed discipline* as we have mentioned, these alone can sufficiently receive and possess all that pertains to a divine destiny. We legally, therefore, ordain, that those who thus labour in these things, both privately and publicly, when they have arrived at old age, ought to possess the greatest authority in cities; and that others should follow these, and should celebrate all the Gods and Goddesses; and lastly, that all of us, in consequence of having examined these things, may, with the greatest propriety, exhort the nocturnal assembly to the pursuit of this wisdom.

[†] Meaning *Dialectic*; for an account of which see my Introduction to the *Parmenides*.

THE TIMÆUS

A DIALOGUE
ON NATURE

INTRODUCTION

The design, says Proclus, of Plato's *Timæus* evidently vindicates to itself the whole of physiology, and is conversant from beginning to end with the speculation of the universe. For the book of Timæus the Locrian concerning nature is composed after the Pythagoric manner; and Plato, thence deriving his materials, undertook to compose the present dialogue, according to the relation of the scurrilous Timon. This dialogue, therefore, respects physiology in all its parts; speculating the same things in images and in exemplars; in wholes and in parts. For it is filled with all the most beautiful modes of physiology, delivering things simple for the sake of such as are composite, parts on account of wholes, and images for the sake of exemplars; and it leaves none of the primary causes of nature unexplored.

But Plato alone, of all the physiologists, has preserved the Pythagoric mode in speculations about nature. For physiology receives a threefold division, one part of which is conversant with matter and material causes; but a second adds an inquiry into form, and evinces that this is the more principal cause; and lastly, a third part manifests that these do not rank in the order of causes, but concauses; and, in consequence of this, establishes other proper causes of things subsisting in nature, which it denominates *producing, paradigmatical,* and *final* causes. But this being the case, all the physiologists prior to Plato, confining themselves to speculations about matter, called this general receptacle of things by different names. For, with respect to Anaxagoras himself, as it appears, though while others were dreaming he perceived that intellect was the first cause of generated natures, yet he made no use of intellect in his demonstrations, but rather considered certain airs and ethers as the causes of the phænomena, as we are informed by Socrates in the *Phædo.* But the most accurate of those posterior to Plato, (such as the more early peripatetics,) contemplating matter in conjunction with form, considered these as the principles of bodies; and if at any time they mention a producing cause, as when they call nature a principle of motion, they rather take away than establish his efficacious and producing prerogative, while they do not allow that he contains the reasons[†] of his productions, but admit that many things are the progeny

---

[†] That Aristotle himself, however, was not of this opinion, I have shown in the Introduction to my Translation of his *Metaphysics.*

of chance. But Plato, following the Pythagoreans, delivers as the concauses of natural things, an all-receiving matter, and a material form, as subservient to proper causes in generation; but, prior to these, he investigates primary causes, i.e. the producing, the paradigmatical, and the final.

Hence, he places over the universe a demiurgic intellect and an intelligible cause; in which last the universe and goodness have a primary subsistence, and which is established above the artificer of things in the order of the desirable, or, in other words, is a superior object of desire. For, since that which is moved by another, or a corporeal nature, is suspended from a motive power, and is naturally incapable either of producing, perfecting or preserving itself, it evidently requires a fabricative cause for the commencement and continuance of its being. The concauses, therefore, of natural productions must necessarily be suspended from true causes, as the sources of their existence, and for the sake of which they were fabricated by the father of all things. With great propriety, therefore, are all these accurately explored by Plato, and likewise the two depending from these, *viz.* form, and the subject matter. For this world is not the same with the intelligible and intellectual worlds, which are self-subsistent, and consequently by no means indigent of a subject, but it is a composite of matter and form. However, as it perpetually depends on these, like the shadow from the forming substance, Plato assimilates it to intelligible animal itself; evinces that it is a God through its participation of good, and perfectly defines the whole world to be a blessed God, participating of intellect and soul.

Such, then, being Plato's design in the *Timæus*, he very properly in the beginning exhibits, through images, the order of the universe; for it is usual with the Pythagoreans,[†] previous to the tradition of a scientific doctrine, to present the reader with a manifestation of the proposed inquiry, through similitudes and images: but in the middle part the whole of Cosmogony is delivered; and towards the end, partial natures, and such as are the extremities of fabrication, are wove together with wholes themselves. For the repetition of the *Republic*, which had been so largely treated of before, and the Atlantic history, unfold through images the theory of the world. For, if we consider the union and multitude of mundane natures, we must say, that the summary account of the *Republic* by Socrates, which establishes as its end a communion pervading through the whole, is an image of its union; but that the

---

† Ειναι γαρ τοις Πυθαγορειοις εθος, προ της επιστημονικης διδασκαλιας προτιθεναι την δια των ομοιων, και των εικονων των ζητουμενων σκεμματων δηλωσιν. Procl. in Tim.

battle of the Atlantics against the Athenians, which Critias relates, is an image of the distribution of the world, and especially so according to the two coordinate oppositions of things. For, if we make a division of the universe into *celestial* and *sublunary*, we must say that the *Republic* is assimilated to the celestial distribution; since Socrates himself asserts that its paradigm is established in the heavens; but that the Atlantic war corresponds to generation, which subsists through contrariety and mutation. And such are the particulars which precede the whole doctrine of physiology.

But after this the demiurgic, paradigmatic, and final causes of the universe are delivered; from the prior subsistence of which the universe is fabricated, both according to a whole and according to parts. For the corporeal nature of it is fabricated with forms and demiurgic sections, and is distributed with divine numbers; and soul is produced from the demiurgus, and is filled with harmonic reasons and divine and fabricative symbols. The whole mundane animal too is connected together, according to the united comprehension which subsists in the intelligible world; and the parts which it contains are distributed so as to harmonize with the whole, both such as are corporeal and such as are vital. For partial souls are introduced into its spacious receptacle, are placed about the mundane Gods, and become mundane through the luciform vehicles with which they are connected, imitating their presiding and leading Gods. Mortal animals too are fabricated and vivified by the celestial Gods; and prior to these, the formation of man is delivered as a microcosm, comprehending in himself partially every thing which the world contains divinely and totally. For we are endued with an intellect subsisting in energy, and a rational soul proceeding from the same father and vivific goddess as were the causes of the intellect and soul of the universe. We have likewise an ethereal vehicle analogous to the heavens, and a terrestrial body composed from the four elements, and with which it is also coordinate. If, therefore, it be proper to contemplate the universe multifariously both in an intelligible and sensible nature, paradigmatically, and as a resemblance, totally and partially, a discourse concerning the nature of man is very properly introduced in the speculation of the universe.

With respect to the form and character of the dialogue, it is acknowledged by all that it is composed according to the Pythagoric mode of writing. And this also must be granted by those who are the least acquainted with the works of Plato, that the manner of his composition is Socratic, philanthropic, and demonstrative. If, therefore, Plato any where mingles the Socratic and Pythagoric property together, this must be apparent in the present dialogue. For it contains, agreeably to the Pythagoric custom, elevation of intellect, together with intellectual and divine conceptions: it likewise suspends every thing from intelligibles, bounds wholes in numbers, exhibits things mystically and symbolically, is full of an elevating property, of that which transcends partial conceptions, and of the enunciative mode of composition. But from the Socratic philanthropy it contains an easy accommodation to familiar discourse, gentleness of manners, proceeding by demonstration, contemplating things through images, the ethical peculiarity, and every thing of this kind. Hence, it is a venerable dialogue, and deduces its conceptions from on high, from the first principles of things; but it mingles the demonstrative with the enunciative, and prepares us to understand physics, not only physically but theologically. For, indeed, Nature herself rules over the universe suspended from the Gods, and directs the forms of bodies through the influence of their inspiring power; for she is neither herself a divinity, nor yet without a divine characteristic, but is full of illuminations from all the various orders of the Gods.

But if it be proper, as Timæus says, that discourses should be assimilated to the things of which they are the interpreters, it will be necessary that the dialogue should contain both that which is physical and that which is theological; imitating by this mean Nature which it contemplates. Further still, since according to the Pythagoric doctrine things receive a triple division, into such as are intelligible, such as are physical, and such as rank in the middle of these, which the Pythagoreans usually call mathematical, all these may very conveniently be viewed in all. For in intelligibles things middle and last subsist in a causal manner; and in mathematical natures both are contained, such as are first according to similitude, and such as are third after the manner of an exemplar. And lastly, in natural things the resemblances of such as are prior subsist. With great propriety, therefore, does Timæus, when describing the composition of the soul, exhibit her powers, and reasons, and the elements of her nature, through mathematical names: but Plato defines the characteristics of these from geometrical figures, and at the same time leaves the causes of all these pre-subsisting in a primary manner in the intelligible intellect, and the intellect of the artificer of the universe.

And thus much for the manner of the dialogue; but its argument or hypothesis is as follows. Socrates coming into the Piræus for the sake of the Bendidian festival, which was sacred to Diana, and was celebrated prior to the Panathenaia,[†] on the twentieth of the month Thargelion or June, discoursed there concerning a republic with Polemarchus, Cephalus, Glauco, Adimantus, and Thrasymachus the sophist. But on the following day he related this discourse in the city to Timæus, Critias, Hermocrates, and a fourth nameless person. On the third day they end the narration; and Timæus commences from hence his discourse on the universe, before Socrates, Critias, and Hermocrates; the same nameless person who was present at the second narration being now absent from the third.

With respect to the term *nature*, which is differently defined by different philosophers, it is necessary to inform the reader, that Plato does not consider either matter or material form, or body, or natural powers, as worthy to, be called nature; though nature has been thus denominated by others. Nor does he think proper to call it soul; but establishing its essence between soul and corporeal powers, he considers it as inferior to the former through its being divided about bodies, and its incapacity of conversion to itself, but as surpassing the latter through its containing the reasons of all things, and generating and vivifying every part of the visible world. For nature verges towards bodies, and is inseparable from their fluctuating empire. But soul is separate from body, is established in herself, and subsists both from herself and another; from another, that is, from intellect through participation, and from herself on account of her not verging to body, but abiding in her own essence, and at the same time illuminating the obscure nature of matter with a secondary life. Nature, therefore, is the last of the causes which fabricate this corporeal and sensible world, bounds the progressions of incorporeal essences, and is full of reasons and powers through which she governs mundane affairs. And she is a goddess indeed, considered as deified; but not according to the primary signification of the word. For the word God is attributed by Plato, as well as by the ancient theologists, to beings which participate of the Gods. Hence every pure intellect is, according to the Platonic philosophy, a God according to union; every divine soul according to participation; every divine dæmon according to contact; divine bodies are Gods as statues of the Gods; and even the souls of the most exalted men are Gods according to similitude; while in the mean time superessential natures only are primarily and properly Gods. But nature governs the whole world by her powers, by her summit comprehending the heavens, but through these ruling over the fluctuating empire of

† Sacred to Minerva.

generation, and every where weaving together partial natures in amicable conjunction with wholes.

But as the whole of Plato's philosophy is distributed into the contemplation of intelligibles and sensibles, and this very properly, since there is both an intelligible and sensible world, as Plato himself asserts in the course of the dialogue; hence in the *Parmenides* he comprehends the doctrine of intelligibles, but in the *Timæus* of mundane natures. And in the former of these dialogues he scientifically exhibits all the divine orders, but in the latter all the progressions of such as are mundane. Nor does the former entirely neglect the speculation of what the universe contains, nor the latter of intelligibles themselves. And this because sensibles are contained in intelligibles paradigmatically, and intelligibles in sensibles according to similitude. But the latter abounds more with physical speculations, and the former with such as are theological; and this in a manner adapted to the persons after whom the dialogues are called: to Timæus on the one hand, who had composed a book on the universe, and to Parmenides on the other, who had written on true beings. The divine Iamblichus, therefore, asserts very properly, that the whole theory of Plato is comprehended in these two dialogues, the *Parmenides* and *Timæus*. For the whole doctrine of mundane and supermundane natures is accurately delivered in these, and in the most consummate perfection; nor is any order of beings left without investigation.

We may behold too the similitude of proceeding in the *Timæus* to that in the *Parmenides*. For, as Timæus refers the cause of every thing in the world to the first artificer, so Parmenides suspends the progression of all things from *The One*. And as the former represents all things as participating of demiurgic providence, so the other exhibits beings participating of a uniform essence. And again, as Timæus prior to his physiology presents us through images with the theory of mundane natures, so Parmenides prior to his theology excites us to an investigation of immaterial forms. For it is proper, after being exercised in discourses about the best polity, to proceed to a contemplation of the universe; and, after an athletic contention through strenuous doubts about ideas, to betake ourselves to the mystic speculation of the unities of beings. And thus much for the hypothesis or argument of the dialogue.

But as a more copious and accurate investigation of some of its principal parts will be necessary, even to a general knowledge of the important truths which it contains, previous to this I shall present the reader with an abstract of that inimitable theory respecting the connection of things, which is the basis of the present work, and of the whole philosophy of Plato. For by a comprehensive view of this kind we shall be better prepared for a minute survey of the intricate parts of the dialogue, and be convinced how infinitely superior the long lost *philosophy* of *Pythagoras* and *Plato* is to the *experimental farrago* of the *moderns*.

Since the first cause is *The Good*,[†] and this is the same with the one, as is evident from the *Parmenides*, it is necessary that the whole of things should be the most excellent, that is, the most united that can possibly be conceived. But perfect union in the whole of things can no otherwise take place than by the extremity of a superior order coalescing, κατα σχεσιν, through habitude or alliance, with the summit of an order which is proximately inferior. Again, with respect to all beings, it is necessary that some should move or be motive only, and that others should be moved only; and that between these there should be two mediums, the self-motive natures, and those which move and at the same time are moved. Now that which is motive only, and consequently essentially immovable, is intellect, which possesses both its essence and energy in eternity; the whole intelligence of which is firmly established in indivisible union, and which though a cause prior to itself participates of deific illumination. For it possesses, says Plotinus, twofold energies; one kind indeed as intellect, but the other in consequence of becoming as it were intoxicated, and deifying itself with nectar. But that which is self-motive is soul, which, on account of possessing its energy in transition and a mutation of life, requires the circulations of time to the perfection of its nature, and depends on intellect as a more ancient and consequently superior cause. But that which moves and is at the same time moved is nature, or that corporeal life which is distributed about body, and confers generation, nutrition and increase to its fluctuating essence. And lastly, that which is moved only is body, which is naturally passive, imbecil and inert.

Now, in consequence of the profound union subsisting in things, it is necessary that the highest beings or intelligibles should be wholly superessential, κατα σχεσιν, according to proximity or alliance; that the highest intellects should be beings, the first of souls intellects, and the highest bodies lives, on account of their being wholly absorbed as it were in a vital nature. Hence, in order that the most perfect union possible may take place between the last of incorporeals and the first of bodies, it is necessary that the body of the world should be

---

[†] See the sixth Book of the *Republic* [509d].

consummately vital; or indeed, according to habitude and alliance, life itself. But it is necessary that a body of this kind should be perpetually generated, or have a subsistence in perpetually *becoming to be*. For after intellect, which eternally abides the same both in essence and energy, and soul, which is eternally the same in essence but mutable in energy, that nature must succeed which is perpetually mutable both in essence and energy, and which consequently subsists in a perpetual dispersion of temporal extension, and is co-extended with time. Such a body, therefore, is very properly said to be generated, at the same time that this generation is perpetual; because, on account of its divisibility and extension, it alone derives its existence from an external cause: likewise, because it is a composite, and because it is not at once wholly that which it is, but possesses its being in continual generation. This body, too, on account of the perpetuity of its duration, though this is nothing more than a flowing eternity, may be very properly called a whole with a total subsistence: for every thing endued with a total subsistence is eternal; and this may be truly asserted of the body of the world, when we consider that its being is co-extended with the infinite progressions of time. Hence, this divine or celestial body may be properly called ολος ολικως, or *a whole totally*, just as the limb of an animal is μερος μερικως, or *a part partially*. But between *whole totally* and *part partially* two mediums are necessarily required, *viz. part totally* and *whole partially* (μερος ολικως and ολος μερικως). The *parts*, therefore, with a *total subsistence* which the world contains, are no other than the celestial orbs, which are consequently eternal and divine, after the same manner as the whole body of the world, together with the spheres of the elements; and the *wholes partially* are no other than the individuals of the various species of animals, such as a man, a horse, and the like.

Now this divine body, on account of its superiority to sublunary natures, was called by Aristotle *a fifth body*, and was said by Plato to be composed for the most part from fire. But in order to a more perfect comprehension of its nature, it is necessary to observe, that the two elements which, according to Plato, are situated in the extremes, are fire and earth, and that the characteristic of the former is *visibility*, and of the latter *tangibility*; so that every thing becomes visible through fire, and tangible through earth. Now the whole of this celestial body, which is called by the ancients heaven, consists of an unburning vivific fire, like the natural heat which our bodies contain, and the illuminations of which give life to our mortal part. But the stars are for the most part composed from this fire, containing at the same time the summits of the other elements. Hence, heaven is wholly of a fiery characteristic, but contains in a causal manner the powers of the other elements; as, for instance, the solidity and stability of earth, the conglutinating and unifying nature of water, and the tenuity and transparency of air. For, as earth comprehends all things in a terrestrial manner, so the heavens contain all things according to a fiery characteristic.

But the following extraordinary passage from Proclus admirably unfolds the nature of this divine body, and the various gradations of fire and the other elements. "It is necessary to understand (says he[†]) that the fire of the heavens is not the same with sublunary fire, but that this is a divine fire consubsistent with life, and an imitation of intellectual fire; while that which subsists in the sublunary region is entirely material, generated and corruptible. Pure fire, therefore, subsists in the heavens, and there the whole of fire is contained; but earth according to cause, subsisting there as another species of earth, naturally associating with fire, as it is proper it should, and possessing nothing but solidity alone. For, as fire there is illuminative, and not burning, so earth there is not gross and sluggish, but each subsists according to that which is the summit of each. And as pure and true fire is there, so true earth subsists here, and the wholeness, ολοτης, of earth;[‡] and fire is here according to participation, and materially, as earth is according to a primary subsistence. So that in heaven the summit of earth is contained, and in earth the dregs and sediment of fire. But it is evident that the moon has something solid and dark, by her obstructing the light; for obstruction of light is alone the province of earth. The stars too obstruct our sight, by casting a shadow of themselves from on high. But since fire and earth subsist in heaven, it is evident that the middle elements must be there also; air first of all, as being most diaphanous and agile, but water, as being most vaporous: each at the same time subsisting far purer than in the sublunary region, that all things may be in all, and yet in an accommodated manner in each.

"However, that the whole progression and gradations of the elements may become apparent, it is necessary to deduce the speculation of them from on high. These four elements, then, fire, air, water, and earth, subsist first of all in the demiurgus of wholes, uniformly according to

---

† In Tim.

‡ For it is necessary that the first subsistence of each of the elements should be, as we have before observed, according to *part total*, in order to the perfect union of the world; and this *part total* is called by the Platonists ολοτης, or *a wholeness*.

cause. For all causes are previously assumed in him, according to one comprehension; as well the intellectual, divine, pure, and vigorous power of fire, as the containing and vivific cause of air; and as well the prolific and regerminating essence of water, as the firm, immutable, and undeviating form of earth. And this the theologist Orpheus knowing, he thus speaks concerning the demiurgus:[†]

> His body's boundless, stable, full of light.

And

> Th' extended region of surrounding air
> Forms his broad shoulders, back and bosom fair.

Again,

> His middle zone's the spreading sea profound.

And

> The distant realms of Tartarus obscure
> Within earth's roots his holy feet secure;
> For these earth's utmost bounds to Jove belong,
> And form his basis, permanent and strong.

"But from these demiurgic causes a progression of the elements into the universe takes place, but not immediately into the sublunary world. For how can the most immaterial things give subsistence to the most material without a medium; or things immovable be immediately hypostatic of such as are moved in all directions? Since the progression of things is nowhere without a medium, but subsists according to a well-ordered subjection; and generations into these material, dissipated, and dark abodes, take place through things of a proximate order. Since, therefore, the elements in the demiurgus are intellects and imparticipable intellectual powers, what will be their first progression? Is it not manifest that they will yet remain intellectual powers, but will be participated by mundane natures? For from imparticipable intellect the proximate progression is to that which is participated. And, universally, progression takes place from imparticipables to things participated, and from supermundane to mundane forms. But what are these things which yet remain intellectual, but are participated, and what subjection do they possess? Is it not evident that they are no longer intellectual (i.e. essentially intellectual)? But I call those natures intellectual which

---

[†] See TTS vol. V, p. 58.

are the forms of intellect, and of a truly intellectual essence. But becoming participated, and being no longer intellectual, it is evident that they are no longer immovable natures. But, not being immovable, they must be self-motive. For these are proximately suspended from immovable natures; and from things essentially intellectual a progression takes place to such as are so according to participation, and from things immovable to such as are self-motive. These elements, therefore, subsist in life, and are self-motive and intellectual according to participation. But the progression from this must be manifest. For the immediate descent from life is to animal; since this is proximate to life. And from that which is essentially self-motive, to that which is self-motive according to a participation of life. For, so far as it proceeds from life to animal, it suffers a mutation. But so far as it proceeds from that which is immaterial to things immaterial,[†] (that is, such as may be called immaterial when contrasted with mutable matter,) and from divine life to a divine essence, it becomes assimilated to them. If, therefore, you take away from hence that which is immaterial and immutable, you will produce that which is mutable and material. And through this, indeed, they are diminished from such as are before them; but on account of the symmetry and order of their motions, and their immutability in their mutations, they become assimilated to them. If, therefore, you take away this order, you will behold the great confusion and inconstancy of the elements; and this will be the last progression, and the very dregs and sediment of all the prior gradations of the elements.

"Of the elements, therefore, some are immovable, imparticipable, intellectual and demiurgic; but others are intellectual and immovable according to essence, but participated by mundane natures. Others again are self-motive, and essentially lives; but others are self-motive and vital, but are not lives. Some again are alter-motive, or moved by another, but are moved in an orderly manner; and, lastly, others have a disordered, tumultuous, and confused subsistence."

Such then is the progression of the elements, and such the nature of a celestial body. But, if the body of the world be spherical, and this must necessarily be the case, as a sphere is the most perfect of figures, and the world the best of effects, there must be some part in it corresponding to a centre, and this can be no other than earth. For, in an orderly progression of things, that which is most distant, and the last, is the worst; and this we have already shown is the earth. But in a sphere,

---

[†] He means the divine bodies of the stars, and the body of the heavens; which, compared with sublunary bodies, may be justly called *immaterial bodies.*

that which is most distant from the superficies is the centre; and, therefore, earth is the centre of the world. This conclusion, indeed, will doubtless be ridiculed by every *sagacious* modern, as too absurd in such an *enlightened* age as the present to deserve the labour of a confutation. However, as it follows by an inevitable consequence from the preceding theory, and this theory is founded on the harmonious union of things, we may safely assert that it is consubsistent with the universe itself. At such a period, indeed, as the present, when there is such a dire perversion of religion, and men of every description are involved in extreme impiety, we cannot wonder that the spirit of profane innovation should cause a similar confusion in the system of the world. For men of the present day being destitute of true science, and not having the least knowledge of the true nature and progressions of things, in the first place make the universe an unconnected production, generated in time, and of course naturally subject to dissolution; and, in the next place, allow of no essential distinction in its principal parts. Hence, the earth is by them hurled into the heavens, and rolled about their central sun in conjunction with the celestial orbs. The planets are supposed to be heavy bodies similar to our sluggish earth; the fixed stars are all so many suns; and the sun himself is a dense, heavy body, occasionally suffering dimness in his light, and covered with dark and fuliginous spots. With respect to this last particular, indeed, they boast of ocular conviction through the assistance of the telescope; and what reasoning can invalidate the testimony of the eyes? I answer, that the eyes in this particular are more deceived when assisted by glasses, than when trusting to their own naked power of perceiving. For, in reality, we do not perceive the heavenly bodies themselves, but their inflammations in the air: or, in other words, certain portions of air enkindled by the swiftness of their course. This at least cannot be denied to be possible; and, if so, it is not at all wonderful that a gross ærial inflammation should, when viewed through a telescope, appear dim and clouded with spots. But this is not an hypothesis of my own invention, but is derived from Ammonius Hermeas, who, as we are informed by Olympiodorus in the *Phædo*, was of this opinion, as also was Heraclitus long before him; who, speaking (says Olympiodorus) in his obscure way concerning the sun, says of that luminary "*enkindling measures and extinguishing measures*," - that is, enkindling an image of himself in the air when he rises, the same becoming extinguished when he sets.

Nor let the moderns fondly imagine that their system of astronomy was adopted by Pythagoras and his followers, for this opinion is confuted by Spanheim and Dickinson; and this, says Fabricius,[†] with no contemptible arguments: and we are informed by Simplicius,[‡] long before them, that the Pythagoreans by the fire in the middle did not mean the sun, but a demiurgic vivific fire, seated in the centre of the earth. The prophecy of Swift, therefore, in his *Gulliver's Travels*, that the boasted theory of gravitation would at one time or other be exploded, may certainly be considered as a most true prediction, at least so far as relates to the celestial orbs.

But to return from this digression. The inerratic sphere, according to the Platonic philosophy, has the relation of a monad to the multitude of stars which it contains; or, in other words, it is the proximate cause of this multitude which it contains, and with which it has a coordinate subsistence. But, according to the same philosophy, all the planets are fixed in solid spheres, in conformity to the motions of which they perpetually revolve; but, at the same time, have peculiar motions of their own besides those of the spheres.[§] These spheres too are all concentric, or have the same centre with the earth and the universe, and do not consist of hard impenetrable matter, as the moderns have ignorantly supposed; for being divine or immaterial bodies, such as we have already described, they have nothing of the density and gravity of this our earth, but are able to permeate each other without division, and to occupy the same place together; just like the illuminations emitted from several lamps, which pass through the whole of the same room at once, and pervade each other without confusion, divulsion, or any apparent distinction. So that these spheres are similar to mathematical bodies, so far as they are immaterial, free from contrariety, and exempt from every passive quality; but are different from them, so far as they are full of motion and life. But they are concealed from our sight through the tenuity and subtility of their nature, while, on the contrary, the fire of the planets which are carried in them is visible through the solidity which it possesses. So that earth is more predominant in the planets than in the spheres; though each subsists, for the most part, according to the characteristic of fire. But let it be carefully remembered, that the peculiarity of all fire is the *being visible*, but that neither heat nor fluidity belongs to every species of fire: and that the property of all

---

[†] Vid. Biblioth. Græc. vol. 1. de Orpheo.

[‡] In Aristot. de Cœlo, lib. 2.

[§] For Plato makes no mention of epicycles and eccentric circles.

earth is the *being tangible*, but that gravity and subsiding downwards do not belong to all.

But, in consequence of each of these spheres being a ολοτης, or *part with a total subsistence*, as we have already explained, it follows that every planet has a number of satellites surrounding it, analogous to the choir of the fixed stars, and that every sphere is full of Gods, angels, and dæmons, subsisting according to the properties of the spheres in which they reside. This theory indeed is the grand key to the theology of the ancients, as it shows us at one view why the same God is so often celebrated with the names of other Gods; which led Macrobius formerly to think that all the Gods were nothing more than the different powers of the sun; and has induced certain superficial moderns, to frame hypotheses concerning the ancient theology so ridiculous, that they deserve to be considered in no other light than the ravings of a madman, or the undisciplined conceptions of a child. But that the reader may be fully convinced of this, let him attend to the following extraordinary passages from the divine commentaries of Proclus on the *Timæus*. And, in the first place, that every planet is attended with a great number of satellites, is evident from the following citation; - "There are other divine animals attending upon the circulations of the planets, the leaders of which are the seven planets; and these revolve and return in their circulations in conjunction with their leaders, just as the fixed stars are governed by the circulation of the inerratic sphere." - Ειδεναι και αλλα ζωα θεια ειη ουρανια συνεπομενα ταις των πλανωμενων περιφοραις, ων ηγεμονες εισιν οι επτα. - Και συμπεριπολει, και συναποκαθισταται ταις εαυτων αρχαις, ωσπερ και τα απλανη κρατειται υπο της ολης περιφορας.[†] And in the same place he informs us, that the revolution of these satellites is similar to that of the planets which they attend; and this, he acquaints us a little before, is according to Plato a spiral revolution. Και γαρ ταυτα τρεπομενα εστι, και πλανην εχοντα τοιαυτην, οιαν ειρηκεν περι των επτα μικρω προτερον. Again, with respect to their number - "about every planet there is a number (of satellites) analogous to the choir of the fixed stars, all of them subsisting with proper circulations of their own." - Εστι γαρ καθ' εκαστην αριθμος αναλογον τω των αστρων χορω, συννφεστος ταις οικειαις περιφοραις. - And if it should be inquired why, with respect to the fixed stars, there is one monad, the *wholeness* (ολοτης) of them; but among the planets there is both a ολοτης, *wholeness* or *totality*, that is the sphere of each, and a leader besides in each, that is the apparent orb; he answers in the same

---

[†] Vid. Procl. in Tim. p. 275.

place, that as the motion of the planets is more various than that of the fixed stars, so their possession of government is more abundant, for they proceed into a greater multitude. He adds - But in the sublunary regions there is still a greater number of governors; for the *monads* (that is, *totalities*) in the heavens generate a number analogous to themselves. So that the planets being secondary to the fixed stars, require a twofold government; one of which is more total and the other more partial.

But with respect to the satellites, the first in order about every planet are Gods; after these, dæmons revolve in lucid orbicular bodies; and these are followed by partial souls such as ours, as the following beautiful passage abundantly evinces. "But that in each of these (the planetary spheres) there is a multitude coordinate to each, you may infer from the extremes. For if the inerratic sphere has a multitude coordinate to itself, and earth is, with respect to terrestrial animals, what the inerratic sphere is to such as are celestial, it is necessary that every *wholeness* should possess certain partial animals coordinate to itself, through which also the spheres derive the appellation of *wholenesses*. But the natures situated in the middle are concealed from our sense, while, in the mean time, those contained in the extremes are apparent; one sort through their transcendently lucid essence, and the other through their alliance to ourselves. But if partial souls are disseminated about these spheres, some about the sun, some about the moon, and others about each of the remaining spheres;[†] and if prior to souls there are dæmons filling up the herds of which they are the leaders; it is evidently beautifully said that each of the spheres is a world. And this is agreeable to the doctrines of theologists, when they teach us that there are Gods in every sphere prior to dæmons, the government of some receiving its perfection under that of others. As for instance with respect to our queen the Moon, that she contains the goddess Hecate and Diana; and with respect to our sovereign the Sun, and the Gods which he contains, theologists celebrate Bacchus as subsisting there,

> The Sun's assessor, who with watchful eye
> Inspects the sacred pole:

They also celebrate Jupiter as seated there, Osiris, and a solar Pan, as likewise other divinities, of which the books of theologists and theurgists are full; from all which it is evident how true it is that each of the

---

[†] This Plato himself asserts in the following dialogue.

planets is the leader of many Gods, which fill up its proper circulation."[†] - Οτι δε και εν εκαστη τουτων πληθος εστιν εκαστη συστοιχον, κατασκευασειας αν απο των ακρων. Ει γαρ η απλανης εχει συστοιχον εαυτη πληθος, και η γη των χθονιων ζωων εστι, ως εκεινη των ουρανιων, αναγκη και εκαστην ολοτητα παντως εχειν μερικα αττα συστοιχα προς αυτη ζωα, δυα και ολοτητες λεγονται. Λανθανει δε ημων τα μεσα την αισθησιν, των ακρων δηλων οντων, των μεν, δια την υπερλαμπρον ουσιαν, των δε δια την προς ημας συγγενειαν. Ει δε και μερικαι ψυχαι περι αυτους εσπαρησαν, αλλαι μεν περι ηλιον, αλλαι δε περι σεληνην, αλλαι δε περι εκαστον των λοιπων, και προ των ψυχων δαιμονες συμπληρουσι τας αγελας ων εισιν ηγεμονες, δηλον οτι καλως ειρηται κοσμον εκαστην ειναι των σφαιρων, και των θεολογων ημας ταυτα διδασκοντων, οποταν περι εκαστους θεους εν αυτοις ειναι, προ των δαιμονων, αλλους υπο των αλλων τελουντας ηγεμονιαν, οιον, και περι της δεσποινης ημων Σεληνης, οτι και η Εκατη θεα εστιν εν αυτη, και η Αρτεμις, και περι του βασιλεως Ηλιου και των εκει θεων, τον εκει Διονυσον υμνουντες, Ηελιος παρεδρος επισκοπεων πολον αγνον, τον Δια τον εκει, τον Οσιριν, τον Πανα τον ηλιακον, τους αλλους, ων οι βιβλοι πληρεις εισι των θεολογων και των θεουργων, εξ ων απαντων δηλον, οπως αληθες, και των πλανωμενων εκαστον αγελαρχην ειναι πολλων θεων, συμπληρουντων αυτου την ιδιαν περιφοραν.

Now, from this extraordinary passage, we may perceive at one view why the Sun in the Orphic hymns is called Jupiter, why Apollo is called Pan, and Bacchus the sun; why the Moon seems to be the same with Rhea, Ceres, Proserpine, Juno, Venus, etc. and, in short, why any one divinity is celebrated with the names and epithets of so many of the rest. For from this sublime theory it follows that every sphere contains a Jupiter, Neptune, Vulcan, Vesta, Minerva, Mars, Ceres, Juno, Diana, Mercury, Venus, Apollo, and in short every deity, each sphere at the same time conferring on these Gods the peculiar characteristic of its nature; so that, for instance, in the sun they all possess a solar property, in the moon a lunar one, and so of the rest. From this theory too we may perceive the truth of that divine saying of the ancients, that all things are full of Gods; for more particular orders proceed from such as are more general, the mundane from the supermundane, and the sublunary from the celestial; while earth becomes the general receptacle of the illuminations of all the Gods. "Hence (says Proclus[‡]) there is a

[†] Procl. in Tim.

[‡] In Tim. p. 282.

terrestrial Ceres, Vesta, and Isis, as likewise a terrestrial Jupiter and a terrestrial Hermes, established about the one divinity of the earth; just as a multitude of celestial Gods proceeds about the one divinity of the heavens. For there are progressions of all the celestial Gods into the earth; and earth contains all things, in an earthly manner, which heaven comprehends celestially. Hence we speak of a terrestrial Bacchus, and a terrestrial Apollo, who bestows the all-various streams of water with which the earth abounds, and openings prophetic of futurity." And if to all this we only add that all the other mundane Gods subsist in the twelve above mentioned, and that the first triad of these is *demiurgic* or *fabricative, viz.* Jupiter, Neptune, Vulcan; the second, Vesta, Minerva, Mars, *defensive*; the third, Ceres, Juno, Diana, *vivific*; and the fourth, Mercury, Venus, Apollo, *elevating* and *harmonic*: I say, if we unite this with the preceding theory, there is nothing in the ancient theology that will not appear admirably sublime and beautifully connected, accurate in all its parts, scientific and divine. Such then being the true account of the Grecian theology, what opinion must we form of the wretched systems of modern mythologists; and which most deserves our admiration, the impudence or ignorance of the authors of such systems? The systems indeed of these men are so monstrously absurd, that we may consider them as instances of the greatest distortion of the rational faculty which can possibly befall human nature, while connected with such a body as the present. For one of these considers the Gods as merely symbols of agriculture, another as men who once lived on the earth,[†] and a third as the patriarchs and prophets of the Jews. Surely should these systems be transmitted to posterity, the historian by whom they are related must either be considered by future generations as an impostor, or his narration must be viewed in the light of an extravagant romance.

I only add, as a conclusion to this sublime theory, that though the whole of the celestial region is composed from the four elements, yet in some places fire in conjunction with earth (i.e. earth without gravity and density) predominates; in others fire, with the summit of water; and in others again fire with the summit of air: and according to each of these an all-various mutation subsists. Hence some bodies in the heavens are visible, and these are such as have fire united with the solid; but others

---

[†] See my notes on the *Cratylus*.

are still more visible,[†] and these are such as have fire mingled with the splendid and diaphanous nature of air. And hence the spheres of the planets, and the inerratic sphere itself, possess a more attenuated and diaphanous essence; but the stars are of a more solid composition. But fire everywhere prevails, and all heaven is characterized through the power of this exalted element. And neither is the fire there caustic (for this is not even the property of the first of the sublunary elements, which Aristotle calls *fiery*, πυροειδες) nor corruptive of anything, nor of a nature contrary to earth; but it perpetually shines with a pure and transparent light, with vivific heat, and illuminating power.

And such are the outlines of the system of the world, according to Pythagoras and Plato; which, strange as the assertion may seem, appears to have been but little known from the æra of the emperor Justinian to the present time. That beautiful mode in which as we have shown the elements subsist both in the heavens and the earth, has not been even suspected by modern natural philosophers to have any existence; and astronomers have been very far from the truth in their assertions concerning the celestial spheres. In consequence of indolence, or ignorance, or prejudice, or from all three in conjunction, the moderns have invented systems no less discordant with the nature of things than different from each other. They have just been able to gain a glimpse of the beautiful union of things in the vegetable and animal tribes belonging to the earth, and have discovered that the lowest of the animal species and the highest of the vegetable approximate so near to each other, that the difference between the two can scarcely be perceived; but this is the very summit of their researches; they are unable to trace the connection of things any further, and rest satisfied in admitting that

The chain continues, but with links unknown.

The divine nature of the celestial bodies cannot be seen through the telescope, and incorporeals are not to be viewed with a microscopic eye: but these instruments are at present the great standards of truth; and whatever opposes or cannot be ascertained by the testimony of these, is considered as mere conjecture, idle speculation, and a perversion of the reasoning power.

But let us now proceed to a summary view of some of the principal parts of this most interesting dialogue. And, in the first place, with

---

[†] That is, in themselves: but they are invisible to us, on account of their possessing but little of the resisting nature of earth; and this is the reason why we cannot see the celestial spheres.

respect to the history which is related in the beginning, concerning a war between the inhabitants of the Atlantic island and the Athenians: Crantor, the most early of Plato's commentators, considered this relation (says Proclus) as a mere history unconnected with allegory; while other Platonists, on the contrary, have considered it as an allegory alone. But both these opinions are confuted by Proclus and the best of the Platonists; because Plato calls it a very wonderful, but at the same time true, narration. So that it is to be considered as a true history, exhibiting at the same time an image of the opposition of the natures which the universe contains. But according to Amelius[†] it represents the opposition between the inerratic sphere and the fixed stars; according to Origen,[‡] the contest between dæmons of a superior and those of an inferior order; according to Numenius, the disagreement between more excellent souls who are the attendants of Pallas, and such as are conversant with generation under Neptune. Again, according to Porphyry, it insinuates the contest between dæmons deducing souls into generation, and souls ascending to the Gods. For Porphyry gives a three-fold distinction to dæmons; asserting that some are divine, that others subsist according to habitude, κατα σχεσιν, among which partial souls rank when they are allotted a dæmoniacal condition, and that others are evil and noxious to souls. He asserts, therefore, that this lowest order of dæmons always contends with souls in their ascent and descent, especially western dæmons; for, according to the Egyptians, the west is accommodated to dæmons of this description. But the exposition of Iamblichus, Syrianus and Proclus is doubtless to be preferred, as more consistent with the nature of the dialogue; which refers it to the opposition perpetually flourishing in the universe between unity and multitude, bound and infinity, sameness and difference, motion and permanency, from which all things, the first cause being excepted, are composed. Likewise, being has either an essential or accidental subsistence, and is either incorporeal or corporeal: and if incorporeal, it either verges or does not verge to body. But bodies are either simple and immaterial, as the celestial bodies, or simple and material, as those of an ærial nature, or composite and material, as those of earth. So that the opposition of all these is occultly signified by that ancient war; the higher and more excellent natures being

---

[†] A disciple of Plotinus contemporary with Porphyry.

[‡] Not the father, of that name, but a disciple of Ammonius Saccas, and contemporary with Plotinus.

everywhere implied by the Athenians, and those of a contrary order by the inhabitants of the Atlantic island.

That the reader, however, may be convinced that Plato's account of the Atlantic island is not a fiction of his own devising, let him attend to the following relation of one Marcellus, who wrote an history of Æthiopian affairs, according to Proclus:[†] "That such, and so great, an island once existed, is evinced by those who have composed histories of things relative to the external sea. For they relate that in their times there were seven islands in the Atlantic sea, sacred to Proserpine: and besides these, three others of an immense magnitude; one of which was sacred to Pluto, another to Ammon, and another, which is the middle of these, and is of a thousand stadia, to Neptune. And besides this, that the inhabitants of this last island preserved the memory of the prodigious magnitude of the Atlantic island, as related by their ancestors; and of its governing for many periods all the islands in the Atlantic sea. And such is the relation of Marcellus in his Æthiopic history." Οτι μεν εγενετο τοιαυτη τις νησος και τηλικαυτη, δηλουσι τινες των ιστορουντων τα περι της εξω θαλαττης. ειναι γαρ και εν τοις αυτων χρονοις επτα μεν νησους εν εκεινω τω πελαγει Περσεφονης ιερας, τρεις δε αλλας απλετους, την μεν Πλουτωνος, την δε Αμμωνος, μεσην δε τουτων αλλην Ποσειδωνος, χιλιων σταδιων το μεγεθος. Και τους οικουντας εν αυτη μνημην απο των προγονων διασωζειν περι της Ατλαντιδος οντως γενομενης εκει νησου παμμεγαθεστατης, ην επι πολλας περιοδους δυναστευσαι πασων των εν Ατλαντικω πελαγει νησων. Ταυτα μεν ουν ο Μαρκελλος εν τοις Αιθιοπικοις γεγραφεν.

Indeed it is not at all wonderful that so large an island should once have existed, nor improbable that many more such exist at present, though to us unknown, if we only consider the Platonic theory concerning the earth, of which the reader will find an account in the Introduction to the *Phædo*, and which the following extraordinary passage from Proclus[‡] abundantly confirms. "It is here (says he) requisite to remember the Platonic hypotheses concerning the earth. For Plato does not measure its magnitude after the same manner as mathematicians; but thinks that its interval is much greater, as Socrates asserts in the *Phædo*. In which dialogue also he says, that there are

---

† In Tim. p. 55.

‡ In Tim. p. 56.

many habitable parts similar to our abode.[†] And hence he relates that an island and continent of this kind exist in the external or Atlantic sea. For, indeed, if the earth be naturally spherical, it is necessary that it should be such according to its greatest part. But the parts which we inhabit, both internally and externally, exhibit great inequality. In some parts of the earth, therefore, there must be an expanded plain, and an interval extended on high, For, according to the saying of Heraclitus, he who passes through a very profound region will arrive at the Atlantic mountain, whose magnitude is such, according to the relation of the Æthiopian historians, that it touches the æther, and casts a shadow of five thousand stadia in extent; for from the ninth hour of the day the sun is concealed by it, even to his perfect demersion under the earth. Nor is this wonderful: for Athos, a Macedonian mountain, casts a shadow as far as to Lemnos, which is distant from it seven hundred stadia. Nor are such particulars as these, which Marcellus the Æthiopic historian mentions, related only concerning the Atlantic mountain; but Ptolemy also says that the lunar mountains are of an immense height; and Aristotle, that Caucasus is enlightened by the rays of the sun a third part of the night after sun-set, and a third part before the rising of the sun. And if any one considers the whole magnitude of the earth, bounded by its elevated parts, he will conclude that it is truly of a prodigious magnitude, according to the assertion of Plato."

In the next place, by the fable of Phaëton we must understand the destruction of a considerable part of the earth through fire, by means of a comet being dissolved of a solar nature. Likewise, when he mentions a deluge, it is necessary to remember, that through the devastations of these two elements, fire and water, a more prolific regeneration of things takes place at certain periods of time; and that when Divinity intends a

---

[†] The latter Platonists appear to have been perfectly convinced that the earth contains two quarters in an opposite direction to Europe and Asia; and Olympiodorus even considers Plato as of the same opinion, as the following passage from his commentary on this part of the *Phædo* clearly evinces. - "Plato (says he) directs his attention to four parts of the globe, as there are two parts which we inhabit, i.e. Europe and Asia; so that there must be two others. in consequence of the antipodes."

Καταστοχαζεται δε των τεσσαρων (τοπων) επειδη δυο καθ᾽ ημας εισιν, η Ευρωπη και η Ασια, ωστε δυο αλλοι κατα τους αντιποδας. Now in consequence of this, as they were acquainted with Africa, the remaining fourth quarter must be that which we call America. At the same time let it be carefully remembered, that these four quarters are nothing more than four holes with respect to the whole earth, which contains many such parts; and that consequently they are not quarters of the earth itself, but only of a small part of the earth in which they are contained, like a small globe in one of a prodigious extent.

reformation, the heavenly bodies concur with this design in such a manner, that when a conflagration is about to take place, then, according to Berosus[†] the Chaldæan, all the planets are collected together in Cancer; but when a deluge, then the planets meet in Capricorn. With respect to Pallas and Neptune, who are mentioned in this part of the dialogue, as the reader will find an account of these Divinities in the Notes to the *Cratylus*, I shall only add at present, that, according to Proclus, Minerva most eminently presides in the celestial constellation called the Ram, and in the equinoctial circle, where a power motive of the universe principally prevails.

Again, it is necessary to understand, that when the world is said by Plato to be *generated*, this term expresses its flowing and composite nature, and does not imply any temporal commencement of its existence. For, as the world was necessarily produced according to essential power, this being the most perfect of all modes of operation, it is also necessary that it should be coexistent with its artificer; just as the sun produces light coexistent with itself, fire heat, and snow coldness. The reader must, however, carefully observe, that when we say it is necessary that the cause of the universe should operate according to power, we do not understand a necessity which implies violence or constraint; but that necessity which Aristotle[‡] defines as the perfectly simple, and which cannot have a multifarious subsistence. And hence this term, when applied to the most exalted natures, to whom alone in this sense it belongs, signifies nothing more than an impossibility of subsisting otherwise than they do, without falling from the perfection of their nature. Agreeably to this definition, Necessity was called by ancient theologists Adrastia and Themis, or the perfectly right and just: and if men of the present day had but attended to this signification of the word, i.e. if any edition of Aristotle's works, with a *copious index* mentioning this sense of necessity, had fortunately existed, they would not have ignorantly supposed that this word, when applied to divine natures, signified constraint, violence, and over-ruling power. As intellect, therefore, is eternal, both according to essence and energy, and as soul is eternal in essence, but temporal in energy, so the world is temporal both in essence and energy. Hence, every thing prior to soul always *is*, and is never generated; but soul both *is*, and is perpetually generated; and the world never *is*, but is always generated: and whatever

---

[†] Vid. Senec. Natural. Quæst. III.

[‡] Metaphys. lib. 5.

the world contains in like manner never is; but instead of being always generated, like the whole world, is so at some particular time. Because the world therefore is conversant with perpetual motion and time, it may be said to be always generated, or advancing towards being; and therefore never truly is. So that it resembles the image of a mountain beheld in a torrent, which has the appearance of a mountain without the reality, and which is continually renewed by the continual renovation of the stream. But soul, which is eternal in essence, and temporal in energy, may be compared to the image of the same rock beheld in a pool, and which, of course, when compared with the image in the torrent, may be said to be permanently the same. In fine, as Proclus well observes, Plato means nothing more by *generation* than the formation of bodies, i.e. a motion or procession towards the integrity and perfection of the universe.

Again, by the *demiurgus* and *father* of the world we must understand Jupiter, who subsists at the extremity of the *intellectual triad*;[†] and αυτο ζωον, or *animal itself*, which is the exemplar of the world, and from the contemplation of which it was fabricated by Jupiter, is the last of the *intelligible triad*, and is same with the Phanes of Orpheus: for the theologist represents Phanes as an animal with the heads of various beasts, as may be seen in our Notes to the *Parmenides*. Nor let the reader be disturbed on finding that, according to Plato, the first cause is not the immediate cause of the universe; for this is not through any defect or imbecility of nature, but, on the contrary, is the consequence of transcendency of power. For, as the first cause is the same with *The One*, a unifying energy must be the prerogative of his nature; and as he is likewise perfectly superessential, if the world were his immediate progeny, it must be as much as possible superessential and profoundly one: but as this is not the case, it is necessary that it should be formed by intellect and moved by soul. So that it derives the unity and goodness of its nature from the first cause, the orderly disposition and distinction of its parts from Jupiter its artificer, and its perpetual motion from soul; the whole at the same time proceeding from the first cause through proper mediums. Nor is it more difficult to conceive matter after this manner invested with form and distributed into order, than to conceive a potter making clay with his own hands, giving it a shape when made, through the assistance of a wheel, and, when fashioned, adorning it through another instrument with figures; at the same time being careful to remember, that in this latter instance different

---

[†] See the Notes on the *Cratylus* and *Parmenides*.

instruments are required through the imbecility of the artificer, but that in the former various mediums are necessary from the transcendency of power which subsists in the original cause. And from all this it is easy to infer, that matter was not prior to the world by any interval of time, but only in the order of composition; priority here implying nothing more than that which must be considered as first in the construction of the world. Nor was it hurled about in a disordered state prior to order; but this only signifies its confused and tumultuous nature, when considered in itself, divested of the supervening irradiations of form.

With respect to the four elements, I add, in addition to what has been said before, that their powers are beautifully disposed by Proclus as follows, *viz*:

FIRE.	AIR.
Subtle, acute, movable.	Subtle, blunt, movable.
WATER.	EARTH.
Dense, blunt, movable.	Dense, blunt, immovable.

In which disposition you may perceive how admirably the two extremes fire and earth are connected, though indeed it is the peculiar excellence of the Platonic philosophy to find out in every thing becoming mediums through that part of the dialectic art called division; and it is owing to this that the philosophy itself forms so regular and consistent a whole. But I have invented the following numbers for the purpose of representing this distribution of the elements arithmetically.

Let the number 60 represent fire, and 480 earth; and the mediums between these, *viz*. 120 and 240, will correspond to air and water. For as $60 : 120 :: 240 : 480$. But $60 = 3 \times 5 \times 4$. $120 = 3 \times 10 \times 4$. $240 = 6 \times 10 \times 4$. and $480 = 6 \times 10 \times 8$. So that these numbers will correspond to the properties of the elements as follows:

FIRE :	AIR : :
$3 \times \quad 5 \times \quad 4$:	$3 \times \quad 10 \times \quad 4$::
Subtle, acute, movable :	Subtle, blunt, movable.
WATER :	EARTH.
$6 \times \quad 10 \times \quad 4$::	$6 \times \quad 10 \times \quad 8$
Dense, blunt, movable ::	Dense, blunt, immovable.

With respect to fire it must be observed, that the Platonists consider
light, flame, and *a burning coal,* φῶς, φλοξ, ανθραξ, as differing from
each other; and that a subjection or remission of fire takes place from
on high to the earth, proceeding, as we have before observed, from that
which is more immaterial, pure, and incorporeal, as far as to the most
material and dense bodies: the last procession of fire being subterranean;
for, according to Empedocles, there are many rivers of fire under the
earth. So that one kind of fire is material and another immaterial, i.e.
when compared with sublunary matter; and one kind is corruptible, but
another incorruptible; and one is mixed with air, but another is perfectly
pure. The characteristic too of fire is neither heat nor a motion
upwards, for this is the property only of our terrestrial fire; and this in
consequence of not subsisting in its proper place: but the essential
peculiarity of fire is visibility; for this belongs to all fire, i.e. to the
divine, the *mortal,* the *burning,* and the *impetuous.* It must, however, be
carefully observed, that our eyes are by no means the standards of this
visibility: for we cannot perceive the celestial spheres, on account of fire
and air in their composition so much predominating over earth; and
many terrestrial bodies emit no light when considerably heated, owing
to the fire which they contain being wholly absorbed, as it were, in
gross and ponderous earth.

In like manner, with respect to earth, the characteristic of its nature is
solidity and tangibility, but not ponderosity and a tendency downwards;
for these properties do not subsist in every species of earth. Hence,
when we consider these two elements according to their opposite
subsistence, we shall find that fire is always in motion, but earth always
immovable; that fire is eminently visible, and earth eminently tangible;
and that fire is of a most attenuated nature through light, but that earth
is most dense through darkness. So that as fire is essentially the cause
of light, in like manner, earth is essentially the cause of darkness; while
air and water subsisting as mediums between these two, are, on account
of their diaphanous nature, the causes of visibility to other things, but
not to themselves. In the mean time moisture is common both to air
and water, connecting and conglutinating earth, but becoming the seat
of fire, and affording nourishment and stability to its flowing nature.

With respect to the composition of the mundane soul, it is necessary
to observe that there are five genera of being, from which all things after
the first being are composed, *viz. essence, permanency, motion, sameness,
difference.* For every thing must possess *essence;* must *abide* in its cause,
from which also it must *proceed,* and to which it must be *converted;*
must be the *same* with itself and certain other natures, and at the same

time *different* from others and distinguished in itself. But Plato, for the sake of brevity, assumes only three of these in the composition of the soul, *viz. essence, sameness,* and *difference*; for the other two must necessarily subsist in conjunction with these. But by a nature impartible, or without parts, we must understand intellect, and by that nature which is divisible about body, corporeal life. The mundane soul, therefore, is a medium between the mundane intellect and the whole of that corporeal life which the world participates. We must not, however, suppose that when the soul is said to be mingled from these two, the impartible and partible natures are consumed in the mixture, as is the case when corporeal substances are mingled together; but we must understand that the soul is of a middle nature between these, so as to be different from each, and yet a participant of each.

The first numbers of the soul are these: 1, 2, 3, 4, 9, 8, 27; but the other numbers are,

	6
8	9
9	12
12	18
16	27
18	36
24	54
32	81
36	108
48	162

But in order to understand these numbers mathematically, it is necessary to know, in the first place, what is meant by arithmetical, geometrical, and harmonic proportion. Arithmetical proportion, then, is when an equal excess is preserved in three or more given numbers; geometrical, when numbers preserve the same ratio; and harmonic, when the middle term is exceeded by the greater, by the same part of the greater as the excess of the middle term above the lesser exceeds the lesser. Hence, the numbers 1, 2, 3, are in arithmetical proportion; 2, 4, 8, in geometrical, since as 2 is to 4, so is 4 to 8; and 6, 4, 3, are in harmonic proportion, for 4 is exceeded by 6 by 2, which is a third part of 6, and 4 exceeds 3 by 1, which is the third part of 3. Again, sesquialter proportion is when one number contains another and the half of it besides, such as the proportion of 3 to 2; but sesquitertian proportion takes place when a greater number contains a lesser, and besides this, a third part of the lesser, as 4 to 3; and a sesquioctave ratio is when a greater number contains a lesser one, and an eighth part of it besides, as 9 to 8; and this proportion produces in music an entire tone, which is the principle of all symphony. But a tone contains five symphonies, *viz.* the *diatessaron*, or sesquitertian proportion, which is composed from two tones, and a semitone, which is a sound less than a tone; the *diapente*, or sesquialter proportion, which is composed from three tones and a semitone; the *diapason*, or duple proportion, i. e. four to two, which is composed from six tones; the *diapason diapente*, which consists of nine tones and a semitone; and the *disdiapason*, or quadruple proportion, i.e. four to one, which contains twelve tones.

But it is necessary to observe further concerning a tone, that it cannot be divided into two equal parts; because it is composed from a sesquioctave proportion, and 9 cannot be divided into two equal parts. Hence, it can only be divided into two unequal parts, which are usually called semitones; but by Plato λειμματα, or *remainders*. But the lesser part of a tone was called by the Pythagoreans *diesis*, or *division*; and this is surpassed by a sesquitertian proportion by two tones; and the remaining greater part, by which the tone surpasses the less semitone, is called *apotome*, or *a cutting off*.

But as it is requisite to explain the different kinds of harmony, in order to a knowledge of the composition of symphonies, let the reader take notice that harmony receives a triple division, into the Diatonic, Enharmonic, and Chromatic. And the Diatonic genus takes place when its division continually proceeds through a less semitone and two tones. But the Enharmonic proceeds through two dieses. And the Chromatic is that which ascends through two unequal semitones and three semitones; or τριημιτονιον, according to the appellation of the ancient musicians. And to these three genera all musical instruments are reduced, because they are all composed from these harmonies. But though there were many different kinds of instruments among the ancients, yet the Pythagorean and Platonic philosophers used only three-the Monochord, the Tetrachord, and the Polychord; to which three they refer the composition of all the other instruments. From among all these, therefore, Plato assumes the *diatonic* harmony, as more agreeable to nature; in which the tetrachord proceeds through a less semitone and two tones; tending by this means from a less to a greater semitone, as from a more slender to a more powerful matter, which possesses a simple form, and is at the same time both gentle and robust. And hence, as all instruments are conversant with these three kinds of harmony, Plato, says Proclus, in consequence of preferring the diatonic harmony, alone uses two tones when he orders us to fill up the sesquitertian, sesquioctave and semitone intervals.

With respect to the first numbers, which are evidently those described by Plato, the first three of these, 1, 2, 3, as Syrianus beautifully observes, may be considered as representing the soul of the world, abiding in, proceeding from, and returning to, herself, *viz.* abiding according to that first part, proceeding through the second, and this without any passivity or imbecility, but returning according to the third: for that which is perfective accedes to beings through conversion. But as the whole of the mundane soul is perfect, united with intelligibles, and eternally abiding in intellect, hence she providentially presides over secondary natures; in one respect indeed over those which are as it were proximately connected with herself, and in another over solid and compacted bulks. But her providence over each of these is twofold. For those which are connected with her essence in a following order, proceed from her according to the power of the fourth term (4), which possesses generative powers; but return to her according to the fifth (9), which reduces them to one. Again, solid natures, and all the species which are discerned in corporeal masses, proceed according to the octuple of the first part (i.e. according to 8), which number is produced by two, is solid, and possesses generative powers proceeding to all things; but they return according to the number 27, which is the regression of solids, proceeding as it were from the ternary, and existing of the same order according to nature: for such are all odd numbers.

And thus much for the first series of numbers, in which duple and triple ratios are comprehended; but after this follows another series, in which the duple are filled with sesquitertian and sesquialter ratios, and the sesquitertian spaces receive a tone. And here, in the first place, in the duple progression between 6 and 12, we may perceive two mediums, 8 and 9. And 8 indeed subsists between 6 and 12 in an harmonic ratio; for it exceeds 6 by a third part of 6, and it is in like manner exceeded by 12 by a third part of 12. Likewise 8 is in a sesquitertian ratio to 6, but 12 is sesquialter to 8. Besides, the difference between 12 and 8 is 4, but the difference between 8 and 6 is 2. And hence, 4 to 2, as well as 12 to 6, contains a duple ratio: and these are the ratios in which the artifice of harmony is continually employed. We may likewise compare 9 to 6 which is sesquialter, 12 to 9 which is sesquitertian, and 9 to 8 which is sesquioctave, and forms a tone; and from this comparison we shall perceive that two sesquitertian ratios are bound together by this sesquioctave, *viz.* 8 to 6 and 9 to 12. Nor is an arithmetical medium wanting in these numbers; for 9 exceeds 6 by 3, and is by the same number exceeded by 12. And in the same manner we may proceed in all the following duple ratios, binding the duple by the sesquitertian and sesquialter, and connecting the two sesquitertians by a sesquioctave ratio. We may run through the triple proportions too in a similar manner, excepting in the tone. But because sesquitertian ratios are not alone produced from two tones, but from a semitone, and this a lesser, which is deficient from a full tone by certain small parts, hence Plato says, that in the sesquitertian ratios a certain small portion remains.[†] And thus much may suffice for an epitome of the mode in which the duple and triple intervals are filled.

But the words of Plato respecting these intervals plainly show, as Proclus well observes, that he follows in this instance the doctrine of the ancient theologists. For they assert, that in the artificer of the universe there are separating and connecting powers, and that through the former he separates his government from that of his father Saturn, but through the latter applies the whole of his fabrication to his paternal unity; and they call these operations incisions and bonds. Hence the demiurgus, dividing the essence of the soul, according to these powers in demiurgic bounds, is said to cut the parts from their totality, and again to bind the same with certain bonds, which are μεσοτητες, middles or mediums, and through which he connects that which is divided, in the same manner as he divides, through sections, that which is united. And as the first numbers, 1, 2, 3, 4, 9, 8, 27, represented those powers of the soul by which she abides in, proceeds from, and returns to, herself, and causes the progression and conversion of the parts of the universe-so, in these second numbers, the sesquitertian, sesquialter, and other ratios constitute the more particular ornament of the world; and, while they subsist as wholes themselves, adorn the parts of its parts.

I only add, that we must not suppose these numbers of the soul to be a multitude of unities; but we must conceive them to be vital self-motive natures, which are indeed the images of intellectual numbers, but the exemplars of such as are apparent to the eye of sense. In like manner, with respect to harmony, soul is neither harmony itself, nor that which subsists in harmonized natures. For harmony itself is uniform, separate, and exempt from the whole of things harmonized; but that which subsists in things harmonized is dependent on others, by which also it is naturally moved. But the harmony of the soul subsists in the middle

---

[†] The proportion of 256 to 243 produces what is called in music λειμμα, limma, or that which remains.

of these two, imparting harmony to others, and being the first participant of it herself.

In order to understand the figure of the soul, in the first place, mathematically, conceive all the above-mentioned numbers to be described in a certain straight rule, according to the whole of its breadth; and conceive this rule to be afterwards divided according to its length. Then all these ratios will subsist in each part of the section. For, if the division were made according to breadth, it would be necessary that some of the numbers should be.separated on this side, and others on that. Afterwards let the two lengths of the rule be mutually applied to each other, *viz.* in the points which divide these lengths in half: but let them not be so applied as to form right angles, for the intended circles are not of this kind. Again, let the two lengths be so incurvated, that the extremes may touch each other; then two circles will be produced, one interior and the other exterior, and they will be mutually oblique to each other. But one of these will be the circle of *sameness*, and the other of *difference*; and the one will subsist according to the equinoctial circle, but the other according to the zodiac: for every circle of difference is rolled about this, as of identity about the equinoctial. Hence, these rectilinear sections ought not to be applied at right angles, but according to the similitude of the letter X, agreeably to the mind of Plato, so that the angles in the summit only may be equal; for neither does the zodiac cut the equinoctial at right angles. And thus much for the mathematical explanation of the figure of the soul.

But again, says Proclus, referring the whole of our discourse to the essence of the soul, we shall say that, according to the mathematical disciplines, continuous and discrete quantity seem in a certain respect to be contrary to each other; but in soul both concur together, i.e. union and division. For soul is both unity and multitude, and one reason and many; and so far as she is a whole she is continuous, but so far as number she is divided, according to the reasons which she contains. Hence, according to her continuity, she is assimilated to the union of intelligibles; but, according to her multitude, to their distinction. And if you are willing to ascend still higher in speculations, soul, according to her union, possesses a vestige and resemblance of *The One*, but according to her division she exhibits the multitude of divine numbers. Hence we must not say that she alone possesses an arithmetical essence, for she would not be continuous; nor alone a geometrical essence, for she would not be divided: she is therefore both at once, and must be called both arithmetical and geometrical. But so far as she is arithmetical, she has at the same time harmony conjoined with her essence; for the multitude which she contains is elegant and composite, and receives in the same and at once both that which is essential quantity and that which is related. But so far as she is geometrical, she has that which is spherical connected with her essence. For the circles which she contains are both immovable and moved; immovable indeed according to essence, but moved according to a vital energy; or, to speak more properly, they may be said to possess both of these at once, for they are self-motive: and that which is self-motive is both moved and is at the same time immovable, since a motive power seems to belong to an immovable nature. Soul, therefore, essentially pre-assumes all disciplines; the geometrical, according to her totality, her forms, and her lines; the arithmetical, according to her multitude and essential unities; the harmonical, according to the ratios of numbers; and the spherical, according to her double circulations. And, in short, she is the essential, self-motive, intellectual, and united bond of all disciplines, purely comprehending all things; figures in an unfigured manner; unitedly such things as are divided; and without distance such as are distant from each other.

We are likewise informed by Proclus, that, according to Porphyry, a character like the letter X comprehended in a circle was a symbol with the Egyptians of the mundane soul; by the right lines, perhaps (says he), signifying its biformed progression, but by the circle its uniform life and intellective progress, which is of a circular nature. But of these circles the exterior, or the circle of sameness, represents the dianoëtic power of the soul; but the interior, or the circle of difference, the power which energizes according to opinion: and the motion which is perpetually revolved in sameness, and which comprehends the soul, is intellect.

Again, we have before observed that, according to the Platonic philosophy, the planets revolve with a kind of spiral motion; while variously wandering under the oblique zodiac, they at one time verge to the south, and at another to the north, sometimes advance, and sometimes retreat, and being at one time more distant from and at another nearer to the earth. And this motion, indeed, very properly belongs to them, from their middle position, as it is a medium between the right-lined motion of the elements and the circular motion of the inerratic sphere: for a spiral is mixed from the right line and circle. Add too, that there are seven motions in the heavens; the circular, before, behind, upwards, downwards, to the right hand, and to the left. But the spheres alone possess a circular motion. And the stars in the inerratic sphere revolve about their centres; but at the same time have an advancing motion, because they are drawn along towards the west by the sphere in which they are fixed. But they are entirely destitute of the other five motions. On the contrary, the planets have all the seven. For they revolve about their own centres, but are carried by the motions of their spheres towards the east. And besides this, they are carried upwards and downwards, behind and before, to the right hand and to the left. Every star, too, by its revolution about its own centre, imitates the energy of the soul which it contains about its own intellect; but by following the motion of its sphere, it imitates the energy of the sphere about a superior intellect. We may likewise add, that the uniformity in the motions of the fixed stars confers union and perseverance on inferior concerns; but that the manifold and opposite motions of the planets contribute to the production, mingling and governing of things various and opposite.

And here, as the reader will doubtless be desirous of knowing why earth is called by Plato the first and most ancient of the Gods within the heavens, I doubt not but he will gratefully receive the following epitome of the beautiful account given by Proclus of the earth in his inestimable commentaries on this venerable dialogue. - "Earth (says he) first proceeds from the intelligible earth which comprehends all the intelligible orders of the Gods, and from the intellectual earth which is coordinated with heaven. For our earth, being analogous to these, eternally abides, as in the centre of heaven; by which being every way comprehended, it becomes full of generative power and demiurgic perfection. The true earth, therefore, is not this corporeal and gross bulk, but an animal endued with a divine soul and a divine body. For it contains an immaterial and separate intellect, and a divine soul energizing about this intellect, and an ethereal body proximately depending on this soul; and, lastly, this visible bulk, which is on all sides animated and filled with life from its inspiring soul, and through which it generates and nourishes lives of all-various kinds. For one species of life is rooted in the earth, and another moves about its surface. For how is it possible that plants should live while abiding in the earth, but when separated from it die, unless its visible bulk was full of life? Indeed it must universally follow that wholes must be animated prior to parts: for it would be ridiculous that man should participate of a rational soul and of intellect, but that earth and air should be deprived of a soul, sublimely carried in these elements as in a chariot, governing them from on high, and preserving them in the limits accommodated to their nature. For, as Theophrastus well observes, wholes would possess less authority than parts, and things eternal than such as are corruptible, if deprived of the possession of soul. Hence there must necessarily be a soul and intellect in the earth, the former causing her to be prolific, and the latter connectedly containing her in the middle of the universe. So that earth is a divine animal, full of intellectual and animastic essences, and of immaterial powers. For if a partial soul, such as ours, in conjunction with its proper ethereal vehicle, is able to exercise an exuberant energy in a material body, what ought we to think of a soul so divine as that of the earth? Ought we not to assert, that by a much greater priority she uses these apparent bodies through other middle vehicles, and through these enables them to receive her divine illuminations?

"Earth then subsisting in this manner, she is said, in the first place, to be our nurse, as possessing, in a certain respect, a power equivalent to heaven; and because, as heaven comprehends divine animals, so earth appears to contain such as are earthly. And, in the second place, as inspiring our life from her own proper life. For she not only yields us fruits, and nourishes our bodies through these, but she fills our souls with illuminations from her own divine soul, and through her intellect awakens ours from its oblivious sleep. And thus, through the whole of herself, she becomes the nurse of our whole composition.

"But we may consider the poles as powers which give stability to the universe, and excite the whole of its bulk to intelligible love; which connect a divisible nature indivisibly, and that which possesses interval in an united and indistant manner. But the axis is one divinity congregating the centres of the universe, connecting the whole world, and moving its divine circulations; about which the revolutions of the stars subsist, and which sustains the whole of the heavens by its power. And hence it is called Atlas, from the immutable and unwearied energy with which it is endued. Add too that the word τεταμενον, *extended*, signifies that this one power is Titanic, guarding the circulations of the wholes which the universe contains.

"Earth is likewise called the guardian and fabricator of night and day. And that she causes the night indeed is evident; for her magnitude and figure give that great extent to the conical shadow which she produces. But she is the fabricator of the day, considered as giving perfection to the day which is conjoined with night; so that earth is the artificer of both these in conjunction with the sun.

"But she is the most ancient and first of the Gods in the heavens, considered with respect to her stability and generative power, her symphony with heaven, and her position in the centre of the universe. For the centre possesses a mighty power in the universe, as connecting all its circulations; and hence it was called by the Pythagoreans the tower of Jupiter, from its containing a demiurgic guard. And if we recollect the Platonic hypothesis concerning the earth (which we have mentioned before), that our habitable part is nothing but a dark hollow, and very different from the true earth, which is adorned with a beauty similar to that of the heavens, we shall have no occasion to wonder at her being called the first and most ancient of the celestial Gods."

Again, according to the Platonic philosophy, some of the fixed stars are sometimes so affected, that for a considerable space of time they become invisible to us; and in this case, both when they withdraw themselves from our view, and when they again make their appearance, they are said by such as are skilled in these affairs, according to the information of Proclus,[†] both to produce and signify mighty events. But though it is evident from the very words of Plato, in this part of the dialogue, that this opinion concerning certain stars disappearing and becoming again visible was entertained by all the astronomers of his time, and by the Pythagoreans prior to him, yet this most interesting circumstance seems to have been utterly unknown to the moderns. Hence, not in the least suspecting this to be the case, they have immediately concluded from stars appearing of which we have no account, and others disappearing which have been observed in the heavens for many ages, that the stars are bodies, like earthly natures, subject to generation and decay. But this is not wonderful, if we consider that such men as these have not the smallest conception that the universe is a perfect whole; that every thing perfect must have a first, middle, and last; and that, in consequence of this, the heavens alone can rank in the first place, and earth in the last.

As the universe, indeed, as well as each of its principal parts or *wholes*, is *perpetual*, and as this perpetuity being temporal can only subsist by periodical circulation, hence all the celestial bodies, in order that all the possible variety of things may be unfolded, form different periods at different times; and their appearings and disappearings are nothing more than the restitutions of their circulations to their pristine state, and the beginnings of new periods. For according to these especially, says Proclus, they turn and transmute mundane natures, and bring on abundant corruptions and mighty mutations, as Plato asserts in the *Republic*.

In the next place, from the sublime speech of the demiurgus to the junior or mundane Gods, the reader may obtain full conviction that the

---

[†] In Tim. p. 285. And in p. 333 he informs us, that the fixed stars have periods of revolution, though to us unknown, and that different stars have different periods. See also Chalcidius in Plat. Tim. p. 218.

Gods of the ancients were not dead men deified; for they are here represented as commanded by the mundane artificer to fabricate the whole of the mortal race. And with respect to the properties of the sublunary Gods, which Plato comprehends in nine divinities, Proclus beautifully observes that *Heaven* bounds, *Earth* corroborates, and *Ocean* moves, the whole of generation. That *Tethys* establishes every thing in its proper motion, intellectual natures in intellectual, middle natures in animal, and corporeal natures in physical motion; *Ocean* at the same time moving all things collected together in one. But *Saturn* distributes intellectually only, *Rhea* vivifies, *Phorcys* scatters spermatic reasons, *Jupiter* gives perfection to things apparent from unapparent causes, and *Juno* evolves according to the all-various mutations of apparent natures. And thus through this ennead the sublunary world is in a becoming manner distributed and filled; divinely indeed from the Gods, angelically from angels, and dæmoniacally from dæmons. And again, the Gods subsisting about bodies, souls, and intellects; angels exhibiting their providence about souls and bodies; and dæmons being divided about the fabrication of nature, and the care of bodies. But it may be asked, why does Plato comprehend the whole extent of the Gods producing generation, in these nine divinities? Because, says Proclus, this ennead accomplishes the fabrication of generation. For in the sublunary regions there are bodies and natures, souls and intellects, and these both totally and partially. And all these subsist in both respects, that is both totally and partially, in each of the elements, because wholes and parts subsist together. Hence, as each element ranks as a monad, and contains bodies and natures, souls and intellects, both totally and partially, an ennead will evidently be produced in each. But *Heaven* and *Earth* generate the unapparent essences of these, the former according to union, and the latter according to multiplication: but *Ocean* and *Tethys* give perfection to their common and distributed motion; at the same time that the motion of each is different. In like manner, with respect to the wholes which are adorned, *Saturn* distributes things partial from such as are total, but in an intellectual manner. But *Rhea* calls forth this distribution from intellectual natures into all-various progressions, and as far as to the ultimate forms of life, in consequence of her being a vivific Goddess. But *Phorcys* produces the Titanic distinction, as far as to natural reasons. And after these three, the fathers of composite natures succeed. And Jupiter indeed orderly disposes sensible natures totally, in imitation of *Heaven*. For in the intellectual order, and in the royal series, he proceeds analogous to *Heaven*.[†] But Juno moves the wholes, fills them with powers, and unfolds them according to every progression. And the Gods posterior to these fabricate the partial works of sensible natures, according to the characteristics by which they are distinguished; *viz*. the demiurgic, the vivific, the perfective, and the connective, unfolding and distributing themselves as far as to the last of things. For these last are all of them analogous to the Saturnian order, from whose government the distributive characteristic originally proceeds.

Again, by the *Crater* in which the mundane soul was mingled, we must understand the vivific Goddess Juno; by the term *mingling*, a communion of essence; and by a second mixture in a certain respect the same, but yet deficient from the first in a second and third degree, the similitude and at the same time inferiority of partial to total souls, and the order subsisting among partial souls. For some of these are pure and undefiled, associating with generation but for a short time, and this for the Godlike purpose of benefiting more ingenious souls; but others wander from their true country for very extended periods of time. For between souls which abide on high without defilement, and such as descend and are defiled with vice, the medium must be such souls as descend, indeed, but without defilement.

But when the artificer of the universe is said to have distributed souls equal in number to the stars, this must not be understood as if one partial soul was distributed under one of the stars, and that the quantity of souls is equal to that of the starry Gods; for this would be perfectly inconsistent with what Plato asserts a little before, that the artificer disseminated some of these into the earth, some into the sun and some into the moon, thus scattering a multitude into each of the instruments of time. But, as Proclus well observes, equality of number here must not be understood monadically, but according to analogy. For in numbers, says he, ten is analogous to unity, thirty to three, fifty to five, and entirely all the numbers posterior to the decad, to all within the decad. And hence five is not equal to fifty in quantity, nor three to thirty, but they are only equal according to analogy. After this manner, therefore, the equal in number must be assumed in partial souls; since there is a number of these accommodated to every divine soul, and which each divine soul uniformly pre-assumes in itself. And hence,

---

[†] For there are six kings, according to Orpheus, who preside over the universe - Phanes, Night, Heaven, Saturn, Jupiter, Bacchus; and of these Saturn proceeds analogous to Phanes, and Jupiter to Heaven.

when it unfolds this number, it bounds the multitude of partial souls distributed under its essence. Likewise, with respect to these depending souls, such as are first suspended from a divine soul are less in number, but greater in power; but such as are second in progression are less in power, but more extended in number; while at the same time each is analogous to the divine cause from which it proceeds.

Observe, too, that when Plato uses the term *the most pious of animals*, man alone is not implied, but the inhabitants likewise or partial souls of the several spheres and stars: for, says Proclus, between eternal animals,[†] and such as live but, for a short period,[‡] (*viz.* whose periods of circulation are short) it is necessary there should be a species of rational animals more divine than man, and whose existence is of a very extended duration. It is likewise worthy of observation, that the soul is conjoined with this gross body through two vehicles as mediums, one of which is ethereal and the other ærial: and of these the ethereal vehicle is *simple and immaterial*, but the ærial *simple and material*; and this dense earthly body is *composite and material*.

Again, when our souls are represented after falling into the present body as suffering a transmutation into brutes, this, as Proclus beautifully observes, must not be understood as if our souls ever became the animating principles of brutal bodies, but that by a certain sympathy they are bound to the souls of brutes, and are as it were carried in them, just as evil dæmons insinuate themselves into our phantasy, through their own depraved imaginations. And by the circulations of the soul being merged in a profound river and impetuously borne along, we must understand by the river, not the human body alone, but the whole of generation (with which we are externally surrounded) through its swift and unstable flowing. For thus, says Proclus, Plato in the *Republic* calls the whole of generated nature the river of Lethe, which contains both Lethe and the meadow of Ate, according to Empedocles;[§] the devouring jaws of matter and the light-hating world, as it is called by the Gods; and the winding rivers under which many are drawn down, as the

---

[†] i.e. stars and spheres.

[‡] i.e. men.

[§] Εν ῃ και η Ληθη, και ο της Ατης λειμων, ως φησιν Εμπεδοκλης, και το λαβρον της υλης, και ο μισοφανης κοσμος, ως οι θεοι λεγουσι, και τα σκολια ρειθρα, υφ᾽ ων οι πολλοι κατασυρονται, ως τα λογια φησιν. Procl. in Tim. See more concerning this in my *Dissertation on the Eleusinian and Bacchic Mysteries* [TTS vol. VII].

oracles[†] assert. But by the circulations of the soul the dianoëtic and doxastic powers are signified; the former of which, through the soul's conjunction with the body, is impeded in its energies, and the latter is Titanically torn in pieces under the irrational life.

Again, if we consider man with reference to a contemplative life, which is the true end of his formation, we shall find that the head, which is the instrument of contemplation, is the principal member, and that the other members were only added as ministrant to the head. With respect to sight, it must be observed that Democritus, Heraclitus, the Stoics, many of the Peripatetics and ancient geometricians, together with the Platonists, were of opinion that vision subsists through a lucid spirit emitted from the eyes: and this spirit, according to Plato and his followers, is an unburning vivific fire similar to celestial fire, from which it originally proceeds. But this fire, the illuminations of which, as we have already observed, give life to our mortal part, is abundantly collected in the eye as in a fat diaphanous substance, whose moisture is most shining and whose membranes are tender and transparent, but yet sufficiently firm for the purpose of preserving the inherent light. But a most serene ray shines through the more solid pupil; and this ray originates internally from one nerve, but is afterwards derived through two small nerves to the two eyes. And these nerves, through the fat humours of the eyes, winding under the tunics, arrive at length at the pupils. But a light of this kind, thus preserved in the small nerves, and bursting through the narrow pupils as soon as it shines forth into dispersed rays, as it commenced from one ray, so it immediately returns into one, from the rays naturally uniting in one common ray: for the eyes also, on account of their lubricity, roundness, and smooth substance, are easily moved hither and thither, with an equal and similar revolution. This visual ray, however, cannot proceed externally and perceive objects at a distance, unless it is conjoined with external light proceeding conically to the eyes; and hence our ray insinuating itself into this light, and becoming strengthened by the association, continues its progression till it meets with some opposing object. But when this is the case, it either diffuses itself through the superficies of the object, or runs through it with wonderful celerity, and becomes immediately affected with the quality of the object. And a resistance, motion, and affection of this kind produces vision, viz. from the vibration of the ray thus affected gradually arriving at the instrument of sight, and by this means exciting that image of the object which is naturally inherent in

---

[†] *Viz.* the oracles of Zoroaster. [TTS vol. VII]

the instrument, and through which when excited perception ensues. For there are three particulars which belong in general to all the senses; first, an image or mark of the sensible thing impressed in the sensitive instrument; and this constituted both in passion and energy in a certain similitude to the sensible object: but afterwards we must consider an impression of this kind as now perfect, and ending in species, *viz.* in the common composite life: and, in the third place, that inherent reason of the soul ensues, which germinates from the sensitive soul, is accommodated to species of this kind, and is that through which sensitive judgment and cogitation subsist.

But further, the Platonists admit, with Democritus and Empedocles, that certain material images of things flow through the pores of bodies, and preserve, to a certain distance, not only the qualities but likewise the shape of the bodies from which they flow. And these radial images are intimated by Plato in this dialogue, in the *Sophista*, and in the seventh book of his *Republic*; in commenting on the last of which, Proclus observes as follows: "According to Plato, (says he) representations of things are hypostases of certain images fabricated by a dæmoniacal art, as he teaches us in the *Sophista*; for shadows, of which they say images are the companions, possess a nature of this kind. For these are the effigies of bodies and figures, and have an abundant sympathy with the things from which they fall; as is evident from what the arts of magicians are able to effect, and from what they tell us concerning images and shadows. But why should I speak of the powers of magicians, when irrational animals are able to operate through images and shadows, prior to all reason? for they say that the hyæna, by trampling on the shadow of a dog seated on an eminence, will hurl him down and devour him; and Aristotle says, that if a woman, during her menstrua, looks into a mirror, she will defile both the mirror and the apparent image." - Οτι κατα Πλατωνα αι εμφασεις υποστασεις εισιν ειδωλων τινων δαιμονια μηχανη δημιουργουμεναι, καθαπερ αυτος εν τω σοφιστη διδασκει. Και γαρ αι σκιαι αις τα ειδωλα συζυγειν φησι τοιαυτην εχουσι φυσιν. Και γαρ αυται σωματων εισι και σχηματων εικονες, και παμπολυν εχουσι προς τα αφ᾽ ων εμπιπτουσι συμπαθειαν, ως δηλουσι και οσα μαχων (lege μαγων) τεχναι προς τε τα ειδωλα δραν και επαγγελλονται και τας σκιας. Και τι λεγω τας εκεινων δυναμεις α και τοις αλογοις ηδη ζωοις υπαρχη προ λογου παντος ενεργειν. Η γαρ ναινα φασιν την του κυνος εν υψει καθημενου πατησασα σκιαν καταβαλλει, και θοινην ποιηται τον κυνα. Και γυναικος καθαιρουμενης φησιν Αριστοτελης, εις ενοπτρον ιδουσης, αιματουται, το τε ενοπτρον, και το εμφαινομενον ειδωλον.[†] And he likewise informs us in the same place, that these images, on account of their slender existence, cannot otherwise become visible to our eyes, than when, in consequence of being established, restored, and illuminated in mirrors, they again receive their pristine power and the shape of their originals. Hence, says he, density is required in the body which receives them, that the image may not be dissipated from the rarity of the receptacle, and that from many defluxions it may pass into one form. But smoothness likewise is required, lest the asperity of the receptacle, on account of the prominency of some of its parts and the depth of others, should be the cause of inequality to the image. And, lastly, splendour is required; that the image, which naturally possesses a slender form, may become apparent to the sight.

In the next place, with respect to matter, and the various epithets by which Plato calls it in this dialogue, it is necessary to observe, that as in an ascending series of subjects we must arrive at length at something which is better than all things, so in a descending series our progression must be stopped by something which is worse than all things, and which is the general receptacle of the last procession of forms. And this is what the ancients called matter, and which they considered as nothing more than a certain indefiniteness of an incorporeal, indivisible, and intellectual nature, and as something which is not formally impressed and bounded by three dimensions, but is entirely remitted and resolved, and is on all sides rapidly flowing from being into non-entity. But this opinion concerning matter, says Simplicius,[‡] seems to have been adopted by the first Pythagoreans among the Greeks; and after these by Plato, according to the relation of Moderatus. For he shows us - "that, according to the Pythagoreans, there is a *first one* subsisting prior to the essence of things and every substance; that after this, true being and intelligible or forms subsist: and, in the third place, that which pertains to soul, and which participates of *The One* and of intellectual forms. But after this (says he) the last nature, which is that of sensibles, subsists; which does not participate of the preceding natures, but is thus affected and formed according to the representation of these; since the matter of sensible natures is the shadow of that non-being which primarily subsists in quantity, or rather may be said to depend upon, and be produced by, this." Hence Porphyry, in his second book on Matter, says Simplicius,

---

[†] Vid. Procl. in Plat. Polit.

[‡] In Aristot. Phys. p. 50, b.

observes that Plato calls matter, quantity, which is formless, indivisible, and without figure; but capacious, and the receptacle of form, figure, division, quality, and other things of a similar kind. And this quantity and form, considered according to the privation of a uniform reason, which comprehends all the reasons of beings in itself, is the paradigm of the matter of bodies; which, says Porphyry, both Plato and the Pythagoreans call a quantum, not after the same manner as form is a quantum, but according to privation and analysis, extension and divulsion, and its mutation from being. Matter, therefore, according to this doctrine, as Simplicius well observes, is nothing else than the permutation and vicissitude of sensible forms, with respect to intelligibles; since from thence they verge downwards, and extend to perfect non-entity, or the last of things - that is, to matter itself. Hence, says he, because dregs and matter are always the last of things, the Egyptians assert that matter, which they enigmatically denominate water, is the dregs of the first life; subsisting as a certain mire or mud, the receptacle of generable and sensible natures; and which is not any definite form, but a certain constitution of subsistence, in the same manner as that which is indivisible, immaterial and true being, is a constitution of an intelligible nature. And though all forms subsist both in intelligibles and in matter, yet in the former they subsist without matter, indivisibly and truly; but in the latter divisibly, and after the manner of shadows. And on this account every sensible form is dissipated through its union with material interval, and falls from the stability and reality of being.

But the following profound and admirable description of matter by Plotinus (Ennead. 3, vi, TTS vol. III p. 247) will, I doubt not, be gratefully received by the Platonic reader. - "Since matter (says he) is neither soul, nor intellect, nor life, nor form, nor reason, nor bound, but a certain indefiniteness; nor yet capacity, for what can it produce? since it is foreign from all these, it cannot merit the appellation of being; but is deservedly called non-entity. Nor yet is it non-entity in the same manner as *motion* and *permanency* are non-beings, considered as different from being: but it is true non-entity; the mere shadow and imagination of bulk, and the desire of subsistence; remaining fixed without abiding, of itself invisible, and avoiding the desire of him who is anxious to perceive its nature. Hence, when no one perceives it, it is then in a manner present; but cannot be viewed by him who strives intently to behold it. Again, in itself contraries always appear; the small and the great, the less and the more, deficience and excess. So that it is a phantom, neither abiding nor yet able to fly away; capable of no one denomination, and possessing no power from intellect; but is constituted in the defect and shade, as it were, of all real being. Hence, too, in each of its vanishing appellations, it eludes our search: for, if we think of it as something great, it is in the mean time small; if as something more, it becomes less; and the apparent being which we meet with in its image is non-being, and, as it were, a flying mockery. So that the forms which appear in matter are merely ludicrous; shadows falling upon shadow, as in a mirror, where the position of the apparent is different from that of the real object; and which, though apparently full of forms, possesses nothing real and true. But the things which enter into, and depart from, matter, are nothing but imitations of being, and semblances flowing about a formless semblance. They seem, indeed, to effect something in the subject matter, but in reality produce nothing; from their debile and flowing nature being endued with no solidity and no rebounding power. And since matter likewise has no solidity, they penetrate it without division, like images in water, or as if any one should fill a vacuum with forms."

Such, then, being the true condition of matter and her inherent shadowy forms, we may safely conclude that whatever becomes corporeal in an eminent degree has but little power of recalling itself into one; and that a nature of this kind is ready by every trifling impulse to remain as it is impelled; to rush from the embraces of bound, and hasten into multitude and nonentity. Hence, as Plotinus beautifully observes, (Ennead. 3, vi, p. 247) - "those who only place *being* in the genus of body, in consequence of impulses and concussions, and the phantasms perceived through the senses, which persuade them that sense is alone the standard of truth, are affected like those in a dream, who imagine that the perceptions of sleep are true. For sense is alone the employment of the dormant soul; since as much of the soul as is merged in body, so much of it sleeps. But true elevation and true vigilance are a resurrection from, and not with, the dull mass of body. For, indeed, a resurrection with body is only a transmigration from sleep to sleep, and from dream to dream, like a man passing in the dark from bed to bed. But that elevation is perfectly true which entirely rises from the dead weight of bodies; for these, possessing a nature repugnant to soul, possess something opposite to essence. And this is further evident from their generation, their continual flowing and decay; properties entirely foreign from the nature of being, substantial and real."

Lastly, when Plato composes the elements from mathematical planes, it is necessary to observe that, as these are physical planes, they must not only have length and breadth, but likewise depth, that they may be able to subsist as principles in natural effects. - "For the Pythagoreans (says Simplicius†) considered every physical body as a figured quantity, and as in itself matter, but fashioned with different figures. That, besides this, it differs from a mathematical body in being material and tangible, receiving its tangibility from its bulk, and not either from heat or cold. Hence, from the subject matter being impressed with different figures, they assert that the four elements of the elements subsist. For these elements rank more in the nature of principles, as for instance, the cubic of earth; not that earth has wholly a cubic figure, but that each of the parts of earth is composed from many cubes, which through their smallness are invisible to our sight; and in the same manner the other elements from other primary figures. They add too, that from this difference of figures all the other properties of the elements ensue, and their mutations into each other. For, if it is inquired why much air is produced from a little water, they can very readily assign the cause by saying, that the elements of water are many, and that, the icosaedrons of water being divided, many octaedrons, and consequently a great quantity of air, will be produced."

Simplicius likewise informs us, that the more ancient of Plato's interpreters, among which the divine Iamblichus ranks, considered Plato as speaking symbolically in this part concerning the figures of the elements; but the latter Platonic philosophers, among whom Proclus, in my opinion, ranks as the most eminent, explained this part according to its literal meaning. And Simplicius, in the same book, has fortunately preserved the arguments of Proclus in defence of Plato's doctrine respecting these planes, against the objections of Aristotle.

Should it be asked in what this doctrine concerning planes differs from the dogma of Democritus, who asserted that natural bodies were fashioned according to figures, we may answer with Simplicius,‡ that Plato and the Pythagoreans by a plane denoted something more simple than a body,§ atoms being evidently bodies; that they assigned commensuration and a demiurgic analogy* to their figures, which

---

† De Cœlo, lib. iv. p. 139.

‡ De Cœlo, p. 142.

§ *Viz.* than any visible sublunary body.

* i.e. active and fabricative powers.

418

Democritus did not to his atoms; and that they differed from him in their arrangement of earth.

And thus much may suffice at present for an epitome of some of the principal parts of this most interesting dialogue. For, as it is my design at some future period to publish as complete a commentary as I am able from the inestimable commentaries of Proclus on this dialogue, with additional observations of my own, a more copious introduction might at present be considered as superfluous. The difficulty, indeed, of proceeding any further, might alone very well apologise for the want of completion in this compendium. For the commentary of Proclus, though consisting of five books, is imperfect,[†] and does not even extend so far as to the doctrine of vision, which in the present introduction I have endeavoured to explain. I trust, therefore, that the candid and liberal reader will gratefully accept these fruits of my application to the Platonic philosophy; and as this introduction and the following translation were the result of no moderate labour and perseverance, I earnestly hope they may be the means of awakening some few at least from the sleep of oblivion, of recalling their attention from fluctuating and delusive objects to permanent and real being; and thus may at length lead them back to their paternal port, as the only retreat which can confer perfect security and rest.

---

† It is a circumstance remarkably unfortunate, as I have before observed, that not one of the invaluable commentaries of this philosopher has been preserved entire. For that he wrote a complete commentary on this dialogue, is evident from a citation of Olympiodorus on Aristotle's *Meteors* from it, which is not to be found in any of the books now extant. In like manner, his treatise on Plato's theology is imperfect, wanting a seventh book; his commentaries on the *Parmenides* want many books; his scholia on the *Cratylus* are far from being complete; and this is likewise the case with his commentary on the *First Alcibiades*.

THE TIMÆUS

7a   SOC. I see one, two, three, but where, friend Timæus, is that fourth person, who being received by me yesterday at a banquet of disputation, ought now in his turn to repay me with a similar repast?

TIM. He labours, Socrates, under a certain infirmity; for he would not willingly be absent from such an association as the present.

SOC. It remains therefore for you, O Timæus, and the company present, to fill up the part of this absent guest.

TIM. Entirely so, Socrates. And we shall endeavour, to the utmost of our ability, to leave nothing belonging to such an employment unaccomplished. For it would be by no means just that we, who were yesterday entertained by you, in such a manner as guests ought to be received, should not return the hospitality with readiness and delight.

SOC. Do you recollect the magnitude and nature of the things which I proposed to you to explain?

TIM. Some things, indeed, I recollect; but such as I have forgotten do you recall into my memory. Or rather, if it be not too much trouble, run over the whole in a cursory manner from the beginning, that it may be more firmly established in our memory.

SOC. Let it be so. And to begin: The sum of yesterday's dispute was, what kind of republic appeared to me to be the best, and from what sort of men such a republic ought to be composed.

TIM. And by us, indeed, Socrates, all that you said was approved in the highest degree.

SOC. Did we not, in the first place, separate husbandmen and other artificers from those whom we considered as the defenders of the city?

TIM. Certainly.

SOC. And when we had assigned to every one that which was accommodated to his nature, and had prescribed only one particular employment to every particular art, we likewise assigned to the military tribe one province only, I mean that of protecting the city; and this as well from the hostile incursions of internal as of external enemies; but

yet in such a manner as to administer justice mildly to the subjects of
their government, as being naturally friends, and to behave with warlike
fierceness against their enemies in battle.

TIM. Entirely so.

SOC. For we asserted, I think, that the souls of the guardians should
be of such a nature, as at the same time to be both irascible and
philosophic in a remarkable degree; so that they might be gentle to their
friends, and bold and ferocious to their enemies.

TIM. You did so.

SOC. But what did we assert concerning their education? Was it not
that they should be instructed in gymnastic exercises, in music, and
other becoming disciplines?

TIM. Entirely so.

SOC. We likewise established, that those who were so educated should
neither consider gold, or silver, or any goods of a similar kind, as their
own private property; but that rather, after the manner of adjutants,
they should receive the wages of guardianship from those whom they
defend and preserve; and that their recompense should be no more than
is sufficient to a moderate subsistence. That, besides this, they should
use their public stipend in common, and for the purpose of procuring
a common subsistence with each other; so that, neglecting every other
concern, they may employ their attention solely on virtue, and the
discharge of their peculiar employment.

TIM. These things also were related by you.

SOC. Of women too we asserted, that they should be educated in such
a manner, as to be aptly conformed similar to the natures of men; with
whom they should perform in common both the duties of war, and
whatever else belongs to the business of life.

TIM. This too was asserted by you.

SOC. But what did we establish concerning the procreation of
children? Though perhaps you easily remember this, on account of its
novelty. For we ordered that the marriages and children should be
common; as we were particularly careful that no one might be able to
distinguish his own children, but that all might consider all as their
kindred; that hence those of an equal age might regard themselves as
brothers and sisters; but that the younger might reverence the elder as
their parents and grandfathers, and the elder might esteem the younger
as their children and grandsons.

TIM. These things, indeed, as you say, are easily remembered.

SOC. But that they might from their birth acquire a disposition as far
as possible the best, we decreed that the rulers whom we placed over the

marriage rites should, through the means of certain lots, take care that
in the nuptial league the worthy were mingled with the worthy; that no
discord may arise in this connection when it does not prove prosperous
in the end; but that all the blame may be referred to fortune, and not
to the guardians of such a conjunction.

TIM. We remember this likewise.

SOC. We also ordered that the children of the good should be
properly educated, but that those of the bad should be secretly sent to
some other city; yet so that such of the adult among these as should be
found to be of a good disposition should be recalled from exile; while,
on the contrary, those who were retained from the first in the city as
good, but proved afterwards bad, should be similarly banished.

TIM. Just so.

SOC. Have we, therefore, sufficiently epitomized yesterday's
disputation; or do you require any thing further, friend Timæus, which
I have omitted?

TIM. Nothing, indeed, Socrates; for all this was the subject of your
disputation.

SOC. Hear now how I am affected towards this republic which we
have described; for I will illustrate the affair by a similitude. Suppose
then that some one, on beholding beautiful animals, whether represented
in a picture, or really alive, but in a state of perfect rest, should desire
to behold them in motion, and struggling as it were to imitate those
gestures which seem particularly adapted to the nature of bodies; in such
a manner am I affected towards the form of that republic which we have
described. For I should gladly hear any one relating the contests of our
city with other nations, when it engages in a becoming manner in war,
and acts during such an engagement in a manner worthy of its
institution, both with respect to practical achievements and verbal
negotiations. For indeed, O Critias and Hermocrates, I am conscious of
my own inability to praise such men and such a city according to their
desert. Indeed, that I should be incapable of such an undertaking is not
wonderful, since the same imbecility seems to have attended poets both
of the past and present age. Not that I despise the poetic tribe; but it
appears from hence evident, that, as these kind of men are studious of
imitation, they easily and in the best manner express things in which
they have been educated; while, on the contrary, whatever is foreign
from their education they imitate with difficulty in actions, and with
still more difficulty in words. But with respect to the tribe of Sophists,
though I consider them as skilled both in the art of speaking and in
many other illustrious arts; yet, as they have no settled abode, but

wander daily through a multitude of cities, I am afraid lest, with respect to the institutions of philosophers and politicians, they should not be able to conjecture the quality and magnitude of those concerns which wise and politic men are engaged in with individuals, in warlike undertakings, both in actions and discourse. It remains, therefore, that I should apply to you, who excel in the study of wisdom and civil administration, as well naturally as through the assistance˙ of proper discipline and institution. For Timæus here of Locris, an Italian city

20a governed by the best of laws, exclusive of his not being inferior to any of his fellow-citizens in wealth and nobility, has arrived in his own city at the highest posts of government and honours. Besides, we all know that Critias is not ignorant of the particulars of which we are now speaking. Nor is this to be doubted of Hermocrates, since a multitude of circumstances evince that he is both by nature and education adapted

b to all such concerns. Hence, when you yesterday requested me to dispute about the institution of a republic, I readily complied with your request; being persuaded that the remainder of the discourse could not be more conveniently explained by any one than by you, if you were but willing to engage in its discussion. For, unless you properly adapt the city for warlike purposes, there is no one in the present age from whom it can acquire every thing becoming its constitution. As I have, therefore, hitherto complied with your request, I shall now require you to comply with mine in the above-mentioned particulars. Nor have you indeed refused this employment, but have with common consent determined to repay my hospitality with the banquet of discourse. I

c now, therefore, stand prepared to receive the promised feast.

HERM. But we, O Socrates, as Timæus just now signified, shall cheerfully engage in the execution of your desire; for we cannot offer any excuse sufficient to justify neglect in this affair. For yesterday, when we departed from hence and went to the lodging of Critias, where we are accustomed to reside, both in his apartment and prior to this in the way thither we discoursed on this very particular. He therefore related to us a certain ancient history, which I wish, O Critias, you

d would now repeat to Socrates, that he may judge whether it any way conduces to the fulfilment of his request.

CRIT. It is requisite to comply, if agreeable to Timæus, the third associate of our undertaking.

TIM. I assent to your compliance.

CRIT. Hear then, O Socrates, a discourse surprising indeed in the extreme, yet in every respect true, as it was once related by Solon, the

e most wise of the seven wise men. Solon, then, was the familiar and intimate friend of our great-grandfather Dropis, as he himself often relates in his poems. But he once declared to our grandfather Critias, (as the old man himself informed us,) that great and admirable actions had once been achieved by this city, which nevertheless were buried in oblivion, through length of time and the destruction of mankind. In particular he informed me of one undertaking more illustrious than the rest, which I now think proper to relate to you, both that I may repay my obligations, and that by such a relation I may offer my tribute of praise to the Goddess in the present solemnity, by celebrating her divinity, as it were, with hymns, justly and in a manner agreeable to truth.

SOC. You speak well. But what is this ancient achievement which was not only actually related by Solon, but was once really accomplished by this city?

CRIT. I will acquaint you with that ancient history, which I did not indeed receive from a youth, but from a man very much advanced in years; for at that time Critias, as he himself declared, was almost ninety years old, and I myself was about ten. When, therefore, that solemnity was celebrated among us which is known by the name of *Cureotis Apaturiorum*,[1] nothing was omitted which boys in that festivity are accustomed to perform. For, when our parents had set before us the rewards proposed for the contest of singing verses, both a multitude of verses of many poets were recited, and many of us especially sung the poems of Solon, because they were at that time entirely new. But then one of our tribe, whether he was willing to gratify Critias, or whether it was his real opinion, affirmed that Solon appeared to him most wise in other concerns, and in things respecting poetry the most ingenious of all poets. Upon hearing this, the old man (for I very well remember) was vehemently delighted; and said, laughing - If Solon, O Amynander, had not engaged in poetry as a casual affair, but had made it, as others do, a serious employment; and if through seditions and other fluctuations of the state, in which he found his country involved, he had not been compelled to neglect the completion of the history which he brought from Egypt, I do not think that either Hesiod or Homer, or any other poet, would have acquired greater glory and renown. In consequence of this, Amynander inquired of Critias what that history was. To which he answered, that it was concerning an affair the greatest and most celebrated which this city ever performed; though through length of time, and the destruction of those by whom it was undertaken, the fame of its execution has not reached the present age. But I beseech you, O Critias, (says Amynander,) relate this affair from the beginning;

and inform me what that event was which Solon asserted as a fact, and on what occasion, and from whom he received it.

e   There is then (says he) a certain region of Egypt called Delta, about the summit of which the streams of the Nile are divided. In this place a government is established called Saitical; and the chief city of this region of Delta is Sais, from which also king Amasis derived his origin. The city has a presiding divinity, whose name is in the Egyptian tongue Neith, and in the Greek Athena, or Minerva. These men were friends of the Athenians, with whom they declared they were very familiar, through a certain bond of alliance. In this country Solon, on his arrival

22a   thither, was, as he himself relates, very honourably received. And upon his inquiring about ancient affairs of those priests who possessed a knowledge in such particulars superior to others, he perceived, that neither himself, nor any one of the Greeks, (as he himself declared), had any knowledge of very remote antiquity. Hence, when he once desired to excite them to the relation of ancient transactions, he for this purpose began to discourse about those most ancient events which formerly happened among us. I mean the traditions concerning the first Phoroneus and Niobe, and after the deluge, of Deucalion and Pyrrha, (as

b   described by the mythologists,) together with their posterity; at the same time paying a proper attention to the different ages in which these events are said to have subsisted. But upon this one of those more ancient priests exclaimed, O Solon, Solon, you Greeks are always children, nor is there any such thing as an aged Grecian among you! But Solon, when he heard this - What (says he) is the motive of your exclamation? To whom the priest: - Because all your souls are juvenile; neither containing any ancient opinion derived from remote tradition, nor any discipline hoary from its existence in former periods of time.

c   But the reason of this is the multitude and variety of destructions of the human race, which formerly have been, and again will be: the greatest of these, indeed, arising from fire and water; but the lesser from ten thousand other contingencies. For the relation subsisting among you, that Phæton, the offspring of the Sun, on a certain time attempting to drive the chariot of his father, and not being able to keep the track observed by his parent, burnt up the natures belonging to the earth, and perished himself, blasted by thunder - is indeed considered as fabulous,

d   yet is in reality true. For it expresses the mutation of the bodies revolving in the heavens about the earth; and indicates that, through long periods of time, a destruction of terrestrial natures ensues from the devastations of fire. Hence, those who either dwell on mountains, or in lofty and dry places, perish more abundantly than those who dwell near rivers, or on the borders of the sea. To us indeed the Nile is both salutary in other respects, and liberates us from the fear of such-like depredations. But when the Gods, purifying the earth by waters, deluge its surface, then the herdsmen and shepherds inhabiting the mountains are preserved, while the inhabitants of your cities are hurried away to the sea by the impetuous inundation of the rivers. On the contrary, in our region, neither then, nor at any other time, did the waters descending from on high pour with desolation on the plains; but they are naturally impelled upwards from the bosom of the earth. And from these causes the most ancient traditions are preserved in our country. For, indeed, it may be truly asserted, that in those places where neither intense cold nor immoderate heat prevails, the race of mankind is always preserved, though sometimes the number of individuals is increased, and sometimes suffers a considerable diminution. But whatever has been transacted either by us, or by you, or in any other place, beautiful or great, or containing any thing uncommon, of which we have heard the report, every thing of this kind is to be found described in our temples, and preserved to the present day. While, on the contrary, you and other nations commit only recent transactions to writing, and to other inventions which society has employed for transmitting information to posterity; and so again, at stated periods of time, a certain celestial defluxion rushes on them like a disease; from whence those among you who survive are both destitute of literary acquisitions and the inspiration of the Muses. Hence it happens that you become juvenile again, and ignorant of the events which happened in ancient times, as well among us as in the regions which you inhabit.

The transactions, therefore, O Solon, which you relate from your antiquities, differ very little from puerile fables. For, in the first place, you only mention one deluge of the earth, when at the same time many have happened. And, in the next place, you are ignorant of a most illustrious and excellent race of men, who once inhabited your country; from whence you and your whole city descended, though a small seed only of this admirable people once remained. But your ignorance in this affair is owing to the posterity of this people, who were for many ages deprived of the use of letters, and became as it were dumb. For prior, O Solon, to that mighty deluge which we have just mentioned, a city of Athenians existed, informed according to the best laws both in military concerns and every other duty of life; and whose illustrious actions and civil institutions are celebrated by us as the most excellent of all that have existed under the ample circumference of the heavens. Solon, therefore, upon hearing this, said that he was astonished; and, burning with a most ardent desire, entreated the priests to relate accurately all the actions of his ancient fellow-citizens. That afterwards one of the priests replied: - Nothing of envy, O Solon, prohibits us from complying with your request. But for your sake, and that of your city, I will relate the whole; and especially on account of that Goddess who is allotted the guardianship both of your city and ours, and by whom they have been educated and founded: yours, indeed, by a priority to ours of a thousand years, receiving the seed of your race from Vulcan

e and the Earth. But the description of the transactions of this our city during the space of eight thousand years, is preserved in our sacred writings. I will, therefore, cursorily run over the laws and more illustrious actions of those cities which existed nine thousand years ago.

24a For when we are more at leisure we shall prosecute an exact history of every particular, receiving for this purpose the sacred writings themselves. In the first place, then, consider the laws of these people, and compare them with ours: for you will find many things which then subsisted in your city, similar to such as exist at present. For the priests passed their life separated from all others. The artificers also exercised their arts in such a manner, that each was engaged in his own employment without being mingled with other artificers. The same

b method was likewise adopted with shepherds, hunters and husbandmen. The soldiers too, you will find, were separated from other kind of men; and were commanded by the laws to engage in nothing but warlike affairs. A similar armour too, such as that of shields and darts, was employed by each. These we first used in Asia; the Goddess in those places, as likewise happened to you, first pointing them out to our use. You may perceive too from the beginning what great attention was paid by the laws to prudence and modesty; and besides this, to divination and

c medicine, as subservient to the preservation of health. And from these, which are divine goods, the laws, proceeding to the invention of such as are merely human, procured all such other disciplines as follow from those we have just enumerated. From such a distribution, therefore, and in such order, the Goddess first established and adorned your city, choosing for this purpose the place in which you were born; as she foresaw that, from the excellent temperature of the region, men would arise distinguished by the most consummate sagacity and wit. For, as

d the Goddess is a lover both of wisdom and war, she fixed on a soil capable of producing men the most similar to herself; and rendered it in every respect adapted for the habitation of such a race. The ancient Athenians, therefore, using these laws, and being formed by good institutions, in a still higher degree than I have mentioned, inhabited this region; surpassing all men in every virtue, as it becomes those to do who are the progeny and pupils of the Gods.

But though many and mighty deeds of your city are contained in our sacred writings, and are admired as they deserve, yet there is one transaction which surpasses all of them in magnitude and virtue. For these writings relate what prodigious strength your city formerly tamed, when a mighty warlike power, rushing from the Atlantic sea, spread itself with hostile fury over all Europe and Asia. For at that time the Atlantic sea was navigable, and had an island before that mouth which is called by you the Pillars of Hercules. But this island was greater than both Libya and all Asia together, and afforded an easy passage to other neighbouring islands; as it was likewise easy to pass from those islands to all the continent which borders on this Atlantic sea. For the waters which are beheld within the mouth which we just now mentioned, have the form of a bay with a narrow entrance; but the mouth itself is a true sea. And lastly, the earth which surrounds it is in every respect truly denominated the continent. In this Atlantic island a combination of kings was formed, who with mighty and wonderful power subdued the whole island, together with many other islands and parts of the continent; and, besides this, subjected to their dominion all Libya, as far as to Egypt; and Europe, as far as to the Tyrrhene sea. And when they were collected in a powerful league, they endeavoured to enslave all our regions and yours, and besides this all those places situated within the mouth of the Atlantic sea. Then it was, O Solon, that the power of your city was conspicuous to all men for its virtue and strength. For, as its armies surpassed all others both in magnanimity and military skill, so with respect to its contests, whether it was assisted by the rest of the Greeks, over whom it presided in warlike affairs, or whether it was deserted by them through the incursions of the enemies, and became situated in extreme danger, yet still it remained triumphant. In the mean time, those who were not yet enslaved it liberated from danger; and procured the most ample liberty for all those of us who dwell within the Pillars of Hercules. But in succeeding time prodigious earthquakes and deluges taking place, and bringing with them desolation in the space of one day and night, all that warlike race of Athenians was at once merged under the earth; and the Atlantic island itself, being absorbed in the sea, entirely disappeared. And hence that sea is at present innavigable, arising from the gradually impeding mud which the subsiding island produced. And this, O Socrates, is the sum of what the elder Critias repeated from the narration of Solon.

But when yesterday you was discoursing about a republic and its citizens, I was surprised on recollecting the present history: for I perceived how divinely, from a certain fortune, and not wandering from the mark, you collected many things agreeing with the narration of 26a Solon. Yet I was unwilling to disclose these particulars immediately, as, from the great interval of time since I first received them, my remembrance of them was not sufficiently accurate for the purpose of repetition. I considered it, therefore, necessary that I should first of all diligently revolve the whole in my mind. And on this account I yesterday immediately complied with your demands: for I perceived that we should not want the ability of presenting a discourse accommodated to your wishes, which in things of this kind is of principal importance. In consequence of this, as Hermocrates has informed you, immediately b as we departed from hence, by communicating these particulars with my friends here present, for the purpose of refreshing my memory, and afterwards revolving them in my mind by night, I nearly acquired a complete recollection of the affair. And, indeed, according to the proverb, what we learn in childhood abides in the memory with a wonderful stability. For, with respect to myself, for instance, I am not certain that I could recollect the whole of yesterday's discourse, yet I should be very much astonished if any thing should escape my remembrance which I had heard in some past period of time very distant c from the present. Thus, as to the history which I have just now related, I received it from the old man with great pleasure and delight; who on his part very readily complied with my request, and frequently gratified me with a repetition. And hence, as the marks of letters deeply burnt in remain indelible, so all these particulars became firmly established in my memory. In consequence of this, as soon as it was day I repeated the narration to my friends, that together with myself they might be better prepared for the purposes of the present association. But now, with respect to that for which this narration was undertaken, I am prepared, O Socrates, to speak not only summarily, but so as to descend to the particulars of every thing which I heard. But the citizens and city which you fabricated yesterday as in a fable, we shall transfer to reality; considering that city which you established as no other than this d Athenian city, and the citizens which you conceived as no other than those ancestors of ours described by the Egyptian priest. And indeed the affair will harmonize in every respect; nor will it be foreign from the purpose to assert that your citizens are those very people who existed at that time. Hence, distributing the affair in common among us, we will endeavour, according to the utmost of our ability, to accomplish in a becoming manner the employment which you have assigned us. It is requisite, therefore, to consider, O Socrates, whether this discourse is reasonable, or whether we should lay it aside, and seek after another.

SOC. But what other, O Critias, should we receive in preference to this? For your discourse, through a certain affinity, is particularly adapted to the present sacred rites of the Goddess. And besides this, we should consider, as a thing of the greatest moment, that your relation is not a mere fable, but a true history. It is impossible, therefore, to say how, and from whence, neglecting your narration, we should find another more convenient. Hence it is necessary to confess that you have spoken with good fortune; and it is equally necessary that I, on account of my discourse yesterday, should now rest from speaking, and be wholly attentive to yours.

CRIT. But now consider, Socrates, the manner of our disposing the mutual banquet of disputation. For it seems proper to us that Timæus, who is the most astronomical of us all, and is particularly knowing in the nature of the universe, should speak the first; commencing his discourse from the generation of the world, and ending in the nature of men. But that I after him, receiving the men which he has mentally produced, but which have been excellently educated by you, and introducing them to you according to the law of Solon, as to proper judges, should render them members of this city; as being in reality no other than those Athenians which were described as unknown to us in the report of the sacred writings. And that in future we shall discourse concerning them as about citizens and Athenians.

SOC. I seem to behold a copious and splendid banquet of disputation set before me. It is, therefore, now your business, O Timæus, to begin the discourse; having first of all, as is highly becoming, invoked the Gods according to law.

TIM. Indeed, Socrates, since those who participate but the least degree of wisdom, in the beginning of every undertaking, whether small or great, call upon Divinity, it is necessary that we (unless we are in every respect unwise) who are about to speak concerning the universe, whether it is generated or without generation, invoking the Gods and Goddesses, should pray that what we assert may be agreeable to their divinities, and that in the ensuing discourse we may be consistent with ourselves. And such is my prayer to the Gods, with reference to myself; but as to what respects the present company, it is necessary to pray that you may easily understand, and that I may be able to explain my meaning about the proposed subjects of disputation. In the first place, therefore, as it appears to me, it is necessary to define what that is which is always *real being*,[2] but is without generation; and what that is *which is generated indeed*, or *consists in a state of becoming to be*, but which never *really is*.   The former of these indeed is apprehended by *intelligence* in conjunction with *reason*, since it always subsists according to *same*.[3] But the latter is perceived by *opinion* in conjunction with *irrational sense*; since it subsists in a state of generation and corruption, and never truly is. But whatever is generated is necessarily generated from a certain cause. For it is every way impossible that any thing should be generated without a cause. When, therefore, an artificer, in the fabrication of any work, looks to that which always subsists according to *same*, and, employing a paradigm of this kind, expresses the idea and power in his work, it is then necessary that the whole of his production should be beautiful. But when he beholds that which is in generation, and uses a generated paradigm, it is alike necessary that his work should be far from beautiful.

I denominate, therefore, this universe *heaven*, or *the world*, or by any other appellation in which it may particularly rejoice.   Concerning which, let us in the first place consider that which, in the proposed inquiry about the universe, ought in the very beginning to be investigated; whether it always was, having no principle of generation,[4] or whether it was generated, commencing its generation from a certain cause. It was generated. For this universe is visible, and has a body.[5] But all such things are sensible. And sensibles are apprehended by opinion, in conjunction with sense. And such things appear to have their subsistence in becoming to be, and in being generated. But we have before asserted, that whatever is generated is necessarily generated from some cause. To discover, therefore, the *artificer* and *father* of the universe is indeed difficult;[6] and when found it is impossible to reveal him through the ministry of discourse to all men.

Again: this is to be considered concerning him, I mean, according to what paradigm extending himself, he fabricated the world - whether towards an exemplar, subsisting according to that which is always the same, and similarly affected, or towards that which is generated. But, indeed, if this world is beautiful, and its artificer good, it is evident that he looked towards an eternal exemplar in its fabrication. But if the world be far from beautiful, which it is not lawful to assert, he necessarily beheld a generated instead of an eternal exemplar. But it is perfectly evident that he regarded an eternal paradigm. For the world is the most beautiful of generated natures, and its artificer the best of causes. But, being thus generated, it is fabricated according to that

APPOINTMENT CARD

IDENTIFICATION NO.

NAME AND ADDRESS OF VA STATION

VETERAN'S NAME AND ADDRESS

Pence

NOTE: An appointment has been made for you as indicated. If you unable to keep this appointment, please call the number listed here at least 24 hours before the date and time specified.

TELEPHONE NO.

EXTENSION NO.

DATE	TIME	SERVICE	INITIALS
11 3	1030	Flu	

VA FORM DEC 1990 **2502**

SHOW THIS CARD TO RECEPTIONIST WHEN REPORTING AND LEAVING

nce, and which subsists
 hence it is perfectly
ince of something. But
is the greatest of all
tinguish concerning the
he things of which they
we speak of that which
that our reasons should
d as much as possible
ir kind. But that, when
s immutable, we should
the same analogy to the
indeed, as essence[8] is to
t wonder, therefore, O
y concerning the Gods
t be able to produce the
cult a subject. But you
ot employ reasons less
embering, that I who
sess the human nature in
common; so that you should be satisfied if my assertions are but assimilative of the truth.

Soc. You speak excellently well, Timæus; and we shall certainly act in every respect as you advise. This introduction, indeed, of your discourse we wonderfully approve: proceed, therefore, with the subsequent disputation.

TIM. Let us declare then on what account the composing artificer constituted generation and the universe. The artificer, indeed, was good; but in that which is good envy never subsists about any thing which has being. Hence, as he was entirely void of envy, he was willing to produce all things as much as possible similar to himself. If, therefore, any one receives this most principal cause of generation and the world from wise and prudent men, he will receive him in a manner the most perfect and true. For, as the Divinity was willing that all things should be good, and that as much as possible nothing should be evil; hence, receiving every thing visible, and which was not in a state of rest, but moving with confusion[9] and disorder, he reduced it from this wild inordination into order, considering that such a conduct was by far the best. For it neither ever was lawful, nor is, for the best of causes to produce any other than the most beautiful of effects. In consequence of a reasoning process,[10] therefore, he found that among the things naturally visible[†] there was nothing, the whole of which, if void of intelligence, could ever become more beautiful than the whole of that which is endued with intellect: and at the same time he discovered, that it was impossible for intellect to accede to any being, without the intervention of soul. Hence, as the result of this reasoning, placing intellect in soul and soul in body, he fabricated the universe; that thus it might be a work naturally the most beautiful and the best. In this manner, therefore, according to an assimilative reason, it is necessary to call the world an animal, endued with intellect, and generated through the providence of Divinity.

c   This being determined, let us consider what follows; and, in the next place, after the similitude of what animals the composing artificer constituted the world. Indeed, we must by no means think that he fashioned it similar to such animals as subsist in the form of a part, or have a partial subsistence: for, if it had been assimilated to an imperfect animal, it certainly would not have been beautiful. But we should rather establish it as the most similar of all things to that animal, of which other animals, both considered separately and according to their genera, are nothing more than parts. For this, indeed, contains all intelligible animals comprehended in itself; just as this world contains us

d   and the other animals which are the objects of sight. For, the Divinity being willing to assimilate this universe in the most exquisite degree to that which is the most beautiful and every way perfect of intelligible objects, he composed it one visible animal, containing within itself all

31a such animals as are allied to its nature. Do we therefore rightly conclude that there is but one universe; or is it more right to assert that there are many and infinite? But indeed there can be but one, if it be only admitted that it is fabricated according to an exemplar. For that which comprehends all intelligible animals whatever can never be the second to any other. For another animal again would be required about these two, of which they would be parts; and it would be more proper to assert that the universe is assimilated to this comprehending third, rather than to the other two. That the world, therefore, from its being

---

† That is, intelligibles: for that these are visible is evident from the words of Plato further on, where he says - "Whatever ideas intellect perceived in animal itself," etc. But that these are *naturally* visible will be evident, as Proclus beautifully observes, if we consider that some things are visible to us, and others according to nature. And the things, indeed, which are visible to us, are in their own nature dark and obscure; but things naturally visible are truly known, and are resplendent with divine light. And such are intelligibles.

singular or alone, might be similar to all-perfect animal - on this account the artificer neither produced two nor infinite worlds; but heaven, or the universe, was generated and will be one and only begotten.

But since it is necessary that a corporeal nature should be visible and tangible, and since nothing can be visible without fire, and nothing tangible without something solid, and nothing solid without earth - hence the Divinity, beginning to fabricate, composed the body of the universe from fire and earth. But it is impossible for two things alone to cohere together without the intervention of a third; for a certain collective bond is necessary in the middle of the two. And that is the most beautiful of bonds which renders both itself and the natures which are bound remarkably one. But the most beautiful analogy naturally produces this effect. For when either in three numbers, or masses, or powers, as is the middle to the last, so is the first to the middle; and again, as is the last to the middle, so is the middle to the first: then the middle becoming both first and last, and the last and the first passing each of them into a middle position, they become all of them necessarily the same, as to relation to each other. But, being made the same with each other, all are one. If, then, it were necessary that the universe should be a superficies only, and have no depth, one medium would indeed be sufficient, both for the purpose of binding itself and the natures which it contains. But now it is requisite that the world should be a solid; and solids are never harmonized together by one, but always with two mediums. Hence, the Divinity placed water and air in the middle of fire and earth, and fabricated them as much as possible in the same ratio to each other; so that fire might be to air as air to water; and that as air is to water so water might be to earth. And from this conjunction and composition he rendered the world visible and tangible. Hence, from things of this kind, which are four in number, it must be confessed that the body of the universe was generated through analogy, conspiring into friendship with itself from their conjunction, and so aptly cohering in all its parts, as to be indissoluble except by its artificer, who bound it in this union and consent.

The composition of the world, therefore, received one *whole* of each of these four natures. For its composing artificer constituted it from *all* fire, water, air, and earth; leaving no part of any one of these, nor any power external to the world. For by a reasoning process he concluded that it would thus be a whole animal, in the highest degree perfect from perfect parts: that, besides this, it would be one, as nothing would be left from which any other such nature might be produced; and lastly, that it would be neither obnoxious to old age nor disease. For he perceived that the heat and cold from which bodies are composed, and all such things as possess vigorous powers, when surrounding bodies externally, and acceding to them unseasonably, dissolve their union, and, introducing diseases and old age, cause them to perish by decay. Hence, through this cause and this reasoning process, he fabricated the universe one whole, composed from all wholes, perfect, undecaying, and without

b disease. He likewise gave to it a figure becoming and allied to its nature. For to the animal which was destined to comprehend all animals in itself, that figure must be the most becoming which contains within its ambit all figures of every kind. Hence, he fashioned it of a spherical shape, in which all the radii from the middle are equally distant from the bounding extremities; as this is the most perfect of all figures, and the most similar to himself. For he considered that the similar was infinitely more beautiful than the dissimilar.

c Besides this, he accurately polished the external circumference of the spherical world, and rendered it perfectly smooth.[11] Nor was the addition of eyes[12] requisite to the universe; for nothing visible remained external to itself. Nor were ears necessary; as there was nothing externally audible. Nor was the universe invested with surrounding air, that it might be indigent of respiration. Nor, again, was it in want of any organ through which it might receive nutriment into itself, and discharge it when concocted: for there was no possibility that any thing could either accede to or depart from its nature, since there was nothing through which such changes could be produced. For, indeed, the universe affords nutriment to itself through its own consumption; and, being artificially fabricated, suffers and acts all things in itself, and from its own peculiar operations. For its composing artificer considered that it would be much more excellent if sufficient to itself, than if indigent

d of foreign supplies. But he neither thought that hands[13] were necessary to the world, as there was nothing for it either to receive or reject; nor

34a yet feet, nor any other members which are subservient to progression and rest. For from among the seven species of local motion he selected one, which principally subsists about intellect and intelligence, and assigned it to the world as properly allied to its surrounding body. Hence, when he had led it round according to *same*, in *same*, and in itself, he caused it to move with a circular revolution. But he separated the other six motions from the world, and framed it void of their wandering progressions. Hence, as such a conversion was by no means indigent of feet, he generated the universe without legs and feet. When, therefore, that God who is a perpetually reasoning divinity cogitated about the God who was destined to subsist at some certain period of b   time, he produced his body smooth and equable; and every way from the middle even and whole, and perfect from the composition of perfect bodies. But, placing soul in the middle of the world, he extended it through the whole; and besides this, he externally invested the body of the universe with soul; and, causing circle to revolve in a circle, established the world one single, solitary nature, able through virtue to converse with itself, indigent of nothing external, and sufficiently known and friendly to itself. And on all these accounts he rendered the universe a happy[14] God. But indeed the artificer did not produce soul,

c   as we just now began to say, junior to body: for he who conjoined these would never permit that the more ancient nature should be subservient to the younger. But we, as being much conversant with that which casually occurs, assert things of this kind in an assimilative way; while, on the contrary, the artificer of the world constituted soul both in generation and virtue prior to, and more ancient than, body, as being the proper lord and ruler of its servile nature; and that in the following manner:

5a   From an essence impartible,[15] and always subsisting according to sameness of being, and from a nature divisible about bodies, he mingled from both a third form of essence, having a middle subsistence between the two. And again, between that which is impartible and that which is divisible about bodies, he placed the nature of *same* and *different*. And taking these, now they are three, he mingled them all into one idea. But as the nature of *different* could not without difficulty be mingled in *same*, he harmonized them together by employing force in their conjunction. But after he had mingled these two with essence, and had

b   produced one from the three, he again divided this whole into becoming parts; at the same time mingling each part from *same*, *different*, and *essence*. But he began to divide as follows: In the first place, he received one part from the whole.[16] Then he separated a second part, double of the first; afterwards a third, sesquialter of the second, but triple of the first: then a fourth, double of the second; in the next place a fifth, triple of the third; a sixth, octuple of the first; and lastly a seventh, twenty-seven times more than the first. After this, he filled up the

6a   double and triple intervals, again cutting off parts from the whole; and placed them so between the intervals, that there might be two mediums in every interval; and that one of these might by the same part exceed one of the extremes, and be exceeded by the other; and that the other part might by an equal number surpass one of the extremes, and by an equal number be surpassed by the other. But as from hence sesquialter, sesquitertian, and sesquioctave intervals were produced, from those b   bonds in the first spaces, he filled with a sesquioctave interval all the sesquitertian parts, at the same time leaving a part[17] of each of these. And then again the interval of this part being assumed, a comparison is from thence obtained in terms of number to number, subsisting between 256 and 243. But now the whole of that mixture from which these were separated was consumed by such a section of parts. Hence he then cut the whole of this composition according to length, and produced two from one; and adapted middle to middle, like the form of the letter X.

c   Afterwards he bent them into a circle, connecting them, both with themselves and with each other, in such a manner that their extremities might be combined in one directly opposite to the point of their mutual intersection; and externally comprehended them in a motion revolving according to sameness, and in that which is perpetually the same. And besides this, he made one of the circles external, but the other internal; and denominated the local motion of the exterior circle, the motion of that nature which subsists according to *sameness*; but that of the interior one, the motion of the nature subsisting according to *difference*. He likewise caused the circle partaking of *sameness* to revolve laterally towards the right hand; but that which partakes of *difference* diametrically towards the left. But he conferred dominion on the circulation of that which is *same* and *similar*: for he suffered this alone

d   to remain undivided. But as to the interior circle, when he had divided it six times, and had produced seven unequal circles, each according to the interval of the double and triple; as each of them are three, he ordered the circles to proceed in a course contrary to each other: - and three of the seven interior circles he commanded to revolve with a similar swiftness; but the remaining four with a motion dissimilar to each other, and to the former three; yet so as not to desert order and proportion in their circulations.

  After, therefore, the whole composition of the soul was completed according to the intention of its artificer, in the next place he fabricated within soul the whole of a corporeal nature; and, conciliating middle

e   with middle, he aptly harmonized them together. But soul[†] being every

---

  [†] Soul proceeding supernally as far as to the last recesses of the earth, and illuminating all things with the light of life, the world being converted to it, becomes animated from its extremities, and also according to its middle, and the whole of its interval. It also externally enjoys the intellectual illumination of soul. Hence soul is said to obtain the middle of the universe, as depositing in it its powers, and a symbol of its proper presence. It is also said to extend itself to the extremities of heaven, as vivifying it on all sides; and to invest the universe as with a veil, as possessing powers exempt from divisible bulks.

way extended from the middle to the very extremities of the universe, and investing it externally in a circle, at the same time herself revolving[†] within herself, gave rise to the divine commencement of an unceasing and wise life, through the whole of time. And, indeed, the body of the universe was generated visible; but soul is invisible, participating of a rational energy and harmony,[‡] and subsisting as the best of generated natures, through its artificer, who is the best of intelligible and perpetual beings. Since, therefore, soul was composed from the mixture of the three parts *same*, *different*, and *essence*, and was distributed and bound according to analogy, herself at the same time returning by a circular energy towards herself; hence, when she touches[18] upon any thing endued with a dissipated essence, and when upon that which is indivisible, being moved through the whole of herself, she pronounces concerning the nature of each - asserts what that is with which any thing is the same,[19] from what it is different, to what it is related, where it is situated, how it subsists; and when any thing of this kind happens either *to be* or *to suffer* both in things which are generated and in such as possess an eternal sameness of being. Reason indeed, which is *becoming to be*[20] true according to sameness, when it is conversant as well with *different* as *same*, evolving itself without voice or sound in that which is moved by itself; when in this case it subsists about a sensible nature, and the circle characterized by *difference* properly revolving, enunciates any circumstance to every part of the soul with which it is connected; then stable and true opinions and belief are produced. But when again it evolves itself about that which is logistic,[21] and the circle of *sameness* aptly revolving announces any particular thing, intellect and science are necessarily produced in perfection by such an operation. Whoever,

---

[†] Plato here evidently evinces, that the conversion of the soul to herself is a knowledge of herself, of every thing which she contains, and of every thing prior to and proceeding from her. For all knowledge may be said to be a conversion and adaptation to that which is known; and hence truth is an harmonious conjunction of that which knows with the object of knowledge. Conversion, however, being twofold, one as to *The Good*, and the other as to *being*, the vital conversion of all things is directed to *The Good*, and the gnostic to *being*.

[‡] Harmony has a threefold subsistence; for it is either *harmony itself*, i.e. ideal harmony in a divine intellect; or *that which is first harmonized, and is such according to the whole of itself*; or *that which is secondarily harmonized, and partly participates of harmony*. The first of these must be assigned to intellect, the second to soul, and the third to body.

therefore, asserts that this[†] is ingenerated in any other nature than soul, asserts every thing rather than the truth.

But when the generating father understood that this generated resemblance of the eternal Gods[‡] moved and lived, he was delighted with his work, and in consequence of this delight considered how he might fabricate it still more similar to its exemplar. Hence, as that is an eternal animal, he endeavoured to render this universe such, to the utmost of his ability. The nature indeed of the animal its paradigm is eternal, and this it is impossible to adapt perfectly to a generated effect. Hence he determined by a dianoëtic energy to produce a certain movable image of eternity: and thus, while he was adorning and distributing the universe, he at the same time formed an eternal image flowing according to number, of eternity abiding in one;[22] and which receives from us the appellation of time. But besides this he fabricated the generation of days[23] and nights, and months and years, which had no subsistence prior to the universe, but which together with it rose into existence. And all these, indeed, are the proper parts of time. But the terms *it was* and *it will be*, which express the species of generated time, are transferred by us to an eternal essence, through oblivion of the truth. For we assert of such an essence that it *was*, *is*, and *will be*; while according to truth the term *it is* is alone accommodated to its nature. But we should affirm, that *to have been* and *to be hereafter* are expressions alone accommodated to generation, proceeding according to the flux of time: for these parts of time are certain motions. But that which perpetually subsists the same and immovable, neither becomes at any time older or younger; neither has been generated in some period of the past, nor will be in some future circulation of time; nor receives

d

e

38a

[†] By *this*, says Proclus, we must understand *intellect* and *science*. Every thing, therefore, which is the recipient of intellect and science, of opinion and faith, is soul. For all the knowledges of the soul are rational and transitive. And because they are rational, indeed, they are exempt from irrational powers; but, because they are transitive, they are subordinate to intellectual knowledge. For, if science and intellect are in intelligibles, they are not *ingenerated* in them, as Plato here says they are in the soul.

[‡] By the *eternal Gods* here we must not understand, as Proclus well observes, the *mundane Gods*; for Plato does not alone speak of the corporeal nature of the universe, but also discourses about it as animated, and an intellectual animal, which comprehends in itself the mundane Gods. We must understand, therefore, that the world is the resemblance of the intelligible Gods: for it is filled from them with deity, and the progressions into it of the mundane are as it were certain rivers and illuminations of the intelligible Gods.

any circumstance of being, which generation adapts to natures hurried away by its impetuous whirl. For all these are nothing more than species of time imitating eternity, and circularly rolling itself according to number. Besides this, we likewise frequently assert that a thing which was *generated*, IS *generated*: that what subsists in BECOMING TO BE, IS *in generation*; that what WILL BE, IS TO BE; and that NON-BEING IS NOT: no one of which assertions is accurately true. But perhaps a perfect discussion of these matters is not adapted to the present disputation.

But time[24] was generated together with the universe, that being produced together they might together be dissolved, if any dissolution should ever happen to these. And time was generated according to the exemplar of an eternal nature, that this world might be the most similar possible to such a nature. For its exemplar is permanent being, through the whole of eternity; but the universe alone *was* generated, *is*, and *will be*, through the whole of time. After this manner, therefore, and from such a dianoëtic energy of Divinity about the generation of time,[25] that he might give birth to its flowing subsistence, he generated the sun and moon, and the five other stars, which are denominated planets, for the purpose of distinguishing and guarding the numbers of time. But the Divinity, as soon as he had produced the bodies of these stars, placed them, being seven in number, in the seven circulations formed by the revolution of the nature distinguished by *difference*. The moon, indeed, he fixed in the first circulation about the earth; the sun in the second above the earth; the star called Lucifer,[†] and that which is sacred to Mercury, in circulations revolving with a swiftness equal to the sun, to whom at the same time they are allotted a contrary power; in consequence of which, these stars, the Sun, Lucifer, and Mercury, mutually comprehend and are mutually comprehended by each other in a similar manner. But with respect to the other stars,[26] if any one should think proper to investigate their circulations, and through what causes they are established, the labour would be greater than that of the discourse itself, for the sake of which they were introduced. An accurate discussion, therefore, of these particulars may, perhaps, be undertaken by us hereafter, if convenient leisure should fall to our lot.

When, therefore, each of the natures necessary to a joint fabrication of time had obtained a local motion adapted to its condition, and their bodies became animals through the connecting power of vital bonds, they then learned their prescribed order; that according to the oblique

[†] Venus.

revolution of the circle of *difference*, which moves in subjection to the circle of *sameness*, these orbs should, by their revolution, partly form a more ample and partly a more contracted circle; and that the orb which formed a lesser circle should revolve swifter; but that which produced a greater, more slow: - but that in consequence of the motion of the circle of *sameness*, the orbs which circulate most swiftly, comprehending other orbs as they revolve, should themselves appear to be comprehended by the revolution of the more slow. But all these circles revolve with a spiral motion, because they are agitated at one and the same time in two contrary directions: and in consequence of this, the sphere endued with the slowest revolution is nearest to that to which its course is retrograde, and which is the swiftest of all. And that these circles might possess a certain conspicuous measure of slowness and swiftness with reference to each other, and that the motion of the eight circulations might be manifest, the Divinity enkindled a light which we now denominate the Sun,[27] in the second revolution from the earth; that the heavens might become eminently apparent to all things, and that such animals might participate of number as are adapted to its participation, receiving numerical information from the revolution of a nature similar and the same. From hence, therefore, night and day arose; and through these revolving bodies the period of one most wise circulation was produced.

And *month* indeed was generated, when the moon having run through her circle passed into conjunction with the sun. But *year*, when the sun had completely wandered round his orb. As to the periods of the other stars, they are not understood except by a very few of mankind; nor do the multitude distinguish them by any peculiar appellation; nor do they measure them with relation to each other, regarding the numbers adapted to this purpose. Hence, it may be said, they are ignorant that the wanderings of these bodies are in reality time; as these wanderings are endued with an infinite multitude, and an admirable variety of motions. But it is easy to conceive, that a perfect number of time will then accomplish a perfect year, when the eight circulations concurring in their courses with each other become bounded by the same extremity; being at the same time measured by the circle subsisting according to sameness. But the stars, whose revolutions are attended with a procession through the heavens, were generated, that the whole of this visible animal the universe might become most similar to the most perfect intelligible animal from an imitation of a perpetual nature. And indeed the artificer fabricated other forms, as far as to the generation of time, according to the similitude of the world's exemplar.

But as the universe did not yet contain all animals in its capacious receptacle, in this respect it was dissimilar to its exemplar. Its artificer, therefore, supplied this defect by impressing it with forms, according to the nature of its paradigm. Whatever ideas, therefore, intellect perceived by the dianoëtic energy in animal itself,[28] such and so many he conceived it necessary for the universe to contain. But these ideas are four:[29] One, the celestial genus of Gods; another, winged and air-wandering; a third, the aquatic form; and a fourth, that which is pedestrial and terrene. The idea, therefore, of that which is divine, or the inerratic sphere, he for the most part fabricated from fire, that it might be most splendid and beautiful to behold. And as he meant to assimilate it to the universe, he rendered it circular; placed it in the wisdom of the best nature; ordered it to become the attendant of that which is best; and gave it a circular distribution about the heavens, that it might be a *true world*, adorned with a fair variety in its every part. But he adapted to each of the divine bodies two motions; one by which they might revolve in *same* according to *same*, by always cogitating the same things in themselves about *same*; the other through which they might be led with an advancing motion from the dominion of the *same* and *similar* circulation. He likewise rendered them immovable and stable as to the other five motions, that each of them might become in an eminent degree the best. And on this account such of the stars as are inerratic were generated, which are divine animals; and, in consequence of this, always abide revolving in that which is *same*. But, the stars, which both revolve and at the same time wander in the manner we have described above, were produced next to these. But he fabricated the earth the common nourisher of our existence; which being conglobed about the pole extended through the universe, is the guardian and artificer of night and day, and is the first and most ancient of the Gods which are generated within the heavens. But the harmonious progressions of these divinities, their concursions with each other, the revolutions and advancing motions of their circles, how they are situated with relation to each other in their conjunctions and oppositions, whether direct among themselves or retrograde, at what times and in what manner they become concealed, and, again emerging to our view, cause terror, and exhibit tokens of future events to such as are able to discover their signification - of all this to attempt an explanation, without inspecting the resemblances of these divinities, would be a fruitless employment. But of this enough; and let this be the end of our discourse concerning the nature of the visible and generated Gods.

But to speak concerning the other dæmons,[30] and to know their generation, is a talk beyond our ability to perform. It is, therefore, necessary in this case to believe in ancient men; who being the progeny

e of the Gods, as they themselves assert, must have a clear knowledge of their parents. It is impossible, therefore, not to believe in the children of the Gods, though they should speak without probable and necessary arguments: but as they declare that their narrations are about affairs to which they are naturally allied, it is proper that, complying with the law, we should assent to their tradition. In this manner, then, according to them, the generation of these Gods is to be described:

That Ocean and Tethys were the progeny of heaven and earth. That from hence Phorcys, Saturn, and Rhea, and such as subsist together with these, were produced. That from Saturn and Rhea, Jupiter, Juno, and

41a all such as we know are called the brethren of these descended. And lastly, others which are reported to be the progeny of these. When, therefore, all such Gods as visibly revolve, and all such as become apparent when they please, were generated, the Artificer of the universe thus addressed them: "Gods of Gods,[31] of whom I am the demiurgus and father, whatever is generated by me is indissoluble, such being my will

b in its fabrication. Indeed every thing which is bound is dissoluble; but to be willing to dissolve that which is beautifully harmonized, and well composed, is the property of an evil nature. Hence, so far as you are generated, you are not immortal, nor in every respect indissoluble: yet you shall never be dissolved, nor become subject to the fatality of death; my will being a much greater and more excellent bond than the vital connectives with which you were bound at the commencement of your generation. Learn, therefore, what I now say to you indicating my desire. Three genera of mortals yet remain to be produced. Without

c the generation of these, therefore, the universe will be imperfect; for it will not contain every kind of animal in its spacious extent. But it ought to contain them, that it may become sufficiently perfect. Yet if these are generated, and participate of life through me, they will become equal to the Gods. That mortal natures, therefore, may subsist, and that the universe may be truly all, convert yourselves, according to your nature, to the fabrication of animals, imitating the power which I employed in your generation. And whatever among these is of such a nature as to deserve the same appellation with immortals, which obtains sovereignty in these, and willingly pursues justice, and reverences you - of this I myself will deliver the seed and beginning: it is your business to accomplish the rest; to weave[32] together the mortal and immortal nature; by this means fabricating and generating animals, causing them d   to increase by supplying them with aliment, and receiving them back again when dissolved by corruption."

Thus spoke the demiurgus; and again into the same crater,[†] in which mingling he had tempered the soul of the universe, he poured mingling the remainder[33] of the former mixture: in a certain respect indeed after the same manner,[34] yet not similarly incorruptible according to the same, but deficient from the first in a second and third degree. And having thus composed the universe, he distributed souls equal in number to the stars, inserting each in each: and causing them to ascend as into a

e   vehicle,[35] he pointed out to them the nature of the universe, and announced to them the laws of fate; showing them that the first generation orderly distributed to all was one, lest any particular soul should be allotted a less portion of generation than another. But when he had disseminated them through the several instruments of time adapted to each, he declared to them it was necessary that an animal the

42a   most religious of all others should make its appearance. But as the human nature is twofold, he showed them that the more excellent kind was that which would afterwards be called man. And as souls are from necessity engrafted in bodies, and as something accedes to and something departs from such bodies, he declared to them that, in the first place, one connate sense[36] produced by violent passions was necessary to all;

b   and, in the second place, love mingled with pleasure and grief. That after these, fear and anger were necessary, with whatever else is either consequent to these, or naturally discordant from a contrary nature. That such souls as subdue these would live justly, but such as are vanquished by them unjustly. And again, that he who lived well during the proper time of his life, should, again returning to the habitation of his kindred star[37], enjoy a blessed life. But that he whose conduct was depraved, should in his second generation be changed into the nature of a woman. * That both these, at the expiration of a thousand years, should return to the allotment and choice of a second life; each soul receiving a life agreeable to its choice. That in this election the human

c   soul should pass into the life of a brute: *[‡] and that in case the inclination to evil should not even then cease, but the defilement of vice remain according to a similitude of the mode of generation, then the soul should be changed into the nature of a brute correspondent to its disposition. And that it should not be freed from the allotment of

---

[†] *Viz.* the vivific Goddess Juno.

[‡] The translation of the part between the two stars is omitted by Ficinus.

labours,[38] till, following the revolution of that *same* and *similar* nature contained in its essence, it vanquishes those abundantly turbulent affections, tumultuous and irrational, adhering to it afterwards from fire, water, air, and earth, and returns to the first and best disposition of its nature.

d   When he had instructed souls in all these particulars, that he might be in no respect the cause of the future evil of each, he disseminated some of them into the earth, others into the moon, and others into the remaining different instruments of time. But after this semination he delivered to the junior Gods the province of fabricating mortal bodies,

e   and generating whatever else remained necessary to the human soul; and gave them dominion over every thing consequent to their fabrications. He likewise commanded them to govern as much as possible in the best and most beautiful manner the mortal animal, that it might not become the cause of evil to itself. At the same time he who orderly disposed all these particulars remained in his own accustomed abiding habit. But in consequence of his abiding, as soon as his children understood the order of their father, they immediately became obedient to this order; and receiving the immortal principle of mortal animal, in imitation of their artificer, they borrowed from the world the parts of fire and earth, water and air, as things which they should restore back again; and

43a   conglutinated the received parts together, not with the same indissoluble bonds which they themselves participated, but gave them a tenacious adherence from thick set nails, invisible through their smallness; fabricating the body of each, one from the composition of all; and binding the circulations of the immortal soul in the influxive and effluxive nature of body.

b   But these circulations,[39] being merged in a profound river, neither govern nor are governed, but hurry and are hurried along with violence: in consequence of which, the whole animal is indeed moved, yet in a disorderly manner: since from every kind of motion its progression is fortuitous and irrational. For it proceeds backwards and forwards, to the right and left, upwards and downwards, and wanders every way according to the six differences of place. For though the inundating[40] and effluxive waves pour along with impetuous abundance, which afford nutrition to the animal, yet a still greater tumult and agitation is produced through the passions arising from external impulsions: and this

c   either when the body is disturbed by the sudden incursion of external fire, or by the solidity of earth, or receives an injury from the whirling blasts of the air. For from all these, through the medium of the body, various motions are hurried along, and fall with molestation on the soul.

But on this account all these were afterwards, and are even now, denominated senses. And these, indeed, both at first and at present,[41] are

d   the sources of an abundant and mighty motion, in conjunction with that perpetually flowing river, moving and vehemently agitating the circulations of the soul, every way fettering the revolution of the nature characterized by *sameness*, through flowing in a contrary direction, and restraining its energies by their conquering and impetuous progressions. But they agitate and tear in pieces the circulation of the nature distinguished by *difference*. Hence, they whirl about with every kind of revolution each of the three intervals of the double and triple, together with the mediums and conjoining bonds of the sesquitertian, sesquialter, and sesquioctave ratios, which cannot be dissolved by any one except the artificer by whom they were bound: and besides this, they induce all the fractures and diversities of circles which it is possible to effect; so that,

e   scarcely being connected with each other, they are borne along indeed, yet in an irrational manner, at one time in a contrary, at another time in an oblique, and then again in a resupine situation. Just as if any one, in an inverted position, should fix his head on the earth and raise his feet on high; for in such a situation both the inverted person and the spectators would mutually imagine the right hand parts to be on the left, and the left to be on the right. So with respect to the circulations of the soul, the very same affections, and others of a similar kind, vehemently

44a   take place; and hence, when this is the case, if any thing external occurs, characterized by the nature of *same* or *different*, they denominate things the same with, or different from, others in a manner contrary to the truth. Hence they become false, and destitute of intelligence; nor is any revolution to be found among them in such a situation which energizes with the authority of a ruler and chief.

But when certain senses, borne along externally, strike against the soul and attract the whole of its receptacle, then the circulations which are

b   in reality in subjection appear to have dominion: and hence, in consequence of all these passions, the soul becomes insane at present, and was so from the first period of her being bound in a mortal body. However, when the river of increase and nutrition flows along with a more gentle and less abundant course, the circulations, being again restored to tranquillity, proceed in their proper path; in process of time become more regular and steady, and pass into a figure accommodated to their nature. Hence, in this case, the revolutions of each of the circles becoming direct, and calling both *same* and *different* by their proper appellations, they render the being by whom they are possessed

c   prudent and wise. If any one, therefore, receives a proper education in conjunction with convenient nutriment, such a one will possess perfect health, and will every way avoid the most grievous disease. But when this is neglected by any individual, such a one, proceeding along the path of life in a lame condition, will again pass into Hades imperfect and destitute of intelligence. These are particulars, however, which happen posterior to the production of mankind. But it is our business at present to discourse more accurately concerning the first composition of our nature, and to show, in the first place, from assimilative reasons, through what cause and providence of the Gods the several members of the body were accommodated to the several employments of the soul.

d   In the first place, then, the Gods bound the two divine circulations of the soul in a spherical body, in imitation of the circular figure of the universe: and this part of the body is what we now denominate the head; a most divine member, and the sovereign ruler of our whole corporeal composition, through the decree of the Gods, who considered that it would participate of all possible motions. Lest, therefore, the head, by rolling like a cylinder on the earth, which is distinguished by
e   all-various heights and depths, should be unable to pass over its inequalities and asperities, the Gods subjected this upright figure of the body, as a pliable vehicle to the head. Hence, in consequence of the body being endued with length, they extended four naturally flexible members; Divinity fabricating a progression through which the body might apprehend any object, might receive a stable support, and might
45a   be able to pass through every place, bearing on high the head, our most divine and sacred habitation. For this purpose, therefore, they furnished us with legs and hands. And as the Gods considered that the anterior parts are more honourable and adapted to rule than the posterior, they gave us a motion for the most part consisting of a forward progression. Beside this, it was requisite that the anterior parts of our body should be divided from each other, and be dissimilar: and on this account they first placed about the cavity of the head the face; fixed in it organs subservient to all the providential energies of the soul, and determined
b   that the natural government of man should consist in this anterior part of the body. But they fabricated the luciferous eyes the first of all the corporeal organs, binding them in the face on the following account. Of that fire which does not burn, indeed, but which comprehends our proper diurnal light, the Gods fabricated the orbs of the eyes. For the fire contained within our body, and which is the genuine brother of this diurnal fire, they caused to flow through the eyes with smoothness, and collected abundance, condensed indeed in the whole, but especially in
c   the middle of these lucid orbs; so as that the more dense fire might

remain concealed within the recesses of the eyes, and the pure might find a passage and fly away. When, therefore, the diurnal light subsists about the effluxive river of the sight, then, similar concurring and being mingled with similar, one domestic body is constituted according to the direct procession of the eyes; and this too in that part where the internally emitted light resists that which is externally adduced. But the whole becoming similarly passive through similitude, when it either touches any thing else or is itself touched by another, then the motion produced by this contact diffusing itself through the whole body of the eye, as far as to the soul, causes that sensation which we denominate sight. But when this kindred fire departs into night, the conjunct on being dissolved, sight loses its power. For in this case, proceeding into a dissimilar nature, it is changed, and becomes extinct: since it is by no means connate with the proximate surrounding air, which is naturally destitute of fire. Hence it ceases from seeing; and, besides this, becomes the introducer of sleep. For the Gods fabricated the nature of the eyelids as a salutary guardian of the sight; that, these being compressed, the inward fiery power of the eye might be restrained from any further emission; that, besides this, they might sprinkle over and equalize the eye's internal motions; and that, when equalized, rest might be produced.

But when much rest takes place, sleep attended with few dreams is produced. On the contrary, if certain more vehement motions remain, then such as is the nature of these relics, and the places in which they were produced, such and so many will be the similar phantasms within, and of which we shall possess the remembrance when we are externally roused. But with respect to the images produced in mirrors, and all such things as are visible in that which is apparent and smooth, there is nothing in these difficult of solution. For, from the communication of the external and internal fire with each other, and from that fire which subsists about the smooth body, and becomes abundantly multiplied, all such appearances are necessarily produced as take place when the fire of the eyes mingles itself with the fire diffused about the smooth and splendid object of vision. But the right hand parts appear to be the left, because a contact takes place between the contrary parts of the sight and the contrary parts of the object, different from the accustomed mode of perception. On the contrary, the right hand parts appear on the right, and the left hand on the left, when the mingled light leaps forth, together with that with which it is mingled. When the smoothness of the mirrors receives this here and there in an elevated manner, it repels the right hand part of the sight to the left of the mirror, and the left to

the right. But if the mirror is turned according to the length of the countenance, it causes the whole face to appear resupine, by repelling the downward part of the splendour towards the upward part, and again
d the upper towards the downward part. All such particulars as these, therefore, are but causal assistants, which the Divinity employed as subservient to rendering the idea of that which is best as far as possible complete. *But the multitude are of opinion that these are not causal assistants, but the real causes of all things; I mean such things as are capable of giving cold and heat, rarity and density, with whatever produces such-like affections, but is incapable of possessing reason and intellect.* For soul must be considered as the only thing among beings by which intellect can be possessed. And this is invisible. But fire and water, air and earth, are
e all of them visible bodies. *It is, however, necessary that the lover of intellect and science should explore the first causes of prudent nature; and that he should consider such things as are moved by others, and at the same time necessarily give motion to other things, as nothing more than secondary causes.* Hence it is proper that we should speak concerning both kinds of causes; separately of such as fabricate things beautiful and good in conjunction with intellect, and of such as, being left destitute of wisdom, produce each particular in a casual and disorderly manner. Concerning the second causes of the eyes, therefore, which contribute to the possession of the power they are now allotted, what has been already said is sufficient.

But the greatest employment of the eyes, with respect to the use for
47a which they were bestowed on us by the Divinity, we shall now endeavour to explain. For, in my opinion, the sight is the cause of the greatest emolument to us on the present occasion; since what we are now discoursing concerning the universe could never have been discovered without surveying the stars, the sun, and the heavens. But now, from beholding day and night, we are able to determine by arithmetical calculation the periods of months and years; to acquire a conception of time, and to scrutinize the nature of the universe. But
b from all this we obtain the possession of philosophy; a greater good than which never was nor ever will be bestowed by the Gods on the mortal race. And this is what I call the greatest benefit of the eyes. But why should I celebrate other particulars of less consequence, which he who is not a philosopher, since destitute of sight, may attempt to explore, but will explore in vain? By us, indeed, it is asserted that Divinity bestowed sight on us for this purpose, that on surveying the circulations of intellect in the heavens we may properly employ the revolutions of our dianoëtic part, which are allied to their circulations; and may recall the

tumultuous motions of our discursive energies to the orderly processions of their intellectual periods. That besides this, by learning these and participating right reason according to nature, and imitating the revolutions of Divinity which are entirely inerratic, we may give stability to the wanderings of our dianoëtic energy.

But concerning voice and hearing, we again assert that they were bestowed on us by the Gods on the same account. For the acquisition of speech pertains to these, and is of the greatest advantage to their possession. And whatever utility musical voice brings to the sense of hearing, was bestowed for the sake of harmony. But harmony, possessing motions allied to the revolutions of our soul, is useful to the man who employs the Muses in conjunction with intellect; but is of no advantage to irrational pleasure, though it appears to be so at present. Indeed, it was given us by the Muses for the purpose of reducing the dissonant circulation of the soul to an order and symphony accommodated to its nature. Rhythm too was bestowed on us for this purpose; that we might properly harmonize that habit in our nature, which for the most part is void of measure, and indigent of the Graces. And thus far, a few particulars excepted, have we shown the fabrications of intellect. But it is likewise requisite to give a place in our discourse to the productions of necessity. For, the generation of the world being mingled, it was produced from the composition of intellect and necessity. But intellect ruling over necessity persuaded it to lead the most part of generated natures to that which is best; and hence necessity being vanquished by wise persuasion, from these two as principles the world arose. If, then, any one truly asserts that the universe was generated according to these, he should also mingle with it the form of an erratic cause, which it is naturally adapted to receive. In this manner then let us return; and, assuming a convenient principle of these, again discourse concerning them as about the former particulars, commencing our discussion from their origin. Let us, therefore, speculate the nature and passions of fire and water, air and earth, prior to the generation of the heavens. No one, indeed, as yet has unfolded the generation of these: but we speak of fire, and the other elements, as if the nature of each was known; and place them as the principles of the universe, when at the same time they ought not to be assimilated to elements, not even as in the rank of syllables, by men who in the smallest degree merit the appellation of wise. But now we shall not speak of the principle or principles, or whatever other denomination they may receive, of all things; and this for no other reason than the difficulty of delivering what appears to be the truth about these in the present mode of disputation. Neither, therefore, is it proper that you should expect me to speak, nor that I should persuade myself into a belief of being able to speak with perfect rectitude on so difficult a subject. But it is proper, as I told you in the beginning of this discourse, that, preserving all the force of assimilative reasons, we should endeavour to deliver that which is not less assimilative of the truth than the doctrine of others; and that in this manner we should discourse from the beginning concerning particulars and the whole. In the first place, therefore, invoking the Divinity who is the saviour of discourse, and beseeching him to lead us from an absurd and unusual exposition to an assimilative doctrine, we shall again begin to speak.

But it is necessary that the beginning of our present disputation should receive a more ample division than the former one. For then we made a distribution into two species: but now a third sort must be added. In the former disputation two species were sufficient; one of which was established as the form of an exemplar, intelligible and always subsisting according to *same*; but the other was nothing more than the imitation of the paradigm, generated and visible. But we did not then distribute a third, because we considered these two as sufficient. However, now reason seems to urge as a thing necessary, that we should endeavour to render apparent by our discourse the species which subsists as difficult and obscure. What apprehension then can we form of its power and nature? Shall we say that it is in an eminent degree the receptacle, and as it were nurse, of all generation? Such an assertion will, indeed, be true; but it is requisite to speak more clearly concerning it. And this will certainly be an arduous undertaking on many accounts, but principally because it will be necessary to doubt previous to its discussion concerning fire and the rest of the elements, why any one of these should be called water rather than fire, or air rather than earth; or why any one should be denominated some definite particular rather than all. For it is indeed difficult to frame any certain opinion, or to employ any stable discourse about such intricate forms. After what manner, then, and in what respect, and what of an assimilative nature shall we assert in this dubious inquiry?

In the first place, then, that which we now denominate water, when it loses its fluidity by concretion, appears to become stones and earth; but, when liquefied and dispersed, it forms vapour and air. Likewise, air when burnt up becomes fire. And, on the contrary, fire becoming concrete and extinct passes again into the form of air. And again, air becoming collected and condensed produces mists and clouds. But from these still more compressed rain descends. And from water, again, earth

and stones derive their subsistence. And thus, as it appears, they
d mutually confer on each other generation in a certain circular
progression. But since these never appear to be the same, who without
being covered with confusion can confidently assert that any one of
these is this rather than that? Certainly, no one. Hence it will be far
the most safe method of proceeding to speak about them as follows:
That the nature which we always perceive becoming something different
at different times, such, for instance, as fire, is not fire absolutely, but
something fiery. And again, that the nature which we denominate water
is not absolutely so, but such-like, or watery; and that it is not at any
time any thing else, as if it possessed any stability of essence. And lastly,
e that they cannot be distinguished by any word, such as we are
accustomed to employ when endeavouring to show that any particular
is either this thing or that. For they fly away, incapable of sustaining
the affirmation which asserts them to be *this thing, of such a nature,
belonging to this*; and all such appellations as would evince them to be
something permanent and real. Hence, we ought not to denominate any
one of these either this, or that; but something such-like, and a
perpetually revolving similitude. Thus, we should assert that fire is
every where *such-like*, and should speak in the same manner of every
50a thing endued with generation. But we should alone distinguish by the
appellations of this, or that, the subject in which each of these appears
to be generated, and again to suffer a dissolution. But this subject is by
no means to be denominated *such-like*, as for instance hot or white, or
any quality belonging to contraries, or any thing which contraries
compose. However, let us endeavour to explain more clearly what we
mean to express. For if any one, fashioning all possible figures from
gold, should without ceasing transform each figure into all; and if,
during this operation, some one who is present should, pointing to one
b of these figures, inquire what it is; it might most safely, with respect to
truth, be replied, that it was gold: but he who should assert that it is a
triangle, or any other of the figures which are continually generated, and
which ought by no means to be denominated beings, would fall from
the truth in the midst of his assertion. But we ought to be content with
that answer as most safe, which denominates it *such-like*, or of such a
determinate nature.

In the same manner we should speak concerning that nature which is
the general receptacle of all bodies. For it never departs from its own
proper power, but perpetually receives all things; and never contracts
any form in any respect similar to any one of the intromitted forms. It
c lies indeed in subjection to the forming power of every nature,

becoming agitated and figured through the supernally intromitted forms: and through these it exhibits a different appearance at different times. But the forms which enter and depart from this receptacle are the imitations of perpetually true beings; and are figured by them in a manner wonderful and difficult to describe, as we shall afterwards relate. At present, however, it is necessary to consider three sorts of things: one, that which is generated; another, that in which it is generated; and

d the third, that from which the generated nature derives its similitude. But it is proper to assimilate that which receives to a mother; that from whence it receives to a father; and the nature situated between these to an offspring. It is likewise necessary to understand that the figured nature can never become distinguished with an all-possible variety of forms, unless its receptacle is well prepared for the purpose, and is

e destitute of all those forms which it is about to receive. For, if it were similar to any one of the supernally intromitted forms, when it received a nature contrary to that to which it is similar, or any form whatever, it would very imperfectly express its similitude, while at the same time it exhibited the very same appearance with the supernally acceding form. And hence it is necessary, that the receptacle which is destined to receive all possible forms should itself be destitute of every form. Just as those who are about to prepare sweet-smelling unguents, so dispose a certain humid matter as the subject of the ensuing odour, that it may possess no peculiar smell of its own; and as those who wish to impress certain figures in a soft and yielding matter, are careful that it may not appear

51a impressed with any previous figure, but render it as much as possible exquisitely smooth. In the same manner, it is necessary that the subject which is so often destined to receive in a beautiful manner, through the whole of itself, resemblances of eternal beings, should be naturally destitute of all that it receives. Hence, we should not denominate this mother and receptacle of that which is generated, visible and every way sensible, either earth, or air, or fire, or water; nor, again, any one of the composites from these, or any thing from which these are generated: but

b we should call it a certain invisible species, and a formless universal recipient, which in the most dubious and scarcely explicable manner participates of an intelligible nature. Of itself, indeed, we cannot speak without deception; but so far as it is possible to apprehend its nature from what has been previously said, we may with the greatest rectitude assert as follows: that fire appears to be its inflamed part; water its moist part; and that earth and air are its parts in a similar manner, so far as it

c receives the imitations of these. But we ought rather thus to inquire about these, distinguishing and separating them by a reasoning process;

whether there is a certain fire, itself subsisting in itself; and whether this is the case with all such particulars which we perpetually assert to subsist from themselves; or whether such things alone as are the objects of sight, and which are perceived through the ministry of the body, possess being and truth; so that nothing besides these has in any respect any subsistence; that we in vain assert there is a certain intelligible form of each of these; and that all such forms are nothing but words. Indeed, whether such a doctrine is true or not, must not be asserted rashly and without examination: nor is it proper to add to the present disputation, which is naturally prolix, any thing tedious and foreign from the purpose. But if any definition can be employed in this affair, comprehending things of great moment in a short compass, such a one will be very opportune to our present design. In this manner then I shall relate my opinion on the subject.

d

If intellect and true opinion are two kinds of things, it is every way necessary that there should be forms, subsisting by themselves, which are not the objects of sense, but which are apprehended by intelligence alone. But if, as appears to some, true opinion differs in no respect from intellect, every thing which is perceived through body is to be considered as possessing the most certain and stable nature. But in reality these ought to be denominated two distinct things, because they are generated separate from each other, and are dissimilar. For the one of these subsists in us through learning, but the other through persuasion. And the one is indeed always attended with true reason, but the other is irrational. The one is not to be moved by persuasion; the other, on the contrary, is subject to this mutation. And lastly, of true opinion every man participates; but of intellect all the Gods, and but a few of mankind. Such then being the case, we must confess that the form which subsists according to *same*, is unbegotten and without decay; neither receiving any thing into itself externally, nor itself proceeding into any other nature. That it is invisible, and imperceptible by sense; and that this is the proper object of intellectual speculation. But the form which is synonymous and similar to this, must be considered as sensible, generated, always in agitation, and generated in a certain place, from which it again recedes, hastening to dissolution; and which is apprehended by opinion in conjunction with sense. But the third nature is that of place; which never receives corruption, but affords a seat to all generated forms. This indeed is tangible without tangent perception; and is scarcely by a certain spurious reasoning the object of belief. Besides, when we attempt to behold this nature, we perceive nothing but the delusions of dreams, and assert that every being must necessarily be

e

52a

b

somewhere, and be situated in a certain place: and we by no means think that any thing can exist, which is neither in the earth nor comprehended by the heavens. All these, and all such opinions as are the sisters of these, we are not able to separate from our cogitation of that which subsists about a vigilant and true nature: and this because we

c   cannot rouse ourselves from this fallacious and dreaming energy, and perceive that in reality it is proper for an image to subsist in something different from itself; since that in which it is generated has no proper resemblance of its own, but perpetually exhibits the phantasm of something else; and can only participate of essence in a certain imperfect degree, or it would become in every respect a perfect non-entity. But to true being, true reason bears an assisting testimony, through the accuracy of its decisions; affirming, that as long as two things are different from each other, each can never become so situated in either, as to produce at the same time one thing, and two things essentially the same.

d   This, then, is summarily my opinion: - that, prior to the generation of the universe, these three things subsisted in a triple respect, *viz.* being, place, and generation. And that the nurse of generation, fiery and moist, receiving the forms of earth and air, and suffering such other passions as are the attendants of these, appeared of an all-various nature

e   to the view. But because it was neither filled with similar powers, nor with such as are equally balanced, it possessed no part in equilibrium; but through the perfect inequality of its libration it became agitated by these passions, and again through its motion gave agitation to these. But the parts in motion, being separated from each other, were impetuously hurried along in different directions, similar to the agitations and ventilations which take place in the operations of textorial instruments,

53a   and such as are employed in the purgation of corn. For in this case the dense and the heavy parts are borne along one way, and the rare and the light are impelled into a different seat. In the same manner, these four natures being agitated by their receptacle tumultuously moving like the instrument of corn, such as were dissimilar became far separated from each other, and such as were similar became again amicably united. And hence they passed into different seats before the universe was from the mixture of these distributed into beautiful order; but at the same time they all subsisted irrationally, and without the limitation of measure.

b   But when the artificer began to adorn the universe, he first of all figured with forms and numbers fire and earth, water and air, which possessed indeed certain traces of the true elements, but were in every respect so constituted, as it becomes any thing to be from which Deity is absent. But we should always persevere in asserting that Divinity rendered them as much as possible the most beautiful and the best, when they were in a state of existence opposite to such a condition. I shall now, therefore, endeavour to unfold to you the distribution and generation of these by a discourse unusual indeed, but, to you who have trod in all the paths of erudition, through which demonstration is necessarily obtained, perspicuous and plain. In the first place, then, that fire and earth, water and air, are bodies, is perspicuous to every one. But every species of body possesses profundity; and it is necessary that every depth should comprehend the nature of a plane. Again, the rectitude of the base of a plane is composed from triangles. But all triangles originate from two species; one of which possesses one right angle, and the other two acute angles. And one of these contains one right angle distributed with equal sides; but in the other unequal angles are distributed with unequal sides. Hence, proceeding according to assimilative reasons, conjoined with necessity, we shall establish a principle of this kind, as the origin of fire and all other bodies. The supernal principles of these indeed are known to Divinity, and to the man who is in friendship with Divinity.

But it is necessary to relate by what means four most beautiful bodies were produced; dissimilar indeed to each other, but which are able from certain dissolutions into each other to become the sources of each other's generation. For, if we are able to accomplish this, we shall obtain the truth concerning the generation of earth and fire, and of those elements which are situated according to analogy between these. And then we shall not assent to any one who should assert that there are visible bodies more beautiful than these, each of which subsists according to one kind. We must endeavour, therefore, to harmonize the four sorts of bodies excelling in beauty; and to evince by this means that we sufficiently comprehend the nature of these. Of the two triangles indeed the isosceles is allotted one nature, but the oblong or scalene is characterized by infinity. We ought therefore to choose the most beautiful among infinites, if we wish to commence our investigation in a becoming manner. And if any one shall assert that he has chosen something more beautiful for the composition of these, we shall suffer his opinion to prevail; considering him not as an enemy, but as a friend. Of many triangles, therefore, we shall establish one as most beautiful (neglecting the rest); I mean the equilateral, which is composed from three parts of a scalene triangle. To assign the reason of this would indeed require a prolix dissertation; but a pleasant reward will remain for him who by a diligent investigation finds this to be the case. We have, therefore, selected two triangles out of many, from which the body of fire and of the other elements is fabricated; one of which is isosceles, but the other is that which always has its longer side triply greater in power than the shorter.

c But that which we formerly asserted without sufficient security, it is now necessary more accurately to define. For it appeared to us, though improperly, that all these four natures were mutually generated from each other: but they are in reality generated from the triangles which we have just described: three of them, indeed, from one triangle containing unequal sides; but the fourth alone is aptly composed from the isosceles triangle. All of them, therefore, are not able, by a dissolution into each other, to produce from many small things a mighty few, or the contrary. This indeed can be effected by three of them. For, as all the three are naturally generated from one triangle, when the greater parts are dissolved, many small parts are composed from them, receiving

d figures accommodated to their natures. And again, when the many small parts being scattered according to triangles produce a number of one bulk, they complete one mighty species of a different kind. And thus much may suffice concerning their mutual generation.

It now remains that we should speak concerning the quality of each of their kinds, and relate from what concurring numbers they were collected together. The first species indeed is that which was composed from the fewest triangles, and is the element of that which has its longer

e side twice the length of the shorter side, which it subtends. But two of these being mutually placed according to the diameter, and this happening thrice, the diameters and the shorter sides passing into the same, as into a centre, hence one equilateral triangle is produced from six triangles. But four equilateral triangles being composed, according to three plane angles, form one solid angle; and this the most obtuse of

55a all the plane angles from which it is composed. Hence, from four triangles of this kind receiving their completion, the first solid species was constituted, distributive of the whole circumference into equal and similar parts. But the second was formed from the same triangles, but at the same time constituted according to eight equilateral triangles, which produced one solid angle from four planes: so that the second body received its completion from the composition of six triangles of

b this kind. And the third arose from the conjunction of twice sixty elements, and twelve solid angles, each of which having twenty equilateral bases is contained by five plane equilateral triangles. In this manner, then, the other elements generated these. But the isosceles triangle, being constituted according to four triangles, and collecting the right angles at the centre, and forming one equilateral quadrangle, generated the nature of the fourth element. But six such as these being conjoined produced eight solid angles, each of which is harmonized together, according to three plane right angles. Hence the figure of the body thus composed is cubical, obtaining six plane quadrangular equilateral bases. There is also a certain fifth composition, which Divinity employed in the fabrication of the universe, and when he delineated those forms the contemplation of which may justly lead some one to doubt whether it is proper to assert that the number of worlds is infinite or finite; - though indeed to affirm that there are infinite worlds, can only be the dogma of one who is ignorant about things in which it is highly proper to be skilful. But it may with much less absurdity be doubted whether there is in reality but one world, or whether there are five. According to our opinion, indeed, which is founded on assimilative reasons, there is but one world: though some one, regarding in a certain respect other particulars, may be of a different opinion. But it is proper to dismiss any further speculations of this kind.

Let us now, therefore, distribute the four sorts of things which we have generated, into fire, earth, water, and air. And to earth indeed let us assign a cubical form: for earth is the most immovable of all these four kinds, and the most plastic, or adapted to formation, of all corporeal natures. But it is in the most eminent degree necessary that this should be the case with that which possesses the most secure and stable bases. Among the triangles, indeed, established at the beginning, such as are equilateral possess firmer bases than such as contain unequal sides. And hence, among the plane figures composed from each, it will be found that the isosceles is necessarily more stable than the equilateral, and the square than the triangle, both when considered according to parts and to the whole. On this account, by distributing this figure to the earth, we shall preserve an assimilative reason. This will be the case too by assigning to water that figure which is more difficultly movable than the other three; to fire, the most easily movable form; and to air, that figure which possesses a middle nature. Besides this, we should assign the smallest body to fire, the greatest to water, and one of a middle kind to air. And again, the most acute body to fire, the second from this to air, and the third to water. But, among all these, it is necessary that the body which possesses the fewest bases, should be the most easily movable: for, being every way the most acute, it becomes the most penetrating and incisive of all. It is likewise the most light, because composed from the fewest parts. But that which is second to this, possesses these properties in a secondary respect; and that which ranks as the third, in a third gradation. Hence, according to right and assimilative reason, the solid form of the pyramid is the element and seed of fire. But we must assign that form which is second according to

c generation to air; and that which is the third to water. And it is necessary to consider all these such, with respect to their smallness, that no one of the several sorts can be discerned by us, on account of its parvitude; but that, when many of them are collected together, their bulks become the objects of our perception. And besides this, all these were accurately absolved and harmonized by the Divinity, both as to their multitude, motions, and powers, in such a proportion as the willing and persuaded nature of necessity was able to receive.

d But, among all those natures whose kinds we have above related, the following circumstances appear to take place. And first with respect to earth: when it meets with fire, becoming dissolved by its acuteness, it is borne along; and remains in this dissolved state either in fire, or in the bulk of air, or in that of water - till its parts, associating themselves together, and again becoming mutually harmonized, produce again a body of earth; for it can never pass into another form. But water, when it is distributed into parts by fire or air, when its parts become again

e collected, produces one body of fire, but two bodies of air. And the sections of air form from one dissolved part two bodies of fire. Again, when fire receives into itself either air or water, or a certain earth, and, being itself small, is moved in many natures; and besides this, when, through opposing, being vanquished by the agitated forms, it becomes broken in pieces, then two bodies of fire coalesce into one form of air. And when air becomes vanquished and separated into parts, then, from two wholes and a half, one whole form of water is produced. But,

57a again, let us consider this matter as follows: When any one of the other forms, becoming invested by fire, is cut by the acuteness of its angles and sides, then, passing into the nature of fire, it suffers no further discerption. For no species is ever able to produce mutation or passivity, or any kind of alteration, in that which is similar and the same with itself: but as long as it passes into something else, and the more imbecil contends with the more powerful, it will not cease to be dissolved.

b Again, when the lesser are comprehended in the greater many, and the few being lacerated are extinguished, - if they are willing to pass into the idea of the conquering nature, they cease to be extinguished, and air becomes generated from fire, and water from air. But if, when this transition is accomplished, the composite opposes any of the other species, the agitated parts will not cease to be dissolved, till, on account of their dissoluble subsistence being every way impelled, they fly to their kindred nature; or being vanquished, and becoming one from many, similar to their vanquisher, they abide with the victor in amicable conjunction. But, in consequence of these passions, they all of them mutually change the receptacles which they once possessed. For the multitude of each kind is distinguished, according to its proper place, through the motion of its recipient seat. But such as become dissimilar to each other are borne along through the agitation to the place of the natures to which they are similar. Such bodies, therefore, as are unmixed, and the first, are generated from such causes as these. But that other genera are naturally inherent in these forms, is owing to the composition of each element; which not only from the first produces a triangle, together with magnitude, but also such things as are greater and less: and this so many in number as there are different kinds in the forms themselves. And hence, these being mingled in themselves, and with each other, produce an infinite variety; which it is proper he should contemplate who is about to employ assimilative reasons in the investigation of nature. He, therefore, who does not apprehend in what manner, and in conjunction with what particulars, the motion and composition of these take place, will find many impediments in the remaining part of this disputation. And these indeed we have already partly discussed; but a part still remains for our investigation.

And, in the first place, motion is by no means willing to reside in smoothness: for it is difficult, or rather impossible, that a thing in motion should subsist without a mover, or a mover without that which is in motion. Hence, it is impossible that these should be at any time equable and smooth. And, in consequence of this, we should always place an abiding nature in smoothness, and motion in that which is unequal and rough. Inequality, indeed, is the cause of roughness: and we have already treated concerning the generation of inequality. But we have by no means explained how the several sorts, being undistributed according to their kinds, cease to be moved and borne along through each other. This, therefore, must be the subject of our present discussion. The circulation then of the universe, since it comprehends the different sorts of things in its circumference, being of a circular form, and naturally desiring to pass into union with itself, compresses all things within its spacious receptacle, and does not suffer a void place any where to subsist. On this account, fire in the most eminent degree penetrates through all things; and air next to this, ranking as the second to fire, on account of the subtility and tenuity of its parts. And the same reasoning must be extended to the other elements, which are posterior to these. For such as are composed from the greatest parts leave also the greatest vacuity in their composition; but, on the contrary, such as are the smallest leave the least vacuity. But the coalition of compression thrusts the small parts into the void spaces of the large; and on this account, the small parts being placed with the large, and the former separating the latter, but the larger being mingled with the c smaller, all of them are borne upwards and downwards to their respective places of abode. For each, upon changing its magnitude, changes also its situation. Hence, through these causes the generation of a nature contrary to smoothness being always preserved, affords a perpetual motion of these, both at present and in all future periods of time.

But, in the next place, it is necessary to understand that there are many kinds of fire: as for instance, flame, and that which is enkindled from d flame; which burns, indeed: but exhibits no light to the eyes - and which, when the flame is extinguished, abides in the ignited nature. In like manner, with respect to air, one kind is most pure, which is denominated ether; but another most turbulent, and at the same time obscure and dark; and after this another nameless kind is produced, through the inequality of the triangles. But, with respect to water, it is in the first place twofold; one kind of which is humid, but the other fusile. The humid, therefore, through its participating such parts as are e small and unequal, becomes movable, both from itself and another, through inequality and the idea of its figure. But that which is composed from large and smooth parts is more stable than this kind of water, and coalesces into a heavy body through smoothness and equality of parts. But through fire entering into and dissolving its composition, in consequence of losing its equability and smoothness, it participates more of a movable nature. Hence, becoming easily agile, driven about by the proximate air, and extended over the earth, it liquefies, which is denominated a purification of bulk, and falls upon the earth, which is 59a called a defluxion. Again, fire flying upwards from hence, since it does not depart into a vacuum, the proximate air being agitated, impels the moist bulk as yet movable into the seats of fire, with which at the same time it mingles itself. But when the bulk becomes collectively thrust downwards, and again receives equability and smoothness of parts, then† fire, the artificer of inequality, departing, the whole mass passes into a sameness with itself. And this departure of fire we denominate

---

† Instead of ουτε, in this part read ατε.

refrigeration; but the coalition which takes place when fire is absent we call a concretion, and cold rigidity. But among all those which we denominate fusile waters, that which, becoming most dense from the most attenuated and equable parts, is of a uniform kind, and participates a splendid and yellow colour, is that most honoured and valuable possession gold, which is usually impelled through a rock. And a branch of gold, on account of its density most hard and black, is called a diamond. But that which contains parts proximate to gold, which possesses more than one species, surpasses gold in density, and participates but a small and attenuated part of earth, so that it becomes of a harder nature, but from its internally possessing great intervals is lighter; - this is one kind of splendid and concrete waters, and is denominated brass. But when an earthly nature, being mingled with this, is through antiquity separated from other parts of the brass, and becomes of itself conspicuous, it is then denominated rust. In a similar manner other particulars of this nature may be investigated without much labour by the assistance of assimilative reasons. And if any one, for the sake of relaxation, omitting for a while the speculation of eternal beings, should pursue the assimilative arguments concerning generation, and should by this means possess a pleasure unattended with repentance, such a one will establish for himself in life a moderate and prudent diversion.

This being admitted, let us run over the assimilative reasons concerning the particulars which yet remain for discussion. When such water then as is attenuated and moist is mingled with fire, (being denominated moist through its motion and rolling progression on the earth, and likewise soft, because its bases being less stable than those of earth easily yield to impulsion,) this, when separated from fire and deserted by air, becomes more equable, and through the departure of these is compelled into itself: and being thus collected, if it suffers this alteration above the earth, it becomes hail; but if upon the earth, ice; which then takes place in consequence of extreme congelation. But when it is less congealed, if this happens above the earth, it becomes snow; but when upon the earth, and this from collected dew, it then becomes frost. But when many species of water are mingled with each other, the whole kind, which is strained from the earth through plants, is called moisture or liquor. These liquors, being dissimilar on account of their mixtures, exhibit many other nameless kinds: but four, which are of a fiery species, and which become in an eminent degree diaphanous, are allotted appellations. And that which heats the soul in conjunction with the body is called wine. But that which is smooth, and segregative of the sight, and on this account splendid, refulgent, and unctuous to the view, is an oleaginous species, and is pitch, gum, oil, and other things endued

b with a similar power. Again, that which possesses a power of diffusing the things collected about the mouth, and this as far as nature will permit, at the same time bringing sweetness with its power, is generally denominated honey. And lastly, that which dissolves the flesh by burning, is of a frothy nature, and is secreted from all liquors, is called juice. But the species of earth strained through water produces a stony body in tile following manner: - When collected water fails in mingling,

c it passes into the form of air; but, becoming air, it returns to its proper place. Hence, as there is no vacuum, it impels the proximate air; and this, if the impulsion is weighty, being poured round the bulk of earth, becomes vehemently compressed, and betakes itself to those seats from whence the new air ascended. But earth, when indissolubly associated with water, through the ministry of air composes stones: the more beautiful sort indeed being such as are resplendent from equal and plane parts, but the deformed being of a contrary composition. But when all the moisture is hurried away by the violence of fire, and the body by

d this means becomes more dry, then a species of earth which is denominated fictile is produced. Sometimes, likewise, when the moisture is left behind, and the earth becomes fusile through fire, then through refrigeration a stone with a black colour is generated. But when this species of strained earth in a similar manner through mixture is deprived of much moisture, but is composed from more attenuated parts of earth, is salt and semiconcrete, and again emerges through water; then it is partly called nitre, a cathartic kind of oil, and earth, and partly salt, a substance most elegantly and legitimately adapted to the common

e wants of the body, and most grateful to divinity. But the parts common to both these are not soluble by water, but through some such thing are thus collected together by fire. Again, fire and air do not liquefy the bulk of earth. For since these naturally consist of parts smaller than the void spaces of earth, they permeate through its most capacious pores without any violence, and neither subject it to dissolution nor liquefaction. But the parts of water, because they are greater and pass

61a along with violence, dissolve and liquefy the mass of earth. Hence, water alone dissolves earth when violently composed, but fire alone when it is properly composed; for an entrance in this case is afforded to nothing but fire.

Again, fire alone permeates the most violent association of the parts of water; but both fire and air diffuse themselves through its more debile collection; air through its void, and fire through its triangular spaces.

But nothing is capable of dissolving air when collected together by violence, except it operates according to an element: but when it coheres together without force, it is resolved by fire alone. Again, bodies which are so composed from water and earth that the water compressed by force obstructs the void spaces of earth, cannot in this case afford an ingress to the water externally approaching; and in consequence of this, the water flowing round such a body suffers the whole mass to remain without liquefaction. But the parts of fire entering into the void spaces of water, as water into those of earth, and influencing water in the same manner as fire influences air, become in this case the causes of liquefaction to a common body. But these partly possess less water than earth; such as the whole genus of glass, and such stones as are denominated fusile: and partly, on the contrary, they possess more of water; such as all those bodies which coalesce into waxen and vaporific substances. And thus we have nearly exhibited all those species, which are varied by figures, communications and mutations into each other; but it is now necessary that we should endeavour to render apparent the causes through which the passions of these are produced.

In the first place, then, sense ought always to be present with discourses of this kind. But we have not yet run through the generation of flesh, and such things as pertain to flesh, together with that part of the soul which is mortal. For all these are inseparable from the passions subsisting with sense, and cannot without these passions be sufficiently explained; though, indeed, even in conjunction with these, it is scarcely possible to unfold their production. We should, therefore, first of all establish other things; and then consider such things as are consequent to these. That in our disputation, therefore, the passions themselves may follow the genera in succession, let our first investigations be concerning such things as pertain to body and soul. Let us then first of all inquire why fire is called hot. And the reason of this we shall be able to perceive by considering the separation and division of fire about our bodies: for that this *passion* is a certain sharpness is nearly evident to all. But we ought to consider the tenuity of its angles, the sharpness of its sides, the smallness of its parts, and the velocity of its motion, through all which it becomes vehement and penetrating, and swiftly divides that with which it meets; calling to mind for this purpose the generation of its figure. For fire, indeed, and no other nature, separating our bodies and distributing them into small parts, produces in us that *passion* which is very properly denominated heat. But the *passion* contrary to this, though sufficiently manifest, ought not to pass without an explanation. For the moist parts of bodies larger than our humid

parts, entering into our bodies, expel the smaller parts; but, not being
able to penetrate into their receptacles, coagulate our moisture, and cause
it through equability to pass from an unequable and agitated state into
one immovable and collected. But that which is collected together
contrary to nature, naturally opposes such a condition, and endeavours
by repulsion to recall itself into a contrary situation. In this contest and
agitation a trembling and numbness takes place; and all this *passion*,
together with that which produces it, is denominated cold. But we call
that hard to which our flesh gives way; and soft, which yields to the
pressure of our flesh. And we thus denominate them with reference to
each other. But every thing yields to pressure which is established on
a small base. But that which rests on triangular[†] bases, on account of
its being vehemently firm, is of a most resisting nature; and, because it
is dense in the highest degree, strongly repels all opposing pressure.

Again, the nature of heavy and light will become eminently apparent,
when investigated together with upwards and downwards. But indeed
it is by no means rightly asserted that there are naturally two certain
places distant by a long interval from each other: one denominated
downwards, to which all bodies tend endued with bulk, but the other
upwards, to which every thing is involuntarily impelled. For, the whole
universe being spherical, all such things as by an equal departure from
the middle become extremes, ought to become naturally extremes in a
similar manner. But the middle, being separated from the extremes
according to the same measures, ought to be considered as in a situation
just opposite to all things. Such, then, being the natural disposition of
the world, he who places any one of the above-mentioned particulars
either upwards or downwards, will justly appear by such appellations to
wander from the truth. For the middle place in the universe cannot be
properly called either naturally downwards or upwards, but can only be
denominated that which is the middle. But that which environs is
neither the middle, nor contains any parts in itself differing from each
other with reference to the middle, nor does it possess any thing
corresponding to an opposite direction. But to that which is every way
naturally similar how can any one with propriety attribute contrary
names? For, if there be any thing solid, and endued with equal powers,
in the middle of the universe, it will never tend to any part of the
extremities, through the perfect similitude which they every where
possess. But if any one moves about this solid in a circle, he will often

---

[†] The word *triangular* here appears to be a mistranslation: the text reads τετραγωνος
- four-angled. Jowett has *quadrangular* here. PT.

stand with his feet in opposite directions, and will denominate the same part of himself both upwards and downwards. Since the universe, therefore, as we have just observed, is of a spherical figure, it is not the part of a prudent man to assert that it has any place which is either upwards or downwards. But from whence these names originate, and, in what things existing, we transfer them from thence to the universe, it is our business at present to investigate. If any one then should be seated in that region of the world which for the most part belongs to the nature or fire, and to which it on all sides tends, and if such a one should acquire a power of taking away the parts of fire, and of causing them to balance; or, placing the parts in a scale, should violently seize on the beam, and, drawing out the fire, hurl it downwards into dissimilar air - it is evident that in this case a less portion of fire would be more easily compelled than a greater. For, when two things are at the same time suspended from one power, it is necessary that the less quantity should more easily, and the greater with less readiness, yield to the oppressive force. Hence, the one is called heavy, and tending downwards; but the other light, and tending upwards. The same thing happens to us who inhabit this terrestrial region. For, walking on the earth, and separating the terrene genera from each other, we sometimes violently hurl a fragment of earth into its dissimilar the air, and this with a motion contrary to its nature; each region at the same time retaining that to which it is allied. But the less portion, being more easily impelled into a dissimilar place than the larger, first of all yields to the violence: and this we denominate light, and call the place into which it is violently hurled, upwards. But the passion contrary to this we denominate heavy and downwards. Hence it is necessary that these should mutually differ from each other; and this through the multitude of genera obtaining contrary situations. For that which is light in one place is contrary to that which is light in a contrary situation: likewise the heavy to the heavy, the downward to the downward, and the upward to the upward. For all these will be found to be contrary, transverse, and every way different from each other. One thing however is to be understood concerning all these, that the progression of each, tending to its kindred nature, renders the proceeding body heavy, and the place to which it tends, downwards. But this progression influences in a different manner such as are differently affected. And thus have I unfolded the causes of these passions.

But again, any one who beholds the cause of the *passion* of smoothness and roughness may be able to disclose it to others. For hardness mingled with inequality produces the one, and equality with density the other. But among the common *passions* which subsist about the whole body, that is the greatest which is the cause of pleasure and pain: to which may be added, such as through the parts of the body detain the senses, and have in these pleasures and pains as their attendants. In this manner, then, we should receive the causes of every passion, both sensible and insensible, calling to mind the distinctions which we b formerly established concerning the easily and difficultly movable nature. For in this manner we ought to pursue all such things as we design to apprehend. Thus, with respect to that which is naturally easily movable, when any slender passion falls upon it, the several parts give themselves up to each other in a circular progression, producing the same effect; till, having arrived at the seat of prudence, they announce the power of that by which the passion was induced. But that which is affected in a contrary manner, being stable and without a circular progression, alone suffers; but does not move any of the parts to which it is proximate. Hence, the parts not mutually giving themselves up to c each other, and the first passion in them becoming immovable with respect to the whole animal, that which suffers is rendered void of sensation. This last case indeed happens about the bones and hairs, and such other parts of our composition as are mostly terrene. But the circumstances belonging to the easily movable nature take place about the instruments of sight and hearing, through their containing the most abundant power of fire and air. But it is necessary to consider the peculiarities of pleasure and pain as follows: When a *passion* is produced d in us contrary to nature, and with violence and abundance, then it becomes the occasion of pain. And again, when a *passion* conformable to our nature is excited, and this with abundance, it causes pleasure and delight. But that which is contrary to these produces contrary effects. But a *passion*, the whole of which is induced with great facility, is eminently indeed the object of sensation, but does not participate of pleasure and pain. And of this kind are the *passions* subsisting about the sight; to which, as we have above asserted, our body is allied. For such objects as exhibit sections and burnings, and other *passions* of a similar kind, do not cause pain to the sight; nor; again, does the sight receive e pleasure when it is restored to the same form as before. But the most vehement and clear sensations influence it with pain, so far as it suffers any thing, strikes against, or comes into contact with, any object. For no violence subsists in the separation or concretion of the sight. But such bodies as are composed from larger parts, and which scarcely yield to impulsion, when they transfer the induced motions to the whole body, contain in themselves pleasures and pains; when varied, indeed, a   pains, but, when restored to their pristine situation, pleasures. Again, whatever bodies in a small degree receive departures and evacuations of themselves, accompanied at the same time with abundant repletions, - since such bodies have no sense of evacuation, but are sensible of repletion, they do not affect the mortal part of the soul with any pain, but, on the contrary, influence it with the greatest delight. And the truth of this is manifest from the sensation of sweet odours. But such bodies as suffer an abundant variation, and are scarce able to be restored in a small degree to their pristine situation, are totally affected in a manner contrary to those we have just described. And the truth of this is manifest in the burnings and sections of the body. And thus have we nearly discussed the common passions of the whole body, and the appellations assigned to the causes by which they are produced.

Let us now endeavour to explain those passions which take place in particular parts of our bodies, and relate from whence they arise, and by what causes they are induced. In the first place, let us if possible complete what we formerly left unfinished concerning humours; since these are passions subsisting about the tongue. But these, as well as many other things, appear to be produced by certain separations and concretions; and, besides this, to employ smoothness and roughness more than the rest. For certain small veins extend themselves from the tongue to the heart, and are the messengers of tastes. And when any thing falls upon these so as to penetrate the moist and delicate texture of the flesh, which through its terrestrial nature is moderately liquefied, it then contracts and dries the veins. Hence, if these penetrating substances are of a more rough nature, they produce a sharp taste; but, if less rough, a sour taste. But such things as are purgative of these veins, and which wash away whatever is found adhering to the tongue, if they accomplish this in an immoderate degree, so as to liquefy something of the nature of the tongue, such as is the power of nitre; - all such as these are denominated bitter. But whatever is subordinate to this property of nitre, and purges in a more moderate degree, appears to us to be salt, without the roughness of bitterness, and to be more friendly to our nature. Again, such things as, communicating with the heat of the mouth, and being rendered smooth by it, heat also in their turn the mouth - and which through their lightness are elevated towards the senses of the head, at the same time dividing whatever they meet with in their ascent; - all these, through powers of this kind, are denominated sharp. But sometimes these several particulars, becoming attenuated through rottenness, enter into the narrow veins, and compel the interior parts, as well the terrene as those containing the symmetry of air, to be mingled together by moving about each other; and when mingled cause some of the parts to glide around, some to enter into others, and when entered to render them hollow and extended; and this

b   in the place where a hollow moisture is extended about the air. This moisture too being at one time terrene and at another pure, a moist orbicular receptacle of air is produced from the hollow water. But that which is produced from pure water is on all sides diaphanous, and is called a bubble. On the contrary, that which owes its subsistence to a more earthly moisture, and which is at the same time agitated and elevated, is denominated fervid, and a fermentation. But the cause of all these passions receives the appellation of acute. And a passion contrary to all that has been asserted concerning these proceeds from a contrary

c   cause. But when the composition of the things entering into moist substances is naturally accommodated to the quality of the tongue, it polishes and anoints its asperities, and collects together or relaxes such parts as were either assembled or dissipated contrary to nature, and restores them to their proper and natural habit. Hence, all such substances are pleasant and friendly to every one, become the remedies of violent passions, and are denominated sweet. And thus much may suffice concerning particulars of this kind.

d   There are, however, no species about the power of the nostrils: for all odours are but half begotten. But it happens to no species to be commensurate with any odour. And our veins, with respect to particulars of this kind, are too narrow to admit the genera of earth and water, and too broad to receive those of fire and air; and hence no one ever perceives an odour of any one of these. But odours are always produced from the malefaction, corruption, liquefaction or evaporation

e   of the elements. For, water becoming changed into air, and air into water, odours are generated in the middle of these. And all odours are either smoke or mists. But, of these, that which passes from air into water is a mist; but that which is changed from water into air, smoke. And hence it comes to pass that all odours are more attenuated than water, and more dense than air. But the truth of this is sufficiently evident when any one, in consequence of a disagreeable smell, violently draws his breath inwards; for then no odour is washed off, but breath

67a   alone follows unattended by smell. On this account, the varieties of these subsist without a name; as they are neither composed from many nor from simple species. But two of these alone receive an appellation, the pleasant and the disagreeable: the latter of which disturbs and violently assaults all that cavity which lies between the top of the head and the navel; but the former allures this part of the body, and by its amicable ingress preserves it in a condition accommodated to its nature. But we ought to consider the third sensitive part of our composition, hearing, in such a manner that we may explain through what causes the passions with which it is conversant subsist. We ought, therefore, entirely to define voice a certain pulsation of the air, penetrating through the ears, brain, and blood, as far as to the soul: and we should call the motion arising from hence, which commences from the head and ends in the seat of the liver, hearing. When this motion is swift, a sharp sound is produced; but, when slow, a flat sound. And the former of these is equal and smooth, but the latter rough. Many voices too produce a great sound, but a small sound is the result of a few. But it is necessary that we should speak about the symphonies of these in the subsequent part of this discourse. The fourth sensitive genus now remains for our discussion; which contains in itself an abundant variety, all which are denominated colours. But colour is a flame flowing from bodies, and possessing parts commensurate to the sight with respect to perception. But we have already considered the causes from which sight is produced. It appears then that we may now speak of colours according to assimilative reasons as follows:

Of things which, proceeding from other parts, fall on the sight, some are greater, others less, and others equal to the parts of the sight. Such as are equal, therefore, cannot be perceived; and these we denominate diaphanous. But, among such as are larger or smaller, some of these separate, but others mingle the sight, similar to the operations of heat and cold about the flesh, or to things sour, acute and hot about the tongue. But things which affect the sight in this manner are called black and white; which are indeed the passions of those particulars we have just related, being their sisters, as it were, and the same with them in a different genus; but which, nevertheless, through these causes appear to be different. We should, therefore, speak of them as follows: That the colour which is segregative of the sight is white; but that which produces an effect contrary to this, black. But when a more acute motion, and of a different kind of fire, falls upon and separates the sight, as far as to the eyes, at the same time violently propelling and liquefying the transitions of the eyes, then a collected substance of fire and water flows from thence, which we denominate a tear; but the motion itself is a fire meeting with the sight in an opposite direction. And, indeed, when a fire, leaping as it were from a certain corruscation, becomes mingled with another fire, penetrating and extinguished by moisture, from this mixture colours of all-various kinds are produced. In this case we call the passion a vibrating splendour, and that which produces it b fulgid and rutilating. But a kind of fire which subsists in the middle of these, arriving at the moisture of the eyes, and becoming mingled with it, is by no means splendid: but in consequence of the rays of fire being mingled through moisture, and producing a bloody colour, we denominate the mixture red. And when splendour is mingled with red and white, it generates a yellow colour. But to relate in what measure each of these is mingled with each, is not the business of one endued with intellect, even though he were well informed in this affair; since he would not be able to produce concerning these either a necessary or an assimilative reason. But red, when mingled with black and white,

c produces a purple colour. And when to these, mingled and burnt together, more of black is added, a more obscure colour is produced. A ruddy colour is generated from the mixture of yellow and brown; but brown from the mixture of black and white. A pallid colour arises from the mingling of white and yellow. But that which is splendid conjoined with white, and falling upon abundance of black, gives completion to an azure colour. And azure mingled with white generates a grey colour. But from the temperament of a ruddy colour with black, green is

d produced. All the rest will be nearly evident from these, to any one who, imitating the former mixtures, preserves assimilative reasons in his discourse. But if any one undertakes the investigation of these, for the sake of the things themselves, such a one must be ignorant of the difference between a divine and human nature: since a God is indeed sufficient for the purpose of mingling many things into one, and of again dissolving the one into many, as being at the same time both knowing and able: but there is no man at present who is able to accomplish either of these undertakings, nor will there ever be one in

e any future circulation of time. But all these which thus naturally subsist from necessity, were assumed in the things which are generated by the artificer of that which is most beautiful and best, when he produced a self-sufficient and most perfect God; employing, indeed, causes which are subservient to these, but operating himself in the best manner in all generated natures. On this account it is requisite to distinguish two species of causes; the one necessary, but the other divine. And we

69a should inquire after the divine cause in all things, for the sake of obtaining a blessed life in as great a degree as our nature is capable of receiving it; but we should investigate the necessary cause for the sake of that which is divine. For we should consider, that without these two species of causes, the objects of our pursuit can neither be understood nor apprehended, nor in any other way become participated. But since to us at present, as to artificers, matter lies in subjection, the genera of causes serving as prepared materials from which the remaining discourse is to be woven, let us again return with brevity to our first discussions, and swiftly pass from thence to the place at which we are now arrived; by this means endeavouring to establish an end and summit to our disputation, which may harmonize with its beginning.

Indeed, as we asserted towards the commencement of our discourse, when all sensible natures were in a disordered state of subsistence, Divinity rendered each commensurate with itself, and all with one another, and connected them as much as possible with the bands of analogy and symmetry. For then nothing participated of order except by accident; nor could any thing with propriety be distinguished by the appellation which it receives at present, such for instance as fire, water, and the rest of this kind. But the demiurgus in the first place adorned all these, afterwards established the world from their conjunction, and rendered it one animal, containing in itself all mortal and immortal animals. And of divine natures, indeed, he himself became the author; but he delivered to his offspring the junior Gods the fabrication of mortal natures. Hence, these imitating their father's power, and receiving the immortal Principle of the soul, fashioned posterior to this the mortal body, assigned the whole body as a vehicle to the soul, and fabricated in it another mortal species of soul, possessing dire and necessary passions through its union with the body. The first indeed of these passions is pleasure, which is the greatest allurement to evil; but the next is pain, which is the exile of good. After these follow boldness and fear, those mad advisers; anger, hard to be appeased; hope, which is easily deceived; together with irrational sense, and love, the general invader of all things. In consequence, therefore, of mingling these together, the junior Gods necessarily composed the mortal race. And religiously fearing lest the divine nature should be defiled through this rout of molestations more than extreme necessity required, they lodged the mortal part, separate from the divine, in a different receptacle of the body; fabricating the head and breast, and placing the neck between as an isthmus and boundary, that the two extremes might be separate from each other.

In the breast, therefore, and that which is called the thorax, they seated the mortal genus of the soul. And as one part of it is naturally better, but another naturally worse, they fabricated the cavity of the thorax; distributing this receptacle in the woman different from that of the man, and placing in the middle of these the midriff or diaphragm. That part of the soul, therefore, which participates of fortitude and anger, and is fond of contention, they seated nearer the head, between the midriff and the neck; that becoming obedient to reason, and uniting with it in amicable conjunction, it might together with reason forcibly repress the race of desires, whenever they should be found unwilling to obey the mandates of reason, issuing her orders from her lofty place of abode.

b But they established the heart, *which is both the fountain of the veins, and of the blood, which is vehemently impelled through all the members of the body in a* CIRCULAR PROGRESSION, in an habitation corresponding to that of a satellite; that when the irascible part becomes inflamed, reason at the same time announcing that some unjust action has taken place externally, or has been performed by some one of the inward desires, then every thing sensitive in the body may swiftly through all the narrow pores perceive the threatenings and exhortations, may be in every respect obedient, and may thus permit that which is the best in all these to maintain the sovereign command.

c But as the Gods previously knew that the palpitation of the heart in the expectation of dreadful events, and the effervescence of anger, and every kind of wrathful inflation, would be produced by fire, they implanted in the body the idea of the lungs, artificially producing them as a guardian to the heart. And, in the first place, they rendered them soft and bloodless, and afterwards internally perforated with hollow pipes like a sponge; that through their receiving spirit and imbibing moisture, they might become themselves refrigerated, and might afford

d respiration and remission to the heart in its excessive heat. Hence they deduced the arteries as so many canals through the substance of the lungs; and placed the lungs like a soft thicket round the heart, that when anger rages in it with too much vehemence it may leap into submission, and becoming refrigerated may be subject to less endurance, and may be able together with anger to yield with greater facility to the authority of reason. But they seated that part of the soul which is desiderative of meats and drinks, and such other things as it requires through the nature

e of body, between the præcordia and the boundary about the navel; fabricating all this place as a manger subservient to the nutriment of the body, and binding in it this part of the soul as a rustic and savage animal. But it is necessary that this part should nourish its conjoined body, if the mortal race has a necessary existence in the nature of things. That this part, therefore, might be always fed at the manger, and might

71a dwell remote from the deliberative part, molesting it in the smallest degree with its tumults and clamours, and permitting it, as that which is most excellent in our composition, to consult in quiet for the common utility of the whole animal; on this account the Gods assigned it such a subordinate situation.

However, as the Divinity perceived that this part would not be obedient to reason, but that it would naturally reject its authority in consequence of every sensible impression, and would be animastically hurried away by images and phantasms both by day and night - considering this, he constituted the form of the liver, and placed it in the habitation of this desiderative part; composing it dense and smooth, splendid and sweet, and at the same time mingled with bitterness; that the power of cogitations, descending from intellect into the liver as into a mirror receiving various resemblances and exhibiting images to the view, might at one time terrify this irrational nature by employing a kindred part of bitterness and introducing dreadful threats, so that the whole liver being gradually mingled might represent bilious colours, and becoming contracted might be rendered throughout wrinkled and rough; and that, besides this, it might influence its lobe, ventricle, and gates, in such a manner, that by distorting and twisting some of these from their proper disposition, and obstructing and shutting in others, it might be the cause of damages and pains. And again, that at another time a certain inspiration of gentleness from the dianoëtic power, by describing contrary phantasms and affording rest to bitterness, through its being unwilling either to excite or apply itself to a nature contrary to its own; and besides this, by employing the innate sweetness of the liver, and rendering all its parts properly disposed, smooth, and free, might cause that part of the soul which resides about the liver to become peaceful and happy, so that it might even refrain from excess in the night, and employ prophetic energies in sleep: since it does not participate of reason and prudence. For those who composed us, calling to mind the mandate of their father, that they should render the mortal race as far as possible the best, so constituted the depraved part of our nature that it might become connected with truth; establishing in this part a prophetic knowledge of future events. But that Divinity assigned divination to human madness may be sufficiently inferred from hence; that no one while endued with intellect becomes connected with a divine and true prophecy; but this alone takes place either when the power of prudence is fettered by sleep, or suffers some mutation through disease, or a certain enthusiastic energy: it being in this case the employment of prudence to understand what was asserted either sleeping or waking by a prophetic and enthusiastic nature; and so to distinguish all the phantastic appearances as to be able to explain what and to whom anything of future, past, or present good is portended. But it is by no means the office of that which abides and is still about to abide in this enthusiastic energy, to judge of itself either concerning the appearances or vociferations. Hence it was well said by the ancients, that to transact and know his own concerns and himself, is alone the province of a prudent man. And on this account the law orders that the race of prophets should preside as judges over divine predictions; who are indeed called by some diviners - but this in consequence of being ignorant that such men are interpreters of ænigmatical visions and predictions, and on this account should not be called diviners, but rather prophets of divinations. The nature, therefore, of the liver was produced on this account, and seated in the place we have mentioned, *viz.* for the sake of prediction. And besides this, while each of such like parts is living, it possesses clearer indications; but when deprived of life it then becomes blind, and the divination is rendered too obscure to signify any thing sufficiently clear. But an intestine which subsists for the sake of the liver, is placed near it on the left hand, that it may always render the liver splendid and pure, and prepared like a mirror for the apt reception of resemblant forms. On this account, when certain impurities are produced about the liver through bodily disease, then the spleen, purifying these by its rarity, receives them into itself from its being of a hollow and bloodless contexture. Hence, being filled with purgations, it increases in bulk, and becomes inflated with corruption. And again, when the body is purified, then becoming depressed it subsides into the same condition as before. And thus we have spoken concerning both the mortal and divine part of the soul, and have related where they are situated, in conjunction with what natures, and why they are separated from each other. That all this indeed is unfolded according to indisputable truth, can only be asserted when confirmed by the vocal attestation of a God: but that it is spoken according to assimilative reasons, we should not hesitate to evince both now and hereafter by a more diligent discussion of what remains.

It is proper to investigate in a similar manner the subsequent part of our disputation; and this is no other than to relate how the other members of the body were produced. It is becoming, therefore, in the most eminent degree that they should be composed as follows: Those artificers then of our race well knew that we should be intemperate in the assumption of meats and drinks, and that we should often through gluttony use more than was moderate and necessary. Hence, lest sudden destruction should take place through disease, and the mortal race thus becoming imperfect should presently cease to exist; the Gods previously perceiving this consequence, fabricated in the lower parts a hollow receptacle for the purpose of receiving a superabundance of solid and liquid aliment; and, besides this, invested it with the spiral folds of the intestines, lest, the assumed nutriment swiftly passing away, the body should as swiftly require an accession of new aliment; and, by producing an insatiable appetite through gluttony, should render our whole race void of philosophy and the muses, and unobedient to the most divine part of our composition. But the nature of the bones and flesh, and other things of this kind, was constituted as follows: In the first place, the generation of the marrow serves as a principle to all these. For the bonds of that life which the soul leads through its conjunction with the body, being woven together in the marrow, become the stable roots of the mortal race. But the marrow itself is generated from other particulars. For, among the triangles, such as are first, being unbent and smooth, were particularly accommodated to the generation of fire and water, air and earth; and the Divinity separating each of these apart from their genera, and mingling them commensurate with each other, composing by this means an all-various mixture of seeds for the mortal race, produced from these the nature of the marrow. But afterwards disseminating in the marrow, he bound in it the genera of souls. Besides, in this first distribution, he immediately separated as many figures and of such kinds as it was requisite the marrow should possess. And he fashioned indeed that part of the marrow in which as in a cultivated field the divine seed was to be sown, every way globular, and called it ἐγκέφαλον, or the brain; because in every animal, when it has acquired the perfection of its form, the receptacle of this substance is denominated the head. But he distinguished with round and at the same time oblong figures, that receptacle of the body which was destined to contain the remaining and mortal part of the soul; and was willing that the whole should receive the appellation of marrow. And besides this, hurling from these as anchors the bonds of all the soul, he fabricated the whole of our body about the substance of the marrow, and invested it on all sides with a covering of bones.

But he thus composed the nature of the bones. In the first place, bruising together pure and smooth earth, he mingled and moistened it with marrow; after this he placed it in fire, then merged it in water, then again seated it in fire, and after this dipped it in water. And thus, by often transferring it into each, he rendered it incapable of being liquefied by both. Employing therefore this nature of bone, he fashioned like one working with a wheel a bony sphere, and placed it round the brain; leaving a narrow passage in the sphere itself. And besides this, forming certain vertebrae from bone about the marrow of the neck and back, he extended them like hinges, commencing from the head and proceeding through the whole cavity of the body. And thus he preserved all the seed, by fortifying it round about with a stony vestment. He likewise added joints, for the purpose of motion and inflection, employing the nature of that which is distinguished by *difference* in their fabrication, as this is endued with a certain middle

b capacity. But, as he thought that the habit of the bony nature would become more dry and inflexible than it ought to be, and that, when it became heated and again cooled, it would in consequence of ulceration swiftly corrupt the seed which it contained, on this account he fashioned the genus of nerves and flesh; that the nerves, by binding all the other members, and becoming stretched and remitted about those hinges the vertebrae, might render the body apt to become inflected and extended as occasion required: but that the flesh might serve as a covering from the heat and a protection from the cold; and, besides this, might defend

c it from falls, in the same manner as external supports, gently and easily yielding to the motions of the body. He likewise placed a hot moisture in the nature of the flesh, that, becoming in summer externally dewy and moist, it might afford a kindred refrigeration to the whole body; and that again in winter, through its own proper fire, it might moderately repel the externally introduced and surrounding cold. When, therefore, the plastic artificer of our bodies had perceived all this through a dianoëtic energy, having mingled and harmonized together

d water, fire, and earth, and added to the mixture a sharp and salt ferment, he gradually composed soft and succulent flesh.

But he mingled the nature of the nerves from bone and unfermented flesh, composing one middle substance from the power of both, and tingeing it with a yellow colour. And on this account it comes to pass that the power of the nerves is more intense and viscous than that of the flesh, but more soft and moist than that of the bones. Hence, the Divinity bound the bones and marrow to each other with the nerves, and afterwards invested them all supernally with the flesh, as with a

e dark concealing shade. Such of the bones, therefore, as were the most animated he covered with the least flesh; but such as were the least animated he invested with flesh the most abundant and dense. And, besides this, he added but a small quantity of flesh to the joints of the bones, except where reason evinces the necessity of the contrary: and this lest they should be a hindrance to the inflections, and retard the motions of the body; and again, lest in consequence of their being many and dense, and vehemently compressed in one another, they should cause through their solidity a privation of sense, a difficulty of recollection, and a remission of the dianoëtic energy. On this account

75a he invested with abundance of flesh the bones of the groin, legs, loins, the upper part of the arms, and that part which extends from the elbow to the wrist, and such other parts of our bodies as are without articulation, together with such inward bones as through the paucity of soul in the marrow are destitute of a prudential energy. But he covered with a less quantity of flesh such bones as are endued with prudence: unless, perhaps, the fleshy substance of the tongue, which was produced for the sake of sensation, is to be excepted. In other parts, the case is such as we have described. For a nature which is generated and nourished from necessity can by no means at one and the same time receive a dense bone and abundant flesh, united with acuteness of sensation. But this would be most eminently the case with the composition of the head, if all these were willing to coalesce in amicable conjunction: and the human race, possessing a fleshy, nervous, and robust head, would enjoy a life twice as long, or still more abundantly extended, healthy and unmolested, than that which we at present possess.

Again, in consequence of those artificers of our generation considering whether they should fabricate our race possessing a life more lasting indeed but of a worse condition, or of a shorter extent but of a more excellent condition, it appeared to them that a shorter but more excellent life was by all means to be preferred to one more lasting but of a subordinate condition. Hence they covered the head with a thin bone, but did not invest it with flesh and nerves, because it was destitute of inflections. On all these accounts, therefore, the head was added to the body as the most sensitive and prudent, but at the same time by far the most imbecil part of all the man. But through these causes, and in this manner, the Divinity placing the nerves about the extreme part of the head, conglutinated them in a circle about the neck, (after a certain similitude), and bound with them those lofty cheekbones situated under the countenance; but he disseminated the rest about all the members, connecting joint with joint. Besides, those adorners of our race ornamented us with the power of the mouth, teeth, tongue, and lips, and this for the sake of things which are at the same time both necessary and the best; producing ingression for the sake of necessaries, but egression for the sake of such as are best. Every thing, indeed, which being introduced affords nutriment to the body, is necessary; but the stream of words flowing forth externally, and becoming subservient to prudence, is the most beautiful and best of all effluxions. Besides, it was not possible that the head could remain without any other covering than that of a naked bone, through the extremities of heat and cold in the different seasons; nor, again, could it become the instrument of knowledge when invested with darkness, dulled, and without sensation, through the perturbation of flesh. Hence, a part of a fleshy nature, not entirely dried, and surpassing the residue, was separated from the rest; and which is now denominated a membrane. This membrane passing into union with itself, and blossoming about the moisture of the brain, circularly invests the head. But the moisture flowing under the sutures of the head irrigates this membrane, and, causing it to close together at the crown, connects it, as it were, in a knot. But an all-various species of sutures is generated through the power of the circulations and the nutriment; the variety becoming greater when these oppose each other with greater violence, but less when they are in a state of less opposition. All this membrane the divine artificer of our bodies circularly pierced with fire. And hence, becoming as it were wounded, and the moisture externally flowing through it, whatever is moist, hot, and pure, passes away; but whatever is mingled from the same natures as the membrane itself, this, in consequence of receiving an external production, becomes extended into length, and possesses a tenuity equal to the punctuation of the membrane. But this substance, from the slowness of its motion, being continually thrust back by the externally surrounding spirit, again revolves itself under the membrane, and there fixes the roots of its progression. Hence, from these passions the race of hairs springs up in the membrane of the head, being naturally allied to, and becoming, as it were, the reins of this membrane, at the same time that they are more hard and dense through the compression of cold. For every hair, when it proceeds beyond the membrane, becomes hardened through cold. After this manner, then, the artificer planted our head with hairs, employing for this purpose the causes which we have mentioned.

But at the same time he understood by a dianoëtic energy, that instead of flesh a light covering was necessary for the security of the brain; which might sufficiently shade and protect it like a garment from the extremities of heat and cold, but by no means hinder the acuteness of sensation. But that comprehension of nerve, skin, and bone about the fingers, being a mixture of three substances, and becoming of a drier nature, produced one common hard membrane from the whole. These indeed were the ministrant causes of its fabrication; but the most principal cause consists in that cogitation which produced this membrane for the sake of future advantage. For those artificers of our nature well knew that at some time or other women and other animals would be generated from men; and that nails would be of the greatest advantage in many respects to the bestial tribes. Hence they impressed in men the generation of nails, at the very period of their production. But from this reason, and through these causes, they planted the skin, hairs, and nails in the members situated at the extremities of the body. However, as all the parts and members of a mortal animal were generated in alliance with each other, and necessarily possessed their life in the union of fire and spirit, lest the animal becoming resolved and exhausted by these should swiftly decay, the Gods devised the following remedy: For mingling a nature allied to the human with other forms and senses, they planted, as it were, another animal; such as those mild trees, plants, and seeds, which, being now brought to perfection through the exercise of agriculture, are friendly to our nature; though prior to this they were of a rustic kind, being more ancient than such as are mild. For whatever participates of life we may justly and with the greatest rectitude denominate an animal. But this which we are now speaking of participates the third species of soul, which we place between the præcordia and the navel: and in which there is neither any thing of opinion, reason, or intellect; but to which a pleasant and painful sense, together with desires, belongs. For it continually suffers all things. But when it is converted in itself, about itself, and, rejecting external, employs its own proper motion, it is not allotted by its generation a nature capable of considering its own concerns by any thing like a reasoning energy. On this account it lives, and is not different from an animal; but, becoming stably rooted, abides in a fixed position, through its being deprived of a motion originating from itself.

But when those superior artificers of our composition had implanted all these genera for the purpose of supplying nutriment to our nature, they deduced various channels in our body as in a garden, that it might be irrigated as it were by the accession of flowing moisture. And, in the first place, they cut two occult channels under the concretion of the skin and flesh, *viz.* two veins in the back, according to the double figure of the body on the right hand and the left. These they placed with the spine of the back, so as to receive the prolific marrow in the middle, that it might thus flourish in the most eminent degree; and, by copiously flowing from hence to other parts, might afford an equable irrigation. But after this, cutting the veins about the head, and weaving them with each other in an opposite direction, they separated them; inclining some from the right hand to the left hand parts of the body, and some from the left to the right, that the head, together with the skin, might be bound to the body, as it is not circularly divided with nerves about its summit; and besides this, that the passion of the senses might from each of these parts be deduced on all sides through the whole of the body. In this manner, then, they deduced an aqueduct from hence; the truth of which we shall easily perceive by assenting to the following position. That all such things as are composed from lesser parts are able to contain such as are greater; but such as consist from greater cannot invest those composed from lesser parts. But fire, among all the genera of things, is constituted from the smallest parts. Hence, it penetrates through water, earth, and air, and the composites from these; and this in such a manner, that nothing can restrain its pervading power. The same must be understood of that ventricle our belly; that it is able to retain the intromitted meat and drink, but cannot stay spirit and fire, because these consist of smaller parts than those from which the belly is composed. These, therefore, the Divinity employed for the purpose of producing an irrigation from the belly into the veins; weaving from fire and air a certain flexible substance like a bow-net, and which possesses a twofold gibbosity at the entrance. One of these he again wove together, divided into two parts; and circularly extended these parts from the curvatures like ropes through the whole body, as far as to the extremities of the net. All the interior parts therefore of the net-work he composed from fire; but the gibbosities and the receptacle itself from air. And lastly, receiving these, he disposed them in the animal new formed as follows: In the first place, one of the gibbous parts he assigned to the mouth; but, as the gibbosity of this part is twofold, he caused one part to pass through the arteries into the lungs, but the other along with the arteries into the belly. But having divided the other gibbous part according to each of its parts, he caused it to pass in common to the channels of the nose, so that, when the one part does not reach the mouth, all its streams may be filled from this. But he placed the other cavity of this gibbous substance about the hollow parts of the body; and caused the whole of this at one time to flow together gently into the gibbous parts, as they were of an ærial texture, and at another time to flow back again through the convex receptacles. But he so disposed the net, as being composed from a thin body, that it might inwardly penetrate and again emerge through this substance. Besides this, he ordered that the interior rays of fire should follow in continued succession, the air at the same time passing into each of the parts; and that this should never cease to take place as long as the mortal animal continued to subsist. But, in assigning an appellation to a motion of this kind, we denominate it expiration and respiration. But all this operation and the whole of this passion in our nature take place in the body by a certain irrigation and refrigeration conducive to our nutriment and life. For, when the breath passes inwardly and outwardly, an interior fire

attends it in its course; and being diffused through the belly, when it
meets with solid and liquid aliments, it reduces them to a state of
fluidity; and, distributing them into the smallest parts, educes them as
from a fountain through the avenues of its progression: pouring these
small particles into the channels of the veins, and deducing rivers
through the body as through a valley of veins.

But let us again consider the passion of respiration, and investigate
through what causes it was generated, such as we perceive it at present.
We should consider it, therefore, as follows: As there is no such thing
as a vacuum into which any thing in motion can enter, and as breath
passes from us externally, it is evident to every one that it cannot
proceed into a void space, but must thrust that which is nearest to it
from its proper seat; that again the repulsed nature must always expel its
neighbour; and that from a necessity of this kind every thing which is
impelled into that seat from which the emitted breath is excluded, must,
when it has entered into and filled up this space, attend on the breath
in its progression. And all this must take place like the revolution of a
wheel, through the impossibility of a vacuum. Hence, when the breast
and the lungs externally dismiss the breath, they are again replenished
through the air which surrounds the body entering into and riding
round the avenues of the flesh. But the air being again externally
dismissed, and flowing round the body, impels the respiration inward,
through the passages of the mouth and nostrils.

But we should establish the following as the cause from which the
origin of these was derived. Every animal belonging to the universe
possesses a heat in the veins and the blood, like a certain fountain of
fire; and this heat we compared to a bow-net, extended through the
middle of the body, and wholly woven from fire; all such things as are
external being composed from air. But it must be confessed that heat
naturally proceeds externally into a region to which it is allied. But as
there are two progressions, one according to the body externally, but the
other again according to the mouth and nostrils, hence, when the breath
is impelled inward, it again thrusts back that by which it was impelled.
And that which is drawn back, meeting with fire, becomes heated; while
that which is exhaled becomes refrigerated. In consequence, therefore,
of the heat being changed, and such things as subsist according to the
other transition becoming more hot, and that again which is more fervid
verging to its own nature, - hence, one thing strikes against and repels
another in its course; and as they always suffer and mutually influence
each other in the same manner, leaping this way and that in a circular
progression, they give birth to the expiration and respiration of the

breath. But in this manner also we should investigate the causes of those passions which arise from medical cupping-glasses, from drinking, from things violently hurled, whether upwards or on the ground; together with such sounds as appear swift and slow, sharp and flat, and which are at one time borne along unharmoniously, through the dissimilitude of the motion which they cause within us, and at another time attended with harmony, through the similitude of motion which they produce. For, the motions of such sounds as are prior and swifter ceasing, and proceeding to a nature similar to their own, are comprehended by such as are slower, which now succeed to the swifter, and set them again in motion. But during their comprehension of these they do not disturb them by introducing another motion, but lead on the beginning of the slower lation in conformity to that of the swifter. And these, adapting to themselves a similitude of the ceasing motion, mingle together one passion from the union of sharp and flat. From whence they afford pleasure to the unwise, but joy to the wise, through the imitation of divine harmony subsisting in mortal motions. And, indeed, with respect to all effluxions of water, the falling of thunder, and the wonderful circumstances observed in the attraction of amber, and of the Herculean stone; - in all these, nothing in reality of attraction takes place: but, as a vacuum cannot any where be found, and these particulars mutually impel each other, - hence, from the individuals when separated and mingled together tending to their proper seats, and from these passions being interwoven with each other, such admirable effects present themselves to the view of the accurate investigator. And indeed respiration (from whence our discourse originated) is generated from these causes, and after this manner, as we asserted above. For fire, dividing the aliment and becoming elevated internally, attending at the same time the breath in its ascent, fills the veins from the belly by this joint elevation; and this in consequence of drawing upwards from thence the dissected parts: so that by this means, through the whole body of every animal, the streams of nutriment are abundantly diffused. But the parts which are recently dissected and separated from their kindred natures, some of which are fruits and others grass, and which were produced by Divinity for the nourishment of our bodies, possess all-various colours through their mixture with each other: but for the most part a red colour predominates in them, whose nature is fabricated from a section of fire, and an abstersion in a moist substance. And hence, the colour of that which flows about the body is such as appears to the sight, and which we denominate blood; being the pasture of the

1a   flesh and of the whole body; from whence an irrigation becoming every where diffused, it copiously replenishes all the exhausted parts.

But the manner of impletion and evacuation is produced in the same way as in the universe the lation of every thing takes place, *viz.* from that cause through which every kindred nature tends to itself. For the natures by which we are externally invested perpetually liquefy and distribute our bodies, dismissing every species to its kindred form. But the sanguineous parts, being distributed and comprehended within us,

b   as is the case with every animal constituted under the heavens, are compelled to imitate the local motion of the universe. Each, therefore, of the divided parts within us, being borne along to its kindred nature, replenishes again that which is void. But when the effluxions surpass the accessions, a corruption of the whole animal ensues; and when the contrary takes place, it receives an increase. The recent composition, therefore, of every animal possessing new triangles, like ships formed from timbers unimpaired by age, causes a strong enclosure of them within each other: but the whole of its delicate bulk unites in amicable

c   conjunction, as being generated from most recent marrow, and nourished in milk. These triangles, therefore, from which the liquid and solid aliments are composed, approaching externally, and being received into the animal, as they are more ancient and imbecil than its own proper triangles, are vanquished and cut in pieces by the new triangles: and the animal is rendered of a large size, through its being nourished from a multitude of similar parts. But when it relaxes the root of its triangles, in consequence of becoming wearied and tamed, through many contests with many particulars in a long course of time; then it is no

d   longer able to reduce by section the received aliment into a similitude of itself, but its own parts become easily dissipated by the natures which are externally introduced. Hence the whole animal, becoming by this means vanquished, decays; and the passion itself is denominated old age. But the end of its existence then arrives, when the jointly harmonized bonds of the triangles about the marrow no longer possess a detaining power, but becoming separated through the weariness of labour, desert the bonds of the soul. The soul, however, in this case being concealed in a state according to nature, flies away with pleasure and delight. For every thing contrary to nature is painful; but that which happens naturally is pleasant. Hence, the death which is produced through wounds and disease is painful and violent; but that which is caused from old age, proceeding to an end according to nature, is of all deaths the most free from labour, and is rather accompanied with pleasure than pain.

82a But it must be obvious to every one from whence diseases are produced. For, since there are four genera from which the body is composed, *viz.* earth, fire, water, and air, the unnatural abundance and defect of these, and a translation from their own proper to a foreign seat, in consequence of which each of these does not receive that which is accommodated to its nature, together with all such circumstances as

b these, produce contentions and disease. For, each of these subsisting and being transferred in a manner contrary to nature, such things as were formerly heated become cold, such as were once dry become moist, such as were light heavy, and every thing receives all possible mutations. For we assert that when the same thing approaches to, and departs from, the same, in the same manner, and according to analogy, then alone it permits that which is the same to abide healthy and safe. But that which inordinately wanders, either in acceding or departing, produces all-various mutations, diseases, and infinite corruptions. Likewise a

c second apprehension of diseases may be obtained by any one who is so disposed, from the second compositions of things constituted according to nature. For, since the concretion of marrow, bone, flesh, and nerve, is derived from these, as likewise the blood, though from a different mode of coalition, hence many events happen in the same manner as those we have mentioned above; but the greatest and most severe diseases subsist as follows: When the generation of these second compositions takes place inversely, then they become subject to corruption. For the flesh and nerves are naturally generated from blood: the nerves indeed from fibres, through the alliance subsisting between

d these; but the flesh from the coalition of that which when separated from the fibres passes into a state of concretion. But that substance again which arises from nerves and flesh, being glutinous and fat, increases at the same time by nutrition the flesh, which for the most part subsists about the nature of the bones; and likewise the bone itself, with which the marrow is surrounded. And again, that which trickles through the density of the bones, being the most pure kind of the triangles, and the most smooth and unctuous, while it drops and distils

e from the bones, irrigates the marrow. And hence, when each particular subsists in this manner, a healthy condition of body is produced; but a diseased condition when the contrary is the case. For, when the flesh becoming liquefied again transmits the consumption into the veins, then the blood, together with spirit, becoming abundant and all-various in the veins, diversified with colours and density, and infected with acid and salt qualities, generates all-various bile, corruption, and phlegm. And all these, being again thus generated and corrupted, in the first place destroy

3a   the blood itself; and this, no longer affording nutriment to the body, is every where borne along through the veins, without observing a natural order in its circulations. But these indeed are unfriendly to each other, because they derive no mutual advantages from the properties with which each is endued. They likewise war upon the natural habit of the body, and its perseverance in its proper state, by introducing dissolutions and liquefactions.

A most ancient portion of flesh, therefore, when it is liquefied and rendered difficult of digestion, grows black through ancient burning; but

b   through its being entirely macerated it becomes bitter, and adverse to all the other parts of the body which are not yet infected with corruption. And then indeed the black colour possesses sharpness instead of bitterness; that which was bitter becoming more attenuated: and the bitterness, being again tinged with blood, possesses a redder colour; but, from the black which is mingled with this, becomes of a bilious nature. But, besides this, a yellow colour is mingled with bitterness, when the

c   new flesh liquefies through the fire subsisting about flame. And, indeed, either some physician will assign to all these the common appellation of bile, or some one who is able to consider things many and dissimilar, and to behold one genus in many particulars deserving one denomination. But such other things as are called species of bile receive an appellation peculiar to each, according to colour. But corruption (ιχωρ), which is the defluxion or whey of the blood, is gentle and mild: but that which is the sediment of black and sharp bile is of a ferocious and rustic nature, when it is mingled through heat with a saline power. And a substance of this kind is denominated acid phlegm. But a portion of recent and delicate flesh is often liquefied together with the air, and

d   is afterwards inflated and comprehended by moisture: and from this passion bubbles are produced, which taken separately are invisible on account of their smallness, but which, when collected into a large bulk, become conspicuous, and possess a white colour on account of the generation of froth. And we denominate all this liquefaction of delicate flesh, and which is woven together with spirit, white phlegm. But we

e   call the sediment of recent phlegm tears and sweat; together with every thing of that kind into which the body is every day resolved. And all these, indeed, become the instruments of disease, when the blood does not naturally abound from liquid and solid aliment, but increases from

4a   contraries in such a manner as to violate the laws of nature. When, therefore, any part of the flesh is cut off, but at the same time the foundation of it remains, the calamity possesses but half its power; for it is capable of being easily recovered. But when that which binds the flesh to the bones becomes diseased, and the blood flowing from it and the nerves no longer nourishes the bones and binds the flesh, but, instead of being fat, smooth, and glutinous, becomes rough and salt through bad diet; then, in consequence of suffering all this, and being separated from the bones, it is refrigerated under the flesh and nerves.

b For the flesh, falling from its roots, leaves the nerves bare, and drenched in a salt humour; and hence, gliding again into the circulation of the blood, it increases the number of the diseases we have already described. And these passions, indeed, which subsist about the body, are of a grievous nature: but those which precede these are still more afflictive and troublesome. But this takes place when the bone through the density of the flesh does not admit sufficient respiration, but, being

c heated through filthiness, becomes rotten, receives no nutriment, but falls upon the flesh, which is on the contrary refrigerated; and the flesh again falls on the blood, so that by this means diseases more severe than the former are produced. But the extremity of all maladies then happens, when the nature of the marrow becomes diseased through some defect or excess: for then it produces the most vehement and fatal diseases; as the whole nature of the body is in this case necessarily dissipated and dissolved.

But it is requisite after this to understand that the third species of diseases receives a tripartite division. For one of the divisions is

d produced by spirit, the other by phlegm, and the other by bile. For when the lungs, those distributive guardians of the breath, being obstructed by defluxions, cannot afford a free passage to the breath; then, as there is no emission of the breath in one part, and more is received into another part than is requisite, the parts without refrigeration become rotten; but that which is received in too great abundance passing through the veins, distorts them and liquefies the diaphragm situated in the middle of the body: and thus ten thousand grievous diseases arise from hence, together with an abundance of sweat.

e But often, when the flesh becomes separated within the body, breath is produced; and this being incapable of departing externally, causes the same torments as the breath when entering from without, It produces, however, the greatest pains, when surrounding the nerves and neighbouring veins it inflates them, and stretches and distorts the ligaments and nerves continued from the back. And these diseases, from the stretching and inflating passion, are denominated tensions and contortions from behind; and of which it is difficult to find a cure. For, fevers taking place dissolve these diseases in a most eminent degree. But

85a the white phlegm possessing a difficulty of respiring externally, through the spirit of the bubbles, variegates the body indeed in a milder nature, yet sprinkles it with white spots, and generates other diseases of a similar kind. But when this white phlegm is mingled with black bile, and becomes dissipated about the circulations of the head, which are of a most divine nature, then it disturbs these circulations; and if this happens in sleep, the perturbation is less violent; but if to those who are awake, it cannot without difficulty be expelled. And as this is a disease of a sacred nature, it is most justly denominated a sacred disease.

A sharp and salt phlegm is the fountain of all such diseases as are produced by a defluxion of humours: and because the places into which this phlegm flows possess an omniform variety, it generates all-various diseases. But whatever parts of the body are said to be inflated are thus affected from the inflammation of bile: which, when it expires, produces externally various tumours from its fervid nature; but, when inwardly restrained, generates many inflammatory diseases. It is, however, then greatest, when, being mingled with pure blood, it removes the fibres from their natural order, which are scattered into the blood for this purpose, that it may possess tenuity and density in a commensurate degree; and that it may neither through heat (as it is of a moist nature) flow from the thin body, nor, when becoming more dense, and of consequence more unadapted to motion, may scarcely be able to flow back again through the veins. The fibres, therefore, are very serviceable on this occasion, which if any one should collect together in the blood when dead, and in a state of frigidity, all the remaining blood would become diffused; and when poured forth they would be swiftly coagulated, together with the cold by which they are surrounded. But as the fibres possess this power in the blood, and the bile naturally becomes ancient blood, and is again liquefied from flesh into this, such things as are hot and moist falling gradually the first of all, hence it becomes collected together through the power of the fibres. When the bile is coagulated and violently extinguished, it causes a tempest and tremour within. But when it flows more abundantly, vanquishing the fibres by its own proper heat, and becoming fervid in an inordinate degree, it then preserves the body: and if it retains its conquering power to the end, it penetrates into the marrow; and burning the bonds of the soul, as if they were the cables of a ship, dissolves her union, and dismisses her from thence entirely free. But when it flows with less abundance, and the body becoming liquefied opposes its passage, then finding itself vanquished, it either falls through the whole body, or, being compelled through the veins into the upper or lower belly, like one flying from a seditious city, it escapes from the body and introduced defluxions, dysenteries, or gripings of the intestines, and all diseases of a similar kind. When the body, therefore, is eminently diseased through excess of fire, it then labours under continued burnings and fever; but when through excess of air, under quotidian fevers; under tertian through water, because water is more sluggish than fire and air; under quartan, through excess of earth. For earth, being the most sluggish of all these, is purified in quadruple periods of time; and on this account introduces quartan fevers, which it is scarcely possible to disperse. And in this manner are the diseases of the body produced.

b

But the diseases of the soul, which subsist through the habit of the body, are as follow: - We must admit that the disease of the soul is folly, or a privation of intellect. But there are two kinds of folly; the one madness, the other ignorance. Whatever passion, therefore, introduces either of these must be called a disease. And we should establish excessive pleasures and pains as the greatest diseases of the soul. For, when a man is too much elevated with joy or depressed with grief, while he hastens immoderately either to retain the one or to fly from the other, he is not able either to perceive or hear any thing properly, but is agitated with fury, and is very little capable of exercising the reasoning power. But he who possesses a great quantity of fluid seed about the marrow, and who, like a tree laden with a superabundance of fruit, riots in the excess, - such a one being influenced by many pains and pleasures in desires, and their attendant offspring, will be agitated with fury for the greatest part of his life through mighty pleasures and pains: and though the soul of such a one will be diseased and unwise, from the body with which it is connected, yet it will be falsely considered not as diseased, but as voluntarily bad. But in reality venereal intemperance for the most part becomes a disease of the soul, through a habit of one kind, from the tenuity of the bones, in a body fluid and moist. And, indeed, it may be nearly asserted, that all intemperance of pleasures of whatever kind, and all disgraceful conduct, is not properly blamed as the consequence of voluntary guilt. For no one is voluntarily bad: but he who is depraved becomes so through a certain ill habit of body, and an unskilful education. But these two circumstances are inimical to all, and productive of a certain ill. And again, the soul, when influenced by pain, suffers much depravity from this through the body. For, when sharp and salt phlegm, and likewise bitter and bilious humours, wandering through the body, are prevented from passing forth externally, but, revolving inwardly, mingle their exhalations with the circulation of the soul; in this case they produce all-various diseases of the soul, in a greater and less degree, and less and more numerous.

c

d

e

87a

They are introduced, indeed, to three seats of the soul; and according to the diversity of the place, each generates all-various species of difficulty and sorrow, of boldness and timidity, and, still further, of oblivion and indocility. But, besides this, the vicious manners of cities, and discourses both private and public, often contribute to increase this malady: nor are any disciplines taught in the early part of life, which might serve as remedies for such mighty ills. And thus all such as are vicious are so through two involuntary causes; the existence of which we should always rather ascribe to the planters than to the things planted, and to the educators rather than to the educated. We should, therefore, endeavour to the utmost of our ability, by education, studies, and disciplines, to fly from vice, and acquire its contrary, virtue. But these particulars, indeed, belong to another mode of discourse.

Again, therefore, with respect to the contrary of these, it is now proper to explain in a becoming manner by what culture, and from what causes, we may preserve both the body and dianoëtic energies of the soul. For it is more just to discourse concerning good things than of such as are evil. But every thing good is beautiful; and that which is beautiful is not destitute of measure. An animal, therefore, which is about to be beautiful and good, must possess commensuration. But, perceiving certain small particulars of things commensurate, we syllogize concerning them; while at the same time we are ignorant of such as are greatest and the chief. For, indeed, no symmetry and immoderation is of greater consequence with respect to health and disease, virtue and vice, than that of the soul towards the body. But we consider no circumstance of these; nor do we perceive that when a more imbecil and inferior form is the vehicle of a robust and every way mighty soul, and when, on the contrary, these two pass into a state of concretion, then the whole animal cannot subsist in a beautiful manner: for it is incommensurate through the want of the greatest symmetry. But the animal whose composition is contrary to this, affords a spectacle to him who is able to behold it, of all spectacles the most beautiful and lovely. When the body, therefore, possesses legs immoderately large, or any other member surpassing its just proportion, and becomes through this incommensurate with itself, it is rendered at the same time base, in the endurance of labour suffers many molestations and many convulsions, and through an aggregation of accidents becomes the cause of innumerable maladies to itself. The same too must be understood concerning that composition of body and soul which we denominate an animal. As, for instance, that when the soul in this composite is more robust than the body, and possesses ie raging and transported, then the soul, agitating the whole of it, inwardly fills it with diseases; and, when she vehemently applies herself to certain disciplines, causes it to liquefy and waste away. Lastly, when the soul employs herself in teaching and literary contests, both in public and private, through a certain ambitious strife, then inflaming the body, she dissolves its constitution; and besides this, introducing distillations of humours, she deceives the most part of those who are called physicians, and induces them to consider these effects as proceeding from contrary causes.

b But again, when a mighty body and above measure frigid is conjoined with a small and imbecil dianoëtic part, since there are naturally twofold desires in man, one of aliment through the body, but the other of prudence through the most divine part of our nature; - in this case, the motions of that which is more powerful prevail, and increase that which is their own: but render the dianoëtic part of the soul dull, indocile, and oblivious, and thus produce ignorance, which is the greatest of all diseases. But this one thing alone is the health and safety of both - neither to move the soul without the body, nor the body without the soul; that, being equally balanced in their mutual contentions, the health

c of the whole composite may be preserved. Hence, he who vehemently applies himself to the mathematics, or to any other dianoëtic exercise, should also employ the motion of the body, and be familiar with gymnastic. And again, he who is careful in forming his body aright should at the same time unite with this the motions of the soul, employing music and all philosophy; if he is to be rendered such a one as can be justly called beautiful, and at the same time truly good. In the

d same manner, too, we ought to take care of the parts of the body, imitating the form of the whole. For when the body, through such things as are introduced from without, is inflamed and refrigerated, and is again rendered dry and moist by externals, and suffers every thing consequent to these affections; then, if any one in a quiet state gives up his body to motions, he will be vanquished by them and dissolved. But if any one imitates that nature which we called the nourisher of the universe, so as never to suffer the body to be in a state of rest, but perpetually moves and agitates it throughout, he will then assist the

e internal and external motions according to nature; and, in consequence of a moderate agitation, will reduce into order and adorn the wandering passions and parts of the body, according to their alliance with each other. Such a one, indeed, as we said in our former discourse about the universe, will not, by placing foe against foe, suffer war and disease to be produced in the body; but, combining friend with friend, will thus render the body healthy and sound. But, of all motions, that is the best a in any nature which takes place in itself from itself: for this is particularly allied to the dianoëtic motion of the universe. But that motion is of the worse kind which is produced by another. And that is the worst of all motions, when the body, being in a recumbent and quiet state, is moved by others according to parts. And hence, of all the purgations and concretions of the body, that is the best which subsists through gymnastic. The next to this is that which takes place through easy carriage, whether in a ship or any other convenient vehicle. But the third species of motion is only to be used when vehemently necessary, and at no other time by any one endued with intellect: and this is that medical motion which is performed by pharmaceutical purgations. For diseases, unless they are extremely dangerous, are not to be irritated by medicines. For every composition of diseases is in a certain respect similar to the nature of animals. And indeed the association of the animal nature is allotted stated periods of life; both the whole genus, and every individual, containing in itself a fatal term of living, separate from the passions which necessity produces. For the triangles, which from the very beginning possessed the power of each animal, are sufficiently able to cohere together for a certain time: but life beyond this period cannot be extended to any one. The same mode of composition likewise subsists about diseases; which if any one destroys by medicine before the fated time, he will only produce great diseases from small ones, and many from a few. On this account it is necessary to discipline all such maladies by proper diet, according as every one's leisure will permit; and to avoid irritating by medicines a most difficult disease. And thus much may suffice concerning the common animal and its corporeal part; and how these may be disciplined and governed in such a manner as to produce a life according to reason in the most eminent degree.

But that which is destined to govern, ought much more and by far the first to be furnished as much as possible with such materials as may render it capable of disciplinative sway, in a manner the most beautiful and the best. To discuss accurately indeed particulars of this kind would require a treatise solely confined to such a discussion: but if any one slightly considers this affair in a manner consequent to what has been above delivered, such a one by thus proceeding will not unseasonably arrive at the end of his pursuit. We have often then previously asserted that there are three species of soul within us, triply distributed; and that each has its own proper motions. And we shall now, therefore, briefly affirm, that when any one of them is in a torpid state, and rests from its own proper motions, it necessarily becomes most imbecil; but that, when it is employed in convenient exercises, it becomes most vigorous and robust. We should, therefore, be careful that the several species may preserve their motions, so as to be commensurate to each other.

With respect, however, to the most principal and excellent species of the soul, we should conceive as follows: that Divinity assigned this to each of us as a dæmon; and that it resides in the very summit of the body, elevating us from earth to an alliance with the heavens; as we are not terrestrial plants, but blossoms of heaven. And this indeed is most truly asserted. For, from whence the first generation of the soul arose, from thence a divine nature being suspended from our head and root, directs and governs the whole of our corporeal frame. In him, therefore, who vehemently labours to satisfy the cravings of desire and ambition, all the conceptions of his soul must be necessarily mortal; and himself as much as possible must become entirely mortal, since he leaves nothing unaccomplished which tends to increase his perishable part. But it is necessary that he who is sedulously employed in the acquisition of knowledge, who is anxious to acquire the wisdom of truth, and who employs his most vigorous exertions in this one pursuit; - it is perfectly necessary that such a one, if he touches on the truth, should be endued with wisdom about immortal and divine concerns; and that he should participate of immortality, as far as human nature permits, without leaving any part of it behind. And besides, as such a one always cultivates that which is divine, and has a dæmon most excellently adorned residing in his essence, he must be happy in the most eminent degree. The culture of all the parts is indeed entirely one, and consists in assigning proper nutriment and motion to each. But the motions which are allied to the divine part of our nature are the dianoëtic energies and circulations of the universe. These, therefore, each of us ought to pursue; restoring in such a manner those revolutions in our head (which have been corrupted by our wanderings about generation), through diligently considering the harmonies and circulations of the universe, that the intellective power may become assimilated to the object of intelligence, according to its ancient nature. For, when thus assimilated, we shall obtain the end of the best life proposed by the Gods to men, both at present and in all the future circulations of time. And now that disputation which we announced at the beginning concerning the universe, as far as to the generation of man, has almost received its consummation. For we shall briefly run over the generation of other animals, and this no further than necessity requires: for thus any one may appear to himself to preserve a convenient measure in such a disputation. Let us, therefore, speak concerning these as follows:

a   Those who on becoming men are timid, and pass through life unjustly, will according to assimilative reasoning be changed into women in their second generation. And at the same time through this cause the Gods devised the love of copulation; composing an animal or animated substance, and placing one in us, but another in the female nature. But they produced each in the following manner. That procession of liquid aliment which passes through the lungs under the reins into the bladder, and which being compressed by the breath is emitted externally, - this the Gods receiving, they deduced it after the manner of a pipe into the concrete marrow, through the neck and spine of the back: and this is what we called seed in the former part of our discourse. But this, in consequence of being animated and receiving respiration, produces in the part where it respires a vital desire of effluxion; and thus perfects in us the love of begetting. On this account, that nature which subsists about the privy parts of men, becoming refractory and imperious, and as it were an animal unobedient to reason, endeavours through raging desire to possess absolute sway. In like manner the privities and matrix of women, forming an animal desirous of procreating children, when it remains without fruit beyond the flower of its age, or for a still more extended period, suffers the restraint with difficulty and indignation; and wandering every way through the body, obstructs the passage of the breath, does not permit respiration to take place, introduces other extreme difficulties, and causes all-various diseases; till the desire and love of the parts educe seed like fruit from a tree: but, when educed, they scatter it into the matrix as into a field. Hence women conceive animals invisible at first through their smallness, rude and unformed; when they become large, through dispersion of the seed, nourish them within; and, lastly, leading them into light perfect the generation of animals. In this manner, therefore, is the generation of women and every thing female performed. But the tribe of birds succeeds in the next place, fashioned from men, and receiving wings instead of hairs. These are produced from such men as are indeed innocent, but inconstant and light; who are curious about things situated on high; but are so infatuated as to think, from the testimony of the sight, that demonstrations about things of this kind are the most firm and incontrovertible of all. But the pedestrian and savage tribe of animals was generated from men,† who being

---

† Plato here generating mortal animals through the human soul, after its polity in the heavens, leads it into the pedestrian genus, that he may completely produce man; and after this has acted erroneously, he again leads it into the winged, and into the pedestrian and savage genus, and afterwards into the aquatic.

entirely destitute of philosophy, never elevated their eyes to any object in the heavens; and this because they never employed the circulations in the head, but followed the impulse of those parts of the soul which rule in the belly and breast. Hence from studies of this kind drawing the anterior members and head to the ground, they fix them through proximity of nature in the earth. Besides this, they possess long and all-various heads; as the circulations of each are through idleness compressed and broken: and by this means their race becomes quadruped and multiped; the Divinity assigning many feet to such as are more unwise, that they may be more strongly drawn towards the earth. But the most unwise of these, and every way extending all their body on the earth, as if there was no longer any occasion of feet, the Gods generated without feet, and destined them to creep on the earth. The fourth genus is the aquatic, which was produced from such men as were stupid and ignorant in the most remarkable degree; and whom those transformers of our nature did not think deserving of a pure respiration, on account of their possessing a soul in an unpurified state, through extreme transgression. And hence they impelled them into the turbid and profound respiration of water, instead of the attenuated and pure respiration of air: from whence the genus of fish and oysters, and the multitude of all aquatic animals arose; and who are allotted habitations in the last regions of the universe, as the punishment of extreme ignorance. And thus after this manner, both formerly and now, animals migrate into each other; while they are changed by the loss and acquisition of intellect and folly. Our discourse, therefore, concerning the universe has now obtained its conclusion. For this world, comprehending and receiving its completion from mortal and immortal animals, is thus rendered a visible animal containing visible natures, the image of an intelligible God, sensible, the greatest and best, the most beautiful and perfect; being no other than this one and only-begotten heaven.

92a

b

c

Additional Notes

to

THE TIMÆUS

1. (See page 423, line 21b) The *Apaturia*, according to Proclus and Suidas, were festivals in honour of Bacchus, which were publicly celebrated for the space of three days. And they were assigned this name, δι απατη, that is, on account of the deception through which Neptune is reported to have vanquished Xanthus. The first day of these festivals was called δορπεια, in which, as the name indicates, those of the same tribe feasted together; and hence (says Proclus) on this day ευωχιαι και δειπνα πολλα, splendid banquets and much feasting took place. The second day was called αναρρυσις, *a sacrifice,* because many victims were sacrificed in it; and hence the victims were called αναρρυματα, because ερυομενα ανω εθυετο, *they were drawn upwards,* and *sacrificed.* The third day, of which Plato speaks in this place, was called κουρεωτης, because on this day κουροι, that is, boys or girls, were collected together in tribes, with their hair shorn. And to these some add a fourth day, which they call επιβδα, or *the day after.* Proclus further informs us, that the boys who were collected on the third day were about three or four years old.

2. (See page 430, line 27d) It is well observed here by Proclus, that Plato, after the manner of geometricians, assumes, prior to demonstrations, definitions and hypotheses, through which he frames his demonstrations, and previously delivers the principles of the whole of physiology. For, as the principles of music are different from those of medicine, and those of arithmetic from those of mechanics, in like manner there are certain principles of the whole of physiology, which Plato now delivers: and these are as follow. *True being is that which is apprehended by intelligence in conjunction with reason: that which is generated, is the object of opinion in conjunction with irrational sense: every thing generated is generated from a cause: that which does not subsist from a cause is not generated: that of which the paradigm is eternal being, is necessarily beautiful: that of which the paradigm is generated, is not beautiful: the universe is denominated heaven, or the world.* For from these principles he produces all that follows. Hence, says Proclus, he appears to me to say *what* eternal is, and *what* that which is generated is, but not to say *that* each of them is. For the geometrician also informs us *what* a point is and *what* a line is, prior to his demonstrations, but he by no means teaches us *that* each of these has a subsistence. For how will he act the part of a geometrician, if he discourses about the existence of his proper principles? After the same manner the

physiologist says *what* eternal being is, for the sake of the future demonstrations, but by no means shows *that* it is; since in so doing he would pass beyond the limits of physiology. As, however, Timæus being a Pythagorean differs from other physiologists, and Plato in this dialogue exhibits the highest science, hence he afterwards, in a manner perfectly divine, proves *that* true being has a subsistence; but at present he employs the definition of *what* it is, preserving the limits of physiology. He appears, indeed, to investigate the definition of eternal being, and of that which is generated, that he may discover the causes which give completion to the universe, *viz.* form and matter: for that which is generated requires these. But he assumes the third hypothesis, that he may discover the fabricative cause of the universe; the fourth, because the universe was generated according to a paradigmatic cause; and the fifth concerning the name of the universe, that he may investigate the participation of *The Good* and *the ineffable* by the world.

3. (See page 430, line 27d) *The former of these is, indeed, apprehended by intelligence in conjunction with reason.*

Let us, in the first place, consider how manifold intelligence is, and collect by reasoning its various progressions. The first intelligence, therefore, is intelligible, which passes into the same with the intelligible, and is in no respect different from it. This is essential intelligence and essence itself, because every thing in the intelligible subsists after this manner, *viz.* essentially and intelligibly. The second is that which conjoins intellect with the intelligible, possessing an idiom connective and collective of the extremes, and being life and power; filling, indeed, intellect from the intelligible, in which also it establishes intellect. The third is the conjoined intelligence in a Divine intellect itself, being the energy of intellect, through which it embraces the intelligible which it contains, and according to which it understands and is what it is: for, it is energy and intelligence itself, not indeed intelligible, but intellectual intelligence. The intelligence of partial intellects possesses the fourth order; for each of these contains all things partially, *viz.* intellect, intelligence, the intelligible, through which it is conjoined with wholes, and understands the whole intelligible world. The fifth intelligence is that of the rational soul; for as the rational soul is called intellect, so its knowledge is intelligence, *viz.* a transitive intelligence, with which time is connate. In the sixth place, you may rank, if you please, phantastic knowledge, which is by some denominated intelligence, and the phantasy itself is called a passive intellect, because it knows whatever it knows inwardly, and accompanied with types and figures. For it is common to all intelligence to possess the objects of its knowledge inwardly, and in this it differs from sense. But the highest kind of intelligence is the thing known itself. The second is that which sees the first totally, and is the thing known secondarily. The third is the thing known partially, but perceives wholes through that which is partial. The fourth sees wholes indeed, but partially, and not collectively. And the fifth is a vision accompanied with passivity. Such, therefore, are the diversities of intelligence.

At present, however, neither phantastic intelligence must be assumed; for this is not naturally adapted to know true being, because it is indefinite, and knows the imaginable accompanied with figures. Eternal being, however, is unfigured; and, in short, no irrational knowledge is capable of beholding being itself, since neither is it naturally adapted to perceive universal. Nor does Plato here signify the intelligence in the rational soul; for this does not possess collective vision, and that which is coordinated with eternal natures, but proceeds according to time. Nor yet are total intelligences to be here understood; for these are exempt from our knowledge; but Timæus coordinates intelligence with reason. The intelligence, therefore, of a partial intellect must now be assumed; for it is this in conjunction with which we once saw true being. For as sense is below the rational soul, so intelligence is above it. For a partial intellect is proximately established above our essence, which it also elevates and perfects; and to which we convert ourselves when we are purified through philosophy and conjoin our intellectual power with its intelligence. This partial intellect is participated by all other proximate dæmoniacal souls, and illuminates ours, when we convert ourselves to it, and render our reason intellectual. It is this intellect which Plato in the *Phædrus* calls the governor of the soul, and says that it alone understands true being, which is also perceived in conjunction with this intellect, by the soul which is nourished with intellect and science. In short, as every partial soul is essentially suspended from a certain dæmon, and every dæmon has a dæmoniacal intellect above itself, hence, every partial soul will have this intellect ranked prior to itself as an impartible essence. Of this intellect, therefore, the first participant will be a dæmoniacal soul, but the second, the partial souls under this, which likewise makes them to be partial. It also appears that the intellect immediately above every dæmon, so far as it is a whole and one, is the intellect of the dæmon which proximately participates it, but that it also comprehends the number of the souls which are under it, and the intellectual paradigms of them. Every partial soul, therefore, will have as an indivisible essence its proper paradigm, which this intellect contains, and not simply the whole intellect, in the same manner as the dæmon which is essentially its leader. Hence, the impartible belonging to every partial soul, may be accurately defined to be the idea of that soul, comprehended in the one intellect which is destined to be the leader of the dæmoniacal series, under which every such soul is arranged. And thus it will be true that the intellect of every partial soul is alone supernally established among eternal entities, and that every such soul is a medium between the impartible above it and the partible nature below it. This, then, is the intelligence prior to the soul, and which the soul participates when its intellectual part energizes intellectually. Hence, in the latter part of this dialogue, Plato says, that this intelligence is in the Gods, but that it is participated by a few only of the human race.

It likewise appears that Plato, unfolding the knowledge of eternal being, calls it at first intelligence, but he also conjoins with intelligence reason. For, when reason understands perpetual being, as reason it energizes transitively, but as perceiving intellectually it energizes with simplicity, understands each particular so far as simple at once, but not all things at once, but passing from one to another, at the same time intellectually perceiving every thing which it transitively sees, as one and simple.

In the next place, let us consider what reason is, and how it is connate with intelligence. Reason, therefore, is threefold, doxastic, scientific, and intellectual. For since there are in us opinion, the dianoëtic part, and intellect, which last is the summit of the dianoëtic part, and since the whole of our essence is reason, in each of these parts reason must be differently considered. But neither is opinion naturally adapted to be conjoined with the intelligence of intellect in energy; for, on the contrary, it is conjoined with irrational knowledge, since it only knows *that* a thing is, but is ignorant of *the why*. Nor is the dianoëtic part, so far as it proceeds into multitude and division, capable of recurring to an intellect above the human soul, but on the contrary, it is separated through the variety of its reasons from intellectual impartibility. It remains, therefore, that the summit of the soul, and that which is most characterized by unity in the dianoëtic part, must be established in the intelligence of a partial intellect, being conjoined with it through alliance. This, then, is the reason which understands in us intelligibles, and an energy which Socrates in the *Republic* calls intelligence, in the same manner as he calls the dianoëtic power a knowledge subsisting between intelligibles and objects of opinion. In a subsequent part of this dialogue, Plato says, that this reason, together with science, is ingenerated in the soul when revolving about the intelligible. Science, however, has a more various energy, exploring some things by others; but the energy of intellect is more simple, surveying beings by an immediate projection of its visive power. This highest, therefore, and most indivisible part of our nature, Plato now denominates reason, as unfolding to us intellect and an intelligible essence. For, when the soul abandons phantasy and opinion, together with various and indefinite knowledge, and recurs to its own impartibility, according to which it is rooted in a partial intellect, and when recurring it conjoins its own energy with the intelligence of this intellect, then, together with it, it understands eternal being, its energy being both one and twofold, and sameness and separation subsisting in its intellections. For then the intelligence of the soul becomes more collected, and nearer to eternal natures, that it may apprehend the intelligible together with intellect, and that our reason, like a lesser, may energize in conjunction with a greater, light.

But how is true being comprehended by a partial intellect, or by reason? For true being is superior to all comprehension, and contains in itself all things with an exempt transcendency. In answer to this it may be replied, that intellect possessing its own intelligible, is on this account said to comprehend the whole of an intelligible essence; but reason, through an intellect coordinate to itself receiving conceptions of real beings, is thus through these said to comprehend being. Perhaps, also, it may be said that reason running round the intelligible, and energizing, and being moved as about a centre, thus beholds it; intelligence, indeed, knowing it without transition and impartibly, but reason circularly energizing about its essence, and evolving the united subsistence of all things which it contains.

Let us, in the next place, consider what opinion is. According to Plato, then, the doxastic power comprehends the reasons of sensibles, knows the essence of these, and *that* they are, but is ignorant of the cause of their existence: the dianoëtic power, at the same time, knowing both the essences and the causes of sensibles, but sense having no knowledge of either. For it is clearly shown in the *Theætetus* that sense is ignorant of essence, being perfectly unacquainted with the cause of what it knows. Hence it is necessary that opinion should be ranked in the middle, and that it should know the essences of sensibles through the reasons or productive principles which it contains, but be ignorant of their causes. For in this right opinion differs from science, that it alone knows *that* a thing is, science being able to speculate the cause of its subsistence. Sense follows opinion, and is a medium between the organ of sense and opinion. For the organ of sense apprehends sensibles with passivity; and on this account it is destroyed when they are excessive. But opinion possesses a knowledge unattended with passion. Sense participates in a certain respect of passion, but has also something gnostic, so far as it is established in the doxastic nature, is illuminated by it, and becomes invested with reason, being of itself irrational. In this the series of gnostic powers is terminated, of which intelligence is the leader, being above reason and without transition. But reason has the second order, which is the intelligence of our soul, and transitively passes into contact with intelligibles. Opinion is in the third rank, being a knowledge of sensibles. And the fourth in gradation is sense, which is an irrational knowledge of sensibles. For the dianoëtic power subsisting between intelligence and opinion, is gnostic of middle forms, which require an apprehension more obscure than that of intelligence, and more clear than that of opinion. Hence opinion must be placed next to reason, because it possesses gnostic reasons of essences, but is otherwise irrational, as being ignorant of causes. But sense must be considered as entirely irrational. For, in short, each of the senses knows the passion subsisting about the animal from a sensible nature. Thus, for instance, with respect to an apple, the sight knows that it is red from the passion about the eye; the smell, that it is fragrant from the passion about the nostrils; the taste, that it is sweet; and the touch, that it is smooth. What then is it which says that this thing which thus affects the different senses, is an apple? It is not any one of the partial senses; for each of these knows one particular thing pertaining to the apple, but does not know the whole. Nor yet is this effected by the common sense; for this alone distinguishes the differences of the passions; but does not know that the thing which possesses such an essence is the whole. It is evident, therefore, that there is a certain power better than the senses, which knowing the whole prior to those things which are as it were parts, and beholding the form of this whole, is impartibly connective of these many powers. Plato calls this power opinion; and on this account he denominates that which is sensible, the object of opinion.

Further still, as the senses frequently announce to us things different from what they are in reality, what is it which judges in us, and says, that the sight, when it asserts that the diameter of the sun is no more than a foot in length, is deceived, and that this also is the case with the taste of the diseased, when honey appears to it to be bitter? For it is perfectly evident that in these, and all such like cases, the senses announce their passion, and are not entirely deceived. For they assert the passion which is produced about the instruments of sense, and which is such as they announce it to be; but that which declares the cause, and forms a judgment of the passion, is different. There is therefore a certain power of the soul which is better than sense, and which no longer knows sensibles through an organ, but through itself, and corrects the gross and inaccurate information of sense. This power which subsists as reason with respect to sense, is irrational with respect to the knowledge of true beings; but sense is simply and not relatively irrational. Hence Socrates in the *Republic* shows, that opinion is a medium between knowledge and ignorance. For it is a rational knowledge, but is mingled with irrationality, in consequence of knowing sensibles in conjunction with sense. Sense, however, is irrational alone; in the first place, because it subsists in irrational animals, and is characteristic of every irrational life; and in the second place, because contrary to all the parts of the irrational soul, it is incapable of being persuaded by reason. For the irascible and desiderative parts, submit to reason, are obedient to its commands, and receive from it instruction. But sense, though it should ten thousand times hear reason asserting, that the sun is greater than the earth, would at the same time see it of the dimension of a foot, and would not announce it to us in any other way. In the third place, sense is irrational alone, because it does not know that which it perceives: for it is not naturally adapted to perceive the essence of it. Thus, for instance, it does not know what a white thing is, but it knows that it is white through passion. It is also distributed about the instrument of sense, and on this account therefore is irrational. In the fourth place, this is true of sense, because it is the boundary of all the series of knowledge, possesses an essence most remote from reason and intellect, belongs to things external, and makes its apprehension through body: for all these particulars indicate its irrational nature. Every thing generated, therefore, is apprehended by opinion, in conjunction with sense; the latter announcing the passions, and the former producing from itself the reasons of generated natures, and knowing their essences. And as reason, when in contact with intelligence, sees the intelligible, so opinion, coordinated with sense, knows that which is generated. For the soul being of a middle essence, fills up the medium between intellect and an irrational nature: for by her summit, or the vertex of the dianoëtic part, she is present with intellect, and by her extremity she verges to sense. Hence Timæus, in the former conjunction, ranked intelligence before reason, as being more excellent; but in the second conjunction he places opinion before sense. For there reason is posterior to intelligence, as being a lesser intellect; but here opinion is prior to sense, as being rational sense. Opinion, however, and reason bound the whole extent of the rational essence; but as the great Plotinus says, intellect is our king, and sense our messenger. And reason indeed, together with intellect, sees the intelligible; but by itself it speculates the middle reasons of things. Opinion, together with sense, sees that which is generated; but by itself it considers all the forms which its own essence contains.

4. (See page 430, line 28b) That is denominated generated, says Proclus (in Tim.) which has not the whole of its essence or energy established in one, so as to be perfectly immutable. And of this kind are, this sensible world, time in things moved, and the transitive intellection of souls. But that every motion subsists according to a part, and that the whole of it is not present at once, is evident. And if the essence of the world possesses generation, and the perpetuity of it is according to a temporal infinity, it may be inferred, that between things eternally perpetual, and such as are generated in a part of time, it is necessary that nature should subsist which is generated infinitely. It is also requisite that a nature of this kind should be generated infinitely in a twofold respect, viz. either that the whole of it should be perpetual through the whole of time, but that the parts should subsist in the parts of time, as is the case with the sublunary elements, or that both the whole and the parts of it should be co-extended with the perpetuity of all time, as is the case with the heavenly bodies. For the perpetuity according to eternity is not the same with the perpetuity of the whole of time, as neither is the infinity of eternity and time the same; because eternity is not the same with time, the former being infinite life at once total and full, or, the whole of which is ever present to itself, and the latter being a flowing image of such a life.

Further still, says Proclus, the term generated has a multifarious meaning. For it signifies that which has a temporal beginning, every thing which proceeds from a cause, that which is essentially a composite, and that which is naturally capable of being generated, though it should not be generated. The term generated, therefore, being multifariously predicated, that which is generated according to time possesses all the modes of generation. For it proceeds from a cause, is a composite, and is naturally capable of being generated. Hence, as that which is generated in a part of time begins at one time, and arrives at perfection in another, so the world, which is generated according to the whole of time, is always beginning, and always perfect. And it has indeed a certain beginning of generation, so far as it is perfected by its cause, but has not a certain beginning so far as it has not a beginning of a certain partial time.

5. (See page 430, line 28b - c) *It was generated. For this universe is visible, and has a body, etc.*

As the demiurgus of wholes looking to himself, and always abiding after his accustomed manner, produces the whole world totally, collectively, or at once, and with an eternal sameness of energy, so Timæus being converted to himself, lays down the whole theory, recurring to intellect from the dianoëtic power, and proceeding into reasoning from intellect. Doubting therefore, and interrogating himself, he energizes according to the self-moved nature of the soul; but answering, he imitates the projection of intellect. In the first place, therefore, he comprehends the dogma in one word γεγονεν, *it was generated*, and enunciates the conclusion prior to the demonstration, directly after the manner of those that energize enthusiastically, who perceive the whole collectively, and contract in intellect the end previous to the digression, in consequence of seeing all things at once. But in the second place syllogizing, he descends from intellect to logical evolutions, and an investigation through demonstration of the nature of the world. In a perfectly divine manner, therefore, he indicates from hypotheses the whole form of the universe. For if the world is visible and tangible, and has a body, but that which is visible, tangible, and has a body, is sensible, and that which is sensible, and the object of opinion in conjunction with sense, is generated: the world therefore is generated. And this he shows demonstratively from the definition: since geometricians also use demonstrations of this kind. And thus much concerning the form of these words.

It is however evident that Timæus, in giving a certain generation to the world, establishes it at the same time remote from temporal generation. For if the world has a *certain*, and not *every* principle of generation, but that which is generated from time has the principle of *all* generation, the world is not generated from time. Further still, let us attend to the wonderful hypothesis of Atticus, who says, that what according to Plato was moved in a confused and disordered manner is unbegotten; but that the world was generated from time. Since then Plato admits that there is a cause of generation, let us see what he asserts it to be. For the world is sensible and tangible. Whether therefore was every thing sensible generated from time, or not every thing? For if every thing, that which was moved in a confused and disordered manner was also generated from time: for he says, that this likewise was visible. But if not every thing, the reasoning is unsyllogistic, according to Atticus, and concludes nothing. Unless indeed Atticus should say that the world is visible and tangible, but that what was moved in a confused and disordered manner is not *now* visible, but *was* so prior to the fabrication of the world, since Plato thus speaks, "Every thing which *was* visible, being moved in a confused and disordered manner;" but here he says, "The world *is* visible and tangible, and has a body." Plato therefore shows that every thing which *is* visible and tangible is generated, but not every thing which *was* so. Should Atticus then thus speak, (for the man is skilful is taking up one word in the place of another,) we must say, that in the definition of what is generated, there is nothing of this kind, but it is simply said, that every thing generated is the object of opinion, in conjunction with irrational sense; so that if any thing is perfectly sensible, it will also be generated. But every thing visible is sensible, so that what was moved with confusion and disorder was generated. Nor is it proper to say that it was unbegotten according to time, but that the universe was generated in time; since either both were generated, or both are unbegotten. For both are similarly called visible and generated by Plato. But if both were generated, prior to this the world was changed into disorder: for generation to a contrary is entirely from a contrary. And if the maker of the world is good, how is it possible that he should not harmonize it beautifully; or that having beautifully harmonized it, he should destroy it? But if he was not good, how not being good, did he make it to be orderly and elegantly arranged? For to effect this is the work of a beneficent artificer. But if being visible and generated, it is not generated according to time, it is not necessary immediately to assign to the universe a temporal generation, because it is said to be visible and generated. And thus much in reply to Atticus.

Let us however return to our principles, and inquire whether the world always was, as being eternal, or is not eternal, but consubsistent with time, and whether it is self-subsistent, or produced by another. Such then is the inquiry. The answer to which is, that it was produced by another, and is consubsistent with time. But a thing of this kind is generated. For if it has a composite form, it has generation in consequence of its composition. And if it alone subsists from another cause, it is generated, as not producing itself. And if it is eternal, it has its whole subsistence coextended with time. For it was fabricated with reference to something else, and it was generated as a flowing image of real being. As therefore that which is composite is to that which is simple, and as time is to eternity, so is generation to essence. If then a simple and uniform essence is eternal, an essence composite, multiform, and conjoined with time, is generation. Hence Plato divinely inquires, whether the world originated from a *certain* principle. For that which was *once* generated, originated from a temporal, fabricative, final, material, and formal principle. For principle being predicated multifariously, that which is produced in time originates according to all these modes. But the world originated from a *certain*, and not from *every* principle. What then was this principle? It was not temporal: for that which originates from this, is also allotted the principle of its generation from all the others. It originated indeed from that most leading and proper principle, the final, as Plato himself teaches us in the course of this Dialogue. For it was generated through *The Good*, and this is the principle of generation from which it originated. In the first place, therefore, he shows that the world is generated, from its composition: for it is tangible and visible. These then are the extremities of the universe: for heaven is visible, but earth is tangible; and the visible is in earth, so far as it participates of light, and the tangible in heaven, so far as a terrene nature is comprehended in it according to cause. In short he says that the world has a body, that we may also take into account the middle perfections of the universe. And in this Plato speaks agreeably to the oracle, which says, "The world is an imitation of intellect, but that which is fabricated possesses something of body." So far therefore as the universe has something corporeal, it is generated, for according to this it is both visible and tangible. But every thing visible and tangible is sensible: for *sense is touching and feeling*. But that which is sensible is the object of opinion, as being mingled with dissimilars, and as incapable of preserving the purity of intelligible forms. And every thing of this kind is generated, as having a composite essence. Plato therefore does not subvert the perpetuity of the universe, as some have thought he does, following Aristotelic hypotheses: and that this is true, we may easily learn as follows.

Time, says Plato, was generated together with heaven, or the universe. If therefore time is perpetual, the universe also is perpetual. But if time has a temporal beginning, the universe also has a temporal beginning; though it is of all things most absurd that time should have a beginning. But the advocates for the temporal origin of the world say, that time is twofold, one kind being disordered, and the other proceeding according to number; since motion is twofold, one disordered and confused, and the other orderly and elegant; and time is coordinate with each of these motions. But it is possible indeed for body to be moved equably or unequably, but impossible to conceive time equable and unequable: for thus the essence of time would be a composite. Though, indeed, why do I thus speak? for when motion is unequable, time is equable. Now, therefore, there are also many motions, some more swift, and others more slow, and one of which is more equable than another, but of all of them there is one continued time, proceeding according to number. Hence it is not right to make this twofold time. But if time is one and continued, if it is unbegotten, the universe also is unbegotten, which is consubsistent with time. But if time is generated, an absurdity will ensue; for time will require time in order to its being generated, and this when it has not yet a being; since when time was generated, time was not yet.

Further still, Plato conjoins the soul of the universe, immediately on its generation with the body of the universe, and does not give to it a life prior to that of the corporeal nature. Soul however ranks, according to him, among perpetual beings. If therefore soul is consubsistent with body, but soul has a perpetual subsistence, body also is perpetual according to Plato: for that which is consubsistent with a perpetual nature is unbegotten.

Again, Timæus here says, that the soul is generated, but Socrates in the *Phædrus* says, that it is unbegotten. Hence he calls that which is clearly unbegotten according to time, after another manner begotten. Again, Plato calls the world incorruptible, in the same manner as those who contend that it was generated in time. But in the *Republic* he clearly asserts, or rather the Muses and not Plato, that every thing which is generated according to time is corruptible. But from these things you may understand what I say: for the world is shown by them to be unbegotten. For if the world is incorruptible, but nothing generated according to time is incorruptible, the world is not generated according to time. But why is a syllogism of this kind necessary, since Plato clearly says in the *Laws*, that time is infinite according to the past, and that in this infinity myriads on myriads of fertile and barren periods of mankind have taken place? Or rather, that we may reason from what we have at hand, Plato a little before, in this very dialogue, says, "that in those places where neither intense cold nor immoderate heat prevails, the race of mankind is *always* preserved, though sometimes the number of individuals is increased, and sometimes suffers a considerable diminution. But if the race of mankind *always* is, the universe also must necessarily be perpetual.

Again, therefore, if the demiurgus of the universe ranks among eternal beings, he does not at one time fabricate, and at another not; for he would not possess a sameness of subsistence, nor an immutable nature. But if he always fabricates, that which he produces always is. For what could be his intention, after having been indolent for an infinite time, in converting himself to fabrication? Shall we say that he apprehended it was better so to do? Was he then ignorant before that this was better or not? For if he was ignorant, he will, though a pure and divine intellect, be deprived of knowledge, which is absurd to suppose. But if he knew that it was better, why did he not before begin to generate and make the world? In another respect also, those appear to me to sin against the demiurgus of the universe, who say that the world once was not. For if the world once had no existence, the demiurgus once did not make it: since that which is made and the maker subsist together. But if he once did not make, he was then a maker in capacity; and if in capacity, he was then imperfect, and afterwards perfect, when he made the world. If, however, prior and posterior subsist about him, it is evident that he does not rank among beings who eternally energize, but among those that energize according to time, passing from not making to making. However, he produces time. How therefore, possessing an energy indigent of time, did he through this energy produce time? For he once made time, of which notwithstanding he is in want, in order that he may make time.

How therefore may the world be said to be generated? We reply, as that which always is to be generated, and always will be generated. For a partial body not only *is* to be generated, but there was a time when it *was* generated. But all heaven, or the universe, alone subsists in the being to be generated, or in becoming to be, and is not at the same time that which was generated. For as the solar light proceeds from its proper fountain, so the world is always generated, and always produced, and is as it were always advancing into being.

6. (See page 430, line 28c) *To discover therefore the Artificer and Father of this Universe, etc.*

Father and artificer differ with respect to each other, so far as the former is the cause of being, and the supplier of union, but the latter of powers, and a multiform essence; and so far as the former stably comprehends all things in himself, but the latter is the cause of progression and generation; and so far as the former signifies ineffable and divine Providence, but the latter a copious communication of reasons or productive principles. But *this universe* signifies corporeal masses, the whole spheres, and those things which give completion to each. It also signifies the vital and intellectual powers which are carried in the corporeal masses. It likewise comprehends all mundane causes, and the whole divinity of the world, about which the number of mundane gods proceeds. The one intellect, divine soul, and whole bulk of the universe, and its conjoined, divine, intellectual, psychical, and corporeal number, since every monad has a multitude coordinate with itself, are also to be assumed in the place of the world. For the universe signifies all these. Perhaps too the addition of *this* is significant of the world being in a certain respect sensible and partial. For the whole of an intelligible nature cannot be denominated *this*, because it comprehends all intellectual forms. But to the visible universe the particle τοδε, or *this*, is adapted, in consequence of its being allotted a sensible and material nature. It is difficult therefore, as he says, to find the artificer of this universe. For since, with respect to invention, one kind proceeds from things first according to science, but another from things secondary according to reminiscence, invention from things first may be said to be difficult, because the discovery of the powers which are situated between, is the province of the highest theory, but that from things secondary is still more difficult. For, in order to behold from these the essence of the demiurgus, and the powers which he contains, it is necessary to survey the whole nature of his productions. We must therefore behold all the apparent parts of the world, and its unapparent powers, according to which the sympathy and antipathy of the parts in the universe subsist; and prior to these stable physical reasons and natures themselves, both the more partial and the more total, material and immaterial, divine and dæmoniacal, and those of mortal animals. And further still, we must survey the genera of life, the eternal and the mortal, the undefiled and the material, the total and the partial, the rational and the irrational, and all the completions pertaining to essences more excellent than ours, through which every thing between the gods and a mortal nature is bound together. We must also be able to perceive all various souls, and different numbers of gods, according to different parts of the universe, together with the ineffable and effable impressions of the world, through which it is conjoined with the father. For he who, without surveying these, attempts the vision of the demiurgus, will, through imperfection, be deprived of the intellectual perception of the father of the universe. But it is not lawful for any thing imperfect to be united with that which is all perfect. It is necessary, indeed, that the soul becoming an intellectual world, and assimilated in her power to the whole and intelligible world, should approach near to the maker of the universe, and through this approximation become familiar with him, through continuity of intellectual projection. For an uninterrupted energy about any thing calls forth and resuscitates our essential reasons. But through this familiarity the soul, being stationed at the gate of the father, will become united with him. For the discovery of him is this, to meet with him, to be united with him, to associate alone with the alone, and to see him with immediate vision, the soul for this purpose withdrawing herself from every other energy. The discovery therefore of the father of the universe is such as this, and not that which is effected by opinion; for such a discovery is dubious, and not very remote from the irrational life. Nor yet is it scientific; for this is syllogistic and composite, and does not come into contact with the intellectual essence of the intellectual demiurgus. But the discovery of which Plato now speaks subsists according to immediate visive projection (κατα την επιβολην την αυτοπτικην), a contact with the intelligible, and an union with the demiurgic intellect. For this may be properly denominated difficult, whether as laborious, and appearing to souls after all the journey of life,[†] or as the true labour of souls. For after the wandering of generation and purification from its stains, and after the light of science, intellectual energy, and the intellect which is in us, will shine forth, establishing as in a port the soul in the father of the universe, purely seating her in demiurgic intellections, and conjoining light with light, not such as that of science, but more beautiful, intellectual, and uniform than this. For this is the paternal port, and the discovery of the father, *viz.* an undefiled union with him.

But when Plato says, "it is impossible to reveal him through the ministry of discourse to all men," it perhaps indicates the custom of the Pythagoreans, who preserved in secrecy assertions respecting divine natures, and did not speak concerning them to the multitude. For, as the Elean guest in the *Sophista* says, "The eyes of the multitude are not sufficiently strong to look to truth." This also, which is a much more venerable assertion, may perhaps be said, that it is impossible for him who has discovered the father of the universe, to speak of him, such as he has seen him. For this discovery was not effected by the soul speaking, but by her being initiated in divine mysteries, and converting herself to the divine light; nor was it in consequence of her being moved according to her proper motion, but from her becoming silent, according to that silence which leads the way. For since the essence of other things is not naturally adapted to be enunciated through names, or through definition, or even through science, but by intelligence alone, as Plato says in his seventh Epistle, after what other manner is it possible to discover the essence of the demiurgus than intellectually? Or how, having thus discovered him, can that which is seen be told through nouns and verbs, and communicated to others? For a discursive energy, since it is attended with composition, is incapable of representing a uniform and simple nature. But here some one may say, Do we not assert many things concerning the demiurgus, and other gods, and concerning *The One* itself, the principle of all things? We reply that we speak *concerning* them, but we do not speak the αυτο, or *the very thing itself*, which each of them is. And we are able indeed to speak of them *scientifically*, but not

---

[†] And this is what Homer divinely insinuates in the Fable of Ulysses.

intellectually: for this, as we have said before, is to discover them. But if the discovery is a silent energy of the soul, how can speech flowing through the mouth be sufficient to lead into light that which is discovered, such as it truly is?

After this, Proclus, following, as he says, the light of science, investigates who the demiurgus of the universe is, and in what order of things he ranks. For Numenius the Pythagorean (says he), celebrating three gods, calls the first *father*, the second *maker*, and the third *work* or *effect* (ποιημα), for the world, according to him, is the third god; so that with Numenius there is a two-fold demiurgus, *viz.* the first and second god, but that which is fabricated is the third divinity. Numenius, however, in thus speaking, in the first place, does not act rightly in connumerating *The Good* with these causes. For *The Good*, or the supreme principle of things, is not naturally adapted to be conjoined with certain things, nor to possess an order secondary to any thing. But with Plato *father* is here ranked after *artificer*. Further still, he coarranges that which is exempt from all habitude, *viz.* the ineffable cause of all, with the natures under, and posterior to, him. But these things ought to be referred to subordinate natures, and all habitude should be taken away from that which is first. That which is paternal therefore in the universe cannot be adapted to the first principle of things. And, in the third place, it is not right to divide father and artificer, since Plato celebrates one and the same divinity by both these names. For one divine fabrication, and one fabricator and father, are every where delivered by Plato.

With respect to Harpocration, it would be wonderful if he were consistent with himself in what he says concerning the demiurgus. For this man makes the demiurgus two-fold, and calls the first god Heaven and Saturn, the second Jupiter and Zena, and the third Heaven and the World. Again, therefore, transferring the first god into another order, he calls him Jupiter, and the king of the intelligible world; but he calls the second, the Ruler; and the same divinity according to him is Jupiter, Saturn, and Heaven. The first god therefore is all these, though Plato in the *Parmenides* takes away from *The One*, or the first god, every name, all discourse, and every habitude. We indeed to not think it proper to call the first even father; but with Harpocration the first is father, son, and grandson.

Again Atticus, the preceptor of Harpocration, directly makes the demiurgus to be the same with *The Good*, though the demiurgus is called by Plato *good* (αγαθος), but not *The Good* (ταγαθον). The demiurgus is also denominated by Plato *intellect*; but *The Good* is the cause of all essence, and is beyond being, as we learn from the 6th book of the *Republic*. But what will he say respecting the paradigm, to which the demiurgus looks in fabricating the world? For it is either prior to the demiurgus, and so according to Atticus there will be something more ancient than *The Good*, which it is not lawful to assert, will be converted to things posterior to itself, and will intellectually apprehend them.

After these men, Plotinus the philosopher places a two-fold demiurgus, one in the intelligible world, and the other the governor of the universe. And he says rightly: for in a certain respect the mundane intellect is the demiurgus of the universe. But the father and artificer, whom he places in the intelligible, is transcendently the demiurgus; Plotinus calling every thing between *The One* and the world intelligible: for there, according to him, the true heaven, the kingdom of Saturn, and the intellect of Jupiter, subsist. Just as if any one should say that the sphere of Saturn, that of Jupiter, and that of Mars, are contained in the heavens: for the whole of an intelligible essence is one many, and is one intellect comprehending many intelligibles. And such is the doctrine of Plotinus. In the next place, Amelius (the disciple of Plotinus) makes a triple demiurgus, three intellects, and three kings, one that *is*, the second that *hath*, and the third that *sees*. But these differ, because the first intellect is truly that which is; but the second is indeed the intelligible which it contains, yet has that which is prior to itself, participates entirely of it, and on this account is the second. And the third is indeed likewise the intelligible which it contains; for every intellect is the same with its conjoined intelligible; but it contains that which is in the second, and sees the first: for that which it possesses is obscure in proportion to its distance from the first. According to Amelius, therefore, these three intellects and artificers are the same as the three kings with Plato, and as Phanes, Heaven, and Saturn, with Orpheus; and that which is especially the demiurgus according to him is Phanes. To Amelius, however, it is proper to say, that Plato is every where accustomed to recur from multitude to the unities from which the order in the many proceeds; or rather prior to Plato, from the very order of things themselves, *the one* is always prior to *multitude*, and every divine order begins from a monad. For it is indeed requisite that a divine number should proceed from a triad,[†] but prior to the triad is the monad. Where therefore is the demiurgic monad, that there may be a triad from it? And how is the world one, not being fabricated by one cause? For it is requisite by a much greater priority that the cause of the world should be united and be monadic, that the world may become only-begotten. Let there then be three artificers; but who is the one prior to the three; looking indeed

---

[†] As all things abide in their causes, proceed from them and return to them, as is demonstrated by Proclus in his *Elements of Theology* [TTS vol. I], this must also be true of the immediate and first procession from the highest god. The first offspring, therefore, from the ineffable principle of things will be an all-perfect triad, the leader of a divine number; and in like manner every divine number will proceed from a triad, and this from a monad: for there is no number prior to three, unity being the principle of number, and the duad partaking of the nature of both unity and number. This will be evident from considering that it is the property of number to receive a greater increase from multiplication than addition, *viz.* when multiplied into itself; but unity is increased by being added to, but not by being multiplied by itself, and two in consequence of its middle nature produces the same when added to, as when multiplied by itself. See the Introduction to the *Parmenides*.

to one paradigm, but making the world only-begotten? It is not proper, therefore, that the demiurgic number should begin from a triad but from a monad.

After Amelius, Porphyry, thinking to accord with Plato, calls the supermundane soul the demiurgus, and the intellect of this soul to which he is converted, animal itself, as being according to him the paradigm of the demiurgus. It is requisite, therefore, to inquire of Porphyry, in which of his writings Plotinus makes soul to be the demiurgus, and how this accords with Plato, who continually denominates the demiurgus a god and intellect, but never calls him soul? How likewise does Plato call the world a god? And how does the demiurgus pervade through all mundane natures? For all things do not participate of soul; but all things partake of demiurgic providence. And divine fabrication indeed is able to generate intellect and gods; but soul is not naturally adapted to produce any thing above the order pertaining to soul. I omit to observe that it is by no means certain that Plato knew any imparticipable soul.

To Porphyry succeeds the divine Iamblichus, who having written largely against the opinion of Porphyry, and subverting it as being Plotinean, delivers to us his own theology, and calls all the intelligible world the demiurgus. If therefore he means that all things subsist demiurgically in the demiurgus, both being itself, and the intelligible world, he accords with himself, and also with Orpheus, who says,

> All that exists in confluent order lies
> Within the belly of the mighty Jove.

Nor is it in any respect wonderful that each of the gods should be the universe, but at the same time each differently from the rest; one demiurgically, another according to connecting comprehension (συνοχικως), another immutably, and another in a still different manner according to a divine idiom. But if Iamblichus means that the whole extent between the world and *The One* is the demiurgus, this indeed is worthy of doubt, and we may reply to the assertion from what he himself has taught us. For where are the kings prior to Jupiter, who are the fathers of Jupiter? Where are the kings mentioned by Plato, whom Iamblichus arranges above the world, and about *The One*? And how can we say that eternal being itself is the first being, but that the demiurgus is the whole intelligible order, who is himself also eternal being as well as animal itself? For shall we not thus be compelled to say that the demiurgus is not eternal being; unless so far as he also is comprehended together with other eternal beings? But that Iamblichus himself, though most prolific in these things, has in some of his other writings more accurately celebrated the demiurgic order, may be inferred from this, that in speaking concerning the fabrication of Jupiter in the *Timæus*, after the intelligible triads, and the three triads of gods in the intellectual hebdomad, he assigns the third order in these processions to the demiurgus. For he says that these three gods are also celebrated by the Pythagoreans, who denominate the first of these intellects, and which comprehends in itself total monads, simple, indivisible, boniform, abiding in and united with itself, and consider it as possessing such like signs of transcendency. But they say that the most beautiful signs of the middle intellect, and which collects together the completion of such like natures, are that which is prolific in the gods, that which congregates the three intellects, replenishes energy, is generative of divine life, and is the source of progression and beneficence to every thing. And they inform us that the most illustrious tokens of the third intellect, which fabricates wholes, are prolific progressions, fabrications and connected comprehensions of total causes, whole causes bounded in forms, and which emit from themselves all fabrications, and other prerogatives similar to these. It is proper, therefore, to judge from these assertions, what the Iamblichean theology is concerning the demiurgus of wholes.

After him Theodorus,[†] following Amelius, says, that there are three artificers; but he does not arrange them immediately after *The One*, but at the extremity of the intelligible and intellectual gods. He likewise calls one of these essential intellect, another intellectual essence, and another the fountain of souls; and says that the first is indivisible, the second is distributed into wholes, and that the third has made a distribution into particulars. Again, therefore, we may say the same things to him as we said to the noble Amelius, that we acknowledge these to be three gods, or analogous to these, but not also three artificers; but we say that one of these is the intelligible of the demiurgus, the second his generative power, and the third that which is truly demiurgic intellect. But it is requisite to consider whether the fountain of souls is to be arranged as the third: for power belongs to the middle, as he also says, and hence the fountain of souls should be partially, and not universally, denominated the fountain of life. For the fountain of souls is only one of the fountains in this middle; since life is not in souls only, nor in animated natures alone, but there is also divine and intellectual life prior to that of the soul, which they say, proceeding from this middle, emits a diversity of life from distributed channels. Such then, in short, are the dogmas of ancient interpreters respecting the demiurgus.

Let us now, therefore, briefly relate the conceptions of our preceptor on this subject, and which we think accord in a very eminent degree with those of Plato. The demiurgus, therefore, according to him, possesses the extremity[‡] of the intellectual divine monads, and the fountains of life, emitting from himself total fabrication, and imparting dominion to the more partial fathers

---

[†] Theodorus, as well as Iamblichus, was the disciple of Porphyry.

[‡] There are three divine orders, which according to ancient theologists are said to comprehend the total orders of the gods, *viz.* the intelligible, (the immediate progeny of the ineffable principle of things,) the intelligible and at the same time intellectual, and the intellectual order. The demiurgus of the universe subsists at the extremity of this last.

of wholes. He is likewise immovable, being eternally established on the summit of Olympus, and ruling over two-fold worlds, the supercelestial and celestial, and comprehending the beginning, middle, and end of all things. For of every demiurgic distribution, one kind is of wholes with a total subsistence, another of wholes with a partial subsistence, another of parts with a total,[†] and another of parts with a partial subsistence. But fabrication being fourfold, the demiurgic monad binds in itself the total providence of wholes, but a demiurgic triad is suspended from it which governs parts totally, and distributes the power of the monad;[‡] just as in the other, or partial fabrication, a monad is the leader of a triad which orderly distributes wholes partially, and parts partially. But all the multitude of the triad revolves round the monad, is distributed about it, divides its fabrications, and is filled from it. If these things then are rightly asserted, the demiurgus of wholes is the boundary of the intellectual gods, being established indeed in the intelligible, but full of power, according to which he produces wholes, and converts all things to himself. Hence Timæus calls him *intellect*, and *the best of causes*, and say *that he looks to* an intelligible paradigm, that by this he may separate him from the first intelligible gods; but by calling him *intellect*, he places him in an order different from that of the gods, who are both intelligible and intellectual: and by the appellation of *the best of causes*, he establishes him above all other supermundane fabricators. He is, therefore, an intellectual god exempt from all other fabricators. But if he was the first deity[§] in the intellectual order, he would possess a permanent characteristic, abiding after his accustomed mode: for this is the illustrious prerogative of the first intellectual god. If he was the second deity[*] of this order he would be particularly the cause of life; but now in generating soul, he energizes indeed together with the crater, but is essentially intellect. He is therefore no other than the third[°] of the intellectual fathers: for his peculiar work is the production of intellect, and not the fabrication of body. For he makes body, yet not alone, but in conjunction with necessity; but he makes intellect through himself. Nor is it his peculiar work to produce soul: for he generates soul together with the crater; but he alone both gives subsistence to and causes intellect to preside over the universe. As he is therefore the maker of intellect, he very properly has also an intellectual order. Hence he is called by Plato, *fabricator and father*; and is neither father alone,

[†] There is wanting here in the original το δε των μερων ολικως.

[‡] Τριαδος is erroneously printed in the original instead of μοναδος.

[§] *Viz.* Saturn.

[*] *Viz.* Rhea.

[°] *Viz.* Jupiter.

nor fabricator alone, nor again, father and fabricator. For the extremes are father[†] and fabricator; the former possessing the summit of intelligibles, and subsisting prior to the royal series, and the latter subsisting at the extremity of the order; and the one being the monad of paternal deity, and the other being allotted a fabricative power in the universe. But between both these are, father and at the same time artificer, and artificer and at the same time father. For each of these is not the same; but in the one the paternal, and in the other the fabricative has dominion; and the paternal is better than the fabricative. Hence the first of the two media is more characterized by *father*; for, according to the Oracle, "he is the boundary of the paternal profundity, and the fountain of intellectual natures." But the second of the media is more characterized by *cator*: for he is the monad of total fabrication. Whence also I think that the former is called *Metis* (μητις) but the latter *Metietes* (μητιετης); and the former is seen, but the latter sees. The former also is swallowed up, but the latter is satiated with the power of the former; and what the former is in intelligibles, that the latter is in intellectuals; for the one is the boundary of the intelligible, and the other of the intellectual gods. Likewise concerning the former Orpheus says, "The father made these things in a dark cavern;" but concerning the latter, Plato says, "Of whom I am the demiurgus and father." And in his *Politicus* he reminds us of the doctrine of the demiurgus and father; because the former of these divinities is more characterized by the paternal, and the latter by the demiurgic peculiarity. But every god is denominated from his idiom, though at the same time he comprehends all things. And the divinity indeed, who is alone *the maker* or artificer, is the cause of mundane natures; but he who is both *artificer* and *father* is the cause of supermundane and mundane natures. He who is *father* and *artificer* is the cause of intellectual, supermundane, and mundane natures; and he who is *father* alone is the cause of things intelligible, intellectual, supermundane and mundane. Plato, therefore, thus representing the demiurgus, leaves him ineffable and without a name, as subsisting prior to wholes, in the allotment of *The Good*. For in every order of gods there is that which is analogous to *The One*; and of this kind is the monad in every world. But Orpheus also gives him a name as being thence moved; and in this he is followed by Plato in other parts of his writings: for the Jupiter with him, who is prior to the three sons of Saturn, is the demiurgus of universe.

After the absorption, therefore, of Phanes, the ideas of all things appeared in Jupiter, as the theologist (Orpheus) says:[‡]

Hence with the universe great Jove contains

[†]   Being itself, or the summit of the intelligible order, is called *father* alone; Phanes, or the extremity of the intelligible order, is called *father and artificer*; Jupiter, or the extremity of the intellectual order, is called *artificer and father*; and Vulcan, who is the fabricator of a corporeal nature, is called *artificer* alone.

[‡]   See TTS vol. V, p. 56 ff.

> Heav'n's splendid height, and æther's ample plains;
> The barren sea, wide-bosom'd earth renown'd,
> Ocean immense, and Tartarus profound;
> Fountains and rivers, and the boundless main,
> With all that nature's ample realms contain;
> And gods and goddesses of each degree,
> All that is past, and all that e'er shall be;
> Occultly, and in confluent order lie
> In Jove's vast womb, the ruler of the sky.

But being full of ideas, through these he comprehends wholes in himself, which also the theologist indicating, adds,

> Jove is the first and last, high thund'ring king;
> Middle and head, and all things spring from Jove.
> King Jove the root of earth and heav'n contains:
> One power, one dæmon is the source of all.
> For in Jove's royal body all things lie,
> Fire, earth, and water, æther, night, and day.

Jupiter, therefore, comprehending wholes, at the same time gives subsistence to all things in conjunction with Night. Hence to Jupiter thus inquiring,

> Tell me how all things will as one subsist,
> Yet each its nature separate preserve?

Night replies,

> All things receive enclos'd on ev'ry side,
> In æther's wide ineffable embrace:
> Then in the midst of æther place the heav'n,
> In which let earth of infinite extent,
> The sea, and stars, the crown of heav'n, be fixt.

And Jupiter is instructed by Night in all the subsequent mundane fabrication: but after she has laid down rules respecting all other productions, she adds,

> But when around the whole your pow'r has spread
> A strong coercive bond, a golden chain
> Suspend from æther.

viz. a chain perfectly strong and indissoluble, proceeding from nature, soul and intellect. For being bound, says Plato, with animated bonds, they became animals,

> .... the golden chain suspend from æther.

The divine orders above the world[†] being denominated Homerically a golden chain. And Plato, emulating Homer, says in this dialogue, "that the demiurgus *binding* intellect in soul, and soul in body, fabricated the universe, and that he gave subsistence to the junior gods, through whom also he adorns the parts of the world." If therefore it is Jupiter who possesses one power, who swallows Phanes in whom the intelligible causes of wholes primarily subsist, who produces all things according to the admonitions of Night, and who confers dominion both on other gods and the three sons of Saturn, he it is who is the one and whole demiurgus of the universe, possessing the fifth order among those gods that rank as kings, as is divinely shown by our preceptor in his Orphic conferences, and who is coordinate with Heaven and Phanes; and on this account he is artificer and father, and each of these totally.

But that Plato also has these conceptions concerning the mighty Jupiter is evident from the appellations which he gives him in the *Cratylus*, evincing that he is the cause and the supplier of life to all things: for, says he, that through which life is imparted to all things is denominated by us δια and ζηνα. But in the *Gorgias*, he coordinates him with the sons of Saturn, and at the same time gives him a subsistence exempt from them, that he may be prior to the three, and may be participated by them, and establishes Law together with him, in the same manner as Orpheus. For, from the admonitions of Night, according to Orpheus, Law is made the assessor of Jupiter, and is established together with him. Further still, Plato in his *Laws*, conformably to the theologist, represents total Justice as the associate of Jupiter: and in the *Philebus* he evinces that a royal soul and a royal intellect presubsist in Jupiter according to the reason of cause; agreeably to which he now also describes him as giving subsistence to intellect and soul, as unfolding the laws of fate, and producing all the orders of mundane gods and animals, as far as to the last of things; generating some of these by himself alone, and others through the celestial gods as media. In the *Politicus* also he calls Jupiter the demiurgus and father of the universe, in the same manner as in this dialogue, and says that the present order of the world is under Jupiter, and that the world is governed according to fate. The world, therefore, living a life under the dominion of Jupiter, has Jupiter for the demiurgus and father of its life. The divine poet Homer likewise represents him fabricating on the summit of Olympus, ("Hear me, all ye gods and goddesses!") and converting the two-fold coordinations of divinities to himself. Through the whole of his poetry, too, he calls him the supreme of rulers, and the father of men and gods, and celebrates him with all demiurgic conceptions. Since, therefore, according to all the Grecian theology, the fabrication of the universe is ascribed to Jupiter, what ought we to think respecting these words of Plato? Is it not that the deity which is celebrated by him as artificer and father is the sovereign Jupiter, and that he is neither father alone, nor father

---

[†]   Instead of των θειων πραξεων υπο των εγκοσμιων, as in the original, it is necessary to read as in our translation των θειων ταξεων υπερ των εγκοσμιων.

and artificer? For the father was the monad, as the Pythagoreans say: but he is this very order of gods, the decad, at which number proceeding from the retreats of the monad arrives, this being a universal recipient, venerable, circularly investing all things with bound, immutable, unwearied, and which they call the sacred decad. After the paternal monad, therefore, and the paternal and at the same time fabricative tetrad, the demiurgic decad proceeds; being *immutable* indeed, because *immutable deity* is consubsistent with it, but *investing all things with bound*, as being the supplier of order to things disordered, and of ornament to things unadorned, and illuminating souls with intellect, as being itself intellect totally; body with soul, as possessing and comprehending the cause of soul; and producing things which are truly generated as middle and last, in consequence of containing in itself demiurgic being.

7. (See page 431, line 29b) That which Plato now calls *stable* and *firm*, he before called eternal being, subsisting after the same manner, and apprehended by intelligence; denominating it *stable* instead of *eternal being*, and *intellectually apparent*, instead of *that which is apprehended by intelligence*. He also says, that the reasonings about it should be *stable* indeed, that through the sameness of the appellation he may indicate the similitude of them to things themselves; but *immutable*, that they may shadow forth the firmness of the thing; and *irreprehensible*, that they may imitate that which is apprehended by intelligence, and may scientifically accede. For it is necessary that reasonings, if they are to be adapted to intelligibles, should possess the accurate and the stable, as being conversant with things of this kind. For, as the knowledge of things eternal is immutable, so also is the *reasoning*; since it is evolved knowledge. However, as it proceeds into multitude, is allotted a composite nature, and on this account falls short of the union and impartibility of the thing, he calls the former in the singular number *stable* and *firm*, and *intellectually apparent*, but the latter in the plural number stable, immutable and irreprehensible *reasons*. And since in *reason* there is a certain similitude to its paradigm, and there is also a certain dissimilitude, and the latter is more abundant than the former, he employs one appellation in *common*, *the stable*; but the other epithets are different. And as, with respect to our knowledge, scientific reasoning cannot be confuted by it, (for there is nothing in us better than science,) but is confuted by the thing itself, as not being able to comprehend its nature such as it is, and as it comes into contact with its impartibility, hence he adds, *as much as possible*. For science itself considered as subsisting in souls is irreprehensible, but is reprehended by intellect, because it evolves the impartible, and apprehends the simple in a composite manner. Since the phantasy also reprehends sense, because its knowledge is attended with passion according to mixture, from which the phantasy is pure; opinion the phantasy, because it knows in conjunction with type and form, to which opinion is superior; science opinion, because the latter knows without being able to assign

the cause, the ability of effecting which especially characterizes the former; and intellect as we have said science, because the latter divides the object of knowledge transitively, but the former apprehends every thing at once in conjunction with essence. Intellect, therefore, is alone unconquerable; but science and scientific reasoning are vanquished by intellect, according to the knowledge of being.

8. (See page 431, line 29c) Plato, says Proclus, had prior to this made two things the leaders, the intelligible and that which is generated, or paradigm and image, and had assumed two things analogous to these, science and probability, or truth and faith, truth being to an intelligible paradigm as faith to a generated image; and now he geometrically adds the alternate proportion. For, if as truth is to the intelligible, so is faith to that which is generated, it will be alternately as truth is to faith, so the intelligible to that which is generated. Plato, therefore, clearly divides reasonings and knowledges with the things known; and Parmenides also, though obscure through his poetry, yet at the same time says, that there are twofold knowledges, truth and faith, of twofold things, *viz.* of beings and non-beings; and the former of these knowledges he calls splendour, as shining with intellectual light, but he deprives the latter of stable knowledge. The faith, however, which Plato now assumes appears to be different from that of which he speaks in the sixth book of his *Republic*, in the section of a line; for that is irrational knowledge, whence also it is divided from conjecture, but is arranged according to sense. But the present faith is rational, though it is mingled with irrational knowledges, employing sense and conjecture; and hence it is filled with much of the unstable. For, receiving *that* a thing is from sense or conjecture, it thus assigns the causes: but these knowledges possess much of the confused and unstable. Hence Socrates in the *Phædo* very much blames the senses, because we neither see nor hear any thing accurately. How then can knowledge, originating from sense, possess the accurate and irreprehensible? For those powers that employ science alone collect with accuracy every thing which is the object of their knowledge; but those powers that energize with sense err and fall off from the accurate, through sense, and through the unstable nature of the thing known. For what can any one assert of that which is material, since it is always changing and flowing, and is not naturally adapted to abide for a moment? And with respect to a celestial nature, in consequence of being very remote from us, it is not easily known, nor scientifically apprehended; but we must be satisfied with an approximation to the truth, and with probability in the speculation of it. For every thing which is in place requires a residence there, in order to a perfect knowledge of its nature. But the intelligible is not a thing of this kind, since it is not to be apprehended by our knowledge in place. For where any one stops his dianoëtic power, there, in consequence of the intelligible being every where present, he comes into contact with truth. And if it is possible to assert any thing stable concerning a celestial nature, this also is possible, so far as it

partakes of being, and so far as it is to be apprehended by intelligence. For it is through geometrical demonstrations, which are universal, that we are alone able to collect any thing necessary concerning it; but, so far as it is sensible, it is with difficulty apprehended, and with difficulty surveyed.

With respect to truth, however, Plato, following the theologists, establishes it as manifold. For one kind of truth is characterized by the nature of *The One*, being the light proceeding from *The Good*, which, in the *Philebus*, he says, imparts purity, and, in the *Republic*, union, to intelligibles. Another kind is that which proceeds from intelligibles, which illuminates the intellectual orders, which an essence unfigured, uncoloured, and untouched first receives, and where also the plain of truth is situated, as it is written in the *Phædrus*. A third kind of truth is that which is connate with souls, which comes into contact with being through intelligence, and science subsisting in conjunction with the objects of science: for the light pertaining to the soul is the third from the intelligible; since the intellectual is filled from the intelligible, and that pertaining to the soul from the intellectual order. This truth, therefore, subsisting in souls, must be now assumed, since we have admitted a corresponding faith, and not that which is irrational, and destitute of all logical consideration; and the one must be conjoined with intelligibles, but the other with sensibles.

9. (See page 431, line 30a) Plato being willing to indicate the providence of the demiurgus pervading the universe, together with the gifts of intellect and the presence of soul, and to show the magnitude of the good which these impart to the world, surveys prior to this the whole corporeal constitution by itself, and how, thus considered, it is confused and disordered; that also, beholding by itself the order proceeding from soul and demiurgic ornament, we may be able to define what a corporeal nature is in itself, and what orderly distribution it is allotted from fabrication. The world, indeed, always had a subsistence, but discourse divides the thing generated from the maker, and produces according to time things which subsist at once together, because every thing generated is a composite. To which we may add, that demiurgic fabrication being twofold, one being corporeal, and the other ornamental, Plato, beginning from the ornamental, very properly represents every thing corporeal moved in a confused and disordered manner, because such is its motion from itself when considered as not yet animated by an intellectual soul.

It also deserves to be noticed that Plato, in giving subsistence to the confused and disordered, prior to the fabrication of the world, imitates the ancient theologists. For, as they introduce the battles and seditions of the Titans against the Olympian Gods, so Plato pre-supposes these two, the unadorned, and the fabricator of the world, that the former may be adorned and participate of order. They, however, introduce these theologically; for they oppose the powers that preside over bodies to the Olympian deities: but Plato philosophically; for he transfers order from the Gods to the subjects of their government.

10. (See page 431, line 30b) The demiurgus of the universe, through the plenitude of his power, fabricates different things by different powers; for, since he comprehends in himself the cause of all fabrications, he after one manner gives subsistence to the whole world, and after another to its parts. Hence, by one intelligence he adorns the whole world, and generates it collectively, according to which energy the world also is one animal; but by reasoning he produces its parts, and these as wholes, because he is the demiurgus of total natures, viz. of total intellect, total soul, and all the bulk of body. In consequence of this, when composing parts, he is said to fabricate by reasoning. For reasoning here signifies a distributive cause of things; since it is not the reasoning of one doubting. For neither does art doubt, nor science; but artists and the scientific then doubt when they are indigent of their proper habits. If these, therefore, do not doubt when they are perfect, can it be supposed that intellect doubts, or the fabricator and father of the universe?

11. (See page 434, line 33c) It is well observed here by Proclus, that, the whole universe being luminous, it is most lucid according to its external superficies, and full of divine splendour. For through this the poets also place Olympus at the extremity of the world, this being entirely luminous and self-splendid.

There a white splendour spreads its radiance round,

says Homer. But of this luminous subsistence smoothness is a symbol. Why, therefore, are the extremities of the universe smooth? We reply, That it may be spontaneously conjoined with soul and intellect, and that it may be harmoniously adapted to supermundane lights, through its similitude to them. Smoothness, therefore, is significant of extreme aptitude, through which the universe is able to receive the illuminations proceeding from intellect and soul; just as mirrors, by their smoothness, receive the representations of things. Proclus further observes, that a mirror was assumed by ancient theologists as a symbol of the aptitude of the universe to be filled with intellectual illumination. Hence, says he, they say that Vulcan made a mirror for Bacchus, into which the God looking, and beholding the image of himself, proceeded into the whole of a divisible fabrication. And you may say that the smoothness of the external surface of the universe, which is now mentioned by Plato, reminds us of the above-mentioned catoptric apparatus. The whole body of the universe, therefore, being externally smooth, becomes connate with its own intellect, and with that of the demiurgus. Hence, poets establish the demiurgus on the lofty summit of the world. which is allotted from him such an aptitude, in order to its participation of intelligible causes.

520

12. (See page 434, line 33c) By these words, says Proclus, Plato appears to do nothing else than to take away from the universe a divisible life, and divisible organs, which being suspended from us descend into generation, or the whole of a visible nature. For, while we remain on high, we are in no want of any one of these multiform lives and divisible instruments; but our lucid vehicle is sufficient, which contains in itself unitedly all the senses. As, therefore, when we are liberated from generation we are purified from every life of this kind, what ought we to think respecting the universe? Is it not this, that it has one simple life, to which the whole of it is excited, and that it is equally on all sides prepared to be filled with one life? Or ought we not much more to admit these things of the universe? For wholes are more divine than parts, and things which comprehend than those which are comprehended.

Plato, however, must not be supposed in what he now says to deprive the world of sense; for, according to him, the world is an animal, and an animal is characterized by sense. In order, therefore, to understand what the nature of that sense is which the world possesses, it will be necessary to make the following division. Of sense, therefore, the first and most principal is that which imitates intellect. For every where things which rank as first possess an imitation of things prior to them. Hence, that is conjoined with first natures which has a sensible perception of itself, comprehended in itself, not passing from one thing to another, for this would be divided sense, nor proceeding to externals, for this is imperfect, but possessing the whole of that which is sensible in itself, and which may be rather called consciousness than sense. The next to this is that which proceeds indeed, and does not abide like the former, but yet proceeds according to a perfect energy, and always, on all sides, similarly apprehends that which is known; which is likewise purified from all passion, and from all that imbecility which is peculiar to divisible and material organs. The third is that which is passive to things external, and is mingled from passion and knowledge; originating, indeed, from passion, but ending in knowledge. The last sense is that with which a most obscure knowledge is present, which is full of passion, and is proximate to physical sympathy, as not knowing the forms of sensibles; as, for instance, that what operates is hot or cold, but that what falls upon it is alone pleasant or painful; for such is the sense of plants, as Timæus informs us in the course of this dialogue, being the apprehension of that which is alone pleasant and painful from things sensible. Sense, therefore, thus supernally proceeding, the world is sensitive according to the first sense. For it is visible, and an eye, according to the whole of itself, since the sun also is called an eye, and each of the stars. The world, therefore, is wholly sight and the thing seen, and is *truly* to be comprehended by sense and opinion. Hence, it contains all-perfect knowledge, indivisible sense, and is itself sensible, the instrument of sense, and sense; just as also its artificer is intellect, intelligence, and the intelligible. And as it comprehends partial bodies in its whole body, so likewise it contains many senses in its total sense.

13. (See page 434, line 33d) These things, says Proclus, are by no means in the universe, though after another manner it contains both sense and motion. For, since every thing sensible is comprehended in it, and it is itself the first sensible, it has also one sense conjoined with sensible of this kind; just as the intelligence of the demiurgus is conjoined with the whole of the intelligible, in consequence of which he is said by Orpheus to absorb the universe in himself. After this manner, therefore, the world absorbs itself by the sensible perception of itself, and comprehends the thing known by a connate knowledge. It also possesses powers which rule over, and are the guardians of, all things; and these are its hands. It likewise possesses perfective orders, which are analogous to nutritive parts; and receives vivific causes which correspond to the members of respiration. Further still, it also contains other powers, some of which fill it with unapparent causes, and others connect it with intelligible light. And of these powers, some are analogous to sight, and others to hearing. With this sense it likewise possesses an analogous motion; for, as it possesses a sensible perception of itself, so also it contains motion in itself, and a revolving about itself; and both these according to the similitude of its paradigm. For in Phanes, or animal itself, there is intelligence verging to itself, a life converted to itself, and a knowledge not subsisting according to transition and division, but self-perfect, and united with intelligibles themselves. For such is the intellect which is there, which in consequence of its being absorbed in superessential light may be said to energize prior to energy; because, according to the Chaldaic oracle, it has not proceeded, but abides in the paternal profundity, and in the adytum, according to a silence which is nourished by Deity.

14. (See page 435, line 34b) The happiness of any being is the proper perfection of that being; and hence, as the perfections of beings differ, so also do their felicities. A felicity, therefore, in the present case must be assumed, adapted to the universe. For, since the world is suspended from a paternal intellect and a total fabricative energy, and lives according to those causes, it is happy in a degree consequent to these. The world, therefore, living according to the will of the father, and preserving immutably the intellectual good which is thence imparted, is very justly said to be happy. But the first form of felicity, says Proclus, and which is all-perfect, is that of the world. The second is that of the mundane Gods, whom Plato in the *Phædrus* calls happy divinities, following the mighty Jupiter. The third is that which subsists in the genera superior to our nature, *viz.* angels, dæmons, and heroes; for the felicity of each of these is different. The fourth is that which subsists in undefiled souls, who make blameless descents into mortality, and exhibit an inflexible and untamed life; such as were the souls of Hercules, Pythagoras, Socrates, Plato, etc. The fifth is the felicity of partial souls; and this is multiform: for a soul the attendant of the moon is not happy after the same manner as the soul that is suspended from the solar order; but as the form of life is different, so also the

perfection is limited by different measures. And the last form of felicity is that which is seen in irrational animals.

15. (See page 435, line 35a) The Orphic writers, says Proclus, (in Tim. p. 184) do not predicate the impartible of every intelligible or intellectual order, but, according to them, there is something better than this appellation; just as, with respect to other names, they do not adapt king and father to all orders. Where, then, shall we first perceive the indivisible according to Orpheus, that we may thus understand the divinely intellectual conception of Plato? Orpheus, therefore, establishing one demiurgus of all divided fabrication, who is analogous to the one father that generates total fabrication, produces from him the whole mundane intellectual multitude, the number of souls, and corporeal compositions. This demiurgus, (viz. Bacchus) therefore, generates all these unitedly; but the Gods who are placed about him divide and separate his fabrications. Orpheus says, that all the other fabrications of this divinity were separated into parts by the distributive Gods, but that his heart alone was preserved indivisible by the providence of Minerva. For, as he gave subsistence to intellects, souls and bodies, and souls and bodies receive in themselves much division and separation into parts, but intellect remains united and undivided, being all things in one, and comprehending in one intelligence total intelligibles, - hence he says, that intellectual essence alone, and an intellectual number, were saved by Minerva. For, says he,

The intellectual heart alone was saved:

openly denominating it intellectual. If, therefore, the indivisible heart is intellectual, it will evidently be intellect and an intellectual number; not that it will, indeed, be every intellect, but that which is mundane; for this is the indivisible heart, since the divided God was the fabricator of this. But Orpheus calls intellect the indivisible essence of Bacchus; and denominates his prolific power that life which is distributed about body, which is physical and productive of seeds, and which he says Diana, who presides over all the generation in nature, and leads into light physical reasons, supernally extends as far as to subterranean natures. All the remaining body of the God is, according to Orpheus, mythologically considered as the composition pertaining to the soul, and is divided into seven parts. "All the parts into which they divided the boy were seven,[†]" says the theologist, speaking concerning the Titans; just in the same manner as Timæus divides the soul into seven parts. And, perhaps, when Timæus says that soul is extended through the whole world, he reminds us of the Orphic Titanic division, through which not only the soul is spread round the universe like a veil, but is also extended through every part of it. With great propriety, therefore, does Plato call that essence

---

[†] Επτα δε παντα μερη κουρου διεμοιρησαντο ψησιν ο θεολογος περι των Τιτανων.

impartible which is proximately placed above soul, following the Orphic fables, and wishing, as it were, to be an interpreter of what is said in the mysteries.

16. (See page 435, line 35b.) *In the first place, he received one part from the whole, etc.*

After Proclus has discussed every thing pertaining to the mathematical speculation of the psychogonic diagram,[†] an epitome of which we have given in the Introduction to this dialogue, he proceeds to a more principal and profound explanation of this part of the *Timæus*, as follows: In the first place, says he, we think it proper to speak about the division of the soul, according to which it is divided in these ratios, and likewise to remove whatever may be an impediment to us in apprehending the truth concerning it. Let no one therefore think that this division is corporeal, for we have before shown that the medium of the soul is exempt from body, and from the whole of that essence which is divided about it. Nor let any one who admits that it is better than body suppose that it ought to be divided after the same manner as the extremes and intervals by which body is measured. For things which possess interval, are not totally through the whole of themselves present to themselves, and when divided are not able to preserve an unconfused union. But soul, participating of an impartible destiny, is united to itself, and exhibits all the same elements subsisting in all the same. Nor again, let any one suppose that this is a section of number. For soul is indeed number, but not that which subsists according to quantity, but that which is essential, self-begotten, uniform, and converted to itself. Nor let any one compare the presence of these ratios in all things to spermatic reasons: for those are imperfect, corporeal and material, and are in every respect surpassed by the immaterial and pure essence of the reasons of the soul. Nor yet let any one assimilate the above-mentioned parts to the theorems of science, in consequence of each possessing the whole: for we do not now consider the knowledge, but the essence of the soul. Nor is it proper to think that diversities of essences are similar to the distinctions of habits: for the latter are all-variously diversified in those that possess them, but the former are established with a sameness of subsistence in demiurgic boundaries. It is requisite, therefore, to suspend the primary principle of the psychogonic division from a demiurgic cause, and from those perfect measures which eternally presubsist in beings, and to which the demiurgus also looking divides the soul. For as he divides this universe by intelligible paradigms, so also he separates the essence of the soul by the most beautiful boundaries, assimilating it to more ancient and principal causes. The mode, therefore, of division is immaterial, intellectual, undefiled, perfective of the essence of the soul, generative of the multitude it contains, collective

---

[†] *Viz.* the diagram pertaining to the generation of the soul.

through harmony into one order, and connective of things divided; at the same time being the cause of the unmingled purity in the soul, and producing a confluent communion of reasons. And the demiurgus appears indeed to consume the whole by dividing it into parts: and thus, after a manner, Timæus also asserts; for he says, that the demiurgus consumed the whole from which he separated these parts. But as he had previously said that soul is not only partible, but also impartible, it is requisite to preserve both, and to consider that while the wholeness remains impartible, a division into multitude is produced: for if we take one of these only, I mean the section, we shall make it only indivisible. The whole, therefore, is divided together with the whole remaining impartible; so that it equally participates of both. Hence it is well observed by the dæmoniacal Aristotle, that there is something impartible in partible natures, by which they are connected;[†] so that it is much more necessary that something impartible should remain in things whose nature is not only partible, but also impartible. For if it should not remain, that which consists from both will be alone partible. But that it is necessary that the whole should remain in the generation of the parts is evident; since the demiurgus is an eternal fabricator. But he constituted the soul one whole prior to its division: for he does not produce at one time and destroy at another; but he always produces every thing, and this eternally; and makes that which is produced to remain such as it is. The wholeness, therefore, is not destroyed in giving subsistence to the parts, but remains and precedes the parts.[‡] For he did not produce the parts prior to the whole, and afterwards generate the whole from these; but, on the contrary, produced the whole first, and from this gave subsistence to the parts. Hence the essence of the soul is at the same time a whole and possesses parts, and is one and multitude. And such is the division which Timæus assumes in the soul.

But let the mode of its explanation accord with the essence of the soul, being remote from apparent harmony, but recurring to essential and immaterial harmony, and sending us from images to paradigms. For the symphony which flows into the ears, and consists in sounds and pulsations, is entirely different

† That which ultimately connects bodies must necessarily be impartible; for if it also consisted of parts, those parts would require something else as the cause of their connection, and this something else, if also partible, another connecting principle, and so on *ad infinitum*. Body, therefore, derives its connection from the presence of something incorporeal.

‡ Whole, as Proclus soon after informs us, has a triple subsistence, prior to parts, in a part, and posterior to parts. We have a beautiful image of the first of these of which Proclus is now speaking, in the centre of a circle considered as subsisting with the extremities of the radii terminating in it. For these extremities, considered as giving completion to the centre, so far as the centre, may be said to be as it were parts of it; but when they are considered as they may be, as proceeding from the centre, they are posterior to it.

from that which is vital and intellectual. Let no one therefore stop at the mathematical speculation of the present passage, but let him excite in himself a theory adapted to the essence of the soul. Not let him think that we should look to intervals, or differences of motions; for these things are very remote, and are by no means adapted to the proposed object of inquiry; but let him consider the assertions essentially, and examine how they indicate the medium pertaining to the soul, and how they exhibit demiurgic providence. In the first place, therefore, since wholeness is triple, one being prior to parts, another subsisting from parts, and another in each of the parts, that wholeness of the soul which is now delivered is that which subsists prior to parts; for the demiurgus made it one whole prior to all division, which, as we have said, remains such as it is, without being consumed in the production of the parts: for to be willing to dissolve that which is well harmonized is the province of an evil artificer. He would however dissolve it, if he consumed the whole in the parts. But Plato insinuates that wholeness which consists from parts, when he represents the demiurgus consuming the whole mixture in the section of the essence of the soul, and renovating the whole of it through the harmony of its parts; this whole receiving its completion from all according parts. And a little further on he will teach us that wholeness which subsists in each of its parts, when he divides the whole soul into certain circles, and attributes all the above-mentioned ratios to them, which he has already rendered apparent; for he says that the three are in each of the parts, in the same manner as in the whole. Every part, therefore, is in a certain respect a triadic whole, after the same manner as the whole. Hence it is necessary that the soul should have three wholenesses, because it animates the universe, which is a whole of wholes, each of which is a whole as in a part. As it therefore animates in a two-fold respect, *viz.* both that which is a whole, and those wholes which are as parts, it requires two wholenesses; and it transcends the natures which are animated, possessing something external to them, so as, in the language of Timæus, to surround the universe as with a veil. Hence by the wholeness prior to parts it entirely runs above the universe, and by the other two connects it, and the natures which it contains; these also subsisting as wholes.

In the next place, we must observe that Plato, proceeding from the beginning to the end, preserves that which is monadic and also that which is dyadic in the soul: for he reduces its hyparxis into essence, sameness, and difference, and bisects number, beginning from one part, into the double and triple; and contemplating the media, he comprehends two in one, and according to each of these unfolds two-fold ratios, the sesquialter and sesquitertian, and again cuts these into sesquioctaves and remainders (λειμματα). In what follows also, he divides one length into two, and one figure of the soul into two periods; and, in short, he very properly never separates the dyadic from the monadic; for to intellect the monadic alone is adapted, on which account it is also impartible, but to body the dyadic; and hence, in the generation of a corporeal nature, he begins from the duad of fire and earth, and arranges two other genera of elements between these. But soul subsisting between body and intellect is at the same time a monad and a duad; and this because in a certain respect it equally participates of bound and infinity; just as intellect is allied to bound, but body more accords with infinity, through its subject matter, and its division *ad infinitum*. And if after this manner some have referred the impartible and partible to the monad and indefinite duad, they have spoken agreeably to things themselves; but if they have considered the soul to be number in no respect differing from monadic numbers, their assertions have been utterly discordant with the essence of the soul. It is therefore at the same time both a monad and duad, resembling by the monadic, intellectual bound, and by the dyadic, infinity; or by the former being the image of the impartible, and by the latter the paradigm of partible natures. This also should be considered, that Timæus here speaks of a two-fold work of the demiurgus: for he divides the soul into parts, and harmonizes the divided portions, and renders them accordant with each other. But in so doing he at the same time energizes both Dionysiacally and Apolloniacally. For to divide and produce wholes into parts, and to preside over the distribution of species, is Dionysiacal; but to perfect all things harmoniously is Apolloniacal. As the demiurgus, therefore, comprehends in himself the cause of both these gods, he divides and harmonizes the soul: for the hebdomad is a number common to both these divinities; since theologists say that Bacchus was divided into seven parts, and they ascribe the heptad to Apollo, as the power that connects all symphonies; for in the monad, duad, and tetrad, from which the hebdomad is composed, the disdiapason first consists. Hence they call the god, the leader of the hebdomad, and assert that the seventh day is sacred to him: for they say that on that day Apollo was born from Latona, in the same manner as Diana on the sixth day. This number, therefore, in the same manner as the triad, accedes to the soul from superior causes; the triad indeed from intelligible, but the hebdomad from intellectual causes.[†] But the hebdomad is derived from these gods, that the division into seven parts may be a sign of the Dionysiacal series, and of that dilaceration which is celebrated in fables. For it is requisite that the soul participating a Dionysiacal intellect, and, as Orpheus says, carrying the god on her head, should be divided after the same manner as he is divided; and that the harmony which she possesses in these parts should be a symbol of the Apolloniacal order. For in the fables[‡] respecting this god, it is Apollo who collects and unites the lacerated members of Bacchus, according to the will of his father.

[†] The number 7, according to the Pythagoreans, is the image of intellectual light; and hence the intellectual order is hebdomadic, consisting of two triads, *viz.* Saturn, Rhea, Jupiter, and the three Curetes, and a separating monad which is called by ancient theologists Ocean. See the fifth book of Proclus on *Plato's Theology* [TTS vol. VIII], and the Introduction and Notes to the *Parmenides*.

[‡] See my *Dissertation on the Eleusinian and Bacchic Mysteries*. [TTS vol. VII].

In the next place, three middles are assumed, which not only in the soul, but also every where shadow forth the daughters of Themis, who are three, as well as these middles: for the geometrical middle is the image of Eunomia; and hence in the *Laws* Plato says, that she governs polities, and is the judgment of Jupiter, adorning the universe, and comprehending in herself the truly political science. But the harmonic middle is the image of Justice, which distributes a greater ratio[†] to greater, and a lesser to lesser terms, this being the employment of Justice. And the arithmetical middle is the image of Peace: for it is she, as he also says in the *Laws*, who attributes to all things the equal according to quantity, and makes people preserve peace with people, for the solid proportion prior to these is sacred to their mother Themis, who comprehends all the powers of these. And thus much generally respecting these three middles.

That we may, however, speak of them more particularly, it is requisite to observe that they are unific and connective of the essence of the soul, *viz.* they are unions, analogies, and bonds. Hence Timæus also calls them bonds. For above, he says, that the geometric middle is the most beautiful of bonds, and that the others are contained in this; but every bond is a certain union. If, therefore, these middles are bonds, and bonds are unions of the things bound, the consequence is evident. These therefore pervade through the whole essence of the soul, and cause it to be one from many wholes, as they are allotted a power which can bind various forms. But these being three, the geometric binds every thing which is essential in souls: for essence is one reason[‡] which pervades through all things, and connects things first, middle, and last, in the same manner as in the geometric middle there is one and the same ratio which perfectly pervades through three terms. The harmonic middle connects all the divided sameness of souls, imparting a communion of reasons to the extremes, and a kindred conjunction; this sameness which it connects being more apparent in more total, but less apparent in more partial souls. And the arithmetic middle binds the all-various difference of the progression of the soul, and is less inherent in things greater according to order, but more in such as are lesser. For difference has dominion in more partial natures, just as sameness has in such as are more total and more excellent. Those middles also may be compared with each other, in the same manner as sameness and difference: and as essence is the monad of these, so the geometric middle of those. The geometric middle therefore is the union of all the essences which are comprehended in the thirty-four terms. The harmonic is the union of equally numerous identities, and the arithmetic of differences; all these middles at the same time being extended through all the terms. For how could a certain

---

[†] Thus in 6, 4, 3, which are in harmonic proportion, the ratio of 6 to 4 is greater than that of 4 to 3.

[‡] Reason must here be considered as signifying a productive and connective principle of things, to which ratio in quantity is analogous.

whole be produced from them, unless they were as much as possible united with each other, essentially indeed by one of these, but variously by the other two? Hence these two become the supplement of the geometric middle, just as sameness and difference contribute to the consummation of essence; for in consequence of their possessing contrariety to each other, the geometric middle conciliates their dissension, and unites their interval. For the harmonic middle, as we have said, distributes greater ratios to greater, and lesser to lesser terms: since it evinces that things greater and more total according to essence are more comprehensive, and transcend in power subject natures. But the arithmetic middle, on the contrary, distributes lesser ratios to greater terms, and greater ratios to lesser terms.[†] For difference prevails more in subordinate natures, as, on the contrary, the dominion of sameness is more apparent in superior than in inferior natures. And the geometric middle extends the same ratio to all the terms, illuminating union to things first, middle, and last, through the presence of essence to all things. The demiurgus, therefore, imparts to the soul three connective unions, which Plato calls middles, because they appear to bind the middle order of the universe. For the geometric collects the multitude of essences, and unites essential progressions; since one ratio is an image of union. But the harmonic binds total identities and their hyparxes into one communion; and the arithmetic conjoins first, middle, and last differences. For, in short, difference is the mother of numbers, as we learn in the *Parmenides*. But in every part there were these three, *viz.* essence, sameness, and difference; and it is requisite that all these should be conjoined with each other through a medium, and binding reasons.

In the next place, we say that the soul is a plenitude of reasons, being more simple indeed than sensibles, but more composite than intelligibles. Hence Timæus assumes seven ratios in it, *viz.* the ratio of equality, multiple, submultiple, superparticular, and superpartient, and the opposites of these, the subsuperparticular and subsuperpartient ratios:[‡] but he does not assume the ratios which are composed from these; since they are adapted to corporeal natures, which are composite and divisible; while on the contrary the ratios in the soul proceed indeed into multitude and division, but at the same time, together with multitude, exhibit simplicity, and the uniform together with division. Neither therefore like intellect is it allotted an essence in the monad and the impartible (for intellect is alone monadic and impartible); nor is it multitude and division alone.

[†] Thus, in the numbers 6, 4, 2, which are in arithmetic proportion, the ratio of 6 to 4, *i.e.* the ratio of the greater terms is less than the ratio of 4 to 2, the ratio of the lesser terms: for the ratio of 6 to 4 is 1½, but that of 4 to 2 is 2.

[‡] For an account of these ratios, see the Notes to the 8th Book of the *Republic* on the Geometric Number, vol i. [TTS vol IX, page 562, *et seq.*]

Again, it is requisite to understand that numbers which are more simple and nearer to the monad have a more principal subsistence than such as are more composite; since Plato also establishes one part prior to all those that follow, refers all of them to this, and ends in those which are especially composite and solid. This then being admitted, I say that equality, and the ratio of equality, have the ratio of a monad to all ratios; and what the monad is in essential quantity, that the equal is[†] in relative quantity. Hence, according to this reasoning, the soul introduces a common measure to all things which subsist according to the same ratios, and one idea bearing an image of sameness; but according to the multiple and submultiple ratio, it governs all series, connects wholes themselves, and exhibits every whole form of mundane natures often produced by it in all things. Thus, for instance, it exhibits the solar and lunar form in divine, dæmoniacal, and human souls, in irrational animals, in plants, and in stones themselves. It possesses therefore the series as one according to multiple ratio, the whole of which repeatedly appears in the same series, and adorns the most universal genera by more partial series. But by superparticular and subsuperparticular ratios it governs things which subsist as wholes in their participants, and are participated according to one of the things which they contain. And, according to superpartient and subsuperpartient ratios, it governs such things as are participated wholly indeed by secondary natures, but in conjunction with a division, into multitude. Thus, for instance, man participates of animal, and the whole form is in him, yet, not alone, but at the same time, the whole is according to one thing, viz. the human form; so that,

---

[†] That all the species of inequality of ratio proceed from equality of ratio may be shown as follows: Let there be any three equal terms, as, for instance, three unities, 1, 1, 1. Let the first therefore be placed equal to the first, viz. 1; the second to the first and second be added together, viz. to 2; and let the third be equal to the first, twice the second, and the third be added together, viz. to 1, 2, 1, or 4. This will produce duple proportion, viz. 1, 2, 4. By the same process with 1, 2, 4, triple proportion will arise, viz. 1, 5, 9; and by a like process with this again, quadruple proportion, and so on. Multiple proportion being thus produced from equal terms, by inverting the order of these terms, and adapting the same process, sesquialter will be produced from duple proportion, sesquitertian from triple, etc. Thus, for instance, let the three terms 4, 2, 1, be given, which form a duple proportion: let the first be placed equal to the first, viz. 4; the second to the first and second, viz. to 6; and the third to the first, twice the second, and the third, viz. to 4, 4, 1, or 9, and we shall have 4, 6, 9, which form a sesquialter proportion; for $6/4 = 1\frac{1}{2} = 9/6$. By a like process with 9, 3, 1, which form a triple proportion, a sesquitertian proportion will arise, viz. 9, 12, 16; and so of other species of superparticular proportion. In like manner, by inverting the terms which compose superparticular proportion, all the species of superpartient proportions will arise. And hence it appears that equality is the principle of all inequalities, in the same manner as the monad of all numbers.

together with the whole, and one certain thing[†] which is a part of it, it is present to its participant. But things which are called common genera, participate indeed of one genus, yet do not participate of this alone, but together with this of many other genera[‡] which are parts, and not a part of that one genus. Thus, for instance, a mule participates of the species, from which it has a mixt generation. Each species therefore either participates of one genus according to one thing, and imitates the superparticular ratio, which contains the whole, and one part of the whole; or it participates of one common genus, and which is extended to many species, and thus imitates the superpartient ratio, which, together with the whole, contains more parts of it than one: and there is not any participation of forms besides these. Looking therefore to these things, we can easily assign the cause of those things which subsist according to one species, as for instance of the sun, the moon, and man; and also of those which subsist according to many species in conjunction with that which is common. For there are many such like natures both in the earth and sea, as, for instance, satyrs and marine nymphs, the upper parts of which resemble the human form, and the lower the extremities of goats and fishes. There is also said to be a species of dragons with the faces of lions, such as these possessing an essence mingled from many things. All these ratios therefore are very properly preassumed in the soul, because they bound all the participations of forms in the universe; nor can there be any other ratios of communion besides these, since all things are deduced into species according to these.

Again, therefore, a hebdomad of ratios corresponds to a hebdomad of parts; and the whole soul through the whole of it is hebdomadic in its parts, in its ratios, and in its circles, being characterized by the number seven. For if the demiurgic intellect is a monad, but soul primarily proceeds from intellect, it will subsist as the hebdomad with respect to it: for the hebdomad is paternal and motherless.[§] And perhaps equality imparts a communion equally to all the ratios of the soul, that all may communicate with all. But multiple ratio indicates the manner in which natures that have more of the nature of unity measure such as are multiplied, wholly pervading through the whole of them; and also the manner in which impartible natures measure such as are more distributed. Superparticular and subsuperparticular ratio appears to signify the differences according to which total reasons do not wholly communicate with

---

[†] Thus in the superparticular ratio of 3 to 2, 2 is contained in 3, and together with it one part of 2, viz. the ½ of it.

[‡] Thus in the superpartient ratio of 10 to 6, 6 is contained in 10, and together with it two parts of 6, viz. 4, which is two-thirds of 6.

[§] The hebdomad is said to be motherless, because in monadic numbers 7 is not produced by the multiplication of any two numbers between 1 and 10.

each other, but possess indeed a partial habitude, yet are conjoined according to one particular thing belonging to them which is most principal. And the superpartient and subsuperpartient ratio indicates the last nature, according to which the communion of the reasons of the soul is divisible, and multiplied through subjection. For the more sublime reasons are wholly united to the whole of themselves; but those of a middle subsistence are not united to the whole of themselves, but are conjoined according to their highest part; and those that rank in the third degree are divisibly connascent according to multitude. Thus, for instance, *essence* communicates with all reasons, measuring all their progressions; for there is nothing in them unessential: but *sameness* being itself a genus, especially collects into one communion the summits of these; and *difference* in a particular manner measures their progressions and divisions. The communion therefore of the ratios of the soul is every where exhibited: for it is either all-perfect, or it alone subsists according to summits, or according to extensions into multitude.

Again, therefore, let us in the next place attend to the manner in which the seven parts subsist.[†] The first part, indeed, is most intellectual and the summit of the soul, being conjoined with *The One*, and the hyparxis of its whole essence. Hence it is called one, as being *uniform*; its number is comprehended in union, and it is analogous to the cause and the centre of the soul. For the soul abides according to this, and subsists in unproceeding union with wholes. And the tetrad indeed is in the first monads, on account of its stability, and its rejoicing in equality and sameness. But the number 8 is in the monads of the second order, through its subjection, and that providence of the soul which extends itself from its supreme part, as far as to the last of things. The triad is in the monads of the third order, through the circular progression of the multitude in it, to the all-perfect. And at the same time it is manifest from these things as images, that the summit of the soul, though it is uniform, is not purely one, but that this also is united multitude, just as the monad[‡] is not without multitude, but is at the same time monad; but the one of the gods is alone *one*. And *the one* of intellect is indeed more one than multitude, though this also is multiplied; but *the one* of the soul is similarly one and multitude, just as *the one* of the natures posterior to soul, and which are divided about bodies, is more multitude than one. And *the one* of bodies is not simply one, but a phantasm and image of *the one*. Hence the Elean guest in the *Sophista* says, that every thing corporeal is broken in pieces, as having an adventitious one, and never ceasing to be divided. The second part multiplies the part prior

---

† Let it be remembered that the first numbers of the soul are, as we have observed in the Introduction to this Dialogue, 1, 2, 3, 4, 9, 8, 27.

‡ In the dissertation on nullities, at the end of my translation of Aristotle's *Metaphysics*, I have demonstratively shown that infinite multitude is contained causally in the monad.

to it by generative progressions, which the duad indicates, and unfolds all the progressions of essence. Hence also it is said to be double of the first, as imitating the indefinite duad and intelligible infinity. But the third part converts the whole soul again to its principle: and it is the third part of it which is convolved to the principles, and which indeed is measured by the first part, as being filled with union from it, but is more partially conjoined to the second part. Hence it is said to be triple of that, but sesquialter of this: for it is indeed contained from the half by the second part, as not possessing an equal power, but is perfectly contained by the first. Again the fourth, and also the fifth part, peculiarly evince that the soul presides over secondary natures: for these parts are intellectual causes of those incorporeals which are divided about bodies, since they are superficies and tetragonic; this being derived from the second, but that from the third part; for the fourth part is the source of progression and generation, and the fifth of conversion and perfection. For both are superficies; but the one subsists twice from the second, and the other proceeds thrice from the third. And it appears that the one,[†] imitating the procession about body, is productive of generative powers, but that the other[‡] is productive of intellectual regressions: for all knowledge converts that which knows to the thing known; just as every nature wishes to generate, and to make a progression downwards. The sixth and seventh parts insert in the soul the primary causes of bodies, and of solid bulks: for these numbers are solid; and the one[§] is derived from the second part, and the other[*] from the third. But Timæus, in what he here says, converting things last to such as are first, and the terminations of the soul to its summit, establishes this to be octuple, and that twenty-seven times, the first. And thus the essence of the soul consists of seven parts, as abiding, proceeding, and returning, and as the cause of the progression and conversion, both of essences divisible about bodies, and bodies themselves.

If you please you may also say, because the soul is allotted an hypostasis between impartible and partible essences, that it imitates the former through the triad, and preassumes the latter from the tetrad. But every soul is from all these terms, because every rational soul is the centre of wholes. The harmonic and arithmetic middles, therefore, fill these intervals, which have an essential subsistence, and are considered according to essence, these as we have said collecting their samenesses, and those their differences.

[†] Viz. 4.

[‡] Viz. 9.

[§] Viz. 8 is derived from 2.

[*] Viz. 27 is derived from 3.

We may likewise, approaching nearer to things themselves, say, that the soul according to one part, *viz.* its summit, is united to natures prior to itself; but that, according to the double and triple parts, it proceeds from intellect and returns to it; and that according to the double of the double, and the triple of the triple, it proceeds from itself, and is again converted to itself; and through its own middle to the principles of its essence; for abiding according to them, it is filled from them with every thing of a secondary nature. And as the progression from itself is suspended from the progression prior to itself, so the conversion to itself depends on that which is prior to itself. But the last parts, according to which the soul gives subsistence to things posterior to itself, are referred to the first part, that a circle may be exhibited without a beginning, the end being conjoined with the beginning, and that the universe may be generated animated and intellectual, solid numbers being coordinated with the first part. From these middles, also, Timæus says that sesquialter, sesquitertian, and sesquioctave ratios result. What else then does he wish to indicate by these things, than the more partial differences of the ratio of the soul? For the sesquialter ratios present us with an image of divisible communion indeed, but according to the first of the parts; but the sesquitertian of communion according to the parts in the middle; and the sesquioctave of that which subsists according to the extremes. Hence the middles are conjoined with each other according to the sesquioctave ratio. For when they are beheld according to opposite genera, they possess the least communion: but each is appropriately conjoined with the extremes. Timæus also adds, that all the sesquitertian ratios are filled with the interval of the sesquioctave together with the leimma, or remainder; indicating by this that the terminations of all these ratios end in more partial hypostases, until the soul has comprehended the causes of things last in the world, and which are every way divisible. For soul has previously established in herself, according to the demiurgic will, the principles of the order and harmony of these. Soul, therefore, contains the principles of harmonious progression and conversion, and of division into things first, middle, and last; and she is one intellectual reason, which is at the same time filled with all reasons.

With these things also accord what we have before asserted, that all its harmony consists from a quadruple diapason, with the diapente and tone. For harmony subsists in the world, in intellect, and in soul; on which account also Timæus says that soul participates of and is harmony. But the world participates of harmony decadically, soul tetradically, and intellect monadically. And as the monad is the cause of the tetrad, and the tetrad of the decad, so also intellectual harmony is the supplier of that which pertains to the soul, and that of the soul is the source of sensible harmony: for soul is the proximate paradigm of the harmony in the sensible world. Since, however, there are five figures[†] and centres[‡] in the universe which give completion to the whole; hence the harmony diapente is the source of symphony according to parts to the world. Again, because the universe is divided into nine parts,[§] the sesquioctave ratio makes its communion commensurate with soul. And here you may see that soul comprehends the world according to cause, and renders it a whole, harmonizing it considered as one, as consisting of four, and of five parts, and as divided into nine parts. For the monad, tetrad, pentad, and ennead, comprehend the whole number according to which all the parts of the world are divided. Hence the ancients considered the Muses, and Apollo the leader of the Muses, as presiding over the universe, the latter supplying the one union of the whole harmony, and the former connecting its divided progression: and the eight Syrens mentioned in the *Republic* appear to give completion to the same numbers. Thus then, in the middle of the monad and ennead, the world is adorned tetradically and pentadically; tetradically indeed, according to the four ideas of animals which its paradigm comprehends, but pentadically according to the five figures through which the demiurgus adorned all things, introducing as Timæus says a fifth idea, and arranging this harmonically in the universe.

Again, therefore, let us say from the beginning, that the demiurgus possessing twofold powers, the one being productive of sameness, and the other of difference, as we learn in the *Parmenides*, he both divides and binds the soul. And he is indeed the final cause of these, that the soul may become the middle of wholes, being similarly united and divided; since two things are prior to it, the gods as unities, and beings as united natures; and two things are posterior to it, *viz.* those natures which are divided in conjunction with others[*] and those which are perfectly divisible.[°] You may also say that *The One* is prior

---

[†] Proclus here means the five regular bodies, *viz.* the dodecahedron, the pyramid, the octahedron, the icosahedron, and the cube. It is a remarkable property of these figures, that the sum of their sides is the same as that of their angles, and that this sum is pentadic; for it is equal to 50. Thus the dodecahedron contains 12 sides, the pyramid 4, the octahedron 8, the icosahedron 20, and the cube 6; and $12 + 4 + 8 + 20 + 6 = 50$. In like manner, with respect to their angles, the dodecahedron has 20, the pyramid 4, the octahedron 6, the icosahedron 12, and the cube 8; and $20 + 4 + 6 + 12 + 8 = 50$.

[‡] *Viz.* the northern, southern, eastern and western centres, and that which subsists between these.

[§] *Viz.* into the five centres and the four elements considered as subsisting every where.

[*] *Viz.* corporeal forms and qualities.

[°] *Viz.* bodies.

to the former, *viz.* to the gods and beings, and that *matter* is posterior to the latter; that sameness and difference which are the idioms of the demiurgic order are effective; and that the sections and bonds of the father are paradigmatic. For he first among the gods cuts and binds with infrangible bonds; theologists obscurely signifying these things when they speak of Saturnian exsections, and those bonds which the fabricator of the universe is said to hurl round himself, and of which Socrates reminds us in the *Cratylus*. We may also consider numbers as having a formal power with respect to divisions; for the parts of the soul are separated according to these. But the middles and the ratios which give completion to these are analogous to bonds: for it is impossible to consider concauses, which have the relation of matter, in souls which have an incorporeal essence. These things being premised, it is evident how the demiurgus of all division, energizing with two-fold powers, the dividing and the binding, divides from primary causes the triform nature and triple mixture of the soul, the whole soul at the same time remaining undiminished. For since he constituted the soul as a medium between an impartible essence, and that nature which is divided about bodies, and since an impartible essence is triple, abiding, proceeding and returning, hence he established a similitude of this in three parts; adumbrating its permanency by the first part, its progression by the second, and its conversion by the third. And perhaps on this account the second is said to be double of the first: for every thing which proceeds has also that which abides subsisting prior to its progression. But the third part is said to be triple of the first: for every thing which is converted proceeds also and abides. Since also soul produces the essence posterior to itself, it likewise contains in itself the whole of this essence. Hence it contains every incorporeal essence, but which is at the same time inseparable from bodies, according to the fourth and fifth parts; but every corporeal essence according to solid numbers, *viz.* the sixth and seventh parts. Or, it produces and converts itself to itself, according to square numbers, since it is self-subsistent[†] and self-energetic, but every divisible essence posterior to itself according to cube numbers. The one ratio of geometric analogy essentially binds these parts, divided as we have said into three and seven. But the harmonic middle binds them according to sameness, and the arithmetic according to difference. These two likewise lie between the geometric middle, and are said to fill the double and triple intervals, because all sameness and all difference are uniformly comprehended under essence and the harmony pertaining to it. But from these middles the multitude of sesquialter, sesquitertian, and sesquioctave ratios becomes apparent;

[†] Even square numbers are beautiful images of self-subsistence. For that which produces itself effects this by its hyparxis or summit, since the being of every thing depends on its principal part, and this is its summit. But the root of a number is evidently analogous to hyparxis; and consequently an even square number will be an image of a nature which produces itself. And hence self-production is nothing more than a involution of hyparxis.

which multitude is indeed binding and connective, as well as the middles, but is of a more partial nature, because each of these is a certain ratio; but each of the middles consists from many ratios, either the same or different. And as analogy or proportion is more comprehensive than ratio, so the above-mentioned middles afford a greater cause to the soul of connecting the multitude which it contains, this cause pervading intellectually through the whole of it. The sesquialter, sesquitertian, and sesquioctave ratios are, therefore, certain bonds of a more partial nature, and are comprehended in the middles, not according to different habitudes of them with respect to the extremes, for this is mathematical, but according to causal comprehension and a more total hypostasis.

Again, these bonds contain the second and third progressions of the ratios; the sesquialter compressing through five centres the harmony of the ratios; the sesquitertian, through the four elements which subsist every where, evincing their power, and rendering all things known and allied to each other; and the sesquioctave harmonizing the division into nine and eight. Hence the ancients at one time, considering the parts of the world as eight, and at another as nine, placed over the universe eight Syrens, and nine Muses, from whom harmony is derived to wholes. The sesquitertian and sesquialter ratios, therefore, are more total than the sesquioctaves; and hence they are the suppliers of a more perfect symphony, and comprehend the harmonious section of the world in less numbers. Here therefore the divisions in the participants are distant from each other, but in the incorporeal ratios of the soul the more total comprehend the more partial. But since the sesquioctaves are the causes of a more partial symphony, hence that which is posterior to these is justly said to be thrust down into the extremity of the universe. Nor is it discordant to the whole of things, that divisible defluxions from each of the elements should be driven into the subterranean region. For since the elements subsist in many places, in the heavens, and in the regions under the moon, the ratio posterior to the sesquioctave collecting the last sediment of them in the subterranean region, conjoins them with wholes, that from the union of both the whole harmony of the universe may be complete. Hence we have said that the harmony of the soul is perfectly intellectual and essential, preceding according to cause sensible harmony, and that Timæus, wishing to exhibit this through images, employed harmonic ratios, presupposing that there are certain causes in the soul more comprehensive than others, and which subsist prior to every form and to all the knowledge of the soul. On this account I think it is not fit to discuss things of this kind, by explaining the parts, or the ratios, or the analogies, but we should contemplate all things essentially, according to the first division and harmony of the soul, and refer all things to a demiurgic and intellectual cause. Hence we should comprehend the sesquioctaves and remainders (λείμματα) in the sesquitertian and sesquialter ratios, these in the middles, and the middles in that one middle which is the most principal of all of them; and should refer more partial to more total causes, and consider the former as derived from the latter. And thus much concerning harmonic ratios.

17. (See page 436, line 36b) It is well observed here by Proclus, (in Tim.) that from each of the spheres from which the universe consists there are certain defluxions which extend as far as to the subterranean regions, and also certain dregs mingled together, of the elements themselves, possessing much of the tumultuous, dark and material, but at the same time contributing to the whole composition and harmony of the world. Plato (says he) placing the cause of this in the soul of the universe calls it a remainder (λειμμα), a term significant of ultimate subjection.

Proclus further observes, "that theologists also establish about subterranean places the powers of the highest Gods; and that Jupiter himself is represented by them as adorning those places in order to adapt them to the participation of such mighty Gods. That, if this be the case, we ought much more to think, concerning the soul of the universe, that it adorns every thing which appears to have a disordered subsistence, possesses the cause of its existence, and arranges it in a becoming manner according to this cause. For, how can it govern the universe, or conduct all things according to intellect, unless it orderly disposes that which is disordered, and coharmonizes things last with the one life of the world? If also the causes of these presubsist in the demiurgus, as Orpheus says, what wonder is it that the whole soul which possesses all such things in a manner adapted to itself, as a divine intellect possesses demiurgically, should also comprehend the cause of things last in the world, and of that which is as it were the sediment of wholes? For soul prior to the apparent and sensible comprehends an unapparent world."

Proclus concludes with observing, that the whole number of the essential monads in the soul is 105,947;[†] the soul thus proceeding according to all the orders of numbers. For it proceeds decadically indeed, that it may become the mundane soul; since the decad is the number of the world: but pentadically, that it may be converted to itself; for the pentad is self-convertive. It also proceeds enneadically (or according to the number 9), that it may not only connect the universe monadically, but may proceed to the last of things after departing from the monad: tetradically, as collecting the quadripartite division of things into one, and hebdomadically (or according to the number 7), as converting all things to the monad, to which the hebdomad is alone referred, this number being motherless and masculine. And the whole of this number is indeed in the soul of the world totally, viz. has a total subsistence; but in divine souls, as energizing towards the mundane soul, it is contained totally and partially. In dæmoniacal souls, as energizing yet more partially, it subsists on the contrary partially and totally; and in human souls partially and gnostically alone.

[†] In the original μυριαδες δεκα, χιλιαδες πεντε, εκατονταδες τεσσαρες; but from what Proclus immediately after observes, it is evident that instead of εκατονταδες τεσσαρες we should read εννεακονταδες τεσσαρακοντες.

18. (See page 437, line 37a) Plato calls the gnostic motions of the soul *touchings*, indicating by this their immediate apprehension of the objects of knowledge, and their impartible communion with them. Since, however, one of the circles, *viz*. the dianoëtic power, knows intelligibles, and the other, i.e. the doxastic power, sensibles, what is it which says that these objects are different from each other, and that the one is a paradigm, but the other an image? We reply, that in the same manner as the common sense knows visibles and audibles, the former through sight, and the latter through hearing, and, in consequence of asserting that these are different from each other, must necessarily have a knowledge of both, - so this reason of which Plato now speaks, being different from the two circles, asserts through the whole soul some things concerning intelligibles, and others concerning sensibles. For, in as much as the soul is one essence, she possesses this one gnostic energy, which he calls reason: and hence we simply say that the whole soul is rational. This reason then is the one knowledge of the soul, which through the circle of sameness understands an impartible essence, and through the circle of difference that which is dissipated.

19. (See page 437, line 37b) The soul of the world, says Proclus (in Tim.) comprehends all sensibles, together with every thing which they either do or suffer. For, since the universe is one animal, it sympathizes with itself, so that all generated natures are parts of the life of the world, as of one drama. Just as if a tragic poet should compose a drama in which Gods make their appearance, and heroes and other persons speak, and should permit such players as were willing, to utter the heroic speeches, or the speeches of other characters, he at the same time comprehending the one cause of all that is said. Thus ought we to conceive respecting the whole soul: that giving subsistence to all the life of the world, this life being one and various, and speaking like a many-headed animal with all its heads, partly in Grecian and partly in Barbaric language, it comprehends the causes of all generated natures; knowing particulars by universals, accidents by essences, and parts by wholes, but all things simply by the divinity which it contains. For a God so far as a God knows things partial, contrary to nature, and in short all things, even though you should say matter itself. For every thing, whatever it may be, is one, so far as it proceeds from *The One*. The knowledge, therefore, of all things simply and directly, is divine.

20. (See page 437, line 37b) This reason is the one power of the essence of the soul, according to which the soul is one, just as it is twofold according to *the same* and *different*. This reason, therefore, being one, knows according to *sameness*. For it does not at one time know the intelligible, and at another time a sensible nature, like our reason, which is unable to energize about both according to the same. Plato very properly says of this reason, that it is

becoming to be true (αληθες γιγνομενος) about intelligibles and sensibles, but is not *absolutely* true like intellect, in consequence of its transitive knowledge according to both these. Hence, by asserting that it knows according to *sameness*, he signifies the difference between the knowledge of a divine and partial soul; but when he says that it is *becoming to be* true, he indicates the difference between the knowledge of soul and intellect. You may also say, that it is *becoming to be* true, as being transitive in its twofold knowledges; but that it is true *according to the same*, as always comprehending the whole form of every thing which it knows, and not like our reason evolving every form, but with respect to every thing which it sees beholding the whole at once. For we see every thing according to a part, and not according to sameness.

21. (See page 437, line 37c) It appears from the comment of Proclus on this part, that we should read λογιστικον, and not λογικον as in all the printed editions of the *Timæus*. Proclus also well observes, that by *logistic*, here, we must understand *the intelligible*; for Plato opposes this to *the sensible*. He adds, that Plato appears to call *the intelligible the logistic*, after the same manner as he afterwards calls *the sensible, sensitive*, (το αισθητον, αισθητικον). For *the sensible* is motive of sense, and *the intelligible* of the reasoning of the soul. After this he observes as follows: "By *aptly revolving* we must understand the intellectual, the unimpeded in transition, the circular, and the consummation of vigour, perfection in intellections, the energizing about a divine nature, the beneficent, and moving about the intelligible as a centre;" - "hastening to conjoin yourself with the centre of resounding light," says some one of the Gods. By *intellect* Plato here signifies intellect according to habit. For intellect is threefold: the first, that which is divine, such as the demiurgic; the second, that which is participated by the soul, but is at the same time essential and self-perfect; and the third, that which subsists according to habit, and through which the soul is intellectual. *Science* here signifies the first knowledge filled from intelligibles, and which has an undeviating and immutable subsistence. But it differs from intellect, so far as intellect is beheld in simple projections alone of the soul; for through this the soul understands at once the whole of every thing which is the object of intellection. For an energy at once collective is the peculiarity of intellect; but that of science consists in a knowledge from cause; since the composition and division of forms constitute the idiom of science.

22. (See page 438, line 37d) *He at the same time formed an eternal image flowing according to number of eternity abiding in one.*

That eternity then, says Proclus, is more venerable, has a more principal subsistence, and is as it were more stable than animal itself, though this is the most beautiful and perfect of intelligible animals, as Plato has informed us in the first part of this dialogue, is entirely evident. For if the eternal is said to be and is eternal, as that which participates, but eternity is neither said to participate of animal itself, nor to receive its appellation from it, it is evident that the one is secondary, but the other more simple and primary. For neither does eternity participate of animal itself, because it is not an animal, nor is time a visible animal, nor any other animal. For it has been shown that animal itself is only-begotten and eternal; and hence eternity is more excellent than animal itself; since the eternal is neither that which eternity is, nor is better than eternity. But as we all acknowledge that what is endued with intellect, and that what is animated, are posterior to intellect and soul, in like manner the eternal is secondary to eternity. But here some one may say, what can be more venerable than animal itself, since it is said by Plato to be the most beautiful of intelligibles, and according to all things perfect? We reply, that it is most beautiful from receiving the summit of beauty, through vehement participation of it, but not from its transcendent participation of *The Good*. For it is not said to be the *best* of intelligibles. To which we may add, that it is not simply the most beautiful of all intelligibles, but of all intelligible animals. Eternity, therefore, is not any animal, but infinite life. In the next place, it is not necessary, that what is every way perfect should be the first. For the perfect possesses all things; so that it will contain things first, middle, and last. But that which is above this division will be super-perfect. Nothing therefore hinders, but that eternity may be superior to the most beautiful and in every respect perfect animal, since intelligible animals are many, if it is the best, and super-perfect.

If these things then are rightly asserted, eternity will neither be one certain genus of being, as some have thought it to be, such as essence, or permanency, or sameness: for all these are parts of animal itself, and each of these possesses as it were an opposition, *viz.* essence, non-being; permanency, motion; sameness, difference; but nothing is opposed to eternity. All these therefore are similarly eternal, *viz.* the same, the different, permanency, motion; but this would not be the case if eternity were one of these. Eternity, therefore, is not opposed to any thing either of these, or to any of the things posterior to itself: for time, which may seem to subsist dissimilarly to eternity, in the first place, does not revolve about the same things with it, but about things which do not receive their continuous coherence from eternity; and in the next place it is an image of, and is not opposed to eternity, as Plato now says, and as we shall shortly demonstrate. Eternity, therefore, will not be any one genus, nor the whole collection of the genera of being: for again, there would be multitude in it, and it would require the union of that which abides in one. But it is itself that which abides in one; so that it would abide, and yet not abide in one. It would abide indeed as eternity, and as the cause of union to beings, but it would not abide as being composed from multitude. To all which we may add, that it is intellect which comprehends the genera of being, and that the conception of intellect is different from that of eternity, in the same manner as the conception of soul from that of time: for the energy of intellect is intransitive intelligence, but of eternity, impartible perpetuity.

What then will eternity be, if it is neither any one of the genera of being, nor that which is composed from the five, since all these are eternal, and eternity has a prior subsistence? What else than the monad[†] of the intelligible unities? But I mean by unities, the ideas of intelligible animals, and the genera of all these intelligible ideas. Eternity is the one comprehension, therefore, of the summit of the multitude of these, and the cause of the invariable permanency of all things, not subsisting in the multitude of intelligibles themselves, nor being a collection of them, but in an exempt manner being present to them, by itself disposing and as it were forming them, and making them to be wholes. For perfect multitude is not unfolded into light, nor is the all-various idea of intelligibles produced immediately after *The Good*; but there are certain natures between, which are more united than all-perfect multitude, but indicate a parturiency and representation of the generation of wholes, and of connected comprehension in themselves. How many, and of what kind these are, the gods know divinely, but the mystic doctrine of Parmenides will inform us in a human and philosophic manner, to which dialogue we shall refer the reader for accurate instruction in these particulars. For we shall now show that eternity is above all-perfect animal, and that it is proximately above it, from the very words of the philosopher.

Because animal itself, therefore, is said to be eternal, it will be secondary to eternity; but because there is nothing eternal prior to it, it will be proximately posterior to eternity. Whence then is this evident? Because, I say, neither is there any thing temporal prior to the world, the image of animal itself, but the world is the first participant of time, and animal itself of eternity. For if as eternity is to time, so is animal itself to the world, then, as geometricians would say, it will be alternately as eternity is to animal itself, so is time to the world. But time is first participated by the world; for it was not prior to the orderly distribution of the universe: and hence eternity is first participated by animal itself. And if time is not the whole sensible animal (i.e. the world), for it was generated together with it, and that which is generated with a thing is not that thing with which it is generated, if this be the case, neither will eternity be intelligible animal, so that neither will it be an animal, lest there should be two intelligible animals: for Plato has before shown that animal itself is only begotten (μονογενες). Hence we must not say that eternity is an animal, but different from animal itself. Neither, therefore, in short, is it an animal: for it is either an animal the same with or different from animal itself, neither of which, as we have shown, can be asserted. It is not the latter, because animal itself is only begotten, nor the former, because neither is time the same with

---

[†] Μονας is omitted in the original; but the sense requires that either this word, or the word αιτια, cause, should be inserted.

that which is temporal. But if it is participated by and does not participate of intelligible animal, it will be a god prior to it, intelligible indeed, but not yet an animal. The order of eternity, therefore, with respect to animal itself, is apparent: for it is evident that it is higher, and proximately higher, and that it is the cause to intelligibles of a subsistence according to the same things, and after the same manner. It has indeed been said to be permanency, but this is a coordinate cause, and rather affords sameness of subsistence about energy; but eternity is an exempt cause. It is also evident that it is the comprehension and union of many intelligible unities; and hence it is called by the oracles *father-begotten light*,[†] because it illuminates all things with unific light. "For," says the Oracle, "this alone, by plucking abundantly from the strength of the father, the flower of intellect, is enabled by intellection to impart a paternal intellect to all the fountains and principles: together with intellectual energy and a perpetual permanency according to an unsluggish revolution." For, being full of paternal deity, which the Oracle calls the flower of intellect, it illuminates all things with intellect, together with an eternal sameness of intellection, and an amatory conversion and energy about the principle of all things. These things, however, I revolve in the inaccessible adyta of the dianoëtic part.

Again, investigating on all sides the intellectual conception of the philosopher about eternity, let us consider what is the meaning of its abiding in *one*. For we inquire, in what *one*? Shall we say, in *The Good*, as it has appeared to the most theological of the interpreters? But neither does *The Good* abide in itself, through its simplicity, as we learn in the first hypothesis of the *Parmenides*, and therefore much less does any thing else abide in it. For, in short, nothing is in it, nor with it, in consequence of its being exempt from coordination with any thing. Hence it is not usually called good, or one, but *The Good* and *The One*, that we may understand its monadic transcendency, and which is beyond every nature that is known. But now eternity is not said to abide in *The One*, but in one; so that neither does it abide *The Good*. Shall we say then, that by eternity abiding in one, its united nature as it were, its permanency in its own one, and its subsisting as one multitude, are implied? Or, in short, the number of that which does not proceed, that it may be the cause of union to the multitude of intelligibles? Shall we say that this also is true, that it may impart to itself the stable and the whole prior to things eternal? For to abide in one,

---

† This is one of the Chaldean Oracles, which, as I have shown in my collection of them [TTS vol. VII], were delivered by Chaldean Theurgists under the reign of Marcus Antoninus. The original is as follows:

Πατρογενες φαος· πολυ γαρ μονος
Εκ πατρος αλκης δρεψαμενος νοου ανθος,
Εχει τω νοειν πατρικον νουν ενδιδοναι
Πασαις πηγαις τε και αρχαις·
Και το νοειν, αει τε μενειν αοκνω στροφαλιγγι.

is to have the whole and the same hyparxis invariably present at once. Every divine nature, therefore, begins its energy from itself, so that eternity also establishes itself in one prior to things eternal; and in a similar manner connects itself. Hence being is not the cause of permanency, as Strato[†] the natural philosopher says it is, but eternity;[‡] and it is the cause of a permanency, not such as is always in generation, or becoming to be, but which, as Timæus says, invariably subsists in one. But if eternity unfolds a duad, though we are often studious to conceal it; for the ever is conjoined with being, according to the same, and *eternity* is *that which always is* (εστιν αιων, ο αει ων); if this be the case, it appears to have the monad of being prior to it, and the one being, *viz.* the highest being, and to abide in this one, agreeably to the doctrine of our preceptor, that the first being may be one prior to the duad, as not departing from *The One*. And the duad indeed in eternity, which causally unfolds multitude, is united to the first being in which eternity[§] abides; but the multitude of intelligibles is united to eternity itself, which in a transcendent and united manner comprehends and connects all their summits. For that the conception of the first being is different from that of eternity is evident; since to be for ever is perfectly different from simply to be. If therefore any thing is *eternal*, this also *is*; but the contrary does not follow, that if any thing *is*, this also is *eternal*. Hence, *to be* is more total and generative than *to be for ever*, and on this account is nearer to the cause of all beings, of the unities in beings, of generation itself, of matter, and, in short, of all things. These three, therefore, orderly succeed each other; *the one being*,[*] as the monad of beings; *eternity* as the duad, together with being possessing *the ever*; and *the eternal*, which participates both of being and the ever, and is not primarily eternal being, like eternity. And *the one being* is alone the cause of being to all things, whether they are truly or not truly beings; but eternity is the cause of permanency in being. And this is what Strato ought rather to have said, and not to have defined being to be the permanency of things, as he writes in his book *Concerning Being*, transferring the idiom of eternity to being.

[†] Strato was a philosopher of Lampsacus. He was the disciple and successor of Theophrastus; and flourished 289 years before Christ.

[‡] For eternity is stability of being; and in like manner immortality is stability of life, and memory of knowledge.

[§] As the intelligible triad, or the first procession from the ineffable cause of all, consists, as will be shown in the Introduction to the *Parmenides*, of *being, life* and *intellect*, eternity forms the middle of this triad, being, as Plotinus divinely says, infinite life, at once total and full, and abides in the summit of this triad, *i.e.* in being itself or the first and intelligible being.

[*] To εν ον, *viz.* being characterized by and wholly absorbed in *The One*; for such is the first being.

Let us now attend to the following admirable account of time, by Proclus.

How then is time said by Plato to be an image of eternity? Is it because eternity abides in *one*, but time proceeds according to *number*? These things however rather indicate their dissimilitude than similitude to each other. For Plato nearly opposes all things to all, *proceeding, to abiding, according to number, to one, the image to the thing itself*. It is better, therefore, to say, that divinity produced these two as the measures of things, I mean eternity and time, the one of intelligible and the other of mundane beings. As the world, therefore, is said to be the image of the intelligible, so also the mundane measure is denominated the image of the intelligible measure. Eternity, however, is a measure as the one, but time as number: for each measures the former things united, and the latter things numbered: and the former measures the permanency of beings, but the latter the extension of generated natures. But the apparent oppositions of these two, do not evince the dissimilitude of the measures, but that secondary are produced from more ancient natures. For progression is from *abiding*, and number from *The One*. May we not therefore say, that time is on this account an image of eternity, because it is productive of the perfection of mundane natures, just as eternity connectedly contains, and is the guardian of beings. For as those natures which are unable to live according to intellect, are led under the order of Fate, lest by flying from a divine nature they should become perfectly disordered; in like manner things which have proceeded from eternity, and are unable to participate of a perfection, the whole of which is established at once, and is always the same, end indeed in the government of time, but are excited by it to appropriate energies, through which they are enabled to receive the end adapted to their nature, from certain periods which restore them to their ancient condition.

But how is time said to be a moveable image of eternity? Shall we say because the whole of it is in motion? Or is this indeed impossible? For nothing is moved according to the whole of itself, not even such things as are essentially changed: for the subject of these remains. Much more therefore must that which is moved, according to other motions, abide according to essence, and this if it be increased, and changed, and locally moved. For if it did not abide according to something, it would at the same time cause the motion to be evanescent; since all motion is in something. Nothing, therefore, is as we have said moved according to the whole of itself, and especially such perpetual natures as it is fit should be established in their proper principles, and abide in themselves, if they are to be continually preserved. But in a particular manner the image of eternity ought in a certain respect to possess perpetuity according to sameness, and stability; so that it is impossible that time should be moved according to the whole of itself, since neither is this possible to any thing else. Something of it, therefore, must necessarily remain, since every thing which is moved is moved in consequence of possessing something belonging to it which abides. The monad of time, therefore, abides suspended from the demiurgus; but being full of measuring power, and wishing to measure the essential motions of the soul, together with physical and corporeal motion, and also being, energies and passions, it proceeds according to number. Hence time, abiding by its impartible and inward energy, and being participated by its external energy, and by the natures which are measured proceeds according to number; i.e. it proceeds according to a certain intellectual number, or rather according to the first of beings, presides over intellectuals, in the same manner as the first being presides over intelligibles. Time, therefore, proceeds according to that number; and hence it distributes an accommodated measure to every mundane form.

You may also say still more appropriately, that time which is truly so called proceeds according to number, numbering the participants of itself, and being itself that intellectual number, which Socrates obscurely indicates when he says that swiftness itself and slowness itself are in true number, by which the things numbered by time differ, being moved swifter or slower. Hence Timæus does not speak with prolixity about this true number, because Socrates had previously in the *Republic* perfectly unfolded it, but he speaks about that which proceeds from it. For that being true number, time, says he, proceeds according to number. Let then true time proceed according to intelligible number, but it proceeds so far as it measures its participants, just as the time of which Timæus now speaks proceeds as that which is numerable, possessing yet an image of essential time, through which it numbers all things with greater or lesser numbers of their life, so that an ox lives for this and man for that period of time, and the sun and moon and the other stars accomplish their revolutions according to different measures. Time, therefore, is the measure of motion, not as that by which we measure, but as that which produces and bounds the being of life, and of every other motion of things in time, and as measuring them according to and assimilating them to paradigms. For as it refers itself to the similitude of eternity which comprehends paradigmatic causes, in like manner it sends back to a more venerable imitation of eternal principles things perfected by it, which are circularly convolved. Hence theurgists say that time is a god, and deliver to us a method by which we may excite this deity to render himself apparent. They also celebrate him as older and younger, and as a circulating and eternal God; not only as the image of eternity, but as eternally comprehending it prior to sensibles. They add further, that he intellectually perceives the whole number of all the natures that are moved in the world, according to which he leads round and restores to their ancient condition in swifter and slower periods every thing that is moved. Besides all this, they celebrate him as interminable through power, in consequence of infinite circulation. And lastly, they add that he is of a spiral form, as measuring according to one power things which are moved in a right line, and those which are moved in a circle, just as the spiral uniformly comprehends the right line and the circle.

We must not, therefore, follow those who consider time as consisting in mere naked conceptions, or who make it to be a certain accident; nor yet must we assent to those who are more venerable than these, and who approach nearer to reality, and assert with them that the idiom of time is derived from the soul of the world energizing transitively. For Plato, with whom we all desire to accord respecting divine concerns, says that the demiurgus gave subsistence to time, the world being now arranged both according to soul and according to body, and that it was inserted in the soul by him, in the same manner as harmonic reasons. Nor again, does he represent the god fashioning and generating time in the soul, in the same manner as he says the Divinity fabricated the whole of a corporeal nature within the soul, that the soul might be the despot and governor of it; but having discoursed concerning the essence, harmony, power, motions, and all various knowledges of the soul, he produces the essence of time, as the guardian and measurer of all these, and as that which assimilates them to paradigmatic principles. For what benefit would arise from all mundane natures being well-conditioned, without a perpetual permanency of subsistence; and in imitating after a manner the idea of their paradigm, but not evolving to the utmost of their power the whole of it, and in receiving partibly impartible intelligence? Hence the philosopher places a demiurgic cause and not soul over the progression of time.

In the next place, looking to things themselves, you may say that if soul generated time, it would not thus participate as being perfected by it; for that soul is perfected by time, and also measured by it according to its energies, is not immanifest, since every thing which has not the whole of its energy collectively and at once, requires time to its perfection and restoration, through which it collects its proper good, which it was incapable of acquiring impartibly, and without the circulations of time. Hence, as we have before observed, eternity and time are the measures of the permanency and perfection of things; the former being the one simple comprehension of the intelligible unities, and the other the boundary and demiurgic measure of the more or less extended permanency of the natures which proceed from thence. If, therefore, soul, after the same manner with intellect and the gods, apprehended every object of its knowledge by one projecting energy, and always the same, understanding immutably, it might perhaps have generated time, but would not require time to its perfection. But since it understands transitively, and according to periods by which it becomes restored to its pristine state, it is evidently dependant on time for the perfection of its energy.

After this, it is requisite to understand that inanimate natures also participate of time, and that they do not then only participate of it when they are born, in the same manner as they participate of form and habit, but also when it appears that they are deprived of all life; and this not in the same manner, as they are even then said to live, because they are coordinated with wholes, and sympathize with the universe, but they also peculiarly and essentially participate of a certain time, so far as they are inanimate, continually dissolving as far as to perfect corruption. To which we may add, that since the mutations, motions and rests pertaining to souls and bodies, and, in short, all such things as rank among opposites in mundane affairs, are measured by time, it is requisite that time should be exempt from all these; for that which is participated by many things, and these dissimilar, being one and the same, and always presubsisting by itself, is participated by them conformably to this mode of subsistence; and still further, being in all things, it is every where impartible, so that it is every where one thing, impartible according to number, and the peculiarity of no one of the things which are said to subsist according to it. And this Aristotle also perceiving, demonstrates that there is something incorporeal and impartible in divisible natures, and which is every where the same, meaning by this the *now* in time. Further still, time not being essence, but an accident, it would not thus indicate a demiurgic power, so as to produce some things perpetually in generation, or becoming to be, but others with a more temporal generated subsistence; and some things more slowly proceeding to being than these, but swifter than more imbecil natures; at the same time distributing to all things an accommodated and proper measure of permanency in beings. But if time is a demiurgic essence, it will not be the whole soul, nor a part of soul; for the conception of soul is different from that of time, and each is the cause of different and not of the same things. For soul imparts life, and moves all things, and hence the world, so far as it approaches to soul, is filled with life, and participates of motion; but time excites fabrications to their perfection, and is the supplier of measure and a certain perpetuity to wholes. It will not, therefore, be subordinate to soul, since soul participates of it, if not essentially, yet according to its transitive energies. For the soul of the universe is said to energize incessantly, and to live intellectually through the whole of time. It remains, therefore, that time is an essence, and not secondary to that of soul. In short, if eternity were the progeny of intellect, or were a certain intellectual power, it would be necessary to say that time also is something of this kind pertaining to soul: but if eternity is the exempt measure of the multitude of intelligibles, and the comprehension of the perpetuity and perfection of all things, must not time also have the same relation to soul and the animastic order? So that time will differ from eternity, in the same manner as all proceeding natures from their abiding causes. For eternity exhibits more transcendency with respect to the things measured by it than time, since the former comprehends in an exempt manner the essences and the unities of intelligibles; but the latter does not measure the essences of the first souls, as being rather coordinated and generated together with them. Intelligibles also are more united with eternity than mundane natures with time. The union indeed of the former is so vehement, that some of the more contemplative philosophers have considered eternity to be nothing else than one total intellect; but no wise man would be willing to consider time as the same with the things existing in time, through the abundant separation and difference between the two.

If then time is neither anything belonging to motion, nor an attendant on the energy of soul, nor, in short, the offspring of soul, what will it be? For perhaps it is not sufficient to say that it is the measure of mundane natures, nor to enumerate the goods of which it is the cause, but to the utmost of our power we should endeavour to apprehend its idiom. May we not therefore say, since its essence is most excellent, perfective of soul, and present to all things, that it is an intellect, not only abiding but also subsisting in motion? Abiding indeed according to its inward energy, and by which it is truly eternal, but being moved according to its externally proceeding energy, by which it becomes the boundary of all transition. For eternity possessing the abiding, both according to its inward energy, and that which it exerts to things eternal, time being assimilated to it according to the former of these energies, becomes separated from it according to the latter, abiding and being moved. And as with respect to the essence of the soul, we say that it is intelligible, and at the same time generated, partible, and at the same time impartible, and are no otherwise able perfectly to apprehend its middle nature than by employing after a manner opposites, what wonder is there if, perceiving the nature of time to be partly immovable and partly subsisting in motion, we, or rather not we, but prior to us, the philosopher, through *the eternal*, should indicate its intellectual monad abiding in sameness, and through *the moveable* its externally proceeding energy, which is participated by soul and the whole world? For we must not think that the expression *the eternal* simply indicates that time is the image of eternity, for if this were the case, what would have hindered Plato from directly saying that it is the *image*, and not the *eternal image* of eternity? But he was willing to indicate this very thing, that time has an eternal nature, but not in such a manner as animal itself is said to be eternal: for that is eternal both in essence and energy; but time is partly eternal, and partly, by its external gift, moveable. Hence theurgists call it eternal, and Plato very properly denominates it not *only* so, for one thing is *alone* moveable, both essentially and according to the participants of it, being *alone* the cause of motion, as soul, and hence it *alone* moves itself and other things: but another thing is *alone* immovable, preserving itself without transition, and being the cause to other things of a perpetual subsistence after the same manner, and to moveable natures through soul. It is necessary, therefore, that the medium between these two extremes should be that which, both according to its own nature, and the gifts which it imparts to others, is immovable and at the same time moveable, essentially immovable indeed, but moved in its participants. But a thing of this kind is time; hence time is truly, so far as it is considered in itself, immovable, but so far as it is in its participants, it is moveable, and subsists together with them, unfolding itself into them. It is therefore eternal, and a monad, and centre essentially, and according to its own abiding energy; but it is, at the same time, continuous and number, and a circle, according to its proceeding and being participated. Hence it is a certain proceeding intellect, established indeed in eternity, and on this account is said to be eternal. For it would not otherwise contribute to the assimilation of mundane natures to more perfect paradigms, unless it were itself previously suspended from them. But it proceeds and abundantly flows into the things which are guarded by it. Whence I think the chief of theurgists celebrate time as a god, as Julian in the seventh of the Zones, and venerate it by these names, through which it is unfolded in its participants; causing some things to be older, and others to be younger, and leading all things in a circle. Time, therefore, possessing a certain intellectual nature, circularly leads according to number, both its other participants and souls. For time is eternal, not in essence only, but also in its inward energy; but so far as it is participated by externals, it is alone movable, coextending and harmonizing with them the gift which it imparts. But every soul is transitively moved, both according to its inward and external energies, by the latter of which it moves bodies. And it appears to me that those who thus denominated time χρονος, had this conception of its nature, and were therefore willing to call it as it were χορευοντος νους, an intellect moving in measure; but dividing the words perhaps for the sake of concealment, they called it χρονος. Perhaps too, they gave it this appellation because it abides, and is at the same time moved in measure; by one part of itself abiding, and by the other proceeding with measured motion. By the conjunction, therefore, of both these, they signify the wonderful and demiurgic nature of this god. And it appears, that as the demiurgus being intellectual began from intellect to adorn the universe, so time being itself supermundane, began from soul to impart perfection. For that time is not only mundane, but by a much greater priority supermundane, is evident; since as eternity is to animal itself, so is time to this world, which is animated and illuminated by intellect, and wholly an image of animal itself, in the same manner as time of eternity.

Time, therefore, while it abides, moves in measure; and through its abiding, its measured motions are infinite, and are restored to their pristine state. For moving in measure, the first of intellects about the whole fabrication of things, so far as it perpetually subsists after the same manner, and is intellect according to essence, it is said to be eternal; but so far as it moves in measure, it circularly leads souls, and natures, and bodies, and, in short, periodically restores them to their pristine condition. For the world is moved indeed, as participating of soul; but it is moved in an orderly manner, because it participates of intellect; and it is moved periodically with a motion from the same to the same, imitating the permanency of the intellect which it contains, through the resemblance of time to eternity. And this it is to make the world more similar to its paradigm; *viz.* by restoring it to one and the same condition, to assimilate it to that which abides in one, through the circulation according to time. From these things also, you have all the causes of time according to Plato; the demiurgus indeed, as the fabricative cause; eternity as the paradigm; and the end the circulation of the things moved to that which is one, according to periods. For in consequence of not abiding in one, it aspires after that which is one, that it may partake of *The One*, which is the same with *The Good*. For it is evident that the progression of things is not one, and in a right line, infinitely extended as it were both ways, but is bounded and circumscribed, moving in measure about the father of wholes, and the monad of time infinitely evolving all the strength of fabrication, and again returning to its pristine state. For whence are the participants of time enabled to return to their pristine condition, unless that which is participated possessed this power and peculiarity of motion? Time, therefore, the first of things which are moved, circulating according to an energy proceeding to externals, and returning to its pristine state, after all the evolution of its power, thus also restores the periods of other things to their former condition. By the whole progression of itself indeed, it circularly leads the soul which first participates of it; but by certain parts of itself, it leads round other souls and natures, the celestial revolutions, and among things last, the whole of generation: for in consequence of time circulating all things circulate; but the circles of different natures are shorter and longer. For again, if the demiurgus himself made time to be a moveable image of eternity, and gave it subsistence according to his intellection about eternity, it is necessary that what is moveable in time, should be circular and moved in measure, that it may not apostatize from, and may evolve the intelligence of the father about eternity. For, in short, since that which is moveable in time is comprehensive of all motions, it is requisite that it should be bounded much prior to the things which are measured by it: for not that which is deprived of measure, but the first measure, measures things; as neither does infinity bound, but the first bound. But time is moved, neither according to soul, nor according to nature, nor according to that which is corporeal and apparent; since its motions would thus be divisible, and not comprehensive of wholes. It would likewise thus participate of irregularity, either more or less, and its motions would be indigent of time. For all of them are beheld in time, and not in progression, as those which are the measures of wholes, but in a certain quality of life, or lation, or passion. But the motion of time is a pure and invariable progression, equal and similar, and the same. For it is exempt both from regular and irregular motions, and is similarly present to both, not receiving any alteration through the motions themselves being changed, but remaining the same separate from all inequality, being energetic and restorative of whole motions according to nature, of which also it is the measure. It also subsists unmingled with the natures which it measures, according to the idiom of its intellectual energy, but proceeds transitively, and according to the peculiarity of self-motion. And in this respect, indeed, it accords with the order of soul, but is inherent in the things which are bounded and perfected by it according to a primary cause of nature. It is not however similar in all respects to any one thing. For in a certain respect it is necessary that the measure of wholes should be similar to all things, and be allied to all things, but yet not be the same with any one of the things measured.

The motion, therefore, of time proceeds evolving and dividing impartible and abiding power, and causing it to appear partible; being as it were a certain number, divisibly receiving all the forms of the monad, and reverting and circulating to itself. For thus the motion of time proceeding according to the measures in the temporal monad conjoins the end with the beginning, and this infinitely; possessing indeed itself a divine order, not *arranged* as the philosopher Iamblichus also says, but that which *arranges*; nor an order which is attendant on things precedent, but which is the primary leader of effects. This motion is also at the same time measured, not indeed from any thing endued with interval, for it would be ridiculous to say that things which have a more ancient nature and dignity, are measured by things subordinate, but it is measured from the temporal monad alone, which its progression is said to evolve, and by a much greater priority from the demiurgus, and from eternity itself. With relation to eternity, therefore, which is perfectly immovable, time is said to be moveable; just as if some one should say that soul is divisible about bodies, when considered with relation to intellect, not that it is this alone, but that when compared with intellect, it may appear to be such, though when compared with a divisible essence, it is indivisible. Time, therefore, is moveable not in itself, but according to the participation from it which appears in motions, and by which they are measured and bounded; just as if it should be said that soul is divisible about bodies, so far as there is a certain divisible participation of it about these of which it comprehends the cause. For thus also time is moveable, as possessing the cause of the energy externally proceeding from it, and which is divisibly apparent in motions, and is separated together with them. As motions, therefore, become temporal through participation, so time is moveable, through being participated by motions.

23. (See page 438, line 37e) What day and night, month and year, are, says Proclus, and how these are said to be parts of time, but *was* and *will be* species, and not parts, requires much discussion and profound consideration. If then we should say that day is air illuminated by the sun, in the first place, we should speak of something which takes place in day, and not that which day is; for, when we say that the day is long or short, we certainly do not predicate an increase or decrease of the air; and, in the next place, it is difficult to devise how this will be a part of time. But if we say that day is the temporal interval according to which the sun proceeds from the east to the west, we shall perhaps avoid the former objections, but we shall fall into more impervious difficulties. For whether, surveying this interval itself without relation to the sun, we say that it is day, how does it happen, since the same interval is every where according to the same, that day is not every where? And if we consider this interval in connection with the solar motion, if it is simply so considered, day will always be in the heavens, and there will be no night; and how is it possible that a part of time should not be every where? for night, day, and month, are here clearly said to be parts of time. But if we connect this interval with the circulation of the sun, not simply, but assert that day is the portion of the sun's course from east to west, but night that portion which is produced by his course from west to east, the heavens will not possess those nights and days which are said to be parts of time; and it is also evident that neither will they possess months and years. But we assert of time, both considered according to the whole of itself, and every part of its progression, that it is present to the whole world: for one and the same *now* is every where the same. It is necessary, therefore, that day and the other parts of time should be every where the same, though they are participated partibly, and with divulsion by sensible fabrications. Assigning, therefore, to these a more principal subsistence,

conformably to the custom of our father,[†] we must say, that night and day are demiurgic measures of time, exciting and convolving all the apparent and unapparent life and motion, and orderly distribution of the inerratic sphere: for these are the true parts of time, are present after the same manner to all things, and comprehend the primary cause of apparent day and night, each of these having a different subsistence in apparent time; to which also Timæus looking reminds us how time was generated together with the world. Hence he says in the plural number *nights* and *days*, as also *months* and *years*. But these are obvious to all men: for the unapparent causes of these have a uniform subsistence prior to things multiplied, and which circulate infinitely. Things immovable also subsist prior to such as are moved, and intellectual natures are prior to sensibles. Such, therefore, must be our conceptions of night and day according to their first subsistence.

By *month* we must understand that truly divine temporal measure which convolves the lunar sphere, and every termination of the other[‡] circulation. But *year* is that which perfects and connects the whole of middle fabrication, according to which the sun is seen possessing the greatest strength, and measuring all things in conjunction with time. For neither day nor night, nor month, is without the sun, nor much more year, nor any other mundane nature. I do not here speak according to the apparent fabrication of things alone, for the apparent sun is the cause of these measures, but also according to that fabrication which is unapparent. For, ascending higher, we shall find that the more true sun[§] measures all things in conjunction with time, being itself in reality time of time, according to the oracle[*] of the Gods concerning it. For that Plato not only knew these apparent parts of time, but also those divine parts to which these are homonymous, is evident from the tenth book of his *Laws*. For he there asserts that we call hours and months divine, as having the same divine lives, and divine intellects presiding over them, as the universe. But, if he now speaks about the apparent parts of time, it is by no means wonderful; because now his design is to physiologize. Let these, therefore, be the parts of time, of which some are accommodated to the inerratic Gods, others to the Gods that revolve about the poles of the oblique circle, and others to other Gods, or attendants of the Gods, or to mortal animals, or the more sublime or more abject parts of the universe.

---

† Meaning his preceptor Syrianus, as being his true father, the father of his soul.

‡ *Viz.* of the circulation about the zodiac.

§ *Viz.* the sun considered according to its subsistence in the supermundane order of Gods.

* *Viz.* one of the Chaldæan Oracles [See p. 41 TTS vol. VII.]

But Plato says that *was* and *will be* are species and not parts of time, in the same manner as days and nights, and months and years: for by these he represents to us those divine orders which give completion to the whole series of time; and on this account he calls them parts of time. But *was* and *will be* are entirely beheld according to each of these; and hence they are certain species, not having as it were a peculiar matter; I mean a diurnal or nocturnal matter, or any other of this kind. If then these are the species of time which was generated together with the world, there was no generation prior to the world. Neither, therefore, was there any motion: for in every motion there are these species of time, because there are prior and posterior. But, if there was not motion, neither was there inordinate motion. In vain, therefore, do the followers of Atticus say, that there was time prior to the generation of the world, but not subsisting in order: for where time is there also there is past and future; and where these are, *was* and *will be* must likewise be found. But *was* and *will be* are species of time generated by the demiurgus: and hence time was not prior to the fabrication of the world. Proclus after this observes, that *was* indicates the perfective order of time, but *will be* the unfolding, in the same manner as *is*, the connective order of time. For time unfolds things which yet are not, connects things present, and perfects things past, and introduces a boundary to them adapted to their periods.

24. (See page 439, line 38b) Plato, says Proclus, asserts that time was generated together with the universe, animated and endued with intellect, because the world first participates of time according to soul and according to a corporeal nature. But when he says, "that, being produced together, they may together be dissolved, if any dissolution should ever happen to these," he clearly shows that the universe is unbegotten and incorruptible. For, if it was generated, it was generated in time; but, if it was generated together with time, it was not generated in time: for neither is time generated in time, lest there should be time prior to time. If, therefore, the universe was generated together with time, it was not generated:[†] for it is necessary that every thing which is generated should be posterior to time; but the universe is by no means posterior to time. Again, if every thing which is dissolved, is dissolved on a certain time, but time cannot be dissolved in a part of itself, time can never be dissolved; so that neither will the universe be dissolved, since it is indissoluble, as long as time is indissoluble. Time also is indissoluble through the simplicity of its nature, unless some one should denominate the contrariety which arises through its procession from, and regression to, the demiurgus, generation and dissolution: for thus also the universe possesses dissolution and generation according to cause. Just, therefore, as if some one, wishing to indicate that the

---

† *Viz.* it was not generated according to the usual acceptation of the word generated.

circulations of the other nature[†] are odd in number, should say that the heptad is consubsistent with them, that if at any time the heptad should become an even number, those circulations also may become even, signifying that the circulations will never be changed into an even number, - after the same manner must we conceive respecting the all-various indissolubility of the world and of time, in consequence of time possessing an indissoluble nature. One cause, therefore, of time being generated together with the universe is, that the universe may be indissoluble and perpetual; but a second cause is, that it may become most similar to its paradigm. How, therefore, does the universe become more similar to its paradigm animal itself ($\alpha v\tau o$ $\zeta \omega o v$) through time? Because, says Plato, as the intelligibles from which animal itself consists receive all the power of eternity, which is unific, and connective, and subsists at once, collectively and unitedly, so the world receives partibly and divisibly all the measured motion of time; through which it was, and is, and will be, not possessing these three in the whole of time, but each in a part of time.

25. (See page 439, line 38c) The one monad itself of time (says Proclus) is an all-perfect number; but from this monad there is also in each of the celestial revolutions a proper measure, Saturnian, or Jovian, or Lunar, receiving its peculiarity from the soul and motive deity contained in each of the spheres. For one number is adapted to the sun, another to a horse, and another to a plant; but the mundane number is common to all that the world contains. Hence also we say that the same time is every where. For the world has one life, in the same manner as it has one nature, and one intellect. But if it has one life, it has also one temporal measure. And as, with respect to the parts which it contains, each lives according to the nature which subsists in the world as a whole, so also it is measured according to total time; and this is the common measure of all things. But after this monad there is a triad, of which the summit is the measure of the first circulation, viz. of the motion of the inerratic sphere; but the middle is the measure of the revolutions of the planets, (for there is one life, one period, and one time, restoring things to their pristine condition, of all the planets as of one animal), and the third is the measure of the circular motion in generation. For through this the mutations of the elements, and the opposition and regeneration of the things moved, again receive their subsistence. But, after this triad, time proceeds according to different numbers, measuring wholes, and bounding all things by appropriate measures.

26. (See page 439, line 38d) By the *other stars*, says Proclus, Plato means Mars, Jupiter, and Saturn; and by the word *established*, he signifies the perpetual and

---

[†] *Viz.* the circulations about the zodiac.

incorruptible fabrication of them. After this Proclus observes, that it is here requisite to call to mind the order of all the mundane spheres. which is as follows: The inerratic sphere ranks as a monad, being the cause to all mundane natures of an invariable subsistence. But of the triad under this monad, *viz.* Saturn, Jupiter, Mars, the first is the cause of connected comprehension, the second of symmetry, and the third of separation. And again, the moon is a monad, being the cause of all generation and corruption; but the triad consists from the elements[†] in generation under the moon; and the planets whose course is equal[‡] subsist between these. And the Sun, indeed, unfolds truth into light, Venus beauty, and Mercury the symmetry of reasons, or the productive principles of nature. Or, you may say that the Moon is the cause of nature to mortals, she being the self-conspicuous image of fontal[§] nature. But the Sun is the demiurgus of every thing sensible, since he is also the cause of seeing and being seen. Mercury is the cause of the *motions* of the phantasy; for the sun gives subsistence to the phantastic *essence*. Venus is the cause of the appetites of desire; and Mars of all natural irascible motions. Jupiter is the common cause of all vital, and Saturn of all gnostic powers. For all the irrational forms are divided into these, and the causes of these are comprehended in the celestial spheres.

27. (See page 440, line 38b) Plato, says Proclus, here delivers the one and the leading cause of apparent time. For, as the demiurgus gives subsistence to unapparent, so the sun to apparent time, which measures the motion of bodies: for the sun, through light, leads into the apparent every temporal interval, bounds all periods, and exhibits the measures of restorations to a pristine state. Very properly, therefore, does Plato call the sun a *conspicuous measure*, as especially unfolding the progression[*] of time into the universe, according to number. For it has a more accurate period than the five planets, being freed from advancing and receding motions, and also revolves more accurately than the moon, in consequence of always bounding its progressions to the north and south, according to the same sign. But, if it has a more accurate period, it is deservedly said to be the measure of measures, and to know from itself the periodic measures of the other planets, the ratios which they contain, and the swiftness of some of them compared with others. It also imitates in a greater

---

[†] *Viz.* from fire, air, and water.

[‡] *Viz.* Mercury and Venus subsist between the triad Saturn, Jupiter, Mars, and the Moon.

[§] *Viz.* of Nature, considered as subsisting in its divine cause Rhea.

[*] In the original περιοδον, but the sense requires we should read προοδον.

degree than the other planets the permanency of eternity, through perpetually revolving after the same invariable manner. Such then is its difference with respect to the planets.

But the sun is after another manner a more conspicuous measure of the inerratic sphere; since this sphere also has a certain appropriate measure, and an appropriate interval, and one invariable number of its proper motion. The solar light, however, makes this measure, and all the evolution of apparent time, conspicuous and known. Hence Plato says "that these circles might possess a certain conspicuous measure:" for though there is a certain measure in the other stars, yet it is not *conspicuous*. But the sun unfolds into light both other intelligibles and time itself. You must not, however, say, that the solar light was therefore generated for the sake of measuring; for how is it possible that wholes can have a subsistence for the sake of parts, governing natures for the sake of the governed, and things eternal for the sake of such as are corruptible? But we should rather say that light manifests total time, possessing an unfolding power, and calls forth its supermundane monad, and one measure, to a mensuration of the periods of bodies. It is the light of the sun, therefore, which makes every thing that is moved to have a conspicuous measure. And this, indeed, is its total good. But after wholes it also secondarily benefits parts; for it gives the generation of number and a measure to such things as are fit participants of these. For irrational natures are destitute of these; but the genera of dæmons follow the periods of the Gods, and men become partakers of number and measure. The communications, therefore, of the sun, supernally beginning from wholes, descend as far as to parts, conferring good through light. And if, commencing from things apparent, you are willing to speak of things unapparent, the sun illuminates the whole world, makes the corporeal nature of it divine, and the whole of it to be totally filled with life. It also leads souls through undefiled light, and imparts to them an undefiled and elevating power, and by its rays governs the world. It likewise fills souls with empyrean fruits. For the order of the sun proceeds supernally from supermundane natures; and hence Plato does not here give subsistence to its light from a certain place, but says that the demiurgus *enkindled* it, as forming this sphere from his own essence, and emitting from the solar fountain a divulsed and nascent life; which also theologists assert concerning the supermundane firmaments. On this account, also, Plato appears to me to deliver a twofold generation of the sun; one together with the seven governors of the world, when he fashions their bodies and places them in their revolving spheres; but the other the *enkindling* of its light, according to which he imparts to it supermundane power. For it is one thing to generate itself by itself, the whole bulk of the sun, and another to generate it together with a governing idiom, through which it is called the king of every thing visible, and is established as analogous to the one fountain of good. For, as *The Good Itself*, being better than *the intelligible*, illuminates both intellect and the intelligible, so the sun, being better than the visible essence, illuminates sight, and whatever is visible. But if the sun is above the visible essence, it will have a super mundane nature: for the world is visible and tangible, and possesses a body. We must, therefore, survey the sun in a twofold respect; as one of the seven mundane governors, and as the leader of wholes, as mundane and as supermundane, according to which also he illuminates with divine light. For, as *The Good* generates truth, which deifies both the intelligible and intellectual orders; as Phanes, according to Orpheus, emits intelligible light, which fills all the intellectual Gods with intelligence; and as Jupiter enkindles an intellectual and demiurgic light in all supermundane natures, so the sun illuminates every thing visible through this undefiled light. But that which illuminates is always in an order more elevated than the things which are illuminated. For neither is *The Good* intelligible, nor is Phanes intellectual, nor Jupiter supermundane. From this reasoning, therefore, the sun being supermundane emits the fountains of light. And the most mystic of discourses place the *wholeness* of the sun in the supermundane order; for there a solar world and total light subsist, as the oracles of the Chaldæans say, and as I am persuaded. And thus much concerning these particulars.

Proclus afterwards, near the end of his commentary on this part, observes, that if by the heavens here we understand that which is moved in a circle, the sun does not illuminate the whole of this: for there are shadows there, through the obscurations of the stars and the moon. But nothing in the world is pure from shadow, (as neither is there any thing mundane pure from matter, supermundane natures alone being without shadow and immaterial,) except the sun. Hence, the sun is truly shadowless and without generation, every thing else receiving at different times different illuminative additions. Why, then, some one may say, was not the light of the sun enkindled in the first of the periods from the earth? Because, I reply, the effulgence of the sun is of itself incommensurate with generation; but the moon, existing as a medium, and first receiving his light, renders it more commensurate with generation. For, as Aristotle says, the moon is, as it were, a lesser sun. And it is requisite that what is proximately above generation should not be the most splendid and luminous. For it is not lawful that a thing of this kind should approach to that which is dark; but what is proximate to the darkness of generation must necessarily be luminous in a secondary degree, always possessing, indeed, its proper light, but evincing a mutation in its participation of a more excellent light. It is likewise requisite that it should exhibit this mutation in an orderly manner, that through this mutation it may be the paradigm of that very mutable nature which matter introduces to generated things.

But that the stars, and all heaven, receive light from the sun, may be easily perceived. For that which is common in many things derives its subsistence from one cause, which is either exempt or coordinate; and the coordinate cause is that which first participates of that form. But that first participates in which this form especially subsists the first. If, therefore, light especially subsists in the sun, the sun will be the first light, and from this the light in other things will be derived.

28. (See page 441, line 39c) *Whatever ideas, therefore, intellect perceived by the dianoëtic energy in animal itself, etc.*

The demiurgic wholeness, says Proclus[†] (p. 266), weaves parts in conjunction with wholes, numbers with monads, and makes every part of the universe to be a world, and causes a whole and a universe to subsist in a part. For the world is allotted this from its similitude to animal itself, because animal itself is an entire monad and number, an all perfect intelligible intellect, and a plenitude of intelligible causes, which it generated so as to abide eternally in itself. For there is one multitude which abides in causes, and another which proceeds and is distributed; since the demiurgus himself also gives subsistence to some genera of gods in himself, and produces others from himself, into secondary and third orders. His father Saturn likewise generates some divinities as paradigmatic causes of fabrication abiding in himself, and others as demiurgic causes coordinated with wholes. And the grandfather of Jupiter, Heaven, contains some divinities in, and separates others from himself. Theologists also manifest these things by mystic names, such as *concealment, absorption*, and *the being educated by Fate*. But by a great priority to these, intelligible intellect, the father of wholes, generates some causes, and unfolds them into light, in himself, but produces others from himself; containing within his own comprehensions, such as are uniform, whole, and all-perfect, but producing through difference into other orders such as are multiplied and divided. Since therefore every paternal order gives subsistence to things after this manner, this world, which is an imitation of the intelligible orders, and is elevated to them, very properly contains one *allness* prior to partial animals, and another, that which receives its completion from them, and together with the former receives the latter, that it may be most similar both to the demiurgic and paradigmatic cause.

With respect to animal itself, we have before said what it is according to our opinion, and we shall also now say, that of the intelligible extent, one thing is the highest, united and occult; and another is the power of this, proceeding, and at the same time abiding; and another, that which unfolds itself through energy, and exhibits the intelligible multitude which it contains. Of these also, the first is intelligible being, the second intelligible life, and the third intelligible intellect. *Animal itself*, however, cannot be the first being: for multitude is not there, nor the tetrad of ideas, but through its singleness and ineffable union it is called *one* by Plato. And, in short, animal itself is said to participate of eternity, but the first being participates of nothing, unless some one should say

---

[†] The beginning of the Commentary of this part of the *Timæus* is unfortunately wanting in the original; and by a strange confusion, the words και η τριτη, which there form the beginning, are connected with the comment in the preceding text, which comment is also imperfect; and the whole is still more strange, the part which is wanting to the completion of this preceding comment is to be found in p. 270, beginning at the words το δε ουτως, line 11.

it participates of *The One*, which is itself a thing in every respect deserving consideration. For may we not say that what is above being itself, is even more excellent than this appellation *The One?* But that is primarily *one*, which is not such according to participation. Animal itself, therefore, cannot be being itself, through the above-mentioned causes. Neither can it be intelligible life: for animal is secondary to life, and is said to be animal by a participation of life. In short, if animal itself were the second, eternity would be being; but this is impossible: for being itself is one thing, and eternal being another; the former being the monad of being, and the latter the duad, having the ever connected with being. Besides the former is the cause of being to all things, but the latter, of their permanency according to being. If therefore animal itself is neither the one being, nor being itself, nor that which is immediately posterior to this, for eternity is this, being intelligible power, infinite life, and wholeness itself, according to which every divine nature is at once a whole; since this is the case, animal itself must be the remaining third. For animal itself must necessarily in a certain respect be intellect, since the image of it entirely subsists with sense, but sense is the image of intellect; so that in that which is primarily animal, intellect will be primarily inherent. If therefore it is secondary to life, it must necessarily subsist according to intelligible intellect: for being intelligible, and an animal, as Plato says, the most beautiful of intelligibles, and only begotten, it will possess this order. Hence animal itself is intelligible intellect, comprehending the intellectual orders of the gods in itself, of which also it is collective, unific, and perfective, being the most beautiful boundary of intelligibles, unfolding their united and unknown cause to intellectual natures, exciting itself to all-various ideas and powers, and producing all the secondary orders of the gods. Hence also Orpheus calls it the god Phanes, as unfolding into light the intelligible unities, and ascribes to him *the forms of animals*, because the first cause of intelligible animals shines forth in him; and *multiform ideas*, because he primarily comprehends intelligible ideas. He also calls him *the key of intellect*, because he bounds the whole of an intelligible essence, and connectedly contains intellectual life. To this mighty divinity the demiurgus of the universe is elevated, being himself, indeed, as we have before said, intellect, but an *intellectual* intellect, and particularly the cause of intellect. Hence he is said to behold animal itself: for to behold is the peculiarity of the intellectual gods; since the *theologist*[†] also denominates intelligible intellect *eyeless*. Concerning this intellect therefore he says,

> Love, *eyeless*, rapid, feeding in his breast.

For the object of his energy is intelligible. But the demiurgus being intellect, is not a participated intellect,[‡] that he may be the demiurgus of wholes, and

---

[†] *Viz.* Orpheus.

[‡] *Viz.* he is not an intellect consubsistent with soul.

that he may be able to look to animal itself. But being imparticipable, he is truly intellectual intellect. And, indeed, through simple intelligence, he is conjoined with the intelligible, but through various intelligence, he hastens to the generation of secondary natures. Plato, therefore, calls his intelligence *vision*, as being without multitude, and as shining with intelligible light; but he denominates his second energy *dianoëtic*, as proceeding through simple intelligence to the generation of demiurgic works. And Plato indeed says, that he *looks* to animal itself; but Orpheus, that he *leaps to* and *absorbs it*, Night[†] pointing it out to him: for through this goddess, who is both intelligible and intellectual, intellectual intellect is conjoined with the intelligible. You must not however on this account say, that the demiurgus looks to that which is external to himself: for this is not lawful to him; but that being converted to himself, and to the fountain of ideas which he contains, he is also conjoined with the monad of the all-various orders of forms. For since we say that our soul by looking to itself knows all things, and that things prior are not external to it, how is it possible that the demiurgic intellect, by understanding itself, should not in a far greater degree survey the intelligible world? For animal itself is also contained in him, though not monadically, but according to a certain divine number. Hence he is said by theologists, as we have observed, to absorb the intelligible god, being himself intellectual, in consequence of containing the whole of an intelligible essence, formal divisions, and the intelligible number, which Plato indicating denominates the ideas of the demiurgus, *such* and *so many*, by the former of these appellations manifesting *the idioms of causes*, and by the latter, *separation according to number*.

If these things then subsist after this manner, it is not proper to place an infinity of forms in intelligibles: for that which is definite is more allied to principles than the indefinite; and the first natures are always more contracted in quantity, but transcend in power natures posterior to and proceeding from them. Nor must we say with some, that animal itself is separate from the demiurgus, thus making the intelligible to be external to intellect: for we do not make that which is seen subordinate to that which sees, that it may be external, but we assert that it is prior to it: and more divine intelligibles are understood by such as are more various, as being contained in them; since our soul also entering into itself, is said to discover all things, divinity and wisdom, as Socrates asserts. Animal itself therefore is prior and not external to the demiurgus. And there indeed all things subsist totally and intelligibly, but in the demiurgus intellectually and separately: for in him the definite causes of the sun and moon presubsist, and not one idea alone of the celestial gods, which gives subsistence to all the celestial genera. Hence the Oracles assert,[‡] that his

---

[†] Night subsists at the summit of that divine order which is denominated intelligible, and at the same time intellectual.

[‡] *Viz.* The Chaldean Oracles [TTS vol. VII, p. 34.] See the *Parmenides*.

demiurgic energies burst about the bodies of the world like swarms of bees: for a divine intellect evolves into every demiurgic multitude the *total* separation of these energies in intellect.

29. (See page 441, line 40a) *But these ideas are four, etc.*

As with respect to demiurgic intelligence, a monad is the leader of intellectual multitude, and as with respect to paradigm, unical form subsists prior to number, in like manner discourse, the interpreter of divine concerns, shadowing forth the nature of the things of which it is the messenger, first receives the whole of the thing known collectively, and according to enthusiastic projection, but afterwards expands that which is convolved, unfolds the one intelligence through arguments, and divides that which is united; conformably to the nature of things, at one time interpreting their union, and at another their separation, since it is neither naturally adapted, nor is able to comprehend both these at once. Agreeably to this, the discourse of Plato first divinely unfolds the whole number of intelligible ideas, and afterwards distributes into parts the progressions which this number contains: for there intelligible multitude is apparent, where the first monads of ideas subsist. And that this is usual with Plato we have before abundantly shown. Descending therefore from words to things, let us in the first place see what this tetrad itself of ideas is, and whence this number originates, and in the next place what the four ideas are, and they subsist in animal itself, whether so as that its all perfect nature receives its completion from these, or after some other manner, for by thus proceeding we shall discover the divinely intellectual conception of Plato. It is necessary, however, again to recur to the above-mentioned demonstrations, in which we said that the first, united, and most simple intelligible essence of the gods, proceeding supernally from the unity of unities, but according to a certain mode which is ineffable and incomprehensible by all things, one part of this essence ranks as the first, is occult and paternal; but another part ranks as the second, and is the one power, and incomprehensible measure of wholes; and the third part is that which has proceeded into energy and all various powers, and is at the same time both paternal and fabricative. The first of these also is a monad, because it is the summit of the whole intelligible extent, and the fountain and cause of divine numbers; but the second is a duad, for it both abides and proceeds as in intelligible genera, and has *the ever* connected with being; and the third is the tetrad which is now investigated, which receives all the occult cause of the monad, and unfolds in itself its unproceeding power. For such things as subsist in the monad primarily, and with unproceeding union, the tetrad exhibits in a divided manner, now separated according to number, and a production into secondary natures. But since the third possesses an order adapted to it, yet also entirely participates of the causes prior to itself, it is not only the tetrad, but besides this which is still greater, as a monad it is allotted a paternal, and as a duad a fabricative and prolific transcendency. So

562

far therefore as it is called animal itself, it is the monad of the nature of all animals, intellectual, vital, and corporeal; but so far as it comprehends at the same time the male and female nature, it is a duad; for these subsist in an appropriate manner in all the orders of animals, in one way in the gods, in another in dæmons, and in another in mortals; but so far as from this duad, it gives subsistence to the four ideas of animals in itself, it is a tetrad; for the fourfold fabrication of things proceeds according to these ideas, and the first productive cause of wholes is the tetrad. Plato therefore teaching this tetradic power of the paradigm, and the most unical ideas of mundane natures, says, that they are four, comprehended in one animal itself. For there is one idea there, animal itself; and there is also a duad, *viz.* the female and the male, or, according to Plato, possessing genera and species: for he calls two of the ideas genera, *viz.* the intellectual and the air-wandering, but the other two species, as being subordinate to these. There is also a tetrad; and as far as to this, intelligible forms proceed into other productive principles according to a different number. For according to every order there is an appropriate number, the lesser comprehending the more total ideas, but the more multiplied number such as are more partial; since more divine natures being contracted in quantity, possess a transcendency of power; and the forms of second natures are more multiplied than those prior to them; such as are intellectual more than intelligibles, supermundane than intellectual, and mundane than supermundane forms. These then are the forms which proceed to an ultimate distribution, just as intelligibles receive the highest union: for all progression diminishes power and increases multitude. If therefore Timæus discoursed about a certain intellectual order, he would have mentioned another number, as for instance the hebdomadic or decadic; but since he speaks about the intelligible cause of ideas, and which comprehends all such animals as are intelligible, he says that the first ideas are four. For there the tetrad subsists proceeding from the intelligible monad, and filling the demiurgic decad. For "divine number, according to the Pythagorean hymn upon it, proceeds from the retreats of the undecaying monad, till it arrives at the divine tetrad, which produces the mother of all things, the universal recipient, venerable, placing a boundary about all things, undeviating and unwearied, which both immortal gods and earth-born men call the sacred decad."† Here the uniform and occult cause of being‡ is called the undecaying monad, and the retreats of the monad: but the manifestation of intelligible multitude, which the duad subsisting between the monad and tetrad unfolds, is denominated the divine tetrad; and the world itself receiving images of all the divine numbers, supernally imparted

---

† The last line of these verses, *viz.* αθανατοι τε θεοι, και γηγενεεις ανθρωποι, is not in Proclus, but is added from the Commentaries of Syrianus on Aristotle's *Metaphysics*, where alone it is to be found.

‡ *Viz.* The summit of the intelligible triad, or superessential being.

to it, is the decad: for thus we may understand these verses looking to the fabrication of the world. And thus much concerning this tetrad.

In the next place, let us consider what the four ideas are, and what are the things to which they give subsistence: for there are different opinions concerning this, some especial regarding the words of Plato, asserting that the progression is into gods, and the mortal genera, but others looking to things, that it is into gods, and the genera superior to man, because these subsist prior to mortals, and it is necessary that the demiurgus should not immediately produce mortals from divine natures. Others again conjoin both these, and follow what is written in the *Epinomis*, that gods subsist in the heavens, dæmons in the air, demigods in water, and men and other mortal animals in the earth. Such then being the diversity of opinion among the interpreters, we admire indeed the lovers of things, but we shall endeavour to follow our leader.[†] Hence we say that the celestial genus of gods comprehends all the *celestial* genera, whether they are divine, angelic, or dæmoniacal; but the *air-wandering*, all such as are arranged in the air, whether gods, or their attendant dæmons, or mortal animals that live in the air. Again, that the *aquatic* comprehends all the genera that are allotted water, and those natures that are nourished in water; and the pedestrial, the animals that are distributed about the earth, and that subsist and grow in the earth. For the demiurgus is at once the cause of all mundane natures, and the common father of all things, generating the divine and dæmoniacal genera by and through himself alone, but delivering mortals to the junior gods, as they are able proximately to generate them. The paradigm also is not the cause of some, but by no means of other animals, but it possesses the most total causes of all things.

It is also requisite to consider the proposed words in an appropriate manner, according to every order; as, for instance, the genus of gods arranged in the heavens, in one way, in those that are properly called gods, and in another, in the genera more excellent than man. For we say that there are celestial angels, dæmons, and heroes, and that all these are called gods, because the divine idiom has dominion over their essential peculiarity. Again, we must consider the winged and air-wandering in one way in the aërial gods, in another in dæmons, and in another in mortals. For that which is *intellectual* in the gods, is denominated *winged*; that which is *providential, air-wandering*, as pervading through all the sphere of the air, and connectedly-containing the whole of it. But in dæmons, *the winged* signifies rapidity of *energy*; and *the air-wandering* indicates their being every where present, and proceeding through all things without impediment. And in mortals, *the winged* manifests the motion through one organ of those natures that alone employ the circular motion; but *the air-wandering*, the all-various motion through bodies: for nothing hinders partial souls that live in the air from pervading through it. Again, *the aquatic* in divine natures, indicates a government inseparable from water: and hence the oracle

[†] *Viz.* Syrianus, the preceptor of Proclus.

calls these gods *water-walkers*;[†] but in the genera attendant on the gods, it signifies that which is connective of a moist nature. And indeed *the pedestrial*, in one place, signifies that which connectedly contains the last seat of things, and proceeds through it, in the same manner as *the terrestrial*, that which stably rules over this seat, and is perfective of it through all-various powers and lives; but in another place it signifies the government at different times of different parts of the earth, through an appropriate motion. And thus much concerning the names.

But from these things it may be inferred that intelligible animal itself is entirely different from animal itself in the demiurgus; since the former has not definite ideas of mortal animals. For the demiurgus wishing to assimilate what the world contains to every thing in himself, produced mortal animals, that he might make the world all-perfect; but he comprehends the definite ideas of these, producing them from the immortal genera. He knows therefore mortal animals, and it is evident that he knows them *formally*; and he thinks fit that the junior gods, looking to him, and not to animal itself, should fabricate them, in consequence of containing in himself separately the ideas of mortals and immortals. In animal itself, therefore, with respect to the aërial, or aquatic, or terrestrial, there was one idea of each of these, the cause of all aërial, aquatic, or pedestrial animals, but they are divided in the demiurgus; and some are formal comprehensions of immortal aërial, and others of mortal aërial animals; and after the same manner with respect to the aquatic and terrestrial genera. The formal multitude therefore in animal itself, is not the same with that in the demiurgus, as may be inferred from these arguments.

We may also see that Plato makes a division of these genera into monad and triad, (opposing the summit of the celestial genus to the total genera,) and into two duads. For he denominates the celestial and winged, genus, but the aquatic and pedestrial, species; the latter possessing and order subordinate to the former, in the same manner as species to genus. It is likewise requisite to observe that he omits the region of fire in these, because the divine genus comprehends the summit of fire. For of sublunary bodies, fire has not any proper region, but subsists according to mutation alone, always requiring the nourishment of air and water. For its proper place, as fire, is on high: but neither is it there, since it would be seen, being naturally visible; nor can it arrive thither, being extinguished by the surrounding air, which is dissimilar to it. If, therefore, it is requisite that there should be a wholeness of fire, and that possessing a form it should be somewhere, and not alone consist in being generated, and if there is no such fire under the moon, fire will alone subsist in the heavens, abiding such as it is, and always possessing its proper place. For

---

[†] Here, also by an unaccountable mistake, all that follows after the word υδροβατηρας, *water-walkers*, which is in p. 270, and which ought immediately to follow this word, begins near the bottom of p. 272, at the words επι δε των επομενων, etc.

a motion upwards[†] is not the property of fire when subsisting according to nature, but is alone peculiar to fire when subsisting contrary to nature. Thus also the SACRED DISCOURSE of the Chaldeans conjoins things aërial with the lunar ratlings, attributing to fire the celestial region, according to a division of the elements in the world. For the fire in generation is a certain defluxion of the celestial fire, and is in the cavities of the other elements. There is not however a sphere of fire by itself, but the summit of air imitates the purity of supernal fire. And we denominate this sublunary fire, and call the region under the heavens the place of fire: for this is most similar to the celestial profundity, as the termination of air is to water, which is gross and dark. But you should not wonder if the most attenuated and pure fire will be in the summits of air, as the most gross and turbid is in the bosom of the earth; not making this pure fire to be a wholeness different from the whole air, but considering it, being most attenuated, as carried in the pores of the air, which are most narrow. Hence it is not seen through two causes; from not being distinct from the air, and from consisting of the smallest parts: so that it does not resist our sight in the same manner as the light of visible objects. True fire, therefore, subsists in the heavens; but of sublunary fire, that which is most pure, is in the air proximate to the celestial regions, which Plato in the course of this Dialogue calls æther; and that which is most gross, is contained in the recesses of the earth.

30. (See page 442, line 40d) Plato here calls the sublunary Gods who proximately preside over, and orderly distribute, the realms of generation, dæmons; for a God who proximately presides over any thing is a dæmon according to analogy. Proclus, in speaking concerning dæmons who fill up all the middle space between Gods and men, observes as follows: "There is a triad which conjoins our souls with the Gods, proceeding analogous to the three[‡] primary causes of things, though Plato is accustomed to call the whole of it dæmoniacal. For the angelic preserves an analogy to the intelligible, which first unfolds itself into light from the arcane and occult fountain of things; on which account it also unfolds the Gods, and announces their occult nature. The dæmoniacal is analogous to infinite life; and hence it proceeds every where according to many orders, and possesses various species and a multitude of forms. But the heroic subsists according to intellect and a convertive energy; and hence it is the inspective guardian of purification, and a magnificently

---

[†] Agreeably to this, Plotinus observes, that every body, when in its proper place, is either at rest, or moves circularly.

[‡] Viz. *Being, life,* and *intellect,* which considered according to their first subsistence form the intelligible triad, or the first procession from the ineffable principle of things. See the *Parmenides.*

operating life. Again, the angelic proceeds according to the intellectual life of the demiurgus; and hence it also is essentially intellectual, and interprets and transmits a divine intellect to secondary natures. The dæmoniacal governs according to the demiurgic providence and nature of wholes, and rightly gives completion to the order of all the world. But the heroic subsists according to a providence convertive of all these. Hence, this genus is sublime, elevates souls on high, and is the cause of the grand and robust. And such are the triple genera which are suspended from the Gods, viz. from the celestial Divinities, and from the inspective guardians of generation. For about each of these Gods there is an appropriate number of angels, dæmons, and heroes: for each is the leader of a multitude which receives the form of its ruling Deity. And on this account the angels, dæmons, and heroes of the celestial Gods are celestial; of the Gods that preside over generation, they are generative; of those that elevate souls on high, they are anagogic; of I those that are immutable, they are immutable; and so on. And again, in those Gods of an anagogic characteristic, the angels, dæmons, and heroes of the Saturnian Gods are saturnine, but those of the Solar Gods are solar. And in those that are vivific, the attendants of the Lunar Deities are lunar, and of the Mercurial Gods, mercurial: for they derive their appellations from the Deities from which they are suspended, as being continuous with them, and receiving one idea with remission. And why is this wonderful, since partial souls also, knowing their presiding and leading Gods, call themselves by their names? Or, whence did the Æsculapiuses, the Bacchuses, and the Dioscuri receive their appellations? As, therefore, in the celestial Gods, so also in those that preside over generation, it is requisite to survey about each of them a coordinate, angelic, dæmoniacal, and heroic multitude; the number suspended from each bearing the name of its monad, so that there is a celestial God, dæmon, and hero. With respect to Earth, also, Ocean, and Tethys, it is requisite to consider that these proceed into all orders, and in a similar manner other Gods. For there is a Jovian, Junonian, and Saturnian multitude, which is denominated through the same name of life. Nor is there any thing absurd in this, since we call man both intelligible and sensible, though the restoration to their pristine condition is in these more abundant. And thus much in common concerning the generation-producing Gods and dæmons, that, conjoined with the Gods, we may also survey the discourse about dæmons: for Plato comprehends each of the genera in the same names. And he seems to call the same powers both dæmons and Gods on this account, that we may understand that the dæmoniacal genus is suspended at the same time together with these Gods, and that we may also adapt the names as to Gods. This he also does in other places, indicating the every way extended nature of the theory, and the eye of science surveying all things together and in connection."

31. (See page 442, line 41a) The scope of this speech, says Proclus, is, as we have said, to insert demiurgic power and providence in the mundane genera of

Gods, to lead them forth to the generation of the remaining kinds of animals, and to place them over mortals, analogously to the father of wholes over the one orderly distribution of the universe. For it is necessary that some things should be primarily generated by the demiurgic monad, and others through other media; the demiurgus, indeed, producing all things from himself, at once and eternally, but the things produced in order, and first proceeding from him, producing, together with him, the natures posterior to themselves. Thus, for instance, the celestial produce sublunary Gods, and these generate mortal animals; the demiurgus at the same time fabricating these in conjunction with the celestial and sublunary Divinities. For in speaking he understands all things, and by understanding all things he also makes the mortal genera of animals; these requiring another proximate generating cause, so far as they are mortal, and through this receiving a progression into being. But the character of the words is enthusiastic, shining with intellectual intuitions, pure and venerable as being perfected by the father of the Gods, differing from and transcending human conceptions, delicate, and at the same time terrific, full of grace and beauty - at once concise and perfectly accurate. Plato. therefore, particularly studies these things in the imitations of divine speeches; as he also evinces in the *Republic*, when he represents the Muses speaking sublimely, and the prophet ascending to a lofty seat. He also adorns both these speeches with conciseness and venerableness, employing the accurate powers of colons, directly shadowing forth divine intellections through such a form of words. But in the words before us he omits no transcendency either of the grand and robust in the sentences and the names adapted to these devices, or of magnitude in the conceptions and the figures which give completion to this idea. Besides this, also, much distinction and purity, the unfolding of truth, and the illustrious prerogatives of beauty, are mingled with the idea of magnitude, this being especially adapted to the subject things, to the speaker, and to the hearers. For the objects of this speech are, the perfection of the universe, an assimilation to all-perfect animal, and the generation of all mortal animals; the maker of all things at the same time presubsisting and adorning all things, through exempt transcendency, but the secondary fabricators adding what was wanting to the formation of the universe. All therefore, being great and divine, as well the persons as the things, and shining with beauty and a distinction from each other, Plato has employed words adapted to the form of the speech.

Homer also, when energizing enthusiastically, represents Jupiter speaking, converting to himself the twofold coordinations of Gods, becoming himself, as it were, the centre of all the divine genera in the world, and making all things obedient to his intellection. But at one time he conjoins the multitude of Gods with himself without a medium, and at another through Themis as the medium.

> But Jove to Themis gives command to call
> The Gods to council.

This Goddess pervading every where collects the divine number, and converts it to the demiurgic monad. For the Gods are both separate from mundane affairs, and eternally provide for all things, being at the same time exempt from them through the highest transcendency, and extending their providence every where. For their unmingled nature is not without providential energy nor is their providence mingled with matter. Through transcendency of power they are not filled with the subjects of their government, and, through beneficent will, they make all things similar to themselves; in permanently abiding, proceeding, and in being separated from all things, being similarly present to all things. Since, therefore, the Gods that govern the world, and the dæmons the attendants of these, receive after this manner unmingled purity and providential administration from their father; at one time he converts them to himself without a medium, and illuminates them with a separate, unmingled, and pure form of life. Whence also I think he orders them to be separated from all things, to remain exempt in Olympus, and neither convert themselves to Greeks nor Barbarians; which is just the same as to say, that they must transcend the twofold orders of mundane natures, and abide immutably in undefiled intellection. But at another time he converts them to a providential attention to secondary natures, through Themis, and calls upon them to direct the mundane battle, and excites different Gods to different works. These Divinities, therefore, especially require the assistance of Themis, who contains in herself the divine laws according to which providence is intimately connected with wholes. Homer, therefore, divinely delivers twofold speeches, accompanying the twofold energies of Jupiter; but Plato through this one speech comprehends those twofold modes of discourse. For the demiurgus renders the Gods unmingled with secondary natures, and causes them to provide for, and give existence to, mortals. But he orders them to fabricate in imitation of himself: and in an injunction of this kind both these are comprehended, viz. the unmingled through the imitation of the father, for he is separate, being exempt from mundane wholes; but providential energy, through the command to fabricate, nourish and increase mortal natures. Or rather, we may survey both in each; for in imitating the demiurgus they provide for secondary natures, as he does for the immortals; and in fabricating they are separate from the things fabricated. For every demiurgic cause is exempt from the things generated by it; but that which is mingled with and filled from them is imbecil and inefficacious, and is unable to adorn and fabricate them. And thus much in common respecting the whole of the speech.

Let us then, in the first place, consider what we are to understand by "Gods of Gods," and what power it possesses: for that this invocation is collective and convertive of multitude to its monad, that it calls upwards the natures which have proceeded to the one fabricator of them, and inserts a boundary and divine measure in them, is clear to those who are not entirely unacquainted with such-like discourses. But how those that are allotted the world by their father are called Gods of Gods, and according to what conception, cannot easily be indicated to the many; for there is an unfolding of one divine intelligence in these names. Proclus then proceeds to relate the explanations given by others of these words; which having rejected as erroneous, he very properly, in my opinion, adopts the following, which is that of his preceptor, the great Syrianus. All the mundane Gods are not simply Gods, but they are wholly Gods which participate: for there is in them that which is separate, unapparent, and supermundane, and also that which is the apparent image of them, and has an orderly establishment in the world. And that, indeed, which is unapparent in them is primarily a God, this being undistributed and one; but this vehicle which is suspended from their unapparent essence is secondarily a God. For if, with respect to us, man is twofold, one inward, according to the soul, the other apparent, which we see, much more must both these be asserted of the Gods; since Divinity also is twofold, one unapparent and the other apparent. This being the case, we must say that "Gods of Gods" is addressed to all the mundane Divinities, in whom there is a connection of unapparent with apparent Gods; for they are Gods that participate. In short, since twofold orders are produced by the demiurgus, some being supermundane and others mundane, and some being without and others with participation, - if the demiurgus now addressed the supermundane orders, he would have alone said to them, "Gods:" for they are without participation, are separate and unapparent: - but since the speech is to the mundane Gods, he calls them Gods of Gods, as being participated by other apparent Divinities. In these also dæmons are comprehended; for they also are Gods, as to their order with respect to the Gods, whose idiom they indivisibly participate. Thus also Plato, in the *Phædrus*, when he calls the twelve Gods the leaders of dæmons, at the same time denominates all the attendants of the Divinities Gods, adding, "and this is the life of the Gods." All these, therefore, are Gods of Gods, as possessing the apparent connected with the unapparent, and the mundane with the supermundane.

32. (See page 442, line 41d) It is well observed here by Proclus, that the animal spirit (το πνευμα) comprehends the summits of the irrational life, which summits subsist eternally with the vehicle of the soul, as being produced by the demiurgus; but that these, being extended and distributed, make this life which the junior Gods weave together, being indeed mortal, because the soul must necessarily lay aside this distribution, when, being restored to her pristine state, she obtains purification, but subsisting for a much longer time than the life of this body; and that, on this account, the soul also in Hades chooses a life of this kind. For, in consequence of verging to a corporeal nature, she receives this mortal life from the junior Gods. If these things then be admitted, the demiurgus gives subsistence to the *summit* of the irrational life, but does not produce this life; since, giving subsistence to dæmons, he certainly also produces the irrational life which they contain, but not this life which the junior Gods weave together in us; for this is alone adapted to souls falling into generation. The mundane Gods, therefore, illuminate their depending vehicles with rational

lives; for they possess intellectual souls. But those dæmons who are properly defined according to reason use irrational powers. which they keep in subjection; but our souls much more possess a life in the vehicle, which is irrational with relation to them. It superabounds however by receiving another irrational life, which is an apostasy from that life in the vehicle which was woven by the junior Gods. All *that* is immortal, therefore, which souls possess according to an imitation of wholes, but the addition of the secondary life is mortal. If, therefore, in the summit of the irrational life, there is one impassive sense, this in the pneumatic vehicle will generate one passive sense; and this latter will produce in the shelly body many and passive senses. The orectic or appetitive power, also, in this summit, will produce many orectic powers in the spirit, possessing something separate from the shelly body, and capable of being disciplined; and these will produce in the body ultimate and material appetitive powers.

33. (See page 443, line 41d) It is well observed here by Proclus, that souls possess essential differences, and not differences according to energies only. For, says he, some souls look to total and others to partial intellects; and some employ undefiled intellections, but others at times depart from the contemplation of true beings. Some perpetually fabricate and adorn wholes, but others only sometimes revolve with the Gods. And some always move and govern fate, but others sometimes subsist under the dominion of fate, and are subject to its laws. Some are the leaders to intelligible essence, and others are sometimes allotted the order of those that follow. Some are divine only, and others are transferred into a different order, dæmoniacal, heroical, human. Some employ horses that are good, but others such as are mingled from good and evil. And some possess that life alone which they received from the one fabrication of things, but others the mortal form of life, which was woven to their nature by the junior Gods. Some energize according to all their powers, but others at different times draw forth different lives. By no means, therefore, do our souls possess the same essence with divinity: for the rational nature is different in the two, being in the Gods intellectual, but in our souls mingled with the irrational; and in the middle genera it is defined according to their middle subsistence. In like manner, with respect to every thing else, such as reasons, the form of life, intelligence and time, these subsist divinely in divine souls, but in a human manner in ours.

Proclus also further observes, that the common definition of all souls is as follows: Soul is an essence subsisting between true essence and generation, being mingled from middle genera, divided into essential number, bound with all media, diatonically harmonized, living one and a twofold life, and being gnostic in one and a twofold manner.

34. (See page 443, line 41d) Timæus, says Proclus, by these words indicates the similitude, subjection and different progression of partial to total souls. For he not only describes their difference together with their alliance, according to first and second demiurgic energy, nor alone according to their union with and separation from the crater of life, nor yet alone according to excess or defect of genera, but also according to the mode of mixture, which is the same, and yet not the same. For neither is the temperament of the genera similar, nor the unmingling of difference; since this is more abundant in partial souls. Hence, of the horses in these, one is good, but the other contrary, and consisting from contraries, as it is said in the *Phædrus*, in consequence of difference having dominion. For the whole mixture is no longer incorruptible, according to the same, and after the same manner, but in a second and third degree; since in these there are subjection and order. But by *incorruptible*, here, we must understand the immutable, the undeviating, the inflexible, the immaculate form of essence, that which is not converted to secondary natures, and which does not receive mutation, or subjection of life, that which is established beyond the reach of mortality, and that which is exempt from the laws of fate: for these things are common to every genus of souls which perpetually transcend generation. But the contraries of these are adapted to powers which descend into generation, *viz.* a mutation of life from intelligence to action, the becoming sometimes subject to fate, and the being mingled with mortal affairs. Neither is the immovable present with these according to the same, since they sometimes proceed into generation, nor, when it is present, is it present after the same manner: for that which always understands is better than that which sometimes departs from its proper intellection. Since, however, in these souls also there is an order, and some are undefiled, rarely associating with generation and deserting their own order, but others are rolled in all-various flowers, and wander myriads of periods, - hence Timæus indicates the difference of these, when he says "in a second and third degree." For souls which descend, and become defiled with evil, are very much separated from those that perpetually abide on high, and are free from evil: but souls of a middle order are such as descend indeed, but are not defiled. For, vice versa, it is not lawful to be defiled, and yet abide on high; since evil is not in the Gods, but in the mortal place, and in material things.

Again, therefore, from these things it appears that the first genus of souls is divine; for every where that which is the recipient of deity has a leading order, in essences, in intellects, in souls and in bodies. But the second genus is that which is perpetually conjoined with the Gods, that, through this, souls which sometimes depart from may again be recalled to the Gods. The third genus is that which falls into generation, but descends with purity, and changes a subordinate for a more divine life, but is exempt from vice and passions; for this genus is continuous with souls that perpetually abide on high, and are perpetually undefiled. But the fourth and last genus is that which abundantly wanders, which descends as far as to Tartarus, and is again excited from its dark profundities, evolving all-various forms of life, employing various manners, and at different times different passions. It also obtains various forms of animals, dæmoniacal, human, irrational, but is at the same time corrected by Justice, returns from earth to heaven, and is circularly led from matter to intellect, according to certain orderly periods of wholes. By the words, therefore, "in a certain respect indeed after the same manner, yet not similarly incorruptible according to the same," he signifies that partial souls are in a certain respect incorruptible, as for instance, according to their essence alone, but that in a certain respect they are not incorruptible, *viz.* being mingled in their energies with all-various destinies, and conversant with mortal things, and not possessing these energies with invariable sameness, and entire, but sometimes more, and at others less, an all-various inequality subsisting in souls, according to their habitude to mortal natures, from which they derive the privation of incorruptibility according to life.

35. (See page 443, line 41e) Vulcan, who is the artificer of the whole of a corporeal essence, gives subsistence to the vehicles of the soul; for he receives souls sent into the world from the intelligible region, and gives different habitations to different souls. The demiurgus of all things also gives subsistence to these vehicles; for he is the fabricator of animals, and the completions of the universe, so that he not only produces souls, but also produces them with their proper vehicles. As Proclus likewise well observes, the conception of Plato here is truly wonderful: for he does not represent the demiurgus as fashioning these vehicles from the *wholenesses* which are now produced, but he says that he makes these, the junior Gods lending parts, and from them composing bodies. But this is an evident argument, that each of these vehicles is in a certain respect self-composed, and not fabricated by an ablation from other things, lest it should require to be again poured back into something else. For every thing which subsists by an abscission from other things, being cut off with a diminution of the whole to which it belonged, must necessarily be returned to the whole from which it was cut off. For it is necessary that every whole in the universe should perpetually remain a whole: and hence every such vehicle is perpetual, and the same vehicle is always suspended from the soul. Besides, how can the soul be any longer said to be mundane, if its vehicle is corrupted? for that of which there is nothing in the universe cannot be mundane. For, if partial souls are superior to a life in conjunction with vehicles, they will also be superior to divine souls: but if they are inferior to such a life, how does the demiurgus immediately after their generation introduce them into these vehicles? And how can they use them in Hades, and in the Heavens, unless they had them perpetually suspended from their essence? For, that they use them in Hades, is evident from what Socrates says in the *Phædo,* *viz.* that souls ascending into their vehicles proceed to Acheron: and that they also use them in the Heavens, is evident from the *Phædrus,* in which Socrates says that the vehicles of the Gods proceed equally balanced, but those of the attendants of the Gods, with great difficulty.

From this, also, we may perceive the difference between partial and divine souls: for with respect to the latter the demiurgus is said to place their bodies in their souls, as being every way comprehended by them, these souls not being converted to the objects of their government, but employing one immutable intellection: but, with respect to partial souls, he is said to cause these to ascend into their vehicles; for these are naturally adapted to be frequently in subjection to bodies, and to convert themselves to the subjects of their government; when they also become parts of the universe as well as their vehicles, act in subserviency to the laws of fate, and no longer live with purity under the divine light of Providence. It must likewise be observed, that the demiurgus among other causes contains that of Nature in himself, to which also he converts souls. For, by showing Nature to souls, he also beholds it himself. But he alone beholds things prior to and in himself. Now, therefore, he beholds Nature in himself, which he comprehends supernaturally, or according to cause.

36. (See page 443, line 42a) The demiurgus, says Proclus, comprehends the whole of a material and mortal life in three boundaries, and establishes the causes of it in souls, that they may obtain dominion over it: for dominion is not derived from any thing else than essential precedency. The irrational life, therefore, subsists *intellectually* in the demiurgus, but *rationally* in souls. Nor is this wonderful, since body also subsists incorporeally in the intelligible causes of all things. But this connate sense produced by violent passions, of which Plato now speaks, is that corporeal life which is gnostic of things falling upon it externally, which produces this knowledge through instruments, does not subsist from itself, but from the natures by which it is used, is mingled with material masses, and knows what it knows with passion. For it is necessary to sensation, that a certain agitation should be produced about the instruments of sense; since neither do the motions in the soul pervade every where, and as far as to the body, but there is a motion of the soul belonging to itself by itself, such as is that which is intellectual; nor does every thing about the body extend as far as to the soul; but there is also a certain corporeal passion, which through its obscurity is not able to move the soul. Sense, therefore, is produced not from all passions, but from such as are violent, and which are attended with much agitation. And this is corporeal sense, which is divisible and material, and forms its judgment mingled with passions. But there is another sense prior to this, in the vehicle of the soul, which with respect to this is immaterial, and is a pure impassive knowledge, itself subsisting by itself, but which is not liberated from form, because it also is corporeal, as being allotted its subsistence in body. And this sense, indeed, has the same nature with the phantasy; for the being of both is common; but externally proceeding it is called sense, and abiding internally, and surveying in the spirit (εν τῳ πνευματι) forms and figures, it is called phantasy. So far also as it is divided about the spirit, it is sense. For, again, the basis of the rational life is opinion; but the phantasy is

the summit of the second, or the irrational life. Opinion also and phantasy are conjoined with each other, and the second is filled from the more excellent with powers. But the middle of the irrational life does not receive the impression of the natures superior to it, but is alone the recipient of things external. It is common, however, to this also to know that which is sensible with passivity: but external sense alone pertains to things externally falling upon and moving it, not being able to possess spectacles in itself, since it is partible and not one; for it is distributed about the organs of sense. There is one sense, therefore, which is impassive and common, another which is common and passive, and a third which is distributed and passive. The first of these belongs to the first vehicle of the soul, the second, to the irrational life, and the third, to the animated body.

After sense, Plato arranges desire. And this indeed is life, and is also corporeal; but it is a life which perpetually unweaves the body, and affords a solace to its wants, and about which pleasure and pain are beheld. For these passions are also present to other parts of the soul; since you may perceive pleasures and pains, both in reason and anger. But corporeal pleasure and pain are produced according to desire. For, with respect to the body, a way contrary to nature, and a privation of life, produce pain in it; but a regression according to nature, and an adaptation to life, are the sources of its pleasure. And that which is afflicted or delighted in these is the desiderative part of the soul. But since these two passions are primary, and the fountains of the other passions, as Plato says in the *Philebus* and the *Laws*, through the mixture of these giving a generation to the other passions he also denominates love a mixture of pleasure and pain. For, so far as it is conversant with the lovely, it is present with pleasure, but, so far as it is not yet present with it in energy, it is mingled with pain. But he characterizes all the life of desire through love, because this passion is most vehement about it.

In the third place, therefore, he enumerates anger. Anger then is also life, but a life which removes every thing painful, and which disturbs the body. Excess and defect also are surveyed about it, such as rashness and timidity, and the things consequent to these, ambition and contention, and all such particulars as take place about mortal concerns. And such is the order of these three generated powers. For as soon as the body is formed it participates of sense: since it would not be an animal, nor would possess appetite, if it were not sensitive. For appetites subsist in conjunction with sense, but the senses are not entirely in conjunction with appetites; and hence the animal is more characterized by the sensitive than by the appetitive nature. But after the possession of sense the animal appears to be pleased and pained, afflicted by the cold, but cherished by the bandages, and led to a condition according to nature. After desire, as age advances, the animal is angered: for anger is the power of a more robust nature. Hence also, among irrational animals, such as are more material alone live according to desire, and partake of pleasure and pain; but such as are more perfect are allotted a more irascible life. But prior to these appetites, as we also said of sense, there is a certain summit of them in the spirit of the soul, which summit is a power impulsive and motive of the spirit, guarding and connecting its essence, at one time extending and distributing itself, and at another being led to bound and order, and measured by reason.

37. (See page 443, line 42b) Since Plato now discourses concerning souls that are restored to their pristine state in their legitimate star, after their first generation, and says that on leaving the body they possess a happy life, it may be asked how this accords with what is said in the *Phædrus?* For, there, he who chooses a philosophic life is restored to his pristine state through three lives. We reply, with Proclus, that Plato does not here assert that the soul passes into that very state whence it came, for this is accomplished through three chiliads of periods, but that the soul returns to the star under which it was essentially arranged, and leads a life in common with it. For it is possible for those that are not philosophers to be elevated by Justice to a certain place in the heavens, and there to live in a manner adapted to their life while in a human form: for this is asserted in the *Phædo* respecting the souls of such as are not philosophers; since the restoration to the same condition again is one thing, and the ascent to the kindred star another. And the former of these requires three periods, but the latter may be effected by one period. The former also leads back the soul to the intelligible, from which it descended, but the latter to a subordinate form of life. For there are measures of felicity, and the ascent is twofold; one, of those that have yet to ascend still higher, and the other, of those that have no further flight to take. So that it is possible for the soul having arrived at its kindred star, either to be conjoined with the mundane powers of its God, or to proceed still higher; but to be led back to the intelligible requires a period of three thousand years. For through this the highest flight is accomplished.

38. (See page 444, line 42c) The one safety of the soul herself, says Proclus, which is extended by the demiurgus, and which liberates her from the circle of generation, from abundant wandering, and an inefficacious life, is her return to the intellectual form, and a flight from every thing which naturally adheres to us from generation. For it is necessary that the soul which is hurled like seed into the realms of generation, should lay aside the stubble and bark, as it were, which she obtained from being disseminated into these fluctuating realms; and that, purifying herself from every thing circumjacent, she should become an intellectual flower and fruit, delighting in an intellectual life instead of doxastic nutriment, and pursuing the uniform and simple energy of the period of sameness, instead of the abundantly wandering motion of the period which is characterized by difference. For she contains each of these circles and twofold powers. And of her horses, one is good, and the other the contrary: and one of these leads her to generation, but the other from generation to true being; the one also leads her round the circle of sense, but the other round an

intellectual essence. For the period of the same and the similar elevates to intellect, and an intelligible nature, and to the first and most excellent habit. But this habit is that according to which the soul being winged governs the whole world, becoming assimilated to the Gods themselves. And this is the universal form of life in the soul, just as that is the partial form when she falls into the last body, and becomes something belonging to an individual instead of belonging to the universe. The middle of these also is the partial universal, when she lives in conjunction with her middle vehicle, as a citizen of generation. Dismissing, therefore, her first habit, which subsists according to an alliance to the whole of generation, and laying aside the irrational nature which connects her with generation, likewise governing her irrational part by reason, and extending intellect to opinion, she will be circularly led to a happy life, from the wandering about the regions of sense; which life those that are initiated by Orpheus in the mysteries of Bacchus and Proserpine pray that they may obtain, together with the allotments of the sphere, and a cessation of evil. But if our soul necessarily lives well, when living according to the circle of sameness, much more must this be the case with divine souls. It is, however, possible for our soul to live according to the circle of sameness, when purified, as Plato says. Cathartic virtue, therefore, alone must be called the salvation of souls; since this cuts off and vehemently obliterates material natures, and the passions which adhere to us from generation, separates the soul, and leads it to intellect, and causes it to leave on earth the vehicles with which it is invested. For souls descending receive from the elements different vehicles, ærial, aquatic, and terrestrial; and thus at last enter into this gross bulk. For how, without a medium, could they proceed into this body from immaterial spirits? Hence, before they come into this body, they possess the irrational life, and its vehicle, which is prepared from the simple elements, and from these they enter into the tumultuous, which is so called as being foreign to the connate vehicle of souls, composed from all-various vestments, and causing souls to become heavy. In short, the connate vehicle makes the soul mundane, the second vehicle, a citizen of generation, and the shelly body, (το οστρεωδες) terrestrial.

39. (See page 444, line 43b) Plato, says Proclus, immediately conjoining the soul to the body, omits all the problems pertaining to the descent of the soul, such as the prophet, the allotments, the lives, the elections, the dæmon, the residence in the plain of oblivion, the sleeping, the oblivious potion, the thunders, and all such particulars as the fable in the *Republic* discusses. But neither does he here deliver such things as pertain to the soul after its departure from the body, such as the terrors, the rivers, Tartarus, those savage and fiery dæmons, the thorns, the bellowing mouth, the triple road, and the judges, concerning which the fable in the *Republic*, in the *Gorgias*, and in the *Phædo*, instructs us. What, then, you will say, is the cause of this omission? We reply, Because Plato preserves that which is adapted to the design of the dialogue. For

here he admits whatever is physical in the theory respecting the soul, and its association with the body.

It is requisite, however, to inquire why souls fall into bodies. And we may reply, with Proclus, Because they wish to imitate the providential energies of the Gods, and on this account proceed into generation, and leave the contemplation of true being: for, as Divine perfection is twofold, one kind being intellectual, and the other providential, and one kind consisting in an abiding energy, and the other in motion, hence souls imitate the prolific, intellectual, and immutable energy of the Gods by contemplation, but their providential and motive characteristic through a life conversant with generation. As the intelligence, too, of the human soul is partial, so likewise is her providence; but, being partial, it associates with a partial body. But still further, the descent of the soul contributes to the perfection of the universe; for it is necessary that there should not only be immortal and intellectual animals, such as are the perpetual attendants of the Gods, nor yet mortal and irrational animals only, such as are the last progeny of the demiurgus of the universe, but likewise such as subsist between these, and which are by no means immortal,[†] but are capable of participating reason and intellect. And in many parts of the universe there are many animals of this kind; for man is not the only rational and mortal animal, but there are other such-like species, some of which are more dæmoniacal, and others approximate nearer to our essence. But the descents of a partial soul contribute to the perfect composition of all animals, which are at the same time mortal and rational.

Should it be again asked, Why, therefore, are partial souls descending into generation filled with such material perturbation, and such numerous evils? we reply, that this takes place through the inclination arising from their free will; through their vehement familiarity with body; through their sympathy with the image of soul, or that divisible life which is distributed about body; through their abundant mutation from an intelligible to a sensible nature, and from a quiet energy to one entirely conversant with motion; and through a disordered condition of being, naturally arising from the composition of dissimilar natures, *viz.* of the immortal and mortal, of the intellectual and that which is deprived of intellect, of the indivisible and that which is endued with interval. For all these become the cause to the soul of this mighty tumult and labour in the realms of generation; since we pursue a flying mockery which is ever in motion. And the soul, indeed, by verging to a material life, kindles a light in her dark tenement the body, but she herself becomes situated in obscurity; and by giving life to the body, she destroys herself and her own intellect, in as great a degree as these are capable of receiving destruction. For thus the mortal nature participates of intellect, but the intellectual part of death, and the whole becomes a prodigy, as Plato beautifully observes in his *Laws*, composed of the

---

[†] For the whole composite which we call man is not immortal, but only the rational soul.

mortal and immortal, of the intellectual, and that which is deprived of intellect. For this physical law, which binds the soul to the body, is the death of the immortal life, but is the cause of vivification to the mortal body.

40. (See page 444, line 43b) The philosopher here, says Proclus, refers the whole of this tumult to two causes, viz. the nutritive and sensitive life; and these are the appetitive and gnostic powers of all the irrational part, into which we are accustomed to divide all the powers of the soul, asserting that some of them are vital, and others gnostic. For the nutritive life, verging to bodies, produces in them an abundant flux; through their material moisture sending forth a great efflux, and through vital heat receiving an influx of other things. But the sensitive life suffers from the external bodies of fire and air, earth and water, falling upon it; and, considering all the passions as mighty, through the vileness of its life, causes tumult to the soul. And to all these things, indeed, those that are arrived at maturity are accustomed; but to those that are recently born, the smallest things, through their being unusual, become the causes of astonishment. For, what a great fire is to the former, that the flame of a lamp is to the latter; and what the magnitude of the highest mountains is to men, that the smallest stone in the fields is to infants. And what whirlwinds and cataracts of rain are to others, that a weak motion of the air, or the falling of a little moisture, is to those that are recently born. For sense, being agitated by all these particulars, astonishes the soul of infants, and leads them to desperation and tumult. These, then, in short, are the causes of the disturbance of souls, viz. the motions of the nutritive part, and the impulses of sense. We must not, however, suppose that the soul suffers any thing through these particulars. For, as if some one standing on the margin of a river should behold the image and form of himself in the floating stream, he indeed will preserve his face unchanged, but the stream being all-variously moved will change the image, so that at different times it will appear to him different, oblique and upright, and perhaps divulsed and continuous. Let us suppose, too, that such a one, through being unaccustomed to the spectacle, should think that it was himself that suffered this distortion, in consequence of surveying his shadow in the water. and, thus thinking, should be afflicted and disturbed, astonished and impeded. After the same manner the soul, beholding the image of herself in boᴅy, borne along in the river of generation, and variously disposed at different times, through inward passions and external impulses, is indeed herself impassive, but thinks that she suffers, and, being ignorant of, and mistaking her image for, herself, is disturbed, astonished, and perplexed. This passion particularly takes place in infants: but it is also seen in the dreams of those that have arrived at maturity; as when some one, in consequence of nature being wearied in the concoction of food, thinks in a dream that he is wearied through long journeys, or carrying heavy burdens, or suffers something else of this kind. But to return to the words of Plato, the *waves* do not signify, says Proclus, the externally blowing wind, as some say, but the collected

agitation, and abundant influx and efflux which take place in youth. But the *inundation* first strikes upon and makes the pneumatic vehicle heavier, for it is this which expresses stains and vapours; and in the second place it strikes upon the soul, for she also is disturbed by the collected and the sudden.

41. (See page 445, line 43d) Sense, says Proclus, is of the present, in the same manner as memory is of the past, but hope of the future. Sense, therefore, excites souls in the present time, and this in conjunction with the nutritive power, which by influxions applies a remedy to the perpetual effluxions of the body, and again composes what was analyzed, after the manner of Penelope's web. For this is the perpetually flowing river, which is properly so called, as being a part of the whole river of generation. Hence, in conjunction with this, it agitates and disturbs the periods of the immortal soul, and *fetters*, indeed, the circle of *sameness*, but *agitates* the circle of *difference*. For, as there are twofold circles in the soul in imitation of divine souls, the dianoëtic circle, which contemplates intelligibles, is only restrained in its energy, but sustains no distortion: but the doxastic circle is distorted; and this very properly, since it is possible to opine not rightly, but it is not possible to know scientifically falsely. If it should be said that the dianoëtic part may be ignorant in a twofold respect, and that a thing which suffers this is distorted; we reply, that twofold ignorance does not simply belong to the dianoëtic part, but, originating indeed from thence, is implanted in the doxastic part. For, so far as it is ignorance, and a privation of science, so far, being an immobility of the scientific power, it originates from the dianoëtic part. For science and ignorance subsist about the same thing. But, so far as it also adds a false opinion of knowledge, it subsists in the doxastic part. And ignorance is the insanity of the dianoëtic part, possessing, indeed, but concealing, the productive principles of knowledge; but false conception is the insanity of opinion, of which it is also the distortion. For, being false, it also depraves its possessor; since what vice is in action, that falsehood is in knowledge. The period of sameness, therefore, is alone fettered, and is similar to those that are bound, and on this account are impeded in their energies; but the period of difference is agitated, being filled with false opinions. For its proximity to the irrational nature causes it to receive a certain passion from externals.

Note to the Classical Journal on

Important Additions to the *Timæus* of Plato

published in volume XXI, June 1820.

The following omissions in the *Timæus* of Plato have been unnoticed by all the editors, in consequence of not having compared the manuscript and printed copies of that dialogue with the text in the Commentaries of Proclus.

After the words[39a], then, κατα δη την θατερου φοραν πλαγιαν ουσαν, δια της ταυτου φύσεως ιουσαν τε και κρατουμενην, το μεν μειζονα αυτων, το δε ελαττω κυκλον ιον· θαττον μεν, τα τον ελαττω, τα δε τον μειζονα βραδυτερον περιϊοντα, (see vol. ix p. 320 of the Bipont edition,) the following passage occurs in the Commentaries of Proclus, (vol 2, p. 235.) Κινειται τα επτα σωματα, τα μεν βραδυτερα οντα, τα δε θαττω. τα μεν, ελαττω περιϊοντα κυκλον, θατερον (lege θαττον) περιεισιν· ο δε κρονος μειζω περιων βραδυτερον. On these words Proclus comments as genuine, in his usual admirable manner. They are also unnoticed by Ficinus, though he appears to have frequently consulted the Commentaries of Proclus; and of course, he did not find them in his manuscript.

In the following passage,[42c-d] (p. 328 of the Bipont edition,) Αλλαττων τε ου προτερον πονων ληξει, πριν τη ταυτου και ομοιου περιοδω τη εν αυτω συνεπισπωμενος, τον πολυν οχλον, και υστερον προσφυντα εκ πυρος και υδατος και αερος και γης, θορυβωδη και αλογον οντα λογω κρατησας, εις το της πρωτης και αριστης αφικοιτο ειδος εξεως, it appears from the Commentaries of Proclus, (vol. 2, p. 415) that there is an omission after τον πολυν οχλον, of the word εξωθεν. For Proclus observes, that Timæus δια του προσφυντα φαναι, και του κατα παντας τους βιους εξαψαι το αλογον τουτο της ψυχης, διεστησεν αυτο τουδε του σωματος, και της ιδιας τουτο ζωης. δια δε του εξωθεν, και του υστερον αυτο προσθειναι, του συμφυους οχηματος, εν ω κατιουσαν αυτην εποιησεν ο δημιουργος.

THE CRITIAS

or

ATLANTICUS

INTRODUCTION

It is a singular circumstance, that though there is not, perhaps, any thing among the writings of the ancients which has more generally attracted the attention of the learned in every age than the Atlantic history of Plato, yet no more than one single passage of about twenty or thirty lines has, prior to my translation of the *Timæus*, appeared in any modern language. Much has been said and written by the moderns respecting the Atlantic island; but the extent of the original source has not even been suspected.

That the authenticity of the following history should have been questioned by many of the moderns, is by no means surprising, if we consider that it is the history of an island and people that are asserted to have existed NINE THOUSAND years prior to Solon; as this contradicts the generally-received opinion respecting the antiquity of the world. However, as Plato expressly affirms, that it is a relation in *every respect true*,[†] and, as Crantor,[‡] the first interpreter of Plato, asserts, "that the following history was said, by the Egyptian priests of his time, to be still preserved inscribed on pillars," it appears to me to be at least as well attested as any other narration in any ancient historian. Indeed, he who proclaims that "truth is the source of every good both to Gods and men," and the whole of whose works consists in detecting error and exploring certainty, can never be supposed to have wilfully deceived mankind by publishing an extravagant romance as matter of fact, with all the precision of historical detail.

Some learned men have endeavoured to prove that America is the Atlantic island of Plato; and others have thought that the extreme parts of Africa towards the south and west were regarded by Plato in this narration. These opinions, however, are so obviously erroneous, that the authors of them can hardly be supposed to have read this dialogue, and the first part of the *Timæus*; for in these it is asserted that this island, in the space of one day and night, was absorbed in the sea. I only add, that this dialogue is an appendix, as it were, to the *Timæus*, and that it is not complete, Plato being prevented by death from finishing it, as we are informed by Plutarch in his life of Solon.

[†] Πανταπασι γε μην αληθης.

[‡] Ο πρωτος του Πλατωνος εξηγητης Κραντωρ. Procl. in Tim. p. 24 et mox - Μαρτυρουσι δε και οι προφηται φησι των Αιγυπτιων εν στηλαις ταις ετι σωζομεναις ταυτα γεγραφθαι λεγοντες.

THE CRITIAS

or

ATLANTICUS

PERSONS OF THE DIALOGUE

TIMÆUS SOCRATES
CRITIAS HERMOCRATES

06a TIM. As pleasant, Socrates, as is rest after a long journey, so pleasing to me is the present liberation from an extended discourse. But I beseech THE WORLD, that God, which was in reality generated formerly, though but recently in our discussion, to preserve those things which we have asserted with rectitude, but to inflict on us a becoming punishment if we have involuntarily said any thing discordant. But the proper punishment of him who acts disorderly and inelegantly, is to make him act with order and elegance. That we may, therefore, after this speak rightly respecting the generation of the Gods, let us beseech THAT DIVINITY, THE WORLD, to impart to us *the medicine science, which is the most perfect and best of all medicines.* But having prayed, let us deliver, according to our agreement, the following discourse to Critias.

CRIT. I receive it, O Timæus: and as you, at the beginning of your discussion, entreated pardon, as being about to speak of great things; in like manner, I at present entreat the same. Indeed I think that I ought

07a to solicit pardon in a still greater degree for the ensuing discourse, though I nearly know that this my request is very ambitious, and more rustic than is proper; but, at the same time, let us begin the discourse. For who endued with a sound mind will attempt to say that the things which have been asserted by you have not been well said? But that the particulars which remain to be discussed require greater indulgence, as being more difficult, this I will endeavour to show. For he, O Timæus, who discourses concerning the Gods to men, may more easily appear to speak all that is sufficient than he who discourses concerning mortals to you. For the unskilfulness and vehement ignorance of the auditors about things of this kind afford a great *copia verborum* to him who enters on the discussion of them: but we know how we are circumstanced with respect to the Gods. However, that I may more plainly evince what I say, thus attend to me in what follows: It is requisite that all we shall say should become in a certain respect an imitation and a resemblance. But we see the facility and subtilty which

c take place in the representation exhibited by pictures of divine and human bodies, in order that they may appear to the spectators to be apt imitations. We likewise see, with respect to the earth, mountains, rivers, woods, all heaven, and the revolving bodies which it contains, that at first we are delighted if any one is able to exhibit but a slender representation to our view; but that afterwards, as not knowing any

d thing *accurately* about such-like particulars, we neither examine nor blame the pictures, but use an immanifest and fallacious adumbration respecting them. But when any one attempts to represent our bodies, we acutely perceive what is omitted, through our continual and familiar animadversion of them, and we become severe judges of him who does not perfectly exhibit all the requisite similitudes. It is likewise necessary to consider the same thing as taking place in discourse. For, with respect to things celestial and divine, we are delighted with assertions concerning them that are but in a small degree adapted to their nature;

e but we accurately examine things mortal and human. And hence it is requisite to pardon whatever in the ensuing discourse may be delivered in an unbecoming manner. For it is proper to think, that to assimilate

108a mortal concerns to opinion, is not an easy but a difficult task. I have said all this, Socrates, being willing to remind you, and to solicit not less but greater pardon for the following discourse. But if my request shall appear to you to be just, do you willingly impart this gift.

Soc. Why should we not, O Critias, impart it? And besides this, the same pardon must be granted by us to a third. For it is evident that Hermocrates,[†] who is to speak shortly after, will make the same request. That he, therefore, may make a different exordium, and may not be obliged to repeat what you have said, let him know that pardon

b is granted him, and let him, therefore, prepare to speak. But I previously announce to you, friend Critias, the conceptions of the theatre.[‡] For the poet has approved in a wonderful manner the person who spoke in it before; so that you will require abundant pardon in attempting to discharge the office of his successor.

[†] This speech of Hermocrates is not extant.

[‡] *Viz.* the persons of the dialogue.

HERM. You announce the same thing to me, Socrates, as to him. But desponding men, Critias, never erect a trophy. It is, therefore, requisite to proceed in a virile manner to the discourse, and, invoking Pæan and the Muses, to exhibit and celebrate ancient citizens who were excellent men.

CRIT. O friend Hermocrates, as you are to speak on the following day, having another to speak before you, on this account you are courageous. But he will, perhaps, manifest to you how this is to be accomplished. You, therefore, thus exhorting and encouraging me, I shall obey; and besides those Gods which you have mentioned, I shall invoke others, and especially Mnemosyne. For nearly the greatest reasons and discussions are contained for us in this Divinity. If, then, we can sufficiently remember and relate the narration which was once given by the Egyptian priests, and brought hither by Solon, you know that we shall appear to this theatre to have sufficiently accomplished our part. This, therefore, must now be done, and without any further delay.

But first of all we must recollect, that the period of time from which a war is said to have subsisted between all those that dwelt beyond and within the pillars of Hercules, amounts to nine thousand years: and this war it is now requisite for us to discuss. Of those, therefore, that dwelt within the pillars of Hercules, this city was the leader, and is said to have fought in every battle; but of those beyond the pillars, the kings of the Atlantic island were the leaders. But this island we said was once larger than Libya and Asia, *but is now a mass of impervious mud, through concussions of the earth; so that those who are sailing in the vast sea can no longer find a passage from hence thither.* The course of our narration, indeed, will unfold the many barbarous nations and Grecian tribes which then existed, as they may happen to present themselves to our view: but it is necessary to relate, in the first place, the wars of the Athenians and their adversaries, together with the power and the polities of each. And in discoursing of these we shall give the preference to our own people.

b   The Gods, then, once were locally allotted[†] the whole earth, but not with contention: for it would be absurd that the Gods should be ignorant of what is adapted to every one, or that, knowing that which rather belongs to others, they should endeavour, through strife, to possess what is not their own. Likewise, receiving places agreeable to them, from the allotments of justice, they inhabited the various regions of the earth. In consequence of this, too, like shepherds, they nourished

c   us as their possessions, flocks, and herds; with this exception, however, that they did not force bodies to bodies in the same manner as shepherds, who, when feeding their cattle, compel them to come together with blows: but they considered us as a docile and obedient animal; and, as if piloting a pliant ship, employed persuasion for the rudder; and with this conception as the leader, they governed the whole mortal race. Different Gods, therefore, being allotted, adorned different places. But Vulcan and Minerva,[‡] who possess a common nature, both because they are the offspring of the same father, and because, through

---

† As, according to the theology of Plato, there is not one father of the universe only, one providence, and one divine law, but many fathers subordinate to the one first father, many administrators of providence posterior to, and comprehended in, the one universal providence of the demiurgus of all things, and many laws proceeding from one first law, it is necessary that there should be different allotments, and a diversity of divine distribution. The allotment, however, of a divine nature is a government exempt from all passivity, and a providential energy about the subjects of its government.

---

‡ Vulcan is that divine power which presides over the spermatic and physical reasons, or productive principles, which the universe contains: for whatever Nature accomplishes by verging towards bodies, Vulcan performs in a divine and exempt manner, by moving Nature, and using her as an instrument in his own proper fabrication; since natural heat has a Vulcanian characteristic, and was produced by Vulcan for the purpose of fabricating a corporeal nature. Vulcan, therefore, is that power which perpetually presides over the fluctuating nature of bodies; and hence, says Olympiodorus, he operates with bellows ($\epsilon\nu$ $\phi\upsilon\sigma\alpha\iota\varsigma$); which occultly signifies his operating in natures ($\alpha\nu\tau\iota$ $\tau o\upsilon$ $\epsilon\nu$ $\tau\alpha\iota\varsigma$ $\phi\upsilon\sigma\epsilon\sigma\iota$). But by *earth* we must understand *matter*, which was thus symbolically denominated by the ancients, as we learn from Porphyry de Antr. Nymph [TTS vol. II.] By Minerva we must understand the summit ($\kappa o\rho\upsilon\phi\eta$) of all those intellectual natures that reside in Jupiter, the artificer of the world: or, in other words, she is that deity which illuminates all mundane natures with intelligence. The Athenians, therefore, who are souls of a Minerval characteristic, may be very properly said to be the progeny of Vulcan and the Earth, because Vulcan, who perpetually imitates the intellectual energy of Minerva in his fabrication of the sensible universe, imparts to them through this imitation those *vehicles*, and those *spermatic reasons*, through which in conjunction with *matter* they become inhabitants of this terrestrial abode.

philosophy and the study of arts, they tend to the same things; - these, I say, in consequence of this, received one allotment, *viz.* this region, as being naturally allied and adapted to virtue and prudence. But these Divinities having produced worthy, earth-born men, arranged in their intellectual part the order of a polity. Of these men the names are preserved; but their works, through the extinction of those that received them, and length of time, have disappeared. For the surviving race of men, as has been observed before, are always mountaineers, and void of discipline, who have only heard the names of men that were powerful in the region, and who, besides this, have been acquainted but with few of the transactions of the country. In consequence, therefore, of loving these ancient men, they gave the names of them to their children: but they were ignorant of the virtues and laws of those before them; for of these they knew nothing, but what they gathered from certain obscure rumours; and as for many generations they were in want of necessaries, both they and their children directed their attention to the particulars of which they were destitute, discoursed about these, and neglected past and ancient transactions. For mythology, and an investigation of ancient affairs, commence in cities in conjunction with leisure, when the necessaries of life are procured; but not before. On this account the names of ancient transactions were preserved, without any account of the transactions themselves. But I infer that this was the case, said Solon, because those priests, in their narration of the war at that period, inserted many names similar to those that were adopted afterwards, such as Cecrops, Erechtheus, Erichthonius, Erisichthon, and many other of those names which are commemorated prior to Theseus. This was likewise the case with the names of the women. The figure too and statue of Minerva evinced, that at that period the studies of women and men with respect to war were common, as an armed image was then dedicated to the Goddess; this serving as a document, that among animals of the same species both male and female are naturally able to pursue in common every virtue, which is adapted to their species. But at that time many other tribes of citizens dwelt in this region, who were skilled in the fabricative arts, and in agriculture. The warlike tribe, however, lived from the first separate from divine men, and possessed every thing requisite to aliment and education. None of them, however, had any private property; for all of them considered all things as common. They likewise did not think it worth while to receive from other citizens beyond a sufficiency of nutriment; and they engaged in all those pursuits which we related yesterday as pertaining to the guardians of our republic. It was likewise plausibly and truly said of our region,

that, in the first place, at that time its boundaries extended, on one side to the Isthmus, and on the other to Epirus, as far as to Cithæron and
e Parnethe. These boundaries are on the descent, having Oropia on the right hand, and limiting Asopus toward the sea on the left. It is likewise said that the whole earth was vanquished by the valour of this region; and that on this account it was at that time able to support the numerous army formed from the surrounding inhabitants. But this it is said was a mighty proof of virtue. For what is now left of this country may contend with any other in fertility of soil, in the goodness
111a of its fruits, and in pastures accommodated to every species of animals. But then it produced all these, not only thus beautiful, but likewise in the greatest abundance. But how is this credible? And by what arguments can it be shown that these are the remains of the land that then existed? The whole of this region is situated like a long promontory, extending into the sea, from the other continent. This the profound receptacle of the sea every way surrounds. *As, therefore, many and mighty deluges happened in that period of nine thousand years (for so many years have elapsed from that to the present time)*, the defluxions of
b the earth at these times, and during these calamities, from elevated places, did not, as they are elsewhere wont to do, accumulate any hillock which deserves to be mentioned, but, always flowing in a circle, at length vanished in a profundity. The parts, therefore, that are left at present are but as small islands, if compared with those that existed at that time; and may be said to resemble the bones of a diseased body; such of the earth as was soft and fat being washed away, and a thin body
c of the country alone remaining. But at that time the land, being unmingled, contained mountains and lofty hills; and the plains, which are now denominated Phellei, were then full of fat earth; and the mountains abounded with woods, of which there are evident tokens even at present. For there are mountains which now only afford nutriment for bees, but formerly, and at no very distant period, the largest trees were cut down from those mountains, as being adapted for buildings; and of these edifices, the coverings still remain. There were likewise many other lofty domestic trees; and most fertile pastures for
d cattle. This region, too, every year enjoyed prolific rain, which did not then, as now, run from naked earth into the sea, but, being collected in great abundance from lofty places, and preserved for use in certain cavities of the earth, diffused copious streams of fountains and rivers to every part of the country; the truth of which is confirmed by certain sacred remains which are still to be seen in the ancient fountains. And
e such was the natural condition of this region formerly; besides which,

it was cultivated, as it is reasonable to suppose it would be, by real husbandmen, who were men of elegant manners, and of a disposition naturally good; who possessed a most excellent soil, most abundant streams of water, and a most salubrious temperament of air.

But the city at that time was built in the following manner: In the first place, the Acropolis was not then, as it is at present. For now one rainy night having softened the bare land round about, in a remarkable degree, at the same time produced an earthquake; *and thus there happened a* THIRD *fatal inundation of water,* PRIOR *to the deluge of Deucalion.*[†] But prior to this, the magnitude of the Acropolis extended as far as to Eridanus and Ilissus, comprehended within itself Pnyx, and Lycabetus, and was bounded in a direction opposite to Pnyx. All the land too was glebous, except a few places in a more elevated situation which were plain. Its exterior parts on the left hand were inhabited by artists and husbandmen, who cultivated the neighbouring land. But the warlike tribe alone inhabited the elevated parts, about the temple of Minerva and Vulcan, being distributed in one enclosure round the garden as it were of one edifice. For those who raised public buildings, and common banquets for the winter season, together with whatever is adapted to a common polity, and who furnished both these, and temples themselves, without gold and silver, all of this description dwelt in the northern parts of this region. For gold and silver were not employed by any one at any time; but, pursuing a middle course between arrogance and illiberality, they built moderate houses, in which both they, and the offspring of their offspring growing old, they always left them to others like themselves. But in summer they used gardens, gymnasia, and public banquets, in places situated towards the south. There was likewise one fountain in the place where the Acropolis is now situated, which having been exhausted by earthquakes, small circulating streams alone remain at present. But at that time every part was abundantly supplied with springs of water, which were of a salutary temperament both in summer and winter. In this manner, then, these places were formerly inhabited; and the men of whom we have been speaking were guardians of their own citizens, but leaders of the other willing Greeks. They likewise were especially careful that there might always be the same number of men and women who by their age are able to fight, and that this number might not be less than twenty thousand. These men, therefore, being such as we have described, and always justly administering in this

---

[†] The deluge of Deucalion appears to be the same with that which is mentioned by Moses; but the Jews had no knowledge of any other.

manner both their own affairs and those of all Greece, they were esteemed and renowned beyond every other nation by all Europe and Asia, both for the beauty of their bodies and the all-various virtue of their souls.

In the next place, I shall communicate to you from the beginning the particulars respecting the adversaries of these men, if I am able to recollect what I heard when I was a boy. But, some what prior to this narration, it is proper to observe, that you must not be surprised at often hearing me mention Grecian names of barbarous men. For the cause of this is as follows: Solon intending to insert this narration into his verses, investigated for this purpose the power of names, and found that those first Egyptians who committed these particulars to writing transferred these names into their own tongue. He, therefore, again receiving the meaning of every name, introduced that meaning into our language. And these writings were in the possession of my grandfather, and are now in mine: they were likewise the subject of my meditation while I was a boy. If, therefore, in the course of this narration you hear such names as subsist among us at present, you must not be surprised; for you know the cause. But it will require a long discourse to speak from the beginning, as I did before, concerning the allotment of the Gods, and to show how they distributed the whole earth, here into larger, and there into lesser allotments, and procured temples and sacrifices for themselves. Neptune, indeed, being allotted the Atlantic island, settled his offspring by a mortal woman in a certain part of the island, of the following description. Towards the sea, but in the middle of the island, there was a plain, which is said to have been the most beautiful of all plains, and distinguished by the fertility of the soil. Near this plain, and again in the middle of it, at the distance of fifty stadia, there was a very low mountain. This was inhabited by one of those men who in the beginning sprung from the earth, and whose name was Evenor. This man living with a woman called Leucippe had by her Clites, who was his only daughter. But when the virgin arrived at maturity, and her father and mother were dead, Neptune[†] being captivated with her beauty had connection with her, and enclosed the hill on which she dwelt with spiral streams of water; the sea and the

---

[†] A dæmoniacal Neptune, or a dæmon belonging to the order of Neptune, by contributing to the procreation of the offspring of Clites, is, in mythological language, said to have been captivated with her beauty, and to have had connection with her. See the first note to the Life of Plato by Olympiodorus [TTS vol IX.]

land at the same time alternately forming about each other lesser and larger zones. Of these, two were formed by the land, and three by the sea; and these zones, as if made by a turner's wheel, were in all parts equidistant from the middle of the island, so that the hill was inaccessible to men. For at that time there were no ships, and the art of sailing was then unknown. But Neptune, as being a divinity, easily adorned the island in the middle; caused two fountains of water to spring up from under the earth, one cold and the other hot; and likewise bestowed all-various and sufficient aliment from the earth. He also 4a begat and educated five male twins; and having distributed all the Atlantic island into ten parts, he bestowed upon his first-born son his maternal habitation and the surrounding land; this being the largest and the best division. He likewise established this son king of the whole island, and made the rest of his sons governors. But he gave to each of them dominion over many people, and an extended tract of land. Besides this, too, he gave all of them names. And his first-born son, indeed, who was the king of all the rest, he called Atlas, whence the whole island was at that time denominated Atlantic. But the twin son that was born immediately after Atlas, and who was allotted the extreme parts of the island, towards the pillars of Hercules, as far as to the region which at present from that place is called Gadiric, he denominated according to his native tongue Gadirus, but which we call in Greek Eumelus. Of his second twin offspring, he called one Ampheres, and the other Eudæmon. The first-born of his third offspring he denominated Mneseus, and the second Autochthon. The elder of his fourth issue he called Elasippus, and the younger Mestor. And, lastly, he denominated the first-born of his fifth issue Azaes, and the second Diaprepes. All these and their progeny dwelt in this place, for a prodigious number of generations, ruling over many other islands, and extending their empire, as we have said before, as far as to Egypt and Tyrrhenia. But the race of Atlas was by far the most honourable; and of these, the oldest king always left the kingdom, for many generations, to the eldest of his offspring. These, too, possessed wealth in such abundance as to surpass in this respect all the kings that were prior to them; nor will any that may succeed them easily obtain the like. They had likewise every thing provided for them which both in a city and every other place is sought after as useful for the purposes of life. And they were supplied, indeed, with many things from foreign countries, on account of their extensive empire; but the island afforded them the greater part of every thing of which they stood in need. In the first place, the island supplied them with such things as are dug out of mines in a solid state, and with such as are melted: and orichalcum,[†] which is now but seldom mentioned, but then was much celebrated, was dug out of the earth in many parts of the island, and was considered as the most honourable of all metals except gold. Whatever, too, the woods afford for builders the island produced in abundance. There were likewise sufficient pastures there for tame and savage animals; together with a prodigious number of elephants. For, there were pastures for all such

115a animals as are fed in lakes and rivers, on mountains, and in plains. And, in like manner, there was sufficient aliment for the largest and most voracious kind of animals. Besides this, whatever of odoriferous the earth nourishes at present, whether roots, or grass, or wood, or juices, or gums, flowers, or fruits, - these the island produced, and produced them well. Again, the island bore mild and dry fruits, such as we use for food, and of which we make bread, (aliment of this kind being denominated by us leguminous,) together with such meats, drinks, and

b ointments, as trees afford. Here, likewise, there were trees, whose fruits are used for the sake of sport and pleasure, and which it is difficult to conceal; together with such dainties as are used as the remedies of satiety, and are grateful to the weary. All these an island which once existed, bore sacred, beautiful, and wonderful, and in infinite abundance.

c The inhabitants, too, receiving all these from the earth, constructed temples, royal habitations, ports, docks, and all the rest of the region, disposing them in the following manner: - In the first place, those who resided about the ancient metropolis united by bridges those zones of the sea which we before mentioned, and made a road both to the external parts and to the royal abode. But the palace of the king was from the first immediately raised in this very habitation of the God and

d their ancestors. This being adorned by one person after another in continued succession, the latter of each always surpassing the former in the ornaments he bestowed, the palace became at length astonishingly large and beautiful. For they dug a trench as far as to the outermost zone, which commencing from the sea extended three acres in breadth, and fifty stadia in length. And that ships might sail from this sea to that zone as a port, they enlarged its mouth, so that it might be sufficient to

e receive the largest vessels. They likewise divided by bridges those zones of the earth which separated the zones of the sea, so that with one three-banked galley they might sail from one zone to the other; and covered the upper part of the zones in such a manner that they might sail under them. For the lips of the zones of earth were higher than the

---

[†] It is uncertain what this orichalcum was: perhaps it was the same with *platina*.

sea. But the greatest of these zones, towards which the sea directed its course, was in breadth three stadia: the next in order was of the same dimension. But, of the other two, the watery circle was in breadth two stadia; and that of earth was again equal to the preceding circle of water: but the zone which ran round the island in the middle was one stadium in breadth. The island which contained the palace of the king was five stadia in diameter. This, together with the zones, and the bridge which was every way an acre in breadth, they inclosed with a wall of stone, and raised towers and gates on the bridges according to the course of the sea. Stones, too, were dug out from under the island, on all sides of it, and from within and without the zones: some of which were white, others black, and others red: and these stone quarries, on account of the cavity of the rock, afforded two convenient docks. With respect to the edifices, some were of a simple structure, and others were raised from stones of different colours; thus by variety pursuing pleasure, which was allied to their nature. They likewise covered the superficies of the wall which inclosed the most outward zone with brass, using it for this purpose as an ointment; but they covered the superficies of that wall which inclosed the interior zone with tin: and lastly, they covered that which inclosed the acropolis with orichalcum, which shines with a fiery splendour.

The royal palace within the acropolis was constructed as follows: In the middle of it there was a temple, difficult of access, sacred to Clites and Neptune, and which was surrounded with an inclosure of gold. In this place assembling in the beginning, they produced the race of ten kings; and from the ten divisions of the whole region here collected every year, they performed seasonable sacrifices to each. But the temple of Neptune was one stadium in length, and three acres in breadth; and its altitude was commensurate to its length and breadth. There was something, however, barbaric in its form. All the external parts of the temple, except the summit, were covered with silver; for that was covered with gold. With respect to the internal parts, the roof was entirely formed from ivory, variegated with gold, silver, and orichalcum; but as to all the other parts, such as the walls, pillars, and pavement, these were adorned with orichalcum. Golden statues, too, were placed in the temple; and the God himself was represented standing on a chariot, and governing six-winged horses; while, at the same time, through his magnitude, he touched the roof with his head. An hundred Nereids upon dolphins were circularly disposed about him; for at that time this was supposed to be the number of the Nereids. There were likewise many other statues of private persons dedicated within the temple. Round the temple, on the outside, stood golden images of all the women and men that had descended from the ten kings: together with many other statues of kings and private persons, which had been dedicated from the city, and from foreign parts that were in subjection to the Atlantic island. There was an altar, too, which accorded in magnitude and construction with the other ornaments of the temple; and in like manner, the palace was adapted to the magnitude of the

117a empire, and the decorations of the sacred concerns. The inhabitants, likewise, used fountains both of hot and cold water, whose streams were copious, and naturally salubrious and pleasant in a wonderful degree. About the fountains, too, edifices were constructed, and trees planted, adapted to these fontal waters. Receptacles of water, likewise, were

b placed round the fountains, some of which were exposed to the open air, but others were covered, as containing hot baths for the winter season. Of these receptacles, some were appropriated to the royal family, and others, apart from these, to private individuals; and again, some were set apart for women, and others for horses and other animals of the yoke; a proper ornament at the same time being distributed to each. They likewise brought defluent streams to the grove of Neptune, together with all-various trees of an admirable beauty and height, through the fecundity of the soil: and thence they derived these streams to the exterior circles, by conducting them through channels over the bridges.

c But in each island of these exterior circles there were many temples of many Gods, together with many gardens, and gymnasia apart from each other, some for men, and others for horses. But about the middle of the largest of the islands there was a principal hippodrome, which was a stadium in breadth, and the length of which extended round the whole circle, for the purpose of exercising the horses. On all sides of the hippodrome stood the dwellings of the officers of the guards. But the

d defence of the place was committed to the more faithful soldiers, who dwelt in the smaller circle, and before the acropolis; and the most faithful of all the soldiers were assigned habitations within the acropolis, and round the royal abodes. The docks, likewise, were full of three-banked galleys, and of such apparatus as is adapted to vessels of this kind. And in this manner the parts about the royal palaces were disposed. But having passed beyond the external ports, which were

e three in number, a circular wall presented itself to the view, beginning from the sea, and every way distant from the greatest of the circles and the port by an interval of fifty stadia. This wall terminated in the mouth of the trench which was towards the sea. The whole space, too, inclosed by the wall was crowded with houses; and the bay and the greatest harbour were full of ships and merchants that came from all parts. Hence, through the great multitude that were here assembled, there was an all-various clamour and tumult both by day and night. And thus we have nearly related the particulars respecting the city and the ancient habitation, as they were then unfolded by the Egyptian 8a priests. In the next place, we shall endeavour to relate what was the nature, and what the arrangement, of the rest of the region.

First, then, every place is said to have been very elevated and abrupt which was situated near the sea; but all the land round the city was a plain, which circularly invested the city, but was itself circularly inclosed by mountains which extended as far as to the sea. This plain too was smooth and equable; and its whole length, from one side to the other, was three thousand stadia; but, according to its middle from the sea upwards, it was two thousand stadia. The whole island, likewise, was situated towards the south, but from its extremities was exposed to the north. Its mountains were then celebrated as surpassing all that exist at present in multitude, magnitude, and beauty; and contained many villages, whose inhabitants were wealthy. Here, too, there were rivers, lakes, and meadows, which afforded sufficient nutriment for all tame and savage animals; together with woods, various both in multitude and kind, and in abundance adequate to the several purposes to which they are subservient. This plain, therefore, both by nature and the labours of many kings in a long period of time, was replete with fertility. Its figure, too, was that of a square, for the most part straight and long; but on account of the trench which was dug round it, it was deficient in straightness. The depth, breadth, and length of this trench are incredible, when compared with other labours accomplished by the hands of men: but, at the same time, we must relate what we have heard. Its depth was one acre; and its breadth every where a stadium. And as it was dug round the whole plain, its length was consequently ten thousand stadia.[†] This trench received the streams falling from the mountains, and which, circularly flowing round the plain towards the city, and being collected from different parts, at length poured themselves from the trench into the sea. Ditches one hundred feet in breadth, being cut in a right line from this part, were again sent through the plain into the trench near the sea: but these were separated from each other by an interval of one hundred stadia. The inhabitants brought wood to the city from the mountains, and other seasonable

---

[†] That is, 1250 miles. This trench, however, was not a more surprising effort of human industry than is the present wall of China.

articles, in twofold vessels, through the trenches; for the trenches intersected each other obliquely, and towards the city. Every year, too, they twice collected the fruits of the earth; in winter using the waters from Jupiter, and in summer bringing the productions of the earth through the streams deduced from the trenches. With respect to the multitude of men in the plain useful for the purposes of war, it was

119a ordered that a commander in chief should be taken out of each allotment. But the magnitude of each allotted portion of land was ten times ten stadia; and the number of all the allotments was sixty thousand. There is said to have been an infinite number of men from the mountains and the rest of the region; and all of them were distributed according to places and villages into these allotments, under their respective leaders. The commander in chief, therefore, of each division was ordered to bring into the field of battle a sixth part of the war-chariots, the whole amount of which was ten thousand, together with two horses and two charioteers: and again, it was decreed that he

b should bring two horses yoked by the side of each other, but without a seat, together with a man who might descend armed with a small shield, and who after the charioteer might govern the two horses: likewise, that he should bring two heavy-armed soldiers, two slingers, three light-armed soldiers, three hurlers of stones, and three jaculators, together with four sailors, in order to fill up the number of men sufficient for one thousand two hundred ships. And in this manner were the warlike affairs of the royal city disposed. But those of the other nine cities were disposed in a different manner, which it would

c require a long time to relate. The particulars respecting the governors were instituted from the beginning as follows: Each of the ten kings possessed absolute authority both over the men and the greater part of the laws in his own division, and in his own city, punishing and putting to death whomsoever he pleased. But the government and communion of these kings with each other were conformable to the mandates given by Neptune; and this was likewise the case with their laws. These mandates were delivered to them by their ancestors inscribed on a pillar of orichalcum, which was erected about the middle of the island, in the

d temple of Neptune. These kings, therefore, assembled together every fifth, and alternately every sixth year, for the purpose of distributing an equal part both to the even and the odd; and, when assembled, they deliberated on the public affairs, inquired if any one had acted improperly, and, if he had, called him to account for his conduct. But when they were about to sit in judgment on any one, they bound each other by the following compact. As, prior to this judicial process, there were bulls in the temple of Neptune, free from all restraint, they selected ten of these, and vowed to the God, they would offer a sacrifice which should be acceptable to him, *viz.* a victim taken without iron, and hunted with clubs and snares. Hence, whatever bull was caught by them they led to the pillar, and cut its throat on the summit of the column, agreeably to the written mandates. But on the pillar, besides the laws, there was an oath, supplicating mighty imprecations against those that were disobedient. When, therefore, sacrificing according to their laws, they began to burn all the members of the bull, they poured out of a full bowl a quantity of clotted blood for each of them, and gave the rest to the fire; at the same time lustrating the pillar. After this, drawing out of the bowl in golden cups, and making a libation in the fire, they took an oath that they would judge according to the laws inscribed on the pillar, and would punish any one who prior to this should be found guilty; and likewise that they would never willingly transgress any one of the written mandates. They added, that they would neither govern, nor be obedient to any one who governed, contrary to the prescribed laws of their country. When every one had thus supplicated both for himself and those of his race, after he had drunk, and had dedicated the golden cup to the temple of the God, he withdrew to the supper, and his necessary concerns. But when it was dark, and the fire about the sacrifice was abated, all of them, invested with a most beautiful azure garment, and sitting on the ground near the burnt victims, spent the whole night in extinguishing the fire of the sacrifice, and in judging and being judged, if any person had accused some one of them of having transgressed the laws.

When the judicial process was finished, and day appeared, they wrote the decisions in a golden table, which together with their garments they dedicated as monuments, in the temple of the God. There were also many other laws respecting sacred concerns, and such as were peculiar to the several kings; but the greatest were the following: That they should never wage war against each other, and that all of them should give assistance if any person in some one of their cities should endeavour to extirpate the royal race. And as they consulted in common respecting war and other actions, in the same manner as their ancestors, they assigned the empire to the Atlantic family. But they did not permit the king to put to death any of his kindred, unless it seemed fit to more than five out of the ten kings. Such then being the power, and of such magnitude, at that time, in those places, Divinity transferred it from thence to these parts, as it is reported, on the following occasion. For many generations, the Atlantics, as long as the nature of the God was sufficient for them, were obedient to the laws, and benignantly affected toward a divine nature, to which they were allied. For they possessed true, and in every respect magnificent conceptions; and employed mildness in conjunction with prudence, both in those casual circumstances which are always taking place, and towards each other. Hence, despising every thing except virtue, they considered the concerns of the present life as trifling, and therefore easily endured them; and were of opinion that abundance of riches and other possessions was nothing more than a burthen. Nor were they intoxicated by luxury, nor did they fall into error, in consequence of being blinded by incontinence; but, being sober and vigilant, they acutely perceived that all these things were increased through common friendship, in conjunction with virtue; but that, by eagerly pursuing and honouring them, these external goods themselves were corrupted, and, together with them, virtue and common friendship were destroyed. From reasoning of this kind, and from the continuance of a divine nature, all the particulars which we have previously discussed, were increased among them. But when that portion of divinity, or divine destiny, which they enjoyed, vanished from among them, in consequence of being frequently mingled with much of a mortal nature, and human manners prevailed, - then, being no longer able to bear the events of the present life, they acted in a disgraceful manner. Hence, to those who were capable of seeing, they appeared to be base characters, men who separated things most beautiful from such as are most honourable: but by those who were unable to perceive the true life, which conducts to felicity, they were considered as then in the highest degree worthy and blessed, in consequence of being filled with an unjust desire of possessing, and transcending in power. But Jupiter, the God of Gods, who governs by law, and who is able to perceive every thing of this kind, when he saw that an equitable race was in a miserable condition, and was desirous of punishing them, in order that by acquiring temperance they might possess more elegant manners, excited all the Gods to assemble in their most honourable habitation, whence, being seated as in the middle of the universe, he beholds all such things as participate of generation: and having assembled the Gods, he thus addressed them: * * *